Van Lingle Mungo
THE MAN, THE SONG, THE PLAYERS

Edited by Bill Nowlin
Associate Editors: James Forr and Len Levin

Society for American Baseball Research, Inc.
Phoenix, AZ

Van Lingle Mungo: The Man, The Song, The Players
Edited by Bill Nowlin
Associate editors: James Forr and Len Levin
ISBN 978-1-933599-76-2
(Ebook ISBN 978-1-933599-77-9)
Design and Production: Gilly Rosenthol, Rosenthol Design

Photo Credits:
Front and back covers: Cover elements courtesy of David Rosner and Darville Music, LLC d/b/a F Seven Music,
with the exception of the photographs of Van Lingle Mungo, which come from the collection of Bill Nowlin.
The photograph of Dave Frishberg on page 8 is courtesy of Dave Frishberg, with thanks to Bob Russon.
National Baseball Hall of Fame and Library: pages 23, 39, 55, 81, 93, 99, 135, 145, 152, 158, 162, 176, 202, 208, 214, 220, 231, 236, and 246.
Retro Images Archive (George Brace Collection): pages 13, 17, 33, 59, 66, 76, 89, 113, 119, 123, 130, 140, 171, 182, 191, 227, 255, and 259.
Collection of Bill Nowlin: 45, 48
Courtesy of Johnny Pesky: 28
Public domain: 105

The Society for American Baseball Research, Inc.
4455 E. Camelback Road, Ste. D-140
Phoenix, AZ 85018
Phone: (800) 969-7227 or (612) 343-6455

Web: www.sabr.org
Facebook: Society for American Baseball Research
Twitter: @SABR

Table of Contents

Introduction

WHY THIS BOOK OF BIOGRAPHIES

centered around Van Lingle Mungo?

Well, why not?

In the past dozen years, since 2002 when Mark Armour first announced BioProject at the Boston convention, and the goal of writing a brief biography of every former major-league baseball player, SABR members have responded. Some people didn't take BioProject seriously at first; it aspired to an unrealistic goal—to organize the writing of something like 17,000 biographies.

With the publication of this book, and several others which will bear 2014 publication dates, the collective and collaborative efforts of SABR members have brought us very close to 3,000 biographies. Many players who never could have expected an appreciation of their lives are now subject of a BioProject profile. Some members have deliberately sought out the least-celebrated among the players.

BioProject's "team books" no doubt have helped accelerate the process. The Boston Chapter's David Southwick conceived of a book of bios celebrating the 1975 Red Sox and embarked upon the process of lining up authors. The resultant book *'75: The Red Sox Team That Saved Baseball* (Rounder Books, 2005, edited by Bill Nowlin and Cecilia Tan) gave biographers and editors the opportunity to contribute to a common effort; some 32 SABR members collaborated to make the book happen.

The idea of assembling a collection of biographies into a book was not a new one. SABR itself had published *Deadball Stars of the National League* (edited by Tom Simon) just the year before, 2004. And Tom Simon himself had edited *Green Mountain Boys of Summer*, the collaborative work of 24 members of SABR's Larry Gardner (Vermont) Chapter. That book was published by The New England Press of Shelburne, Vermont in 2000.

The Boston Chapter followed up in 2007 with *The 1967 Impossible Dream Red Sox: Pandemonium on the Field* (edited by Bill Nowlin and Dan Desrochers and published by Rounder Books.)

By 2009, there had been a few others books—one on the 1948 Boston Braves and Boston Red Sox, one on the 1918 Red Sox, and books on the 1968 Detroit Tigers, the 1969 New York Mets, the 1939 Red Sox, the 1959 Chicago White Sox, and *Minnesotans in Baseball*, edited by Stew Thornley, which followed the geographic focus of the Vermont book. Beginning with the 1975 Red Sox book through September 2014, there have been 25 books published. This book is #26.

And this book takes a different focus.

BioProject has grown to embrace biographies of ballparks, and a variety of people associated with the game besides the players—owners, broadcasters, reporters, etc. *New Century, New Team: The 1901 Boston Americans* also featured two biographies of prominent "fans"—Joanne Hulbert's biography of Arthur "Hi-Hi" Dixwell and Pete Nash's biography of Mike "Nuf Ced" McGreevy.

There are any number of themes around which a collection of biographies can be based. Witness this book. SABR's Lyle Spatz was editor of 2012's *The Team That Forever Changed Baseball* and *America: The 1947 Brooklyn Dodgers* (University of Nebraska Press) and 2013's *Bridging Two Dynasties: The 1947 New York Yankees* (also published by Nebraska). He is also chair of SABR's Baseball Records Research Committee. And in an August 11, 2013 e-mail to Mark Armour, Paul Rogers, and Bill Nowlin, Lyle wrote: "For an offbeat idea how about a 'team book' on the Dave Frishberg song. Perfect for Bill, I would think."

Dave Frishberg's song listed 37 ballplayers in the lyrics. That's a good number to build a book around. And Dave himself was still around—and a SABR member for 25 years. Four days later, on August 15, Bill Nowlin interviewed him by telephone. Why was the book "perfect for Bill"? Well, I'm Bill, and Lyle knew that I'd been active in the music business since co-founding Rounder Records with Ken Irwin and Marian Leighton Levy back in 1970. That was, by pure coincidence, the year after Dave wrote "Van Lingle Mungo." Rounder went on to release over 3,000 record albums, with special attention to documenting America's musical heritage and "roots music and its contemporary off-shoots."

As it happens, Rounder was acquired by the Concord Music Group—and "Van Lingle Mungo" is one of 17 songs included on Dave Frishberg's album *Classics*, released on Concord Records in 1991.

Lyle's idea did appeal to me, and—in just under a year—here is the result, thanks to the hard work and dedication of 31 SABR members.

We all hope you enjoy this offbeat idea. There are opportunities for other quirky projects to come, as well as a continuing series of "team books"—all of which are completely free to all 6,000-plus SABR members in digital editions, and available to the general public as well in both digital and hardcopy Print on Demand versions.

—Bill Nowlin

The Recording

By Bill Nowlin

THE SONG ITSELF WAS RELEASED ON A 45 rpm single in 1970. It ran 2:45 and was the "A side" of CTI 509 — Creed Taylor Inc., from East 57ᵗʰ Street in Manhattan. It was produced by David Rosner and Margo Guryan for Daramus, Inc. The publishing was registered to Red Day Music, Inc., ASCAP.

The single came from a CTI album by Dave Frishberg, *Oklahoma Toad* (CTI SR-3306), released in 1970. The "B side" was the lead track on the album, "Nasty, Nasty Habit."

Daramus itself was an acronym derived from David A. Rosner's initials and the first three letters of the word "music." Rosner writes in an e-mail, "We initially did the sessions for ABC Records, and my partners, at the time Neil Diamond and Tom Catalano, negotiated out of that deal, allowing me to submit the album to Creed. We recorded at Associated Studios on 7th Avenue in Manhattan, and it became Dave's first as a featured artist and very different from all his subsequent albums."

Personnel on the album session were:

Dave Frishberg, keyboards and vocals

Herb Lovelle, drums

Russell George, bass

Stuart Scharf, guitar

Al Cohn, tenor saxophone

Sol Schlinger, baritone saxophone

Garnett Brown, trombone

Bill Berry, trumpet

Not all songs featured all the instruments.

Red Day Music morphed over time into F7 Music.

The song was re-cut in 1981 by Omnisound as *The Dave Frishberg Songbook, Volume 1* (Omnisound N-1040), with a smaller combo. The album was a Grammy finalist for Best Jazz Vocal. These sessions were held in East Stroudsburg, Pennsylvania and featured:

Dave Frishberg, piano and vocals

Bill Goodwin, drums

Steve Gilmore, bass

The Dave Frishberg Songbook, Volume 2 was released in 1983 and also attracted a Grammy nomination.

The two Omnisound albums are out of print but were combined into one and re-released by Concord Jazz in 1991 as *Dave Frishberg Classics* (Concord Jazz CCD-446.)

David Rosner is Dave Frishberg's publisher.

Margo Guryan is a songwriter and singer with many recordings to her credit. She and David Rosner have been married for 44 years. David provides a little more information on the two:

"Margo worked for Creed in the early sixties, both at ABC Records (coincidentally) and at Verve. She was at ABC when Creed started the Impulse label. In about 1965-6, she was looking for a publisher, and Creed suggested April/Blackwood, where I was what was then called Professional Manager. We — April/Blackwood (the publishing arm of Columbia Records) — had a string of hits including "Wild Thing" and "Angel Of The Morning." I took a few songs from Margo and then signed her as a staff writer. In 1968, she introduced me to Dave [Frishberg]. She met Dave at the Half Note, a Greenwich Village jazz club. At the time they met, she was married to valve trombonist Bob Brookmeyer who, with Clark Terry, played the club regularly. Dave was playing piano for Al Cohn and Zoot Sims, who also were club regulars. Margo had a Spanky And Our Gang hit in early `68 with «Sunday Morning»; then, almost two years later, with Oliver, same song. She did an album for Bell Records (later renamed Arista). The album bombed because she wasn't a performer and didn't tour in support. Thirty years later, it was pirated on CD in Japan, which led to legitimate releases in Asia, the U.S. and Europe. She's also released a demos album.

"I worked for Dick James in 1970-1 representing, among others, the Beatles catalog, and later Elton John. Dick was Elton's publisher, record company and manager, so I was significantly involved in EJ's introduction to this country. In fact, Margo and I, then still in New York, flew to Los Angeles, to shepherd 'the lads' through their first U.S. gig at The Troubador. Between sets one night, she and I rushed back to our hotel to

4

see Dave and VLM on Cavett, then back to the club. I, Margo and I having moved to L.A., formed The Bicycle Music Company, where I represented the songs of, among others, George Harrison in the 70's, Robbie Robertson and, most significantly, Neil Diamond, whose catalogs I represented since late '71. I sold Bicycle in 2005."

NOTE: The Concord Jazz album is available both as a compact disc and in digital format on iTunes.

Thanks to David Rosner for e-mails in August 2013 and in subsequent months.

Dave Frishberg's website is: http://davefrishberg.net/

Van Lingle Mungo: The Lyrics

Words and music by Dave Frishberg

Heenie Majeski, Johnny Gee
Eddie Joost, Johnny Pesky, Thornton Lee
Danny Gardella
Van Lingle Mungo

Whitey Kurowski, Max Lanier
Eddie Waitkus and Johnny Vandermeer
Bob Estalella
Van Lingle Mungo

Augie Bergamo, Sigmund Jakucki
Big Johnny Mize and Barney McCosky
Hal Trosky

Augie Galan and Pinky May
Stan Hack and Frenchy Bordagaray
Phil Cavaretta, George McQuinn
Howie Pollett and Early Wynn
Art Passarella
Van Lingle Mungo

John Antonelli, Ferris Fain
Frankie Crosetti, Johnny Sain
Harry Brecheen and Lou Boudreau
Frankie Gustine and Claude Passeau
Eddie Basinski
Ernie Lombardi
Hughie Mulcahy
Van Lingle…Van Lingle Mungo

Mungo on "Mungo"

WHAT DID VAN LINGLE MUNGO THINK of the song?

Dave Frishberg recalled meeting him when both appeared in 1969 on ABC's *The Dick Cavett Show*. Frishberg, a SABR member from way back, once wrote to SABR's listserve. He mentioned meeting Eddie Basinski, but then added, "The only other guy from the song I ever met was Mungo himself, who arrived from Pageland, South Carolina, to be on the Dick Cavett show and listen to me sing the song. This was 1969, when Cavett had a nightly show in New York. Backstage, Mungo asked me when he would see some remuneration for the song. When he heard my explanation about how there was unlikely to be any remuneration for anyone connected with the song, least of all him, he was genuinely downcast. 'But it's my name,' he said. I told him, 'The only way you can get even is to go home and write a song called Dave Frishberg.' He laughed, and when we said goodbye he said, 'I'm gonna do it! I'm gonna do it!' If he did it, The Baseball Almanac doesn't mention it."[1]

Frishberg hadn't expected Mungo to be there. "When I showed up, I was surprised to find Mungo there. When I got to my dressing room, I found out I was sharing it with him, so we met in the dressing room, waiting to go on. We talked affably. He was a cheerful guy. He gave me a big pat on the back. He said, 'I'm going to go home and write a song called 'Dave Frishberg.' I'm still waiting."[2]

Several years later UPI ran a piece purporting to recount the story of a woman who phoned from Detroit to Pageland and the conversation was said to begin thusly:

"Are you Van Lingle Mungo?"

"Yes."

"You're not dead, are you?"

"Well, I'm talking to you, aren't I?"

"How do you like the song?"

"What song?"

"You mean you haven't heard the song, 'Van Lingle Mungo,' the one they named after you. They've been playing it all over the country. I'm crazy about it."

Mungo's wife Eloise told the reporter, "I like the music and the rhythm, but most of all I like the title because it has to do with my favorite ballplayer." Eloise herself called him "V.L."

Mungo himself added, "I have no idea why it was written. The fellow who wrote it must have mad something in mind."[3]

—BN

NOTES

1 David Frishberg post to SABR-L, March 17, 2005.

2 David Frishberg, interview by Bill Nowlin. August 15, 2013.

3 *Sarasota Journal*, May 18, 1977.

A note about the additional players included in this book

READERS CAREFULLY COMPARING THE "VAN
Lingle Mungo" song lyrics to the biographies in this book will
notice that there are a few players who are in the book, but not
included in the lyrics. That's because the lyrics changed from
one iteration to another, for reasons Dave Frishberg explains
in the biography of him which is included in this volume.

So, in addition to the players mentioned in the song, we also
have biographies of Roy Campanella, Johnny Kucks, and
Virgil Trucks.

—BN

Dave Frishberg

By Stew Thornley

A JAZZ PIANIST AND SONGWRITER WHO
is known to kids for his contributions to the *Schoolhouse Rock!* series, Dave Frishberg is equally prominent with baseball fans for incorporating his boyhood love of the sport into his music, most notably with the song "Van Lingle Mungo."

David Lee Frishberg was born on March 23, 1933, in St. Paul, Minnesota. His father, Harry, worked in the clothing business and later bought a men's store in downtown St. Paul, where his mother, Sarah, worked as the bookkeeper.

Growing up a block from the Mississippi River in St. Paul, Frishberg had three older siblings, a sister, Miriam, and brothers Arnold and Mort (born seven years before Dave). During World War II Arnold was in the South Pacific, and Mort was starting college (he entered the US Navy after the war).

In 1942 Harry took his youngest son to Lexington Park to see the St. Paul Saints of the minor-league American Association. "They were the doormats," Frishberg said of the Saints. "The first year I watched them, Truck Hannah was the manager, and they ended up in last place. The next year Salty Parker was the manager, and they ended up in last place."

Despite the losing ways of the hometown team during the war, Frishberg described himself as "a rabid St. Paul Saint fan." The Saints did better after the war, and in 1946 Frishberg had a special, though brief, role with the team. He had interviewed Dick Siebert, a former major leaguer who was doing the play-by-play announcing for the Saints, and written an article on him for his school's newspaper.

Siebert, who would soon become the baseball coach at the University of Minnesota and lead the team to three national championships, invited Frishberg to sit in the press box and help him with the broadcasts. "I didn't know what he meant by help him. What he figured out was that I could be the statistician, the spotter. There was nothing much to spot, because he knew what was happening. But I would keep the stats

up to date. I had a little slide rule. If someone got a hit, I would figure out what his average was."

However, Frishberg'a job lasted only a few games because of a polio epidemic that year, prompting his parents to keep him away from crowds. "I was broken-hearted, but they asked me not to do that anymore. It wasn't like I had a long relationship with Dick Siebert, but I was impressed with the way he conducted himself and thought he was a nice guy, a real good guy, and a good announcer. I was impressed with the whole thing. I loved sitting there in the press box. It was an interesting place to watch the game. I liked to see the people, what they were doing in the press box."

Empty to crowded is how Frishberg recalled Lexington Park during and after the war. "My memories are that you could go in there and sit anywhere you want [during the war years]. Then the team got good in the late '40s, and I remember then the park was crowded." In 1948 the Saints, by then owned by the Brooklyn Dodgers, made it to the Junior World Series

(formerly the Little World Series) against another Brooklyn farm team, the Montreal Royals of the International League.[1] "The most excitement in Lexington Park was when the Saints were contenders, and there was hysteria in the park at that time. That's the year that they went to the Little World Series.

"The Saints are proud of the fact that [Roy] Campanella played on the team and [Duke] Snider played on the team, but they were only there momentarily. The real Saints that stayed season after season were mainly Eric Tipton, a great player, Johnny Dantonio as a great catcher, and the pitchers, Otho Nitcholas and Harry Taylor and Phil Haugstad. They were with the team over a period of time, and they were great stars. Those Dodgers [Campanella, Snider, et al.] were only down for a cup of coffee with the Saints and they were back up quick."

St. Paul's rival in the American Association was the Minneapolis Millers, who played in Nicollet Park, of similar vintage to Lexington Park but distinct in that, while the distant fence in right at Lexington was a tough target for left-handed hitters, the opposite was true at Nicollet, where the distance down the line was 279 feet with a high fence with double-decked billboards just beyond that. "I saw one game in Nicollet Park," said Frishberg. "Minneapolis versus Columbus. I was about 14 and went over there alone. I wanted to see what the hated Millers looked like at home. I wanted to see what the home uniform looked like, and I wanted to see the famous right-field fence. I scoffed when I saw it, of course."

Despite the rise of the Saints, Frishberg was starting to pay more attention to music than baseball. "I got interested in playing the piano when I was 15. Soon that eclipsed my interest in baseball. I had a year's worth of lessons when I was a kid, but I never played a lot of classical music, never had a lot of classical chops. I stopped playing while I watched the Saints. When I started playing again it was virtually by ear. I came from a different path than most of the music majors."

On his web page, Frishberg wrote, "I recognized notes on the staff but I couldn't read them and execute them quickly. Struggling through piano notation was such an unrewarding process that I lost patience with it. The music died when I tried to read it."

Frishberg had a couple of mentors, one of them his brother. "If I had a question about music or anything else I naturally went to Mort, who was my adviser and authority about everything." Another was Jimmy Mulcrone, a co-worker at the Roycraft Company in Minneapolis, where Jimmy's brother administered the Columbia Records distributorship.

"What Jimmy offered to show me was how to use the piano to deal with music—music theory essentially, or keyboard harmony." Frishberg said Mulcrone's lessons "[were] enough to keep me subsequently occupied for years, sitting at the keyboard discovering how to navigate music by using music theory as an expressive tool."

By the time Frishberg started college, the United States was engaged in another war, this time in Korea. "The idea in those days was to not get drafted. The procedure was stay in college. Plus, join the ROTC, so that when you did have to go into the service, at least you were a commissioned officer—a lot better than being an enlisted man." ROTC paid for his second two years of college at the University of Minnesota, where he was a journalism major.

"In retrospect, I think I took that journalism major just so I could stay in college during the draft years. I did manage to do it. … It seemed like an interesting way to go and not too difficult. I never paid too much attention to it as a vocation." Frishberg took electives in the music department. "I wanted to be a music major, but because I wasn't a legit pianist and had never studied piano, really, I couldn't be a music major. So I took my electives there and got my major in the journalism school."

After college, Frishberg served his two years of active duty in Salt Lake City as an Air Force recruiter, "which I thought was kind of ironic because all I wanted to do was get out."

Done with military obligations, Frishberg moved to New York. "I knew all the time that I wanted to be a bebop piano player, and that's what I did. I went to New York and became a bebop piano player. … My life was a night life, the world of nightclubs and playing for a lot of jazz groups and ensembles and playing for singers, traveling, and stuff like that."

Frishberg's music has been described as "an improbable blend of Hoagy Carmichael, Woody Allen, and Noel Coward." On the piano Frishberg accompanied jazz and bebop legends like Ben Webster, Bobby Hackett, Al Cohn, and Zoot Sims. He also became a prolific songwriter.

He was later described by Mike Joyce in the *Washington Post* as a "genuine wordsmith." In another *Washington Post* review, Steve Futterman wrote, "He sneaks up on a song, relying on sly, dry wit or plain-spoken candor to make his best points."

On his composing, Frishberg said in 1997, "I don't know if you can study it, but I will say this. I'm a better songwriter now than I was then. In a way I did study it, tried to make myself better. I learned on the job. I was lucky enough to be paid for being a songwriter, not anything that was ever approaching a hit. All during my life as a songwriter, I've been hired to do special assignments, to write special material for television, for instance." His gimmick is to "write songs for which there is no audience," and he found his niche by doing what was natural, not what was based on potential for commercial appeal. "I tried to write songs that other people who were hot people would sing. But how could I write those songs? I didn't believe in them. Ultimately, I found myself writing down to my audience. As a result, what I churned out was inferior. If you don't mean it, it can't be good.

"I was always composing. … I became interested in it because I worked for a lot of singers, and I began to get clinically interested in the repertoire. 'This guy's good, and this guy's not that good,' and what makes Frank Loesser's song sound so good and so forth. I got interested in songs from an analytical point of view; then began to write them myself."

In the 1997 interview, Frishberg added, "After I started writing songs that I myself was interested in and let the chips fall, that's, I think, when I began to be a better songwriter. Now a lot of singers are starting to do my stuff, notably Rosemary Clooney, who did four or five songs in the last couple years—'Do You Miss New York?,' 'Sweet Kentucky Ham.'"

After 15 years in New York, Frishberg moved to Los Angeles to write material for a short-lived television comedy series, and 15 years later to Portland, Oregon. "What prompted me to leave LA was that I couldn't stand living there any longer. My wife and I now had two sons [Harry and Max], infants, that were born right around the end there. I decided I don't want them growing up in LA, so we decided to move." He had always liked Portland, Oregon, and it reminded him of St. Paul, "same kind of people, same kind of towns."

While still in New York, Frishberg wrote a melody in a Brazilian vein. "This was 1969 when the bossa nova had broke on my consciousness. I had written a couple lyrics for it, and they had nothing to do with baseball. One of them had to do with Richard Nixon, and one of them had to do with a salmon swimming upstream.

"One night, I said, 'This is terrible,' and in an idle moment I was looking through the *Macmillan Baseball Encyclopedia,* and one of the names fit right with the musical motif I had. In a flurry I assembled a bunch of names that seemed to go together from a certain era when I was a baseball fanatic."

Van Lingle Mungo was a pitcher with the Brooklyn Dodgers and New York Giants, known for a great fastball in the 1930s. After arm surgery in 1940, Mungo switched his pitching style and hung on for a few more years, including one with the Minneapolis Millers in 1942, the year Frishberg saw his first game. He didn't remember if he saw Mungo pitch, "but I certainly remember his name from seeing the newspaper stories, 'Millers Get Mungo.' He was a big name at that time."

"I was such a baseball nut that every one of those names, I could see they guy's face. I knew exactly what Augie Bergamo looked like, and I could pick him out of a lineup. The only one I ever saw that I know of was [Eddie] Basinski. He was a Saint. He qualified for the song because he had gone up with the Dodgers and Pittsburgh."

The same year Frishberg wrote "Van Lingle Mungo," Jim Bouton wrote *Ball Four,* a tell-all diary of his 1969 season pitching for the Seattle Pilots and Houston Astros. As a follow-up to the controversy generated by his book, Bouton wrote a sequel, *I'm Glad You Didn't Take It Personally,* and in it referred to Frishberg's new song and how it caused him to contemplate his own writing. "It's a very pleasant song, sad and haunting," wrote Bouton. "For the first time, listening to that song, I had some twinges of regret about *Ball Four*. I felt perhaps a kid reading it would be turned off to baseball heroes that he would never want to write songs about them when he grew up, that he would never feel nostalgic about them. I wondered if I had really smashed heroes, whether I had ruined the game for the kids and ruined it for baseball fans. … And I decided, no, that's not the way things work."

Bouton soon switched from pitching to broadcasting and made a video of "Van Lingle Mungo," displaying photos of the players in the song. However, the video showed Johnny Antonelli, a left-handed pitcher in the 1950s, rather than the John Antonelli that Frishberg had intended, an infielder during World War II.

"John Antonelli's name is in the song," Frishberg said in a 2013 interview with Bill Nowlin, "and it's really uncomfortable because I didn't realize until later, when it was too late, that there was a more modern John Antonelli, a left-handed pitcher who pitched for the Braves and the Giants. Johnny Antonelli, a left-handed pitcher. I wasn't talking about that guy at all. The guy I'm talking about in my song was an infielder.

"Later, after the song was out and there was no way to undo it, I realized that the name John Antonelli means different things to different people. It was embarrassing that I would confuse the listeners that way. He was a wartime player. The other guy is a much later guy."

Frishberg discovered a few other quirks over the years and revised the lyrics. "You have to rhyme it, and I rhymed it quickly, and that's the first version that came out. Through the years, sitting idly, I'd look and find some names that didn't fit, weren't from that era. [Roy] Campanella's name stuck out. The era I'm talking about there were no black major leaguers. Campanella's name doesn't belong in there. I took him out and put in Art Passarella [an umpire]."

In response to comments and inquiries about the song on SABR-L, a listserv of the Society for American Baseball Research (which Frishberg joined in 1984), he wrote, "Imagine my dismay when I subsequently learned that [Bob] Estalella's name didn't rhyme in the first place, because it was pronounced as in Spanish: 'Estaleya.' So you see, the whole rhyme scheme should have been scrapped, starting with "Danny Gardella," and now I stand facing humiliation in Baseball Songland. What did I know? I never heard his name uttered, only saw it in print. Same goes for Johnny Gee, whose name I mangled with a soft 'g.' There may be other names I'm mispronouncing, but at this stage further corrections would only confuse me."

Frishberg was invited to sing the song on the *Dick Cavett Show*, and Mungo was brought in from Pageland, South Carolina. In the waiting room, Mungo said to Frishberg, "You made me famous back home. When do I get the first payment?"

Frishberg said, "I realized he was serious. He thought he was going to get paid." Frishberg broke the news that he wouldn't get paid and added, "The only way you can get back at me is write a song called Dave Frishberg. He said, 'I understand,' clapped me on the back, and laughed."

The only other player from the song Frishberg met was Basinski, whom Frishberg had watched play in St. Paul. Basinski later played ten seasons with Portland in the Pacific Coast League and settled in the same city where Frishberg took up residence. "When someone introduced me to Basinski, I eagerly recited the entire starting lineup of his teammates, the 1946 St. Paul Saints, and then tried to explain to him that he was in my song, Van Lingle Mungo.' Mr. Basinski looked at me like I was from Mars."

Others weren't clear about the song, either. Some who approached him thought the lyrics were Portuguese.

"That's a wonderful song about your childhood friends," another fan told him. Frishberg said, "I thought, 'This guy's hip. He knows exactly what I'm talking about—my childhood friends.' I was about to compliment him on his acute listening when he says, 'You know, one of those guys was a ballplayer.'"

Frishberg has received requests to substitute other names in place of the ones he used. He said he normally declines. "My answer usually is, 'If you're going to do a parody lyric, at least pick a song that everybody knows, not an esoteric piece of music like "Van Lingle Mungo."'

"I designed the song as a piece of nostalgia. To modernize that would pretty well nullify it. I don't consider it a template for baseball players' names. It just stands by itself as a statement of my own nostalgia for days that are long gone.

"There is something sad about the song, and I think it's the music but even the text is somewhat sad because there are a lot of forgotten names."

One request for different lyrics came from the Los Angeles Dodgers. "I convinced them it was a bad idea and ended up writing a new song for them called 'Dodger Blue,'" a paean containing the names of Dodgers after the team moved to Los Angeles. He was at a Dodgers banquet when the song was sung for the first time. "I watched Walter Alston at a table nearby, and I watched a tear come down his cheek and thought, 'If I can make one ballplayer cry, my life will not have been in vain.'"

As of 2013 Frishberg still performed on the piano and lived in Portland with his wife, April Magnusson. He said he kept an eye on the Seattle Mariners, the team closest to him, but was not much of a sports fan. His baseball interest remained in history, and he collected books and sports periodicals from a hundred years ago. His collection included a Reach baseball guide from 1911. "What I look for when I hit the stores when I'm traveling, I'm looking for stuff that's out of print and from the first part of the century."

"I love the hunt."

SOURCES

Stew Thornley interview with Dave Frishberg, January 25, 1997, on *On Deck Circle* (television show of the Halsey Hall Chapter of the Society for American Baseball Research).

Dave Frishberg telephone interview with Bill Nowlin, August 15, 2013.

Stew Thornley telephone interview with Dave Frishberg, September 18, 2013.

Bouton, *Jim, I'm Glad You Didn't Take It Personally* (New York: Dell Publishing Company, 1971), 136-137.

Chapin, Dwight, "Van Lingle Mungo?! Song Lifts Former Dodger Out of Obscurity," *Los Angeles Times*, September 12, 1970, D1.

Dave Frishberg web page: davefrishberg.net

Futterman, Steve, "The Inimitable Dave Frishberg," *Washington Post*, August 22, 2001, C5.

Joyce, Mike, "Dave Frishberg," *Washington Post*, July 24, 1989, B8.

Okrent, Daniel, "Isn't It Ironic?," *Esquire*, December 1989, 54.

Jazz at the Fitz program, January 25, 1997, Fitzgerald Theater, St. Paul, Minnesota.

NOTES

1   The Saints had a working agreement since 1944 and were purchased by the Dodgers on November 20, 1947. See Joe Hennessy, "Dodgers Purchase St. Paul, Mel Jones Shifted from Royals to Operate Saints," *The Sporting News*, November 26, 1947, 19.

Hank Majeski

By Mark Hodermarsky

MANY BASEBALL ENTHUSIASTS RECALL the bottom-of-the-tenth pinch-hit home run that gave the underdog New York Giants a dramatic win over the Cleveland Indians in Game One of the 1954 World Series. Many remember that Dusty Rhodes was the batter, that Bob Lemon was the pitcher, and that the ball barely cleared the 258-foot-deep right-field wall. And most will not forget how Rhodes' homer and "The Catch" by Willie Mays two innings earlier established the direction and tone of the shocking sweep by the New Yorkers. What a good number of fans don't recollect, however, is the other pinch-hit home run in the Series or, more importantly, the hitter responsible for the round-tripper: Hank Majeski.

Hank Majeski played for the Indians during the twilight of an impressive 13-year major-league career. Before taking up duties as a dependable reserve third baseman and second baseman for the Tribe from 1952 through 1955, Majeski, who debuted in the major leagues in 1939, had strung together five solid seasons at the plate and in the field, most notably for the Philadelphia Athletics.

Heeney—his nickname from childhood—enjoyed his best year in 1948 as the Athletics' third baseman (plus eight games at shortstop). He batted .310, hit 12 home runs, drove in 120 runs, and set a major-league record with six two-base hits in a doubleheader. Considered one of the finest defensive third basemen of his era, in 1947 Majeski committed only five errors and set an American League record with a .988 fielding percentage. (Don Money of the Milwaukee Brewers broke the record in 1974 with a .989 mark.)

In seven minor-league seasons between 1936 and 1942, Majeski never hit less than .303. Playing for Eau Claire of the Class D Northern League on August 3, 1936, he went 7-for-7 (three singles, two doubles, a triple, and a home run). He reached with major leagues with the Boston Bees (the once and future Braves) in September 1939. Though his career numbers don't match those of the future All-Stars and Hall of Famers who also debuted in 1939 (Hal Newhouser, Dizzy Trout,

Mickey Vernon, Ted Williams, and Early Wynn), his career demands respect. In 3,421 at-bats in 1,069 games, Majeski batted .279, collected 956 hits, and knocked in 501 runs. In 1948 he ranked in the top ten in most batting categories. In two consecutive years, 1947 and 1948, he led American league third basemen in fielding percentage. And in 1954 Majeski was a key role player in Cleveland's record-shattering pennant-winning season, in which the Tribe piled up 111 wins and only 43 losses.

Majeski grew up during the Depression on Staten Island, New York, the son of Polish-American parents, and never forgot his roots. Born on December 13, 1916, the son of a factory worker, he became a determined, talented, and humble athlete and later an esteemed coach and steady friend. Except for his baseball travels, he never strayed far from the place he most loved—his home, Staten Island.

By the age of 6, Henry was obsessed with baseball, as were most boys of his generation, and was called

Shorty by neighborhood boys because of his short legs. Later he was nicknamed Heeney for reasons unknown. When Henry was 8, his father, who had worked at the U.S. Gypsum Co. plant on Staten Island making wallboard and paint, died, leaving five children. The oldest brother, Walter, assumed the role of father figure to his brothers Henry and Eddie, and his two sisters, Sadie and Sophie.

Young Henry dreamed of becoming a big leaguer as soon as he discovered baseball. A family friend gave him his first glove, which the man had been saving for a son who had died young. He offered the glove with these prophetic words: "Now you take it and become a big leaguer." When Majeski was in the major leagues, he told a sportswriter he could "never forget" the day his first pair of baseball shoes arrived. He was 11. "It was pouring rain, but I slipped into the kitchen, took some grease, rubbed it on the shoes, and ran around the block five times," he said.[1]

At Curtis High School, the future alma mater of another baseball great, Bobby Thomson, Majeski had not yet achieved a growth spurt and stood only about 5-feet-5. But his coach, Harry O'Brien, believed in him. Majeski said that "in high school I was too small to play anything but baseball. But Harry O'Brien felt I had the stuff to play on the team, and his confidence in me got me started."[2]

After high school, Majeski's sturdy build, with his powerful neck and strong shoulders, made him appear bigger than his actual frame. He eventually grew to 5-feet-9 and 180 pounds. (Al Simmons, a coach with the Athletics when Majeski was on the team, said, "Majeski's power is in his wrists. He snaps that bat pretty quick."[3]) Majeski aroused the interest of major-league scouts with his slashing line-drive hitting, excellent batting eye, and deft fielding at second base.

As with most players coming out of high school during Majeski's time, the road from amateur to professional baseball was winding and bumpy, even for the likes of the gifted Staten Islander. After he had spent two years playing sandlot baseball for the Staten Island team in the Police Athletic League, the Boston Red Sox signed him to a contract in 1935 to play for Class D Eau Claire. The Chicago Cubs picked up the Eau Claire franchise, as well as Majeski, after the 1936 season. In 1937, with Moline in the Class B Three-I League, Majeski hit .345. For Birmingham of the Southern Association in 1938 he batted .325. After that season the Bees bought his contract.

Boston manager Casey Stengel moved Majeski from second base to third in 1939, and that's primarily where he would stay for the duration of his 13-year big-league career. Majeski said Stengel did him a favor with the switch because "I probably could have played fast minor-league ball at second base for the rest of my life, but might never have made the grade in the majors at that spot."[4]

Majeski singled and drove in a run in his May 17 debut for the Bees. He played in 106 games in his rookie season and batted .272; he hit seven home runs, enough to rank him third on the team, though well behind Max West's 19. But a broken toe after the season and a stay in Stengel's doghouse resulted in a demotion to Newark of the International League in 1940. There, Majeski blistered opposing pitching, but he appeared in only three games for Boston. In 1941 he played in 19 games in April and May, but was batting only .145 so was placed at Newark once more. Later in May, the New York Yankees, for whom Newark was a farm team, purchased his contract from the Bees. He remained with Newark in 1942 and batted .345 with 121 RBIs. Never once in Majeski's seven minor-league seasons did he hit below .300.

In 1943 Majeski enlisted in the Coast Guard, and in June of that year he married Margaret McLaughlin, who was employed on Staten Island. Discharged from the Coast Guard, he began the 1946 season with the Yankees, getting into eight games with just one hit, and in June he was sold to the Philadelphia Athletics, where his career blossomed. In what remained of the 1946 season, he hit .250 in 264 at-bats, bumping that up to .280 in 1947 in the course of 141 games.

Majeski enjoyed a brilliant 1948 in which he batted .310, hit 41 doubles, and drove in 120 runs, fifth in the American League. He hit a career-best 12 homers, and placed 11th in league MVP balloting. His production tailed off in 1949, as he batted .277 in 114 games and drove in 67 runs. He missed a month of action after being drilled in the head by an Early Wynn fastball on August 7.[5] In December 1949 Majeski was traded to the Chicago White Sox for pitcher Ed Klieman. In 1950 he batted .309 in 122 games for the White Sox. In early June 1951, Chicago traded Majeski back to Philadelphia; in 89 games for the Athletics, he hit .285.

In 1952 Majeski played in 34 games for Philadelphia and 36 games for Cleveland; his contract had been sold to the Indians on June 10. With the Indians, he assumed a utility role. He hit .296 for the Tribe in those 36 games.

Majeski played in 50 games for Cleveland in '53 and hit for an even .300. In 1954, as the Indians won 111 games and the AL pennant with ease, he played in 57 games, hitting .281 and driving in 17 runs. On winning the pennant, beating the Yankees, Majeski said, "I've been around a long time, and I've been waiting a long time to see those Yankees beaten. Now we've done it. We really broke their backs. … Look around. Look at all these guys. Not one didn't go a great job when we needed him. … I don't think I ever had a day like this one. This is a real team. Greatest team spirit I ever saw."[6]

Majeski's one and only trip to the World Series came in 1954. Al Rosen was Cleveland's starting third baseman, MVP in 1953, and a .300 hitter in 1954. Majeski played in all four World Series games. After the Giants won the first two games, Indians manager Al Lopez tried Majeski against Ruben Gomez in Game Three, but he was 0-for-4 with a strikeout and grounded into a double play.

In Game Four the Giants were on the brink of a sweep, and held a 7-0 lead over the Indians through the top of the fifth inning. After the Indians made two outs in the bottom of the fifth, two consecutive errors put Sam Dente on second and Jim Hegan on first. Lopez had Majeski pinch-hit for pitcher Ray Narleski and on the second pitch he hit a three-run homer to deep left field. It might have inspired a turn in fortunes, but in the end the Giants won, 7-4.

Majeski was hitting only .188 for the Indians in his first 36 games on 1955, and was traded to the Baltimore Orioles on June 27. After about a month, and only 41 at-bats, the Orioles released him, and 38-year-old Majeski's playing career was over.

Majeski became a minor-league manager for the Indians, piloting the Daytona Beach Islanders of the Florida State League in 1956 and the Cocoa Indians (the franchise had moved) for part of 1957. He later managed the Oneonta Yankees (1973), coached at Wagner College on Staten Island, and scouted for several major-league teams. He was a hitting instructor for the Houston Astros and Cincinnati Reds in 1966.

Majeski remained dedicated to baseball. Bill Klapach, a veteran Staten Island umpire and longtime friend of Majeski's, said he always participated in the annual Staten Island old-timer's baseball game and "loved to speak to kids about baseball." Majeski, a member of the Staten Island Sports Hall of Fame, never missed an induction ceremony. Klapach said, "Majeski was a fine gentleman who was proud to be from Staten Island."[7]

Bert Levinson, former baseball coach at Curtis High School on Staten Island, recalled how Majeski would "attend our practices and help the kids out with their batting and infield play. He would also show up when he could for some of our games and sit in the stands near the bench so as not to be a distraction to the team." Levinson added that Majeski would "always be there to distribute awards at the end-of-the-year Baseball Fair." He said Majeski was a father figure to Bobby Thomson.[8]

Perhaps no one else can trace Majeski's rise to the majors and his contribution to Staten Island baseball better than a former minor-league pitcher and close friend of his, Carmine "Lefty" DeRenzo. Living only five doors away from Majeski, DeRenzo eagerly followed his neighbor's progress toward stardom. Once after he injured his foot during spring training, Majeski asked for DeRenzo's help. "To help Heeney get his swing back in shape, we went to Curtis High School where I threw him batting practice four days in a row," DeRenzo recalled.[9]

Although Dusty Rhodes hit the more famous pinch-hit home run in the 1954 World Series, Majeski's blast had to feel extra special to him. His three-run shot in Game Four against Don Liddle with two outs gave the Tribe, down 7-0 at the time, some hope for a comeback.

Majeski died on August 9, 1991, at the age of 74. He was survived by his wife, Margaret; a stepdaughter,

Nanette; a sister, Sophie; four grandchildren; and seven great-grandchildren. He also left behind a host of memories for those lucky enough to have seen him play and to call him a friend.

SOURCES

Aside from the sources indicated in the endnotes, the author also relied on statistics from Baseball-Almanac.com, Baseball-reference.com, and Thorn, John et. al., eds., *Total Baseball, 8th Edition* (Munster, Indiana: Sports Media Publishing, 2004). Thanks to James Forr and Bill Nowlin for additional material.

New York Times, August 14, 1991. (Hank Majeski's obituary)

NOTES

1   Stan Baumgartner, "Meet Majeski—Houdini of the Hot Corner," *Sport Life*, 1949, 74.

2   Ed Rumill, "Majestic Majeski," *Baseball Digest*, July 1948, 43.

3   Ibid.

4   Ibid.

5   *St. Petersburg Times*, August 10, 1949.

6   Jonathan Knight, *Summer of Shadows* (Cincinnati: Clerisy Press, 2011), 375.

7   Telephone interview with Bill Klapach, December 29, 2010.

8   Telephone interview with Bert Levinson, December 27, 2010.

9   Telephone interview with Carmine DeRenzo, December 27, 2010.

Johny Gee

By Armand Peterson

JOHN A. (JOHNNY) GEE, JR. DREW national attention in August 1939 when the Pittsburgh Pirates purchased him for cash and four players from the Syracuse Chiefs of the International League. A front-page story in the September 21 issue of *The Sporting News* stated that the $75,000 price was the "biggest independent deal since 192[4], when Lefty Grove was sold to the A's [for $106,000]."[1] Gee's 6-foot-9 height also drew attention. He became the tallest player in major-league history, and remained so until 6-foot-10 Randy Johnson made his debut in September 1988.[2] Sportswriters couldn't resist making light of Gee's height—"long Johnny," "altitudinous," "mountainous," "Herculean," "sky-scraping," "the whopper," "towering," and "the pitching giraffe" were just a few of the sobriquets chosen.

Johnny Gee (pronounced 'jē' as in "Gee Whiz") was born in Syracuse, New York, on December 7, 1915, to parents John A. and Anna (Nicholson) Gee. His father was superintendent of school buildings and repairs for the Syracuse school district. Johnny had one older sister. He made the Central High School baseball team as a freshman, but didn't become the team's number-one pitcher until his junior year. Because of his height it might be assumed that he played basketball growing up, but in fact he had never played on a varsity team at the time he enrolled at the University of Michigan in the fall of 1933.[3] He played tennis well enough to be a contender for citywide open tournaments.[4]

Gee was recruited to Ann Arbor by Michigan's head baseball coach, Ray Fisher.[5] (Fisher won 100 games in a ten-year major-league career, and was Michigan baseball coach for 38 years, 1921-1958.) Fisher was also the freshman basketball coach and, it was thought, brought his tall pitching recruit to the freshman basketball team tryouts.

Varsity basketball coach Franklin Cappon may have had a hand in recruiting Gee for the basketball team, too. According to an article in the *Ann Arbor Daily News*, Michigan's "B" team had beaten tiny Calvin College (Grand Rapids, Michigan) in 1933, but Cappon had been impressed by Calvin's 6-foot-9 center. "I wonder what would happen if I could get a tall center like that for the Western Conference [Big Ten]," mused Cappon. [College rules at the time called for a center-court jump ball after each basket.] During a walk on campus one day, Cappon noticed a boy—Johnny Gee—"as tall as a telegraph pole," and asked him to join the freshman team.[6]

Gee made the freshman team as the second-string center. "He was awkward, having his gigantic proportions as his only attribute," wrote columnist Art Carstens. "Coach Fisher devoted more time to Gee than any other of the freshmen, and Cappon, determined to utilize his height, worked on him during spring practice."[7] Gee was the starting center the next three years and team captain as a senior. At the time he was the tallest man to have played basketball for Michigan.[8]

Gee also won three letters in baseball, highlighted by the Wolverines winning the Big Ten championship in 1936 and ending a six-year drought for Coach Fisher, whose teams had won six conference championships in the 1920s. Gee received the Big Ten Medal of Honor in 1937. (The medal is awarded annually at each school in the conference to a student in the graduating class who best demonstrates proficiency in scholarship and athletics.) Gee had been at best a good student in high school, but blossomed in college. He was a member of the secret Sphinx Society and Phi Kappa Sigma fraternity, and graduated in 1937 with a bachelor of arts degree in education.

Syracuse Chiefs owner Jack Corbett courted the hometown pitcher while he was still in college. "Three years ago [1934] Corbett 'spotted' Gee as a baseball possibility and persuaded him to pitch batting practice for the Chiefs. He showed enough ability to have Corbett elicit a promise from him that he would report to Syracuse after graduating from Michigan," the *Syracuse Herald* wrote.[9]

Corbett had planned to bring Gee along slowly, perhaps waiting until 1938 to unveil him. Initially, Gee was placed on the ineligible list, but he showed so much in practice that manager Mike Kelly insisted he be placed on the active roster. Gee pitched well in two relief appearances, and then made a big impact with a complete-game, 4-2 exhibition win on July 13 over Cincinnati, the Chiefs' major-league parent club. Gee finished with a 4-3 record and a fine 2.90 ERA. He appeared in 16 games, starting seven.

Gee was the Opening Day starter for the Chiefs in 1938—the first Syracuse native to have that honor. He pitched a complete game to defeat Montreal 3-1 before a large, adoring crowd. He finished the season with a 17-11 record in 30 starts. His 2.71 ERA was second in the league.

Gee started fast in 1939. His record was 16-4 on August 1 when he was purchased by Pittsburgh in the blockbuster $75,000 deal, effective at the end of the International League season. He finished with a 20-10 record and a 3.11 ERA. He made his first start for the Pirates on September 17, losing to the Phillies 7-3 as his new teammates made eight errors. Gee gave up

only six hits in eight innings, and no earned runs. His first taste of major-league baseball was encouraging—he started three games, completed one, and ended up with a 1-2 record and a 4.12 ERA.

Thus, the offseason was full of hope and promise. Gee took a trip back to Ann Arbor to watch a football game, and then returned to Syracuse to prepare to coach and play basketball in a city league. He was a popular guest on radio shows and Hot Stove League dinners. "Just before he headed west with the Pirates," Charles J. Doyle of the *Pittsburgh Sun-Telegraph* wrote in *The Sporting News*, "Johnny attended the annual 'Sports Roundup' of the Pittsburgh baseball writers and made a fine impression. The 6-foot-9 Hercules has unusual grace and poise and inasmuch as he is a graduate of the University of Michigan, he knows the answers to a lot of questions not connected with baseball."[10]

Sadly, Gee did not throw a pitch in a regular season game in 1940. He came down with a sore arm shortly after arriving in the Pirates' training camp in San Bernardino, California. Gee failed to last an inning in his first start, on March 17, and his arm was still a concern as the team broke camp for a series of exhibitions on the way back to Pittsburgh. He was wild in a game against the White Sox in Lubbock, Texas, on April 4, and didn't make it out of the second inning in a start against Evansville of the Class B Three-I League on April 14. A St. Louis specialist said that Gee was suffering from neuritis, and recommended that he rest his arm for a week.[11]

Pittsburgh optioned Gee to Syracuse on May 9. He worked out for several weeks, but did not appear in a game, and the Chiefs canceled his option and sent him back to Pittsburgh. The Pirates then optioned him to Albany of the Class A Eastern League. Gee refused to report, stating that his arm was in no shape to pitch. He left Syracuse to work out with Ray Fisher at his former coach's summer camp in Vermont.[12]

Pittsburgh placed Gee on its 1941 spring-training roster and hoped for the best. Gee had been a durable pitcher and there apparently had been no warning signs about his arm in college or the minors. He had pitched 226 innings with Syracuse in 1938, and 240 innings in 1939, plus 19⅔ innings with the Pirates. Charles Doyle expressed the opinion of many—that the highly publicized rookie tried too hard in spring training to justify the big $75,000 price tag: "Against definite orders, issued by [Pittsburgh manager Frankie] Frisch, that no pitcher throw a curve-ball in the first workout of the season, the highly publicized southpaw proceeded to put his hook on display in San Berdoo and for weeks was well-nigh helpless."[13] Gee later admitted his mistake in a 1944 Associated Press story filed from the Pirates' spring-training camp in Muncie, Indiana. "I guess I just threw too hard too soon, that's all," he recalled.[14]

Pittsburgh sent Gee to training camp ten days early in 1941 to work with a Los Angeles specialist, and he had earlier spent time working out indoors at Ann Arbor with Fisher. Gee said his arm was responding to his former coach's workouts. "I'm placing myself entirely under Fisher's directions," Gee said. "He'll do the pacing and I'll do the pitching. He taught me all I know and he's the one who can straighten me out."[15]

But the 1941 season was another disaster. Gee had a few good outings in spring training, but Frisch farmed him out to Portland of the Pacific Coast League, figuring he would benefit from more regular work than he would get with the Pirates. He pitched in only two games for Portland before being optioned to Dallas of the Texas League. Pittsburgh hoped the hot weather would be good for his arm, but Gee refused to report, citing a contract dispute, and Charles Doyle lamented that the Pirates were having more "Gee trouble."[16] Gee spent some more time working out with Fisher in Ann Arbor, and then agreed to report to Albany. He did not appear in a game there, but was one of four players called up to Pittsburgh in early September. Gee lasted only 1⅓ innings in his first start, and finished with 7⅓ innings in three appearances and a 6.14 ERA.

Major-league teams were starting to lose players to the military draft, making Gee particularly appealing, since men 6-feet-6 or taller were classified 4-F. Nevertheless, Pittsburgh optioned him to Toronto of the International League on February 18, 1942. They hoped he would benefit from the teaching of manager (and future Hall of Fame pitcher) Burleigh Grimes. It looked as though that might work, as a sportswriter observed: "Johnny Gee broke into the victory column

with a win over his home town Syracuse Chiefs. Under Grimes' handling, the big fellow appears to be on the way to pitching greatness."[17]

The apparent improvement was short-lived. After five games Gee was 2-2, but had given up 24 runs in 34 innings pitched. Grimes gave up on Gee, and Pittsburgh optioned him to Atlanta of the Southern Association, once again hoping a steady diet of hot weather would help their ailing pitcher. Gee decided not to report and asked to be placed on the voluntarily retired list. He signed to teach and coach at Adams (New York) High School, and on August 30 married Suzanne Corl of Maumee, Ohio. They'd met while attending the University of Michigan.

But Gee wasn't done with baseball just yet. He tested his arm early in 1943 by pitching batting practice for the Toronto and Syracuse International League teams, and petitioned Pittsburgh president Bill Benswanger for a tryout. Gee looked good in batting practice trials and the team reinstated him to its roster once again.[18] He lasted only 2⅔ innings in his first start, on July 3, and was pummeled for 11 runs in 2⅔ innings by the Dodgers in his next start, but then shut out the Phillies in a seven-inning relief appearance on July 23 to earn his first major-league victory since 1939. Gee followed with complete-game victories over the Giants and Braves, but lost his last three starts to finish at 4-4, with a 4.28 ERA and 82 innings pitched in a half-season of work.

Gee and the Pirates had high hopes heading into 1944. He reported to camp late because of teaching responsibilities, but Charles Doyle reported that "Johnny Gee looks more formidable right now than at any time in his unfortunate career."[19] The old sore arm problem came back again, though, and Gee was unable to make his scheduled start for the second game of the season in St. Louis. He appeared in only four games through the end of May and the Pirates finally gave up on him. They sold Gee to the New York Giants for the $7,500 waiver price on June 12.[20] Gee worked in only four games for the Giants, for a total of five innings.

The 1945 season was even worse—Gee pitched two innings in April and one in May, and asked to be placed once again on the voluntarily retired list. He signed a contract to teach and coach at Waterloo (New York) High School.

When the weather warmed up in 1946, Gee tested his arm and it felt pretty good. He pitched a few games for a semipro team in Palmyra, a short drive from Waterloo, and decided to give Giants manager Mel Ott a call to request another tryout. Gee offered to join the team after the school year, and Ott told him a spot would be open on the roster whenever he was ready. "Gee was given complete charge of his own training," *Syracuse Herald-Journal* sports editor Lawrence J. Skiddy wrote. "He worked himself into shape, told Ott when he was ready, and really went to town."[21] Gee pitched two shutout innings of relief against his old Pittsburgh mates in his first appearance, on July 17. Then he started and pitched 8⅔ innings to beat Cincinnati 2-1 on July 21, and followed that up on July 26 with a complete-game 3-2 win over the Reds.

The tallest pitcher in major-league history couldn't expect to escape the size-oriented nicknames he'd been tagged with, but it finally looked as though, after battling his sore arm for six years, he might erase some of the crueler ones, such as "the $75,000 lemon." But it was not to be. Gee lost his next four starts, and was relegated to the bullpen. He finished the season with a 2-4 record and a 3.99 ERA in 47⅓ innings. He did not pitch in the major leagues again.

Gee returned to Waterloo after the baseball season to resume his teaching career. He signed to play with the 1946-47 Syracuse Nationals of the National Basketball League on a part-time basis, depending on his teaching schedule. He played in 24 of the team's 44 league games, but turned down a chance to play the next season when the team insisted he become a full-time player.

There were rumors, especially in the New York press, that Gee planned to return to the Giants in 1947. One article stated that he would report after the Waterloo High School basketball season was finished.[22] Gee talked to the team, but the two sides could not reach satisfactory terms. He did his pitching the next four years for the semipro Homer (New York) Braves of the Southern Tier League.

Gee returned to organized baseball—controversially, as it turned out—on September 10, 1949, pitching a 3-0 shutout for Geneva against Ogdensburg in the first round of the Class C Border League playoffs.[23] Geneva, the league pennant winner, had signed Gee in August, with the understanding he would report after the completion of Homer's season. He did not pitch a game in the regular season, but led Geneva to the postseason championship with four of the team's eight victories. Geneva had not violated league rules, but Gee's success caused the league to change playoff eligibility requirements before the next season.[24]

Gee played for Homer again in 1950, and then in 1951 returned to the Border League to pitch for Auburn (New York). He stipulated that he would pitch only in home games and in nearby Geneva until the end of the Waterloo school year. It was a troubled year financially for the league, and it disbanded on July 16. Gee finished the shortened season with a 4-2 record and an ERA of 2.49, and quickly found another pitching job with a semipro team in Blacks Harbor, New Brunswick. He brought his family along for an extended vacation.[25]

The family enjoyed a two-month stay at a cabin on Swan Lake in Minnesota in 1952, courtesy of the Fergus Falls Red Sox of the fast semipro West Central Minnesota League. Gee and his family arrived in Fergus Falls just in time for him to pitch a game on July 3. The *Fergus Falls Daily Journal* described his arrival: "Johnny Gee untangled his huge frame … from beneath the steering wheel of his car Thursday evening as he finished the long driving grind from New York state. … It was no easy task for the big lefthander who became stiff and tired from his long journey with his wife and four youngsters, but the former Pittsburgh Pirate chucker wouldn't let the crowd down who came to see him pitch and defeat the Willmar Rails."[26]

Gee's son, John A. Gee, III, remembered a wonderful summer in Fergus Falls. He even enjoyed the nearly 1,300-mile drive, especially the red skies from steel mills in Gary, Indiana, and the restaurant in Eau Claire, Wisconsin, where his parents danced. He remembered beavers in Swan Lake and the time he fell into the Mississippi River. (Of course it was at the source of the river in Lake Itasca, where it is only a shallow stream.)

Young Gee got to play on a peewee baseball team coached by two Fergus Falls players from the University of Southern California, Lou Bishara and Don Herman. "I had a Beaver Cleaver childhood," he said, "based around baseball."[27]

Gee's record was 4-5 at Fergus Falls. He threw seven complete games in ten starts and struck out 80 hitters in 77⅔ innings. Complete ERA records are not available, but if the 30 runs he gave up were all earned, his ERA would have been 3.50.

What had happened to Gee's sore arm? We may never know for sure. It's possible he learned to pace himself, something he did not or could not do in the major leagues, where competition was stronger. It's also possible he figured out how to avoid the muscular stress that caused the sore arm. Harley Oyloe, a Fergus Falls resident and the team's other starting pitcher, said, "Gee threw pretty hard, and had a good curveball. He was a good pitcher and teammate, and I never heard him complain about his arm."[28]

Gee pitched for Homer again in 1953 because his wife was pregnant and the family wanted to stay close to home. They baseball-vacationed for the last time in 1954 when Gee pitched for a Truro, Nova Scotia, semipro team. It was the last time because Gee was made principal at Waterloo High School in 1955, a job that was a year-round assignment.

Gee received a master's degree in education from Syracuse University in 1956, moved to Cortland, New York, in 1960 and was principal there until he retired in 1977. He was one of the area's top football, basketball, and baseball game officials, and an inspiration for a generation of students. He could often be found at Syracuse Chiefs games. In 2014 Ron Gersbacher, the Chiefs' president, said, "Johnny Gee was known as a truly great professional and showed all of us that being an athlete is not enough. You must back it up with education."[29] Gee was posthumously inducted into the Greater Syracuse Sports Hall of Fame on October 26, 1998, and to the Syracuse Baseball Wall of Fame on July 28, 2001.

Perhaps the award that would have pleased Gee the most took place on August 3, 2013, when the Cortland High School Class of 1968 honored him with a plaque

and dedication ceremony to christen the John A. Gee Main Office. "We thought it would be very fitting," said John Woodward, a member of the class who helped plan the dedication. "Our class fared well under his stewardship and we thought a lot of him. We all looked up to him."[30] Gee was also remembered as a stern disciplinarian who could easily silence an uncouth cheering section with his intimidating stature. "If he saw that raucous behavior, all he had to do was look up at the student section with his hands on his hips and it was done," [Bill] Kulikowsky said. "No more booing."[31]

Gee died on January 23, 1988, in Cortland. He and his wife, Suzanne, raised five children: Corlann (born 1943), John A. Gee, III (1946), Nancy (1947), Katherine (1950), and Thomas (1953). All five have college degrees.

SOURCES

Ann Arbor Daily News

Cortland Standard

Fergus Falls Daily Journal

Michigan Alumnus

New York Times

Saskatoon Star-Phoenix

Syracuse Herald

Syracuse Post-Standard

The Sporting News

Watertown (New York) *Daily News*

2014 University of Michigan Baseball Record Book, mgoblue.com/sports/m-basebl/mich-m-basebl-body.html. Last date accessed: February 3, 2014.

2014 University of Michigan Basketball Record Book, mgoblue.com/sports/m-baskbl/mich-m-baskbl-body.html. Last date accessed: November 30, 2013.

baseball-reference.com/

retrosheet.org/

Interviews:

John A. Gee, III

Ron Gersbacher, Syracuse Chiefs president

Jeffrey Morey, SABR member, Cliff Kachline and Luke Easter Chapters

Harley Oyloe, 1952 Fergus Falls Red Sox pitcher

Research assistance:

Debbie Gallagher, Ann Arbor District Library

Sarah Kozma, Onondaga Historical Association

Holly Sammons, Onondaga County Public Library

NOTES

1 "Double-Duty Hurlers from Double A … Which Will Survive Major Test?" *The Sporting News*, September 21, 1939, 1; "Mack Pays $106,000 for Lefty Groves [sic]," *New York Times*, October 11, 1924, 10.

2 "Standing Tall on Hill," *The Sporting News*, October 3, 1988, 20.

3 Gerald Ashe, "Syracuse to Tackle Wolverines Tomorrow," *Syracuse Post-Standard*, January 1, 1935, 16. Many news articles reported incorrectly, even in Syracuse, that Gee was a high-school basketball star, but no mention of his name can be found in stories or box scores of Central High School games while he was a student there.

4 "Gee Opposes Tracy Jones At Onondaga," *Syracuse Herald*, July 24, 1936, 19.

5 John A. Gee, III, telephone interview, January 16, 2014.

6 "Varsity Five Meets Calvin," *Ann Arbor Daily News*, December 1, 1934, 9.

7 Art Carstens, "Star Dust" column, from an unidentified news clipping in a Gee family scrapbook. The information in the article places it between November 24 and December 1, 1934.

8 *Michigan Alumnus*, October 21, 1939, 67.

9 "Baseball Men Whisper That Corbett and Chiefs Have Found the 'Talent Tree' and Will Enjoy Crop of Gold," *Syracuse Herald*, July 25, 1937, 3B.

10 Charles J. Doyle, "Harnessing-Up Time Finds Frisch Frisky," *The Sporting News*, February 29, 1940, 7.

11 Charles J. Doyle, "Later Opening Date Gains Favor in Pitt," *The Sporting News*, April 25, 1940, 1.

12 Jack Durkin, "Gee, Refusing to Join Albany, Asserts $75,000 Arm Is Unfit," *The Sporting News*, July 25, 1940, 5.

13 Charles J. Doyle, "Pair of Big Hurlers Frisch's Biggest 'If,'" *The Sporting News*, December, 26, 1940, 5.

14 "Pitcher John Gee Now Appears Ready," *Saskatoon Star-Phoenix*, March 25, 1944, 13.

15 "Gee's Pitching Arm Has Lost Soreness," *New York Times*, January 21, 1941, 25.

16 Charles J. Doyle, "Injuries Add Grief to Pirate Defeats," *The Sporting News*, May 29, 1941, 3.

17 Bunny Morganson, "Leafs Bud Into Threat By Surge On Home Soil," *The Sporting News*, May 21, 1942, 11.

18 "Landis Reinstates Pitcher Gee," *New York Times*, June 22, 1943.

19 Charles J. Doyle, "Handley Still Lacks Arm of Perfect Picket," *The Sporting News*," March 30, 1944, 17.

20 "Major League Flashes," *The Sporting News*, June 15, 1944, 14.

21 Lawrence J. Skiddy, "Tommy Dugan Puts Official O.K. on Gee," *Syracuse Herald-Journal*, July 30, 1946, 18.

22 James P. Dawson, "Ott Lures Jansen into Giants' Fold," *New York Times*, March 3, 1947, 30.

23 Nat Boynton, "Gee Marks Return to O. B. With Shutout for Geneva," *The Sporting News*, September 21, 1949, 41.

24 "Border League Changes Rules," *Watertown Daily Times*, January 23, 1950, 18.

25 John A. Gee, III, telephone interview, January 16, 2014.

26 "Fergus Red Sox Beat Willmar, 6-5," *Fergus Falls Daily Journal*, July 5, 1952, 6.

27 John A. Gee, III, telephone interview, January 16, 2014.

28 Harley Oyloe, telephone interview, January 4, 2014.

29 Ron Gersbacher, email interview, February 15, 2014.

30 Matt Leader, "Bighearted Principal Honored," *Cortland Standard*, July 31, 2013.

31 Ibid.

Eddie Joost

By Bill Nowlin

ONE THING ABOUT EDDIE JOOST — HE learned how to work a walk. A lifetime .239 hitter over the course of 17 major-league seasons, Joost drew more than 1,000 bases on balls — enough to give him a very good on-base percentage of .361. He hit safely 1,339 times, but reached base via the walk or hit-by-pitch 1,076 times.

He was a two-time All-Star and earned some distinction as the last manager in Philadelphia Athletics history, and only the third one the team had in its 54 years before the franchise moved west to Kansas City.

Joost was born to Emma C. Joost and her husband, Henry, an auto mechanic, on June 5, 1916, in San Francisco. He was the second of five children born to the couple. Emma's parents were both native Californians; Henry's both came from Germany. Henry Joost had played some semipro baseball.[1] His son Edwin David Joost considered himself of German/Dutch ancestry.

Life in the days of the Depression was not easy. "My family wasn't destitute," Joost said, "but it was close to it."[2]

Eddie attended Bryant Elementary School and Horace Mann Junior High, and then graduated from Mission High School, all in San Francisco. He started playing professional baseball early, signing with the Mission Reds of the Pacific Coast League at the age of 16, while still in high school, for $150 a month.[3] The team played at Seals Stadium in San Francisco and Eddie's first season was in 1933 under manager Fred Hofmann. He played as a shortstop, appeared in 25 games, and hit .250. He played with the Mission Reds for four seasons, through 1936 and was the team's principal third baseman in 1935 and 1936, batting .287 and .286 respectively under managers Gabby Street and Willie Kamm.

Joost's contract was sold to the Cincinnati Reds near the end of the 1936 season, and he was a September call-up to the majors. He got into 13 games for manager Chuck Dressen, going 4-for-26 with just one run batted in and one extra-base hit, a double. Nonetheless, he'd gotten his feet wet.

Dressen wasn't all that impressed. Joost later recalled his manager telling him, "What I have seen of you, you will not be a major-league player. ... If we keep you, you'll be a utility player."[4] Joost played for Cincinnati's Syracuse Chiefs affiliate in the International League in 1937, hitting .269 in what was then Double-A ball, and then coming back to the majors (and going 1-for-12) in September.

On October 16, 1937, Eddie married Alice Bernard; the two had met in high school. They had the first of their five sons in September 1939, but lost Edwin Jr. to leukemia in November 1941. The four younger Joosts were David, Dennis, Donald, and Dean.

In 1938 Joost played for the Kansas City Blues, the New York Yankees' farm team in the American Association. He hit .289 for them, with five homers. Though runners-up in the American Association, the Blues beat the Newark Bears and won the Junior World Series in seven games.

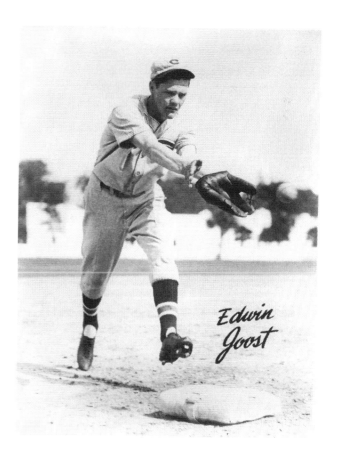

Edwin Joost

From 1939 through 1943, Joost was back in the majors, and with the Reds for the first four of those years, all under Bill McKechnie. He began as a utility infielder. Joost had never been on a pennant-winning team in the minors (though winning the Junior World Series was at least as good), but won back-to-back pennants with Cincinnati in 1939 and 1940, the Reds' world championship season. He appeared in only 42 games in '39 (batting .252), but he played in 88 games in '40, batting .216 while drawing enough walks to bump his on-base percentage up to just over .300. He had a very good .960 fielding percentage. He hit the first of his 134 major-league home runs on June 17, 1940, off Boom-Boom Beck of the Phillies. Following tradition, his teammates pointedly ignored the homer, so when Joost got back on the bench, he loudly applauded for himself.

Joost didn't play in the 1939 World Series, as the Reds were swept by the Yankees. In 1940 he played in all seven games as the team's second baseman. It was his only postseason action. He was 5-for-25 with two RBIs, knocking in the first Reds run in Game Two, a 5-3 victory. The Reds went on to beat the Tigers.

Joost got the opportunity only because an accident had befallen the Reds' regular second baseman, Lonny Frey. A couple of days before the Series, Frey had stopped to get a drink from the dugout water cooler and the heavy iron cover fell on his foot and broke some of his toes. Joost acquitted himself well and in December McKechnie said, "Whoever plays shortstop for the Reds next year will have to beat out Eddie Joost."[5]

When McKechnie greeted Joost the following spring, he congratulated him again on the World Series win. Joost shot back, "If you had played me in the 1939 Series we would have won that one, too." Joost later admitted it wasn't the most tactful thing to say. "Not a great start for the '41 season."[6]

Joost had what was described as "a prickly personality, an aggressive style and strong opinions that often didn't sit too well with the martinets who ran big-league teams at the time."[7] He clashed more than once with McKechnie and, later, Casey Stengel. Though he allowed that McKechnie was "a good manager," he also said that "occasionally he was wrong and sometimes I would tell him that. The next thing you know he and

I just didn't get along." It may have factored into his later trade to the Boston Braves.[8] McKechnie, for his part, seemed to have warm enough feelings for Joost.[9]

There had been some thought that Joost was too slight (he grew to 6-feet even and eventually added 15 pounds to fill out to 175 pounds) and lacked the stamina for regular play; he was sometimes called "The Thin Man." His minor-league record should have disproved that, but his work over the next couple of years finally put the notion to rest.

Joost played almost every game in both 1941 and 1942, batting .253 (.340 OBP) and .224 (.307). He tied a major-league record in the May 7, 1941, game, successfully handling 19 chances at shortstop (he also made an error). The team finished in third place, then fourth place, and in December 1942 ("not a year to brag about") the club traded Joost and pitcher Nate Andrews (and $25,000) to the Braves to acquire shortstop Eddie Miller, who was coming off three All-Star seasons and would go on to four more. Boston sportswriter Al Hirshberg wrote that Alice Joost had wanted to leave Cincinnati, that she couldn't bear to return after the loss of their child there.[10] McKechnie was said to understand and helped facilitate the change of scenery.[11]

Joost was a "sparkplug" early in the season, bringing some fresh competitive fire to the Braves, but cooled off soon. He played in 124 games for the Braves, but hit only .185—though his 68 bases on balls lifted his OBP to .299. An August article in the *Christian Science Monitor* talked about a real change of demeanor in Joost during the season.[12] Manager Casey Stengel seemed to very much rub him the wrong way.

Joost missed all of 1944 due to World War II, although he didn't serve in the war. Though initially rejected by the Army, he passed the second time around and was told by the draft board that he had to do defense work in a meat-packing plant as part of the war effort, or be inducted. One sportswriter characterized the work as "heaving hams in a San Francisco slaughterhouse."[13] He played some industrial league ball on Sundays.

Joost did not get along with Stengel and later called him "one of the worst managers in baseball at the time."[14] When Stengel was giving a talk before a game,

Joost admitted, he would turn his chair away from his manager and read a newspaper. In turn, there was at least one time that Stengel changed the signs for his third-base coach but pointedly told the coach not to let Joost know they had changed.[15] Joost acknowledged that he didn't play well at all for the Braves.

Joost excelled in spring training and played for the Braves again in 1945, hitting .248 through July 19. But on that date he suffered a broken wrist when Billy Jurges slid into third base, kicked at his glove, and hit his wrist instead. He thought he had permission to return home after the injury but may have left the Braves without the proper formalities, and he was declared AWOL and suspended on August 22. "Not a good year. Enough said."

Commissioner Happy Chandler got involved in the dispute regarding Joost's departure from the Braves, and in February 1946 Boston made a deal with the St. Louis Cardinals for Johnny Hopp, giving Joost his outright release to Rochester, the Triple-A International League club of the Cardinals, and sending St. Louis $40,000. Joost initially said he would not report. There had been four clubs that claimed him when the Braves placed him on waivers, and he thought he could still play major-league ball.[16] In the end, Joost did report and had a very good year. He hit 19 homers—more than all his prior years in the minors combined—and batted .276, driving in 101 runs.

The Philadelphia Athletics were interested—the only team that was - and invested $10,000 (and three players) to purchase Joost's contract at the end of September. Connie Mack reportedly told him, "I've heard good reports and bad reports about you, young man. I believe the good ones."[17] One of the bad stories was detailed in *The Sporting News*, something of a guilt-by-association incident that led many in baseball to think Joost had a problem with alcohol. "I'm a high-strung sort of guy," Joost said, "and beer relieves the tension. But I never was drunk in my life."[18]

Joost said that Mack "was a great man, a great person. I don't think in the eight years I was with the A's I ever heard him say an unkind word to anyone."[19]

It proved a good investment for Philadelphia, though Joost's first year with the A's, 1947, was not that suc-

cessful; he struck out a league-leading 110 times and batted only .206. "I had astigmatism," Joost said in 1994, "but I didn't want Mr. Mack to know it because only [one big-league player] wore glasses. But it got worse. … I finally got up the nerve to tell Mr. Mack that I'd probably have to wear glasses."[20] He did, for the rest of his career, and his average jumped back up to .250 (.393 OBP) the following year.

Joost did have his home-run stroke going, though, with 13 in 1947—and his 24 sacrifice hits led the league. It was more than double the number of successful sacrifices in any other year; perhaps he felt more comfortable putting down bunts than swinging away.

Joost spent eight seasons in Philadelphia and was the team's starting shortstop for the first six of those years, 1947 through 1952. He was solid in the field, and during one stretch from late 1947 into June 1948, he played 42 straight error-free games at shortstop, and handled 225 consecutive errorless chances, both records at the time. At least one publication called him a "pepperpot with specs."[21] Shirley Povich of the *Washington Post* wrote that Joost "has been the making of the A's infield."[22]

Joost hit .249 over his eight Athletics seasons but was so patient at the plate that he recorded an on-base percentage of .392. He drew an average of 118 walks per season in the six full seasons he played for the A's. Twice he scored over 100 runs and twice he was in the 90s. His best season was probably 1949, when he hit .263 and got on base at a .429 pace. He drove in a career-high 81 runs (from the leadoff spot) and scored a career-high 128 runs. He was named to the All-Star squad and came in 13th in MVP voting. He and second baseman Pete Suder helped the team turn a record 217 double plays.

In the 1949 All-Star Game, Joost singled to drive in two runs and help the American League win, 11-7. He called it "the greatest single I ever hit in my life. I was so proud to be in the game."[23]

Joost had picked up some power, too, after the wartime work in the meat-packing plant and his year in Rochester. He averaged just over 18 home runs a year in his first six seasons with the Athletics, with a career-high 23 homers in 1949, starting with a home run to help win the home opener. He hit two homers on his birthday, June 5—"the first man ever to bash two homers off the distant left-field [Cleveland Stadium] girders in one game."[24] He'd actually hit one in each game of a doubleheader, against two future Hall of Famers, Bob Feller and Satchel Paige. The homers came early in the year—15 by mid-June. From July 26 on, he hit only two, both in September. Joost's fielding was fairly consistent from year to year, and he wound up with a .956 career fielding percentage.

"During the late 1940s," the *Philadelphia Inquirer* wrote, "Mr. Joost helped the A's achieve one last run of respectability in Philadelphia." After finishing last nine times between 1935 and 1946, they reached the first division—fourth place—in 1948 and 1952, and set an all-time attendance mark in 1947 and then again in 1948. Joost "nearly saved the Philadelphia A's as their spark-plug shortstop," wrote the *Inquirer* in its obituary.[25] He was a fan favorite; a late-season poll of *Philadelphia Bulletin* readers ranked him as the Athletics' most valuable player.[26] Three days later, Joost had five consecutive hits and scored four runs in a 12-2 win over the St. Louis Browns.

Joost's desire to get into games was exemplified in August 1948 when he suffered a jammed thumb and missed a week of games. He was hospitalized for treatment, but worked out an arrangement that allowed him to check out long enough to play in home games but then return to the hospital overnight for further treatment.[27] It was a couple of weeks later that an amusing incident occurred. Billy Goodman of the Red Sox hit a ball to Joost at shortstop—and the ball disappeared. He looked around for it in vain, and then undid his shirt—the ball had rolled up his arm and entered his sleeve and fallen inside his jersey.

In five seasons from 1947 through 1952, excepting only 1950, Joost placed in the top 15 in the voting for American League MVP. Though he never ranked higher than tenth place (1948), his vote totals nonetheless constituted recognition of his excellence. His best day overall was likely June 16, 1951, when he broke out of an 0-for-16 slump and hit two home runs and a game-winning 11th-inning triple. It wasn't uncommon for people to compare his play with that of Phil Rizzuto. And Casey Stengel, Rizzuto's manager with the Yankees,

"pointed to a slim, bespectacled guy who looks more like an accountant than a shortstop and commented, 'There, fellows, is a mighty fine ballplayer.'"[28]

Joost had an appendectomy in February 1953. A serious injury to his right knee brought his 1953 season to an end after the game on June 19. (He hurt the same knee in an automobile crash the following January.) He appeared in only 51 games in 1953, batting .249. In one of those games, on May 10 against the Washington Senators, his was the only base hit of the game for the Athletics. It was—bizarrely—the third time he had deprived Bob Porterfield of a no-hitter, each time the base hit coming in the seventh inning.

Joost didn't play as much in 1954 (19 scattered games, but with a .362 batting average when he did appear) because in November 1953 he was named manager of the team. Connie Mack had managed through 1950 (he'd managed the team since 1901), and Jimmie Dykes from 1951-53. The team apparently did not think "a manager should play 18 holes of golf every day and come into the clubhouse all tired out. We needed a change, some younger blood at the helm."[29] Dykes finished in seventh place in 1953, with 95 losses. Joost had been expected to be a playing manager but the car crash in January left him feeling he'd do better to stick to managing.

Joost hadn't wanted to be manager, Dick Rosen told the *Philadelphia Daily News*. "Rosen said he was told by Spook Jacobs, who played for the Athletics in the mid-1950s, that Joost was named manager because the Athletics simply took the highest-paid player and promoted him to save money. 'They gave him added duties without giving him added salary. They were financially down. ... He didn't want to be the manager, he had to be the manager."[30] His salary that year was the most he ever earned, $30,000.[31] One of his coaches was former Negro League star Judy Johnson, the first African American coach in major-league history. Unfortunately, the Athletics lost 103 games and ended up in last place.

In 1955 the franchise moved to Kansas City and Lou Boudreau became the manager. Joost was not part of the sale and was released in November 1954 by the relocated and renamed team. He tried out with

Cleveland during spring training, and was offered a contract but he had kept in touch with old friend Joe Cronin, the GM of the Boston Red Sox. At the end of March 1955, the Red Sox signed Joost to fill in for the injured Milt Bolling. He played well in spring training, hitting .340, and made the team, but it was an engagement that lasted just the one season; he was released on October 3. He suffered two broken bones when he was hit on the left hand in late April and lost playing time. He played shortstop and second base, appearing in 55 games over the course of the year, batting .193 and yet again reaching base nearly 30 percent of the time (.299 OBP). It was his last season in the majors.

In December Cronin asked Joost (both of them native San Franciscans) to manage and play for the Red Sox-affiliated San Francisco Seals in 1956. He was managing a few years after the immensely popular Lefty O'Doul and those were hard shoes to fill. Joost played in only six games, and the team underperformed in the early going. On June 9 he was replaced by Joe Gordon. It was his final year as either player or manager in Organized Baseball.

Though he'd said he wanted to stay in the game, Joost did not. Instead he took up work as an automobile salesman in San Francisco, and later opened a sportswear shop in nearby Burlingame. In 1961 he told an inquiring reporter that he'd go right back to work in baseball if someone were to call and offer him another opportunity to manage.[32]

Eddie's son Dean Joost played three years of minor-league ball in the Athletics, Angels, and Indians systems, from 1970-72, never rising about Single-A. He was a third baseman who played a few games in the outfield.

Joost remained very popular with A's fans from Philly days and attended Philadelphia Athletics Historical Society events as late as 2009.

Joost died during his sleep on April 12, 2011, in Shingle Springs, near Fair Oaks, California, at the age of 94.

SOURCES

In addition to the sources noted in this biography, the author also accessed Joost's player file and player questionnaire from the National Baseball Hall of Fame, the *Encyclopedia of Minor League Baseball*, Retrosheet.org, and Baseball-Reference.com.

NOTES

1   Philadelphia Athletics 1948 press release in Joost's Hall of Fame player file. See also *The Sporting News*, June 22, 1949. Henry Joost had been a catcher.

2   Eric Ahlqvist, "Joost still has lots of juice," *Cooperstown Crier*, August 14, 2008.

3   *San Francisco Examiner*, February 24, 1991.

4   Handwritten notes by Eddie Joost in his player file at the National Baseball Hall of Fame, and Rich Marazzi, "Joost spins a tale of two careers," *Sports Collectors Digest*, July 2, 1999.

5   Cincinnati Reds press release, December 1940, from Joost's Hall of Fame player file.

6   Joost's handwritten notes in his player file. A couple of the brief quotations that follow are Joost's, from these notes.

7   *San Francisco Examiner*, February 24, 1991.

8   *Sports Collectors Digest*, July 2, 1999.

9   *Christian Science Monitor*, August 9, 1943.

10 Unidentified article in Joost's Hall of Fame player file.

11 *Hartford Courant*, December 9, 1942.

12 *Christian Science Monitor*, August 9, 1943.

13 Roger Birtwell in the *Boston Globe*, April 6, 1945.

14 Ibid.

15 *Cooperstown Crier*, August 14, 2008.

16 *Los Angeles Times*, February 7, 1946.

17 *San Francisco Examiner*, February 24, 1991.

18 *The Sporting News*, May 26, 1948.

19 Ibid.

20 *Philadelphia Inquirer*, April 14, 2011.

21 Unidentified article in Joost's Hall of Fame player file.

22 Shirley Povich, *Washington Post*, May 7, 1948.

23 *Sports Collectors Digest*, July 2, 1999.

24 *The Sporting News*, June 22, 1949.

25 *Philadelphia Inquirer*, April 14, 2011.

26 As reported by the Associated Press on September 11, 1948.

27 *New York Times*, August 20, 1948.

28 *Hartford Courant*, August 16, 1951.

29 *The Sporting News*, November 11, 1953.

30 *Philadelphia Daily News*, April 14, 2011.

31 *San Francisco Examiner*, February 24, 1991.

32 *Hartford Courant*, June 13, 1961.

Johnny Pesky

By Bill Nowlin

JOHNNY PESKY'S CAREER GOT OFF TO
an unparalleled start, and could have propelled him
into the Hall of Fame had World War II not pulled
three prime years out. Pesky set a rookie record with
205 hits his freshman year (1942) but then served in the
Navy for the next three years. When he came back, he
twice more produced over 200 hits, in the Red Sox
pennant-winning year of 1946 and in 1947. Had he
managed over 200 hits for each of his three missing
years, there is every possibility this lifetime .307 hitter
could have made the Hall.

Born John Michael Paveskovich in Portland, Oregon,
on February 27, 1919, Johnny Pesky (he changed his
name legally in 1947) was the son of Croatian immigrants. His father, Jakov, never did really understand
baseball, but he and Johnny's mother, Marija, were both
supportive of their middle of three sons when he took
to hanging around the Portland Beavers ballpark, a few
blocks from the family home. Johnny was just one of
the kids around the park, but groundskeeper Rocky
Benevento invited him in and put him to work. Before
too long, Johnny was one of the visitors' clubhouse
kids—and clearly recalled hanging up the laundry of
Pacific Coast League players only a year or two older
than himself—players with names like Ted
Williams and Bobby Doerr.

Johnny had an older brother, Anthony,
a younger brother, Vincent—who spent a
little bit of time in the New York Yankees'
system—and three sisters: Anica (Ann),
Milica (Millie), and Danica (Dee). Jakov
worked in the sawmills until asthma forced
him to retire. The older children took jobs;
Vincent was the youngest and Johnny next-
to-youngest. There was enough money
coming in that it freed up the two boys to
play some baseball.

From an early age, Johnny was doing
everything he could to better himself at
baseball. The young middle infielder also
played American Legion ball, and on a

number of city teams in Portland, as well as on some
semipro teams. Before he graduated from Lincoln High
School in Portland, he spent the summer of 1937 with
the Bend Elks in the town of Bend, Oregon, and led
the league with a .543 batting average. The team won
the state league title. The summers of 1938 and 1939
were spent with the Silverton Red Sox. Both the Bend
and Silverton teams were summer-league teams associated with local timber companies. Surprisingly, Boston
Red Sox owner Tom Yawkey owned the Silver Falls
Timber Company, so Johnny was actually with the Red
Sox (albeit the Silverton Red Sox) even before Boston's
scout Ernie Johnson signed him. Twice Pesky was part
of a Northwest team that went to the semipro tournament in Wichita and competed nationally. The Silverton
team won 34 games and lost two, and sometimes played
exhibition games against touring teams like the House
of David aggregation and the Negro League Kansas
City Monarchs.

Pesky was offered $2,500 as a bonus by the St. Louis
Cardinals, but signed with Boston for $500, because
Johnson had so impressed his parents. They felt he'd
look out for Johnny if he signed with the Red Sox.
Johnson had offered an additional $1,000 if Johnny

stayed in the organization for two years. His pay was $150 per month, and the Red Sox sent him the full thousand after just his first year.

Johnny's first year in pro ball, after signing with Boston, was 1940 in Rocky Mount, North Carolina, playing for the Rocky Mount Red Sox of the Piedmont League, under manager Heinie Manush, whom Johnny credited as a major influence. He hit a club-leading .325. He had 55 runs batted in but, ever the table-setter, scored 114 times. Pesky led the league with 187 hits and 16 triples. That .325 average placed him third in the league.

In 1941 Pesky progressed from Class B ball in Rocky Mount to Louisville, where he played for the Colonels, again hitting .325. Louisville was a Double-A team in the American Association, managed by Bill Burwell. Pesky hit for precisely the same average — .325, and once again led the league in hits, this time with 195. He won the MVP award in the American Association for 1941.

By year's end, Pesky was bound for Boston, offered $4,000 for his first year's salary. He joined the Sox for spring training just three months after the Japanese attack on Pearl Harbor. War loomed large over all of baseball, and during Pesky's rookie year; he spent three evenings a week beginning in May taking classes for the United States Navy, where he was in training to become a naval aviator, in the same program as teammate Ted Williams. Pesky won the shortstop spot in spring training and was assigned number 6. Despite the need to balance baseball with naval training, Johnny Pesky finished the season with a .331 batting average, second only to Williams (.356) in the American League. He led the league in sacrifice hits. There was no "rookie of the year" award yet. That same year, *The Sporting News* named Johnny the shortstop on its All Star Major League team. And he came in third in the MVP voting, behind Joe Gordon and Ted Williams.

Tom Yawkey had his own prize for Pesky. At season's end, there was a $5,000 bonus for the rookie shortstop — enough to buy his parents a home in Portland. Johnny Pesky never forgot Tom Yawkey's generosity at a time when Johnny was off to military service, perhaps never to return. Yawkey won fierce loyalty from many

of his players; with gestures like this, one can understand why.

World War II took three years out of Pesky's baseball career, but while in the Navy he met his future wife, Ruth Hickey. She was a WAVE whom Johnny met while serving as an operations officer in Atlanta. Ruthie and Johnny remained very happily married for more than 60 years. In 1953 they adopted a five-month-old son through Catholic Charities — David Pesky, who was born in December 1952. Like a lot of ballplayers, Johnny had many opportunities to play baseball during the war and even played in the AL vs. NL All-Star Game at Furlong Field, Honolulu, in 1945.

In 1946, the war over, Johnny and the Red Sox won the pennant, and took the fight right down to the ninth inning of the seventh game of the World Series against the St. Louis Cardinals. Johnny hit safely a league-leading 208 times that season, with a .335 average (third in the league), scoring 115 times (second behind Ted's 142.) The Series was a disappointing one for Pesky, as it was for two other players, named Musial (who batted .222 in Series play) and Williams (.200). And generations of baseball aficionados have heard that "Pesky held the ball" on a key play in the eighth inning of Game Seven, allowing Enos Slaughter to score the winning run from first base on Harry Walker's hit to left center. Cardinals 4, Red Sox 3. Films of the play do not show a clear hesitation, and perhaps sportswriter Bob Broeg was right in arguing that credit should go to Slaughter for his "mad dash" around the bases rather than blame being assigned Pesky for what was, at most, momentary surprise that Slaughter was streaking toward the plate rather than secure at third.

The following year, Pesky again collected his 200 hits (207 this time around) — the third year in a row he'd led the league. He and Dom DiMaggio were the table-setters for Ted Williams, and the speedy Pesky was usually discouraged from stretching a single into a double, because a double just meant the other team would walk Ted to fill the unoccupied sack at first. Pesky was a clever infielder as well; three times he pulled the rare hidden-ball trick, and would have done so a fourth time had the pitcher not stepped off the rubber at the wrong moment.

The Red Sox came within a game of winning the pennant in 1948 and 1949, and were only four games behind in 1950. These were some great Red Sox teams. Pesky's place, though, never seemed secure—a strange spot to be in for a top-ranking shortstop. When Johnny joined the team for spring training in '48, he was unsure where he'd be playing, since Boston had acquired Vern Stephens from the St. Louis Browns and it looked as if Billy Goodman—another infielder—would make the team. Stephens contributed 137 RBIs in '48; clearly manager Joe McCarthy's decision to play him proved wise. (Stephens led the league in RBIs in '49 and '50. Goodman stuck, and hit .310. In 1950 he won the AL batting title with a .354 average—with a bit of an assist from Pesky. Johnny approached 1950 manager Steve O'Neill late in the season and offered to take himself out of the lineup so that Goodman could accumulate the necessary at-bats to qualify.)

The problem was an embarrassment of riches. There were just too many good hitters on these Red Sox teams. Johnny Pesky's average fell off sharply in 1948, down to .281. Almost certainly part of the reason was that McCarthy slotted Stephens in at short, and shuffled Pesky over to third. He put a brave "team face" on it, but being asked to learn a new position was unsettling. So, too, was the pay cut Joe Cronin imposed on him after the 1947 season. All he'd done was led the league in hits for each of his first three years, but Cronin cut his $20,000 pay to $17,500 for 1948. "They asked me how many home runs I hit and how many runs I had knocked in," Johnny explained 50 years later. This was certainly a discouraging situation, and Pesky did pop a career-high three home runs in 1948. He may have been pressing more than a little.

The 1949 season saw a bit of a rebound, Pesky's average back up to .306 and, with an even 100 walks, an on-base percentage of .408. Johnny, always a team booster, allowed, "What a lucky guy I am. Instead of wearing these shoes, I'd probably be shining them for some other guy in the Coast League." There were endless rumors, though, about trades said to feature Pesky. From time to time, he admitted, these rumored trades proved distracting for him.

The 1950 season was a tremendous year offensively for Boston. Pesky hit .312, walked 104 times, and boosted his OBP to a solid .437. His fielding at third base drew frequent accolades in the Boston press. Scoring 112 runs, he joined teammate Ted Williams as the only other player to have scored 100 or more runs each of his first six seasons of major-league ball. This was the year Pesky, in effect, took himself out of the lineup so that Billy Goodman could have a shot at the batting title. *Boston Herald* sportswriter Bill Cunningham wrote, "The sporting part about his gesture is that he made it for the man who took the job away from him." Years later, in 1985, the *Lynn Sunday Post* editorialized that Johnny Pesky led the majors in "Most Friends."

By 1951, though, the bloom was off the rose, and when the Marines called Williams back in 1952 to fly combat in Korea, the golden days were gone. There were signs that Pesky was slowing a bit. He stole only two bases each in '50 and '51, down somewhat from earlier years. He maybe wasn't getting to as many balls as an infielder as he had earlier. Lou Boudreau had been brought in by Yawkey, and was projected as the shortstop. Even though Pesky's career .316 average at the time ranked him fifth among active players, here he was—once again—having to fight for a spot. Johnny got off to a slow start, but wound up the season at .313. Boudreau hit .267.

Johnny's 1952 season began poorly, and he was hardly ever used by Boudreau, now the manager and seeking a "youth movement" in Boston. Hampered by injuries, he was hitting a pitiful .149 when he was traded to the Tigers in a monster deal. Boston sent five players to Detroit, a full 20 percent of the 25-man roster. In exchange for Pesky, Walt Dropo, Fred Hatfield, Don Lenhardt, and Bill Wight, they got four Tigers (Hoot Evers, George Kell, Johnny Lipon, and Dizzy Trout). Johnny pulled it together a bit and hit .254 for Detroit. It truly was a subpar season.

Pesky cracked 300 at-bats in 1953, and hit .292 but he was in decline. After appearing in 20 games for the Tigers in '54, he was traded to Washington, where he finished his playing career with a .246 mark between the two teams.

Johnny Pesky wound up his major-league career with a .307 average, and an on-base percentage of .394.

His life in baseball, though, was just entering a new phase. Johnny coached with the Denver Bears in the Yankees organization in 1955, then managed five different minor-league teams for the Detroit Tigers from 1956 to 1960.

Most of Pesky's 60-plus years in baseball, however, were with the Red Sox. After his years managing for Detroit, the Red Sox called him back after the 1960 season. Johnny managed the Sox' Seattle minor-league team in 1961 and 1962, and managed the big-league Red Sox in '63 and '64. As manager, he brought some fire to the position, after years of yawns under the likes of Pinky Higgins. Some felt Pesky was a little too fiery; he had a few run-ins with "Dr. Strangeglove" Dick Stuart, who committed 29 errors at first base in 1963, but hit 42 homers and collected a league-leading 118 runs batted in. He also clashed with Carl Yastrzemski a number of times, and Carl made clear his discontent. As much as anything, that may explain Yawkey's refusal to find a position for Pesky within the organization when Higgins (by then the general manager) finally dismissed him late in 1964. Yaz was like a son to Yawkey, and Higgins was one of Yawkey's drinking buddies. Pesky had originally been brought in as manager despite Higgins' opposition.

When relieved as manager, Pesky hooked on with the Pirates and served as a major-league coach for three years, then managed the Pirates' Columbus club for a fourth.

From 1969 to 1974, he served as a broadcaster for Boston, working with Ken Coleman and Ned Martin as a color commentator. Though he worked hard at improving himself, Johnny never felt comfortable except during rain delays when he could really stretch out with stories about players from his era.

During the same period, Pesky called on clients for the Sox, initiating a fledgling marketing department for the club, working in tandem with former catcher Bob Montgomery. Pesky probably appeared at more banquets and events around New England than any other figure in Red Sox history.

He's also one of the few people in baseball to have a part of a ballpark named after him. Fenway Park's famed Pesky Pole—the right-field foul pole—was given the nickname by Red Sox broadcaster Mel Parnell. A former teammate, Parnell was poking a little fun at Johnny's lack of power—he hit just 17 home runs, and only six at Fenway—every one of which went out past the right-field foul pole, as of 2014 the shortest distance for a home run in major-league ball.

From 1975 to 1984, Pesky was first-base coach under Red Sox skippers Darrell Johnson, Don Zimmer, and Ralph Houk. From 1985 until his passing, Johnny was listed as a special-assignment instructor, evaluating players at lower levels in the Red Sox system, but also working with generations of Red Sox players at spring training and at Fenway Park. As late as 2003, Johnny Pesky—"Mr. Red Sox" in the eyes of decades of New Englanders—could be found on the field at Fenway before games, hitting fungoes to infielders and generally serving as a goodwill ambassador throughout the region.

It was a good year in 2004. Not only did Johnny enjoy some extra attention when his biography *Mr. Red Sox* was published, but he was able to revel in the Red Sox finally attaining the Holy Grail of Baseball, a world championship. For three years he proudly wore the championship ring the Red Sox presented him on the day that he and Carl Yastrzemski walked across the field to hoist the 2004 World Series banner on the Fenway Park flagpole. After the Red Sox won the Series again in 2007, he sported a second companion ring.

Johnny Pesky is a charter member of the Boston Red Sox Hall of Fame.

"Mr. Red Sox" died on August 13, 2012, in Danvers, Massachusetts.

This biography originally appeared in the book *Spahn, Sain, and Teddy Ballgame: Boston's (almost) Perfect Baseball Summer of 1948*, edited by Bill Nowlin and published by Rounder Books in 2008.

SOURCES

Most of the information for this article was gleaned from many hours of conversation with Johnny Pesky, who gave unsparingly of his time as I worked on the book *Mr. Red Sox: The Johnny Pesky Story*, published by Rounder Books in 2004, with a new edition published in 2012, In addition to the newspapers cited in the text, I consulted *Total Baseball*

(7th edition) for statistics, and the microfilmed records of the *Boston Globe* newspaper for the years of Pesky's career. Other information was provided by personal interviews with Ken Coleman, Bob Montgomery, and Vincent Paveskovich.

Thornton Lee

By Gregory H. Wolf

WHEN THE CHICAGO WHITE SOX acquired him before the 1937 season, Thornton Lee was a hard-throwing but wild 30-year-old southpaw with just 12 victories in three-plus seasons for Cleveland. But under the aegis of manager Jimmy Dykes and coach Muddy Ruel, Lee developed into one of the best left-handers in the big leagues and the anchor of the White Sox pitching staff on weak-hitting teams from 1937 to 1941. Averaging 15 wins and 243 innings per year during that stretch, Lee enjoyed one of the best years in franchise history in 1941, completing 30 of 34 starts and winning 22 games.

Thornton Starr Lee was born on September 13, 1906, in Sonoma, California, north of San Francisco. Thornton derived his middle name from his father, Starr Lee, a farmer and employee of the Southern Pacific Railroad. His mother, Celia Lenice (Steinhoff) Lee, was a homemaker who raised four children (Laura, Thelma, Thornton, and Willard) born in the first decade of the 20th century. By 1909 the Lees had moved to Willcox, Arizona, a stop on the Southern Pacific Railroad east of Tucson, to try their luck as homesteaders. Finding it difficult to eke out an existence in the brutal climate, the Lees returned to California and settled in Oceano in San Luis Obispo County, about 190 miles northwest of Los Angeles.[1] A bright and athletic youngster, Thornton attended Arroyo Grande High School and upon graduation in 1925 entered California Polytechnic State University in San Luis Obispo intending to become a teacher or coach.

Big for his day, about 6-feet-3 and 180 pounds in college (though he got bigger as a professional ballplayer), Thornton was a legendary athlete at Cal Poly. He was a track star who competed in the javelin, discus, and shot put; a center on the basketball team; and an end on the football team. But his passion was baseball. The lithe left-hander was a hard thrower who once struck out 19 batters in a game against San Jose State and began attracting professional scouts during his sophomore year.[2] Denny Long, a scout for the Chicago White Sox, offered him a contract, but was spurned by

Lee, who wanted to get his degree.[3] In 1928 he was signed by Dan Sheehe, a scout for the San Francisco Seals of the Pacific Coast League.[4]

Lee progressed slowly and methodically through the minor leagues for six years, flashing signs of brilliance tempered with inconsistency and bouts of wildness. Lee's first assignment was with the Salt Lake City Bees in the Class C Utah-Idaho League. He roomed with another promising left-hander, Vernon "Lefty" Gomez.[5] Finding a chance to pitch for the eventual league champs in a short season proved difficult. Lee won one of four decisions and posted a 6.51 ERA in 37⅓ innings. Dropped to Class D for the 1929 season, Lee was able to pitch regularly for the Globe Bears (who actually played their games in Miami, Arizona), evenly splitting his 22 decisions, but leading the league in walks (118) and posting a 5.71 ERA. When the Seals

did not exercise their option on the young hurler, the Tampa Smokers of the Class B Southeastern League drafted Lee on umpire George Blackburne's recommendation.[6]

Lee enjoyed a breakout season in Tampa, where he developed a reputation as a strikeout artist, whiffing a league-record 14 batters in one game and tossing a no-hitter in another.[7] Acting on the advice of scout Bill Rapp, the Cleveland Indians purchased the hot prospect for a reported $10,000, although his tantalizing potential (a league-high 145 strikeouts) was matched by his control problems.[8] The Indians assigned Lee to the New Orleans Pelicans of the Class A Southern Association, where he struggled for the remainder of the 1930 season.

Following his first taste of the big leagues at the Indians' spring training in 1931, Lee was optioned to the Shreveport Sports of the Class A Texas League, where his record (7-14) was more an indicator of his poor team (66-94) than of his ability. Lee was promoted to the Toledo Mud Hens of the American Association in 1932, but his "arm went lame" after he had logged just 38 innings.[9] After resting for several weeks, he was dropped two classifications to the Class B Wilkes-Barre Barons of the New York-Penn League. There he won 14 games despite pitching in pain all season. Back with the Mud Hens in 1933, Lee proved that he was major-league-ready by harnessing his speed and winning 13 games.

Six days after his 27th birthday, Lee made his major-league debut for the Cleveland Indians on September 19, 1933. In relief of starter Clint Brown, Lee struck out the only batter he faced in a 4-3 loss to the Boston Red Sox at Fenway Park. Five days later, in his first start, he tossed a complete game to defeat the Chicago White Sox, 12-6, despite issuing a career-high nine walks. Lee "looked the part of a top-notcher" in his late-season trial, wrote *The Sporting News*.[10]

Lee was groomed for three years (1934-1936) as the Indians' much-needed left-handed starter but had trouble finding consistent opportunities to demonstrate his ability. He logged just 85⅔ innings as primarily a long reliever in 1934 for manager Walter Johnson, whose confidence was notoriously difficult to earn. Indians

beat reporter Gordon Cobbledick wrote that baseball sage Connie Mack of the Philadelphia Athletics encouraged the Indians to keep pitching the young left-hander despite his control problems, reminding them that left-handers develop more slowly than right-handers.[11]

Praised for the "fastest ball in camp," Lee was widely expected to win 15 or 20 games in 1935.[12] "Lee has all the assets — height, weight, strength, a blazing fastball and a fast breaking curve," wrote *The Sporting News*, puzzled at how Johnson used Lee.[13] When Steve O'Neill replaced Johnson as the Indians' manager after 94 games, Lee finally had the chance to start regularly and relieve intermittently. In the last two months of the season, he won six of 11 decisions, completed five of 12 starts, posted a respectable 3.71 ERA in 99⅓ innings, and finished the season with a 7-10 record and a solid 4.04 ERA. It appeared as though Cleveland's long hunt for a left-handed starter was over.

By Lee's third full season with the Indians (1936), he had been described as a " 'comer' for so long that he seems something of a veteran."[14] Manager O'Neill became exasperated by the lefty's lack of control and banished him to the bullpen for much of the season. Lee pitched in a career-high 43 games, but started just eight times and finished with only three wins in eight decisions. At the baseball winter meetings, Lee was sent to the Chicago White Sox as part of a three-team trade involving the Washington Senators (who shipped pitcher Earl Whitehill to the Cleveland Indians) and the White Sox (who dealt pitcher Jack Salveson to the Senators).

Considering his pedestrian 12-17 record in just over three big-league seasons, expectations were minimal for the 30-year-old Lee in 1937, but he landed in an ideal situation, with manager Jimmy Dykes and coach Muddy Ruel both known for their reclamation projects. Lee's former manager O'Neill looked like a genius when the Indians clobbered the left-hander in his first start with the White Sox.[15] Undeterred, Dykes sent Lee to the mound against the predominantly left-handed-hitting Yankee lineup four times in his first six starts. He was victorious each time. The third of Lee's four victories over the Yankees (a complete game on June

8) pushed the upstart White Sox into a tie for first place, the first time the club had been in first place so late in the season since 1920. Dykes employed six regular starters and continued using Lee against clubs that relied on left-handed power (18 of 25 starts came against New York, Cleveland, and Washington). In a four-game span in July, Lee tossed back-to-back ten-inning complete games to defeat the Senators and the Yankees (his fifth consecutive triumph over the club) followed by a five-hit shutout against the Senators. "One must have control and confidence in himself," said Lee after the season. "A big fellow like me needs more work. Manager Dykes instilled the confidence."[16] Lee concluded the season with a resounding 11-inning shutout over the St. Louis Browns to finish with a 12-10 record and a 3.52 ERA (sixth best in the league).

It was the best season for the White Sox since 1920, and evoked hopes and dreams for an even better campaign in 1938, but instead the team dropped to sixth place. In an oft-repeated refrain throughout Lee's most productive years with the White Sox, his record (13-12) did not reflect how well he pitched. The "tall southpaw [was] held largely responsible for the quaint notion that the New York Yankees couldn't hit left-handed pitching," wrote an Associated Press correspondent in light of Lee's 1.61 ERA against the champions.[17] The big lefty, an able-bodied hitter throughout his career with a respectable .200 average (167-for-835), belted all four of his career home runs, including two against the Yankees, in 1938.

Lee was one of the biggest pitchers in his era and was affectionately known as Goon or Goon-man for his enormous size and physical strength. "When I was with the Indians," he said, "I weighed about 190 pounds. Now I am over the 220-pound mark. After I quit smoking I couldn't keep my head out of the icebox. The extra weight gave me more stamina and increased my speed."[18] Lee was the staff workhorse in 1939, tying for the team lead with 15 victories and leading the club in innings (235). Noting the "paucity of left-handed talent" in the big leagues, The Sporting News wrote, "In probably no year since the American League came into existence at the turn of the century have the left-handed pitchers of the two majors been as mediocre a lot as this season,"

and counted Lee, along with Lefty Gomez and the aged Lefty Grove among the exceptions.[19]

Lee's success rested with a blazing, sinking fastball, a sharp-breaking overhand curveball, and his control. Syndicated sportswriter Harry Grayson wrote, "[Lee] did little more than rear back and pump the pill in there" as a member of the Indians, but Muddy Ruel transformed him into one of game's best left-handers.[20] "Ruel took me in hand and cured my wildness," said Lee. "He picked out flaws in my delivery and pretty soon I had better than average control."[21] Over the course of several years, Ruel instructed Lee to shorten his long stride in order to stay on top of the ball and help his curveball break more sharply. On top of that was his unflappable mound presence. "Lee has one quality which great pitchers must have," said teammate Ted Lyons. "He's the coolest pitcher in baseball when under fire. Load the bases, get a count of three balls on the batter, and the Goon is like cucumbers on ice."[22]

Lee's commanding four-hit complete game against the Cleveland Indians in his first start of the 1940 season inaugurated a dominating two-year stretch during which he completed 54 of 61 starts. The White Sox finished in fourth place again in '40, and Lee finished with a losing record (12-13), primarily due to poor run support. His 24 complete games trailed only Bob Feller's 31. What might he have done had he started more than 27 times? Dykes continued to juggle his six primary starting pitchers so that Lee could face the left-handed sluggers on the Indians and Yankees (15 of his 27 starts were against them).

In 1941 Lee had one of the best years any White Sox pitcher has experienced in the lively-ball era. On a team that ranked last in runs scored, Lee posted a career-high 22 wins, led the American League with a 2.37 ERA, topped the major leagues with 30 complete games (in a career-high 34 starts), and logged 300⅓ innings. Through much of May and into June, the White Sox pitchers kept the team in second place as close as a half-game out. "[Lee's been] carrying Dykes' hitless hitters on his back all season," wrote The Sporting News.[23] Often a tough-luck loser, Lee was locked in a scoreless duel with Red Ruffing of the New York Yankees through ten innings in the Bronx on July 13.

In the top of the 11th inning, Lee surrendered a run to lose, 1-0. In Lee's 11 losses, the White Sox scored just 27 runs combined and were shut out four times. "I've had the misfortune to stack up against pitchers on their good days," said Lee.[24] Often pitching on short rest during the final seven weeks of the season, Lee finished in a flurry, winning ten of 13 decisions. For the only time in his career, he was named to the American League All-Star team. In Briggs Stadium in Detroit, he pitched the fourth through sixth innings, surrendering four hits and a run in the junior circuit's exciting 7-5 victory, which came courtesy of Ted Williams's dramatic walk-off three-run home run.

Widely regarded as the best left-handed pitcher in baseball in 1941, Lee saw his career come crashing down as a series of injuries limited him to just ten victories and 41 starts over the next three seasons. He was sidelined with "torn shoulder ligaments" until July 5 in 1942;[25] shoulder and back pain plagued him through the remainder of the season, limiting him to just eight starts and a 2-6 record. Forced to sign a "$1-a-year"[26] contract for 1943 with the option of earning a full-fledged backdated contract, Lee suffered an additional setback when he was diagnosed in early May with three bone chips and a growth in his left elbow, which cast doubts on his future. He opted against potentially season-ending surgery in order to concentrate on his still aching shoulder. He underwent treatment involving a "gallows-like neck-pulling gadget" that supposedly stretched his shoulder and broke the adhesions.[27] Lee's return (he won four of five decisions over a five-week stretch from late May to July) created optimism and earned him a full contract; however, he struggled thereafter and finished with a 5-9 record.

After the season Lee underwent two operations to revive his career. In one he had bone chips removed from his elbow; the other operation involved severing a tendon in his neck that affected his shoulder. "It seems like the tendon becomes taut with age," Lee said. "In some way [it] shut off the flow of blood to my arm when I raised it above my shoulder. This explains why I was good for just a few innings last year. … By the fifth inning or so my fingers would start getting numb.

A lot of the times I couldn't even tell if I had the ball in my hands."[28]

The 37-year-old Lee returned in 1944 as a once-a-week pitcher, but the only breaks he encountered were bad ones. In his second start of the year, he tossed a career-best 12 innings in a 2-0 loss to the Tigers. In a relief appearance against the Philadelphia Athletics on July 9, Lee was hit on the lower arm near the wrist by a screeching liner from Bobby Estalella; Lee picked up the ball and threw Estalella out, but the damage was done. Lee had suffered a broken forearm.[29] He was expected to miss the rest of the season, but returned to hurl two complete-game victories in September, finishing the season on a positive note and providing a glimmer of hope for 1945 despite his 3-9 record.

After three years of frustrating injuries, Lee made a remarkable comeback in 1945, going 15-12, completing 19 of 28 stars and posting the AL's fifth lowest ERA (2.44). He made his first and only Opening Day start that season, earning the victory against the Indians, 5-2, and pitched consistently all season against competition that was admittedly depleted due to the war. On June 12 at Comiskey Park, he hurled arguably the best game of his career, an overpowering three-hitter against the Indians with a career-high 13 strikeouts. Though the sixth-place White Sox surprisingly led the AL in batting average for the first time since 1919, their bats were often silent in Lee's losses; they scored two or fewer runs in ten of his 12 defeats.

The excitement resonating from Lee's comeback dissipated soon after the start of his 14th season in the big leagues. Lee fought through early-season elbow pain, but ultimately succumbed to bone chips after just his seventh start of the season, on June 16. He was placed on the voluntary retired list, returned to Phoenix for rest and treatment and eventually had elbow surgery.[30] Lee made an auspicious return in 1947, shutting out the St. Louis Browns on two hits and hurling a complete-game victory over the Yankees in his first two starts. His success proved illusory, though, and he would win just one more start that season, his final one in Chicago. At the age of 40 and with a long history of arm woes, Lee was relegated to the role of spot starter and reliever.

The White Sox released Lee after the 1947 season. In April 1948 he signed with the New York Giants, but his big-league career came to its conclusion when the Giants let him go on June 19. In 16 seasons in the major leagues, Lee's record stood at 117-124; he posted an impressive 3.56 ERA in 2,331⅓ innings.

Lee had a short, unsuccessful stint with the Oakland Oaks before retiring to Phoenix. Since the mid-1930s he and his wife, Esther Mae Ellis (whom he met while playing in Miami, Arizona, and married in 1929), had called the desert their home. They had one son, Don, a right-handed pitcher who won 40 games in a nine-year big-league career from 1957 to 1966. Ted Williams homered off both Thornton (in 1939) and Don (in 1960), making him the only player to hit a round-tripper off a father and son. Thornton was lured out of retirement in 1949 by the Phoenix Senators of the Class C Arizona-Texas League, for whom he made 11 appearances. He went on to manage the Globe-Miami Browns in that league in 1950. Lee then had a prosperous career for more than 25 years as a businessman, most notably with Phoenix-based Garrett AiResearch, a producer of turboprop engines. He was inducted into the Arizona Sports Hall of Fame in 1960 and the Cal Poly Sports Hall of Fame in 1988.[31]

The big left-hander never lost his passion for baseball. For almost four decades, he served as a part-time scout for a number of teams, including the St. Louis Cardinals, Washington Senators, and San Francisco Giants, retiring when he was 80 years old. An active outdoorsman, Lee maintained his stout physique his entire life. At the age of 90, Thornton Lee died from complications related to Parkinson's disease.[32] At the request of the family, no services were held.[33]

SOURCES

Websites

Ancestry.com

BaseballAlmanac.com

BaseballCube.com

BaseballLibrary.com

Baseball-Reference.com

SABR.org

Newspapers

Arizona Republic (Phoenix)

Chicago Daily Tribune

Cleveland Plain Dealer

New York Times

The Sporting News

Other

Thornton Lee player file, National Baseball Hall of Fame, Cooperstown, New York.

NOTES

1   Thornton Starr Lee obituary. *Arizona Republic*, June 11, 1997.

2   Cal Poly Mustangs. gopoly.com/inside_athletics/hof/Lee_Thornton.

3   Henry P. Edwards, press release, American League Service Bureau, released on December 19, 1937. Appeared syndicated as "Thornton Lee Took Years to 'Get Right.' Now He's Chisox Star," *San Antonio Light*, December 19, 1937, 18.

4   Press release, American League Service Bureau, released in 1937, in Lee's Hall of Fame file.

5   Veronica Gomez and Lawrence Goldstone, *Lefty: An American Odyssey* (New York: Ballantine Books, 2013), 220.

6   Thornton Lee, American League press release, 1937, in Lee's Hall of Fame file.

7   Ed Bang, "Thornton Lee Looms Up Like Good Prospect," *Cleveland News*, January 30, 1931.

8   Henry P. Edwards, "Thornton Lee Took Years to 'Get Right.' Now He's Chisox Star," *San Antonio Light*, December 19, 1937, 18.

9   Billy Evans, "Building the Indians. Is This Lee's Year?" February 10, 1936. (Unknown source, in Lee's Hall of Fame file).

10 *The Sporting News*, October 5, 1933, 1.

11 Gordon Cobbledick, "Mack Advises Evans To Keep Lee on Roster," *Cleveland Plain-Dealer*, September 16, 1934. Player's Hall of Fame file.

12 Gordon Cobbledick, "Lee Displays Fastest Ball in Tribe Camp. *Cleveland Plain-Dealer*, no date. (in Lee's Hall of Fame file).

13 *The Sporting News*, August 28, 1935, 1.

14 Ibid.

15 Irving Vaughan, "'My Lefty Lee' is Prof. Dykes Latest Sox Hit," *Chicago Daily Tribune*, March 5, 1937, 29.

16 Henry P. Edwards, "Thornton Lee Took Years to 'Get Right.' Now He's Chisox Star," *San Antonio Light*, December 19, 1937, 18.

17 Associated Press, "White Sox Again Trounce Cubs to Take Series Lead," *Sarasota* (Florida) *Herald*, October 9, 1937, 6.

18 Eugene J. Whitney, "Bust With Tribe, Lee Travels on 20-Victory Road." (Unknown source, in Lee's Hall of Fame file).

19 *The Sporting News*, August 24, 1939, 4.

20 Harry Grayson, News Enterprise Association, "Ruel Rebuilds
    Chisox Hurlers With Instructions in Delivery," *Arizona Republic*,
    June 9, 1941, II, 2.

21 Eugene J. Whitney, "Bust With Tribe, Lee Travels on
    20-Victory Road."

22 *The Sporting News*, April 2, 1947, 5.

23 *The Sporting News*, July 10, 1941, 14.

24 *Eugene J. Whitney*, "Bust With Tribe, Lee Travels on
    20-Victory Road."

25 "Thornton Lee Ready to Join Sox in St. Louis," *Chicago Daily
    Tribune*, May 8, 1942, 25.

26 *The Sporting News*, May 13, 1942, 10.

27 *The Sporting News*, June 24, 1943, 14.

28 "Lee, of White Sox, OK After Slit Throat." (Unknown source, in
    Lee's Hall of Fame file).

29 Edward Burns, "Dietrich Whips A's, 4-3; Grove Defeated, 8-2,"
    Chicago Daily Tribune, July 10, 1944, 17.

30 *The Sporting News*, August 7, 1846, 9.

31 Phoenix Regional Sports Commission, phoenixsports.org/hall-of-
    fame/history-of-the-hall-of-fame/; Cal Poly Mustangs, gopoly.com/
    inside_athletics/hof/Lee_Thornton.

32 Bill Lee, *The Baseball Necrology* (Jefferson, North Carolina:
    McFarland, 2009), 232.

33 Thornton Starr Lee obituary, *Arizona Republic*, June 11, 1997 (in Lee's
    Hall of Fame file).

Danny Gardella

By Charlie Weatherby

TODAY'S MULTIMILLIONAIRE PLAYERS probably don't know Danny Gardella or the impact the wartime New York Giants outfielder had on their high salaries. Gardella's brief adventure in the Mexican League and his challenge to baseball's reserve clause was one of the first steps toward modern-day free agency.

At a "not much taller than a fire hydrant" 5-feet-7 and a heavily-muscled 160 pounds, the left-handed pull hitter played all but one of his 169 major-league games in 1944-45, hitting .267 with 24 home runs and 85 RBIs.[1]

Gardella was a singular character in the annals of baseball, one who earned a long list of nicknames: The Ignited Italian; Dauntless/Dangerous/Desperate Danny; the Mighty Midget; the Magnificent Busher; and the Little Philosopher.

Gardella was eccentric, colorful, and articulate, and his teammates never knew what he would do or say next. A voracious reader who often carried poetry anthologies, psychiatry tomes, and novels on road trips, he could quote Plato and philosophize for anyone who would listen. He was a fan favorite wherever he played, and often sang opera in a resonant baritone voice. Physically gifted, Gardella possessed enormous strength and could have been a professional acrobat. He could walk up stairs on his hands, do a triple midair twist while bursting into song, execute one-armed handstands, and do a two-legged split in the shower room. On long train rides, he would sometimes climb into a luggage rack above the seats and strap himself in with his belt for a nap.

A New York City native, Daniel Lewis Gardella was born on February 26, 1920. His father, Albert, was a mason who specialized in fancy inlaid marble floors for banks. His mother, Henrietta, an immigrant who arrived from Italy in 1912, stayed at home with Danny's older siblings, Lillian and Alfred, and his younger sister, Rita. The Gardellas lived in the Fordham Road section of the Bronx; Danny attended Paul Hoffman Junior High and Roosevelt High School, and worked as a shipyard roustabout after school.

Danny and his brother Al (who also became a major leaguer) grew up playing with Bronx sandlot and club teams. Both signed contracts with Detroit before the 1938 season and were sent to Beckley, West Virginia, to play in the Class D Mountain State League. The second-place Bengals (61-52) upset pennant-winning Logan in the President's Cup Playoffs. Danny hit .263 with four home runs in 113 games.

In 1939 Gardella was with the Class D Northeast Arkansas League's Newport Tigers; his .352 average was fifth in the league after 35 games. Less than two weeks later, he was sent to the Kitty League's Fulton Tigers, where he hit .227 in 75 contests.

Gardella's Southern Class D league tour continued in 1940, first with Salem-Roanoke of the Virginia League, a Cleveland affiliate. After hitting .213 in 11 games, he was shipped to last-place Shelby (Tar Heel League), a Washington Senators farm, where he hit .252 with two homers in 37 games and place in the league's All-Star game. He finished the year at

Williamston, North Carolina (Coastal Plain League), where his average improved to .299 in 38 games. Gardella was so popular with local fans that special bleachers were constructed behind him in left field. However, by season's end, Gardella could see the handwriting on the wall and, encouraged by manager Dixie Parker, decided to quit professional baseball.[2] Other managers had previously told him that he would never make good in the game.

Gardella easily found work when he returned to New York. Over the next three years, he was an elevator operator and house detective at the New Yorker Hotel, a railroad yard freight handler, and a shipyard stevedore, and turned his physical-fitness fixation into a position as a trainer and masseuse at Al Roon's Gym, sometimes helping chorus girls work off extra weight. Gardella had a short amateur boxing career and reached the 1940 Golden Gloves welterweight semifinals with four knockouts.

Gardella continued to play baseball, first for the New Yorker Hotel team in 1941 and then in the semipro Consolidated Shipyard League, where he hammered the ball throughout the summer of 1943. His manager, New York Giants scout Joe Birmingham, a former major-league player and manager, recommended him to Giants manager Mel Ott; Gardella was 4-F due to a punctured eardrum and couldn't serve in the military. He signed a Giants contract on January 31, 1944. It was an opportunity he would have never received if there weren't a wartime shortage of capable players.

At spring training in Lakewood, New Jersey, Gardella soon became known for walking the resort town's streets loudly singing operatic arias in a rich baritone voice. Before an exhibition game on April 6, a number of baseballs were dropped from a Navy blimp from a height of 400 feet; Gardella caught one, which the *New York Times* called "no mean feat considering the near-freezing temperatures and a biting wind."[3]

Mel Ott kept Gardella on the Giants bench for the season's first ten games before sending him to Jersey City on May 1. He hit .263 in five games with the Little Giants, driving in eight runs, before Ott brought him back as a replacement for injured outfielder Bruce Sloan. Gardella made his major-league debut on May 14 at Pittsburgh, going 0-for-4 in the first game of a double-header as Rip Sewell blanked the Giants, 1-0. He got his first hit, a triple off Nick Strincevich, in the nightcap. According to the *Times*, "Gardella … found himself up to his elbows in tough chances … in perhaps the most difficult right field pasture in either major loop."[4] He started again on the 16th, and the *Times* remarked that "Gardella almost flattened himself into eternity against the tricky right field wall in the second in a futile attempt to snare [Johnny] Barrett's three-bagger, but the plucky little fellow bounced back to give better than he received before it was over," smashing a double in the first and an RBI single in the sixth.[5] Back at the hotel after the game, Gardella donned a sports jacket, crashed a high-school prom, acquainted himself with the orchestra, and began to sing "Indian Love Call" to his startled audience before being ejected by the school principal.

In Chicago on May 17, Gardella was 3-for-4 with three runs, a triple, and two RBIs in a 10-6 win. By the time the Giants concluded their Western swing, Gardella sported a gaudy .375 average in eight games.

Fielding was another story. Gardella had never used sunglasses; during his first attempt, instead of flipping them down, he pulled his cap over his eyes, blinded himself, and almost got beaned. On another occasion, his pants were too loose, so he unbuckled his belt, only to look up and see a fly ball headed his way, which he ran after while holding up his pants with one hand, eventually picking up the ball with the other. He was particularly atrocious in a July 20 doubleheader in New York, misplaying three St. Louis balls into triples. Those he managed to snare kept the crowd on the edge of their seats. One sportswriter observed that "Gardella is the first guy since Babe Herman who provides more entertainment muffing a fly than catching it."[6] On another occasion, *The Sporting News* wrote, "Gardella caught Litwhiler's fly, unassisted."[7] Nevertheless, Danny, who had a .957 lifetime fielding percentage, was so popular that a large contingent of fans always hung a "Danny Gardella" banner from the Polo Grounds' upper left-field balcony, which became known as Gardella Gardens.

Gardella also pulled pranks; a memorable one occurred during a July trip to St. Louis. Danny and Nap Reyes returned to their hotel room; Reyes adjourned to the bathroom to shave. Minutes later, noticing a strange silence, Reyes opened the door and found a note on his dresser: "I'm bored with life. So long. Danny." The window was wide open and a frantic Reyes was horrified before checking it. There was Danny, hanging by his fingers from the window ledge, grinning as though it were a big joke. According to *The Sporting News*, "Other Giants, when they learned of the episode, shuddered, for the window was several stories up."[8]

After playing on a regular basis through June 4, Gardella was a pinch-hitter or pinch-runner in 19 straight appearances from June 11 to July 9. Then he started in three more games, but on July 24, Gardella was optioned to Jersey City because of his fielding woes. In a brief return to the Giants, he played two games in Philadelphia on September 15 and 16. On September 17, Ott suspended Gardella for the rest of the season for breaking curfew; Gardella told Ott he disapproved of curfews. His season ended with a .250 average, 6 homers, and a .912 fielding percentage in 47 games.

Although the Giants, in the *Times'* opinion, viewed Gardella as "something of a problem child"[9] in 1944, he was back on the team in 1945. He continued to pinch-hit for his first ten appearances but made the case for more playing time on May 24 by smashing a two-run pinch homer in the eighth, securing a 7-6 win at Cincinnati. Other notable performances followed: 3-for-4 with four RBIs in a 7-2 victory over Philadelphia on June 16, another 3-for-4, four-RBI game on the strength of homers in two consecutive innings against Boston on June 20, and another two-homer, four-RBI game in a July 7 win against Cincinnati. Eleven days later, Gardella's three-run, eighth-inning homer was the difference in a 6-3 victory at Pittsburgh.

On July 15 the *Times* offered this assessment: "Dauntless Danny right now is going great guns no matter where you play him. ... (T)he conviction is growing that ... for all his queer antics and occasional mental lapses, [Gardella] has the makings of an excellent ball player. He still runs the bases like an unbridled bronco on the range, but he does possess a powerful

throwing arm, fields capably wherever he is played—they have now had him in left, right and first base—and his hitting has been no flash in the pan."[10] During a 15-game Western swing from July 12 to 24, Danny hit .317, socked three homers, and knocked in 14 runs.

On May 16 the Giants purchased Al Gardella's contract from Jersey City; he made his major-league debut the next day, in the first of 14 games he and Danny played together before Al was optioned to Birmingham of the Southern Association on July 7. They were one of nearly 100 sets of brothers who played together in the major leagues.

After a 6-3 win at Cincinnati on July 21, Gardella offered his opinion on the state of the game. "Baseball today ... is too stereotyped. Everything is precision play and while the technique improves, the individual dash and verve of players which once made them standouts has disappeared. Take [Van Lingle] Mungo. ... [S]ure he is a much smarter pitcher than he was ten years ago. But at the same time he no longer is the colorful guy he was ten years ago when every one came out to see him pitch."[11]

Gardella specialized in game-winning homers during the season's final two months. His two-run clout in the 13th secured a 4-2 win over Philadelphia on August 5. A week later, another two-run shot was the difference in edging Cincinnati, 3-2. On September 22, he broke a 2-2 tie with a walk-off, upper-deck wallop off Boston's Don Hendrickson.

By season's end Gardella had played in 121 games and posted a .272 average. His 18 homers were eighth in the National League. His .954 fielding percentage was an improvement from 1944, but his nine errors as an outfielder (fourth in the NL, despite playing only 94 games in the outfield) showed that he was still a liability afield.

Even with players returning from the war, the Giants offered Gardella a $5,000 contract for 1946. He had earned $1,900 in 1944, started 1945 at $2,200, and was boosted to $5,000 in midseason. Unhappy with the offer and believing he deserved a modest raise, Gardella missed the train to the Giants' Miami training camp in 1946 and paid his own way, arriving in a foul mood. Shortly thereafter, he loudly clashed with Giants traveling secretary Eddie Brannick over a rule requiring a jacket and tie in the team dining room. Admonished by Mel Ott, Danny exited the premises vowing to leave the Giants in favor of playing in Mexico. Then, a few hours later, he was back, announcing that he was ready to sign the original offer. By this time, Ott had heard enough and washed his hands of the matter. Before leaving camp, Gardella told reporters, "You may say for me, that I do not intend to let the Giants enrich themselves at my expense by sending me to a minor-league club. They have treated me shabbily. I have decided to take my gifted talents to Mexico. … I would have accepted this figure had they not started to push me around."[12]

Frustrated, Gardella immediately contacted Jorge Pasquel, a wealthy Mexican customs broker he had met at Roon's Gym during the winter. Pasquel was surprised that Gardella earned so little playing baseball that he needed winter work. He was in the process of organizing his Mexican League and offered Gardella a contract to play for Veracruz, giving him $5,000 to sign, an $8,000 salary, and an option for two more seasons. Another 21 major-league players followed, including fellow Giants Nap Reyes, Adrian Zabala, Ace Adams, and Sal Maglie. On April 16 the Giants placed Gardella on the ineligible list.

On Opening Day Gardella hit a two-run homer as Veracruz took a 12-5 victory over Mexico City; two losses followed when he lost two drives in the sun. He continued to hit well during the season's first half, capping it by slugging two home runs in the Mexican League All-Star Game. By late June most American players in Mexico had become disillusioned. Mexican players resented the high salaries received by the Americans, who were dissatisfied with field and living conditions. In late June *The Sporting News* reported that "Danny Gardella [is] about the only happy player in Mexico."[13] His play fell off during the second half; Veracruz slumped to the bottom of the standings. Lonesome, Gardella asked his girlfriend, Katherine Bonaventura, to join him from New York; the couple soon married in Mexico City. In 100 games, Gardella hit .275 with 13 home runs and 64 RBIs. A few hours after the final game, Pasquel told him that he would

cut salaries for the 1947 season; revenues had failed to meet his projections.

In June baseball Commissioner A.B. "Happy" Chandler had barred any player who jumped to the Mexican League from returning to the major leagues for five years. He cited the reserve clause in the standard player contract, which bound a player to a team for life unless the team traded or released him.

Gardella and Katherine returned to New York after the Mexican League finale. Then he went to Cuba, where he hit .217 and was a reserve first baseman for Cienfuegos in the Cuban Winter League.

Back in New York during the summer of 1947, Gardella played for the Gulf Oilers, a Staten Island semipro team. Before a game with the Cleveland Buckeyes of the Negro American League, Commissioner Chandler sent a telegram to the stadium that was read over the loudspeaker: Any player caught participating in a game with Gardella or any other former Mexican League player would be banned from the major leagues for life. None of the Buckeye players was willing to take the risk and the game was canceled.

Disgusted and humiliated, Gardella hired lawyer Frederic Johnson, who was interested in his case because Gardella was blacklisted for violating the reserve clause rather than a player contract. Johnson and his family had ties to baseball going back to the 1880s and he had once written a *United States Law Review* article on baseball law. In October Gardella sued Major League Baseball, charging conspiracy to restrain free trade and using the reserve clause to deprive him of his right to make a living. Jumpers Max Lanier, Fred Martin, and Maglie filed suit shortly thereafter.

Banned from playing in the 1947-48 Cuban Winter League, Gardella returned to the island to play for the Cuba club in the Cuban Players League (also called Players Federation League), where he hit .250 and led the four-team circuit with ten homers. At home in New York, he earned a living with various blue-collar jobs, including factory work, truck driving, street sweeping, and working for a moving company.

In 1948 Gardella toured with Max Lanier's All-Stars, a club that won all of its 80 games; he sang "Danny Boy" and opera pieces at many of the stops. Later in the season, and in 1949, he played for Drummondville (Quebec) of the independent Provincial League and had his best year (.283, 17 homers, 80 RBIs) for the league champion Cubs, whose lineup included such major leaguers as Lanier, Maglie, Vic Power, Tex Shirley, Roy Zimmerman, and Negro League all-star Quincy Trouppe. Gardella played in the league All-Star game, and in the playoff finals his first-inning grand slam cemented a 7-0 victory over Farnham in a series Drummondville won, five games to four.

Meanwhile, in July 1948, Gardella's suit had been rejected by a federal judge who cited the 1922 Supreme Court decision that baseball was not subject to laws governing interstate commerce. In February 1949 a federal appeals court overturned the judge's ruling and ordered a jury trial. The baseball establishment, fearing a negative outcome, launched a war of words. Branch Rickey told a congressional committee that Gardella and others who opposed efforts to strengthen baseball's antitrust exemption were persons of "avowed Communist tendencies", and added, "Without the reserve clause, baseball cannot endure."[14] Many journalists shared this opinion. According to author Ron Briley, "Dan Daniel asserted that abolishing the reserve clause would bring chaos, while Shirley Povich of the *Washington Post* insisted that players were "delighted with the high salaries paid by MLB and wanted no government interference with the game.""[15]

Sensing that the owners' cause was doomed, on June 5, 1949, Chandler allowed the jumpers to return to the major leagues in return for dropping their litigation. Lanier and Martin complied, but Gardella refused. Johnson, Gardella's lawyer, questioned Chandler in a pretrial deposition on September 19, and got him to concede that baseball earned $750,000 from radio rights and $65,000 from television. After a second day of questioning, a defensive Chandler and other baseball officials approached Johnson and Gardella with a proposed settlement. On October 8 the owners announced that the case had been settled; Gardella dropped his suit in exchange for a cash payment. The amount was not announced, but in November 1951 Gardella said it was $60,000, half of which went to his lawyer. At the time, Gardella was employed as a $36-a-week hospital

orderly in Mount Vernon, New York. Upon receipt of the money, he bought a house in Yonkers so his growing family could move out of his father-in-law's home. He was reinstated to the Giants on November 3, 1949, and released to the St. Louis Cardinals the same day.

Gardella's hope for a continued major-league career ended abruptly. After one pinch-hitting appearance, the Cardinals sent him to the Texas League's Houston Buffaloes, where he played in 39 games, batting .211 with two homers; he was placed on Houston's inactive list on June 15. During Gardella's stay, team president Allen Russell sometimes recruited him to sing to the fans before games. In August he was picked up by brother Al, manager of Bangor (Pennsylvania) of the North Atlantic League, where he hit .337 in 26 games.

In mid-October, Gardella announced, "No more baseball for me—from now on I'm a singer,"[16] and signed to tour the vaudeville circuit, singing songs from Broadway shows. He would start in Gloversville, New York. If all went well, he planned make a career of it. It didn't go well; Gardella later claimed that someone associated with Organized Baseball tried to block his entertainment career.

Gardella signed with Brooklyn's semipro Bushwicks in April 1951. In mid-May, his brother Al, now manager of Three Rivers (Provincial League), signed him as an outfielder/first baseman. After hitting .178 in 42 games, he was released by new manager Del Bissonette. It was Gardella's last stop in Organized Baseball.

Gardella had a number of occupations during his post-baseball career. After his release by Three Rivers he joined the athletic staff at the Concord Hotel in Kiamesha Lake, New York. In 1952 he was a drill press operator for the Otis Elevator Company. Gardella was reported to be broke after his New York restaurant failed in 1955. After a stint on a construction project, he worked as a warehouseman for Western Electric for more than two decades.

Gardella's gamily grew to ten children, three boys and seven girls. Later in life, as baseball's free-agency era began, he was frequently interviewed by sportswriters about his fight with baseball. "If I didn't sue, they would have destroyed my spirit," he told the *New York Daily News* in 1994. "In some ways, I considered the settlement a sellout, a moral defeat. I think they would have lost if the case went all the way to the Supreme Court. … But my lawyer told me they would delay it for years, and still find a way to keep me out of the game. I loved playing for the Giants. They were my home team. I still feel as though I beat them."[17]

One Mets game per year satisfied Gardella's need to watch live baseball; his primary sports interest in 1966 was watching pro football on television. During the 1960s he became friends with newspaper columnist Maury Allen; they would often jog ten miles, sometimes stopping to discuss old tales of the game. In May 1975, still focused on physical fitness, Gardella ran in the Yonkers Marathon.

Katherine Gardella died on August 30, 2004. Danny followed her six months later, on March 6, 2005, when he died of congestive heart failure at a hospice in Yonkers, New York. He was 85 years old. His ten children and 27 grandchildren survived him. He is buried at Mt. Hope Cemetery, Hastings-on-Hudson, New York. In Maury Allen's view, "The baseball establishment didn't make much of a fuss over Gardella when he left us. But remember this. He led the league in laughter in his time. That's Hall of Fame stuff in my book."[18]

NOTES

1   The "fire hydrant" quote comes from Jimmy Powers, "The Powerhouse," *New York Daily News*, February 10, 1949.

2   Dan Parker, "Young Fella, Gardella, Lifts Giants Out of Cella'," *New York Daily Mirror*, June 3, 1944.

3   John Drebinger, "Ott's Team Victor With 12 Hits, 12-3," *New York Times*, April 7, 1944, 24.

4   John Drebinger, "Sewell Halts Giants in Tenth, 1-0; Pirates Also Take 8-2 Nightcap," *New York Times*, May 15, 1944, 22.

5   John Drebinger, "Weintraub's Four Hits Lead Giants to Uphill 8-7 Victory Over Pirates," *New York Times*, May 16, 1944, 25.

6   J.G.T. Spink, "Looping The Loops," *The Sporting News*, June 15, 1944, 2.

7   Ibid.

8   Oscar Ruhl, "From The Ruhl Book," *The Sporting News*, July 13, 1944, 14.

9   James P. Dawson, "Medwick, Rucker Sign With Giants," *New York Times*, March 6, 1945, 26.

10 John Drebinger, "Ott Shifts Line-Up To Bolster Giants," *New York Times*, July 15, 1945, 1, 3.

11 John Drebinger, "Mungo Of Giants Checks Reds, 6-3," *New York Times*, July 22, 1945, 49.

12 "A Jolly Good Fellow, *Baseball Magazine*, February 1946, 29.

13 "Most US Players Disillusioned in Mexico, *The Sporting News*, June 26, 1946, 14.

14 Stephen Miller, "Danny Gardella, 85, N.Y. Giant," *New York Sun*, March 10, 2005.

15 Ron Briley, "Danny Gardella and Baseball's Reserve Clause: A Working-Class Stiff Blacklisted in Cold War America," *Nine*, Fall 2010.

16 "Gardella Opens Singing Career Here; Is Through With Baseball, He Says," *Gloversville* (New York) *Morning Herald*, October 14, 1950, 7.

17 Jim Callaghan, "Baseball Rebel: Ex-Giant Took On Owners in '40s," *New York Daily News*, September 18, 1994.

18 Maury Allen, "Danny Gardella: Baseball's King of Laughter," thecolumnists.com/allen/allen68.html.

Van Lingle Mungo

By Alan Cohen

"HE IS ANOTHER VANCE, ANOTHER Dazzy, I'm telling you. Hasn't the best disposition in the world. You know some of those Carolina fellows get funny ideas sometimes, but he certainly can buzz that ball over. Best young pitcher I've seen since Rube Marquard. Only he is faster than Rube was. Say, maybe he is another Walter Johnson. I'll bet he will be winning 20 to 25 games a year for this club for a long time."[1] So said manager Wilbert Robinson late in the 1931 season when a young Van Lingle Mungo joined the Dodgers for the first time.[2]

It wasn't long before the Brooklyn populace became obsessed with the young phenom. "I was paying more attention to Van Lingle Mungo than I was to Moses," said Bill Mazer, reminiscing about his days in a Brooklyn yeshiva during the 1930's.[3]

And sportswriter Jimmy Cannon, in 1970, wrote about those days in Brooklyn. "The Dodgers traveled around the league in ridiculed obscurity. But Mungo was famous and exciting, and they would bring him into a city advertised to pitch against the other club's best. All over Brooklyn, people would stop ball writers. 'How's the arm?' they would ask. They seldom mentioned Mungo's name. There was only one arm in Brooklyn."[4]

Mazer also noted, "It was a constant struggle for Mungo. He had all the equipment, but he was like Sisyphus in the Greek myth. He kept rolling the stone uphill, and it kept rolling back."[5]

Van Lingle Mungo was born in Pageland, South Carolina, on June 8, 1911, to Henry Van and Martha Charlotte (Lingle) Mungo. Van's middle name was his mother's maiden name. His father, a cotton grower and retailer, had himself been a pitcher, plying his trade in the Sally League during the early years of the 20th century. Van's father gave him his first big break in 1926, and Van, at age 15, pitched the Pageland town team to victory in its most important game of the year. Having defeated every other town team in the area, there was only one team left to conquer—Cheraw. Cheraw's star pitcher was Buck (aka Bobo) Newsom, who went

on to pitch in the major leagues from 1929 through 1953. Mungo's father managed the team, and at stake were 13 bales of cotton.[6] Van was one of two children. His sister, Lucille, was born in 1908, and as an adult worked as a saleswoman in the family's retail store.

Mungo graduated from Pageland High School in 1928 and began his career in 1929, pitching for Fayetteville, North Carolina, in the Class D Eastern Carolina Association and going 10-9. Late that season he pitched in one game for Charlotte in the Class B South Atlantic (Sally) League.

Mungo spent most of 1930 with Winston-Salem in the Class C Piedmont League, going 11-11, and his work impressed George Napoleon "Nap" Rucker, who was scouting the South for the Robins. Brooklyn acquired his contract from Winston-Salem at the end of the season, and assigned him to its affiliate in the Eastern League, the Hartford Senators, in 1931.

Mungo's first appearance of the 1931 season was not particularly auspicious. In the season opener, on April

27 at New Haven, Hartford had taken a 10-3 lead into the ninth inning against the Bulldogs. Hartford's starter, Johnny Krider, got into difficultly and Mungo came into the game with none out, the bases loaded, and the score 10-4. Van sandwiched two strikeouts around a walk but an error by the shortstop and another walk made the score 10-7, and Mungo's day was over. New Haven continued its rally against two other pitchers and won the game, 11-10.[7] The team rebounded from this start to post a 97-40 record. The 20-year-old Mungo was 15-5 and led the league with 151 strikeouts in 191 innings pitched. His 2.12 earned-run average was third best in the league.

At the end of the season, Mungo was called up to Brooklyn, and posted a 3-1 record. He shined in his debut, shutting out the Boston Braves, 2-0, on three hits on September 7. At the plate he singled and tripled. Before the game Mungo had split the sole of one of his baseball shoes. The only shoes that fit him belonged to Dazzy Vance, Brooklyn's star pitcher of the 1920s, who was, at age 40, nearing the end of his career.[8] That being the case, Mungo stepped into Vance's shoes literally as well as figuratively.

Mungo was the only quality pitcher on some very bad Dodgers teams in the 1930s. In his first full season with Brooklyn he went 13-11 in 1932 as the Dodgers finished third in the league with an 81-73 record for new manager Max Carey. During each of the next six seasons, the Dodgers lost more games than they won. Before each season Mungo would promise to anyone and everyone that he would win 20 games. And each season, the promise of spring met up with the reality of summer, and Mungo never won more than 18 games.

Eloise Clamp of Salley, South Carolina, was teaching school in Mount Croghan, ten miles east of Pageland. One day she was en route to the post office in Pageland when Mungo drove by with some friends. One look was all that was needed. The car stopped and Van met Eloise. The two fell in love, but Eloise's father, Ernest, who worked for the post office, frowned on his daughter marrying a "celebrity." Nonetheless, Van and Eloise were secretly married on December 10, 1932. They welcomed their first child, Pamela, in 1934. Van Jr., known as Sonny, followed in 1937, and their youngest child,

Ernest, came along in 1943. Ernest played outfield in the minor leagues from 1962 through 1964, making it as far as Class A. Eloise went on to teach for 28 years, and remained devoted to her husband, despite the fact that over the years, as legend has it, many females caught the eye of Van Lingle Mungo.

In 1933 Mungo went 16-15 with a 2.72 ERA as the Dodgers finished in sixth place with a 65-88 record. Then in 1934, Mungo was named to the All-Star team for the first time. It was the game in which Carl Hubbell struck out five future Hall of Famers in succession (Ruth, Gehrig, Foxx, Simmons, and Cronin). Mungo did not fare as well. He entered the game in the top of the fifth inning with his National Leaguers leading 4-2. Lon Warneke had walked the first two batters in the inning, and Mungo was summoned from the bullpen. In his inning of pitching, he allowed three singles and a double and the American League scored six runs, four of which were charged to Mungo, as he was tagged with the loss.

Mungo was a workhorse that season, leading the league in games started (38) and innings pitched (315⅓). But his last start was his most important. Before the season, Giants manager Bill Terry famously asked whether the Dodgers were still in the league. Casey Stengel was now the Dodgers manager, and the Dodgers made it their mission to derail New York as the Giants contended with the St. Louis Cardinals for the National League pennant. The Cardinals and Giants were tied going into the last weekend of the season. The Giants' last two games were against the Dodgers. On Saturday, September 29, manager Stengel handed the ball to Mungo. The ace went the distance, allowing only five hits, to gain his 18th win of the season (against 16 losses) and the Cardinals passed the Giants in the standings. In the 5-1 game, Mungo starred at the plate as well, hitting two singles, scoring the Dodgers' first run and driving in the second, which was all Brooklyn would need.[9] Mungo's ninth-inning performance put the icing on the cake. After the first two batters reached base, he struck out Travis Jackson, George Watkins (who had homered earlier for the Giants' sole tally), and pinch-hitter Lefty O'Doul, all on called third strikes, to end the game. Fifty years later, Mungo looked back on that moment as the highlight of his career.[10]

After his 18-win season in 1934, Mungo felt he was due a more significant salary than the Dodgers were offering, and he elected to hold out for a better deal in 1935, not reporting until the end of February. Any number of sources quoted any number of figures ranging from $10,500 to $13,000. That year Mungo posted a 16-10 record, including a league-leading four shutouts. On September 29 he struck out 15 Philadelphia Phillies en route to his final win of the season.

He might have reached the elusive 20-win mark but for an injury that resulted in his not starting a game for close to eight weeks during July and August. The injury to his middle finger was initially sustained on May 12 when it was struck by a line drive off the bat of Sam Byrd of Cincinnati. The finger was placed in a cast for two weeks and he made five relief appearances, none longer than 3⅓ innings, between July 4 and August 26.[11]

Not only did Mungo have a great year on the mound, but he excelled at the plate as well. During spring training, Stengel encouraged Mungo to stop swinging for the fences and to concentrate on singles. During the early part of the season, he went on a tear. Through five games, he was batting .474 (9-for-19) with two doubles and eight RBIs.[12] His batting average remained north of .300 through mid-September, and he wound up the season batting .289 (26-for-90).

At the end of the 1935 season, Mungo made his way back to Pageland by car with his batterymate, Al Lopez. Lopez would drop Mungo off en route to his home in Tampa, Florida. Mungo was quick to credit his catcher with a very large share of his success. Unfortunately for Van, this was their last trip together, as Lopez was traded to the Boston Braves over the winter. The new Brooklyn catcher was Babe "Blimp" Phelps, and Mungo did not think particularly highly of Phelps, who would find himself consistently among the league leaders in passed balls.

There was no love lost between New York's National League teams in the more than 60 years that they shared Gotham, and tempers flared anew in 1936. In just the second game of the season, on April 15, Mungo was pitching for the Dodgers at the Polo Grounds and threw a pitch in the general direction of Dick Bartell's head. On the next pitch, Rowdy Richard bunted toward first base. Mungo ran to cover first, but Giants first baseman Buddy Hassett made the unassisted putout. During the play, Mungo bumped the smaller Bartell and sent him sprawling. A fight ensued, both players were ejected, and each was subsequently fined $25.[13]

But this was 1936 and the Dodgers were still quite the daffy bunch. The next day, Mungo came on in relief of Ed Brandt with two outs in the fifth inning. The Dodgers rallied to take a 6-5 lead into the bottom of the ninth inning. There were two outs before the Giants could mount a rally, but mount one they did. They had runners on first and second when Hank Lieber strode to the plate. Lieber was coming off a season in which he had batted .331 with 22 homers, but Mungo induced Lieber to hit a popup that sailed into short left field. Left fielder Freddie Lindstrom was poised to make the catch, as was shortstop Jimmy "Lord" Jordan. After the ensuing collision, the ball fell to the ground, as did Lindstrom and Jordan. Both runners scampered home for a 7-6 Giants win, and Mungo was off to a 0-2 start.[14]

The fun was just beginning. By early June the Dodgers were giving Mungo little support, offensively or defensively, and after two June losses took his record to 6-8 (five of the losses by one run), he demanded to be traded. A sportswriter, Eddie Zeltner, smelled a good story, and arranged for airfare to get Mungo out of town, which in this case was Pittsburgh. Mungo, not one to turn down a favor, temporarily left the team on June 10, much to the consternation of manager Stengel.[15] He returned after three days, joining the club in Cincinnati and receiving a $600 fine. From that point on, as noted by Tommy Holmes of the *Brooklyn Eagle*, Mungo was "likely to become the center of a number of wild reports every time somebody sees him, or thinks they see him, drink a glass of beer."[16]

On June 25, 1936, Mungo pitched a masterpiece—and lost. Against the Cincinnati Reds, he struck out a record seven consecutive batters, 11 in all, but the Dodgers lost, 5-4. Only three of the runs scored against him were earned. It was the first of six times that Mungo struck out ten or more batters in a game in 1936. The workhorse

of the Dodgers staff started a league-leading 37 games that year, posted an 18-19 record, and led the league with a career-high 238 strikeouts. He was named to his second All-Star team, but did not appear in the game.

Despite Mungo's efforts, the Dodgers lost far more than they won, finishing with a 67-87 record. The seventh-place finish did not enthrall the Dodger faithful and it came as no surprise that Casey Stengel did not return for 1937.

Before the 1937 season, Mungo once again expressed dissatisfaction with his contract and once again the number of different estimates correlated with the number of newspapers in the New York area. In any event, he signed for an estimated $15,000 and got to play for his fourth manager in his years with the Dodgers, Burleigh Grimes.

Mungo was unquestionably an outstanding pitcher for the Dodgers. But his violent temper continued to overshadow his talent. In 1937, after a slow start, he was turning his season around and took a streak of four straight wins into the May 16 contest at Boston. The third of those wins came against Pittsburgh at Ebbets Field on May 6. (During the game, the Hindenburg,

a giant dirigible, hovered overhead, but the fans took little notice — the Arm was pitching. Later that day, in Lakehurst, New Jersey, the airship burst into flames.)

On May 16, in a tight game, the Dodgers and Bees were knotted, 2-2, as the game entered the 11th inning. Teammate Tom Winsett snuffed out Mungo's hopes for his fifth victory in succession. He singled to right field with one out in the top of the inning. The next batter hit what appeared to be a single to right but somehow Winsett lost track of the ball and was forced at second base, stopping the rally in its tracks. The Bees won the game in their half of the inning.[17] Mungo completely lost it, ranting and raving and questioning Winsett's ancestry. Usually players cool down as quickly as they heat up. Not Van Lingle Mungo. He walked several blocks to a telegraph office, fuming all the way, and sent the following wire to his wife. "Pack up your bags and come to Brooklyn, honey. If Winsett can play in the big leagues, it's a cinch you can too."[18]

One other off-the-field caper would define Mungo's season and contribute to his legend as one of the true characters of the game. It also showed that he did not react well to adversity. On May 21 he called his wife in Pageland only to find out that his infant son, Van Jr., was critically ill after surgery.[19] The news prompted Mungo to an evening of drinking. In the early morning hours of May 22, he broke into the hotel room occupied by teammates Woody English and Jimmy Bucher in St. Louis, ostensibly looking for a pinochle game. Bucher confronted Mungo and the latter began throwing furniture over the room. Bucher then sent his fist into Mungo's face, giving him a black eye. Mungo was fined $1,000 for his extracurricular activities. He then returned home for a short spell to tend to his ailing son, who did recover.

In the soap opera that was Mungo's career, he then proceeded to win his next four starts, going the distance each time, to bring his record to 8-4. Dodger fielding lapses halted his streak as they fell to Pittsburgh 6-4 on June 18.

On July 4, 1937, while pitching against the Giants, Mungo was forced to leave the game in the eighth inning when he pulled a muscle in his side. He had been chosen for the All-Star team and joined the NL team to Washington. Brooklyn skipper Grimes instructed National League All-Stars manager Bill Terry not to use Mungo in the game. To ensure that Van, who had been known to misbehave, would control himself, the Dodgers sent along their road secretary, Babe Hamberger, a good friend of Van's, to serve as his manager, valet, trainer, and announcer (spokesman).[20]

Three days later Mungo, who had a 9-7 record at the time, was at his third All-Star Game. At game time, he and Dizzy Dean were arguably the best two right-handed pitchers in the National League. After that day, neither would ever again pitch effectively in the major leagues. Dean started the game for the National League and in the third inning was hit on the foot by a line drive off the bat of Earl Averill. In his haste to return to action later that season, Dean altered his delivery and damaged his arm. A few innings after Dean's departure, Terry, despite Grimes's instructions, inserted Mungo into the game. He aggravated his injury and developed a sore shoulder while pitching the sixth and seventh innings. To make things worse, Grimes did not rest his star and handed Mungo the ball on July 11.[21] He lasted only four ineffective innings that day and proceeded to lose his last four decisions in 1937.

Not only was Mungo having arm problems, but he also had tonsillitis. He did not start between July 19 and August 14, as he had his tonsils removed and he rested in Pageland. At the end of August, not long after he came back, Grimes, skeptical of Mungo's claims of a sore arm, suspended him. Mungo pitched in pain for the balance of his time with the Dodgers, and his blazing fastball was rarely seen again.

Before the 1938 season, before the full extent of Mungo's arm injuries was known, several teams expressed interest in obtaining his services, including the St. Louis Cardinals and the Chicago Cubs. But Mungo, who had some differences with Grimes in 1937 and led the team in fines, returned to the Dodgers for the 1938 season, promising a return to the form he had displayed before the 1937 All-Star Game. Newly appointed Dodgers executive vice president Larry MacPhail, so convinced that Mungo would be his former self, turned down an offer from the Cubs that included four players and $75,000 in cash. (Ultimately, the Cubs acquired

Dizzy Dean from the Cardinals for $185,000.). Mungo returned to the Dodgers in 1938 with a renewed determination—again.

On the eve of the season, Mungo had a sobering moment. A man of many moods, he displayed his kinder side when he visited young Jackie Bruger. The six-year-old, who idolized Mungo, had suffered severe burns after falling into a bonfire and had been hospitalized for five months. The boy was in pain, and missing the scheduled exhibition between the Yankees and the Dodgers was, in actuality, the least of his problems. After 13 transfusions, his survival was in question. But his hero, "My friend Mun," was there. Mungo autographed a ball for the ever-optimistic youngster and was emotionally overcome as he departed. Through tears he exclaimed, "I think I have troubles. But look at that family."[22]

By the end of April 1938, Mungo's arm problems re-emerged. His fastball was not in evidence as he lost his first three decisions. His first win of the season was a 7-0 shutout of the Cubs on May 11. It was vintage Mungo. At the plate he went 2-for-4 with a double, and he struck out nine batters in the cold Chicago air. The effort brought his ERA for the season to 1.91. Hope was renewed, but Mungo would not regain the form that placed him among the elite pitchers in the game. He would never again strike out as many as nine in a game.

Mungo would never win 20 games. His longtime pitching coach, Otto Miller, thinking that Mungo had more gas left in his tank, felt that he should have thrown his fastball more often in 1938. Mungo's speed, in his prime, was as good as that of anyone, but he would use his curve when the count went to 3 and 2. On June 17, 1938, the Dodgers were facing Cincinnati and had staked Mungo to a lead going into the ninth inning in a game at Ebbets Field. Ernie Lombardi worked the count to 3 and 2 and walloped a homer to tie the game. The game went into extra innings and Ival Goodman's homer off Mungo gave the visiting Reds the victory. The whole episode infuriated Larry MacPhail. He addressed Mungo directly, in front of the team, between games and angrily voiced his disappointment with his falling star. He committed himself toward cutting

Mungo's salary if his record, then standing at 2-7, did not improve. Mungo finished the season at 4-11, and his salary was cut from $15,000 to $5,000 prior to the 1939 season.

There was one more glimpse of what might have been. On June 30, 1938, Mungo pitched a one-hitter against the Boston Bees. Reflecting on his effort he stated, "The truth is my arm ached from the first inning to the last. I really wasn't fast. Only occasionally, I would throw a fast one. But when I threw a curve, it was terrible. I thought it would pull the arm out by the roots."[23]

When manager Burleigh Grimes sent Mungo out for his next start, on July 4, the Giants needed only five batters to end Van's day. Lou Chiozza greeted him with a home run to the right-field upper deck and three of the next four batters walked. Mungo retired only one batter before exiting. After he left, things really got out of hand. Each of the men he walked came home on a grand slam by Dick Bartell and the Giants went on to win, 16-1.

By this point, as noted in an article in the *New York World Telegram*, "It is no longer a question of whether Van wants to pitch for the Dodgers — it's a question of whether the Dodgers want Mungo to pitch for them."[24]

Grimes was dispatched after the 1938 season. During Mungo's final years with the Dodgers, when his talent had eroded and promise evolved into disappointment, his manager was Leo Durocher. Durocher said of Van Lingle Mungo that he "sounded like Edgar Bergen doing Mortimer Snerd (Bergen's none-too-articulate dummy) from the bottom of a well."[25] Durocher first joined the Dodgers in 1938 when Mungo went 4-11, and was the player-manager during Mungo's last three years with Brooklyn.

The annual hyperbole concerning Mungo's prospects became part of the national baseball fabric. In December 1938, an Associated Press article proved that hope is eternal: "The Brooklyn baseball club has made the approach of a new year official by issuing its annual announcement that Van Lingle Mungo, the big fireball pitcher with the ailing arm and sultry disposition, will not be sold or traded 'because we expect him to win 20

games for us next season.' This statement, delivered solemnly about this time of year by each succeeding Brooklyn manager, is becoming part of the language, like the Gettysburg address."[26]

When he took over the managerial reins in 1939, Durocher had hopes that he could "handle" Mungo and see a return to form. On May 4 Durocher used Mungo in relief of Cletus Elwood "Boots" Poffenberger. Boots had not been able to last the first inning. Mungo came on with one run in, none out, and the bases filled with Cubs. He got out of the jam by striking out two and inducing Billy Herman to hit a popup, and he did not allow a run until the ninth inning, when he showed signs of tiring. At the plate, he went 2-for-3 with a double and a pair of RBIs as the Dodgers won the game, 6-2.[27] Durocher inserted him in the rotation and by the end of May his record stood at 3-3 with a 2.79 ERA. After May, Mungo was largely ineffective and his season ended on July 23, when he broke his ankle sliding into second base while being used as a pinch-runner. His record for the season was 4-5 with a 3.26 ERA in only 77⅓ innings.

The Dodgers were impressed with Mungo's efforts during the season, although he won only four games. He was used as a pinch-hitter and pinch-runner, and even took a turn in left field. For the season, Mungo's batting average was .345. After the season Larry MacPhail rewarded him with a bonus for his efforts.[28]

When 1940 rolled around, Mungo came to camp determined to turn things around — again. His contract for the season called for a $7,500 salary and he was most definitely a team man. But as Tom Meany of the *World Telegram* noted, "It would be ironic if when the spirit was finally willing, the flesh, so strong all these years, suddenly was found weak."[29]

In 1940, Mungo's role with the Dodgers was that of a relief pitcher. He was doing well in his new role. In his first four appearances, he pitched a total of 14 innings and did not yield a run. But his arm problems re-emerged and his season ended on June 24. His only decision was a win on June 2. He came into the game in the eighth inning with the Dodgers trailing 2-1. He was the beneficiary of two ninth-inning runs, and left the game with one out in the bottom of the ninth. The Dodgers held on to the lead to win, 3-2.

After Mungo was dropped from the Dodgers' active list, it was decided that surgery was the best option to restore the strength to his arm. The Dodgers, under Durocher, were being transformed from the Daffiness Boys into a contender, and on July 1, 1940, Mungo underwent an operation to remove calcium deposits from his shoulder. He came to spring training in 1941 ready to pitch.

And then came a series of off-the-field incidents that would permanently cast a shadow over any of Mungo's accomplishments. Always known for his lack of sobriety, he had sworn off alcohol and even elected to room with the quieter Whitlow Wyatt as the Dodgers trained in Havana. On Saturday, March 8, things took a definite downturn. Mungo was scheduled to pitch that day, but the game was rained out and he found himself with some idle time. Accompanied by Lady Ruth Vine, the mistress of ceremonies for the floor show at the Hotel Nacional, he went for some "malt and merriment" and became inebriated.[30] Lady Ruth was not of nobility. She was from a Nashville family and her first name was really Lady.

After midnight, no longer in the company of Lady Ruth, Mungo found his way into the bar at the Hotel Nacional, and offered to buy a round of drinks for everyone there. He told the bartender not to "skip those two fellows up at the end of the bar. They look like a couple of regular guys." Those regular guys, unfortunately for Van, were Durocher and coach Chuck Dressen. Durocher, not in the least amused by the incident, ordered Mungo to retreat to his room.[31] The next day, Mungo went to the ballpark ready to pitch the opener of the March 9 doubleheader against the Cleveland Indians. Larry MacPhail and Durocher had other ideas. They fined Mungo $200 for drinking and had him banished from training camp. Mungo was assigned to the Dodgers affiliate in the International League and ordered to depart Havana via a Sunday evening boat (along with the visiting Cleveland squad), and to join the Montreal Royals at their Macon, Georgia, training base.

But the Sunday night boat left Havana Harbor without Mungo. After leaving the ballpark that afternoon, he resumed his drinking and set about to destroy everything in sight. After he missed the 7:00 P.M. boat, arrangements were made to have him take a flight out of Havana the following morning.[32] The Dodgers went so far as to have a detective keep an eye on Van as he had dinner and went back to his room to rest up for the 10:00 A.M. flight.

And then everything completely unraveled.

Sometime after midnight, Van was joined once again by Lady Ruth and she brought along Miriam Morgan, the female half of the dance duo of Gonzalo and Cristina. Cristina, prior to taking to a life in show business, had been the petite Miriam Morgan of Wilkes-Barre, Pennsylvania. The trio took in the Havana nightlife.

By 6:00 A.M. on Monday, the drunken Mungo and the women had found their way to Room 273 of Hotel Nacional. This happened to be the room of Lady Ruth. Lady and Cristina were on one bed, and Van Lingle Mungo was in the other. Gonzalo was in Room 272. His real name was Francisco Callada Carreno, and in another life, he had been a matador. He was quite annoyed to discover that his wife, the aforementioned Cristina, was not occupying her proper bed. He made his way to the next room and, by his account, found his wife attired in a blue negligee. The former Dodger ace was in the room with the ladies and had on not a stitch of clothing. Fisticuffs ensued and Gonzalo came out on the short end. Van, who had done some prizefighting in his younger days, displayed his skills, despite being somewhat incapacitated by the alcohol he had consumed.

There were many versions of what happened. Robert Sullivan in the *New York Daily News* wrote that the ladies contended that they were "doing a Samaritan act, seeking to sober Van up on milk and other health-giving elements full of Vitamin B-1. This work at last proved so tiring that the ladies, not knowing otherwise how to get rid of Van, dumped him into one of Lady's beds. They fell into the other, knowing nothing more until the before mentioned dawn."[33]

At 10:00 A.M. that same day, Mungo, in the company of the ever vigilant Babe Hamberger, was deposited on an airplane and flown back to the United States. Gonzalo, Cristina, and Lady Ruth Vine were fired by the hotel. Gonzalo and Cristina proceeded to divorce court. Gonzalo sued the hotel for $100,000 for breaking up his act and Van Lingle Mungo $20,000 for breaking up his marriage.

In an exhibition outing on April 12, Mungo started and pitched an effective four innings against the Yankees, striking out six and allowing only two hits, and at the Dodgers Welcome Home dinner on April 14, manager Durocher said that "Mungo is the key to success of the club this year."[34] Despite this, Mungo's Dodger days were effectively over. He made two brief appearances without a decision before being sent to Montreal on May 15.

Mungo was traded to the Giants' American Association affiliate at Minneapolis before the 1942 season. An 11-3 record with the Millers earned him a call-up to the Polo Grounds and during the spring of 1943, Giants manager Mel Ott became afflicted with what sportswriter Joe Williams called the "Mungo Daze." Mungo thought so highly of his manager that he named his second son Ernest Melvin Mungo.

No sooner had Ott been "exposed to the sight of the pitcher whamming his fastball into a warmup catcher's glove than (he) would develop that dreamy glint and predict that this was 'the year, yes sir, this was the year old Van Lingle was going to win 20 games, for sure.'"[35] Mungo posted a 3-7 record in 1943. He entered the Army early in 1944 and served stateside for nine months, missing the entire season. After nine months in the Army, he received a medical discharge on October 19, 1944.

Mungo returned to the Giants in 1945, once again sober and once again promising to make good — this time at age 33. He did not touch so much as a drop of alcohol in training camp, and he excelled in an exhibition performance against the Yankees in Atlantic City on April 1. This prompted Dick Young of the *Daily News* to state that "Van Lingle Mungo, who at one time might have inspired a little ditty called 'Rum and Coca-Cola,' is now working for the Giant dollah — but

good. Van is bearing down with an unprecedented determination that augurs the long-promised brilliant season."[36]

With determination, sobriety, and a sinker pitch alleged to contain a certain amount of foreign substance, Mungo posted a 14-7 record in 1945 for the Giants. His 101 strikeouts were his most since 1937. He had an outside shot at the elusive 20-win plateau until he was sidelined by a shoulder separation on September 2. After his performance in 1945, he elected to hold out. He was re-signed by the Giants for $12,000, but during spring training, his sobriety, which had been a key to his 1945 success, was questioned by manager Ott. Mungo was suspended and subsequently released.[37]

For his career, Mungo was 120-115 with an ERA of 3.47. The workhorse of the Brooklyn Dodgers led the league in games started on two occasions and in innings pitched on one occasion. During his time in Brooklyn, he did have control issues. Although he led the National League in strikeouts with 238 in 1936, he also led the league in walks with 118 that very same season. He also led the league in walks in 1932 and 1934.

Late in June 1946, Mungo signed on with Clinton (North Carolina) in the Class D Tobacco State League, where he recorded a 1-1 record in five appearances and batted a remarkable .471 (24-for-51). He became the team's manager as well, but his season ended abruptly when he got into an altercation with opposing manager Gus Brittain of Wilmington in a game on August 13. Brittain had himself gotten into a serious argument with the umpires, and in short order, Mungo and Brittain were exchanging blows. The matter was referred to the league office and Mungo was suspended for the balance of the season on August 30. He returned as player-manager in 1947. He was no longer pitching, but as an outfielder and pinch-hitter, he batted .362 (46-for-127) with three homers in 33 games.

After his playing days, Mungo stayed in his childhood home of Pageland, where he owned a movie theater. He opened the Ball Theater to people of color. To accomplish this and still comply with the prevailing policy of segregation, he had a balcony built in the theater for the black audience, previously denied access to the facility. The other theater in town was closed to blacks. Mungo also continued his family's involvement in cotton, owning a cotton gin, and continued to operate the retail store that had been started by his father.

One of his other businesses was a trucking concern. However, the company was not properly insured and when one of his drivers was involved in a major accident, the resulting lawsuits caused the business to fail.

Like many a player, Mungo would often be reunited with old teammates. On one occasion, in 1965, he was part of the Old-Timer's festivities at Shea Stadium, home of the New York Mets. In those days, the Mets, in only their fourth year of existence, had few of their own "old-timers" and called upon former Dodgers and Giants to appear. Mungo, garbed in Dodger Blue, served up a home run to Bobby Thomson. The next batter was Johnny Mize. The competitive juices were still flowing and Van's first pitch was in the general direction of Mize's back. Mize noted, "That's the way he pitched."[38]

On May 17, 1974, Mungo was inducted into the South Carolina Athletic Hall of Fame.

Mungo suffered a heart attack and died in Pageland on February 12, 1985, at the age of 73. He was preceded in death by his daughter, Pamela, who died of breast cancer in 1982 at the age of 48. His son, Van, died in 2002 from lung cancer and his wife, Eloise, passed away on October 8, 2002.

Mungo's business enterprises foundered. The Ball movie theater was ruined by a fire in 1957, and the cotton gin and business fell victim to the changing economy. Nevertheless, Mungo forever remained the pride of Pageland, and if you drive through Chesterfield County, South Carolina, you may very well find yourself on the Van Lingle Mungo Boulevard.

SOURCES

Anderson, Dave, *Pennant Races: Baseball at its Best* (New York: Doubleday, 1994).

Durocher, Leo, with Ed Linn, *Nice Guys Finish Last* (New York: Simon and Schuster, 1975).

Goldstein, Richard, *Superstars and Screwballs: 100 Years of Brooklyn Baseball* (New York: Dutton, 1991).

Hynd, Noel, *The Giants of the Polo Grounds: The Glorious Times of Baseball's New York Giants* (New York: Doubleday, 1988).

Lee, Bill, and Jim Prime, *Baseball Eccentrics: A Definitive Look at the Most Entertaining, Outrageous, and Unforgettable Characters in the Game* (Chicago: Triumph Books, 2007).

Long, Robert, *New York World Champions: 1933* (Victoria, British Columbia: Trafford, 2003).

Mazer, Bill, *Bill Mazer's Amazin Baseball Book* (New York: Kensington Publishing Corporation, 1990).

Nestor, Bob A., *Pride of Pageland* (Taylors, South Carolina: Faith Printing Company, 2002).

Vitti, Jim, *Brooklyn Dodgers in Cuba* (Charleston, South Carolina: Arcadia Publishing, 2011).

Newspaper Articles:

Drebinger, John, "Giants Lose to Dodgers and Now Trail Cardinals by Game in Pennant Race," *New York Times*, September 30, 1939, S1.

Fraley, Oscar, "Slants on Sports," *Niagara Falls* (New York) *Gazette*, September 9, 1961, 12.

Holmes, Tommy, "At 16, His Dad Tossed Him In to Twirl Game Down South—He Won," *Brooklyn Daily Eagle*, May 27, 1934, D-3.

Holmes, Tommy, "Brooklyn's New Dazzy Vance," *Brooklyn Daily Eagle*, May 1935.

Keane, Albert W., "Four Hartford Hurlers Lose Control in Ninth and Senators Bow to New Haven," *Hartford Courant*, April 28, 1931, 15.

Kerkhoff, Johnson D., "Jackie, Who Doesn't Know He May Die, Can't Go to Game, so Dodgers Ace Goes to Him," *New York Journal American*, April 15, 1938, 1.

McCullough, Bill, "Yen for Curves Mungo's Failing," *Brooklyn Daily Eagle*, March 7, 1939, 14.

McGowen, Roscoe, "Van Mungo Leaves Camp of Dodgers," *New York Times*, March 11, 1941, 32.

Meany, Tom, "Bartell, Van Mungo Each Fine $25 for Fight on Field," *New York World Telegram*, April 16, 1936, 33.

Meany, Tom, "They're at It Again: The Giants and the Dodgers: Another Round in the Forty-Year Brawl Opens Tuesday," *New York World Telegram Weekend Magazine Section*, April 17, 1937, 1–3, 12.

Parker, Dan, "Pitcher Mungo's 'Woo-Pitching' Woes From Down Havana Way," *New York Journal-American*, May 25, 1941.

Sullivan, Robert, "The Ballplayer and the Ladies: Van Lingle Mungo Mingles, Bungles," *New York Daily News*, March 30, 1941, 52–53.

Turkin, Hy, "Havana Havoc Brings Mungo Big Love Suit," *New York Daily News*, March 12, 1941.

"Mungo Fined $200, Sent Back to U.S. for Buying 2 Too Many," *New York Herald Tribune*, March 10, 1941, 21.

Others:

Ancestry.com

Baseball-Reference.com

FultonHistory.com

GoogleNewsSearch.com

NewspaperArchive.com

Sanders, Alex, "Cards Against the Wall," documentary, 2012.

Van Lingle Mungo player file, Baseball Hall of Fame library, Cooperstown, New York.

Interview with Ernest Melvin Mungo, March 12, 2014.

NOTES

1   Arch Ward, "Mungo in Eclipse as Dodgers Sun Rises," *The Sporting News*, July 4, 1940, 4.

2   The team was known as the Brooklyn Robins at the time.

3   Bill Mazer, *Bill Mazer's Amazin Baseball Book*, 145.

4   Jimmy Cannon, "Van Lingle Mungo Is Set to Music," *New York Post*, August 4, 1970.

5   Mazer, 381-382.

6   Tommy Holmes, *Brooklyn Eagle*. Undated clipping from May 1935 in Mungo's Hall of Fame player file.

7   Albert W. Keane, *Hartford Courant*, April 28, 1931, 15.

8   Holmes, *Brooklyn Eagle*. Undated clipping from May 1934 in Mungo's Hall of Fame player file.

9   Dave Anderson, *Pennant Races: Baseball at Its Best*, 92.

10   Steve Calhoun, "Where Are They Now: Van Lingle Mungo," *Dodger Blue*, January, 1984.

11   Bill McCullough, *Albany Times Union*, July 13, 1935.

12   Tommy Holmes, "Mungo Proves Pitcher Can Learn How to Hit," *The Sporting News*, May 9, 1935, 3.

13   Tom Meany, N*ew York World Telegram*, April 16, 1936, 33.

14   Noel Hynd, *The Giants of the Polo Grounds: The Glorious Times of Baseball's New York Giants*, 300.

15   Dan Parker, *New York Journal American*, May 25, 1941.

16   Tommy Holmes, "Mungo Puts Lie to Hub Yarn," *Brooklyn Daily Eagle*, July 19, 1936.

17   Roscoe McGowen, "Bees Down Dodgers in 11th, 3-2, To Snap Four Game Winning Streak," *New York Times*, May 17, 1937, 24.

18   Bill Lee and Jim Prime. *Baseball Eccentrics: A Definitive Look at the Most Entertaining, Outrageous, and Unforgettable Characters in the Game*, 80.

19   Bob Nestor, *Pride of Pageland*, 73-74.

20   John Lardner, *Hartford Courant*, July 11, 1938, 10.

21   Tommy Holmes, "Van Mungo Makes Headlines Again," *Brooklyn Eagle*, March 16, 1945. 15.

22   Johnson D. Kerkhoff, *New York Journal American*, April 15, 1938, 1.

23   Unattributed newspaper clipping in the Van Lingle Mungo player file, Baseball Hall of Fame, Cooperstown, New York.

24   "Van Mungo More Than Ever Problem Child of Dodgers; 'The Arm' Goes and So Does Pitcher," *New York World Telegram*, July 5, 1938, 22.

25   Leo Durocher with Ed Linn. *Nice Guys Finish Last*, 170.

26   Associated Press. "Brooklyn Dodgers will Keep Van Lingle Mungo—As Usual," *Spokane Daily Chronicle*, December 28, 1938.

27   Pat McDonough. "Mungo Toast of Flatbush," May 5, 1939.

28   "Mungo in Fine Trim, He Writes Dodgers," *New York Times*, November 16, 1939, 32.

29   Tom Meany, "Mungo Still Problem Child of Dodgers," *New York World Telegram*, February 19, 1940, 21.

30   Hy Turkin, *New York Daily News*, March 12, 1941.

31   Dan Parker, *New York Journal American*, May 25, 1941.

32   Roscoe McGowen, *New York Times*, March 10, 1941, 22.

33   Robert Sullivan, *New York Daily News*, March 30, 1941, 53.

34   "Mungo Praised at Dinner," *New York Times*, April 15, 1941, 28.

35   Joe Williams. "Mungo Daze!", *Pittsburgh Press*, March 26, 1943, 41.

36   Dick Young, "Unveil 'New' Mungo; Onlookers Impressed," *New York Daily News*, April 3, 1945, 34.

37   Joe King, "Ott Suspends Mungo as Giants' Discontent Grows," *New York World Telegram*, April 11, 1946, 39.

38   Jimmy Cannon, "Van Mungo's Creed: Pitchin to Hit Em," *Oneonta (New York) Star*, August 3, 1965, 8

Whitey Kurowski

by Rick Swaine

WHEN WHITEY KUROWSKI WAS 7 YEARS old in Reading, Pennsylvania, he fell off a fence and landed in a pile of broken glass, cutting his right arm. Blood poisoning developed and turned into osteomyelitis, an infection of the bone. Doctors feared they would have to amputate the youngster's arm, but they saved it by removing about four inches of infected bone and tissue from the ulna, the inside and longer of the two bones in the forearm. The result was a deformed, misshapen limb that was several inches shorter than his left arm when Kurowski grew to adulthood.

After his injury Whitey simply wouldn't allow his wounded arm to keep him from playing ball and he developed powerful muscles to compensate for the missing bone. He played softball five nights a week and played baseball on weekends from morning till night. In high school and American Legion baseball he concentrated on third base despite the fact that the position requires a better throwing arm than most others.

Because his right arm was shorter than his left, the right-handed hitter had difficulty reaching pitches on the outside part of the plate. He had to crowd the plate, and as a result was plunked frequently by inside pitches. The disfigurement also forced him to turn his right wrist over when he swung the bat, making him a dead pull hitter; second basemen often played him on the shortstop side of the base when he reached the major leagues.

George John "Whitey" Kurowski was born in Reading on April 19, 1918, to Anthony and Victoria Kurowski, the sixth of ten children. (He got his nickname early in his life when his hair turned white prematurely.) Reading was in the middle of the Pennsylvania coal-mining region, and his father was a miner. Like many other young men raised in the area, Whitey wanted no part of the mines, especially after his older brother was killed in a mine cave-in when Whitey was a teenager. Baseball seemed to be his ticket out, but scouts were leery of his maimed throwing arm. Initially he didn't get any offers after high school. But in 1937 Harrison Wickel, a native of the Reading area and the

manager of the Caruthersville team in the Class D Northeast Arkansas League, gave the 19-year-old a shot. A .339 batting average started him on his way, and a league-leading .386 mark the next year for Portsmouth in the Mid-Atlantic League solidified his status as a prospect in the St. Louis Cardinals farm system.

Kurowski, who developed into a stocky 5-foot-11, 193-pounder with thick legs and surprising speed, spent the next three years as the regular third baseman for the Rochester Red Wings in the Double-A (the equivalent of Triple-A) International League hitting .291, .279, and .288, stealing 47 bases and belting 39 homers. In the closing weeks of the hotly-contested 1941 pennant race, he was called up along with Rochester teammate Stan Musial to join the parent Cardinals for the stretch run. But Musial's .426 average and Kurowski's .333 mark in limited action weren't enough for the Cards to catch the Brooklyn Dodgers.

In the spring of 1942, while Whitey was fighting to win his first big-league job, his father died of a heart

attack. The 24-year-old had to leave the team to attend to funeral arrangements in the middle of spring training, but he returned to wrest the third-base job from veteran Jimmy Brown. With Musial taking over in left field, the two rookies helped drive the Cardinals to the National League pennant and a World Series victory over the heavily favored New York Yankees.

Kurowski was the Series hero. He blasted a home run off future Hall of Famer Red Ruffing in the top of the ninth inning to break a 2-2 tie in the deciding fifth game. After the Cardinals' victory, Whitey led the celebration by playfully ruffling the proud white mane of the commissioner of baseball, Judge Kenesaw Mountain Landis, and tearing National League President Ford Frick's hat to shreds. He also led the team in a rousing chorus of "Pass the Biscuits, Mirandy," their victory anthem that season.

Kurowski was integral to a Cardinals dynasty that brought world championships to St. Louis in 1942, 1944, and 1946. He was part of a wave of young stars who emerged from the organization's vast farm system in the early 1940s. The group included Musial, Marty Marion, Walker and Mort Cooper, Max Lanier, Ernie White, Johnny Beazley, Murry Dickson, Howie Pollet, Johnny Hopp, Ray Sanders, Harry Walker, Harry Brecheen, and others.

From 1943 through 1947 Kurowski established himself as one of the finest third basemen in baseball and made the National League All-Star team every year except 1945, when the All-Star Game was suspended because of World War II. He was, however, named to the 1945 major-league all-star team selected by *The Sporting News*.

The gritty, underrated third baseman also made his mark as a consummate team player. Cardinals owner Sam Breadon was a notorious skinflint when it came to player salaries, and before the 1946 season Kurowski was involved in a bitter pay dispute before finally accepting the club's offer. Meanwhile, the outlaw Mexican League had begun raiding major-league rosters. The league's owners, the Pasquel brothers, had targeted the Cardinals because of the club's abundance of talent and low salaries. In May their star lefty Lanier, second baseman Lou Klein, and rookie pitcher Fred Martin took off for Mexico, and rumors were flying that Kurowski, Stan Musial, and other Cardinal stars would soon follow.

Kurowski took it upon himself to call a clubhouse meeting to clear the air. He told his teammates that he'd talked to Mexican League representatives and that he believed in getting every cent he was worth, but he felt honor-bound to fulfill his St. Louis contract. He urged them to put the Mexican League business behind them and concentrate on winning the pennant. The players knew that Kurowski was no front-office lackey, that he had battled the club and was dissatisfied with his salary. So his words meant something, and they apparently took them to heart. The Cardinals overtook the Dodgers to capture the National League pennant and then went on to defeat the powerful Boston Red Sox in the 1946 World Series.

Because Kurowski's osteomyelitis made him ineligible for military service, he is sometimes erroneously tagged as a wartime player who benefited from a lower level of competition. But 1947—when the "regular" players had returned from the war—was actually his best year, even though the Cardinals had to settle for a second-place finish. With future Hall of Fame teammates Musial, Red Schoendienst, and Enos Slaughter having offseasons, Kurowski carried the Cards' offense much of the time. In 146 games he hit .310 and compiled a .420 on-base percentage, second highest in the league behind his former teammate, batting champ Harry Walker of the Philadelphia Phillies. He slammed 27 homers, scored 108 runs, drove in 104 and walked 87 times—all career highs. In the National League Most Valuable Player voting that year, Boston Braves third baseman Bob Elliott captured the award with numbers that were remarkably similar to Kurowski's. Elliott batted .317, hit 22 homers, scored 93 runs, drove in 113, and drew 87 bases on balls for the third-place Braves. In addition, Elliott's .956 fielding average was only slightly better than Kurowski's .954 percentage. But for some reason Whitey finished a distant ninth in the MVP balloting.

That was Kurowski's last full season as a big-league player. Although it was not publicized, his patched-up throwing arm had bothered him throughout his career.

The condition caused pinched nerves and muscle damage, and he underwent 13 operations on the arm so he could continue playing. But in 1948 his arm problems became so severe that he was limited to just 65 games in the field and a disappointing .214 batting average.

Kurowski's favorite saying, "Putting We Ahead of I," was put to the test in the spring of 1949. During his injury-plagued 1948 season, word had filtered down through the Cardinals farm system that they were looking for a replacement at the hot corner. One of the top prospects, Eddie Kazak, a second baseman for six minor-league campaigns, was shifted to third base when Kurowski started to falter. Despite the fact that Kazak was competing for his job, Whitey worked hard to teach the rookie the finer points of third-base play and was rewarded when Kazak was named the National League's starting third baseman for the 1949 All-Star Game.

While his protégé was starring in St. Louis, Kurowski spent most of the 1949 campaign trying to rehabilitate his arm with Houston in the Texas League, but it failed to come around. For the season he hit only .143 in 10 games with the Cardinals and .233 for Houston. At age 31, when many players are still in their prime, his big-league career was over.

Kurowski accepted an offer to manage the Cardinals' Lynchburg farm club in the Piedmont League in 1950, thus beginning a long and successful career as a minor-league manager and coach. He worked in the Cardinals' organization for more than a decade before moving to the New York Mets chain shortly after the franchise started. Although he was basically through as an active player after 1949, he made occasional minor-league appearances up until the 1959 season. That year his successful pinch-hitting appearance for Billings at the age of 41 gave him a 1.000 batting average for his final season as a player.

Kurowski's managing career included a stint as skipper of his hometown Reading club in the Cleveland Indians system and ended in 1972 after a disappointing season in the Carolina League. After leaving baseball, he worked for Berks County as the sealer of weights and measures before retiring from that post in 1980.

In retirement Kurowski lived in Shillington, a suburb of Reading. He was an avid golfer and a tireless autograph signer who took great pleasure in signing for fans. He died on December 9, 1999, leaving behind his wife of nearly 60 years, Joan (Setley) Kurowski; two sons; two daughters; nine grandchildren; and six great-grandchildren.

During his career with the Cardinals, Kurowski never played on a team that finished lower than second place. His lifetime batting average was a fine .286, with a career high of .323 in 1945 that tied for the fourth highest mark in the major leagues. From 1943 through 1947 he finished among the top ten in the league in home runs each season, and from 1945 through 1947 he finished among the top ten hitters in batting average, on-base percentage, slugging, total bases, and runs batted in every year. He led National League third sackers in putouts three times, in fielding twice, and in assists and double plays once. He forged a 22-game hitting streak in 1943 and was a hero of the 1946 playoff victory over the Dodgers for the pennant. Although known as a free swinger throughout his career, he posted respectable bases-on-balls totals. Despite these accomplishments Kurowski was overshadowed by more illustrious teammates, and his best finish in balloting for the National League Most Valuable Player Award was fifth place in 1945.

Kurowski held the Cardinals' record for most homers in a month with 12 until Mark McGwire came along. His three years with Rochester resulted in his selection as the third baseman on the all-time Rochester Red Wing squad. He was inducted into the Pennsylvania Sports Hall of Fame and the Polish-American Sports Hall of Fame.

This biography is an adaptation of a Whitey Kurowski profile from *Beating the Breaks: Major League Ballplayers Who Overcame Disabilities* by Rick Swaine (Jefferson, North Carolina: McFarland & Co., Inc., 2004).

SOURCES

Books

Craft, David, and Tom Owens, *Redbirds Revisited: Great Memories and Stories from St. Louis Cardinals* (Chicago: Bonus Books, 1990).

Gilbert, Bill, *They Also Served: Baseball and the Home Front 1941-45* (New York: Crown, 1992).

Golenbock, Peter, *The Spirit of St. Louis: A History of the St. Louis Cardinals and Browns* (New York, Harper Collins, 2000).

Mead, William B., *The 10 Worst Years of Baseball: The Zany, True Story of Baseball in the Forties* (New York: Van Nostrand, Reinhold, 1978).

Rains, Rob, *The St. Louis Cardinals: 100th Anniversary* (New York: St. Martin's Press, 1992).

Swaine, Rick, *Beating the Breaks: Major League Ballplayers Who Overcame Disabilities* (Jefferson, North Carolina: McFarland & Co. Inc., 2004).

Turner, Frederick, *When the Boys Came Back: Baseball and 1946* (New York: Henry Holt & Company, 1996).

Westcott, Rich, *Diamond Greats: Profiles and Interviews with 65 of Baseball's History Makers* (Westport, Connecticut: Meckler Books, 1988).

Articles

Manning, Gordon, "Kazak Spelled Backwards is Kazak." *Collier's*, September 17, 1949.

"Whitey Kurowski, All-Star ballplayer." (obituary) *Reading Eagle/Reading Times*, December 10, 1999.

Other

Family background information supplied by Whitey Kurowski's son George J. Kurowski.

Max Lanier

By Gregory H. Wolf

A HARD-THROWING SOUTHPAW AND two-time All-Star, Max Lanier won 45 games and posted an impressive 2.47 earned-run average from 1942 to 1944 for the St. Louis Cardinals, who captured three consecutive National League pennants and two World Series championships in those seasons. At the height of his career, in 1946, Lanier stunned baseball by breaking his contract with the Cardinals and jumping to the Mexican League. Suspended for five years from Organized Baseball, Lanier challenged baseball's reserve clause in federal court. He dropped his lawsuit when he was reinstated in 1949. But in large part because of chronic elbow problems that developed early in his career, he never regained the form that had made him one of the big leagues' best left-handed pitchers.

Hubert Max Lanier was born on August 18, 1915, the fifth of sixth children of Stephen Ashley and Mittie Celina (Morris) Lanier, and was raised on his parents' farm in Denton, North Carolina, located in the fertile grounds of central North Carolina about 70 miles northeast of Charlotte. Lanier was not a natural left-hander. When he was about 8 years old he broke his right arm above the elbow. His doctor set it incorrectly, requiring that it be broken again and reset. Once it healed, young Max returned to the pastures and fields to help his family on the farm and to the sandlots in his small town to play baseball. When he shattered his arm again at age 12, at the exact same spot, by cranking an old Model T Ford, the injury was more serious. With his right arm in a cast for months and immovable after that, Lanier began to throw with his left hand, though he continued to bat right-handed. "As far as I can remember," Lanier once said about learning to pitch left-handed, "I always did the pitching. I could throw pretty hard as a kid, could strike out a lot of other boys, so my team always wanted me to pitch."[1] An athletic adolescent, Lanier earned letters in basketball, baseball, and track at Denton High School.

Despite his father's protestations that baseball was a waste of time, Lanier played whenever he could and attracted the attention of scouts. Frank Rickey, the brother of St. Louis Cardinals general manager Branch Rickey, signed Lanier at the age of 17 while he was still in high school. Upon graduation in 1934, Lanier showed a glimpse of the independence, stubbornness, and concern for his own financial well-being that led to his jump to the Mexican League 12 years later. Desiring a fast track to the big leagues, Lanier balked at the idea of being sent to Martinsville in the Class D Bi-State League, claiming that he could earn more money playing semipro ball in North Carolina. The Cardinals relented and assigned him to the Greensboro Patriots in the Class B Piedmont League, but Lanier left the team after pitching just a third of an inning in two appearances, surrendering three earned runs and walking four.

For the next 2½ seasons Lanier played semipro baseball in nearby Emmons Township and Asheboro, North Carolina, in the highly competitive Carolina Textile League for $240 a month.[2] "It was really a matter of money," Lanier said several years later. "I could make a lot more pitching for the Asheboro mill team … than

I could get from the Cardinals."[3] A local pitching legend of sorts, Lanier supposedly won 16 consecutive games in 1936, and again attracted the attention of big-league scouts. Chick Doak, the baseball coach at North Carolina State University and a part-time scout for the Philadelphia Athletics, recommended to manager-owner Connie Mack that he sign the hard-throwing 21-year-old. Mack approached Branch Rickey, since the Cardinals still owned the rights to Lanier. Mack's interest rekindled Rickey's curiosity, and the general manager sent his brother Frank to Denton in the spring of 1937 to persuade Lanier to reconsider professional ball. Promised an assignment with the Cardinals' top affiliate, the Columbus Red Birds in the American Association, Lanier readily agreed to the new favorable terms.

Reporting to manager Burt Shotton's Red Birds, Lanier impressed the Cardinals in his first full season of professional baseball. He made 38 appearances, including 12 starts, won ten of 14 decisions, and posted the league's second-best ERA (3.06) in 147 innings. Lanier also won a game in the team's seven-game Junior World Series loss to the International League's Newark Bears. The Cardinals purchased Lanier's contract after the season and invited him to his first big-league spring training in 1938.

Still a raw pitcher, Lanier struggled with control but his fastball and sweeping curve suggested unlimited potential. Lanier earned a spot in the bullpen for Frankie Frisch's Cardinals and made his major-league debut on April 20, 1938, in the second game of the season, relieving starter Si Johnson and pitching two unspectacular innings (four hits and two runs) in a 9-4 loss to the Pittsburgh Pirates at Sportsman's Park. With a 4.38 ERA in 15 appearances (including two brief, ineffective starts), Lanier was optioned to Columbus to work on his control. He earned a September call-up on the strength of a stellar 2.25 ERA over 44 innings, but finished winless in three decisions in his rookie season.

Lanier started the 1939 season with Columbus, which staggered to a 62-82 record, the Red Birds' worst season since 1927.[4] Depressed about his demotion, Lanier struggled with his control and concentration, and felt his dreams of the big leagues slipping away. A teammate, pitcher Max Macon, suggested that he start golfing to escape the pressure of pitching. The solitude, the concentration on the links, and an emphasis on hand-eye coordination helped. Despite 16 losses (fourth highest in the league) and a league-leading 105 walks in 200 innings, Lanier showed flashes of dominance, attested by his circuit-best 148 strikeouts. In another September call-up, he was thrust into a tight pennant race with the Cincinnati Reds. In his first start, on September 5 against the Reds, Lanier gave up two runs in the tenth inning and was charged with the 3-1 loss. On the 19th he tossed a complete-game five-hitter, and rapped two hits to earn his first big-league victory in a 6-1 win over the Dodgers that put the Cardinals 2½ games behind the Reds. Described as a "late-season sensation," Lanier posted an impressive 2.39 ERA in 37⅔ innings in September.[5] The Sporting News compared the young lefty to former Red Sox star pitcher Dutch Leonard, saying, "[Lanier] is a well-constructed athlete with a lot of poise and judgment. He whips the ball."[6]

Even before he arrived at spring training in 1940, the press touted Lanier as the Cardinals' number-one southpaw. The Sporting News called him the "best among newcomers" in camp, a group that included Frank Barrett, Harry Brecheen. Murry Dickson, Preacher Roe, and Ernie White.[7] Laboring through most of the season as a spot starter and reliever, Lanier was just 2-5 at the beginning of July and was described as the "biggest disappointment" in midseason for the underachieving Cardinals, who were 14 games below .500 on July 11. Unexpectedly, Billy Southworth, the team's third manager of the season, transformed the Cardinals into the hottest team in the National League. They played at a 57-28 clip to salvage the season and finish in third place. Lanier concluded his season by pitching three consecutive complete-game victories, including a 12-inning 4-3 win over the Chicago Cubs in front of just 1,623 fans at Sportsman's Park on September 28. He finished with a 9-6 record and a 3.34 ERA in 105 innings.

In 1941 Lanier developed elbow problems that he contended with for the rest of his career. His season was as erratic as it was frustrating. Through the first five weeks of the season he was limited to just 18 innings (and two starts, one of which was a complete-game victory). When healthy, Lanier pitched well. Beginning on May 27, he commenced his best stretch of the year, completed five of six starts, posted a 2.08 ERA in 52 innings, and proved that he was one of the most unhittable pitchers in the league (batters hit just .204 against him). Then, starting in late July, Lanier went almost two months without winning a start before concluding with a complete-game victory over the Braves on September 17 and a shutout over the Pirates on the 23rd. All the while, the Cardinals and Dodgers battled in an exciting pennant race that the Dodgers won by 2½ games. For the season, despite his elbow miseries, Lanier posted a 10-8 record and a stellar 2.82 ERA in 153 innings. Among his 35 appearances were 18 starts. Lanier's tender elbow and inconsistency, coupled with 24-year-old left-hander Ernie White's breakout season (17-7 and a 2.40 ERA) tempered the club's expectations from him.

In 1942 the Cardinals began spring training in St. Petersburg, Florida, with the big leagues' deepest pitching staff, boasting at least eight legitimate starters; all but 33-year-old Lon Warneke were products of the team's farm system. Mort Cooper, Murry Dickson, Howie Krist, Lanier, Howie Pollet, White, and rookie Johnny Beazley all made at least 26 appearances and pitched at least 109 innings during the season. The Cardinals set a post-Deadball Era National League record for lowest team ERA (2.55), led by MVP Cooper's league-leading 1.78 mark. Lanier's 2.96 ERA was the highest of the home-grown group.

Elbow miseries limited Lanier to 11 appearances (seven starts) and extended periods of inactivity through June. In just his second start in five weeks, he tossed a six-hit shutout over Boston on July 24 to keep the Cardinals within seven games of the streaking Dodgers. With a healthy elbow at last, Lanier won his last three decisions in July and six of his first seven in August while the red-hot Cardinals went 22-9 in July and 25-8 in August to set the stage for a dramatic September. On September 12 Lanier held the Dodgers to five hits in a 2-1 victory at Ebbets Field in the final meeting of the two rivals. It was Lanier's fifth victory against the Dodgers and gave the Cardinals a share of the lead. St.

Louis won 12 of the remaining 14 games to capture the pennant by two games and set a franchise record with 106 victories.

Though Lanier distinguished himself in World Series competition over the years by posting an excellent 1.71 ERA in 31⅔ innings, his first appearance in the fall classic, in 1942, was a forgettable one. Facing the New York Yankees in relief, Lanier, pitching the ninth inning in Game One, made two throwing errors and issued a walk in a 7-4 loss. He redeemed himself in Game Four. Entering a game tied 6-6, Lanier held the Yankees scoreless over the final three innings and drove in a run to earn the victory in the Cardinals' comeback 9-6 win. Johnny Beazley won the next day to secure the Redbirds' first championship since the Gashouse Gang in 1934.

During the offseason, Lanier tended his family's farm in Denton. He married high-school sweetheart Lillian Bell (Doby) in 1934 shortly before he began his professional career. They had three children, Maxine, Betty, and Hal, who had a ten-year big-league career (1964-73) as an infielder for the Giants and Yankees. Lillie, Max's wife, died on December 24, 1948, when her car skidded off an icy road. In October 1949 Lanier married Betty Cunningham, with whom he had two children, Terry and Ruth.

Lanier was an avid hunter, fisher, golfer, and basketball fan. He played for the McCrary Eagles, a semipro basketball team from Asheboro, and competed against local colleges and other semipro teams in hoops-crazed North Carolina. A county boy at heart, Lanier was said to have a "fine moaning mountaineer hillbilly voice," and enjoyed singing and playing the guitar and harmonica.[8] When he came up with the Cardinals he played in Pepper Martin's Mudcat Band, a bluegrass group made up of players. Later in his career with the Cardinals, he was known for monopolizing the clubhouse record player and playing country music before home games.

Lanier's success in 1942 reignited discussions that he "could be the best southpaw in baseball" if he could stay healthy.[9] The Sporting News wrote that Lanier "had more stuff than any other left-hander in the league."[10] He had a powerful overhand delivery to right-handers and dropped to a three-quarters to side-arm delivery to left-handers, making his curveball even more unhit-table. He had a "blazing fastball" and effective change of pace, and beginning in 1942 a deceptive hard knuckleball.[11]

A victim of poor run support to start the 1943 season, Lanier lost two consecutive hard-luck complete games in May, a 13⅓-inning effort against the Cubs (2-1) and a 9⅔-inning outing against the Braves (4-3) by sur-rendering walk-off hits. After receiving extra time between starts to ensure that his elbow remained healthy, Lanier hurled his third extra-inning complete game of the month on May 28. He limited the Braves to five hits and scored the winning run himself in the bottom of the tenth on Lou Klein's triple in a 2-1 victory. Boasting a 5-4 record and a 2.56 ERA, Lanier was named to the NL All-Star team for the first of two times in his career. Other Cardinals on the squad managed by Billy Southworth were Marty Marion, Stan Musial, Mort Cooper, and Howie Pollet. Lanier did not see action in the game.

The reigning world champions began a surge in July, winning 68 games and losing just 25 through the rest of the season. After the All-Star Game, Lanier (10-3 with a 1.51 ERA) was arguably the best pitcher in the major leagues, and with Mort Cooper (10-3, 2.68 in the second half) formed the most formidable lefty-righty combo in baseball. Lanier ended the season by tossing four consecutive complete-game victories and saving a game in relief. At season's end he had a career-low and NL-leading 1.90 ERA. He surrendered just three home runs all season. The Cardinals had lost Harry Gumbert and Ernie White to injuries and phenom Pollet to the military, but reloaded with Harry Brecheen and Al Brazle and again led the league in team ERA (2.57).

In a rematch against the Yankees, Lanier started Game One of the 1943 World Series, which was played in a 3-4 format (with just one travel day) due to wartime travel restrictions. Lanier limited New York to seven baserunners (seven hits and no walks) over seven innings, but was undone by his own mistakes, as the Cardinals absorbed a 4-2 loss. His error on Frank Crosetti's infield hit led to two unearned runs in the fourth inning; a wild pitch in the sixth inning allowed

Crosetti to score and Billy Johnson to scamper from first to third (he later scored on a single by Bill Dickey). Lanier took the mound again in Game Four in St. Louis with the Cardinals down two games to one. He pitched seven strong innings, surrendering just four hits and one run, but did not get the decision in the Cardinals' 2-1 loss. In the Yankees' Game Five Series-clinching win, Lanier pitched 1⅓ innings of scoreless relief. New York limited the Cardinals, who led the NL in hitting (.279) and were second in runs scored (679), to nine runs in the Series.

Touted as a future 20-game winner, Lanier began the 1944 season by hurling complete-game victories in six of his first seven starts. Included were three dominat-ing shutouts: a two-hitter against the Pirates, a three-hitter versus the Cubs, and an overpowering three-hitter against the Giants on May 20 when he struck out a career-high 11 batters. After losing four starts, Lanier enjoyed a career-best ten-game winning streak in July and August while the Redbirds built an insurmountable lead for the second consecutive year. On July 2, Lanier tossed a career-high 14-inning complete game to beat the arch-rival Dodgers, 2-1. (From 1942 through 1944, no pitcher had more success against the Dodgers than Lanier, who defeated them five times each year and lost only three total.) Lanier was named to the All-Star team again, but Southworth chose not to pitch him, undoubtedly hoping to spare his elbow. The stocky lefthander concluded one of the most dominating extended stretches in his career (85⅔ innings and a 1.37 ERA) by tossing his fifth and final shutout of the season (a five-hitter against the Giants) followed by his only career one-hitter in a 2-1 defeat of the Braves on August 22. It was Lanier's 17th and last win of the season. Suffering from terrible swelling in his elbow, a pulled muscle in his back, and excruciating stomach pains (later determined to be a severe case of appendicitis requiring surgery), Lanier lost seven consecutive starts to end the season.

Despite fears that Lanier would miss the World Series against the surprising St. Louis Browns, with whom the Cardinals shared Sportsman's Park, the feisty North Carolinian started Game Two and limited the Browns to five hits and two runs in seven innings, his longest outing in almost three weeks. The Cardinals won, 3-2, on Ken O'Dea's pinch single in the 11th inning. In Game Six, Lanier fought back pain to pitch 5⅓ innings of three-hit ball, surrendering one run, before yielding to Ted Wilks, who pitched 3⅔ hitless innings to save the 3-1 victory that gave the Cardinals their second championship in three seasons. With the victory, Lanier improved his record to 2-1 in World Series competition.

Like all major-league teams, the Cardinals lost players to military service during World War II. When Lanier passed his Army physical in December 1944, it was assumed that he would be called to active service before spring training, joining Cardinal hurlers Beazley, Brazle, Ken Burkhart, Dickson, Krist, Red Munger, Pollet, Fred Schmidt, and White in the military. Said Cardinals owner Sam Breadon, "I have a better pitching staff in the service than Billy Southworth can put on the field."[12] Lanier's record was 2-2 with a 1.73 ERA when he was inducted into the Army at Fort Bragg on May 24, 1945.[13] He remained stateside during his abbreviated stint in the service, pitching and playing outfield on his camp team. The war ended in August and Lanier was discharged in October as a "hardship case" which eventually led to claims that he had received special treatment.[14] After investigating, the military called the charges baseless.[15]

Throughout Lanier's career, he battled with Breadon over salary. A contentious dispute after the 1944 season heightened the tensions and in early 1946 *The Sporting News* said there was a "strong feeling" that Lanier would be traded.[16] Saying he was dissatisfied with the Cardinals' contract offer, Lanier held out at the start of spring training and reported to camp late.[17] The holdout apparently had no ill effects. Described as "faster than Feller" and in great shape, Lanier began the season with six consecutive complete-game victories, including two shutouts and an 11-inning effort against the Dodgers at Ebbets Field.[18] Then the unthinkable happened. At the peak of his career, Lanier jumped to the Mexican League.

Jorge Pasquel, the president and leading promoter of the Mexican League, and his four brothers poured millions of dollars into the upstart league in an attempt to create a viable rival to the major leagues. Pasquel had successfully lured stars from the Negro Leagues in the early 1940s, and in 1946 actively recruited big leaguers with promises of exorbitant salaries to "jump" to his league. On May 23 news broke that Lanier, Fred Schmidt, and Lou Klein of the Cardinals had accepted Pasquel's contract offers. "I can make more money down there in a few seasons than I could in a lifetime in St. Louis," Lanier supposedly told his roommate Red Schoendienst.[19] Unsubstantiated reports circulated that Lanier had received a $50,000 bonus and a five-year contract worth $30,000 a year. (Almost all major leaguers at the time signed one-year contracts and Lanier reportedly earned about $11,000.)[20] Other big leaguers followed, among them All-Star catcher Mickey Owen and pitcher Sal Maglie. Commissioner Happy Chandler summarily suspended all "Mexican jumpers" from Organized Baseball for five years.[21]

By the time Lanier was reinstated in June 1949, he had lost three years of his prime (ages 30-32) while pitching in Mexico, winter ball in Cuba, in an independent league in Canada, semipro ball in the US, and as the leader of a barnstorming team. He admitted that his jump to the Mexican League was not what he expected, despite the immediate financial rewards. "I thought the conditions would be better," he said, referring to poor fields and lighting, and unprofessional behavior.[22] Pitching for the Veracruz team, he suffered from bursitis in his left elbow and inflamed muscles in his first season, and was ineffective.[23] Throughout his season and a half in Mexico, he fought with the Pasquel brothers about his contract and extra pay during the postseason in 1946, and abruptly quit the league in 1947 after playing less than two months.[24] Lanier was excoriated in the American press as an egotistical money-grubber who turned his back on his teammates. Reports published in *The Sporting News* about his struggles as a pitching nomad read like opening warnings to players against challenging the authority of baseball.

In 1948 Commissioner Chandler, and team owners vowed not to soften their stance against the 22 big-league "jumpers" Chandler had banned.[25] In March 1949 Lanier and teammate Fred Martin filed lawsuits seeking $2.5 million in damages. They charged that baseball was a monopoly and the reserve clause was illegal, and requested immediate reinstatement. After two judicial rulings against reinstatement, it appeared as though Lanier and Martin might have their day in court; but rather than risk a test of the legality of the reserve clause, Chandler offered general amnesty to all the jumpers in June 1949. Lanier withdrew his lawsuit, citing exceptional "treatment and consideration" by the Cardinals organization in accepting him.[26] The "game needs a reserve clause," Lanier said publicly. "[It] preserves order [and] aids competition."[27]

When Lanier returned to the Cardinals on June 24, 1949 (after playing briefly for Drummondville, Quebec, in the independent Provincial League), the 33-year-old had not pitched a full season in the big leagues since 1944, and had lost almost four years to the military and his suspension. Age and the years away had taken their toll. Before jumping, Lanier had a career record of 74-47 with a 2.63 ERA; after his return he was 34-35 and his ERA was a run higher (3.64).

The Cardinals were a team in transition when Lanier returned. Sam Breadon's sale of the team to Fred Saigh and minority partner Robert Hannegan after the 1947 season had ended a long, successful run dating back to 1926. Lanier joined the Redbirds in an exciting pennant race in 1949, but it was the last time the team seriously contended until 1957, and the only time they finished higher than third place from 1950 to 1962.

In 1950 and 1951 Lanier won 11 games and lost 9 each season with ERAs (3.13 and 3.26 respectively) much better than the league average, but he was no longer a front-line starter. And the Cardinals' pitching staff, always a strength during the Rickey years, had grown old. Lanier (35 years old), Brecheen (36), Brazle (37), Munger (32), and Wilks (35) had been largely together for almost a decade. With 23 starts among his 31 appearances in 1951, Lanier closed out his tenure with the Cardinals with a dominating stretch, evoking memories of 1943 and 1944. Beginning with a commanding two-hit shutout over the Reds on August 11, he hurled six consecutive complete-game victories, concluding with a ten-inning, 2-1 victory over the Pirates on September 9. It was Lanier's last win in a Cardinals uniform. In December he was traded along

with utilityman Chuck Diering to the New York Giants for infielder and player-manager Eddie Stanky, who succeeded Marty Marion as manager, the first skipper from outside the organization since Jack Hendricks in 1918.

The second-place Giants went 92-62 in 1952, but Lanier pitched inconsistently. In his debut he surrendered a career-high ten earned runs in a loss to the Dodgers, the team he had always dominated and one of the reasons manager Leo Durocher wanted to acquire him. Relegated to the bullpen and spot starting duty for much of May and June, he reeled off a streak of 22⅔ scoreless innings, highlighted by his last big-league shutout (in a start against the Phillies on July 6) which earned him another chance in the rotation. With the Giants attempting to mount a challenge to the league-leading Dodgers, Lanier tossed a complete-game four-hitter to beat the Boston Braves on September 1. It proved to be his last win in the major leagues.

Described as a "flop" with the Giants in 1952, Lanier was released on May 15, 1953, and was picked up by Bill Veeck and the St. Louis Browns two weeks later.[28] Reunited with Marty Marion (the Browns' manager) and Harry Brecheen (in his last season), the 37-year-old Lanier was worn out. With a 7.25 ERA in 22⅓ innings, he was released in July and his 14-year big-league career came to an end. He finished with 108 wins and a 3.01 ERA. His career 126 ERA+ (also called adjusted ERA, a metric that compares a pitcher's ERA to the league's ERA and adjusts it for ballpark factors) ranks him right behind Bob Gibson, Tom Seaver, and six others.

After being released, Lanier pitched in the Texas League with Shreveport (1953) and Beaumont (1954). In 1956 he attempted a comeback, first with the Philadelphia Phillies and then with the Miami Marlins of the International League, but was among the last players cut on each team.

Lanier settled in St. Petersburg, Florida, where he had been living with his wife, Betty. He was involved in varied business interests, including a restaurant called the Diamond Café, before returning to baseball in 1961 when the San Francisco Giants hired him as a scout, roving pitching instructor, and all-around trouble-shooter. Throughout the 1960s and early 1970s, he managed several low-level farm teams in the Giants, Phillies, and Tigers farm systems. In 1967 he was named manager of the year for the Batavia (New York) Trojans in the short-season New York-Pennsylvania League.

After his baseball days, Max and Betty retired to Dunnellon, Florida, about 100 miles north of St. Petersburg. He died on January 30, 2007, at the age of 91, and is buried in the Dunnellon Memorial Gardens.

SOURCES

Newspapers

New York Times

The Sporting News

Online Sources

Ancestry.com

BaseballLibrary.com

Baseball-Reference.com

Retrosheet.com

Other

Max Lanier player file at the National Baseball Hall of Fame, Cooperstown, New York

NOTES

1   *The Sporting News*, September 17, 1942, 3.

2   Dr. Harold and Dorothy Seymour, *Baseball: The People's Game* (New York: Oxford University Press, 1990), 252.

3   *The Sporting News*, September 17, 1942, 3.

4   The Red Birds' .403 winning percentage was their lowest since 1927, when they went 60-108 (.357). Bill O'Neal, *The American Association. A Baseball History 1902-1991* (Austin, Texas: Eakin Press, 1991).

5   *The Sporting News*, January 4, 1940, 10.

6   *The Sporting News*, September 28, 1939, 3.

7   *The Sporting News*, March 7, 1940, 1.

8   *The Sporting News*, August 10, 1944, 3.

9   *The Sporting News*, April 1, 1943, 6.

10   *The Sporting News*, June 17, 1943, 1.

11   *The Sporting News*, August 10, 1944, 3.

12   *The Sporting News*, May 31, 1945, 8.

13   Ibid.

14   *The Sporting News*, October 25, 1945, 6.

15   *The Sporting News*, December 20, 1945, 6

16   *The Sporting News*, January 17, 1946, 14

17   *The Sporting News*, February 21, 1946, 6.

18   *The Sporting News*, April 11, 1946, 13.

19   *The Sporting News*, June 5, 1946, 7.

20   Mike Eisenbath, *The Cardinals Encyclopedia* (Philadelphia: Temple University Press, 1999), 224.

21   *The Sporting News*, August 21, 1946, 2.

22   Rich Westcott, *Splendor on the Diamond: Interviews with 35 Stars of Baseball's Past* (Gainesville, Florida: University of Florida Press, 2000), 228.

23   *The Sporting News*, August 14, 1946, 6.

24   *The Sporting News*, October 13, 1947, 1.

25   *The Sporting News*, January 28, 1948, 2; February 11, 1948, 1.

26   *The Sporting News*, September 7, 1949, 14.

27   *The Sporting News*, September 28, 1949, 1.

28   The "Flop" characterization appeared in *The Sporting News*, January 28, 1953, 8.

Eddie Waitkus

by C. Paul Rogers III

EDDIE WAITKUS WAS A SLICK-FIELDING first baseman who in an 11-year big-league career for three teams batted a solid .285 and struck out only 204 times in 4,681 plate appearances. Although a fine ballplayer, he would today likely be little remembered but for what happened to him on June 14, 1949, in a room at the Edgewater Beach Hotel in Chicago. That evening a young, obsessed female fan named Ruth Steinhagen lured Waitkus to her hotel room with a cryptic note and then shot him in the chest, critically wounding him.

The Waitkus shooting is said to have inspired Bernard Malamud to write his iconic baseball novel, *The Natural*, which he published in 1952 and which was later immortalized in the Robert Redford movie by the same name in 1984.[1]

Waitkus managed to survive the shooting after enduring four operations, and returned to the major leagues in 1950, playing a key role in the Philadelphia Philles Whiz Kids' rush to the National League pennant. But the story does not have a happy ending. Waitkus was never really able to recover emotionally from the shooting, and his post-baseball career was particularly difficult. He battled depression and alcoholism and endured a nervous breakdown before succumbing to cancer just after his 53rd birthday.

Life began for Eddie Waitkus on September 4, 1919, in Cambridge, Massachusetts. He was born to Veronica and Stephen Waitkus, Lithuanian immigrants who met and fell in love on their passage to America. Eddie grew up, with younger sister Stella, in a modest flat in East Cambridge. He first learned to play baseball at Cambridge Field, a neighborhood park just a block from his home. He was a natural right-hander and liked to pitch, but didn't have a glove, so he first played bare-handed.[2]

When Eddie was 8, his father, a butcher by trade who was an accomplished swimmer but knew nothing about baseball, brought home a first baseman's glove for his son. Young Eddie was thrilled but didn't have the heart to tell his father that he was a pitcher, not a first baseman, and that the glove was for a left-handed thrower. Instead, he just taught himself how to throw left-handed and became a first baseman.[3]

At Cambridge Field, Waitkus came under the tutelage of Jack Burns, who played first base in the big leagues for seven years with the St. Louis Browns and Detroit Tigers. Burns, whose big-league career was ending in 1936 just as Waitkus was preparing for his senior year of high school, taught Eddie the finer points of first-base play.[4]

Eddie's life was to be full of hardships and the first occurred when he was only 14. His mother was hospitalized with pneumonia and died just days later.

Despite the tragedy, Waitkus went on to become an honor student at Cambridge Latin High, where he studied foreign languages, was a star debater, and graduated sixth in a class of 600. When he was a sophomore he walked into a baseball practice with his trusty first baseman's mitt, only to be told by the coach that the team already had a first baseman. Eddie asked the coach to at least let him take a few grounders and after he

scooped up everything hit his way, was told to grab a bat. Waitkus proceeded to smack line drives all over the park and all of a sudden Latin High had a new first baseman.[5]

By the time Waitkus graduated, he was a legend on the baseball field as well as in the classroom. He hit .600 his senior year, including a prodigious home-run blast that landed on the top of a three-story apartment building beyond the right-field fence. He was named to every All-Scholastic team in the Boston area in 1937 and that summer played in the semipro Suburban Twilight League. He considered accepting a scholarship to play baseball at either Harvard, Holy Cross, or Duke but playing for the Worumbo Indians of Lisbon Falls, Maine, in the fast Maine League during the summer of 1938 changed any college plans.[6]

Waitkus played exceptionally well and became the top prospect in New England that summer. His club won the Maine championship and qualified for the National Baseball Congress tournament in Wichita, Kansas, where it won two games before being eliminated. Waitkus hit over .500 in Wichita and fielded flawlessly. After the young first baseman was named by major-league scouts to an All American semipro team, Boston sportswriter Fred Barry proved prescient when he wrote, "These big league 'wise men' viewed the left-handed batting and throwing of 19-year-old Waitkus and termed him a 'natural.'"[7]

Ralph Wheeler, the high-school sports editor for the *Boston Herald*, had close ties with the Chicago Cubs and arranged for Waitkus to work out for Cubs manager Gabby Hartnett on Chicago's last trip to Boston to play the Bees. That led to a contract and a $2,500 bonus from the Cubs, who assigned him to the Moline Plow Boys of the Class B Three-I League for the 1939 season.[8]

Eddie got off to slow start at Moline, perhaps because he had never played night baseball before, and after eight weeks was hitting only .189. But then he hit his stride and finished with a .326 batting average and a dozen triples, making the league's All-Star team while playing for a seventh-place team.

That performance earned Waitkus a promotion to the Tulsa Oilers of the Class A Texas League for 1940. He adjusted to the faster league quite well, batting .303

in 162 games and leading the league in hits with 192. Dizzy Dean, who was trying to rehab a sore arm, spent much of the summer with the Oilers and roomed with Waitkus when the team was on the road. While it would seem that the 30-year-old Southern country boy Dean and the 20-year-old kid from Boston would have little in common, they became fast friends. In fact, Dean became one of Waitkus's biggest supporters.

In 1941 the Cubs invited Eddie to Catalina Island for spring training, where Dean continued to sing his praises. Waitkus didn't disappoint and made an impact that spring. When the season opened on April 15 in cold and windy Wrigley Field, he was the Cubs' starting first baseman. Hitting second in the lineup, he slapped a single in four-at-bats and recorded 13 putouts at first base as the Cubs defeated the Pirates 7-4.

But both the Cubs and Waitkus struggled thereafter with the team settling in the second division and Eddie garnering only four singles in 21 at-bats in part-time duty for the first month of the season. In the middle of May, he was returned to Tulsa, where he finished the season, hitting .293 in 125 games.

As a result of that solid performance, the Cubs assigned Waitkus to the Los Angeles Angels of the Pacific Coast League for 1942. This time he didn't miss a beat stepping up to tougher competition and in 175 games and 766 plate appearances he batted .336 to finish near the top of the league in batting average. In fact, he led the league with 235 hits for the season. In spite of that, the year ended on a sour note as the Angels blew a four-game lead over the Sacramento Solons in the last five days of the season to finish in second place by a game. Waitkus, the team's leading hitter all summer, slumped as well, failing to drive in a run in the season-ending series.[9]

During his year with the Angels, Waitkus got a taste of Hollywood, appearing in several action scenes batting and at first base during the filming of *Pride of the Yankees*. Apparently the movie's producers thought that his swing and fielding more resembled Lou Gehrig's than did Gary Cooper's.[10]

One would normally expect that Waitkus would be back in Catalina Island with the Cubs in 1943. World War II, however, intervened, as it did for so many, and

Eddie spent that spring in Army basic training in Fort Devens, Massachusetts. He was assigned to the 544th Engineering Boat and Shore Regiment and on May 2, 1944, shipped overseas from San Francisco to Oro Bay, New Guinea. Over the next 17 months Waitkus would see heavy combat on New Guinea, Morotai, Bougainville, and Luzon.[11] He survived bloody initial beach landings on Morotai, Bougainville, and the Phillipines, where he narrowly escaped being taken prisoner by the Japanese.[12]

After Manila was secured, Waitkus worked with his outfit to repair Rizal Stadium, which could hold up to 30,000 GIs. After the booby-traps and a corpse were removed and foxholes and bomb craters were filled in, he and his mates played games in T-shirts, fatigues, and combat boots.[13] Waitkus later remembered that soldiers from his unit wagered $60,000 against soldiers of the 594th Regiment for a game between the two.[14] In September 1945, while the Cubs were winning the National League pennant, he and the rest of the 544th were among the first troops ashore at Wakayama, Japan.

Waitkus finished the war with ten meritorious service awards, including four bronze stars and four overseas bars.[15]

Eddie was 26 years old when he reported to Catalina Island for the Cubs' 1946 spring training after 34 months in the service. The only problem was that the Cubs had a first baseman, Phil Cavarretta, who was coming off a batting championship (.355) and a National League Most Valuable Player Award. When Waitkus arrived, manager Charlie Grimm, also a former slick-fielding first baseman, told him to go to first and take some groundballs. For a full 15 minutes Grimm futilely tried to smash a ball past Waitkus, but could not. Before long, the question was not whether Eddie would make the team, but when and where the team would move Cavarretta to make room for him at first base.[16]

Once the season began, Bill Nicholson, the Cubs' right fielder, continued his slump from the previous year, and on April 25 manager Grimm benched Nicholson, moved Cavarretta to right field, and inserted Waitkus at first base. Batting sixth, Waitkus singled twice, doubled, and drove in two runs in his first game as a starter. Thereafter the job was his. By mid-June he

was hitting .310 and fielding flawlessly. On June 23 Eddie got into the major-league record book when fellow rookie Marv Rickert and he hit back-to-back inside-the-park home runs in the Polo Grounds against the Giants. They were the first duo ever to accomplish the feat.

Waitkus finished the season with a .304 batting average, the only Cub regular to hit over .300, as the team slipped to third place, 14½ games behind the pennant-winning Cardinals. In 106 games at first base he committed only four errors for a .996 fielding average. The Chicago chapter of the Baseball Writers Association of America named him Rookie of the Year ahead of Del Ennis of the Phillies. He even finished 13th in the balloting for National League MVP, an unusual accolade for a rookie. According to Charlie Grimm, he was "easily the best all-round first sacker in our league."[17]

Now entrenched as the Cubs' first baseman, Waitkus battled injuries early in 1947, but when he was in there he still hit for a solid average, typically batting second in the batting order. He slumped in late May and early June, dropping to .244, but steadily improved his average the rest of the year. He had a big day at the plate on September 14 with a triple and two singles against the Boston Braves. For the season, he finished at .292 in 130 games, third best on a team that slipped to sixth place with a 69-85 record.

Waitkus and two other bachelors on the Cubs, Rickert and pitcher Russ Meyer, enjoyed the Chicago nightlife together since the Cubs played all day games at Wrigley. Eddie was known as a very sharp dresser whom the ladies much admired. Sometimes after dinner the threesome would go bowling or hit a nightclub. A favorite was the 5100 Club, where they would sometimes have ringside seats when comedian Danny Thomas performed.[18]

The Cubs continued their downward slide in 1948, finishing in the National League basement with a 64-90 record. It was hard to fault Waitkus, however, as he turned in another solid season, batting .295 in 139 games. He was even named to the National League All-Star team to back up starting first baseman Johnny Mize. Eddie walked in his only appearance, pinch-hitting for Johnny Sain in the sixth inning. Late in the season,

Charlie Grimm, trying something new, even sent Waitkus to the outfield for 20 games. It was the only time in his career that he played a position other than first base.[19]

After the season the Cubs were on the trade market to try to resurrect the franchise, and found a willing partner in the sixth-place Philadelphia Phillies, who under new ownership were eager to turn their team into a contender. At the winter meetings in December, the two clubs announced a blockbuster trade with the Cubs sending Waitkus and pitcher Hank Borowy to the Phillies in exchange for pitchers Dutch Leonard and Walt Dubiel. Although trade rumors had Waitkus headed to the Giants or Dodgers, he was happy with the deal in part because he would be rejoining teammates Russ Meyer and Bill Nicholson, whom the Cubs had dealt to the Phillies earlier in the offseason.

Rogers Hornsby, the outspoken former Cubs manager, was not so thrilled. According to the Rajah, "The Cubs have two real ballplayers—Andy Pafko and Eddie Waitkus. They can't trade the best first baseman in the business." But of course they did and, as it turned out, the Phillies got a key component of their Whiz Kids club that would win the 1950 National League pennant.[20]

The slick-fielding Waitkus had an immediate impact on the longtime doormat Phillies in '49 as the club flirted with the first division for much of the early season. By the first week of May, he was batting third in the order and hitting over .300. His teammates tabbed him "the Fred Astaire of first basemen," and manager Eddie Sawyer compared him to George Sisler and Joe Kuhel, two of the top glove men of all time at first.[21]

Waitkus continued to enjoy the nightlife while with the Phillies, particularly with his old Cubs teammates Meyer and Nicholson, who was his roommate on the road. On June 14 the Phillies had just begun a 15-day road trip and had defeated the Cubs at Wrigley Field that afternoon, 9-2 behind Meyer's complete-game pitching. Waitkus was enjoying his best year in the big leagues, hitting .306 and leading in the balloting for the All-Star Game.

That evening Waitkus went out for dinner and drinks with Nicholson and Meyer, Russ's fiancée, Mary, and Meyer's parents, visiting from nearby Peru, Illinois. After dinner, Nicholson and Waitkus took a cab separate from Meyer back to the Edgewater Beach Hotel, where the Phillies were staying.

When they arrived, Eddie suggested that Nicholson go down to the Beachwalk to find Meyer and ask him to join them for a nightcap. In the meantime, a bellhop approached Waitkus and told him that he had a note from a girl in his mailbox at the front desk. Eddie retrieved the note and read it while walking through the lobby. The writer identified herself as Ruth Anne Burns and gave her room number as 1297-A. She wrote, "It's extremely important that I see you as soon as possible. We're not acquainted but I have something of importance to speak to you about. I think it would be to your advantage to let me explain it to you." The note concluded by saying, "Please come soon. I won't take much of your time."

Waitkus returned to the front desk and asked who was registered in room 1297-A. The clerk told him that the registration was to a Ruth Anne Burns from Portland Street in Boston. That information made Waitkus a little uneasy, as he had grown up on Portland Street in East Cambridge. Eddie decided that he should find Nicholson and Meyer for that drink and joined them at a small table at the back of the Beachwalk. He showed his teammates the strange note and finally decided he should call on Ruth Anne Burns, thinking she might be a family acquaintance who was in need of help.

He first called the room, and it seemed to him that Ruth Anne may have been asleep. But she urged him to come up and at about 11:30 he knocked on her room door. Ruth Ann opened the door and bade him come in. Waitkus entered the room and walked past her in the tiny room and sat down in a small armchair by the window.

The girl, who was in reality 19-year-old Ruth Ann Steinhagen of Chicago, appeared from behind the door brandishing a .22-caliber rifle and said, "I have a surprise for you. You are not going to bother me anymore."

Waitkus stiffened immediately and said, "What goes on here? Is this some kind of joke? What have I done?"

She answered by shooting Waitkus once in the abdomen. As Eddie slumped down he said over and over, "Oh baby, why did you do that?"

Steinhagen at first wasn't convinced she'd shot Waitkus, but eventually stepped over Eddie, returned the gun to the closet, and called the front desk, saying that she had just shot a man in her room.

That call probably saved Waitkus's life. He was near death when he was taken to the Illinois Masonic Hospital. The bullet had pierced a lung and was lodged near his spine. He would undergo two operations at Masonic before being transferred to Billings Memorial Hospital on the University of Chicago campus, where he had a third operation. There he developed a persistent fever and it was determined that he needed a fourth operation to remove the bullet.

After being indicted for attempted murder, Ruth Ann Steinhagen was declared mentally ill and committed to the Kankakee State Hospital. She had been obsessed with Waitkus since she first saw him play for the Cubs in April of 1947. Although she had never met him, she attended all the Cubs games and would wait for him to pass by outside the clubhouse after the games. Her room was a virtual shrine to Waitkus and she ultimately decided that if she couldn't have him, nobody could.[22]

Waitkus's recovery was near miraculous. He spent a month in the hospital before returning to Philadelphia by air on July 17, where 500 fans braved the pouring rain to greet him. By early August the Phillies were in their worst slump of the season, having lost five games in a row and ten of 13. Waitkus was restless convalescing in his Philadelphia apartment and, accompanied by Babe Alexander of the Phillies' front office, flew to Pittsburgh, where the Phillies were playing the Pirates. He walked unannounced into the Phillies clubhouse, where his teammates were shocked at how much weight he had lost. But his visit must have helped because the Phillies beat the Pirates and began playing better.

On August 19 the club had a "Welcome, Eddie Waitkus" night at Shibe Park, where Waitkus was greeted with a standing ovation from nearly 20,000

fans. He wore his Phillies uniform, although his jersey hung loosely from his frame, and received a new Dodge convertible, a television set, golf clubs, a full wardrobe including about ten suits, a two-week vacation to Atlantic City, and many other gifts. Dick Sisler, who had replaced Waitkus at first base, presented a tearful Eddie with a gift from the team, a bronzed first baseman's glove and two silver baseballs mounted on a velvet-covered plaque. "You put me on the spot on June 14," Sisler said, "so I hope you have a speedy recovery and come back and take the job away from me."[23]

The Phillies continued to play inspired baseball for the rest of the year and finished in third place with 81 wins. After the season, Waitkus spent four months, beginning in November, in Clearwater Beach, Florida, working out under the guidance of Phillies' trainer Frank Wiechec. There under the taskmaster Wiechec, Waitkus ran on the beach each day and went through demanding physical training to get back into baseball shape. Later Waitkus called his time in Florida "the four most horrible months of my life. Worse than anything in the Army—worse than New Guinea or anyplace in the Philippines."[24] But all of that hard work most certainly saved his baseball career.

While in Clearwater Beach, Waitkus also met Carol Webel, a pretty 20-year-old blonde from Albany, New York, who was vacationing with her family. Carol became an important part of Waitkus's support system in his recovery from the shooting. He frequently observed that the shooting had almost cost him his life but it also caused him to find the future Mrs. Waitkus. After carrying on a long-distance relationship, they were married in November 1951 in Albany's St. Patrick Roman Catholic Church. Teammate Bill Nicholson served as best man.[25]

A couple of years later Waitkus had an off-season radio show near their home in Albany called "The Sports Review." The show consisted of his telling sports stories and highlighting the top athletes of the day. His broadcast on his second wedding anniversary, however, was a touching personal reminiscence, delivered in the third person, of how he had met Carol and how she had ultimately helped his recovery, mentally and physically. He described the grueling workouts in Clearwater and

Then, he met a girl. A girl who knew nothing of baseball. . . Their few "Hellos" on the beaches grew to infrequent dates. Slowly he started to withdraw from his shell and lose the fear he had developed of people. Slowly, through her influence, he started to take interest again in the world around him. And with her quiet confidence to help him, he went into his training with renewed interest. She had faith he could come back, so he HAD to do it, for her sake. When the going got rough, she was always there to cheer him up. When he felt like quitting, she was there to prod him on. . . . With her comforting presence in the background, he went on to a great season and a World Series.

That year the newspapers called his the Comeback of the Year, but he didn't do it alone. The season ended and the companionship grew into something deeper. As it happens in fiction, they were married, and went back to baseball together…[26]

Waitkus's recovery, while long and arduous, was nothing short of miraculous. He was in the Whiz Kids' Opening Day lineup in 1950, playing first base and batting third against the Brooklyn Dodgers. For the day in the Phillies' 9-1 win, Eddie was 3-for-5 with a run batted in. He went on to start all 154 games at first as the Phillies nosed out the Dodgers for their first pennant in 35 years.

His Whiz Kids teammates respected and admired the veteran Waitkus in the clubhouse and off as well as on the field. Steve Ridzik, who was a 20-year-old rookie pitcher, remembered that in spring training Waitkus and Bill Nicholson would invite rookies to eat with them and always picked up the check. After dinner Waitkus and Nicholson would put the rookies in a cab back to the hotel while they went clubbing. Bubba Church, another rookie pitcher, recalled how Eddie's calm demeanor when he would come to the mound in a tight spot always settled him down. Waitkus would

say, "Hey, sweets, let's slow that engine down just a bit. Let's get it back together."

Robin Roberts recalled how Waitkus was always upbeat in the clubhouse, although he wasn't overly loud or talkative. His favorite sayings were "How goes the battle?" and "Keep the faith." Rookie Paul Stuffel remembered Waitkus singing "My Heart Goes Where the Wild Goose Goes," in the shower after a Phillies victory.[27]

Waitkus played a key role in the Phillies' pennant-clinching victory over the Dodgers in Ebbets Field on the last day of the season, hitting a Texas League single in the top of the tenth, eventually scoring the winning run on Dick Sisler's three-run homer, and then squeezing the final out, a popup from Tommy Brown, in the bottom of the tenth to clinch the pennant.[28]

For the season he went to the plate 702 times, scored 102 runs, and hit a solid .284. He even garnered some votes for Most Valuable Player, finishing 24th,' and won the Associated Press's Comeback Player of the Year Award in a landslide.

The long season and the World Series, however, wore Waitkus down physically and emotionally. It's difficult to know if there was any carryover affect for the 1951 season, but it was a disappointment for both the Phillies, who slumped to fifth place with a sub-.500 record, and Waitkus, who hit only .257, his lowest full-season average by 27 points. With rumors flying that the Phillies wanted to trade him, Eddie rebounded in 1952 to hit .289 as the Phillies improved to fourth place, finishing 20 games over .500. On June 22 in Shibe Park, Waitkus had one of the best days of his career, going 6-for-9 in a doubleheader, including a perfect 4-for-4 in the second game.

On the final day of the 1951 season Waitkus was involved in a controversial play that is still talked about today. The Phillies were playing the Dodgers in Philadelphia in a game Brooklyn had to win to tie the resurgent New York Giants, who had trailed the Dodgers by 13 ½ games on August 26, for the pennant. The Dodgers fell behind 6-1 and then 8-5 before rallying to tie the score 8-8 in the ninth. In the bottom of the 12th the Phillies had the bases loaded with two outs when Waitkus smashed a low line drive up the middle that second baseman Jackie Robinson dove for and appeared to trap behind second base. The winning run scored as Robinson, momentarily stunned, rolled over on the ball. Except that umpire Lon Warneke signaled that Robinson had caught the ball, ending the inning. The protestations of the Phillies were to no avail and the game continued into the 14th inning when Robinson hit a home run off Robin Roberts to send the Dodgers into a three-game playoff against the Giants. But for that controversial call the Giants would have won the pennant outright and Bobby Thomson would not have had the chance to hit his "Shot Heard Round the World" a couple of days later.[29]

Waitkus rebounded from 1951 even though Ruth Steinhagen was declared sane and released from the mental hospital just after the 1952 season got under way.[30] He confided in Russ Meyer that her release made him very uneasy because she had apparently told the Chicago police after her arrest in 1949 that she would kill him for sure if he ever got married.[31]

Phillies manager Steve O'Neill, who had replaced Eddie Sawyer in June of 1952, batted Waitkus eighth in the batting order after the All-Star break, in spite of his solid average. Then, in February of 1953 the Phillies acquired Earl Torgeson from the Boston Braves, another left-handed first baseman who had twice hit more than 20 home runs in a season. It was clear that the Phillies wanted more pop from first base, even at the expense of defense.[32] As a result, Eddie played only 59 games at the position. He was also 7-for-20 as a pinch hitter and batted .291 for the season.

Waitkus became disgruntled riding the bench and began to drink more heavily. In late September with the Phillies battling for first place, he left the team without permission, ostensibly to visit his ailing father in Boston. His father, it turned out, was not seriously ill, although Waitkus apparently thought he was. Phillies owner Bob Carpenter was furious and suspended Waitkus without pay for the last week or so of the season. Waitkus later admitted making a mistake and admitted that the Phillies were fully justified in suspending him.[33]

The Phillies mailed Waitkus a contract for 1954 that included a substantial pay cut. Waitkus wrote "N.S.F."

on the contract, for "not sufficient funds," and mailed it back. He also included a personal letter of apology to Carpenter for jumping the team. It apparently did not assuage Carpenter, who had announced that Waitkus would go to the highest bidder.

After rejecting a second contract offer, Waitkus finally signed for 1954 and reported to Clearwater. Manager O'Neill, however, did not play Waitkus in a single exhibition game that spring, much to Eddie's disgruntlement. When he finally demanded to know why from Carpenter, he was told that he just been sold to the Baltimore Orioles.[34]

The 34-year-old Waitkus was sad to leave the Phillies but hopeful of being able to play every day again with the Orioles. His main competition at first base was power-hitting Dick Kryhoski. As luck would have it, Kryhoski broke his wrist when hit by a pitch in a spring-training game just after Waitkus was purchased. As a result, Waitkus started the season playing regularly. He got off to a poor start, however, and was hitting only .170 in early May, prompting manager Jimmy Dykes to insert Kryhoski into the lineup upon his return.

Although Kryhoski hit fairly well, after three weeks Dykes inserted Waitkus back at first base, with good results. By early June Waitkus was hitting .290 when he sprained an ankle in Boston while running the bases. He missed two weeks and for the rest of the season alternated with Kryhoski.[35] For the year Waitkus batted .283 in 95 games and 349 plate appearances for the seventh-place Orioles. Most impressive, however, was his 1.000 fielding average: In 78 games at first base Eddie did not make a single error.

Although Waitkus rarely complained about it, he was increasingly bothered by lower-back spasms, apparently related to adhesions from the surgery to remove the bullet. He began the 1955 season on the disabled list and thereafter played sparingly, appearing in only 38 games by late July. The Orioles under new manager Paul Richards were headed into a youth movement and on July 25 gave Waitkus his unconditional release.

Five days later the Phillies signed Waitkus to spell struggling rookie Marv Blaylock at first base. Waitkus joined his old club in Cincinnati and smacked a pinch-hit single in his first game back. He went on to play in

33 games for the Phillies in the last two months of the season, batting .280.

On September 20 in Ebbets Field in Brooklyn, the 36-year-old Waitkus played his last major-league games as the Phillies lost a doubleheader to the Dodgers. In the fourth inning of the first game, Eddie smashed a home run over the billboards in right field off Don Newcombe to tie the score, 1-1. It was his second home run of the season and only the 24th of his career. Although it was out of character, Waitkus tipped his hat to his wife, Carol, in the stands after crossing home plate.[36] In the third inning of the second game Waitkus lined a single to center field off Roger Craig for the last of the 1,214 base hits in his career. He finished with lifetime batting average of .285.

The Phillies released Waitkus in October and he decided to retire rather than try to hang on another year in the majors or play back in the Pacific Coast League. He obtained a job in marketing and sales with Eastern Freightways, a New Jersey-based trucking firm. He and his family, which now included daughter Ronni and son Ted, were soon relocated to Buffalo, New York. Without baseball, Waitkus's drinking became more of a problem as did his depression, which he had battled since the shooting. Now he self-medicated his deepening depression with alcohol.

All of this took a toll on his family and in 1960 Carol took the kids and moved to Albany to be near her family. Eastern Freightways transferred him to Camden, New Jersey, and Waitkus continued his downward spiral. Finally, in late February 1961 he was admitted to the Veterans Hospital in Philadelphia with a nervous breakdown. He spent several days there, but apparently did not follow up on the prescribed counseling after his release.[37]

Waitkus did not return to the trucking company, but instead took a job in sales at Wanamaker's Department Store in Philadelphia. One of baseball's sharpest dressers was now selling men's clothing. By the time of a Whiz Kids' reunion in 1963 Waitkus had moved to Waltham, Massachusetts, to live with his sister Stella and work selling sporting goods at the Grover Cronin department store.

Shortly thereafter, Waitkus moved out of his sister's home and rented a room on the second floor of a home on Fayette Street close to Harvard University in his hometown of Cambridge. There he lived alone for the rest of his life. Those years were very quiet ones. Waitkus shied away from much contact with baseball or his old schoolboy chums, although he did talk baseball with the neighborhood kids.

The one real positive of Waitkus's later years began in 1967 when he started working during the summers as a baseball coach and counselor at the Ted Williams Baseball Camp in Lakeville, about 45 minutes south of Boston. Waitkus connected with the campers, many of whom didn't even know that he was a former big leaguer. He acquired a great admirer in Ted Williams, who later said, "I always knew Eddie Waitkus was a great ballplayer, but he was a hell of a man, too. The kids at camp loved him. He was magnificent with them, and we were truly lucky to have him. He was a classy-looking hitter and a classy-looking fielder. I loved that camp, being around the kids, teaching baseball. And I know Eddie did too."[38]

In June 1969 Waitkus took time out from his duties at camp to travel to Philadelphia, where he was honored at a Phillies game for the fans' selection of him as the greatest first baseman in Phillies history. He beat out controversial slugger Dick Allen, who was still with the Phillies in 1969, for the honor. According to Eddie, "It was a popularity contest. In essence, it proved one thing—the love affair between the people of Philadelphia and the Whiz Kids does not die quickly."[39]

In the fall of 1971, Waitkus fractured his hip when he fell while installing storm windows on the second story of the house where he rented a room. Although he had quit drinking, he continued to be a heavy smoker. According to his son Ted, who attended the Ted Williams camp with his dad in the summers, "His Benson and Hedges Menthol 100s never left his side." Eddie walked with a pronounced limp and used a cane that summer at the baseball camp, but still taught kids how to hit.

He felt so poorly, however, that he left camp about a week early and drove back to Cambridge. Within days of returning home, he entered the VA Hospital in Jamaica Plain with pneumonia. He was soon diagnosed with esophageal cancer and would never leave the hospital. He died on September 16, 1972, and was just 53 years old.

Waitkus was a card-carrying member of what has become known as the Greatest Generation. But the horrors of his war experience and then his almost fatal shooting took a large toll on him. His drinking, depression, and anxiety issues would now be recognized as post-traumatic stress disorder and surely contributed to his early death. But he will always be remembered as a key member of the 1950 Whiz Kids and as one of the smoothest fielding first baseman of his or any time.

SOURCES

Beverage, Richard E., *The Angels—Los Angeles in the Pacific Coast League 1919-1957* (Placentia, California: The Deacon Press, 1981).

Gold, Eddie, and Art Ahrens, *The New Era Cubs: 1941-1985* (Chicago: Bonus Books, 1985).

Goldstein, Richard, *Spartan Seasons—How Baseball Survived the Second World War* (New York: Macmillan Publishing Co., 1980).

Greenberg, Robert A., *"Swish" Nicholson—A Biography of Wartime Baseball's Leading Slugger* (Jefferson, North Carolina: McFarland & Co., Inc., 2008).

Johnson, Lloyd, and Miles Wolff, eds., *The Encyclopedia of Minor League Baseball* (2nd ed.) (Durham, North Carolina: Baseball America, Inc. 1997).

Marshall, William, *Baseball's Pivotal Era: 1945-1951* (Lexington, Kentucky: The University Press of Kentucky, 1999).

McGuire, Mark, and Michael Sean Gormley, *Moments in the Sun: Baseball's Briefly Famous* (Jefferson, North Carolina: McFarland & Co., Inc. 1999).

Orodenker, Richard, ed., *The Phillies Reader* (Philadelphia: Temple Univ. Press, 1996).

Paxton, Harry T., *The Whiz Kids the Story of the Fightin' Phillies* (New York: David McKay Company, Inc., 1950).

Roberts, Robin, and C. Paul Rogers, III, *My Life in Baseball* (Chicago: Triumph Books, 2003).

Roberts, Robin, and C. Paul Rogers, III, *The Whiz Kids and the 1950 Pennant* (Philadelphia: Temple Univ. Press, 1996).

Spalding, John E., *Pacific Coast League Stars, Vol. II—Ninety Who Made It In the Majors, 1903 to 1957* (Manhattan, Kansas: Ag Press, 1997).

Theodore, John, *Baseball's Natural: The Story of Eddie Waitkus* (Carbondale, Illinois: Southern Illinois University Press, 2002).

Westcott, Rich, and Frank Bilovsky, *The New Phillies Encyclopedia* (Philadelphia: Temple University Press, 1993).

Alexander, Charles C., "Eddie Waitkus and Bernard Malamud: Life versus Art," *Nine: A Journal of Baseball History and Social Policy Perspectives*, Spring, 1998.

Burnes, Robert L., "Why the Waitkus Deal?," *Baseball Digest*, March, 1949.

Clayton, Skip, "Eddie Waitkus—Slick Fielding First Baseman Came Back from Shooting Incident," *Phillies Report*, undated copy.

Fay, William, "Lionized Cub—Eddie Waitkus Lives Up to the Chicago Tradition of Great First Sackers," *Sportfolio*, July, 1947.

Fay, William, "They Woke Up the Busher," *Baseball Digest*, May, 1947.

Rogers, C. Paul, III, Book Review, "An American Tragedy," *Elysian Fields Quarterly*, Spring 2003.

Rumill, Ed, "The Only Cub Regular Who Hit .300 in 1946, *Baseball Magazine*, March, 1947.

Visco, Ron, and Bruce Markusen, "Fatal Attraction: The Woman Who Shot Eddie Waitkus, *Elysian Fields Quarterly*, Fall 1999.

Yeutter, Frank, "They Can't Bump Off Waitkus," *Baseball Digest*, September 1953.

"Ed Waitkus: Comeback of 1950," *Sport Life*, August, 1950.

Eddie Waitkus clippings file, National Baseball Library, Cooperstown, New York.

NOTES

1   Charles C. Alexander, "Eddie Waitkus and Bernard Malamud: Life Versus Art," *Nine—A Journal of Baseball History and Social Policy Perspectives*, Spring, 1998, 15.

2   John Theodore, *Baseball's Natural—the Story of Eddie Waitkus*, 22.

3   Theodore, 22.

4   Burns would go on to play in five more years in the minors, mostly with the Toronto Maple Leafs and San Francisco Seals.

5   Theodore, 23-24.

6   Ed Rumill, "The Only Cub Regular Who Hit .300 in 1946," *Baseball Magazine*, March 1947, 330.

7   Theodore, 24-25.

8   Theodore, 25.

9   Richard E. Beverage, *The Angels—Los Angeles in the Pacific Coast League 1919-1957*, 135-137; Theodore, 28.

10 Theodore, 27.

11 Theodore, 29-30, 115-119.

12 Theodore, 116-118.

13 William Fay, "They Woke Up the Busher," *Baseball Digest*, May 1947, 41; Richard Goldstein, *Spartan Seasons—How Baseball Survived the Second World War*, 243.

14 Waitkus had encountered the Cardinals' Fred Martin, whom he knew from his Texas League days and managed to get him assigned

for rations and quarters to the 544th so that he could pitch for his
unit. He won, 1-0. Goldstein, 244.

15   Theodore, 29.

16   Eddie Gold and Art Ahrens, *The New Era Cubs: 1941-1985*, 47;
Theodore, 31-33.

17   Rumill, 329.

18   Theodore, 36-37.

19   Robert L. Burnes, "Why the Waitkus Deal?," *Baseball Digest*,
March, 1949, 62.

20   Theodore, 38.

21   Theodore, 40.

22   The account of the Waitkus shooting is taken largely from Robin
Roberts and C. Paul Rogers, III, *The Whiz Kids and the 1950 Pennant*,
174-177; Robert A. Greenberg, *Swish Nicholson — A Biography of
Wartime Baseball's Leading Slugger*, 194-196; Mark McGuire and
Michael Sean Gromley, *Moments in the Sun — Baseball's Briefly
Famous*, 102-104; Ron Visco and Bruce Markusen, "Fatal Attraction:
The Woman Who Shot Eddie Waitkus," *Elysian Fields Quarterly*,
Fall 1999, 28-31; Alexander, 16-18; and Theodore, 2-5.

23   Theodore, 50-51.

24   "Ed Waitkus: Comeback of 1950," *Sport Life*, August, 1950, 16;
Alexander, 20..

25   Theodore, 54, 84-85, 88.

26   McGuire and Gormley, 106-107.

27   Roberts and Rogers, 169, 269. The name of the song is actually "Cry
of the Wild Goose."

28   Roberts and Rogers, 13-15.

29   Carl Lundquist, "Drama in Philadelphia," *The Baseball Research
Journal*, 1997, 3-4. The Phillies believed that Robinson trapped the
ball for the rest of their days. Robin Roberts saw Jackie Robinson
at a banquet that winter and said to Robinson, "Jackie, you didn't
catch that ball." Robinson replied, "What did the umpire say?" Robin
Roberts and C. Paul Rogers III, *My Life in Baseball*, 104-105.

30   Steinhagen lived a very quiet, almost reclusive life in North Chicago,
not far from Wrigley Field. She died on December 29, 2012, at 83,
although her death went unreported in the press until March 15, 2013.
Bruce Weber, "Ruth Steinhagen is Dead at 83; Shot a Ballplayer,"
New York Times, March 24, 2013, A22.

31   Theodore, 89-90.

32   Frank Yeutter, "They Can't Bump Off Waitkus," *Baseball Digest*,
September 1953, 45-46.

33   Theodore, 101-103.

34   Theodore, 103-104.

35   Both Waitkus and Kryhoski were left-handed hitters and alternated
as the regular first baseman the rest of the year.

36   Theodore, 109.

37   Theodore, 113-114.

38   Theodore, 124-125.

39   Theodore, 128.

Johnny Vander Meer

By James W. Johnson

CINCINNATI REDS PITCHER JOHNNY Vander Meer was close to achieving baseball immortality, but he didn't know it. It was June 15, 1938, and he was on the mound in Brooklyn's Ebbets Field with the bases loaded, two outs, and a 1-and-1 count on the irrepressible Dodgers shortstop Leo Durocher. One more out and his name would go into the record books as the first major-league player to pitch back-to-back no-hitters.

Durocher, who was hitting just .250 but was tough in the clutch, dug in against the often-wild Vander Meer, who had walked eight that night but was comfortably ahead, 6-0. The left-hander reared back, kicked his leg high, and fired. Durocher hit a ball deep to right field that brought the crowd to its feet. It curved foul. The crowd let out a collective sigh of relief.

On the next pitch Vander Meer thought he caught the edge of the plate for strike three, but umpire Bill Stewart called it a ball, sending catcher Ernie Lombardi into a near rage. Hoots and catcalls rained from the Reds' dugout. Vander Meer shrugged the call off and delivered again. This time Durocher lofted an easy fly ball to the sure-handed center fielder Harry Craft.

Teammates mobbed Vander Meer as he hurried off toward the clubhouse to avoid fans who ran on the field to congratulate him. Only in the dugout did he learn he had accomplished what no other pitcher in major-league baseball had: back-to-back no-hitters. And as of 2013, 75 years later, the feat has never been duplicated.[1]

John Samuel "The Dutch Master" or "Double No-Hit" Vander Meer was born on November 2, 1914, to deeply religious immigrant Dutch parents, Jacob and Katie Vander Meer, in Prospect, New Jersey. He grew up in Midland Park, New Jersey, about 30 miles from New York City. There he learned to play baseball.[2] His interest in the game began at the age of 8 when he listened on the radio as the New York Giants swept the New York Yankees in the 1922 World Series. He began playing at 10 as a first baseman for his school at

Stumps Oval, so named because of its shape and the stumps left sticking up when trees were leveled.[3]

Vander Meer played ball every chance he could get. Then at 14 he came down with peritonitis, an abdominal inflammation that nearly killed him. He was hospitalized for eight weeks and spent five more at home.[4] When he recovered, high school had already started so he dropped out. He went to work as an apprentice engraver at the factory where his father worked—and he continued to play baseball.

After his illness, Vander Meer's weight shot up from 110 pounds to 175 by the time he was 17. (He eventually stood 6-feet-1 and weighed 190 pounds as a big leaguer.) He also moved from first base to the pitching mound. He played semipro ball for the Midland Park Rangers, who rarely lost when he was pitching, although he was cursed by wildness that would plague him throughout his baseball career. In 1932 Vander Meer pitched five no-hitters for Midland Park and finished the season 14-1.[5]

Vander Meer was hoping for a major-league career not only because of his love of the game but also because he knew that without a high-school diploma chances were slim for him to make a good living.[6]

Vandy caught the interest of a scout who arranged a tryout for him with the Giants, but he failed to attract much attention. He received a second chance, however, when National League officials began looking for a "typical American boy" to star in a film designed to promote baseball. His wholesome look was what they needed. A Dodgers official, Dave Driscoll, said Vander Meer, who they planned to give a tryout, fit that profile. League officials agreed and the Dodgers sent him to Florida, where the documentary was filmed. Again he failed to attract interest during the tryout– except from veteran pitcher Joe Shaute, who urged the Dodgers to give him a chance.[7] They relented and sent the 18-year-old Vander Meer off to pitch for the Dayton Ducks in the Class C Middle Atlantic League. His manager was the flamboyant Ducky Holmes and he was paid $125 a month.[8]

In his first season, 1933, Vander Meer posted an 11-10 record with a 4.28 earned-run average. He struck out 132 and walked 74 in 183 innings. The Dodgers had first rights to Vander Meer, but when they inquired about him, Holmes recommended that keep neither him nor first baseman Frank McCormick, whom the Reds later picked up and who went on to win the MVP in 1940.[9]

Vander Meer wound up being sold to the Scranton Miners in the Class A New York-Penn League, where he improved, posting an 11-8 record with a 3.73 ERA in 164 innings. Wildness was becoming inherent in his pitching. In one game that he won 2-1, he walked 16 batters. It was at Scranton that Vander Meer hurt his pitching shoulder in a fall, an injury that he said delayed his promotion to the major leagues.[10]

Although the Dodgers earlier had lost interest in Vander Meer, after his stint in Scranton they put in a claim that Dayton's sale of the young lefty to Scranton was illegal. Baseball Commissioner Kenesaw Mountain Landis, however, ruled that the Dodgers only showed renewed interest in Vander Meer when he started pitching better.[11]

Vander Meer stayed in Scranton but hurt his arm in the first game in 1935 and wound up with a 7-10 record and a 5.35 ERA, striking out 88 and walking 90 in 133 innings. It was in Scranton that Vander Meer met his future wife of more than 50 years.

Before the 1936 season Scranton traded Vander Meer to Durham, a Cincinnati affiliate in the Class B Piedmont League. There he experienced a breakthrough. He was 19-6 with a 2.65 ERA although his walks sky-rocketed to 116 in 214 innings. He was named *The Sporting News'* Minor League Player of the Year. The paper said the speed of his fastballs "makes it appear as though they're hummingbird eggs."[12] The performance earned Vander Meer a late-season promotion to Nashville in the Southern Association, an A-1 league, where he went 0-1 in ten games with 25 walks and a 7.25 ERA in 22⅓ innings.

One apocryphal story had it that when Vandy was just missing the outside corner of the plate, Durham manager Johnny Gooch moved the plate overnight before Vander Meer's scheduled outing the next day. His accuracy improved and then that night the plate was moved back.[13]

The Reds liked what they saw at Durham and invited Vander Meer to spring training in 1937. The *Atlanta Constitution* welcomed the pitcher with the headline, "Johnny May Cause Fans to Forget about Bob Feller in '37."[14]

Vander Meer was thrilled to reach the big leagues. But he didn't last long. He didn't think he was pitching enough, and he didn't get along with manager Charlie Dressen. General manager Warren Giles agreed to send Vander Meer to Syracuse to work on his game. After a late-season recall, he finished his rookie season with a record of 3-5 and a respectable ERA of 3.85, with 52 strikeouts and 69 walks in 84 innings.[15] In Syracuse, in the Double-A International League, he posted a 5-11 record despite a respectable 3.34 ERA—although he walked 80 in 105 innings. He called his wildness "the old bugaboo."

During the winter Vander Meer wrote to Giles: "I know I'm a better ballplayer than the showing I made during the past season." Giles thought so too and again Vander Meer was invited to spring training.[16]

When he arrived in Tampa for spring training in 1938 he found a new manager, future Hall of Famer Bill McKechnie, who had replaced the fired Dressen. McKechnie was a godsend for Vander Meer. McKechnie was a player's manager. Pitchers said fondly of him, "If you can't pitch for McKechnie, you can't pitch for anyone."[17]

That spring McKechnie and coach Hank Gowdy discovered a key to making Vander Meer a better pitcher: throwing overhand with a three-quarters delivery. They also got future Hall of Famer Lefty Grove to work with Vandy. McKechnie's patience pleased Vander Meer. "I was able to concentrate on exactly what he told me," he said. "I knew I didn't have to rush or be afraid if I took my time."[18]

As the season opened, Vander Meer figured that if he didn't stick with the Reds this time, he would hang up his spikes.[19] In his first outing he lost to the Pittsburgh Pirates 7-4, prompting McKechnie to put him in the bullpen, where he pitched in two games. Back as a starter, Vandy beat the Pirates this time 8-6 but had to hang on after holding an 8-2 lead going into the ninth inning. An error and three hits knocked him out of the game, but he earned his first win. He lost his next game 2-0 to the Philadelphia Phillies, but pitched a complete game. Next he blew a 5-1 lead against the Cardinals in a game that ended in a 7-7 tie. Then Vander Meer turned it around with a 4-0 blanking of the Giants in the Polo Grounds. That started him on a nine-game winning streak. In the start before his first no-hitter, he beat the Giants again, 4-1, giving up only three hits, two in the first inning and a bloop single in the ninth.

On June 11 Vander Meer took the mound at home against the Boston Bees, the worst-hitting team in the National League with a .245 batting average. He was 5-2 and leading the league with 52 strikeouts. In pitching a no-hitter, Vander Meer gave up only four hard-hit balls; one was a liner by Vince DiMaggio that ricocheted off his glove to third baseman Lew Riggs, who threw DiMaggio out. Teammates carried the 23-year-old rookie off the field after the 3-0 shutout. "He's a real pitcher," Bees manager Casey Stengel said. "You watch him from now on. They'll have trouble beating him."[20]

In his next outing, on June 15, Vander Meer and the Reds visited Ebbets Field for the first night game in New York City. It was a banner night for the Dodgers with fireworks, a band, and Olympic star Jesse Owens racing against ballplayers. Five hundred fans from Vander Meer's hometown, Midland Park, joined the festivities.

Vander Meer was going to put a damper on Brooklyn's big celebration. Inning after inning he shut the Dodgers down to the point that even Brooklyn fans rooted for him to throw a second no-hitter. Once Durocher flied out, a new celebration was on. "If I'd known it had never been done before," Vander Meer said, "it would have put more heat on me."[21]

Vander Meer took his time showering with the hope that fans who might linger after the game to see him leave the park had given up and gone home. He told sportswriters he was going fishing the next day.

Up to that point only three pitchers before Vander Meer had thrown two no-hitters in their careers, Ted Breitenstein, Cy Young, and Christy Mathewson. Did he think he could throw three in a row? "I can't say I'll be out there for another no-hitter next time," he told sportswriters. "I'll just start out like I did last night and pitch my natural game. Then we'll have to see what happens."[22]

Before his next start, Vander Meer was feted by his hometown, was offered lucrative endorsement packages, received a salary boost, was lauded in poetry, and was named the honorary mayor of Tampa, Florida, the home of the Reds' spring-training site.

His next start was against the same Bees team he had beaten in his first no-hitter, but this time the game was in Boston. With Cy Young looking on—he had pitched 23 hitless innings spread out over several games—Vandy pitched 3⅓ more hitless innings until Debs Garms hit a single. That ended his hitless string at 21⅔ innings.

Vander Meer was glad it was over. "The pressure had become too much and I was glad to get out from under it. Enough was enough," he said. "I think if I'd have had a $10 bill in my baseball pants I'd have gone over to first base and handed it to Garms."[23] The Reds won 14-1 and Vandy went the distance, allowing four hits.

On the basis of his nine-game winning streak with the no-hitters sandwiched in between, Vander Meer was selected to be the starting pitcher in the annual All-Star Game, this one at his home park, Crosley Field. He pitched three scoreless innings and gave up only one hit, to Joe Cronin. In addition to Cronin, the American League roster featured Charlie Gehringer, Jimmie Foxx, Joe DiMaggio, Bill Dickey, and Lou Gehrig. The American Leaguers were impressed. "He's wicked," said DiMaggio.[24] Vander Meer was the winning pitcher as the National League prevailed, 4-1.

Vander Meer finished the season 15-10 with an ERA of 3.12, striking out 125 and walking 103. He was named *The Sporting News'* Major League Player of the Year.

The Reds had high hopes for Vander Meer in 1939. But it was not to be. A series of illnesses and arm troubles put a crimp in his pitching, although probably for sentimental reasons he was selected to again appear in the All-Star Game. He finished the season 5-9 with a 4.67 ERA. The Reds reached the World Series but the Yankees swept them. Vander Meer didn't pitch an inning.

The 1940 season was not much better. He was sent down to pitch at Indianapolis in the middle of the year with the hope that he could return to help the Reds to another pennant. And that he did. He came back in September, pitched a couple of good games, and then Bill McKechnie picked him to pitch against the Phillies on September 18 in a game to possibly clinch the pennant. He pitched 12 innings of the 13-inning game and scored the tiebreaking run of the 4-3 game on a sacrifice fly.

Vander Meer was hoping to start a World Series game, but McKechnie used him only in relief. He pitched three scoreless innings in a mop-up role in Game Five. The Reds beat the Tigers in seven games.

The next year Vandy ran up a 16-13 record and a 2.82 ERA with a one-hitter thrown in, on June 6, when he shut out the Phillies, 7-0. "It was the best game he ever pitched," catcher Ernie Lombardi said. Except for a disputed scratch hit, Vander Meer would have had his third no-hitter.[25] On August 20 Vander Meer was half

of a pitching duo that accomplished a rare feat in a doubleheader against the Philadelphia Phillies. He and Elmer Riddle threw back-to-back shutouts, Vandy winning 2-0 and Riddle 3-0. That feat had been accomplished only 39 times in the American League and 58 in the National League since 1900. That was followed by an 18-12 year in 1942, and then 15-16 in 1943. On September 26 of that year, Vander Meer and Riddle matched their 1941 feat during another doubleheader in which they blanked their opponents, this time the Boston Braves. Riddle won the first game this time, 2-0, and Vander Meer the second, 1-0—only the second time ever that the same two pitchers accomplished this feat.[26]

Vander Meer made the National League All-Star teams again in 1942 and '43. In 1944-45, during World War II, he served in the Navy, joining other major leaguers who played in all-star games to entertain US troops.

After the war ended and he returned to baseball, Vander Meer was pretty much a mediocre pitcher, with a record of 44-55 with three teams. He was purchased by the Chicago Cubs in 1950 and joined the Cleveland Indians in 1951 after being released by the Cubs. He was 3-4 with Chicago and in his only appearance for the Indians gave up six runs in three innings and was released. Vander Meer's career major-league record was 119-121. He walked 1,132 batters and struck out 1,294. He pitched 29 shutouts.

He spent the rest of 1951 pitching for Oakland in the Pacific Coast League, where his record was 2-6 in 13 games. Vandy was out of baseball at the age of 37, but then Gabe Paul, the Reds' general manager, offered him a contract to pitch and serve as pitching coach for Tulsa in the Double-A Texas League. Vander Meer saw it as a chance to get back to the major leagues. He finished the season 11-10 with a 2.31 ERA, including a no-hitter. Still, no big-league team picked him up.

Vander Meer continued in the game as a manager for ten years, mostly with teams in the South, then family pressures led him to retire from baseball for good. "I enjoyed the hell out of [baseball]," he said, "but I had to get into the business world."[27] Among the players he managed who became notable major-league players were Pete Rose, Jim "The Toy Cannon" Wynn, Jim Maloney, and Lee May.

After baseball Vander Meer worked for Schlitz Brewing Co. for 15 years. He also spent time playing in old-timer's games, attending autograph signings, and fishing. He spent his final years devastated by loss his wife, Lois, who died of a stroke in 1988, and his two daughters, Shirley, 41, of complications of diabetes, and Evelyn, of an aneurysm at the age of 32. He died on October 6, 1997, in Tampa, Florida, at the age of 82. He was survived by a sister and two grandchildren. He was buried holding a baseball in his left hand.

NOTES

1   James W. Johnson, *Double No-Hit: Johnny Vander Meer's Historic Night under the Lights* (Lincoln: University of Nebraska Press, 2012), 89-91, 98-99.

2   Johnson, 31.

3   Cynthia J. Wilber, *For the Love of the Game: Baseball Memories From the Men Who Were There* (New York: William Morrow, 1992), 141.

4   Johnny Vander Meer and George Kirksey, "Two Games Don't Make a Pitcher," *Saturday Evening Post,* August 17, 1938, 41.

5   Johnson, 35.

6   *Kansas City Star,* May 29, 1983.

7   Newspaper clipping, June 23, 1938, Vander Meer player file, Baseball Hall of Fame, Cooperstown, New York.

8   *Paterson* (New Jersey) *Evening News,* June 18, 1938.

9   *New York World-Telegram and Sun,* July 6, 1938.

10 Gordon Campbell, *Famous American Athletes Today,* Ninth Series (Boston: L.C. Page and Co., 1945), 53.

11 Johnson, 53.

12 *The Sporting News,* November 5, 1936.

13 *Washington Post,* March 4, 1959.

14 *Atlanta Constitution,* January 24, 1937.

15 Johnson, 58-59.

16 Vander Meer and Kirksey, 43.

17 United Press, September 19, 1940.

18 Vander Meer and Kirksey, 44.

19 *New York World-Telegram,* January 28, 1939.

20 North American Newspaper Alliance, January 6, 1939.

21 From video included in James Buckley, Jr. and Phil Pepe, *Unhittable: Reliving the Magic and Drama of Baseball's Best-Pitched Games* (Chicago, Triumph Books, 2004).

22 *New York Times,* June 17, 1938.

23 David N. Keller, "Oh, Johnny: Forgotten Baseball Legend," *Timeline* (a publication of the Ohio Historical Society), March/April 1999, 42.

24 Associated Press, July 7, 1939.

25 International News Service, April 30, 1941.

26 James Watkins and Paul Doherty, "The Double Whammy," *Baseball Research Journal,* 4 (1975); research.sabr.org/journals/double-whammy.

27 Bill Ballew, "Johnny Vander Meer Discusses His Baseball Career," *Sports Collectors Digest,* May 25, 1990, 245.

Roberto Estalella
El Tarzán

By Joanne Hulbert

"Estalella was a pudgy, happy-go-lucky sort of a guy who struck people the right way."
—Ossie Bluege, Washington Senators third baseman, 1922—1939, Washington Senators Manager, 1943—1947.

THE 12TH PLAYER AMONG THOSE IN DAVE

Frishberg's "Van Lingle Mungo" lyrics lineup is Roberto Estalella, and he is united by rhyme with Danny Gardella, the song's sixth man.[2] There may not have been anything intentional about it, but nonetheless, they encountered each other elsewhere in the arts as well as on the ballfield. Baseball fans are now more familiar with his namesake grandson Bobby Estalella, who debuted in major-league baseball in 1996, playing for the Phillies, Giants, Yankees, Rockies, Diamondbacks, and Blue Jays. Less is remembered about the original Roberto Estalella, who graced the infield and outer garden of the Washington Senators, the St. Louis Browns, and the Philadelphia Athletics between 1935 and 1949, with a brief hiatus spent in the Mexican League. But like many lesser-known players, he is the star of a monumental saga, and like many other players who have left indelible impressions and memories, he accumulated nicknames, attesting to his popularity with fans and reporters: "El Tarzán," "Cuba's Gift to the Washington Senators," "The Hotcha Kid," "Esty," and "Cheese and Crackers." Sportswriters routinely called him "Bob" and "Bobby." Roberto Estalella's story begins in 1933 with the Washington Senators, Clark Griffith, and baseball scout Joe Cambria.

Estalella explained that he learned how to bat and take a terrific cut at a ball by swinging a bat in the same arc as cutting sugar cane. He was born on April 25, 1911, in Cardenas, Cuba, where he played baseball on a company team comprising workers from the sugar fields, deep within a culture rich with baseball talent. Cuba had been known for decades as fertile territory for American baseball organizations seeking raw young players, but there were a few bothersome problems. There was the language barrier. Cuban players rarely knew even a little English and there was no organized effort to teach them once they arrived here. American scouts, Joe Cambria included, were not inclined to learn Spanish. And then there was the pigmentation issue.

Everybody having a known trace of Negro blood in his veins—no matter how far back it was acquired—is classified as a Negro. No amount of white ancestry, except one hundred per cent, will permit entrance to the white race.
—Gunnar Myrdal, *An American Dilemma*, Vol. I, 1944.

When Roberto Estalella debuted with the Washington Senators in 1935, his introduction included

the remark that he was "born of Spanish parents in Havana," and, adding a note of poverty-stricken innocence, that "he never wore a pair of shoes until he was 11 years old."[3] His arrival in the United States inspired a rags-to-mythical-riches tale guaranteed to delight fans.

He had played baseball in Cuba with the amateur and semipro teams Club Deportivo Cardenas and Central Hershey.[4] Cambria, known as the "laundry man" for his side job of providing laundry services around Baltimore, an enterprise that employed some of his acquisitions in the offseason, heard about Estalella in 1933 from Albany outfielder Ismael Morales, Estalella's teammate in Cuba's winter league.[5] "He hit good, he field all right, he good arm and he pretty fast. You better take a look at him queek before some other club pick heem up," Morales advised Cambria.[6] Estalella hit a "crucial late-inning home run" which won the season's final game for Havana's Leones in the 1932-33 winter season, bringing about a tie with the rival Alacranes.[7] Estalella had hit .351 in the 1931-32 season and .317 in 1932-33.[8] Almost every year from 1936-37 through 1953, he played winter ball in Cuba. Using Morales as the go-between, Cambria offered Estalella $150 a month, which was attractive money for an apprentice machinist earning $1.20 a day at a Cuban sugar refinery. Transportation and a meal allowance were sent to Estalella's home in Cardenas.

"I [made] myself plenty [of] trouble," Estalella said when he recalled that July day in 1934 when he arrived by boat from Havana at Key West with a ticket pinned to the lapel of his coat with the instruction: "Albany, New York. Please deliver to the baseball park."[9] The customs officer, realizing the young man could not speak any English at all, handed him a slip of paper and told him to keep it in his hand at all costs. At Jacksonville, Florida, he encountered difficulty finding something to eat. The food seemed familiar to him but he didn't know how to ask for anything. He pointed at a bottle of milk and then noticed a man enjoying a slice of pie, so he thought that might do for him, too. Unfortunately it was peach pie. "I no like peaches," he recounted later. "But I was so hungry I eat all the pie—one hand, too, because I hold slip in other hand."[10]

The train brought Estalella as far as Washington D.C., and not knowing what else to do in this bewildering situation in which he found himself, he espied the sign "Information," and, figuring it was close enough to "Información," he took a chance and indicated to the woman at the booth that he needed help. With rudimentary hand signals and drawings she made him understand that the bus he was to board would leave at 10:45. A porter was summoned to escort him to the bus. All that kindness of strangers succeeded in getting him to Albany, where he arrived 72 hours later, not having slept the entire time. Once there, Estalella showed that critical slip of paper in his hand to a policeman who put him in a taxi and sent him to the ballpark. Cambria had expected him to arrive in May, but instead Estalella appeared unexpectedly in midseason and consequently did not appear in a game until September 5, 1934. His story continued to be nothing less than classic baseball history.

Local cuisine continued to be a problem. The manager of the Albany club took Estalella out to breakfast and ordered up a plate of ham and eggs. Estalella, considering the dish acceptable, remembered the three words and over the next month ate nothing else for breakfast, lunch, and dinner. This illustrated how Roberto Estalella acquired much of his English—picking up words casually and inserting them into his mental dictionary. His fractured English was a source of amusement among sportswriters, managers, and fellow players, and he was accused of hiding behind a feigned ignorance of the English language. And yet, when it came to needing someone to bridge the language gap, Estalella was called upon to intervene. Clark Griffith, president of the Washington Senators, the team that Estalella joined in 1935, said he regretted releasing Moe Berg in 1934, for in that day and age, learning even a little Spanish was never considered practical by managers or players except, perhaps, for Moe Berg.

"He's just the man to talk to some of these foreigners,"[11] Griffith lamented, pointing out that he had Roberto Ortiz, a Cuban pitcher who spoke no English; pitcher Rene Monteagudo, who spoke very little English; and Venezuelan Alejandro Carrasquel, whose name was so confounding to Griffith that he renamed him Al Alexander. And there was Joe Krakauskas, a Canadian of Lithuanian descent who did speak English—with an accent—but when overly excited, Griffith couldn't understand at all what language he spoke. "The way things are going now, we sound like a row in the League of Nations."[12] With no formal English-language classes, players had to pick up whatever they could hear. Joe Cambria did not think players should learn English and believed the Latin recruits would get along better if they were not able to express any opinions or complaints or let on that they knew what was going on when the manager bawled them out.[13]

The story of Estalella's arrival in America served to entertain readers, but the tale also portrayed a stereotypical ignorant immigrant, while overlooking the fact that it took Estalella a great deal of wit and creativity to travel alone from Cuba to Key West and all the way to New York and actually arrive at the intended destination.

Roberto Estalella's professional career began in earnest in 1934 in Albany. Cambria, actually owned the Albany Senators of the International League, the minor-league team that served as the portal for raw talent intended for the Washington Senators. He moved on through the minor-league ranks to the Harrisburg team—also owned by Cambria—of the New York-Penn League in 1935, hitting .316 with a league-leading 18 home runs.[14] August 9, 1935, was "Bobby Estalella Night" at Harrisburg's Island Park, a tribute to how far he had come in winning the esteem of fans. By this time Estalella had been dubbed "Tarzan" for the yell he belted out every time he stepped up to the plate, described as akin to that heard in the popular Tarzan movies starring Johnny Weissmuller.

Reports conflicted about how much Estalella was improving. Local baseball fans supported him while *Harrisburg Telegraph* columnist Nobe Frank remained a skeptic: "Call it a hunch or whatever you will, I cannot see Bobby Estalella staying up there in the big leagues. Of course, the type of team that the Washington Senators have been sporting the past few years cannot exactly be classed as big league."[15]

The subsequent backlash from fans was unrelenting, but Frank was still not convinced of Estalella's impending greatness, and wanted him banished from Harrisburg. As he saw it: "Estalella has been spoiled by the fans' hero worshipping adulation. He has come to think that everything he does is O.K., whether he swings three times and misses or loses one over the fence. He has that inherent flair for color and the bizarre.… He struts to that plate like Casey at the bat, and as many times does the same as Casey in the clutch, but he has the mistaken impression that as long as he swings heftily, though breezily, and gives the fans a treat, everything is O.K. for Bobby."[16]

Mr Frank: Personally I think your article in the paper Monday night was terrible, and that you are more detrimental than anything we know by attempting to write an article of that sort. The only time the games have any pep whatsoever is when Bob is playing.

Signed: Two Lady fans that have never missed a game.[17]

On September 7, one month after Frank's tirade, Estalella made his major-league debut at third base with the Washington Senators. He appeared in 15 games near the end of the 1935 season, hit .314 with two home runs, had a .485 on-base percentage, and immediately became the idol of the Washington fans. Years later, in 1949, Shirley Povich wrote that fans would call the ballpark to see if he was in the lineup before deciding whether they would come to the game.

Estalella later recalled an incident where he was suddenly introduced to Goose Goslin. "I play third base while I was with Washington, and one afternoon de player named Goosie Gooslin slid into the base and I tagged him out. He got mad and kicked at me and I kicked back. He get up and poosh me and I pooshum back. I couldn't speak over 20 words in English and when the umpire came up and asked what was the matter, I couldn't tell him. I got mad and just said quack, quack, quack."[18]

Estalella returned to the Senators in 1936, making only 13 plate appearances. Manager Bucky Harris noticed that he was using a cheap, inferior glove, and once provided with a professional mitt, his fielding dramatically improved. Also improved, as Harris observed, was Estalella's English-language proficiency. Yet, he still had to win over the Senators staff even when fans and other observers applauded his ability and charisma. While at batting practice at Fenway Park in April, 1936, Senators southpaw Earl Whitehill was tossing a few warm-up pitches. Not until Estalella stepped up to bat did he actually ramp it up and let loose with his best stuff. He threw all his best fastballs and curves at Bobby, seemingly determined to make him look bad, but Estalella dug in and, much to the amusement of the spectators, he hit three consecutive pitches over the left-field wall.

Estalella's work at third base during that game at Fenway Park caught the attention of reporters and fans, but apparently not that of his manager or the team owner. The team continued to harbor doubts about his defense, so he was returned to Joe Cambria in Albany on condition that he get more playing time and a trial in the outfield. While there, he hit .331 with 14 home runs. He started the 1937 season with Chattanooga and maintained a .299 average before the Senators shifted him to the Charlotte club of the Piedmont League.

Estalella's fielding was apparently a source of some amusement in D.C. at the time. Peter Bjarkman writes, "Washington fans of the late thirties had so much fun watching the gritty Estalella knock down enemy grounders with every part of his anatomy save his glove hand that they often phoned the park in advance to find out if the handsome swarthy Cuban was in the lineup before making the trek out to the usually sparsely populated Griffith Stadium grandstands."[19]

From 1936 through 1938, Roberto Estalella wandered around minor-league baseball. He continued to be a fan favorite and he also built a reputation among baseball players he encountered along the way. His statistics continued to reflect a player with good potential, but always something would interfere with his return to the Senators. He was called a "notoriously slow starter at bat … a weak sister with the stick during the first month of the season."[20]

"Estalella can powder a ball and can really toss an agate around but he just doesn't seem to be major league timber," wrote Al Clark, sports editor of the *Harrisburg Telegraph*, in April 1938. What one needed to fulfill that requirement is lost in the fog of Estalella's minor-league statistics. What was it that he lacked in the eyes of coaches, managers, and club owners? Bucky Harris considered him a very bad fielder, and his arm was suspect, but he could hit,. Estalella would have made it on the roster if the decision had been left in the hands of the fans, who adored him. At the end of the 1938 season in Charlotte, his batting average was .378, better than his 1937 average of .349, and he had won the batting crown for the Hornets for the second year in a row, despite being out for part of the season with a broken jaw caused by a fungo bat thrown by a teammate.

Bats were not the only object Estalella had to beware of while playing with minor-league teams in the South. He was known to rocket line drives that traveled back toward the pitcher, some of whom refused to throw batting practice to him. One incident so angered a pitcher that he grabbed a ball and threw at Estalella's head, dropping him to the ground. Such incidents became routine and pitchers in the Piedmont League had a field day knocking Bobby down for nearly two years and peppering him with epithets disparaging his ethnic origin. Despite the controversies, he was named by *The Sporting News* as the Most Valuable Player in the Piedmont League in 1938 by one point over Phil Rizzuto of the Norfolk Tars. "He's learned a lot since I saw him last," said Harris. "He isn't a bad fielder at all and he's fairly fast. Best of all, he's got a great arm and plenty of power at bat."[21]

Two impressive years in minor-league baseball earned Estalella a return trip to Washington, where other issues came up. Calvin Griffith had to keep him on the roster in 1939 or lose him because he was out of options. In order to make room for Estalella on the roster, Griffith traded Zeke Bonura to the Giants and sold Al Simmons to the Boston Bees, a move that shocked many. Griffith said he did so because Simmons had "used profane language in front of ladies at the park last year. I won't stand for a player of mine cursing fans, and when Simmons did it, he washed himself up as far as my club was concerned."[22] Griffith also denied that he made the Bonura-Simmons moves because he could drop $25,000 in salaries to make room for the cheaper Estalella, who was paid $2,750 in 1939. Griffith was also accused of using the Cuban players on his roster for publicity purposes to hide a bad ballclub behind "circusy press notices."[23]

The 1939 season appeared to be Estalella's best chance of returning to the Senators roster, and the way looked clear for him to inherit the left-field position. He finished the season with the Senators with a "disappointing" .275 average in 82 games. Doubt and skepticism remained. "Estalella cowhides minor league pitching, but they say he doesn't like the high hard one inside."[24] Bucky Harris still expressed concerns, for in early in spring training, he noticed that the star hitter of the Piedmont League seemed to be having difficulty hitting curveballs. Despite making progress and getting extra batting practice from the Senators pitching staff, he was sent back down to the minors, to Minneapolis in the American Association, because, Griffith explained, "the American Association will give Estalella the kind of minor league experience he needs. It's lots faster than the Piedmont."[25]

At Minneapolis in 1940, Estalella maintained a .341 average and hit 32 home runs. In 1941 the St. Louis Browns, his next major-league experience, gave him the chance to compete for the right-field job. Tom Sheehan, who had managed the Minneapolis team where Estalella had played the previous year, was convinced the "Cuban thunderbolt" had solved his problems with curveballs.[26] He received a raise to $3,500, but appeared in only 46 games, mainly as a pinch-hitter. His baseball career again stalled, as he was sent back down to the minors, this time to Toledo.

World history changed the course of Estalella's career when the United States entered World War II. Once again Clark Griffith acquired him from the Browns, for $7,500 — and paid him a $3,500 salary — and was interested in adding him to the Senators roster, but it was not merely because of Estalella's continued minor-league accomplishments that the Old Fox wanted him back. By March 1942, 13 Washington players had been drafted or had enlisted in the armed forces; the Cuban players were granted six-month visas and called "entertainers," which exempted them from the draft. Estalella was also outhitting any other prospect

available at the time, and Bucky Harris acknowledged that the time spent playing winter baseball in Havana had given him a big advantage.

The fans still loved Estalella, and his English language skills still fascinated: "Estalella, a squatty number built closer to the ground than a flat tire, wields one of the few big bats on the weak-hitting Washington squad. Bobby is the club's 'chatter guy.' His scrambled Cuban-English has the crowds in the aisles. Here are a few samples of Bobby's repertoire. 'Hong rong' is home run. 'Tubeis' means a double. 'Mata el arbitro' translates as kill the umpire and 'keche' is the Cuban for catcher."[27] Not everyone was amused. Harris complained that Joe Cambria was inflicting him with the painful duty of looking after a bunch of temperamental players. "Bah! Cuban ballplayers. Haven't I enough troubles without Cambria bringing me some more of those rhumba dancers to look over."[28]

The 1942 season turned out to be Estalella's most productive year to that point in the majors, as he hit .277 with an on-base percentage of .400 in 133 games, while playing mostly third base and left field. His baseball career took a major turn during the 1943 season, when he was traded to the Philadelphia Athletics, who sent Bob Johnson to the Senators after he and Connie Mack couldn't agree on the bonus Johnson said he had coming to him. Although Mack lost an All-Star player, he was relieved of the $10,000 salary he was paying Johnson, and acquired Estalella, whom he paid $4,000.

Johnson's and Estalella's stats were not very different over the remainder of their careers, but Mack would eventually lament that after all was said and done it was not a good deal, and said he truly missed Johnson after he was gone. Johnson, with the Senators that year, appeared in 117 games. His batting average was .265, his OBP was .362, and he hit seven home runs. In 1943 Estalella also played in 117 games, batted .259 .352 OBP), and hit 11 home runs. He also brought his flamboyant personality to the ballpark and continued his knack for putting fans in the seats. He finished the 1943 season as the leading hitter on the Athletics. What was not to like? Estalella did spend a brief exile in the minors again. Despite the .259 average, Mack sent him to Indianapolis for Jo-Jo Moore, the veteran Giant outfielder, but Moore was inducted into the Army and Roberto was back up again.

It was not just language that set Roberto Estalella apart from his teammates. He was a different sort of player than what Americans were used to. Exuberant at the plate, irrepressible on the field, and relentlessly noisy in the clubhouse, he arrived in the US bringing with him a style of baseball that was lost in translation by the American managers, magnates, and teammates.

Roberto Estalella lamented that in the eight years that he been playing baseball, he had always been with clubs deep in the second division. When he joined the Philadelphia Athletics, Connie Mack heard about his lament and chuckled: "Don't worry sonny," he told him. "We'll probably make you feel right at home. [You've] come to the right place to keep that record intact."29

Estalella arrived at spring training in Frederick, Maryland, in 1944, just back from another winter playing ball in Havana, waving the new bat he predicted was going to "show zem somesing weeth thees thees year."30 The majagua wood bat, from the tropical pariti tiliaceum tree, would surely improve his game and bring him luck. "Nine years and never weeth a contender," Roberto said, his brown eyes flashing "Always eet was the second deevision—and sometimes even the third deevision. But thees year he's deferent. I theenk we have thee chance for thee pennant. Meester Mack he says so and I think heem right."31

Shortly after the 1944 season opened, the Detroit Tigers came to Shibe Park. The players of the two teams exploded into a punchless melee around the pitcher's mound with the requisite pushing and shoving. Estalella was in the middle of it, making himself useful by picking up cast-off baseball caps, dusting them off and handing them back to the players. "Bending down, working off my stomach," he explained, that the extra exercise was intended to decrease the weight that was affecting his batting average. He proudly reported that he had lost 30 pounds since 1943, when he weighed 210 pounds, and his batting average had increased in 1944 by as many points as pounds he lost.

By mid-May Connie Mack admitted that Estalella was not only hot, but also the "most improved" player in the major leagues. By then he was hitting .343 and

his fielding had improved significantly. "It's fruit that did it," said Mack. "Fruit and changing his playing position. He never played center field before. The position is made for him."32 There was no mention whether the majagua bat was a hit, but Bobby shed another 20 pounds.

Estalella was truly hot during the 1945 season. He finished with a .299 batting average and felt the ire of the Detroit Tigers, who held him personally responsible for their unfortunate finish the previous September, accused him of having a jinx bat33 and held him responsible for misjudging a fly ball that allowed the St. Louis Browns to overtake them in the standings and win the 1944 pennant. They also condemned him for hitting a line drive that fractured the leg of Tigers pitcher Al Benton, who had just returned from several years in the service. And then to add insult to injury, he also spoiled a one-hit shutout by Tigers pitcher Prince Henry Kauhane Oana by driving in the tying run with a ninth-inning double on a 3-and-2 pitch with two outs. The Athletics went on to win the game, 3-2, in 16 innings when once again Estalella doubled to bring home the winning run. The United Press reporter who wrote the story advised, "the Tigers best bet where the bothersome Cuban is concerned appears to be to buy the fellow."34

With the end of World War II, the players who had spent years in the service contended that the GI Bill entitled them to return to the jobs they held before the war, and many of those players who were on teams during the war now found themselves back in the minors or out of a job. Players also came back from the war with a heightened awareness of dealing with the owners in regard to contract negotiations and pay. Then along came the Pasquel brothers of the Mexican League with mountains of money and promises of wealth and glory. At the start of spring training in 1946, Connie Mack, despite the rumors, still expected Estalella show up. Bobby told Mack he was examining a big wage offer from the Pasquel brothers. Mack waited. Roberto did not report.

Major League Baseball called the Mexican League the greatest threat since the Federal League.35 Estalella joined several popular players, among them Mickey

Owen, Sal Maglie, Ace Adams, Max Lanier, and Danny Gardella—his eventual rhyme scheme partner in "Van Lingo Mungo." Their adventures in Mexico were also recounted in the novel *Vera Cruz Blues* by Mark Winegardner.

Gordon Cobbledick of the *Cleveland Plain Dealer* condemned the "contract jumpers." He wrote, "The Americans could afford to be complacent—though they were not conspicuously so—in the face of the desertion of such second-raters as Roberto Estalella, Alejandro Carrasquel and Danny Gardella, whose Latin antecedents fitted them naturally into the Mexican picture."[36] Estalella was the home-run leader of the Mexican League, slamming four homers in his first five games. His batting average in April 1946 was .471.

Eighteen players from the major leagues went to Mexico, and were punished for it with five-year suspensions handed out by a very unhappy Commissioner A.B. "Happy" Chandler. The hardships of playing in uncomfortable circumstances – along with the Pasquel brothers' fright-inducing business practices and their army of gun-toting bodyguards – compelled the players to come straggling back. A few were welcomed by their former teams but many, including Roberto Estalella, looked elsewhere to play ball. In 1947 he returned to winter ball for Marianao, Cuba, and was the center fielder for Pasquel's Los Tuneros de San Luis Potosí in Mexico during the summer. "Tarzan" Estalella continued to thrill fans with his signature flamboyant, vociferous presence at the plate and in center field.

In 1948 Estalella was the left fielder for the Havana team and played great baseball, but no one in the major leagues was paying much attention. Hoping that all had been forgiven, he tested Connie Mack's mood. Mack commented that he would expect to "dispose of" Estalella if he applied for reinstatement.[37] But Mack did not dispose of him immediately. Bobby returned to the Philadelphia A's in 1949, near the end of the season, appearing in eight games, with 20 at-bats and five hits. He was paid $2,604. In November 1949 the Browns purchased Estalella from the Athletics and sent him to their San Antonio farm club of the Texas League. After appearing in a few games with the San Antonio Missions, Estalella was sold to the Havana team of the Class B Florida International League in June 1950, after being placed on the waiver list.

Estalella's playing days over, he returned to Washington and worked as a butcher, but he was not far from baseball. In 1955 Senators manager Chuck Dressen hired him to teach English to the next generation of Cuban players on the team—Carlos Paula, Pedro Ramos, Juan Delis, and Camilo Pascual. He appeared at old-timer's games and events that celebrated the veteran Cuban players. When Luis Tiant, Sr. was allowed to come to the United States in 1975 to see his son pitch in the World Series, he also wanted to visit his friends and fellow players from the old Cuban teams. His list included Roberto Estalella.

Major-league teams of the 1930s, mindful of baseball's unwritten color-line, had been walking a thin line in order not to cause controversy and also not to rile other players who might abuse a new player with darker skin. If Clark Griffith was curious, he never outwardly appeared to be concerned. A few American-born players cast the usual epithets, and other Cuban players who knew Estalella considered him to be of mixed-race heritage and had little interest or concern about his skin color. Many baseball historians contend that Estalella slipped under the discriminatory barrier that kept many great players with darker skin from reaching the major leagues before Jackie Robinson.

Author and academic Roberto Gonzalez Echeverria writes that Estalella was "a very light mulatto …white enough to play in the American League and in Organized Baseball."[38] Throughout his career in major-league baseball, questions about his ancestry were a shadow behind the headlines. Many of his teammates and a few prominent sportswriters of the era considered him to be black. Shirley Povich wrote that there was blatant racism: "Estalella was the first of the Cubans in the American League in a couple of decades and it was a tribute to him that he did hit .400 one season while ducking dust-off pitches from guys who didn't cotton to his particular pigmentation." Decades later, when asked to comment about it, Estalella simply answered, "It was only an issue for the Americans."[39]

Estalella handed down his love of baseball to his son, Victor, and grandson Robert, who was a catcher for six major-league teams over a career that spanned 1996-2004. "The reason I wear my stirrups so high is because my grandfather did. It's to honor his memory," The younger Estalella said in 1998. "Up until last year I always wore No. 26 because that was his number. Then I reached a point where I knew I'd have to get a number [27] for myself. But still, I respect everything about my grandfather's career."

Roberto Estalella died on January 6, 1991, in Hialeah, Florida. when his grandson was a junior in high school. Selected by the Philadelphia Phillies in the 23rd round of the 1992 draft, Bobby said, "… and I know he knows what I'm doing."[40]

SOURCES

Other than those referenced in the endnotes, the author consulted the following sources:

Myrdal, Gunnar, *An American Dilemma*, Vol. I (New York: Harper and Brothers, 1944)

Wallace, Steve, "Jazz, Baseball, Life and other Ephemera." wallacebass. com, May 2, 2013.

Silary, Ted, philly.com, August 4, 1998

baseball-reference.com

baseballalmanac.com

Welch, Matt, "The Cuban Senators," espn.com

Heuer, Robert, "Minnie," chicagoreader.com

Graham Jr., Frank, "The Great Mexican War of 1946." si.com

NOTES

1   Robert Heuer, "Minnie," chicagoreader.com, May 7, 1987.

2   Frishberg did not pronounce Estalella's name correctly in the song; see his explanation in the BioProject biography of Dave Frishberg.

3   *The Sporting News*, November 17, 1938.

4   Roberto Gonzalez Echeverria, *The Pride of Havana: A History of Cuban Baseball* (New York: Oxford University Press, 1999), 264.

5   *The Sporting News*, April 16, 1936.

6   *The Sporting News*, July 20, 1944. The fractured English was typical of the time.

7   Peter C. Bjarkman, *A History of Cuban Baseball 1864-2006* (Jefferson, North Carolina: McFarland, 2007), 119.

8   Jorge S. Figueredo, *Who's Who in Cuban Baseball 1878-1961* (Jefferson, North Carolina: McFarland, 2003), 145.

9   Ibid.

10 Ibid.

11 *Canton* (Ohio) *Repository*, February 26, 1939.

12 Ibid.

13 *New Orleans Times-Picayne*, April 45, 1953.

14 *The Sporting News*, April 16, 1936.

15 *Harrisburg Telegraph*, October 19, 1935.

16 *Harrisburg Telegraph*, August 5, 1935.

17 *Harrisburg Telegraph*, August 9, 1935.

18 *Richmond* (Virginia) *Times Dispatch*, August 30, 1937.

19 Bjarkman, 331.

20 *The Sporting News*, April 27, 1939.

21 *The Sporting News*, February 23, 1939. Later that year, on December 2, in a game pitched for Havana by Luis Tiant (father of the major-league pitcher), Estalella hit a ball so deep to left field at La Tropical that, though his ball was caught, baserunner Frank Crespi tagged up and scored from second base, giving Tiant another run with which to work. See Echeverria, 265.

22 *The Sporting News*, April 27, 1939.

23 Ibid.

24 *Richmond Times Dispatch*, September 13, 1939.

25 Ibid.

26 *The Sporting News*, March 21, 1941.

27 *Rockford (Illinois) Morning Star*, May 9, 1942.

28 *Dallas Morning News*, March 15, 1940.

29 *Kansas City Star*, April 6, 1943.

30 *Richmond Times*, March 24, 1944.

31 Ibid.

32 *Augusta (Georgia) Chronicle*, May 16, 1944.

33 United Press, Springfield (Massachusetts) Republican, September 19, 1945.

34 Ibid.

35 *Baton Rouge Advocate*, April 3, 1947.

36 *Cleveland Plain Dealer*, May 28, 1946.

37 *Terre Haute Star*, June 7, 1949.

38 Echeverria, 264.

39 Baseball-Reference.com.

40 Silary, Ted, philly.com, August 4, 1998.

Augie Bergamo

By Gregory H. Wolf

WHEN BIG-LEAGUE PLAYERS HEEDED
the call of duty during World War II, many teams were left scrambling to find replacement players. One such wartime player was slap-hitting Augie Bergamo, who debuted with the St. Louis Cardinals in 1944 after six years in the minor leagues. A versatile outfielder and pinch-hitter with a good eye, Bergamo batted .304 as a part-time starter in 1944 and 1945. Despite his success, after the war ended he went unclaimed on waivers by all 16 major-league teams, and returned to the minors in 1946.

August Samuel Bergamo was born on Valentine's Day 1917 in Detroit. His parents, Joseph and Jennie (Dasaro) Bergamo, were both born in Italy and came to America at the turn of the 20th century. Like many of the millions of unskilled immigrants who poured into urban areas all over the rapidly developing country, Joseph found employment in construction and listed his job as "cement finisher" in a city directory at the time. The Bergamos lived in the Elmwood Park neighborhood, just east of the city center in Detroit, and raised at least six children born in the US.

By all accounts, Augie was an athletic youngster whose first introduction to baseball came on the sandlots that dotted his neighborhood. He attended Eastern High School (now named Martin Luther King High School), where he played basketball, earning honorable mention in the *Detroit News* during his senior year in 1936. He was also a champion table-tennis player. After graduation, Bergamo took a job at a local roller-bearing company and played semipro baseball on the weekends. Standing just 5-feet-9 and weighing only 165 pounds, the left-handed Bergamo established a reputation as a clever pitcher. He later developed arm problems and switched to the outfield.

Bergamo seemed destined to spend his life in a factory, but he had an understanding boss, Norman Phillips, who recognized his passion for baseball. Phillips encouraged Bergamo to attend a tryout camp the St. Louis Cardinals conducted in Flint, about 70 miles north of Detroit. "There were about 800 kids

there," said Bergamo. "I was put under contract, and hustled to another elimination tryout camp in Pine Bluff, Arkansas."[1]

The 21-year-old Bergamo began his professional career with the Paducah (Kentucky) Indians of the Kentucky-Illinois-Tennessee (Kitty) League, one of the 13 Class D affiliates among the Cardinals' 27 farm teams. The speedy left-hander batted a league-best .355 to earn a promotion to the Columbus (Georgia) Red Birds of the Class B South Atlantic (Sally) League in 1939. Described as a "wiry little star," Bergamo batted .345 and led the circuit with 190 hits and 18 triples.[2]

After jumping two classes, Bergamo spent the next four seasons (1940-1943) with two of the Cardinals' three top minor-league teams, the Rochester Red Wings of the International League and the Columbus (Ohio) Red Birds of the American Association. In his season

and a half with Rochester, Bergamo played for four different managers, including his future big-league skipper, Billy Southworth. In 1940 he was lauded for his "brilliant" defensive work in the outfield (he could play all three positions), and batted a robust .286 against more seasoned competition, many of whom had big-league experience.[3] He smashed a home run on September 13 to help the Red Wings clinch the regular-season title.

In mid-1941, Bergamo was transferred to Columbus, where he was platooned in 1941 and 1942. Manager Burt Shotton piloted the Red Birds, arguably the most stacked team in the entire minor leagues, to the league title in 1941 and then to the Junior World Series title over the Montreal Royals of the IL. The following season, Bergamo improved his average from .266 to .303 while playing for manager Eddie Dyer. After a third-place regular-season finish, the Red Birds were on the brink of elimination in Game Seven of their first-round playoff series against Kansas City. In the bottom of the 13th inning of a game tied 3-3, Bergamo singled off the Blues' ace, 21-game winner Butch Wensloff, to score Jim Gleeson for a dramatic, walk-off series-clinching upset.[4] Columbus then beat the Toledo Mud Hens for the league championship and the IL's Syracuse Chiefs to capture another Junior World Series title.

Bergamo finally cracked the starting lineup in 1943. The Red Birds had their third manager in three years, but the results were the same. They captured the league title (despite a third-place finish) and then beat the Chiefs again for their third consecutive Junior World Series title. Bergamo proved to be an effective slap hitter who had a knack for finding the outfield gaps. He batted .324 (fifth best in the AA) and tied for the league lead with 35 doubles. He continued to prove his patience and discerning eye at the plate by drawing a league-best 109 bases on balls while striking out just 41 times in a career-high 626 plate appearances.

Major-league teams saw their rosters depleted in 1943 as players enlisted or were drafted en masse for the war effort at home and abroad. With their deep farm system, the Cardinals were in a perfect position to adjust to the new reality. In October 1943 they pur-chased Bergamo's contract and added him to their 40-man roster. Described as an "outfield star" by the Associated Press,[5] Bergamo was classified as 4-F (medically unfit to serve) and was viewed as an excellent replacement for outfielder Harry Walker, who was soon to be serving Uncle Sam.[6]

Bergamo reported to Cardinals spring training, held in Cairo, Illinois, due to wartime travel restrictions. The two-time reigning NL champions had won 106 and 105 games respectively in 1942 and 1943, and were widely considered the favorites again in 1944. An Associated Press report predicted that Bergamo would make an "emphatic bid for a regular playing berth" as camp opened.[7] Notwithstanding the Cardinals' veteran roster, Bergamo distinguished himself with his hustle and timely hitting, prompting The Sporting News to christen him the "outstanding rookie in camp."[8]

Bergamo's six-year wait to play in a big-league game ended on April 25 when he pinch-hit against the Cincinnati Reds at Crosley Field. He picked up his first hit in his next pinch-hit appearance, on May 4 against the Pittsburgh Pirates at Forbes Field, connecting for a single off Max Butcher. Given the Cardinals' depth in the outfield (Stan Musial, Johnny Hopp, and Danny Litwhiler), Bergamo played sparingly prior to the All-Star break, but batted a robust .324 (11-for-34) as a pinch-hitter and late-inning defensive replacement at all three outfield positions. "I was amazed by the power displayed when I saw him hit his first ball here," said manager Southworth. "It's all in his shoulders. Augie won't be a home-run hitter, but he'll hit plenty of line drives off the fences."[9]

Bergamo proved his mettle over a nine-game span in late July when he effectively replaced an injured Litwhiler in left field. He pounded out 12 hits in 35 at-bats, scored nine times, whacked his only two home runs of the season, and drove in eight runs. His success led to 13 more starts in August (11 in left field and two in right). Despite a shaky end to the regular season (14-19), St. Louis cruised to its third consecutive pennant with a 105-49 record. Bergamo wielded a Rogers Hornsby model, 33-ounce Louisville Slugger bat and finished the season with an impressive .286 batting average (55-for-192). He "would probably have won a regular job in most outfields," wrote *The Sporting News*, which named him to its All-Rookie team, joining Andy Pafko and 40-year-old Chuck Hostetler in the outfield.[10]

The "Trolley World Series" of 1944 pitted the St. Louis Cardinals against the St. Louis Browns with all games played at Sportsman's Park, which both teams called home (but was owned by the Browns). In Game One, Bergamo walked in the bottom of the seventh inning pinch-hitting for second baseman Emil Verban, and then replaced Litwhiler in left field to start the eighth inning. With the Cardinals down 2-0 with no outs in the ninth inning, Bergamo advanced Marty Marion from second to third on a groundout. Marion later scored the Redbirds' only run in the team's surprising 2-1 loss. Bergamo started Game Two in left at batted leadoff. Though he went 0-for-5 in the Cardinals' dramatic 11-inning, 3-2 victory, his sharp grounder to second base in the third inning drove in Verban and accounted for the team's first run. His last appearance in the Series occurred when he drew a walk pinch-hitting for pitcher Freddy Schmidt in Game Three. In an unexpectedly competitive World Series, the Cardinals won the last three games to capture their second title in three years.

With the loss of Stan Musial to the military, Bergamo was the Opening Day starter in right field in 1945 and batted leadoff. He started 20 of the team's first 21 games until he injured a tendon sliding into third base against the Boston Braves on May 16. The Cardinals reconfigured their outfield in his absence, eventually moving Hopp to right field. Relegated to the role of backup for the remainder of the season, Bergamo served as a valuable replacement when Hopp went down with an injury, and also made seven starts in left field and even one at first base. Bergamo enjoyed one of the most productive doubleheaders in Cardinals history on July 4 facing the New York Giants at the Polo Grounds. In the first game, he went 3-for-5 with a triple, scored twice, and drove in one run in the Cardinals' 8-4 victory. He supplied the fireworks in the nightcap by banging out five hits in six at-bats, scoring four times and driving in eight runs. "[Bergamo's] display of pyrotechnics left a trace of destruction," wrote *The Sporting News*.[11] He belted two home runs, including his only grand slam, in that 19-2 thrashing of the Giants. Bergamo finished

the season with a .316 batting average (96-for-304), 44 RBIs, and 43 walks. His .401 on-base percentage was the best on the club for players with at least 150 at-bats. The Cardinals won 95 games but finished runner-up to the pennant-winning Chicago Cubs.

Immediately after the season, the press and Cardinal fans speculated about what the Cardinals would do with their deep outfield with the expected return of Musial and Walker for the 1946 season. Bergamo was placed on waivers, but not one of the 16 big-league teams placed a claim. "Frankly I was surprised that no one put in a bid for Bergamo," said Cardinals owner and president Sam Breadon. "With our crack outfielders returning, we had no room for Augie."[12] Upon news that he had been assigned to Columbus, Bergamo threatened to quit baseball, claiming he was unjustly demoted.[13]

Just 29 years old, Bergamo was not yet ready to give up on another shot at making the big leagues. He batted .302 and was named to the American Association all-star team for the Red Birds in 1946, but also battled nagging shoulder and leg injuries that ultimately affected his play in subsequent seasons. In the following three campaigns (1947-1949), Bergamo played for five different minor-league teams in four organizations, and saw his average dip and his playing time reduced. After spending the 1949 season in Double-A, he retired. Injuries derailed an abbreviated comeback in 1951. In his two-year big-league career, he batted .304 with a .400 on-base percentage over 174 games. He batted .301 during his 11 seasons in the minor leagues.

A Detroit lifer, Bergamo lived in the Motor City in the offseasons during his playing career. He settled down with his wife, Clara Frances "Fran" (Dunn) Bergamo, in nearby Grosse Pointe, and worked as a manufacturer's representative for the Condamatic Company. Bergamo maintained a connection to baseball by participating in annual Major League Baseball golf tournaments in Florida through the mid-1960s. He also attended the Cardinals' 20th-anniversary celebration of the 1944 World Series championship.

On August 19, 1974, Augie Bergamo died at the age of 57 at Bon Secour Hospital in Grosse Point. The cause of death was pancreatic cancer; he also suffered from diabetes.[14] He was survived by his wife and daughter, Kimberly, and was buried at Forest Lawn Cemetery in Detroit.

SOURCES

New York Times

The Sporting News

Ancestry.com

BaseballLibrary.com

Baseball-Reference.com

Retrosheet.com

NOTES

1   Sam Davis, "Augie Bergamo Makes Good in Card Outfield" (NEA), *Wisconsin Rapids Daily*, August 6, 1944, 4.

2   *The Sporting News*, April 6, 1939, 3.

3   *The Sporting News*, September 12, 1940, 2.

4   *The Sporting News*, October 1, 1942, 18.

5   Associated Press, "Cards Get Bergamo," *Palm Beach* (Florida) *Post*, September 28, 1943, 14.

6   *The Sporting News*, October 21, 1943.

7   Associated Press, "Considering Veteran Squad, Cards Are Best Bet For Flag," *Troy* (New York) *Record*, March 3, 1944, 32.

8   *The Sporting News*, March 30, 1944.

9   Chip Royal, "Verban, Bergamo produced By Red Bird Farm System," *Charleston* (West Virginia) *Gazette*, May 12, 1944, 17.

10 *The Sporting News*, October 19, 1944, 5.

11 *The Sporting News*, July 12, 1945, 21.

12 *The Sporting News*, January 24, 1924, 6.

13 *The Sporting News*, February, 1946, 17.

14 Certificate of Death, *DeadBallEra.Com*. thedeadballera.com/ DeathCertificates/Certificates_B/Bergamo.Augie.DC.pdf

Sig Jakucki

By Gregory H. Wolf

BIG RIGHT-HANDER SIG JAKUCKI WAS once described as having a "$100,000 arm and a million-dollar thirst."[1] Converted to a pitcher while a minor leaguer, Jakucki had a cup of coffee as a 27-year-old with the St. Louis Browns in 1936. Out of Organized Baseball for almost six years, Jakucki returned to the Browns in 1944, surprisingly won 13 games, and pitched the most important game in the club's history, a complete-game victory over the New York Yankees on the last day of the regular season to give the Browns their only pennant. But a penchant for drinking and fighting made Jakucki an unpredictable and divisive player. His big-league career came to an end when the Browns suspended him less than a year after his greatest achievement. "He was a mean son of a bitch, a big strong bastard that would turn over a juke joint every night if he could," teammate Ellis Clary said of Jakucki. "But you could not help but like him if he was on your side."[2]

A life in professional baseball could not have been foretold when Sigmund Jakucki was born on August 20, 1909, in Camden, New Jersey, across the Delaware River from Philadelphia. His parents, John and Johanna (Opszynski) Jakucki, were Polish immigrants who arrived in the United States at the turn of the century looking for a better life. According to US Census reports, John found work as a blacksmith at the Penn Shipyards and later in wool and soap factories; Johanna was a homemaker who raised four children, Henry, Sigmund, Theodore, and Florentina, born between 1908 and 1914. Growing up with limited means in the predominantly Polish-immigrant neighborhood of Liberty Park, Jakucki reportedly left school after the seventh grade and found piecemeal work.[3] By all accounts athletic, strong, and big for his age, Jakucki probably got his formal introduction to baseball with the Polish Citizens Club, associated with the family's parish, St. Joseph's Catholic Church.[4] Jakucki played shortstop and the outfield for the club and competed against semipro teams in southern New Jersey and Philadelphia.

With limited education and a burning desire to see the world, Jakucki enlisted in the US Army in 1927 and spent the following four years (1927-1931) stationed primarily with the 11th Field Artillery at the Schofield Army Barracks in Honolulu, Hawaii. The burly 6-foot-2, 200-pound Jakucki established a local reputation as a slugging sensation for his base team. Jakucki received an early medical discharge from the Army during his second tour; according to some sources, a local baseball promoter helped secure Jakucki's release[5] or "bought his release."[6] In any case, Jakucki joined the semipro Honolulu Braves, a team consisting of "Hawaiian born Japanese and Chinese, a few Portuguese, two native Hawaiians, and two players from the American mainland."[7] A shortstop, outfielder, and occasional pitcher, Jakucki gained additional exposure when he played against a squad of major-league stars (including Lefty Grove, Lou Gehrig, Al Simmons, and Mickey Cochrane) organized by "Baseball's Ambassador to the Orient," promoter Herb Hunter.[8] A fan favorite, Jakucki

reportedly clouted three home runs in a game in Tokyo on one of the two trips he made with the Honolulu Braves to Japan to compete against local professional and semipro teams.[9] He also played for Asahi in Honolulu, a semipro team made up of Hawaiian Japanese.

Jakucki was spotted by Bill Inman, a scout for the San Francisco Seals of the Pacific Coast League. In spring of 1934, Jakucki traveled to San Francisco (by one account fans collected money to pay for his expenses) for a tryout.[10] Unable to handle the Seals' mature hurlers in spring training, Jakucki was eventually sent across the bay to the PCL's Oakland Oaks. After he batted just .202 (17-for-84) as an outfielder, the Oaks sold him to the Galveston Buccaneers of the Class A Texas League, where manager Bill Webb converted the hard-throwing right-hander into a pitcher. Jakucki thrived in his new role, winning 10 of 17 decisions in 28 games accompanied by a 3.20 ERA in 138 innings for the league champions. "I guess being sent to Galveston was a good break for me," he said in 1944. "I could play shortstop or in the outfield good enough to stand out in Hawaii. ...I could hit that kind of competition, but when I got into Class AA or A ball, well, you had to have more to get by."[11]

In three seasons with the Buccaneers (1934-1936) Jakucki proved to be a durable, hard-throwing moundsman with a proclivity for wildness—and not just on the baseball diamond. In 1935, his first full season as a pitcher, the 25-year-old led the Texas league with 51 appearances and won 15 games, but walked 117 batters on 279 innings. He beaned 23-year-old Johnny Keane (a future big-league manager), who was in a coma for a week. The following season provided a glimpse into Jakucki's violent and often uncontrollable temper. In Houston to play the Buffaloes, Jakucki charged into the stands and started pummeling fans who had been riding him throughout the game. He and catcher-manager Jack Mealey, who also went into the stands, were suspended indefinitely.[12] Although Jakucki was uniformly castigated by the press, he was reinstated a week later.

Jakucki struggled for most of 1936, but caught fire in the last six weeks of the season. He tossed a seven-inning no-hitter against Oklahoma City on July 16,

and soon had the attention of major-league scouts. On the recommendation of scout Bobby Goff, the St. Louis Browns purchased Jakucki's contract on August 18, and Jakucki joined the Browns.[13]

Known to his teammates as Jack or Sig, the big right-hander made his major-league debut in the second game of a double header against the Washington Senators on August 30. He yielded only four hits in six innings but walked seven, surrendered five runs (four earned), and was collared with the loss, 7-4. He finished the season with an unsightly 8.71 ERA in 20⅔ innings and lost all three of his decisions.

Jakucki was fiercely independent and unpredictable, and kept his own council. In 1937, at the conclusion of what proved to be his last big-league spring training for seven years, Jakucki went AWOL when the Browns optioned him to Galveston. Jakucki and manager Rogers Hornsby (a noted teetotaler) clashed because of the pitcher's excessive drinking.[14] Jakucki eventually reported to Galveston, but was a "bitter disappointment," winning just three games, losing six, and posting a 5.70 ERA. He was sold to the New Orleans Pelicans in the Class A-1 Southern Association where he found his groove, won 12 games, and secured the third-best ERA in the league (2.75). The Pelicans also got Jakucki's fighting side—on and off the field. In an episode described by the New York Times' Arthur Daley, Jakucki and teammate Chief Euel Moore attended a wrestling match in Atlanta where they got into a brouhaha with the referee (whom Jakucki "flattened"), the wrestlers, and fans, and ultimately ended up in jail.[15] The Pelicans' exasperated owner, Larry Gilbert, let Jakucki spend a few days behind bars before he sent him to the Los Angeles Angels in a multiplayer trade in the offseason.

Jakucki wore out his welcome with the Angels after just 25 innings and was sent to the Shreveport Sports in the Texas League. After three appearances, Big Jack quit the team and returned to Galveston, his hometown since 1934.

Jakucki was out of Organized Baseball from 1938 through 1943. He worked as a painter and paper hanger as well as in the shipyards, and played semipro baseball. He played in the national semipro tournament in Wichita, Kansas, for three consecutive years (1940-1942), causing an uproar each season for different reasons. Jakucki was the pitching sensation for a Houston-based team in 1940; then was disqualified in 1941 when it was discovered that he had signed contracts with two teams (the Bona Allens from Buford, Georgia, and the Waco Dons). After losing a 2-1 game in the 1942 tournament, an inebriated Jakucki confronted the home-plate umpire, whom he later dangled over a bridge, threatening to drop him before he was arrested at gunpoint.[16] Ray Dumont, president of the National Semi-Pro Conference, called Jakucki the "most persistent problem child in the ten-year history" of the association.[17] A legend of sorts whom home fans loved and visitors despised, Jakucki was elected to the National Baseball Conference Sandlot Hall of Fame in 1942 in spite of his off-the-field excesses.[18]

Like most major-league teams during World War II, the St. Louis Browns fielded a talent-depleted squad consisting of aged veterans, 4-F (medically unfit to serve) players, and prematurely promoted minor leaguers to compensate for the veterans lost to the war effort. In March 1944 Jakucki was surprised to receive a letter from Browns general manager Bill DeWitt inviting the 34-year-old to spring training, which was conducted in Cape Girardeau, Missouri, under wartime travel restrictions. Praised for his "fast one," Jakucki made the team.[19] The press often referred to Jakucki as the "three-cent stamp pitcher" in reference to the price of a stamp needed to acquire Big Jack.[20]

In what proved to be his only full season in the big leagues, Jakucki played on the most memorable Browns team ever and starred in the most important game in the franchise's history. Along the way he also demonstrated that he was one of the strongest, toughest, and meanest players baseball had seen in quite some time. With his large, work-hardened hands, Jakucki impressed teammates by warming up with iron bearings shaped like baseballs on days he pitched; he claimed that the baseball felt light after such a workout.[21]

In his first big-league game since 1936, Jakucki tossed a complete game to defeat the Detroit Tigers, 8-5, on April 20 and notch his first major-league win. Used a starter and reliever in May, Jakucki was firmly ensconced as a starter by June. On June 17 and 23 he tossed con-

secutive shutouts over the Tigers, surrendering seven and five hits respectively to extend his winning streak to four games. Against the Philadelphia Athletics at Shibe Park on July 4, he hurled his third shutout (an eight-hitter) in four starts. Described by *The Sporting News* as a "sensation on the mound," Jakucki was one of the biggest surprises in all of baseball. The Browns, historically the worst team in the history of the AL, were in an unexpected pennant race and led by a strong pitching corps including Jack Kramer, Nels Potter, Bob Muncrief, and Denny Galehouse. "Finding Jakucki was a tremendous break," suggested *The Sporting News* in August. "It looks like he might have made the difference between success and failure."[22]

Jakucki's excessive drinking and fighting have attained legendary if not mythical stature. "I wouldn't say that [Jakucki] was an alcoholic, but he drank a lot," said fellow right-hander Galehouse. "He was the barfly."[23] Big Jack's two seasons with the Browns are filled with stories about his excesses. "I got sick in Boston," said Jakucki, recalling an episode at Fenway Park. "I threw up right there on the mound. I went in and got a glass of water and came back out."[24] "I don't know how you classify people like him," said Jimmy Outlaw of the Tigers. "He was a kind of a tough guy. He was ready to fight at any time."[25] Browns backup catcher Joe Schultz said many years later, "Jakucki used to spit on your shoes and dare you to do something about it."[26] According to teammate Ellis Clary, he and Jakucki were drinking at a bar across the street from the New Yorker Hotel in Manhattan when they got into fight with a supposed mobster who pulled a gun on Jakucki. Big Jack grabbed the gun and knocked the gangster unconscious. "He was into something every night," said Clary. "Jakucki, goddamn, he was like Al Capone rolling around at night."[27]

In the final week of the most exciting season in Browns history, Jakucki tossed a five-hitter to defeat the Boston Red Sox 1-0 on September 26 at Sportsman's Park (his fourth shutout of the season) and kept the Browns in a tie for first place with the Detroit Tigers, with the reigning champion New York Yankees lurking just three games back. As fate would have it, the Browns' pennant hopes were decided on the last weekend of the season in a four-game series with the Yankees. The Browns won the first three games, holding New York to just one run, and set up what *New York Times* sportswriter John Drebinger called the "most dramatic finish any championship campaign has ever seen."[28]

Entering the last day of the season tied with the Tigers, Browns manger Luke Sewell chose Yehoodie (his pet name for Jakucki) to start the season finale.[29] Recognizing the significance of the game, Browns players pleaded with Jakucki to refrain from drinking the night before he pitched. But Jakucki had other plans. "They knew I wasn't gonna be in my room," he said years later. "I went to bed at 6 in the morning and the game didn't start until 1:30. I was there."[30] In front of a record crowd of 35,518 spectators in Sportsman's Park, Jakucki pitched a six-hitter to defeat the Yankees, 5-2. The Browns' victory, coupled with the Tigers' 4-1 loss to the Washington Senators, gave the long-suffering club their first and only pennant in St. Louis. "Drunk or not," wrote longtime St. Louis sportswriter Bob Broeg, "big Sig was competitive."[31] Jakucki finished the season with 13 victories, completed 12 of 24 starts (35 appearances), and carved out a 3.55 ERA in 198 innings.

The "Trolley World Series" pitted the Browns against the St. Louis Cardinals. For the first time since the New York Giants and the New York Yankees battled in the Polo Grounds in 1922, all of the World Series games were played in one ballpark, Sportsman's Park, which was owned by the Browns; the Cardinals were tenants. The Browns won Game One, but lost four of the next five to the heavily favored Redbirds. Jakucki squared off against Harry Brecheen in Game Four, but lasted only three innings, surrendering five hits and four runs (three earned) and was saddled with the 5-1 loss.

Named Opening Day starter in 1945, Jakucki tossed a six-hitter to defeat Detroit, 7-1. On June 1, he blanked the Philadelphia A's on three hits to keep the Browns just 4½ games off the AL lead. He concluded the first half of the season by winning six consecutive decisions (including five complete games) to improve his record to 9-5. However, Jakucki's behavior was increasingly erratic and his boiling point seemingly had become lower. On June 20 Jakucki was involved in the "Battle of the Dugout," one of the most brutal brawls in major-

league history, when he and several Browns players charged into the White Sox dugout at Sportsman's Park and savagely pummeled Karl Scheel, Chicago's batting-practice pitcher, who had been riding the Browns throughout the game. Scheel landed in the hospital; Jakucki (who was not pitching that day) was not suspended.[32] Jakucki struggled after the All-Star break, losing five of seven decisions as the team drifted off the lead. While tensions in the clubhouse intensified, Jakucki often took out his frustrations on teammates, especially one-armed outfielder Pete Gray, whom he harassed viciously.[33]

Jakucki's tenure with the Browns came to an abrupt end on Saturday, September 1, when he arrived drunk at Union Station in St. Louis as the team prepared to depart to Chicago. Jakucki and Sewell's relationship had deteriorated and hit its nadir in Jakucki's last start, a miserable outing lasting just 2⅓ innings.[34] According to several eyewitnesses, Sewell prohibited Jakucki from boarding the train, whereupon the stout pitcher challenged his manager and coaches Fred Hoffmann and Zach Taylor to fight. Jakucki nonetheless boarded the train, but was escorted off by police at the Delmar station, about five miles away. Bob Bauman, the Browns' longtime trainer, reported that Jakucki hopped a freight train and arrived at the team's hotel in Chicago demanding a room, but was denied one. Finally GM Dewitt suspended him indefinitely, on the spot, and his major-league career was at an end.[35] The Browns were only four games out of first place at the time, leading Bob Broeg to speculate that the team might have won a second pennant had Jakucki not been so unpredictable and violent.[36] Big Jack finished the season with a 12-10 record, completed 15 of 24 starts, and posted a 3.51 ERA in 192⅓ innings.

The Browns reinstated Jakucki in the offseason, paving the way for his sale to the San Antonio Missions of the Texas League when not one major-league team expressed interest in acquiring him.[37] At the age of 36, Jakucki had arguably his best year in Organized Baseball with San Antonio, winning 15 games and putting up an impressive 2.16 ERA. But when his team needed him most, he "took a powder" and went AWOL during the league playoffs.[38]

Running out of options and with too many burned bridges in the Texas League, Big Jack signed with Seattle of the PCL in 1947. The Rainiers employed him as a starter and occasional reliever, then traded him the Sacramento Solons on July 31, but rather than report, Jakucki jumped the team and returned home to Galveston. [39] He subsequently was suspended and never played professional baseball again.

For a brief moment, Sig Jakucki was the biggest name in St. Louis baseball. He concluded his three-year big-league career with 25 wins, 22 losses, and a respectable 3.79 ERA. He won 77 games in his seven-year minor-league career.

In Galveston Jakucki lived the rest of his life in relative obscurity. He continued working odd jobs, mainly painting, and also in the shipyards in the 1950s. Jakucki gradually lost contact with baseball, save for his teammate Frank Mancuso, who was active as a city councilman in Houston in the 1970s. In his later years, Jakucki suffered from emphysema brought on by years of smoking three packs of cigarettes a day, as well as cirrhosis of the liver, likely due to his years of alcohol abuse. [40]

Destitute, Jakucki was found dead in his room at a flophouse, the Panama Hotel, on May 29, 1979. He was 69 years old and had no survivors. [41] Services were held at the J. Levy and Brothers Funeral Home, and he was buried at the Calvary Cemetery in Galveston. On his gravestone, his name is misspelled as Jackucki.

SOURCES

Broeg, Bob, *One Hundred Greatest Moments in St. Louis Sports* (St. Louis: Missouri Historical Society Press, 2000).

Gaus, Ed, *Beerball: A History of St. Louis Baseball* (Lincoln, Nebraska: iUniverse, 2001).

Goldman, Steve, ed., *It Ain't Over Till It's Over* (Philadelphia: Perseus, 2007).

Heidenry, John, and Brett Topel, *The Boys Who Were Left Behind. The 1944 World Series Between the Hapless St. Louis Browns and the Legendary St. Louis Cardinals* (Lincoln, Nebraska: University of Nebraska Press, 2006).

Heller, David Alan, *As Good As It Got: The 1944 St. Louis Browns* (Charleston, South Carolina: Arcadia, 2003).

Mead, William M., *Baseball Goes to War. Stars Don Khakis, 4Fs Vie for Pennant* (Washington, D.C.: Broadcast Interview Source, 1998).

Mead, William M., *Even the Browns: Baseball During World War Two* (Chicago: Contemporary, 1978).

Swaine, Rick, *Beating the Breaks. Major League Ballplayers Who Overcame Disabilities* (Jefferson, North Carolina: McFarland, 2004).

Galveston Daily News

New York Times

The Sporting News

Ancestry.com

BaseballAlmanac.com

BaseballCube.com

BaseballLibrary.com

Baseball-Reference.com

SABR.org

St. Louis Browns Historical Society (thestlbrowns.com/)

Sig Jakucki player file, National Baseball Hall of Fame, Cooperstown, New York.

NOTES

1   *The Sporting News*, July 28, 1979, 50.

2   David Alan Heller, *As Good As It Got: The 1944 St. Louis Browns* (Charleston, South Carolina: Arcadia, 2003), 101.

3   *The Sporting News*, June 22, 1944, 3.

4   The Polish Citizens Club changed its name in 1928 to Polish American Citizens Club. See the club's website at dvrbs.com/camden/CamdenNJ-PolishAmericanCitizensClub.htm.

5   Heller, 102.

6   *The Sporting News*, June 22, 1944, 3.

7   Ibid.

8   Bill Nowlin, "Herb Hunter," SABR BioProject, sabr.org/bioproj/person/06f2e2e9

9   W.J. McGoogan, "Jakucki, Who Had Trial with Club in 1937, Says He'll Win 12 or 15 Games," *St. Louis Post-Dispatch*, 1944 [no date] (Jakucki's Hall of Fame file.)

10 *The Sporting News*, June 22, 1944, 3; Harry Rasmussen, "Local Boy Makes Good in Pacific Coast League," *Camden Courier-Post*, May 2, 1934)Jakucki's Hall of fame file).

11 *The Sporting News*, June 22, 1944. 3.

12 *The Sporting News*, June 4, 1936, 1.

13 *The Sporting News*, August 27, 1936, 5.

14 William B. Mead, *Baseball Goes to War. Stars Don Khakis, 4Fs Vie for Pennant* (Washington, D.C.: Broadcast Interview Source, 1998), 116.

15 Arthur Daley, "Sports of the Times," *New York Times*, October 8, 1944, J8.

16 William M. Mead, *Baseball Goes to War*, 117.

17   *The Sporting News*, July 10, 1946, 26; Harry Grayson, "Grayson's Scoreboard. Jakucki Had Flair For Signing Contracts; That Wasn't Why Umpires Kept an Eye on Him; Big Jack Ate Sandlot Veracity for Breakfast," *Burlington* (North Carolina) *Daily Times-News*, October 11, 1944, 8.

18   *The Sporting News*, July 10, 1946, 26.

19   *The Sporting News*, March 30, 1944, 7.

20   *The Sparing News*, October 5, 1944, 2.

21   *The Sporting News*, July 27, 1944, 14.

22   *The Sporting News*, August 17, 1944, 7.

23   Heller, 101.

24   Milton Richman, "Islander Jakucki 's Office Is On Bench in the Park," *Galveston Daily News*, June 6, 1978, 1.

25   Heller, 101.

26   *The Sporting News*, August 24, 1963, 22.

27   Heller, 102.

28   John Drebinger, "Browns Win Flag; Halt Yankees, 5-2," *New York Times*, October 2, 1944, 14.

29   "Sewell Heaps Praise on Kramer; Jakucki to Face Brecheen Today," *New York Times*, October 7, 1944, 12.

30   *The Sporting News*, July 28, 1979, 50.

31   Bob Broeg, *One Hundred Greatest Moments in St. Louis Sports* (St. Louis: Missouri Historical Society Press, 2000), 70.

32   *The Sporting News*, July 5, 1945, 5.

33   Pete Gray could dress, bat, and field with just one arm; however, he needed help with tying his shoes. In one well-documented incident when Gray asked Jakucki for help, Jakucki replied, "Tie your own goddamn shoes, you one-armed son-of-a-bitch," and walked out of the dressing room. William Kashatus, *One Armed Wonder: Pete Gray* (Jefferson, North Carolina: McFarland, 1995), 114.

34   *The Sporting News*, September 6, 1945, 4.

35   William B. Mead, *Baseball Goes to War*, 230.

36   *The Sporting News*, May 7, 1977, 6.

37   *The Sporting News*, March 14, 1946, 17.

38   *The Sporting News*, September 17, 1947, 36.

39   *The Sporting News*, September 17, 1947, 36.

40   Milton Richman, "Islander Jakucki 's Office Is On Bench in the Park," *Galveston Daily News*, June 6, 1978, 1.

41   "Jakucki Services Pending," *Galveston Daily News*, May 31, 1979, 8-A.

Johnny Mize

By Jerry Grillo

IN 1947 JOHNNY MIZE DID SOMETHING unmatched in baseball history. He became the first player to hit 50 or more home runs in a season while striking out fewer than 50 times, one of the game's extraordinary records and a sole distinction Mize still held more than 65 years later.

Few, if any hitters have combined meticulous bat control with brute power the way Mize did in '47, back when the New York Giants carried two trunks of bats when they hit the road. "One trunk was for Johnny Mize," said Buddy Blattner, Mize's roommate on the Giants. "The other was for the rest of the team."

So yes, Mize had plenty of bats, and he knew how to use every one of them. This was his arsenal, his black bag, and throughout a 15-year Hall of Fame baseball career the Georgian used his tools with the precision of a surgeon and the stylistic beauty of an artist. Built like a slugger (6-feet-2, 215 pounds in his prime), Mize was a line-drive hitter who could hit for distance, to all fields, and generally for high average, especially earlier in his career. "Nobody had a better, smoother, easier swing than John," said Don Gutteridge, who roomed with Mize on the Cardinals. "It was picture perfect."

Mize split his career among the St. Louis Cardinals (1936-1941), the Giants (1942, 1946-49), and the New York Yankees (1949-1953), and was a ten-time All-Star who led his league in most major offensive categories at one time or another. A first baseman through most of his career until injuries took their toll, Mize reinvented himself in his late 30s, becoming one of the game's premier pinch-hitters on a Yankee club that won five straight World Series titles.

John Robert Mize was born on January 7, 1913, in Demorest, Georgia, a small college town in the rural Appalachian foothills of Northeast Georgia. He was the second son of Edward Mize, a local merchant and salesman, and Emma Loudermilk, a homemaker who had to go to work in an Atlanta department store after the couple separated.

Johnny stayed with his grandmother in Demorest, and was actually more interested in tennis than baseball as a youngster, winning a county championship with a racket in his hand. Mize may have been a hitter on some molecular level, as if it were in his DNA somehow—a distant cousin was another Georgian of note, Tyrus Raymond Cobb. Mize also was related to the game's greatest hitting star, though not by blood –Clara Mae Merritt, who became better known as Mrs. Babe Ruth, was a cousin.

Between the ages of 13 and 15, Mize grew rapidly and his sweet swing caught the attention of the Piedmont College baseball (and football and basketball) coach Harry Forester, who persuaded the muscular teen to try out for the team. "The fact is, when I was 15 and a sophomore at high school, I played on the varsity baseball team for the college," Mize said in his instructional book, *How to Hit*. "I could do this because Piedmont College didn't belong to any athletic conference and therefore there were no rules governing eligible players."

Mize hit over .400 for Piedmont in his two seasons on the college team while attending the local high school, Piedmont Academy. Stories have been passed down in Demorest of long home runs, baseballs sailing

over the college administration building, and onto or
beyond US Route 441. Mize, as a low-key old man
living back in his hometown, admitted that most of it
was a myth. But tales of his actual prowess—which
probably came from Forester, a former minor-league
pitcher—reached Branch Rickey, general manager of
the St. Louis Cardinals, and he sent his brother Frank
to scout the young slugger.

The college season was over and Mize was playing
semipro ball in nearby Toccoa, Georgia. That's where
Frank Rickey saw a young outfielder, slow-footed, but
quick-minded, playing like a veteran—never swinging
at bad pitches or making mistakes on the basepaths or
throwing to the wrong base. He signed the 17-year-old
Mize after seeing him play just once.

It was 1930, the middle of the baseball season. Mize
was sent to the Class C Greensboro (North Carolina)
Patriots, deep within the Cardinals' vast farm system,
where he got into 12 games and batted .194. The next
season, though, began a string of 14 consecutive seasons
during which Mize hit over .300.

The 18-year-old returned to Greensboro in 1931, and
batted .337. He was promoted to Elmira in the New
York-Penn League in 1932. That year, after consulting
with Elmira manager Clay Hopper, Branch Rickey
decided the ponderous Mize should switch to first base.
It was evident early on that Mize, with his plodding
pace and limited range, would never be a defensive star.
And yet, he always claimed that he earned his famous
nickname, the Big Cat, because of his fielding. The man
supposedly responsible was Cardinals infielder
Joe Orengo.

"One day the infielders were having a pretty bad
time and were making some bad throws to me at first
base," Mize said late in his career. "After digging a few
out of the dirt, Joe Orengo called over to me, 'Atta boy,
John, you look like a big cat.' Some of the writers
overheard the remark and asked Joe about it later. The
nickname has stuck with me ever since."

Others, like St. Louis sportswriter Bob Broeg and
broadcaster Buddy Blattner, maintained that it was sort
of a derisive nickname that described the way Mize
stalked around the bag. Either way, Rickey moved the
19-year-old Mize to first base, and that remained his

regular position for the rest of his career. Certainly,
nobody was complaining about his glove or his range
in 1932, when he batted .326 and drove in 78 runs in
106 games for Class B Elmira.

In spite of that showing, the Cardinals inexplicably
sent Mize back to Greensboro in 1933, and he responded
by hitting .360, with 22 home runs and 104 runs batted
in in just 98 games. He finished the year at Rochester,
one of the Cardinals' top teams, batting .352 with eight
homers and 32 RBIs in 42 games. In St. Louis, however,
the Cardinals already had a hard-hitting first baseman
with a better glove, Ripper Collins. Thus, Mize's eye-
popping offensive numbers didn't seem to be moving
him any closer to the big leagues, though he was becoming a known commodity around major-league
front offices.

But something happened in 1934 that almost ended
his career. While legging out a double for Rochester,
Mize felt a painful snap in his groin. The injury limited
him to 90 games, but he batted .339, drove in 66 runs
and hit 17 homers. It was good enough for the Cincinnati
Reds to buy him from the Cardinals in the spring of
1935 for $55,000 (a sum that qualified as a bona-fide
star investment in the midst of the Great Depression).
But it was a conditional deal—Mize had to prove he
was healthy enough to play. He couldn't.

Spurs had developed on his pelvic bone, a result of
the groin strain months earlier. He couldn't swing a bat
without wincing, couldn't dig out low throws, and ran
even more slowly than usual. So the Reds sent him
back to the Cardinals, whose club surgeon, Dr. Robert
Hyland, said he was fit enough to play the 1935 season
in Rochester. Mize didn't last three months. He was
hitting .317 after 65 games, but the pain and immobility
forced him out of action and he went on the voluntarily
retired list. At the age of 22, he thought his playing
days were over.

Hyland performed a daring bit of surgery that winter,
and by the time spring training began, Mize had made
an amazing recovery. He made the Cardinals' big-league
roster and by midsummer had moved Collins off first
base. Mize's rookie campaign was nothing short of
brilliant—in 126 games he batted .329, with 19 homers
and 93 RBIs. Moreover, he was on pace to lead National

League first basemen in fielding percentage had he played in enough games to qualify. Mize actually led his league in percentage, assists, and putouts twice each. Then again, he also led in errors twice and finished second in that dubious category three other times. "He was a big, lumbering guy, and some groundballs got by him, sure, but if he could reach it, if he ever got his hand on the ball, he held it," Don Gutteridge said.

Proving his rookie season was no fluke, Mize batted a career-high .364 in 1937, second in the league to his teammate and rival, Joe Medwick (who captured the Triple Crown that year). Mize also was second in the NL in on-base percentage, total bases, slugging percentage, and doubles. He belted 25 homers, drove in 113 runs, and made the All-Star team for the first time in his career.

Mize broke in with the St. Louis team known as the Gas House Gang, the Cardinals of Dizzy Dean and Pepper Martin and Leo Durocher. They were World Series champions in 1934, two years before Mize's rookie season, and finished second in Mize's first year with the team. Medwick was another of the team's stars. Mize and Medwick played 5½ seasons together in St. Louis (Medwick was dealt to the Brooklyn Dodgers in June 1940), forming one of baseball's most terrifying tandems. But they didn't get along—hardly anyone on the club got along with Medwick, and there may have been some jealousy between the two sluggers.

"John wanted to drive in runs, and so did Medwick," Gutteridge recalled. "And there was some times when John was on base and Medwick got a hit, and he thought John should have scored. Then, Medwick would get on him. But Joe was kind of arrogant. We called him the Mad Hungarian because he was mad all the time."

Outwardly. Mize was a low-key person, never a rah-rah kind of guy or an emotional team leader. At times he was something of a clubhouse lawyer and salary holdout. But he usually got along well with his teammates and the press. "He is a quiet, pleasant, easy-going giant," wrote Dick Farrington in *The Sporting News* in 1937.

According to Hal Epps, Mize's teammate in St. Louis for two seasons and a fellow native of Northeast Georgia, "Johnny was always smiling, and if he had a bad moment, I didn't know about it. He had a good attitude. Easygoing. Nothing seemed to bother him much."

Instead, Mize bothered National League pitchers. He hit .337 in 1938, led the league in triples, hit 27 homers, and led in slugging percentage, something he also would do the next two seasons. (He won four slugging titles in five seasons). The home runs came in clusters—Mize twice hit three in a game in 1938. (He was the first player to do this, and he did it again in 1940.)

In 1939 Mize finished second in Most Valuable Player voting after leading the National League in batting (.349), home runs (28), total bases, and slugging, hitting a career-high 44 doubles and posting a career-high OPS of 1.070. (That last figure, the sum of Mize's slugging average and on-base percentage, is retrospective; it wasn't compiled in those days.)

Mize recalled arriving for spring training in 1940 at the Cardinals' camp in St. Petersburg, Florida. When he walked into the clubhouse he saw 43 bats lined up along the clubhouse wall—his bats, some left over from the year before, and new ones ordered by the team at his request. The clubhouse man "was most vigorously complaining that they occupied an entire bat trunk. I asked him how he expected me to work without my tools—for which he had no answer," Mize said. Or, as his teammate Gutteridge said, "When you hit .350, they buy you all the bats you want."

So Mize started the 1940 season with 43 bats, and when it was over he'd hit a club record 43 home runs, leading the league in that category and in RBIs (137). "To this day I wonder what would have happened if I had started the season with 61 bats," he mused in *How to Hit*. He eventually would take his shot at Ruth's record of 60 home runs in a season, or as Mize called it, "Cousin George's mark." But it would have to wait until a blockbuster deal sent him to New York City. And then, of course, there was World War II.

"He had bats of different sizes and weights, 34 ounces, 37, 40. The harder the thrower, the lighter the bat," said Don Gutteridge, who remembered an incident when the left-handed-hitting Mize was about to face a tough, hard-throwing left-handed pitcher (Gutteridge could not accurately recall who) who'd been giving him fits. "We were at home in St. Louis, and John says, 'Next time I get up there, I'm gonna get one of those light bats and I'll get around on that high fastball, you watch.' So, next time up he hits the first pitch out onto Grand Avenue outside of old Sportsman's Park. He comes back and says to me, 'See, I told you.'"

In 1941, with most of the Gas House Gang gone, the Cardinals made a serious run at the National League pennant, winning 97 games, but finishing 2½ games behind Brooklyn, which won its first flag since 1920. As it turned out, rookie Stan Musial joined the Cardinals for the final two weeks of the season, batting .426 in 12 games. Mize, who missed the end of the season with a bum leg, complained, "We might have gone ahead and won the pennant" if Rickey had brought Musial up sooner.

Surprisingly, that season was the end of Mize's stint in St. Louis. Back in New York, new manager Mel Ott had his eyes on the Big Cat. Ott, who held the National League record for career home runs at the time with 511, insisted that the Giants make a deal for the 28-year-old slugger. That's exactly what they did, getting Mize from the Cardinals in exchange for $50,000 and three players..

It was big news in baseball, but not particularly earth-shattering considering the times — four days before that deal, the Japanese attacked Pearl Harbor and the US was at war. Mize had one season in a Giants uniform (.305 average, 26 homers, and a league-leading 110 RBIs) before putting on a Navy uniform, which he wore for three years — three prime years, and as has been said about lots of stars of that era, there's no telling how gaudy his career numbers would have been had his career not been interrupted.

Like so many other ballplayers who served during World War II, Mize carried a bat in lieu of a gun. His combat was limited to the baseball diamond, against other professional ballplayers who provided a welcome and entertaining respite for GIs.

Mize returned to the Polo Grounds in 1946 and picked up where he left off, batting .337 with 22 homers in 101 games. In the second Mayor's Trophy game versus the Yankees on August 5, Joe Page broke Mize's hand with a pitch. Mize was out until September 13 and then

promptly broke a toe in his return. Yet he was only setting the stage.

In 1947 the talk was over who would catch the Babe — Mize or Pittsburgh Pirates slugger Ralph Kiner. After Mize hit his 44th home run on August 28, he said, "It dawned on me that I might give that record a scare." Though he finished well shy of Ruth with 51 homers, it was his career high and it tied him with Kiner for the major-league lead. He helped the fourth-place Giants to what was at the time the record for home runs by a team in one year (221). Mize also had career highs in RBIs (138) and runs (137), leading the majors in both categories in 1947. The Giants' big first baseman also hit .just 302 — the lowest mark of his big-league career to that point — but he struck out just 42 times.

Mize tied Kiner for the National League home-run title again in 1948 with 40 blasts (striking out only 37 times). It would be his last full season with the Giants, his last great statistical season as a full-time player. But some of his biggest thrills were ahead.

In 1949 Mize was 36, struggling at the plate, and unhappy playing for Giants manager Leo Durocher. He was about to get a lot happier. In August the Big Cat was sent to the Yankees for $40,000. Although the press criticized the Yankees' wisdom, the move ultimately helped make Casey Stengel a genius as the aging slugger became an important cog in baseball's greatest dynasty, helping the Yankees win a record five straight World Series championships. "Your arm is gone, your legs likewise, but not your eyes, Mize, not your eyes," wrote New York sportswriter Dan Parker, inspired by the aging slugger's ability to drag his bulk to the plate and deposit baseballs anywhere on the field, and often beyond it.

"He didn't run very well and he'd injured his arm so he couldn't throw very well, either, but Mize was an extremely valuable guy on our team, because he was such a dangerous hitter, especially in the clutch," said former Yankee third baseman (and American League president) Bobby Brown. Or, as former Yankees star and teammate Hank Bauer noted, Mize had "an abnormal ability to respond to the most urgent demands."

Nursing an injured shoulder, Mize performed admirably as a pinch-hitter down the stretch as the Yankees nipped the Red Sox in a blistering 1949 pennant race. His two-out, ninth-inning, bases-loaded single broke a tie score and brought the Yankees a critical win over the Dodgers in Game Three of the World Series.

Playing a part-time role in 1950, he put up full-time numbers, with 72 RBIs and 25 homers in only 274 at bats. He was among the leaders in the American League in pinch hits each of the next three seasons and earned the Most Valuable Player Award in the 1952 World Series, as he hit three home runs (and just missed a fourth), batted .400, and led the Yankees in a classic seven-game victory over Brooklyn.

Normally a quiet giant, Mize was nonetheless happy to offer his opinion on hitting. He even wrote about it in *How to Hit*, by Johnny Mize as told to Murray Kaufman, published in 1953. "He's the one guy I'd tell the other guys to imitate at the plate," said Gutteridge. "He was absolutely one of the great students and teachers of hitting."

Sometimes, though, Mize's unsolicited advice backfired. During the 1953 World Series — Mize's last hurrah — Brooklyn pitcher Carl Erskine was throwing a masterpiece in Game Three at Ebbets Field, striking out a horde of Yankees with his sharp-breaking off-speed pitches. As teammate after teammate went down on strikes, and Erskine got closer to a World Series strikeout record, Mize kept grumbling that the Yankees should lay off pitches in the dirt.

"A lot of our players were getting pretty annoyed, they looked at him like he was crazy," said teammate Whitey Ford. "Then Casey (Stengel) sent him up to pinch hit in the ninth. He ends up swinging at a curveball in the dirt, and Erskine set the World Series strikeout record."

Mize was Erskine's record 14th victim, swinging three times at pitches that were down around his ankles. When he returned to the dugout, tight-lipped and none too happy, the Yankees' mouthy second baseman Billy Martin managed to rip Mize's whiff and bad defense in one quip: "What happened, John, that low curve take a bad hop?"

When he left the game following the 1953 season (during which he hit .298 as a pinch hitter and led the league with 17 pinch hits), Mize had 359 home runs, sixth all-time when he retired, and had hit one in all 15 of the ballparks in use at the time. He also had 1,337 RBIs and a .312 batting average, plus a .397 on-base percentage and a .562 slugging percentage (higher than Hank Aaron or Willie Mays). He was the first player to hit three homers in a game six times — a record since matched by Sammy Sosa. His 43 home runs in 1940 remained a Cardinals record until Mark McGwire broke it in 1998.

After retiring as a player, Mize bounced around between businesses in Florida (real-estate development, orange groves, liquor store) and the occasional foray into coaching (New York Giants, Richmond in the minors, and Mexico City, among others).

His wife of 20 years, Jene, died tragically in 1957 — she fell asleep while smoking and later died from the burns suffered in the fire at their Deland, Florida, home. Three months later, however, Mize married Marjorie Pope in Deland, and eventually adopted her children, Jim and Judi. In his later years, Mize played a lot of golf, and attended old-timer's games and baseball card shows, where he signed a lot of autographs — and donated his fee to local Boy Scout troops.

In 1974 the Mizes moved to his boyhood home in Demorest, across the street from Piedmont College, where he died on June 2, 1993. Mize went to bed after watching the Atlanta Braves on TV and never woke up.

The greatest moment of Mize's post-playing career finally came on August 2, 1981, when he was inducted into the Baseball Hall of Fame after waiting nearly 30 years. Bob Broeg and others suggested that Mize's defensive liabilities probably cost him, but many fans, journalists, and baseball people wondered why it took so long. Mize wondered himself, but took it in stride and announced with his typical wry humor on the day of his induction, "Years ago the writers were telling me that I'd make the Hall of Fame, so I kind of prepared a speech. But somewhere along in the 28 years it got lost."

Thanks to my SABR colleague Rory Costello for his support as this story took final form.

SOURCES

Interviews (conducted between 2000 and 2002): Buddy Blattner, Bob Broeg, Bobby Brown, Whitey Ford, Don Gutteridge, and Judi Mize.

Golenbock, Peter, *The Spirit of St. Louis: A History of the St. Louis Cardinals and Browns* (New York: Avon Books Inc., 2000).

Mize, Johnny, *How to Hit* (New York: Henry Holt and Company, 1953).

The Sporting News

Baseball Digest

baseball-reference.com

baseballhall.org

thebaseballpage.com

Barney McCosky

By Jim Sargent

WILLIAM BARNEY MCCOSKY, A Pennsylvania native who grew up in Detroit, was a talented and speedy all-around center fielder who broke into the major leagues with a bang in 1939, hitting .311 for the Detroit Tigers. McCosky stood 6-feet-1 and weighed 185 pounds in his prime, threw right and batted left, and did both with skill, accuracy, and grace. So well did he perform that by July 22 of his rookie season, Joe Williams, a sportswriter for the *New York World-Telegram*, named McCosky to his "Major [League] All-Recruit Team." Williams picked three American Leaguers to his all-rookie outfield: Boston's Ted Williams, batting over .300 at that point with 15 home runs and 80 RBIs, in left field; New York's Charlie Keller, who finished the year averaging .334 with 11 homers and 83 RBIs, in right; and for center field, McCosky, who averaged .311 with four home runs and 58 RBIs. After the season, *The Sporting News*, considered Baseball's Bible in those years, named McCosky the center fielder on its "Freshman Team." Despite such honors, and after 11 years in the major leagues with a career batting average of .312, McCosky remained virtually unknown, except to longtime fans of the Tigers and the Philadelphia Athletics, the team to which he was traded in 1946.

McCosky, a line-drive hitter who seldom pulled the ball, owned one of the sweetest swings in baseball. Many big leaguers of the 1940s suffered major career interruptions during World War II, but Barney endured a second major disruption. He suffered a back injury on June 15, 1948, that finally led to spinal fusion surgery in 1949, and though he played four seasons after the operation, he was no longer the same athlete.

McCosky, one of the great players ever to perform for the Tigers, was a modest, energetic, likeable young man with a smiling disposition, wavy brown hair, and pale blue eyes who was liked

by his veteran Detroit teammates. The modest hometown hero batted .447 in his first nine big-league games, and he never fell below .305 in 1939. Barney made a big hit with the Briggs Stadium bleacherites, who loved cheering for exploits of the local star. By mid-1940, with the world heading toward war, Michigan's factories gearing up for war production, and the Tigers fighting for the American League pennant against the Cleveland Indians and the defending champion Yankees, the Tigers as well as their fans expressed outrage when McCosky was omitted from the All-Star game. At the midseason break, Barney, the speedy, wide-ranging center fielder, was hitting a nifty .346. When the season was over, he had an average of .340 along with league highs in hits with 200 and triples with 19. McCosky, however, displayed only occasional power, and his peak for home runs came with seven in 1942, his last season before joining the Navy.

The youngest of nine children in a Lithuanian-Polish working-class family, McCosky was born in the mining town of Coal Run, Pennsylvania, on April 11, 1917, one week after Congress voted for the United States to enter World War I. When he was 5, his father, seeking a job in Detroit's booming auto industry, moved his

McCosky before a game in Guam.

family to the Motor City. A youngster who excelled at baseball and basketball, Barney was playing the national pastime on sandlots before the Great Depression. Like many boys of his era, he dreamed of playing in the major leagues. His hero was Charlie Gehringer, the Hall of Fame second baseman who starred for the Tigers from 1926 to 1942. McCosky a left-handed hitter, copied Gehringer's left-handed stance, grip, and smooth swing while playing American Legion ball. Moved to the outfield by his high-school coach as a sophomore, McCosky was spotted by Wish Egan, the Tigers' chief scout. Barney recalled batting .457 as a junior and .727 as a senior, but first he wanted to go to college. Egan and the Tigers made the 18-year-old an offer he couldn't refuse: He would play one year in the minors, and if he didn't perform well, Detroit would pay for his four years of college.

The deal paid off for the Tigers after McCosky climbed through the club's farm system in three years. The teenager started the 1936 season with 20 games at Beaumont of the Class A1 Texas League, where he batted just .227 with one double. Three weeks later, Detroit sent him to Charleston, West Virginia, of the Class C Middle Atlantic League. The fleet left-handed hitter starred in center field for the second-place Senators, leading the league in hitting with a .400 mark and making the All-Star team. Talking about that season in a 1991 interview with SABR member Norman Macht, McCosky recalled earning $150 a month and hitting well, but making a few mistakes in the outfield; paying room and board of $7 a week and traveling everywhere by bus; and playing mostly night games under "candlelight." At the time, Barney said, you learned from your mistakes. Players didn't get much coaching, so they had to improve on their own.

McCosky spent the next two seasons back at Beaumont, at that time an important minor-league stop for future Tigers. Beaumont was about 25 miles from the Gulf of Mexico in the southeastern corner of Texas, and the Exporters sweated through hot and humid summers wearing dark red woolen uniforms. In 1937 Barney hit .318, topping the league in four categories: hits with 201, runs with 116, triples with 20, and outfield putouts with 412 in 158 games. In 1938 the Detroiter missed five weeks early with a broken ankle. After the ankle healed, he enjoyed a good season, batting .302. McCosky batted leadoff or second in the order, so his lack of power didn't bother the Tigers. He could, and did, slam doubles and triples into the gaps in right-center and left-center fields, and his speed made him a threat on the basepaths. In the outfield, his arm wasn't strong, but he threw the ball quickly to the cutoff man.

McCosky went to spring training with Detroit in 1939, and he did not hit well in the early exhibition games. Near the end of March, Tigers manager Del Baker was deciding between two left-handed-batting rookies, McCosky and Frank Secory, who hit .323 at Beaumont in 1938. Taking a last look at Barney, Baker put the 22-year-old into an exhibition in the leadoff spot against Brooklyn's veteran right-hander Whitlow Wyatt. McCosky went 3-for-4. That evening McCosky recalled in 1991, Baker told him he had made the team.

Thereafter, Barney was a changed player: His tension was gone, his fielding improved, and he hit over .400 for the rest of the spring. The first graduate of Detroit's sandlots and high schools to play for the Tigers, McCosky displayed his batwork on Opening Day against the Chicago White Sox, rapping a pair of singles. He continued to hit well, partly because he swung only at good pitches and because he seldom tried to slug the ball.

"Rare days that have seen McCosky stopped by a [Bob] Feller or a [Red] Ruffing have served to emphasize a quality responsible for his consistent success," Sam Greene, sports editor of the *Detroit News*, wrote on July 8, 1939. "Failure does not discourage him. Tomorrow always is another day that he greets with determination and poise, unmindful of pop flies or strikeouts that may have spoiled a previous afternoon's work." As if to second that motion, Clark Griffith, owner of the Washington Senators, declared McCosky his choice for "Recruit of the Year." (The major leagues' Rookie of the Year award was not created until 1947.)

Baker's Tigers, however, fell to the second division for the first time since 1933, finishing fifth with an 81-73 mark, 26½ games behind the pennant-winning Yankees (106-45). But Detroit fielded a good-hitting team.

Gehringer, still anchoring the infield, paced the club with a .325 average, including 16 home runs and 86 RBIs. Hank Greenberg, the slugging first baseman, ranked second behind Gehringer in 1939 with a .312 mark, and Greenberg led the Bengals with 33 homers and 112 RBIs. Batting leadoff, McCosky posted the Tigers' third-best batting average at .311. He showed power in the alleys, hitting 33 doubles and 14 triples, and he hit four home runs while producing 58 RBIs. Rudy York, who caught in 67 games and played 19 games at first base, ranked fourth with a .307 mark, but the strong right-handed batter hit 20 home runs and drove in 68 runs. Curveballer Tommy Bridges posted the team's best won-lost record at 17-7. Burly Louis Norman "Buck" Newsom, acquired in a trade with the St. Louis Browns, had a 17-10 mark with Detroit (20-11 overall). Newsom threw a hopping fastball and a slider, but no curve, McCosky recalled.

Reflecting on that season more than 50 years later, McCosky said that Detroit was loaded with veteran players who knew one another. He didn't drink or play cards, two of the favorite pastimes of most major leaguers, so he usually kept to himself. When the Tigers played at home, Barney, who was single, lived with his family. On the road he roomed with rookie right-hander Paul "Dizzy" Trout. Gehringer, Barney's hero, took him under his wing. Also, teams traveled by train in those years, and spending half of the season on the road helped foster camaraderie. As a result, McCosky got to know all of the Tigers as the season progressed.

As a hitter, McCosky remembered planting his front foot up in the batter's box. That kept him from lifting the front foot too soon, or striding too far on a pitch. If he had a question, Barney would ask Gehringer to watch him bat, but the veteran star would often just say, "Keep going." McCosky recalled, "I would just try to meet the ball, not swing hard, just like a pepper game." He attributed his good hitting to his open stance and bat control. His contract called for $500 a month, but due to his success, Detroit raised him on June 15 to $5,000 a year.

McCosky recalled being nervous on his first Opening Day, Tuesday, April 18, 1939, before 47,000 shivering fans on a chilly, windy, rainy day at Briggs Stadium.

The Tigers defeated the White Sox, 6-1, and Barney singled twice in three official at-bats, walking once, scoring once, and driving in one run. In his first major-league at-bat, he faced Chicago right-hander Johnny Rigney. "I got up to the plate leading off, and regardless of where the pitch was, I was taking it," Barney commented. "I took the ball—it was high, under my chin. With that [pitch], everything just dropped [into place]. It seemed like I relaxed, and I was ready." McCosky followed with a single. He remembered the same nervous feeling in the 1940 World Series, but after the first pitch, he was ready.

After his impressive rookie season, McCosky enjoyed a career year in 1940, hitting .340, pacing the league with 19 triples (no Tiger would hit that many for another 67 years), The Tigers' success was boosted by key trades and by a major position shift during spring training: Del Baker persuaded Hank Greenberg to move from first base to left field. Baker shifted slow-footed Rudy York, a 6-foot-1, 209-pounder of Cherokee ancestry who grew up in rural northwest Georgia, to first base. In the end the Tigers fashioned a record of 90-64, one game better than the Cleveland Indians and two ahead of the Yankees. Detroit posted the AL's best batting mark at .286 (tied with Boston) and scored the most runs, 888. Greenberg, who stood 6-feet-3 and weighed 210 pounds, shared the Tigers' hitting honors with McCosky as both averaged .340. Hank didn't like the left field at first, but he adjusted well. Greenberg, later the first Jewish player inducted into the National Baseball Hall of Fame (1956), led the AL with 41 home runs and 150 RBIs. Close behind was York, who batted .316, slugged 33 homers and drove home 134 runs. In addition, Charley Gehringer overcame back problems to average .313 with 10 home runs and 81 RBIs; catcher Billy Sullivan, traded to the Tigers by the Browns, averaged .309; and Pinky Higgins, acquired from the Red Sox in in December 1938, hit .271 with 13 home runs and 76 RBIs.

On the mound, Buck Newsom led the Motor City club with a 21-5 record, giving him three straight 20-win seasons. Also, former ace Lynwood "Schoolboy" Rowe, the 6-foot-4½ Texan who was coming back from arm woes (Rowe was 10-12 in 1939), produced a 16-3 mark,

Tommy Bridges was 12-9, and Detroiter and future Hall of Fame southpaw Hal Newhouser pitched his first full season and went 9-9. Al Benton, the 6-foot-4 reliever who threw a "heavy" sinker, posted a 6-10 record, finished 35 games, and posted a league-best 17 saves.

By mid-1940 Detroit's sportswriters were already comparing McCosky to the Tigers' immortal Ty Cobb in terms of style, speed, and ability. Although he fell short of Joe DiMaggio in the race for the batting title and didn't evidence much power, McCosky led the league with 200 hits. Leading the Indians by two games, Detroit arrived in Cleveland for the final three games of the season. Baker opened with right-hander Floyd Giebell. On September 27, 1940, the tall West Virginia native hurled a shutout, spacing six singles to defeat fireballing Bob Feller, 2-0. Feller allowed just three hits, but in the fourth inning Gehringer walked and York clouted a two-run homer that clinched the pennant. Giebell had been recalled from Buffalo of the International League after September 1, making him ineligible for the World Series.

The Indians won the final two games of the series by one run each, but it hardly mattered, because the surprising Tigers had battled their way into the World Series for the third time in seven years. Many experts figured defending National League champion Cincinnati had the better pitching staff, anchored by Bucky Walters, who posted NL bests with his 22-10 record and 2.48 ERA, and Paul Derringer, with a 20-12 record and a 3.06 ERA. Still, most observers agreed that if the fall classic hinged on hitting, Detroit could win. In particular, the Tigers had the better outfield, with Greenberg in left and McCosky in center. In right field Baker had two choices: veteran Pete Fox, a right-handed batter who averaged .289 with five home runs and 48 RBIs in 1940, and left-handed-hitting Bruce Campbell, a veteran acquired from Cleveland who batted .283 with eight homers and 44 RBIs.

McCosky hit .304 in the World Series, which came to the decisive seventh game tied at three games each. Cincinnati won the finale, 2-1. McCosky, leading off, was hitless in three trips but drew one walk. Newsom pitched against Paul Derringer on one day's rest, while Derringer had two days. Detroit scored once in the

third when Billy Sullivan beat out an infield hit and took second on Newsom's bunt. After Dick Bartell popped out, McCosky walked. Charlie Gehringer smashed a shot to third base, and Billy Werber knocked it down but threw late to first, allowing Sullivan to score on the error. Newsom made the lead stand up until the seventh, when Frank McCormick, the Reds' top power threat with 19 home runs and 127 RBIs, doubled to left. Jimmy Ripple doubled off the top of the right-field screen, and McCormick, who hesitated at second and also at third base, scored when Bartell took the relay from Campbell, but held up before firing home. Evidently crowd noise kept the shortstop from hearing Sullivan's shouts to throw the ball. After a sacrifice bunt and an intentional pass, Billy Myers drove in the Series-winning run with a long fly to McCosky in front of the center-field wall.

McCosky, a fan favorite in Detroit, became an established star in 1940. Further, he gave the Tigers two more stellar years before joining the Navy. During his seven years as a regular, Barney averaged a consistent .316, and he missed the .300 mark only in 1942.

Although McCosky enjoyed another good year in 1941, baseball headlines that season focused on Joe DiMaggio's 56-game hitting streak, Ted Williams's .406 season, and, in Detroit, Hank Greenberg's service in the Army. The Tigers expected to contend, but fell to fifth with a 75-79 record. The big blow occurred when Greenberg, the league's Most Valuable Player in 1940, was drafted in April and sworn into the Army on May 7. Greenberg's importance to baseball was such that he made headlines at Michigan's Fort Custer, for example, when he was promoted to private first class, corporal, and sergeant. On December 5 the 30-year-old Greenberg was mustered out of the Army under a recent ruling that said men over 28 were ineligible to go overseas. Two days later, on December 7, the Japanese bombed Pearl Harbor and propelled the United States into World War II. Greenberg said he would re-enlist for the duration, adding, reported *The Sporting News*, "We are in trouble and there is only one thing for me to do—return to the service."

McCosky averaged .324 in 127 games in 1941, hitting 25 doubles, eight triples, and three home runs. Also, he suffered his first major injury, on May 11 against the White Sox at Chicago's Comiskey Park, when he wrenched his back rounding second base. Teammates had to carry Barney from the field, He was treated at Detroit's Ford Hospital for several days, and he returned to the lineup in early June. Rookie Pat Mullin, a left-handed batter who hit .345 with five homers and 23 RBIs in 1941, took over center field, until he broke his collarbone in early July. McCosky returned to center, and his highlights included leading the Tigers over Bob Feller and the Indians, 4-3, on August 7, rapping three singles in five trips and scoring the game-winner in the 13th inning. On August 20 at Briggs Stadium against the Yankees, he went 2-for-5 with an RBI single in the tenth that won the game, 1-0. Two days later at home, McCosky's only hit was decisive: a ninth-inning three-run homer into the upper deck in right field for a 5-4 victory over Washington. Regardless of how well he batted and fielded, Barney seemed to labor in ob-scurity, which was the irony of his fine career.

In 1942, with the US fully committed to fighting against the Japanese in the Pacific as well as the forces of Nazi Germany and Italy on the other side of the world, McCosky tried to lift the Tigers by focusing more on hitting the long ball. Regardless, Detroit re-mained in fifth place and his average slipped to .293, still the best mark among Tiger regulars. Avoiding injuries, he played the entire 154 games, usually batting third. , Barney stepped up to bat 680 times, his second most plate appearances (he appeared 692 times as a rookie), drawing 68 walks, and producing 176 hits, including 28 doubles, 11 triples, and a career-best seven four-baggers.

On December 10, 1942, just over a year after the Pearl Harbor attack, McCosky was inducted into the Navy, making him the 15th Tiger to enter the armed forces. He served until October 1945, but was unable to return home in time to join his teammates as they defeated the Chicago Cubs in a seven-game World Series. McCosky started out at the Great Lakes Naval Training Center, north of Chicago, and he spent time at the Bainbridge (Maryland) Naval Training Center for advanced training. Later, he was stationed in Hawaii and elsewhere in the Pacific. Wherever he was stationed,

he became a recreation specialist, and as he recalled, "We had to give exercises, umpire ballgames, set up basketball tournaments, be instructors, all this stuff. Everybody played hard, and we really enjoyed playing out there." Also, like most big leaguers, he played service baseball, notably in Hawaii in 1944. During one season in Honolulu, McCosky remembered leading the league with 17 homers, but he hit only .220. Still, players won a free War Bond for each four-bagger, and, he said, "I was going for the downs!"

World War II ended with the surrender of Japan in August 1945, the US began demobilizing the economy and the armed forces, and a host of ballplayers, back from the service, traveled to spring training in 1946. McCosky took the train from his Dearborn, Michigan, home (which he built with his 1940 World Series money), to the Tigers' camp at Lakeland, Florida. Like many ballplayers he was rusty after three years in the Navy. He made the Tigers roster (a federal law required that major-league teams give prewar players their roster spot for at least 30 days), but started slowly, averaging .198 through 25 games.

Detroit had youthful outfielders, including Pat Mullin, who hit .246 with three homers and 35 RBIs in 1946, and 6-foot-2-inch rookie Hoot Evers, a right-handed batter who averaged .266 with four homers and 33 RBIs.

On May 28 Detroit traded the 29-year-old McCosky to the Philadelphia Athletics for 23-year-old third baseman George Kell. Kell, 4-F in wartime, batted .268 and .272, respectively, for the 1944 and 1945 Athletics, and he was a fine third baseman. "As a prewar baseball name, McCosky stands out," concluded New York scribe Dan Daniel. "As an actual asset, he is of doubtful worth. Barney is suffering from a leg injury which is said to be chronic. His Detroit batting average this season is under .200." Calling Kell a "far better fielder" than people realized, Daniel pointed out that the Clifton, Arkansas, athlete led AL third basemen in assists with 345 and in putouts with 186 in 1945.

In 1991 McCosky called the trade a "shock." At the time he had a sore ankle from rolling over his foot rounding third base, so he could not run as well as usual. That afternoon in the locker room at Briggs Stadium, one of the coaches told him, "You've just been traded to Philadelphia."

McCosky moved to the Philadelphia, found an apartment, got married a month later, and rejuvenated his career. His fiancée was Jane Malicki, a Detroit resident he had known for years. Speaking in a 1996 interview, Jane recalled, "Our friendship developed into a serious relationship through the mail during World War II while Barney was in the South Pacific and I was at Michigan State [College]. Truthfully, I focused on him much before that as a high-school teenager, when he and my father used to hunt and fish together. Since there was a seven-year age difference, he considered me a youngster. With the news of his trade, we canceled our wedding plans for October and were married on June 19, 11 days after my graduation from MSU."

For the remainder of the 1946 season McCosky's hitting was as good as ever, but he had occasional back problems. For A's fans, the popular Kell looked great in Detroit, hitting .327 for the rest of the season and batting .322 overall. More important, Kell, who later won the hearts of millions as a down-home broadcaster for the Tigers, went on to enjoy a Hall of Fame career, hitting .306 lifetime, while McCosky, even though he batted a career .312, later would be known in Detroit mostly as the player the Tigers traded to get Kell.

In 1946 Barney averaged .318 overall, but he topped the A's by hitting a sizzling .354 in 92 games, contributing 17 doubles, four triples, one home run, and 34 RBIs. Typical of his good batting eye, he drew 43 bases on balls and fanned only 13 times in Philadelphia (overall he walked 60 times with 22 strikeouts). McCosky's erstwhile teammates in Detroit ranked second with a record of 92-62, 12 games behind pennant-winning Boston (104-50), but five games ahead of third-place New York (87-67). For McCosky, life in the City of Brotherly Love meant more obscurity than he had found in Detroit. The cash-strapped Athletics owner, Connie Mack, was trying to rebuild his team. In 1947, the year Jackie Robinson crossed the "color line" in major-league baseball, the Athletics, riding improved pitching, climbed as high as second place and finished fifth with a 78-76 record, the team's first winning record

since 1933. Mack shifted the speedy Sam Chapman, who led the team with 14 homers, to center field, sent the good-hitting McCosky, who had lost some speed, to left, and kept Elmer Valo in right.

The 1947 season featured McCosky's duel with Ted Williams for the batting championship, eventually won by Teddy Ballgame with an MVP-like performance of .343, plus league highs of 32 home runs and 114 RBIs. Still, McCosky excited Athletics fans with his .328 mark, leaving him second only to Williams. Barney hit just one home run, but he connected for 22 doubles and seven triples, and he scored 77 runs while driving home 52 runs, mostly from the first and second slots. In the league's MVP balloting by sportswriters, Joe DiMaggio won with 202 votes, Williams narrowly missed the honor with 201 votes, and Kell was fifth with 132. McCosky and shortstop Eddie Joost of the A's received 35 votes each.

McCosky, despite a major injury, mirrored his 1947 season in 1948 when Cleveland (97-58) won the AL pennant and Philadelphia made a good run at the flag, finishing fourth with an 84-70 record, six games above the fifth-place Tigers (78-76). Batting .326, but with no home runs, Barney rapped 168 hits (compared with 179 in 1947), slugged 21 doubles and 5 triples (compared with 22 and 7, respectively, in 1947), scored 95 runs (he scored 77 times in 1947), walked 68 times (11 more than 1947), and struck out 22 times (seven fewer than 1947). Ted Williams won the hitting crown again in 1948, averaging a hefty .369. McCosky's average ranked below those of four other good hitters: Williams; Cleveland's Lou Boudreau at .355; Dale Mitchell of the Indians, .336; and Al Zarilla of the Browns, .329.

On June 15, 1948, during the Tigers' first night game at Briggs Stadium, McCosky was injured when, backpedaling for a high home-run ball hit by Dick Wakefield, he hit the concrete-reinforced wall, fell awkwardly on the wooden frame holding the tarpaulin, and twisted his back. Reflecting on the incident in 1991, McCosky, who had a plug of tobacco in his cheek, recalled asking Sam Chapman, the first player on the scene, to pull out the chew. Chapman did, McCosky passed out, and he was carried from the field on a stretcher. Still, baseball is highly competitive, and Barney claimed the injury was not serious, saying he felt good enough to play within a week. On June 21 he entered a game at St. Louis, replacing Chapman in the first inning, and finishing the game, going 0-for-4 in a 9-8 loss. The next day against the Browns he seemed back to normal, going 2-for-5 as Philadelphia topped St. Louis, 7-6. At that point Barney was hitting .259, but he improved steadily to finish at .326, fifth-best in the league

Jane McCosky, speaking in 1996, explained what happened in 1949: "The first day of the '49 spring-training season, Barn bent down to pick up a ball and that was all it took—the pain was so severe, he was unable to play a single game the entire year. When we got back to Philadelphia, he spent weeks in traction and then underwent therapy. Finally in August, Mr. Mack placed him on leave for the rest of the year, and we returned to Michigan. In December, after exploratory surgery at Henry Ford Hospital, it was determined he had a pinched nerve in the last vertebra. The doctors concluded that a fusion [of the lower three vertebrae] was necessary. I credit his extraordinary team of surgeons with his successful recovery, since this type of operation was dangerous and rare at that time."

McCosky arrived at spring training in 1950 in a removable body cast, but he set it aside because it dramatically limited his mobility. Jane recalled, "At the opening game in Washington, he stretched his base hit into a double, sliding in and laying very still at second base, listening to his back clicking away as the adhesions from his surgery broke loose. That evening he received a telegram from his doctor in Detroit wanting to know, 'What the hell are you doing in there?' When the A's arrived in Detroit, he underwent a thorough exam, and although he was OK'd for play, his back never responded with the flexibility he was used to. Because of this, his career was ended too soon."

Having lived his baseball dream successfully for eight seasons, McCosky hated letting it go. As it happened, his back made it so that he could not play a full season as a regular again. For the Athletics in 1950, McCosky, now 33, played in 66 games, including 42 in the outfield, but the onetime speedster compiled his worst average to date, .240. Barney began the 1951 season with Philadelphia, hitting .296 in 12 games, but on May

4 he was sold to Cincinnati, where he averaged .320 in 25 games. Cleveland, with former Tiger Hank Greenberg as general manager, acquired McCosky off waivers on July 21. The Indians wanted him to serve partly as a left-handed pinch-hitter, but Barney averaged only .213 in 31 games. Returning to Cleveland in 1952, McCosky played in 19 games in the outfield and hit .213 again, but he was a solid 9-for-30 off the bench. In 1953 McCosky got into 22 games, all as a pinch-batter, but he averaged just .190. The Indians finally released him on July 14. Greenberg offered his former teammate a coaching job in the minors, but McCosky declined and returned to Dearborn. For several years his work included selling cars for a local Chevrolet dealer.

McCosky was one of the top outfielders in the league before missing 1949 with spinal surgery, and the fact that he overcame that injury and played four more seasons was a tribute to his desire, determination, and fortitude. Greg Kaza, a public-policy researcher, pointed out that compared to active ten-year players in 1953, when he retired, McCosky's lifetime average of .312 left him tied with Johnny Mize, who was inducted into the Hall of Fame in 1981. At the time, Barney trailed only Ted Williams (HOF, 1966, .344) and Stan Musial (HOF, 1969, .331).

McCosky was inducted into the Michigan Sports Hall of Fame in 1995 and as of 2013, his .312 lifetime average ranked 11th best among Tigers with at least 2,000 career at-bats. McCosky, who died in 1996, was a talented all-around athlete with a positive demeanor who was liked and respected by teammates and fans. As a result, the Detroiter represented the kind of ballplayer that fathers, sons, and fans of all ages liked to root for at major-league ballparks like Briggs Stadium and Shibe Park. In addition to enjoying six .300-plus seasons, he was able to live any ballplayer's dream of playing in a World Series. Even though Detroit lost to Cincinnati in 1940, the hometown hero gave the game his best, batting .304 in October. In retrospect, Barney McCosky remains one of the great players ever to wear the Tiger uniform.

SOURCES

Books:

Jordan, David M., *The Philadelphia Athletics: Connie Mack's White Elephants, 1901–1954* (Jefferson, North Carolina: McFarland & Company, Inc., 1999).

Mead, William B., *Baseball Goes to War* (Washington, DC: Farragut Publishing, 1985).

Pattison, Mark, and David Raglin, *Detroit Tigers: List and More* (Detroit: Wayne State University Press, 2002).

Smith, Fred T., *Tiger S.T.A.T.S.: Statistics, Trades, Alumni, Trivia, Stories* (Ann Arbor, Michigan: Momentum Books, Ltd, 1991).

Articles:

"Hank Greenberg, Back to the Colors, Becomes the Hank Gowdy of '41," *The Sporting News*, December 18, 1941, 1.

Daniel, Dan, "Daniel's Dope," *New York World-Telegram*, May 20, 1946.

Dell, Alan, "McCosky Deserves Cooperstown Berth, *Sarasota Herald Tribune*, September 10, 1996.

Farrington, Dick, "Williams and Keller Rated No. 1 Stars of '39 Freshman Team," *The Sporting News* October 19, 1939, 5.

Green, Jerry, "Barney McCosky," in program for State of Michigan Sports Hall of Fame (1995), 17.

Greene, Sam, "Belting Barney: Motor City's Fast-Starting Rookie, *The Sporting News*, May 4, 1939, 1.

Greene, Sam. "McCosky Passes First Test as 'Recruit of the Year,'" July 8, 1939, unidentified clipping in McCosky player file at the National Baseball Hall of Fame.

Greene, Sam, "Tigers Call Barney's Omission Inexcusable," July 2, 1940.

Kaza, Greg, "Forgotten Tiger, 72, Should Be Elected to Hall of Fame," *Midland* (Michigan) *Daily News*, May 6, 1990.

Williams, Joe, "Present Crop of Baseball Recruits Greatest in Years," *New York World-Telegram*, July 23, 1939.

Interviews:

Barney McCosky and Billy Sullivan, by Norman Macht, 1991. McCosky quotes not otherwise cited came from this interview.

Jane McCosky, 1996, by Jim Sargent. Mrs. McCosky, Barney's wife, also sent me statements in 1996 about their marriage in 1946 and about her husband's back injury in 1948, his surgery in 1949, and the aftermath.

Hal Trosky

By Bill Johnson

HAL TROSKY PLAYED FIRST BASE FOR the Cleveland Indians and the Chicago White Sox in the 1930s and 1940s. His career reached its apex in 1936, when he led the American League in runs batted in with 162, yet he has largely been consigned to historical obscurity. This anonymity is not only due to the reality that his career overlapped a triumvirate of Jimmie Foxx, Hank Greenberg, and Lou Gehrig, a triumvirate of future Hall of Fame first basemen who held a virtual lock on the position on the American League All Star teams of the mid-'30s, but also because, at what should have been the peak of his career, Trosky was sidelined with two years of severe migraine headaches, pain so debilitating that he became unable to take the field for days in a row.

Born Harold Arthur, he arrived on November 11, 1912, to John and Mary (née Siepman) Trojovsky. The family, second-generation immigrants from Bohemia, moved to a 420-acre farm outside Norway, Iowa, in 1917. Harold had two sisters, Annette and Esther, and a brother, Victor.

After an impressive schoolboy and amateur career, Hal was courted with varying degrees of intensity by the Philadelphia Athletics, the St. Louis Cardinals, and the Cleveland Indians. Graduating from high school in 1930, he was offered a minor-league contract by the Cardinals. Not sure how to proceed, Trosky called on Bing Miller in nearby Vinton. Miller was then a member of Connie Mack's powerhouse Philadelphia Athletics, who had just played in the second of their three consecutive World Series. Miller was delighted to speak with the boy.

Miller knew Trojovsky's reputation and advised him to do nothing until Miller had had the chance to inform Mr. Mack. Hal drove home quite content, but upon returning to Norway found his father seated in the kitchen with Cleveland Indians scout and Cedar Rapids native Cyril C. "Cy" Slapnicka. Trosky later told Gordon Cobbledick, the baseball columnist for the *Cleveland Plain Dealer*, "I liked Slap, and after we talked baseball for a while he suggested I sign with him."[1] Evidently,

Slapnicka had been aware of Hal's prowess and local reputation, but hadn't felt any urgency in pursuing him until he got wind of the Athletics' and Cardinals' interest.

After almost no deliberation, Hal chose the Indians. He signed his first contract Harold Trojovsky, but from then on used the shorter Trosky, as did his siblings. A contract offer from Connie Mack arrived three days later. Hal returned the unsigned document with a note explaining what had happened and apologizing for the inconvenience. He was touched that Mack took time to respond with his best wishes for the player's future career.

Trosky reported to the Class D Cedar Rapids Bunnies in early 1931, playing for a $65 monthly salary. He was signed primarily as a pitcher, one who had the odd habit of hitting cross-handed from the right side of the plate. Slapnicka, in a visit to the park to check on his prospects, took player and manager aside and suggested that Hal retain his grip but switch to a left-handed batting stance. The change was providential, as

Trosky played 52 Mississippi Valley League games that summer as a converted first baseman and, in 162 at-bats, managed 49 hits (including 3 home runs) for a respectable .302 batting average. He followed that mark in 1932 by hitting .307 in 56 games for Burlington of the Mississippi Valley League, and then .331 after promotion to Quincy in the Class B Three-I League. His 15 home runs in 68 games with Quincy summoned the attention of executives in Cleveland, and in 1933 Trosky began the season as a $200-a-month player with the Toledo Mud Hens of the Double-A American Association, the minors' highest classification.

At the close of the Mud Hens' season Cleveland called, and on September 11, 1933, Trosky started at first in place of Harley Boss. He went 0-for-3 against the Washington Senators' Monte Weaver, and notched his first hit the next day off Monte Pearson. On the 18th he collected his first major-league home run, off the Boston Red Sox' Gordon Rhodes.

The day before that homer, September 17, provided a brush with baseball royalty. In the second game of a doubleheader against the Yankees, Trosky was playing deep behind first base when Babe Ruth hit a screaming line drive down the line that carried the rookie's mitt almost halfway into right field. (Hal later had the glove bronzed for his personal collection.)

After retrieving the glove, the rookie had to sift through the conflicting emotions of awe in the presence of a living legend and of fear in the form of Lou Gehrig striding to the plate. If possible, Gehrig represented an even greater hazard to Trosky's well-being than the Bambino, because Ruth generally hit high, arcing fly balls, while Gehrig could rip a vicious line drive off any pitch.

Trosky had to cover the bag with second base open, but against Gehrig the only chance to reel in a hard drive was found in playing farther back on the outfield grass.

The Babe must have divined Trosky's fielding dilemma, because he whispered out of the side of his mouth, "Don't worry about holding me on, kid. I ain't going noplace. Just drop back a little and play it safe. If he hit one at you up here, it would take your head off."[2] Hal backed off and, true to his word, Ruth stood just a few feet from first and awaited the Yankee onslaught. It wasn't that big a deal to the Babe, but Trosky never forgot that small kindness.

In 44 at-bats that month, spread over 11 games, Trosky hit .295 with a homer, a double, and two triples, and drove in eight runs.

In 1934, Trosky's first full year in the major leagues, he was little short of spectacular. He played every inning of all 154 games, hit .330 with 35 home runs, drove in 142 runs, and posted a slugging percentage of .598. He finished seventh in balloting for American League Most Valuable Player. (Triple Crown winner Lou Gehrig could muster no better than fifth place as the award went to Mickey Cochrane, catcher-manager of the pennant-winning Detroit Tigers.)

The 1935 season proved to be something of a sophomore slump for Trosky, marked by an almost 60-point drop in batting average and a commensurate drop in home runs, from 35 to 26. When mired in a September slump that year, a stretch in which he had exactly one hit in 40 at-bats, coach Steve O'Neill, his former manager at Toledo, suggested that Trosky try hitting from the right side against the Senators. The next day, in the opener of a doubleheader in Washington, Hal came up in the first inning and took a right-handed stance. He stunned his teammates by smoking an Orlin Rogers curve for a single. After a left-handed out in the fifth, he hit from the right side again in the eighth inning and knocked a Leon Pettit pitch into the distant reaches of Griffith Stadium's left-field bleachers for his 23rd home run of the year. Overall in the two games, Trosky punched five hits in ten at-bats. Three singles and a home run came from the right side, and one long double from the left. It proved to be the last time he would try switch-hitting.

The 1934 model Hal Trosky returned for the '36 campaign. Trosky put together a 28-game hitting streak and broke his own team record for home runs in a single season when he hit number 36 against the Senators. Although the AL pennant went to the Yankees, it was a memorable season for Trosky, as he led the league in RBIs (162) and total bases (405). His RBI total over his first three seasons was greater than the totals amassed by Gehrig, Foxx, or Greenberg over their first three years.

After his 1933 call-up, Hal had wed longtime sweetheart Lorraine Glenn (from Norway, Iowa), and in September of 1936 they welcomed their first son, Harold. Baseball ran in the genes. Twenty-two years later Hal Junior made it to the major leagues for a late season two-game cup of coffee as a pitcher with the White Sox.

The years from 1937 to 1939 were relatively stable for both player and team. Rather than succumb to the hyperbole and inflated expectations that followed his 1936 season, Trosky chose to focus on improving his fielding. After achieving the rather dubious distinction of leading American League first basemen in errors in 1934 and 1936, he worked diligently to improve his footwork around the base. Along with the subsequent decline in errors, he sought a better approach at the plate, and elevated his batting average to .334 in 1938 and .335 in 1939. Naturally his home-run totals declined, but he found that he could still drive in more than 100 runs per season by putting a higher percentage of balls into play. Trosky and the Indians continued to win, but were competing with a Yankee juggernaut that dwarfed the rest of the league.

By 1939 the Indians had named Hal team captain. Trosky agreed not only for the extra $500 stipend, but because he felt that he could serve as a buffer between some of the less experienced players and their acerbic manager, Oscar Vitt.

In midseason Trosky lifted himself from the lineup and let understudy Oscar Grimes play a few games at first. Trosky never admitted it to the team, but there were times when his head absolutely throbbed. The season ended with Trosky recording only 448 at-bats, the first season since his 1933 overture that he appeared in fewer than 150 games. It was becoming difficult for him to bring the necessary intensity to the park each day. He was only 26 years old when the season ended, but the pain from the headaches sapped his vigor.

Over the winter the headaches faded. Trosky consulted several doctors in Cleveland and in Cedar Rapids, but none was able to pinpoint the source of his discomfort. As the frequency of attacks decreased, he threw himself into his farming and family life, and by

the end of the offseason, he was eager to return to baseball.

Events in spring training of 1940 provided unmistakable indications of how the Indians would perform on the field, but not even the closest observers could have predicted the off-field show that was gradually unfolding. The players felt that their manager, Vitt, was antagonistic and spiteful, despite the press's portrayal of him as suffering and misunderstood. The first week in June brought the cauldron to a boil.

On June 10, after a week of inconsistent play, the Indians were rained out in Boston and the players spent the day in the hotel lobby dissecting their misfortune. They put the blame for the team's struggles on Vitt. Some of the players advanced the idea of trying to dump the manager, but team captain Trosky counseled patience. The slugger was a proud man, and wanted no part of pointing public fingers at anyone, even though Vitt's words had repeatedly stung him.

The next evening, after an afternoon Red Sox blowout of the Indians, Trosky spoke with Frank Gibbons of the *Cleveland Press*. He told the scribe that the Indians could win the pennant with their current players, but had no chance as long as Vitt was the manager. Gibbons cautioned Hal to wait and see how things turned out before doing anything rash. (It was the same advice Trosky had given his teammates earlier.)

The following morning the players checked out of their rooms early. At breakfast they again discussed solutions for the "Vitt problem." Later, on the train ride from Boston to Cleveland, veterans Ben Chapman and Rollie Hemsley reportedly called Lou Boudreau and Ray Mack to their berth and told the young infielders that some of the players were circulating a petition calling for Vitt's ouster. Boudreau and Mack, along with Al Smith, Beau Bell, Mike Naymick, and Soup Campbell, were excused from participating. In a meeting with the rest of the players, pitchers Mel Harder and Johnny Allen told the team that they would go to owner Alva Bradley alone to discuss the problems, and Harder was appointed the voice for the players. On June 13 tragedy found Trosky. As the team's train pulled into the Cleveland station, Hal received word that his mother had died suddenly in Iowa. Trosky went straight from the train station to the airport, while Harder called Alva Bradley's office seeking an appointment with the owner.

Instead of sending Harder alone, ten more of the dissidents accompanied him to Bradley's office to show him the sincerity of their grievance. The players were all seasoned veterans, men who worked in the offseason not by choice but by necessity, and they were men who understood the consequences of their actions. Clearly, this was no idle grumbling about a stern taskmaster. Vitt had wounded them deeply enough to spur those extraordinary measures.

The players told Bradley that Vitt had to go if the team was to compete. They outlined four specific grievances, each of which Bradley later confirmed as true, and demanded that the owner take action. Trosky even telephoned Bradley from the airport to ensure that his absence wouldn't be misconstrued. Despite his personal misgivings about the action, the team captain would not even consider standing idly by while his teammates pressed the issue.

Bradley told the players that he would look into the matter and warned them that if word of the meeting was released, the players would be ridiculed forever. Gordon Cobbledick of the *Cleveland Plain Dealer* found out almost immediately. The Indians won the game that afternoon, but it was the insurrection that was front-page news in the *Plain Dealer* the next morning. The headline for the story was physically larger on the printed page than that afforded to Hitler's invasion of Paris. Bradley went on the record saying that he would take no immediate action regarding his manager or his players until he had a chance to talk with the team captain.

Trosky's involvement in the "Crybaby" incident, rumored so heavily by the writers, probably was not nearly as great as some supposed. Three days after the story broke, on the back page of the *Plain Dealer*, an apology of sorts was printed that stated that neither Oscar Vitt nor Hal Trosky had ever claimed that Trosky was bent on usurping Vitt's authority.

In 1951 the *Cleveland News* unearthed and published a memo from Alva Bradley concerning the incident. It read in part: "We should have won the pennant. ...

Our real trouble started when a group of 10 players came to my office and made four distinct charges against (Vitt) and asked for his dismissal. The four charges made against Vitt, on investigations I have made, were 100% correct."[3] At the end of the season, Bradley fired Vitt. The latter caught on with the Portland Beavers of the Pacific Coast League the following season, but after finishing 26 games below .500, he resigned rather than await another termination. After managing the Hollywood Stars of the PCL to a seventh-place finish in 1942, Vitt was through as a manager.

On August 11, 1940, in St. Louis, Trosky became the 17th major-league player to clout 200 home runs. He finished the season batting .295. His 93 RBIs marked his first full major-league season in which he failed to drive in at least 100 runs. He hit 39 doubles and a team-leading 25 home runs. The headaches hit hard again in August and September, but Hal loathed missing any game in the tight pennant race. The Indians finished second, one game behind Detroit.

Trosky's migraines proved too much for him in 1941. They were striking with no notice and leaving a wake of debilitating agony. For a hitter who made a living off fastballs, he was powerless against a blurry white apparition that he said sometimes looked "like a bunch of white feathers." He played less and less. The migraines were now almost unbearable. On August 11 Cleveland began a seven-game road trip without their slugger. Trosky was left home with Oscar Grimes assuming first-base duties.

Trosky rejoined the team for its last stop, in Chicago. In the sixth inning of the opener of a doubleheader at Comiskey Park, Trosky's Indian career came to an abrupt end when he fractured his thumb in a collision with White Sox pitcher Ted Lyons. The slugger missed the final 42 games of the season and, as it turned out, never wore Cleveland colors again.

The Indians finished in a tie for fourth place with the Tigers as Trosky drove in only 51 runs in 310 at-bats. In February 1942 he told reporter Gayle Hayes that he wouldn't be playing baseball that year. It was, he was quoted, "for the best interest of the Cleveland club and for myself that I stay out of baseball. ... I have visited various doctors in the larger cities in the United States and they have not helped me. If, after resting this year, I find that I am better, perhaps I'll try to be reinstated. If I don't get better, then my major-league career is over."⁴

Trosky passed 1942 and 1943 on his farm in Iowa. He devoured news of the war, farmed, and despite some interest from the Yankees, waited for a call from the draft board. He was evidently a decent farmer, averaging production of over 90 bushels of corn per acre in a time before the advent of modern farming technology. But he wanted to contribute on the front lines.

Trosky worked out for the White Sox and in November the Indians, perhaps willing to remove a piece of the Crybabies incident and aware that he was not the offensive force he had been earlier, sold his contract to Chicago for $45,000. As if an echo of Cleveland's judgment, the Army officially declared Hal Trosky 4-F, unsuitable for military service, in March 1944, due entirely to his history of migraines. Despite a treatment protocol of vitamin shots, the Army wasn't willing to take a chance on a compromised recruit.

The White Sox took advantage of the Army's concession. Trosky played baseball in 1944 like a man with great talent who had been out of the game for two seasons. In April he logged two multi-RBI games, but he showed no consistency. His play was marked by a succession of solid games followed by mediocre performances.

Migraines notwithstanding, Trosky managed ten home runs in 1944, which was enough to lead his team in that category. Including his 1944 season, Hal led his teams seven times in home runs. According to the *SABR Home Run Encyclopedia*, Trosky homered in nine different parks and off 112 different pitchers during his career; his most frequent victims were Tommy Bridges and Bump Hadley. Of his 228 home runs, 106 were hit on the road, and 122 at home. No one but Earl Averill hit more at Cleveland's League Park.

At the end of 1944, with the White Sox in seventh place after winning only 71 times, Trosky called it quits again. He headed home for some hunting and farming, and to await another possible call-up to support the war effort.

In 1945 Trosky worked at the nearby Amana Refrigeration plant. The headache pain had been, in part, controlled by vitamin B-1 shots and by a significant reduction in his daily intake of dairy products. It was ironic that an Iowa dairy farmer was allergic to the very stuff his animals produced, and that he consumed so frequently in order to maintain his athletic frame. The treatments helped lessen the migraines considerably, and the end of the war presented Trosky with one more opportunity. He accepted a White Sox offer of a contract to play in 1946. Trosky hit only .254 with two home runs and 31 RBIs. Despite Chicago's offer of $25,000 to suit up again in 1947, the 34-year-old Trosky knew it was time to hang up the spikes. His baseball career complete, he was able to devote more of his time to the infinitely greater demands of being a father not only to Hal Junior, but also to sons James and Lynn and to their youngest, daughter Mary Kay.

After his official release as a player in February 1947, Trosky rejoined the White Sox as a scout. Between 1947 and 1950, he traveled the tiny towns of eastern Iowa looking for "the next Trosky." In 1947 he also managed a semipro team, the Amana Freezers, sponsored by Amana Refrigeration. That team consisted largely of former University of Iowa baseball and football players and included future Milwaukee Braves second baseman Jack Dittmer and NFL Hall of Famer Emlen Tunnell. The Freezers went 27-2 and just missed qualifying for the Amateur World Series in Kansas. Trosky left the Freezers the next year, and the White Sox in 1950, to settle down on the farm (he owned two over the next 25 years) before taking up agricultural real-estate sales around Cedar Rapids in 1962.

Trosky was, in many ways, a typical Midwestern man. He raised his family with a firm sense of discipline; he hunted, played cards, and went to church. His primary contact with baseball in his later days came through the Iowa High School Baseball Coaches Association. The archives of that organization, later run by Trosky's nephew Harold "Pinky" Primrose, show that he was an active lecturer for many years until the mid-1970s.

Trosky suffered a heart attack in early 1978 and by 1979 was moving around only with the support of a cane. On June 18, at the age of 66, he collapsed in the kitchen of his Cedar Rapids apartment. The doctors said the heart attack was so massive that Trosky was dead by the time he reached the floor. He is buried in St Michael's Cemetery on a hillside overlooking his hometown of Norway, Iowa.

SOURCES

Schneider, Russell, *Cleveland Indians Encyclopedia* (Champaign Illinois: Sports Publishing, 2001)

Thorn, John et al., eds., *Total Baseball, Completely Revised and Updated: The Ultimate Baseball Encyclopedia* (New York: Warner Books, 2004)

Cleveland News (1933-1941)

Cleveland Plain Dealer

Cleveland Press (1930.1946)

Des Moines Register

The Sporting News

New York Daily News

New York Times

Interviews

Gayle Holt (niece)

Russell Schneider (journalist and team historian)

Lorraine Trosky (widow); additionally, used her archival collections for uncatalogued material

Susan Volz (niece); additionally, used her private collections for uncatalogued material

Bob Feller

Rick Ferrell

Denny Galehouse

Mel Harder

Ralph Hodgin

Willis Hudlin

Roy Hughes

Thornton Lee

NOTES

1 Gordon Cobbledick, *Cleveland Plain Dealer*, clipping from 1935 on file in the archives of the National Baseball Hall of Fame, Cooperstown, New York (date of clipping unavailable).

2 Tait Cummins, *Cedar Rapids Tribune*, June 2, 1949, 8.

3 Tait Cummins, *Cleveland News*, clipping from 1951 in private scrapbook archive of Susan Volz, Norway, Iowa.

4 Tait Cummins, *Cedar Rapids Gazette*, February 19, 1942, 17.

Augie Galan

By Greg King

DONNING THE UNIFORMS OF THE Chicago Cubs and Brooklyn Dodgers for the better part of his career, along with playing short stints for the Reds, Giants, and Athletics, Augie Galan (pronounced "guh-LANN") put together a lifetime .287 batting average in 16 major-league seasons. He reached the .300 plateau six times, played in three World Series, and was named to three All-Star squads.

August John Galan was born in Berkeley, California, on May 25, 1912. Galan's parents had emigrated from France in the late 19th century, and his father operated a French hand laundry on Berkeley's University Avenue. One of eight children, Augie maintained that he would have otherwise been involved in the family business had baseball not become his profession. "If something happened to take me out of baseball, I could make a living in the laundry business. I started working for my father after school hours when I was 12 years old and know every branch of the business," he once said.[1]

It was baseball, however, that drew his early interest, and it was on the local sandlots of the East Bay, especially James Kenney Park, that Galan honed his skills. At about the age of 11, he broke his right elbow when he fell out of a tree. He concealed the extent of his injury, and because he didn't see a physician, the arm healed improperly. As a result, he learned to bat left-handed, a skill that served him well in later years.[2]

After graduation from Berkeley High, where he starred, Galan signed with the San Francisco Seals of the Pacific Coast League in 1931. He was sent to a Class D farm team at Globe in the Arizona-Texas League and the next season was brought up to the Seals camp, where he won the starting shortstop spot and hit a respectable .291. Near season's end, Galan, whose heritage led to him to be called Frenchy during his PCL days, requested permission to join a Seals teammate, Hawaiian-born Prince Oana, on a barnstorming trip back to the islands. With three games left in the season, Vince DiMaggio persuaded Seals manager Ike Caveney to allow his little brother Joe to take over at shortstop while Galan was in Hawaii.[3]

The following season, 1933, Joe took an outfield spot with the Seals, where he batted for a lofty .340 average; only Galan, the cleanup hitter, topped DiMaggio and, in fact, carried the highest average on the team, .356. He led the PCL in runs scored (164) and triples (22); he also swiped 41 bases.

A New York Yankees scout approached Galan after hearing rumors that there might be something wrong with the ballplayer's right arm, and asked to see it. Galan refused. "Well, I was dead either way," he said years later. "So I decided not to remove my coat, and maybe it wouldn't get around and somebody else would take a chance on me." The Chicago Cubs indeed took notice of Galan's fine season and obtained him from San Francisco for $25,000 and seven veteran players.[4]

During the 1934 season, Galan platooned for the Cubs at second base, hitting .260 in 192 at-bats. He quickly earned the name "Goo Goo" from his teammates, due to his "great big round eyes," an endearing moniker that survived throughout his playing career. Second base proved to be a bit of a defensive challenge for the rookie, however, and the following year Cubs manager Charlie Grimm moved Galan to the outfield to take advantage of his speed.[5]

The Cubs' first baseman in 1935, Phil Cavarretta, looked back on that season many years later. "Augie Galan originally was a second baseman, but we had Billy Herman, so Charlie moved him out to center field, because we needed a center fielder, and Augie turned out to be one of the best fielding center fielders I've ever seen. He had a great arm, and he was a good little hitter. He was our leadoff man. Billy Herman was hitting second, and I'm not just saying this just because they were my teammates, but as far as hit-and-run men are concerned, to me Augie Galan and Billy Herman were the best."[6]

The move from second to the outfield paid immediate dividends. In his sophomore year, one in which the Cubs claimed the National League pennant, the switch-hitting Galan hit .314, collected 203 hits, and led the league in both runs scored (133) and stolen bases (22). Galan played the full 154-game schedule (646 at-bats) without hitting into a double play, the first player ever to accomplish the feat. Ironically, however, in an extra-inning affair against the Reds at Wrigley Field on April 21, Galan did line into a triple play.[7]

The 1935 World Series, however, did not end well for Galan, who hit .160 (4-for-25), or, for that matter, for the Cubs. The Detroit Tigers took the fall classic in six games.

As players gathered for spring training in 1936, one reporter considered what Galan meant to the Cubs. "In addition to his value as a ballplayer, Augie was good medicine for the team's morale with his pleasing personality and his infectious smile," the scribe noted. "He went over big with the fans in every city he visited."[8]

"Augie Galan was always happy," remembered Cavarretta. Billy Herman characterized Galan by saying, "He loved to laugh and fool around, and he had a great imagination for practical jokes. His favorite victim was [Chuck] Klein."[9]

On the heels of his tremendous 1935 season, Galan was named to start the All-Star Game in 1936 at Boston's Braves Field. In the fifth inning, he hit the first All-Star home run ever by a Cub, driving a pitch from Detroit's Schoolboy Rowe off the right-field foul pole. But the 1936 and '37 seasons proved disappointing to Galan, who saw his batting average dip to .264 and .252, respectively, though in 1937 the outfielder did hit 18 home runs and his 23 stolen bases led the league. One game in this period stands out. On June 25, 1937, against the Dodgers, Galan accomplished a feat never before witnessed in the National League, and only once before in baseball. He launched home runs from both sides of the plate in the same game: from the left side against Freddie Fitzsimmons and from the right side off Ralph Birkofer; only Wally Schang of the Philadelphia Athletics had accomplished it previously, in 1916.[10]

Galan bounced back in 1938, lifting his average to .286, and he was once again named an All-Star. After looking up in the standings to see the Giants claim first place in 1936 and 1937, the Cubs again hoisted the National League pennant at Wrigley Field in 1938, only to have the Yankees sweep the World Series in four games. Galan saw limited duty due to a knee injury sustained late in the season and went 0-for-2 as a pinch-hitter in the Series.[11]

Galan remained an everyday outfielder for the Cubs and his batting average improved to .304 in 1939, despite his having to play with an ailing knee at the start of the season. Sportswriter Frank Moran characterized Galan as the National League equivalent of the "Iron Horse," in July 1939, with "two twisted knees" and "performing with his leg in a steel brace and his right elbow swollen nearly twice its original size." However, much like the Dodgers' Pete Reiser, Galan did not know how to play with less than full intensity, and he often paid the price. Perhaps the worst injury came in late July 1940, when Galan broke a knee crashing into the outfield wall at Shibe Park. He saw limited duty from then on with the Cubs and some within the front office felt the outfielder's career was just about through. While rehabbing his ailing knees in 1941, Galan was good-naturedly outfitted by the team's trainer with a jockey's cap and a whip for riding the stationary bike in the clubhouse. Galan was known to be a big fan of horse racing, and often carried a racing form under his arms. But he could not hide his general discontent. The Cubs had recently dealt away two of his best buddies on the ballclub, Billy Herman to the Dodgers and Billy Jurges to the Giants. Couple this with his frustrating injury, and the usually good-natured Galan was not happy.[12]

In August 1941, with Galan hitting just .208 in 65 games, the Cubs elected to sell his contract to the Los Angeles Angels of the PCL. Galan refused to go. Instead the Brooklyn Dodgers picked up his contract in exchange for $2,500 and pitcher Mace Brown. According to Brooklyn pitcher Rex Barney, Billy Herman persuaded Dodgers owner Larry MacPhail to take a chance on the oft-injured Galan. He arrived in Brooklyn at the tail end of August, made a spectacular diving catch in center in his first game as a Dodger, and reinjured his knee in the process. Still, he helped Brooklyn win its first pennant since 1920. He was hitless in two World Series at-bats against the Yankees, but the Dodgers liked what they saw and Galan remained with the team for another five seasons, through 1946.[13]

Slated to become a regular in 1942, Galan was stricken with typhoid fever and saw action in only 69 games. He became an everyday player again with the Dodgers in 1943, and over a four-season span hit between .307 and .318. He was selected to be on the All-Star squad in 1943 and 1944; later in '44, he established a Dodger franchise record, later matched by Roy Campanella and Matt Kemp, by driving in a run in nine consecutive games. Rex Barney recounted in his memoirs, "Galan was as selective a hitter as Ted Williams. He swung only at strikes. Even in batting practice, he made the pitchers throw strikes." In fact, with his discerning eye and great patience, Galan twice led the National League in walks during this period (1943 and 1944).[14]

If Galan had his way, however, he would have put his bat and glove aside and joined many of his colleagues in the military service during World War II. But after a physical following the 1942 season, the Selective Service declared him 4-F, unfit for military service, not only due to his baseball-induced knee injuries, but also because of the arm problem caused by his early boyhood tree mishap. Indeed, he was required to freeze his arm before every game. Galan once explained, "By the sixth or seventh inning, the feeling would come back, and if I had to make a throw it would be like somebody sticking needles in me."[15]

Though he hit a robust .310 with the Dodgers in 1946, Galan was traded to the Cincinnati Reds for pitcher Ed Heusser after the season. *Brooklyn Eagle* sportswriter Tommy Holmes wrote that "the deal … does not meet with the unqualified approval of Brooklyn fans. Galan, a grand fellow and a conscientious, capable ball player, is deservedly popular here." The columnist speculated that it was just another instance of Branch Rickey trading or selling a veteran while he still had market value. As a matter of fact, the Dodgers had a surplus of outfielders heading into the 1947 season, including Dixie Walker, Gene Hermanski, Pete Reiser, Carl Furillo, and a young prospect named Duke Snider.[16]

Showing he could still swing the bat, Galan posted a .314 average with Cincinnati in 124 games in 1947 and led the league with a .449 on-base percentage. But his big-league career was clearly winding down, his many knee injuries taking a toll and limiting his playing time. Galan had but 165 plate appearances in his final two seasons, playing with the Reds, New York Giants, and Philadelphia A's. Over a span of 16 seasons, Galan had played every position in the majors except for pitcher and catcher, and had hit for a .287 average, collecting 1,706 hits and amassing an even 100 home runs. His favorite target for home runs had been Bucky Walters, whom he took deep five times.[17]

Galan returned home to the Bay Area and signed with the Oakland Oaks of the PCL. He played first base, third base, and the outfield in 265 games over the 1950 and 1951 seasons, and was a coach for the team in 1952. He took over as manager in 1953, succeeding Mel Ott; the team played poorly, however, and finished seventh, and Galan was fired after just a year at the helm. At the end of the year, he married Shirley Boyle. He accepted a coaching job with the Philadelphia Athletics in 1954. Player-manager Eddie Joost found

Galan to be "knowledgeable, and a good guy, and helpful."[18]

But coaching for a last-place team some 3,000 miles from his home and his new bride was not appealing, and after one year in Philadelphia, Galan retired from the game for good. He returned to the Bay Area to manage a string of butcher shops, a business he had begun during his playing days. Together Augie and Shirley raised four children. On December 28, 1993, one day after their 40th wedding anniversary, Galan died at the age of 81.[19]

NOTES

1   Doug Feldman, *September Streak: The 1935 Chicago Cubs Chase the Pennant* (Jefferson, North Carolina: McFarland and Co., 2003), 29. While a few sources list Galan's birth date as May 23, most sources, ranging from the Sporting News' *Baseball Register* (1945 edition) to MLB.com and the US Social Security Death Index cite May 25.

2   For most of his playing years, Galan was identified as being a switch-hitter. Bob McConnell wrote "Searching Out the Switch Hitters" in the 1973 edition of SABR's *Baseball Research Journal*, Galan, from the start of his major-league career in 1934 through 1940, batted from both sides of the plate. However, he batted only right-handed in 1941, went back to being a switch-hitter from 1942 through 1944, and then batted only left-handed from 1945 through the end of his career in 1949. McConnell said he sent letters to living ballplayers for his research and Galan wrote back that he was a switch-hitter until 1943, when he began batting exclusively left-handed. Yet, reports in the *Brooklyn Eagle* cite at least a couple of exceptions: "Augie Galan went back to switch-hitting, batting right-handed against southpaw Max Lanier. It was on instructions from manager Leo Durocher" (May 13, 1944). A July 31, 1944, article in the *Eagle* stated that Galan had switched sides of the plate in the same at-bat after failing to get down a sacrifice bunt after two strikes in the previous day's game.

3   Kevin Nelson, *The Golden Game: The Story of California Baseball* (Berkeley, California: Heyday Books, 2004), 177.

4   Pete Cava, *Tales from the Cubs Dugout* (Champaign, Illinois: Sports Publishing, 2000), 94; Spalding, 98. The players he was traded for were pitchers Sam Gibson, Win Ballou, Leroy Hermann, and Walter Mails; catchers Larry Woodall and Hugh McMullen; and infielder Lenny Backer.

5   Rex Barney with Norman L. Macht, *Rex Barney's Thank Youuuu* (Centreville, Maryland: Tidewater Publishers, 1993), 42; References to "Goo-Goo" Galan appear in wire-service stories over the years, including the *Nevada State Journal* (Reno), March 29, 1935; *Charleston* (West Virginia) *Daily Mail*, June 5, 1938; and the *Lowell* (Massachusetts) *Sun*, August 3, 1942, among others. Dolph Camilli originated the Goo-Goo nickname when they were Cubs rookie teammates, according to the *Brooklyn Eagle*, July 12, 1942. Newspaper accounts and sports columns also frequently referred to Galan as

"Little Augie Galan" over the years; though he was of slight frame, Galan was listed as just a half-inch short of 6 feet in height.

6   Peter Golenbock, *Wrigleyville: A Magical History Tour of the Chicago Cubs* (New York: St. Martin's, 1999), 253. Actually, Cavarretta's memory had slightly faded. According to Baseball-Reference.com, Galan played in left field exclusively in 1935, as fellow Californian Frank Demaree patrolled center. Galan did play center field in 1936, but then went back to primarily playing in left.

7   *Hammond* (Indiana) *Times*, October 24, 1935.

8   *Berkeley* (California) *Daily Gazette*, February 20, 1936.

9   Golenbock, 253; Donald Honig, *Baseball When the Grass Was Real* (New York: Coward, McCann and Geoghegan, 1975), 146.

10 John Thorn et al., eds. *Total Baseball* (Kingston, New York: Total Sports, 1999 [Sixth Edition]), 288, 875; BaseballLibrary.com; bleed-cubbiesblue.com.

11 *Hutchinson* (Texas) *News*, September 28, 1938.

12 *Lowell Sun*, July 6, 1939; *Nevada State Journal*, April 11, 1939; Barney, 42; *Saratoga Springs* (New York) *Saratogian*, July 1, 1941; Warren Brown, *The Chicago Cubs* (Carbondale, Illinois: Southern Illinois University, 2001 [originally published 1946]), 199-200; Dick Bartell recalled, "Herman, Jurges, and Galan were sort of a club within the club. They did everything together. Galan and Jurges were jokesters." Dick Bartell with Norman L. Macht, *Rowdy Richard* (Berkeley, California: North Atlantic Books, 1987), 228.

13 *Baseball Register* (St. Louis: The Sporting News, 1943), 141. *Lowell Sun*, August 26, 1941; Barney, 42, *Brooklyn Eagle*, March 3, 1942.

14 *Brooklyn Eagle*, April 21, 1943, and July 3, 1944; Spalding, 99; Barney, 42.

15 *Brooklyn Eagle*, February 9, 1943; Cava, 95.

16 *Brooklyn Eagle*, December 10, 1946. Heusser, in fact, never appeared in a single game for the Dodgers.

17 *Brooklyn Eagle*, June 10, 1947, February 20, 1949; Bob McConnell and David Vincent, *SABR Presents the Home Run Encyclopedia* (New York: Macmillan, 1996), 540.

18 Dennis Snelling, *The Pacific Coast League: A Statistical History, 1903-1957* (Jefferson, North Carolina: McFarland and Co., 1995), 185; *Oakland Tribune*, December 29, 1953; Danny Peary, ed., *We Played the Game: Memories of Baseball's Greatest Era* (New York: Black Dog and Leventhal, 1994), 264.

19 *Big Spring* (Texas) *Daily Herald*, March 27, 1945; Spalding, 99; *New York Times*, December 30, 1993.

Pinky May

By Alan Cohen

THOSE WHO SERVED DURING WORLD
War II were collectively known as the Greatest
Generation. Many young, and not so young, men went
into the service during that time and returned home
to resume their lives. But for those whose lives had
been baseball, they often found that their days of playing
major-league baseball were over.

One such player was Merrill Glend "Pinky" May,
who in the five seasons prior to going into the Navy
after the 1943 season had played in more than 100 games
at third base in each season for the Philadelphia Phillies.
They were to be his only seasons at the major-league level.

May was born on January 18, 1911, in Laconia,
Indiana. He was the fifth of six children born to Perry
and Anna May. By the time the United States entered
World War II, May was over 30 and had completed
his third major-league season with the Phillies.

Perry May was a farmer in Laconia and would scold
Merrill for playing ball on weekends, not realizing that
his son could make a living at the game. Merrill graduated from Laconia High School in 1928, and went on
to play at Indiana University. While at Indiana, he was
scouted by Paul Krichell of the New York Yankees.
After May completed his studies in 1932, Krichell signed
him to a Yankee contract. Years later, Pinky looked back
on the signing of his first contract as his biggest thrill.
"As a young boy, I thought that ballplayers were on a
different plateau than ordinary human beings," he said.
"It, being a professional baseball player, was something
that an ordinary person couldn't reach. But I reached
it and was happy just to think I was going to get paid
just to play baseball. I must have set a record for a
long-distance run, because when I signed that first
contract, I was in college and my coach had called me
on the phone to say that Mr. Krichell was in his office
and wanted to sign me to a Yankee contract. I was two
miles away and ran the whole way."[1]

May came to professional baseball without a nickname, but that was about to change. As he told it, "I
got the nickname Pinky when I first got into professional baseball. When I arrived at my first minor-league

team, sportswriters asked me what my nickname was
and I told them I didn't have one. I did tell them that
when I played at Indiana University, that a couple of
the boys on my team did call me Pinky, but the name
never stuck. That was good enough for them because
after that they always wrote my name up as Pinky, and
it's been Pinky ever since."[2] In those college days, May
was so intense that his cheeks would glow bright red
when his temper was not under control. Thus his teammates took to calling him "Pinky."

May's first stop was at Cumberland (Maryland) in
the Class C Middle Atlantic League. In his first minor-
league season, Pinky was playing in West Virginia and
the hotel accommodations were not that good. There
wasn't even a sink in the room. The players were provided
a water basin and a pitcher. When Pinky was finished,
he saw a policeman down below and, very uncharacteristically, deposited the water atop the cop. He quickly
concluded that his prank was not the smartest of ideas.
May hastily departed the room and raced toward the

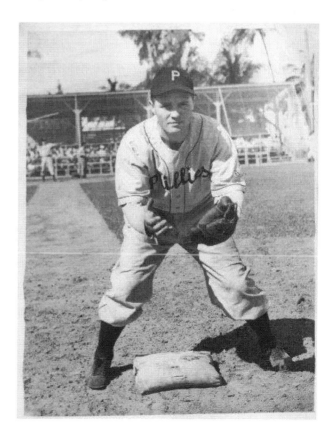

lobby. He mingled with his teammates, waiting for the bus to the ballpark. The enraged patrolman was able to determine that the water came from May's room and went looking for the young player. His fellow players covered for him and off to the ballpark they went.

May batted .264 for Cumberland and was promoted to Durham in the Class B Piedmont League for the 1933 season. Manager Bill Skiff switched him from the outfield to third base.[3] During those early minor-league seasons, May was still under the wing of Paul Krichell, who convinced him that he wouldn't succeed unless he learned to hit to all fields. At Durham, hitting to all fields, he batted .309. However, with the Depression in full swing, times were tough and Pinky and the rest of the team agreed to take a pay cut. "So I ended up playing in 1933 for $150 per month. And, you know, that was enough to get by on."[4]

In 1934 May moved up to Binghamton in the Class A New York-Penn League and batted .301 with 69 RBIs.

His next four years were spent at Double-A which at the time was the highest level of minor-league baseball. Except for most of the 1937 season, which he spent at Oakland (Pacific Coast League), he played with the Newark Bears.[5] At the end of the 1936 season, during which he hit .280 with ten homers and led the league's third basemen in fielding, he was recalled by the Yankees but did not get into any games with New York. At Oakland in 1937, he batted .304 in 120 games.

In 1938, with Newark, May batted.331. He had 53 extra-base hits (including a career-high 12 home runs), and 108 RBIs, but the Yankees, who had just won their third consecutive World Series, were set at third base with Red Rolfe. May had his best game ever on May 1 of that year when, in four trips to the plate, he drove in four runs with two homers, a single, and a double as the Bears defeated Rochester, 12-8.[6]

While May was at Newark in 1935, fellow Laconian Art Funk was playing for Louisville. They got to be friends. On one occasion the two players were driving and Art brought along his 18-year-old niece Veneva Jane Weaver. It was the first meeting for Pinky and Jane. The two were married on February 25, 1939. Pinky and Jane were married for 61 years and had three children (Merrill, Milt, and Mira Jane), five grandchildren,

and 14 great-grandchildren. Pinky would ultimately take over the farm and sold it when his family relocated to St. Petersburg, Florida in 1960.

May was frustrated at being trapped in the Yankee farm system for so long. In those days, only one ballplayer could be drafted off any one minor-league club. The Yankees had Double-A clubs in Newark and Kansas City and a working arrangement with Oakland in the Pacific Coast League. "They put their best players on the Newark roster so when one was drafted, the others were protected," May told a sportwriter.[7]

After the 1938 season, May was drafted by the last-place Philadelphia Phillies, and he finally made it to the majors with Philadelphia in 1939 at the not-so-tender age of 28. "I was fortunate that I got drafted at the end of that 1938 season," he said. "That gave me a chance to play in the major leagues. It didn't bother me that the Phillies were a last-place team. It was still major-league baseball, and I was going to get my chance."[8]

In 1939 May had a good spring with the Phillies, but it briefly appeared that he would be sidelined, as he twisted his spinal column chasing a foul pop on March 30 in an exhibition game. He was hospitalized briefly, but whipped himself back into shape and missed only the season opener.

May's first major-league hit came in a 5-4 12-inning win over Brooklyn on April 23, 1939. His sixth-inning single off Brooklyn's Whitlow Wyatt drove on two runs and gave the Phillies a 3-0 lead. The Dodgers tied the game and the contest went into extra innings. In the decisive 12th inning, May walked and scored the tying run after the Dodgers had taken a 4-3 lead in the top of the inning.

In the very early going, it appeared that the Phillies might escape their doormat status. They won four games in a row from April 22 through April 25 and had a 4-2 record through six games. In the April 25 game, an 8-1 win over the Giants, May went 2-for-4 with an RBI and a stolen base. By May 6 he had six multiple-hit games to his credit, and his batting average stood at .422.

May's first career four-hit game came on June 5, 1939, when he went 4-for-4 with two RBIs in an 8-7 win over the Cubs. His batting average stood at .333.

The following day, with Philadelphia down 8-6 going into the bottom of the ninth, May's hit was the second of five consecutive Phillies singles that allowed them to rally for a 9-8 win.

May was definitely not a home-run threat and his only two round-trippers of 1939 came in back-to-back games on August 12 and 13 against the Giants at the Polo Grounds.

The Phillies, despite May's efforts, slipped into the cellar on May 18 and remained there for the balance of the season. There were few bright spots, as the team went 45-106 for the season, 18 games behind the seventh-place Braves and 50½ games behind the pennant-winning Reds. During each of May's first four seasons with the Phillies, they lost at least 100 games.

For his rookie season, he batted .287 with 67 RBIs. His 41 walks gave him an on-base percentage of .346. He tied for the league lead with 25 sacrifice hits, and posted the best fielding percentage among the National League's third basemen. In his five seasons with the Phillies, he led the league's third basemen in fielding three times. The other two seasons, he finished second.

May was named to the All-Star team in 1940, in his second major-league season. He was part of a Phillies infield (Art Mahan, 1B; Herman Schulte, 2B; Bobby Bragan, SS; and May) that was described as the "Pepper Pots" by sportswriters for their sure-handed fielding.[9] In two plate appearances in the All-Star Game, he flied out and was hit by a pitch, as the National League won 4-0.

The third baseman batted .293 with a career high 147 hits in 1940. Both figures were the best on the Phillies that season and he tied for the team lead in doubles with 24. During the course of the season, he had 11 three-hit games. From August 14 through August 26, May put together a career-best 14-game hitting streak, and his batting average was .300 as late as September 19. A late-season slump sent him below .300. The Phillies finished at 50-103, completing their third consecutive year in the basement.

In 1941 May got off to a terrible start, batting .134 (13-for-97) in his first 26 games. But he turned things around and batted .300 for the balance of the season to wind up with a .267 average (but with no home runs and only 21 extra-base hits). His fielding numbers were the best of his career. He led the National League with career highs in fielding percentage (.972), putouts (194), assists (324), and double plays (31). But the Phillies once again were in the cellar, this time with a 43-111 record, their lowest winning percentage during May's time in the City of Brotherly Love. Teammate Danny Litwhiler remembered, "We all pretty much stuck together. It was a good group of guys. No one got angry with anyone else. We didn't blame each other for what happened. We got on pretty well, considering."[10]

During the 1942 season, May roomed with Ernie Koy, another player whose career was interrupted by the war. Koy, like May, had originally signed with the Yankees, and the two were teammates for four seasons in the Yankee farm system. Koy entered the Navy in 1943. Koy's assessment was that "Pinky May was a great third baseman, but he couldn't run. We would take Pinky down the right-field line before a game and try to teach Pinky to run faster, but he just couldn't. Pinky should have made the majors long before he did."[11]

May had an off-year in 1942, playing in only 115 games and batting .238. The team sank to a new low, winning only 42 games, the least of any Phillies team in the 20th century. Mercifully, three games were postponed and not made up. The manager that year was Hans Lobert, and he was so concerned about the opposition stealing signs that he used a different set of signs for each player on the team. He used word signals, and the bunt sign for May was "Chatfield."[12] If anyone was confused by this, it was most definitely not the opposition.

In 1943 May returned to form, batting .282 in 137 games. The game against the Pirates on October 3 was his last in the majors. His batting average was the second best on the team, and his on-base percentage of .369 led the Phillies. The team improved, too, winning 64 games and climbing out of the cellar after five consecutive eighth-place finishes. Even the players' wives were part of the team's success. Pinky's wife, Jane, along with the wives of Danny Litwhiler, Ron Northey, and Si Johnson, gave up eating steaks, handing over their war ration points to their husbands, so as to make them stronger.[13] Pinky's RBI count increased from 18 to 48, and the team's home run production, with Northey leading the way with 16, jumped from 44 (worst in the league) to 66 (third).

As late as June 30 the Phillies were in fourth place, and within a game of .500. Could this continue? On July 8, the second game of a doubleheader against Cincinnati was a scoreless tie in the bottom of the 14th inning. Dick Barrett, who had not won a game all season, had pitched 14 shutout innings for Philadelphia. With the winning run at third base and two out, manager Bucky Harris summoned May to pinch-hit for his pitcher. May's single scored Coaker Triplett with the winning run. By that point, the Phillies had slipped to fifth place, but were still within 11 games of the league lead. They would not get any closer, although they put together a seven-game winning streak in August. They eventually sank to seventh place, 41 games behind the pennant-winning St. Louis Cardinals.

Bucky Harris had become the Phillies manager at the start of the season. On July 28 he was abruptly fired by team owner William D. Cox. Freddie Fitzsimmons managed the team for the balance of the season. Harris had an impact not only on May the player, but also on May the man. May said Harris had the happy faculty of making the players believe they could win a game that appeared to be hopelessly lost.[14] Harris's record with the Phillies was 39-53.

In that October 3 game, May had four hits as the Phillies swept a twin bill from the Pirates to finish at 64-90. His 4-for-10 day brought his batting average to .282. May, who once again led the league's third basemen in fielding percentage, would never again play an inning of major-league baseball. He enlisted in the Navy after the season, and played for Lieutenant Mickey Cochrane's Great Lakes Naval Station team in 1944, then was sent to Hawaii at the beginning of 1945 as part of the Western Pacific Tour squad that played before fighting troops on Pacific Islands. He was then assigned to the island of Tinian, where the Quonset hut he lived in was less than 100 yards from an airstrip. He spent many evenings watching B-29s take off to bomb Japan.[15] On August 6, 1945, he was watching as the *Enola Gay* took off at 2:45 A.M. and headed toward Hiroshima.

May returned to the Phillies after the war, only to be released on May 7, 1946. He had an opportunity to resume his playing career with the Pirates in 1947; in need of third-base help, they offered him a job. But Pinky elected to forgo playing in the majors, and embarked on a managerial career. In 1947 he joined the Albany Senators, the Pirates' affiliate in the Eastern League, as a player-manager. In his first season, he batted .322 as the team finished in second place with an 80-58 record. In the playoffs the Senators defeated Scranton in seven games before losing to Utica in the final series.

Charles Young, in Albany's *Knickerbocker News*, summed up May's qualities, both as a man and as a manager: "May is serious virtually all the time. No man has more of the will to win spirit in baseball. He talks, eats, and sleeps baseball. Playing for May is a breeze if the players cooperate with him." May didn't expect the player to "do the impossible." On the other hand, he did not have "any use for a player who does not give 100 per cent effort at all times."[16]

May eased himself out of the lineup over the following two seasons (1948-49), playing his final minor-league game (with the exception of a lone pinch-hitting appearance later in his career) in 1949. In 1949 his Albany Senators, led by pitcher Orie "Old Folks" Arntzen's 25-2 record, won the pennant,[17] but lost in the playoffs. In 1950 they slipped to fourth place. Pittsburgh severed its working arrangement with Albany before the 1951 season and May's team finished in eighth place.

May left Albany and moved on to the Cleveland Indians' organization in 1952. His first stop was Spartanburg, South Carolina, in the Class B Tri-State League. He managed the team, which included a young Rocky Colavito, to third place. The following season, May led the Sherbrooke Indians, who finished first in the Provincial League with an 84-41 record but lost in the first round of the playoffs.

After spending 1954 managing Reading in the Eastern League, May moved on to Keokuk, Iowa, where his 1955 team, the Kernels, finished first with a 92-34 record in the Illinois-Indiana-Iowa League, the best winning percentage of May's managerial career, and won the league playoffs. The fans were so elated that they presented him with a thoroughbred heifer for his farm in Indiana.[18] When baseball historians Bill Weiss and Marshall Wright compiled their list of the best 100 teams in minor-league history, the 1955 Kernels ranked 30th.[19] May's star player was 19-year-old Jim "Mudcat" Grant, who posted a 19-3 record in his second professional season.

In 1958 May's Class B Alamance (Burlington, North Carolina) team qualified for the Carolina League playoffs, after being in the cellar on July 8 and in seventh place, just two games ahead of the last-place team at the end of July. The common refrain was "all the way with Pinky May."[20] The team finished fourth with a 70-67 record and won the league championship by defeating Danville and Greensboro in the playoffs. May's top players were pitcher Steve Hamilton and outfielder Walt Bond.[21] At one point during the season, May grabbed his bat for a pinch-hitting appearance, but failed to reach base safely.

May continued to manage in the Indians' organization through 1962. In his third season at Burlington in 1960, he was chosen the Carolina League's Manager of the Year as he brought his team from far behind to win second-half honors with a 41-29 record, and a place in the playoffs against first-half winner Greensboro. Burlington had gone 26-44 to finish dead last during the first half, and were 2-8 after ten games in the second half before storming back to win 39 of their last 60 games. But May's Burlington squad lost the best-of-seven playoff final in five games.

May spent 1961 season with Dubuque in the Class D Midwest League, where his son Milt was the team's batboy. Pinky moved on to the Selma Cloverleafs in the Class D Alabama-Florida League in 1962. His star player, as the team swept through the playoffs to the league championship, was 18-year-old Lou Piniella, who was in his first year of professional ball. Piniella remembered May taking him under his wing when he reported to Selma and got off to a bad start. May's advice to Piniella was, "You have to prove you can hit the fastball. Nobody plays in the big leagues without being able to hit the fastball first. Show us you have power and strength. We'll teach you how to hit a curve ball. I guarantee it. First I want you to hit the fastball, regain your confidence, and get comfortable with your

swing." Piniella was on his way, and in 1969, he was American League's Rookie of the Year. The 1962 season was the last for Selma and for the Alabama-Florida League, as Alabama Governor George Wallace stood in the way of integration when every other league in Organized Baseball accepted black players.[22]

May left the Indians organization and spent the early part of the 1963 season with the Fort Lauderdale Yankees, before being fired on June 26. He was with the Reds organization from 1964 through 1966. His 1965 Tampa and 1966 Peninsula clubs included future stars Bernie Carbo, Johnny Bench, and Hal McRae. In June 1965 he and Jack Cassini switched teams, with May heading from the Tampa Tarpons in the Florida State League to the Peninsula Grays (Hampton, Virginia) in the Carolina League. May took over a team with a 23-31 record. Peninsula went 63-27 the rest of the way to win its division by ten games.

On June 21, 1966, May became the last man to manage Satchel Paige. The Grays brought in Paige as a publicity stunt and the ancient one, then age 59, pitched his last two professional innings.[23]

May returned to the Indians in 1967 and managed at the Class A and Rookie levels through 1972. In 1969, when he managed the Statesville-Monroe team in the Western Carolinas League, the lineup of the opposing Gastonia team featured an 18-year-old catcher in his second year in the minors. The kid got into 86 games and slugged 11 homers, including ten against May's team. The kid happened to be Pinky's son Milt. In a game on June 11, Pinky was ejected from the game for protesting that Milt's inside-the-park homer should have been ruled a ground-rule double as his line drive had become lodged in the batting cage that was being stored down the left-field line. Milt also gunned down three of Pinky's runners who were trying to steal third base.[24]

On July 9 at Gastonia, Milt hit two homers. The next night Milt hit another pair of four-baggers, this time in successive at-bats,[25] and the next time up, Pinky ordered his pitcher to throw at Milt.[26] During the at-bat in the seventh inning, three pitches came at Milt before he was walked. On ball four, he was sprawled in the dirt and looked toward the opposition dugout where his father was smiling. Pinky's wife, Jane, bawled him out for having his pitcher throw at Milt. Unfazed, Milt slammed another pair of homers against Pinky's team on July 25.[27]

In 1970 Pinky managed Reno to a second-place finish in the Class A California League with a 79-61 record. He remained with Reno through 1971 and was with the Indians affiliate in the Gulf Coast League in 1972. He was slated to return that position in 1973, but resigned on February 15.

In his 26-year managerial career, May put together a record of 1698-1580. After retiring from managing, he worked in a chain of liquor stores in the St. Petersburg, Florida, area for about ten years.

In 1986, Pinky and Jane moved to San Antonio, Texas, to be closer to their older children, Merrill and Mira.

The May family was on the verge of having three generations succeed in professional baseball when fate intervened in 1990. Milt's son Scott, a student at Manatee (Florida) High School, was involved in an automobile accident on December 24, 1990, suffering life-threatening head injuries. He recovered and resumed his baseball efforts at Manatee Community College and Carson-Newman (Tennessee) College. In 1996 he was drafted by the Pirates in the 41st round.[28] He batted .250 in 44 games during 1996 and 1997 at Erie in the New York Penn League and Augusta in the Sally League, after which he left baseball and became involved in the family's orange groves in the Bradenton area, as well as coaching high-school and Little League ball.

In his later years, Pinky May returned to Indiana, where he died on September 4, 2000. He was survived by his wife, Jane, and their three children, Merrill, Milt, and Mira Jane. Jane, who spent her last years living with her daughter in San Angelo, Texas, died on September 30, 2010, at the age of 92.

May was inducted into the Indiana Baseball Hall of Fame in 2003. In 2009 his hometown of Laconia, Indiana, honored him, and his son Milt by naming the town's baseball complex in their honor. The renamed May Fields opened on July 4, 2009.

Piniella, Lou, and Maury Allen, *Sweet Lou* (New York: G.P. Putnam's Sons, 1986).

Roberts, Robin, and C. Paul Rogers, III, *The Whiz Kids and the 1950 Pennant* (Philadelphia: Temple University Press, 1996).

Van Blair, Rick, *Dugout to Foxhole: Interviews with Baseball Players Whose Careers were Affected by World War II* (Jefferson, North Carolina: McFarland and Co., 1994).

Cameron, Brad, "Bees Commemorating '55 Keokuk Kernels with Special Jerseys for Tonight's Game, *Daily Gate City* (Keokuk, Iowa), June 21, 2002.

Gaven, Michael F., "Minors Worth Watching," *Newark* (New Jersey) *Star Eagle*, July 7, 1938.

Hunter, Bill, "Pinky Recalls Hamilton, Bond and Playoff Champs of 1958," *Burlington* (North Carolina) *Daily Times-News*, June 10, 1965, 2B.

Young, Charles, "Sports Stadium: Rip Collins and Pinky May Are Compared; Both Managers are Easy on Their Players; Present Albany Boss More Serious Than Jimmy," *Knickerbocker News* (Albany, New York), April 3, 1948, 10-B.

Albany Times-Union

Burlington (North Carolina) *Daily Times-News*

Gastonia (North Carolina) *Gazette*

Hartford Courant

New York Times

The Sporting News

Ancestry.com

FultonHistory.com

GenealogyBank.com

NewspaperArchive.com

Newspapers.com

Baseball-Reference.com

Pinky May file at the Baseball Hall of Fame Library

Interviews with Milt May, February 11 and March 4, 2014.

Interview with Merrill May, March 14, 2014.

NOTES

1   Van Blair, 131, 137.

2   Van Blair, 128.

3   Gaven, July 7, 1938

4   Van Blair, 129

5   At the time, Double B was the highest level of minor-league ball, equivalent to today's Triple A.

6   *New York Times*, May 2, 1938, 21.

7   Van Blair, 129

8   Van Blair, 129

9   Tom Mahon. *Philadelphia Daily News*, July 1, 1993.

10 Ed Hilt, *The Press* (Atlantic City, New Jersey), July 10, 1997.

11 Van Blair, 85

12 Robin Roberts and C. Paul Rogers, III, 23.

13 *Racine* (Wisconsin) *Journal Times*, April 30, 1943, 16

14 Young, April 3, 1948

15 Gary Bedingfield, "Baseball in Wartime," 2008

16 Young, April 3, 1948.

17 *Hartford Courant*, August 28, 1949, 10.

18 Ronald Melcher, "Grist from the Sports Mill," *Hartford Courant*, September 10, 1955, 13.

19 Brad Cameron, June 21, 2002.

20 *Burlington* (North Carolina) *Daily Times-News*, June 8, 1965, 2B

21 Bill Hunter, "Pinky Recalls Hamilton, Bond and Playoff Champs of 1958," *Burlington* (North Carolina) *Daily Times-News*, June 10, 1965, 2B.

22 Lou Pinella and Maury Allen, 33-34.

23 Mike Holtzclaw, *Daily Press* (Newport News, Virginia), August 21, 1994.

24 Dwight Frady, "G-Pirates Roll, 14-1: Bucs Win, So do (Greenwood) Braves," *Gastonia* (North Carolina) *Gazette*, June 12, 1969, 2-B.

25 Neal Patrick, "Milt Hits Two More Homers Against Pop Pinky's Team," *Gastonia* (North Carolina) *Gazette*, July 11, 1969, 2-B.

26 Larry Hug, *Evening Independent* (St. Petersburg, Florida), August 23, 1969, C1.

27 *Gastonia* (North Carolina) *Gazette*, July 26, 1969, 2-B

28 *Bradenton Herald*, June 9, 1996.

Stan Hack

By Eric Hanauer

THERE ARE FEWER THIRD BASEMEN IN the Hall of Fame than players from any other position. One who hasn't made it is Stan Hack, who held down the post for 16 years with the Chicago Cubs, from 1932 through 1947. Yet Bill James ranks him the ninth best all time at the position, well ahead of Pie Traynor, Jimmy Collins, and George Kell, who are enshrined in Cooperstown. Hack retired with a lifetime batting average of .301 and an on-base percentage of .394, drawing 1,092 walks against 466 strikeouts. He was a five-time All-Star and twice finished in the top ten in MVP voting. He played in four World Series with the Cubs, hitting .348 with a .408 on-base percentage.

So why is Stan Hack virtually forgotten today? There are several reasons. He wasn't the archetypical slugging third baseman, essentially a singles hitter who never hit more than eight home runs in a season. He was overshadowed on some strong Cubs teams by the likes of Gabby Hartnett, Kiki Cuyler, Phil Cavarretta, and Bill Nicholson. He was even overshadowed by the shortstop on the other side of town, Luke Appling, a similar player who won a pair of batting championships.

As a leadoff man for most of his career, Hack's job was getting on base and scoring runs. And he did that admirably. For six straight years he scored over 100 runs, tying a National league record. He led the league in hits twice, and in stolen bases twice. (Of course, players didn't run much in the late 1930s. His leading numbers were 16 in 1938 and 17 in 1939.) Defensively, Hack ranked among the best third basemen of his time. At one point he held the record for most consecutive games without an error at third. James retroactively awarded him three Gold Gloves. (The award wasn't introduced until ten years after Hack retired.)

Because of his consistency and good nature, Stan was one of the most popular players on the Cubs. An opposing player once said that Hack "has more friends than Leo Durocher has enemies."[1] From rookie to elder statesman, with good teams and bad ones, Smiling Stan was the same man.

Stanley Camfield Hack was born in Sacramento, California, on December 6, 1909. His father, Charles Hack, worked as department manager in a bank at the time of the 1910 census, but ten years later had taken up farming. His mother, Pearl Hack, also gave birth to Stan's younger brother, Delwyn. At Sacramento High School Stan was the starting third baseman, alongside outfielder Myril Hoag, whose Yankees would sweep Hack's Cubs in the 1932 and 1938 World Series. A left-handed contact hitter at 6 feet and 170 pounds, Stan was a throwback to the third basemen of the Deadball Era. His job was setting the table for the big boppers, getting on base and into position to score. It was a skill set he carried into the major leagues.

After graduation Hack worked as a bookkeeper in a Sacramento bank and played weekends on a semipro team. He attracted the attention of the local Pacific Coast League team, the Sacramento Senators, and in 1931 was signed to a contract. Hack was a star among stars on the Senators, whose roster included future major leaguers Dolph Camilli, Frank Demaree, and Frenchy Bordagaray. At 21, Hack hit .352, with 232 hits in 164 games.

During those Depression years, PCL teams survived by developing players and selling them to the major leagues. Cubs president Bill Veeck, Sr. paid $40,000 for Hack's contract at the end of the season. He also bought Demaree, who became a mainstay later in the decade. Although the Cubs had won the pennant in 1929, the core of that team was on the shady side of 30. Hack Wilson, Rogers Hornsby, Charlie Grimm, Riggs Stephenson, and Kiki Cuyler soon would need to be replaced. So Veeck brought in Hack and Demaree along with Billy Jurges, Billy Herman, and Lon Warneke to fortify the team through the coming decade.

Hack didn't set the National League on fire in his rookie year, 1932. He hit only .236 in 72 games, and his only World Series action was as a pinch-runner. Perhaps one reason was that he replaced Hack Wilson as pitcher Pat Malone's drinking buddy. As he matured, Hack gave up partying and his career flourished. He was the Opening Day third baseman, and for most of the year shared the position with Woody English. He struggled at the plate, but when shortstop Billy Jurges was shot by a spurned girlfriend, English moved to short and Hack got more playing time. Veeck also brought in former Yankees shortstop Mark Koenig, who sparked the Cubs in the dog days of late summer by hitting .353. Manager Rogers Hornsby was fired in August, replaced by Charlie Grimm. The Cubs came from behind to win the pennant, but were swept by the Yankees in the World Series.

Hack topped off that turbulent year on a high note, marrying his teenage sweetheart, Dorothy Weisel. She was a top-ranked tennis player, twice reaching the quarterfinals at the US Nationals and ranking as high as third nationally. At that point, she was a more famous athlete than her husband. They had one child, Stanley Jr., born in 1934.

English was the Cubs' starting third baseman the following year, so Hack was sent off to Albany, where he hit .299. Recalled to Chicago late in the season, he hit .350 in 20 games. Except for his final year at age 37, Hack never hit less than .280 again.

In 1934 Hack established himself as the Cubs' starting third baseman. Three-fourths of the infield of Grimm, Hack, Jurges, and Herman remained intact for the rest of the decade. Only first base changed hands, from Grimm to Cavarretta to Ripper Collins and then to Rip Russell. Behind the scenes, Bill Wrigley and Bill Veeck had died, and the Cubs were inherited by Wrigley's son, Phil. Phil Wrigley had little interest in baseball and kept the Cubs only because they had meant so much to his father. The people he put in charge lacked the elder Wrigley's dedication and Veeck's baseball sense, so the talent flow that made the Cubs contenders during the 1930s began to slow down. In 1935 they had first crack at a San Francisco Seals outfielder but turned him down because of a questionable knee, so Joe DiMaggio was sold to the Yankees. Five years later the Cubs turned down his brother Dom because he was too small and wore glasses.

But the Cubs of the 1930s still managed two more pennants. In September 1935 they won 21 games in a row to overtake the Cardinals and Giants. Hack hit seventh most of the season, batting .311 with 65 walks and only 17 strikeouts. Gabby Hartnett hit .344 and won the MVP award, Billy Herman led the league with 227 hits and 57 doubles.

By this time, Hack had acquired the nickname Smiling Stan because of his good nature and handsome looks. In one of the few promotions of the day, the Cubs handed out mirrors to the fans with his picture on the back. The promotion backfired when fans tried to shine them in the faces of opposing players, and umpires threatened to forfeit the game. That giveaway was the idea of Bill Veeck, Jr., then 21 years old and recently hired into the Cubs' front office. Two years later, a better idea of his took root when he planted ivy on the outfield walls.

The Cubs faced the Tigers in the 1935 World Series. Hack had only five hits in the six games, hitting .227. In Game Six, with the scored tied 3-3, and the Cubs trailing 3 games to 2, Hack led off the ninth inning with a triple. Jurges then struck out on three pitches. Grimm's pitching staff was thin, so he had to let pitcher Larry French bat. French grounded out to the pitcher. Galan ended the frustrating inning by flying out to left field, leaving Hack stranded. In the bottom of the ninth, the Tigers scored on Goose Goslin's single to end the series.

A few years later Hack returned to Briggs Stadium for the All-Star Game. When he arrived, he took a quick look at third base before entering the clubhouse. He explained later, "I just wanted to see if I was still standing out there waiting for somebody to drive me home."[2]

From 1929 through 1938, the Cubs won a pennant every three years. During the seasons of 1936 and 1937, Hack hit .297 and .298, alternating mostly between leadoff and fifth in the batting order. By this time he was considered one of the top third basemen in the National League, but his best years were ahead.

In the pennant-winning year of 1938, Stan was 28 years old, made his first All-Star team, and finished seventh in the MVP voting. He led off for the Cubs most of the season, hit .320 with a .411 OBP and led the league in steals. The Cubs were struggling in July, when Grimm resigned as manager and was replaced by Gabby Hartnett. That set a spark, and slowly they crept up on the league-leading Pirates. Going into a late-September series at Wrigley Field, the Cubs trailed Pittsburgh by 1½ games. Dizzy Dean, pitching on guts and a lame arm, won the first game, 2-1. The second game is legendary in Cubs lore. It was tied 5-5 going into the last of the ninth with darkness descending on the ballpark. That was when Hartnett hit his "Homer in the Gloamin'" to vault the Cubs into first place. As Gabby joked later, his mother could have pitched the next game because the Pirates were done. The Cubs won the final game of the series, 10-1, to all but lock up the pennant.

That won them the chance to become sacrificial lambs to another loaded Yankee team, which swept the

Series in four games. The highlight for the Cubs was Stan Hack, who hit .471. It was the end of the good times for Cubs fans, as the team began a long slide into mediocrity. They dropped to fourth place in 1939, their last winning season until the wartime pennant of 1945. Hack hit .298 in '39, led the league in stolen bases again, and started his second All-Star Game.

Hack was even better in 1940, leading the league in hits and batting .317, along with 21 stolen bases. But the Cubs dropped to fifth place, losing four more games than they won.

Hartnett was fired and Jimmie Wilson hired as the Cubs manager for 1941. It was a great year for baseball, featuring tight pennant races, DiMaggio's 56-game streak, and Ted Williams's .406 average. But it was dreary for the Cubs, as they limped home in sixth place with five fewer wins than the year before. Hack was consistent, though, hitting .317 again, leading the league with 186 hits, and playing in his third All-Star Game.

The 1942 season was the first of the war years. At 32, Hack was too old to be drafted, so he remained in a Cubs uniform. By now his best years were behind him, as his batting averages dropped to .300 and .289. Although Stan kept smiling, the losing was getting to him. At the end of 1943 he'd had enough. He didn't get along with Wilson, and retired at the age of 33. Wilson's Cubs won their opener without Hack at third, but then lost 13 in a row. General manager Jim Gallagher fired Wilson, replacing him with Mr. Cub of that time, Charlie Grimm. One of the first things Grimm did was to call his old infield buddy and talk him out of retirement. Hack debuted on June 18. He was a bit rusty, played in only 98 games, and hit .282.

In 1945 it all came together for the Cubs. They improved from 75 to 98 wins, and won the National League pennant. Travel restrictions resulted in lots of doubleheaders that year, and the Cubs won both ends of 20 of them, as of 2014 still a major-league record. They also beat up on the Cincinnati Reds, winning 21 out of 22 games. Although detractors called their pennant a wartime fluke, the Cubs were a solid ballclub that led the league in team batting average and team ERA. Hack contributed big-time, hitting a career-high .323, with a .420 OBP, and scoring 110 runs. He was selected for his fifth All-Star Game, although the game wasn't played due to wartime travel restrictions. He finished 11th in MVP voting; teammate Phil Cavarretta won the award.

In the World Series the Cubs again faced the Tigers. Chicago sportswriter Warren Brown called it the World's Worst Series, referring to sloppy play from many who wouldn't have been in a big-league uniform if the real players weren't in the military. The Cubs took two of the first three games in Detroit on shutouts by Hank Borowy and Claude Passeau. Passeau's victory was a one-hitter, equaling the Cubs' Ed Reulbach as the best-pitched game in Series history. (This was 11 years before Don Larsen's perfect game.) But the Tigers came back to win the next two games at Wrigley Field. With the Cubs facing elimination in Game Six, Hack hit a 12th-inning line drive that skipped past left fielder Hank Greenberg for a game-winning double.

It was the biggest hit of Hack's career. (He had another great Series, hitting .367 with a .441 OBP.) Grimm started his weary ace, Borowy, in Game Seven. Hank had pitched four scoreless relief innings in Game Six, but with one day's rest had nothing left. When the first three batters got hits, Grimm got the message and pulled him. Before the inning was over, the Tigers had scored five runs and cruised to a 9-3 win.

While other teams got stronger with returning war veterans, the Cubs stood pat and paid the price. Their 82 wins in 1946 were good for third place. It would be their last winning season for 17 years. At the age of 36, Hack hit .285, and 83 walks in 92 games raised his OBP to .431, a career high for a full season. He broke a finger in August, which kept him out of the lineup for a month.

The 1947 season was Hack's last as a player. The Cubs tried several others at third base, limiting him to 76 games. He hit .271 with a .377 OBP. In September the Cubs gave him a car on Stan Hack Day in front of a capacity crowd.

Hack was such a favorite in Chicago that the Cubs offered him a managerial job in their minor-league system. Over the next six years he worked his way up the ladder, from Des Moines to Springfield, and in 1951 to Los Angeles. There he managed the system's first African American player, shortstop Gene Baker. Baker spent four years in Triple-A before being called up, as the Cubs were one of the last teams to integrate.

Phil Cavarretta was managing the major-league team in 1954. During spring training Phil Wrigley asked him how the team was looking. The blunt Cavarretta told him the truth: With the players they had, they were a second-division ballclub. Wrigley fired him for a defeatist attitude. It was the first time a manager had ever been fired in spring training. The only way to defuse a media firestorm was to replace one Cubs icon with another. That was how Stan Hack became manager of the Cubs.

The Cubs had bought Ernie Banks from the Kansas City Monarchs and played him in ten games at the end of the previous year. Hack installed him as the starting shortstop, while Baker moved to second base, and both had strong rookie years. Hank Sauer and Ralph Kiner supplied punch in the outfield, but Cavarretta was right. They lost 90 games and finished in seventh place.

The 1955 Cubs started out strong. Banks became a star, with 44 homers and 117 RBIs. Rookie Bob Speake had a great streak until pitchers caught up with him. Veterans Randy Jackson and Frankie Baumholtz still had something in the tank. The Cubs were 45-38 in early July, but a couple of long losing streaks doomed the season. They finished in sixth place, nine games under .500. The following year Banks played hurt, his production dropped off, and the team finished in the cellar. Hack was fired.

Hack didn't stay unemployed long. Fred Hutchinson hired him as a coach with the Cardinals. Having been a Cubs employee for 24 years, it must have been strange for Stan to don a Redbirds uniform. The Cardinals weren't much better than the Cubs, and Hutchinson was fired with ten games left in the 1958 season. Hack was tabbed to replace him, but won only three of those games.

From that point, Hack bounced around the minor leagues as a manager and coach, finally retiring from baseball in 1966. By this time he and Dorothy had divorced. Stan and his second wife, Glennyce, bought the Landmark Restaurant in Grand Detour, Illinois, about 100 miles west of Chicago. One patron wrote, "In the entrance to the Landmark was the largest collection of Chicago Cub memorabilia I had ever seen: uniforms, photos of players, coaches, radio announcers and executives, scorecards and equipment. Everything there was to collect was there."[3] Hack enjoyed his other passions, golf, fishing, and hunting. In an interview with Chicago sportswriter Jim Enright, he said he had only two wishes. He wished Cubs pitchers had dusted Giants hurler Monty Kennedy, who "used to hit me like I was a dart board." The other was one more victory, because he had 199 as a major-league manager. "On second thought," he said, "I wouldn't want to see Monte or anybody else hurt, and it's too late now to worry about 200 victories."[4]

Stan Hack died in 1979, at 70. In 1996 Lennie Merullo, the last living Cub who played for them in the World Series, described him this way: "Everybody loved Stan Hack. … He hit from foul line to foul line, a line-drive hitter … like Wade Boggs. He didn't have a great arm, but had such a nice, soft throw. It was never off the mark, and he'd always come up with the ball."[5]

Phil Cavarretta added, "Stan never got the credit he deserved. … To me, with his stats and knowing Stan Hack, I can't understand why he isn't in the Hall of Fame."[6]

Hack never had much support for the Hall of Fame, falling off the ballot after about five years. Bill James disagrees with the voters, comparing Hack with Pie Traynor, who was considered the best third baseman of all time before the likes of Eddie Mathews, Ron Santo, and Mike Schmidt came along. Traynor hit .320 against Hack's .301, but Traynor played most of his career in the 1920s, when averages were significantly higher. Traynor drove in more runs, but Hack scored more, seldom hitting from an RBI position in the lineup. James argues that Hack was actually a better hitter on the basis of runs created. Somewhere in that ivy-covered ballpark in the sky, Stan Hack must be smiling over the comparison.

SOURCES:

baseball-reference.com/players/h/hacksto1.shtml Accessed December 5, 2013.

jockbio.com/Classic/S_Hack/S_Hack_bio.html Accessed December 4, 2013.

baseballlibrary.com/ballplayers/player.php?name=Stan_Hack_1909 Accessed December 4, 2013.

Brown, Warren, *The Chicago Cubs* (New York: Putnam, 1946).

Enright, Jim, *Chicago Cubs* (New York: Collier Books, 1975).

Gold, Eddie, and Art Ahrens, *The New Era Cubs* (Chicago: Bonus Books, 1985).

Golenbock, Peter, *Wrigleyville* (New York: St. Martin's Press, 1996).

James, Bill, *The New Bill James Historical Baseball Abstract* (New York: Free Press, 2003).

NOTES

1   *Baseballlibrary.com/ballplayers/player.php?name=Stan_Hack.*

2   Warren Brown, *The Chicago Cubs* (New York: Putnam, 1946), 150.

3   Sandy Goldman, "We're Still Waiting! … the 1945 World Series, *andthatsmyopinion.com.*

4   Jim Enright, *Chicago Cubs* (New York: Collier Books, 1975), 148.

5   Peter Golenbock, *Wrigleyville.* (New York: St. Martin's Press, 1996), 297.

6   Ibid., 251.

Frenchy Bordagaray

By Norm King

"HE'S EITHER THE POOREST GREAT third baseman or the greatest poor third baseman."[1]

In perhaps one of the best non-Yogi-Berra quotes in baseball history, this was Branch Rickey's assessment of Frenchy Bordagaray, a colorful outfielder/third baseman who played for several teams in the 1930s and 1940s. He was free-spirited enough to fit in with both the Gas House Gang St. Louis Cardinals and the daffy Brooklyn Dodgers, and some of his shenanigans, especially those with Brooklyn manager Casey Stengel, are legendary. Some are even true.

Stanley George Bordagaray was born on January 3, 1910, in Coalinga, California, one of seven children born to Dominique and Louise Bordagaray, who were among the original settlers of the San Joaquin Valley. Dominique was a hotel owner and sheep rancher. Bordagaray's family was of Basque descent. (In Europe the Basques inhabit an area of southern France and northern Spain.) Stanley and his six brothers were all nicknamed Frenchy.

Bordagaray played baseball and football and ran track at Coalinga High School. After high school he entered Fresno State College, where he continued playing baseball and football. He also played semipro ball while in school, and it was a semipro connection that led him to entering Organized Baseball.

Army Armstrong, a semipro teammate of Bordagaray's, recommended to the Sacramento Senators of the Pacific Coast League in 1931 that they give him a tryout. Bordagaray impressed team management with his speed and was signed to a contract on July 30 of that year. In his first game he went 2-for-3 against the Oakland Oaks. Frenchy got into 70 games that season, batted .373 with five home runs, and cemented a spot for the following season.

Bordagaray played an exhausting 173 games for the Senators in 1932, batting .322 with 223 hits in 692 at-bats. Frenchy also gave new meaning to the term "horse-racing" when he actually ran a 100-yard race against a horse named Eat 'Em Raw at the California State Fair in Sacramento. Bordagaray ended up eating the horse's

dust, as the nag ran the distance in 8.75 seconds. Frenchy's time was not reported.

Perhaps Sacramento management wasn't happy with the race results, because they offered Bordagaray a pay cut for the 1933 season. In what became a regular rite, Frenchy demanded a pay increase and left spring training on March 14.

"The trouble with Bordagaray is that he thinks he is a Babe Ruth and wants to be paid accordingly," said team owner Lew Moreing. "We can't relish that stuff."[2]

It seems that Moreing could, in fact, "relish that stuff" because Bordagaray was back the next day.[3] He went on to have one of the best seasons of his baseball career, hitting .351 with a career-high 7 home runs in 117 games.

Bordagaray's impressive numbers motivated the Chicago White Sox to purchase his contract for $15,000 before the 1934 season. He made an impressive major-league debut on Opening Day against the Detroit Tigers at Chicago's Comiskey Park, getting a pinch hit and scoring a run in an 8-3 White Sox loss. He went on to appear in 29 games, including 17 as an outfielder, and batted .322 in 87 at-bats. (He was 8-for-12 as a pinch-hitter.) Still, the White Sox returned him to Sacramento on June 9. Accounts differ as to whether the White Sox weren't pleased with Bordagaray's play

or simply decided they wanted their $15,000 back. Either way, he played 117 games for the Senators and despite getting off to a slow start, managed to hit .321.

That season Bordagaray performed the first feat of flakiness that made him a raconteur's delight. In a game against the Portland Beavers, the General, as he was called in Sacramento, evidently forgot to go out with the rest of the troops to his position in right field. None of his teammates noticed until Portland center fielder Nino Bongiovanni hit a double to Frenchy's vacated spot.

Nonetheless, the Brooklyn Dodgers were interested enough in Bordagaray to acquire him after the season in exchange for Johnny Frederick and Art Herring plus cash. Frenchy joined the Dodgers (whose manager was one Charles Dillon "Casey" Stengel) for the 1935 season.

Babe Ruth brought a new era to baseball in the 1920s with his home runs. Stengel and Bordagaray revived an old era when they teamed up, except in this case it was vaudeville. No one would confuse this band of Dodgers with the Boys of Summer teams of the 1950s. The Dodgers of the 1920s and 1930s were a ragtag group. The franchise was mired in debt and playing in a deteriorating Ebbets Field. The team acquired the nickname "The Daffiness Boys" because of the oddball characters and strange plays that made the Dodgers entertaining, even if they weren't successful.

Statistically, Bordagaray's 1935 and 1936 seasons with the Dodgers were pretty good. In his first full campaign as a major leaguer, he hit .282 with one home run, 39 RBIs, and 69 runs scored. He was third in the league with 18 stolen bases. In 1936 he hit .315 with 4 home runs, 31 runs batted in, 63 runs scored, and 12 stolen bases in 125 games. But the numbers don't convey the color that Frenchy brought to the team.

During one exhibition game, Bordagaray's hat fell off while he was chasing a fly ball. Frenchy, being Frenchy, stopped to retrieve the hat, and then continued chasing the ball.

"Stengel stood in the dugout in the dugout with his arms hanging and his mouth open. He couldn't believe what he was seeing," said former Dodger Buddy Hassett. "When Frenchy got back to the dugout, Stengel asked him what he thought he was doing out there. 'The cap

wasn't going anywhere, Bordagaray,' said Stengel, 'but the ball was.' 'I forgot,' Frenchy said."[4]

There was also the time Frenchy was standing on second base when he was suddenly picked off. Stengel went out to argue, to no avail, and when he went back to the dugout he asked Bordagaray what happened. Frenchy explained that he was tapping his toe on the bag and that the infielder caught him between taps.

Another story had Bordagaray tagged out on a play at the plate when he tried to score standing up instead of sliding. His explanation to Stengel was that he didn't slide because he had some cigars in his back pocket that he didn't want to ruin. Stengel fined Bordagaray $50 or $100, depending on who is telling the tale. The next day he hit a home run and slid into every bag on his trip around the bases.[5]

The pièce de résistance had to be the scandal Frenchy caused when he showed up at spring training in 1936 sporting a wispy mustache. After the 1935 season, Frenchy grew the mustache for a small, uncredited part in a film directed by John Ford, *The Prisoner of Shark Island*, and was still wearing it when spring training arrived. This was an era when players were clean-shaven, so the facial hair created a media sensation.

"The new mustache of the noted movie extra is a delicate affair of a distinctly Ronald Colman pattern," wrote Tommy Holmes in the *Brooklyn Eagle*.[6] "Stengel says it was the prettiest he ever saw, but Frenchy says that Casey is jealous and threatens to wear it from now on."[7]

Bordagaray was ahead of his time when it came to self-promotion with the media, and he kept the ink-stained wretches busy writing articles about the mustache. He even arrived at camp one day sporting a monocle to go with the mustache; sort of an Adolphe Menjou meets Colonel Klink. This went on for a while until Stengel finally had enough.

"After I had it about two months, Casey called me into the clubhouse and said, 'If anyone's going to be a clown on this club, it's going to be me,'" Bordagaray said.[8]

Whether Dodgers management was tired of the comedy act or just wanted to make changes, they fired Stengel after the season, and traded Bordagaray to St. Louis.

They may also have traded him simply because he didn't have the baseball smarts that turn a player with his talent into a star. After Frenchy was gone, Holmes remarked that he wasn't a great ballplayer despite talent, speed, charisma, and a good attitude.

"With all those qualities you'd think he'd be a really good ball player," wrote Holmes. "And yet he makes you eat holes in your hat. The reason, it seems to me, is lack of big league instinct in such fundamentals as base running and fly catching."[9]

The St. Louis Cardinals of 1937 were not the powerful Gas House Gang that won the World Series in 1934. They still had some of their stars, including Joe Medwick, Pepper Martin, and Dizzy Dean, but they were no longer a contender. Bordagaray got into 96 games that season, batting .293 with one home run and 37 RBIs. He played 50 games at third base and 28 in the outfield. The man whose father had hoped he would be a violinist also joined teammate Pepper Martin's Mudcat Band as fiddle player and first washboard. The band toured the theater circuit for $50 a show. It was also popular at the Cardinals' 1938 spring-training camp, with Frenchy, of course, wowing them in the aisles.

"Frenchy is the sensation," said an article by the Associated Press. His washboard has a three-tone phone, bicycle bells, and even an electric light for special renditions."[10]

The 1938 Cardinals finished under .500 for the first time in six years with a 71-80 record (plus five ties). On the surface, it would seem that Bordagaray's contribution was ordinary, with a .282 batting average in 81 games, zero home runs and only 21 runs batted in. He did, however, excel in a very difficult role, that of pinch-hitter. He had 20 pinch hits, just two off the record then of 22 set in 1932 by Sam Leslie of the Giants. (As of 2014 the record holder was John Vander Wal of the Colorado Rockies, with 28 in 1995.) Bordagaray's batting average of .465 as a pinch-hitter was at the time the second highest batting average ever for a pinch hitter, behind only the .467 attained by Smead Jolley of the White Sox in 1931 (As of 2014 Ed Kranepool of the 1974 New York Mets holds the single-season record, .486.)[11]

Being a good pinch-hitter apparently wasn't enough for the Cardinals to keep Frenchy on the big-league roster. After the 1938 season, they wanted to send him down to their farm club in Rochester. He refused to report, so the team traded him to the Cincinnati Reds for outfielder Dusty Cooke. The trade worked in Bordagaray's favor because he not only stayed in the big leagues, he also got his first chance to appear in the World Series.

It's safe to say that Bordagaray's contribution was not integral to the Reds' winning the 1939 National League pennant. He batted only .197 in 122 at-bats with no home runs and 12 RBIs. He appeared as a pinch-runner in Games Two and Three of the World Series, and didn't steal any bases or score any runs as the Reds were swept by the New York Yankees.

After the 1939 season, Bordagaray opened a nightclub in Cincinnati called Frenchy's Barn, an event that found its way into the famous column of Walter Winchell: "Frenchy Bordagaray of the pennant-winning Cincinnati Reds team has opened a night club in that city. … Could it be, do you think, that the World Series beating by the N.Y. Yankees has affected his mind?"[12]

Perhaps Winchell had a point, because Frenchy's 1939 statistics didn't guarantee any job security, and he ended up going to the Yankees, along with Nino Bongiovanni, to complete a deal in which the Yankees sent Vince DiMaggio to the Reds in exchange for $40,000 and players to be named later.

A team that had just won four straight World Series wasn't in great need of a .197 hitter, so the Bronx Bombers sent Frenchy to their Kansas City Blues farm club in the American Association. Frenchy tore up the league, pounding out 214 hits for a .358 average and a ticket to the Bronx for 1941.

The 1941 Yankees were a powerhouse team that won the American League pennant by 17 games. They had an outfield of Charlie Keller, Tommy Henrich, and Vince DiMaggio's younger brother, so Bordagaray's playing time was limited to just 16 starts in the outfield and 73 at-bats. He did manage to get a pinch-running appearance in Game Two of the World Series, which the Yankees lost. Perhaps somebody realized that Frenchy's teams always lost in the World Series whenever he pinch-ran, so he stayed on the bench for the next three games, all won by the Yankees, and Frenchy had his one and only championship. Nonetheless, he didn't enjoy playing with the Bronx Bombers. "(I) couldn't have fun with them," he said. "They were too serious. Snooty guys. Except Joe (DiMaggio). He's the only one I got along with."[13]

The Yankees, on the other hand, felt they could get along fine without Bordagaray, and sold him back to the Dodgers after he refused a demotion to Kansas City. Bordagaray spent the rest of his playing career in Flatbush. He played a total of 137 games in 1942 and 1943, batting a respectable .291, with no home runs and 24 RBIs. Wartime player shortages gave Bordagaray more playing time in 1944. He played in 130 games that year and batted .281 with 6 home runs and 51 RBIs, both highs for his major-league career. He also played more games at third base (98) than in any other season and made 15 errors there.

The 1945 season probably had Rickey's opinion leaning toward "poorest great third baseman." Frenchy played the hot corner as if it were the too-hot-to-handle corner, committing 19 errors in 166 chances for a woeful .886 fielding percentage. He batted .256 in 273 at-bats with 2 home runs and 49 RBIs. He played his last game on September 30, 1945. He was released before the start of the 1946 season.

By the end of his playing days, Bordagaray was still fun-loving, but was taking his career more seriously, both on the field and under it. He invested in a company that built cemeteries across the United States and made more money with the company than he did playing baseball. The Dodgers gave him a job as player-manager of the Trois-Rivieres Royals, their affiliate in the Class C Canadian-American League, in 1946. He justified the Dodgers' faith in him by batting .363 and managing the team to the regular-season title with a 72-49 record as well as the league championship.

Bordagaray also played a small role in Branch Rickey's effort to integrate major-league baseball. It is well known that Jackie Robinson broke baseball's color barrier with the Montreal Royals of the International League in 1946, but Rickey had assigned African-American players to other levels as well. Pitchers John

Wright and Roy Partlow had had trials in Montreal, but were sent down to Trois-Rivieres. Partlow went 10-1 and Wright was 12-8, and they both played significant roles in Trois-Rivieres' drive to the championship.

"On the Three Rivers team, we had all nationalities: blacks, whites, Frenchmen, Jewish boys. We had the whole works," Bordagaray noted. "The funny thing about it was I never thought of (Wright, who joined the team before Partlow) as black. I just thought of him as a ballplayer."[14]

Frenchy's success earned him a promotion to player-manager of the Greenville Spinners of the Class A South Atlantic League for 1947. It was there that a promising managerial career came to an end when he punched and spat on an umpire during a dispute in a July 15 game. He was suspended for 60 days and fined $50. The incident happened on the same day he was chosen Most Valuable Player for the 1946 season in the Canadian-American League. He never returned to Organized Baseball.

When told of the fine and suspension, he was quoted as saying, "I deserved something, but this is more than I expectorated."[15]

After leaving baseball, Bordagaray, his wife, Victoria (whom he married in 1940), and their family moved to Kansas City, where he worked in the cemetery business until 1961. They then moved to Ventura, California, where Frenchy worked as sports supervisor for the Ventura Department of Sports and Recreation until 1988.

Looking back, Bordagaray acknowledged that he had fun as a ballplayer, but felt he could have played better. He once said in an interview that he never reached his peak because doctors failed to diagnose that he had hypoglycemia, a blood-sugar disorder that causes weakness.[16]

Bordagaray died in a Ventura nursing home on April 13, 2000, at the age of 90. He left his wife, four children, seven grandchildren, and six great-grandchildren.

SOURCES

Honig, Donald, *Baseball Between the Lines: Baseball in the Forties and Fifties As Told by the Men Who Played It* (Lincoln: University of Nebraska Press, 1993).

Spatz, Lyle, ed., *The SABR Baseball List and Record Book* (New York: Scribner, 2007).

Zubiri, Nancy, *A Travel Guide to Basque America: Families, Feasts and Festivals* (Reno: University of Nevada Press, 1998).

Altoona (Pennsylvania) *Tribune*

Brooklyn Daily Eagle

Burlington (Iowa) *Hawk-Eye*

Fresno (California) *Bee Republican*

Greensboro (North Carolina) *Daily News*

Los Angeles Times

Middlesboro (Kentucky) *Daily News*

Reading (Pennsylvania) *Times*

Sports Illustrated

Baseball-reference.com

IMDB.com

The author wishes to thank Joanne Hulbert and J.G. Preston for providing materials for this article.

NOTES

1 Oscar Fraley, "Bordagaray Succeeds Among Flatbush Flock," *Greensboro* (North Carolina) *Daily News*, June 14, 1944.

2 "Bordagaray Deserts Sacs In Pay Fuss," *Fresno Bee Republican*, March 14, 1933.

3 The account of Bordagaray's return was unclear as to whether he signed at the same amount as he received the previous year or with a slight raise. Anyway, it seems he avoided a pay cut.

4 Donald Honig, *Baseball Between the Lines: Baseball in the Forties and Fifties As Told by the Men Who Played It*, 57.

5 Stengel was reported to have fined Bordagaray $50 in August 1935 for not sliding when he should have, but the story about sliding into every base after hitting a home run the next day may be fictitious. The author could not find newspaper accounts of the incident, and former teammate Buddy Hassett did not mention it in an interview for the Honig book. It's still a great story.

6 Ronald Colman was a British actor who won an Oscar Award for Best Actor in the 1947 film *A Double Life*.

7 Tommy Holmes, "Dodger Recruits Click In Training Workout," *Brooklyn Daily Eagle*, March 7, 1936.

8 Richard Goldstein, "Frenchy Bordagaray Is Dead; The Colorful Dodger Was 90," *New York Times*, May 23, 2000.

9 Holmes, "Lack of Big League Fundamentals Raises Havoc With Bordagaray," *Brooklyn Daily Eagle*, December 15, 1936.

10 "Frankie Frisch Loses Some of His Wrinkles As Cards Become Gashouse Gang of Old," *Altoona* (Pennsylvania) *Tribune*, March 17, 1938.

11 *The SABR Baseball List and Record Book* (New York: Scribner, 2007), 187.

12 Walter Winchell, "Walter Winchell on Broadway," *Reading* (Pennsylvania) *Times*, November 3, 1939.

13 Jeff Meyers, "THE NEWS OF THE DAY: Frenchy Bordagaray, an 82-Year-Old Great-Grandfather Living in Ventura, Shocked the Baseball Establishment in the 1930's With Such Gimmicks as Racing a Horse on Foot and Growing a Mustache, but His Flair Made Him a Media Darling," *Los Angeles Times*, December 25, 1992.

14 Jules Tygiel, "Those Who Came After," *Sports Illustrated*, June 27, 1983.

15 Julian Pitzer, "Sports Briefs," *Middlesboro* (Kentucky) *Daily News*, January 30, 1948.

16 Meyers.

Phil Cavarretta

by Lawrence Baldassaro

IN 1934, AT THE HEIGHT OF THE GREAT Depression, 17-year-old Phil Cavarretta helped support his family by playing professional baseball in the Chicago Cubs organization. At the end of his first and only season in the minor leagues, the Chicago native made his first start in the big leagues two months after his 18th birthday and hit a game-winning home run at Wrigley Field, three miles from his boyhood home and high school. For the next 19 years the first baseman/outfielder was a mainstay of the Cubs. A four-time All Star, he won an MVP Award and a batting title, played in three World Series, and was a player/manager for two-plus seasons. His competitive spirit and relentless hustle made him one of the all-time favorite Cubs players. He was, as many have said, "Mr. Cub" before that title was bestowed upon Ernie Banks.

Before signing with the Cubs, the left-hander had been a star pitcher and first baseman for Lane Tech High School's 1933 city championship team and then had led his American Legion team to a national championship later that summer. "I always loved baseball," said Cavarretta in a 2001 interview, "even in grade school." (As a youngster he would earn free passes to Wrigley Field by helping clean up the park after a game ended; when that opportunity wasn't available, he would sneak in.) "I started by playing 16-inch softball. That was a pretty big target and I wish I was hitting that when I played in the big leagues."[1] But the effects of the Great Depression quickly turned the teenager playing for the love of the game into a professional trying to earn a living.

Philip Joseph Cavarretta was born in Chicago on July 19, 1916, the third child of Joseph and Angela Cavarretta, immigrants from Palermo, Sicily. His older siblings were Michael and Sarah. "All we spoke at home was Italian," said Cavarretta. "I learned English at school." The family was hit hard by the Depression. "We had a tough time getting anything to eat," he recalled. "My dad (who had lost his job as a school janitor) couldn't get a job, my brother couldn't get a job. Things were so tough I'd go down to the coalyards and pick up the droppings from the coal cars and take them home to put in the pot-bellied stove."

When he told Percy Moore, his high school and American Legion coach, that he would have to drop out of school to help support the family, Moore arranged for his young star to have a tryout with the Cubs. The high school senior was not greeted with open arms when he showed up at Wrigley Field in the spring of 1934. "I went out there and I must have weighed all of about 150 pounds," he said. "I'm walking around and, geez, all these players are looking at me and they thought I was a batboy. Someone came up and said, 'Hey, kid, what are you doing here?' and I said, 'I'm here for a tryout.' (Cubs pitcher) Pat Malone, he was a tough guy, he came up and said, 'A tryout? You oughta go get something to eat and put some weight on, kid.' I was scared to death.

"Finally, Charlie Grimm, the Cubs first baseman and manager, came over and said, 'Go get yourself a bat, take a few swings and we'll look at you.' Anyway,

I had a real good batting session. One I hit out of the park. They were saying, 'Look at this guy, he's whacking that pea pretty good. We'd better sign this kid.'"

The Cubs did sign the kid, for $125 a month. Cavarretta's father had not always been fond of his son's love of baseball, a game he considered a frivolous waste of time. But his objections disappeared when he saw what his son would be making as a professional ballplayer.

Initially Cavarretta was assigned to the Peoria Tractors in the Class B Central League. In his first professional game, on May 15, 1934, he hit for the cycle and drove in four runs. When that league folded after Cavarretta had appeared in 23 games, he was sent to the Reading Red Sox in the Class A New York-Pennsylvania League.

After hitting .310 in 108 games in the minors, Cavarretta was called up in mid-September while the Cubs were in Boston to play the Bees. After two hitless pinch-hitting appearances on the road, he made his first start in front of hometown fans at Wrigley Field on September 25. In the second inning, the 18-year-old rookie hit a homer off Reds pitcher Whitey Wistert for the only run in a 1-0 win. He then started at first base in the Cubs' remaining four games, going 8-for-17.

Three games into the 1935 season, Grimm, who had been the Cubs' first baseman for nine years, turned the job over to Cavarretta, who went on to start 145 games. On September 25 the one-year anniversary of his first big-league home run, he again hit a second-inning homer that provided the only run in a 1-0 win, this time over the second-place Cardinals. That victory, the 19th straight for the Cubs, clinched at least a tie for the pennant. In the Cubs' six-game World Series loss to the Tigers, Cavarretta played every inning but managed only three singles in 24 at-bats.

Grimm would later claim credit for creating the nickname that would stick with Cavarretta the rest of his career. "When I first saw Cavarretta in the mid-'30s, I started calling him 'Philibuck,'" said Grimm. "It just came to me and was inspired, if you can call it that, by my reaction that here was a hard-nosed athlete. Phil liked it."[2] According to Len Merullo, the Cubs shortstop from 1942 to '47, he and Cavarretta, his road roommate,

shared a different nickname. "We were two Italian kids, about the same age and we got along great," said Merullo. "Our teammates called us 'The Grand Opera Twins.'"[3]

Cavarretta was again the starting first baseman in 1936, but in 1937 and '38 he played primarily in the outfield, the Cubs having acquired veteran Rip Collins. In 1935 Cavarretta had led the NL in errors by a first baseman, and would again in 1943. Grimm later said, "We moved him off first a couple of times and put him in the outfield when we got such experienced first basemen as Rip Collins and Babe Dahlgren. But Phil gradually mastered the position."[4] The Cubs again won the pennant in 1938 but were swept in the World Series by the Yankees, in spite of Cavarretta's .462 batting performance.

Injuries in 1939 and 1940 limited Cavarretta's playing time to 22 and 65 games respectively. On May 8, 1939, he broke an ankle sliding into second base. He returned on July 25, but appeared in only seven more games. The following season Cavarretta broke the same ankle, again sliding into second, again against the Giants. According to *The Sporting News*, the injury occurred during the July 16 game, *before* Cavarretta drove in both runs in a 2-0 win. The next day Cavarretta scored the Cubs' only run in a loss to the Dodgers. It was not until July 18 that x-rays revealed the injury.[5]

In 1944 Cavarretta, who was exempt from military service because of a perforated eardrum, earned the first of four consecutive All-Star selections. (In the 1944 game he set an All-Star Game record by reaching base five consecutive times, on a triple, single, and three walks.) Playing in all but two games that season, he batted .321, fifth in the NL, and tied Stan Musial for the league lead in hits with 197.

The next year Cavarretta reached the pinnacle of his career, leading the Cubs to their third pennant in 11 years with a league-best batting average (.355) and on-base percentage (.449) while driving in a career-high 97 runs. In the Cubs' seven-game World Series loss to the Tigers he hit .423, with two doubles, one home run, seven runs scored, and five RBIs. Then, in November, he was voted the league's Most Valuable Player by a wide margin. "It was the kind of a year you dream of," said Cavarretta. "Everything has to go your way, your line drives have to drop, your broken-bat hits have to drop."

The Cubs finished third in 1946 before descending into what would become a long stay in the second division. On July 21, 1951, two days after his 34th birthday, the 18-year veteran was named the player/manager of the seventh-place Cubs, replacing Frankie Frisch. The team went 27-47 under their new manager and finished in the cellar.

In 1952 Cavarretta became the first Italian American to manage a major-league club for a full season. That year the Cubs moved up to fifth place with a 77-77 record, their only non-losing record between 1947 and 1962. When I asked him, in 2001, if he was aware of this distinction, the 84-year-old Cavarretta said, "I feel honored. I didn't know that. That's great."[6]

After the Cubs fell back to seventh place in 1953, Cavarretta's tenure as manager came to an abrupt end the following spring. On March 29, 1954, within a few days of telling owner Phil Wrigley that the Cubs would probably finish in the second division, Cavarretta became the first manager ever fired during spring training. The dismissal was all the more bitter for him since it came after an exhibition game in Dallas, where at the time he made his home and owned a children's amusement park.

Wrigley was quoted as saying, "I decided to remove Cav as manager when I learned that he picked everyone else but us to finish in the first division. I did not feel the picture was as bleak as he painted it."[7] However, nearly 50 years later Cavarretta remained convinced that it was the Cubs' general manager, Wid Matthews, who persuaded Wrigley to dismiss him. "I guess my general manager got to Mr. Wrigley and he (Matthews) didn't like what I said," Cavarretta explained in 2001. "We didn't get along together. I was just being honest with Mr. Wrigley, telling him the truth. Before the meeting was over, Mr. Wrigley said, 'This is the first time in all the time I've owned the club that any manager has spoken to me on these grounds. I'm really glad that we talked.' I felt pretty good."

Soon after, Cavarretta was summoned by Matthews. "I figured we were going to go over the roster and see

who we were going to keep and who we were going to release. Well," said Cavarretta with a chuckle, "he released *me*. I couldn't believe it." Wrigley appointed Stan Hack, manager of the Cubs' Pacific Coast League team in Los Angeles, to replace Cavarretta, then asked Cavarretta to replace Hack in Los Angeles. When Cavarretta declined, his 20-year career with the Cubs was over. His tenure as a Cubs player is surpassed in franchise history only by Cap Anson's 22 years.

In a story about Stan Hack's first day as Cavarretta's replacement, the *Chicago Tribune* casually announced that "the Cubs yesterday officially retired Phil Cavarretta's No. 44."[8] For reasons that remain unclear, there never was a formal ceremony to retire the number.[9]

In a column for mlb.com posted on December 24, 2010, former baseball executive Fred Claire suggested that the time had come for the Cubs to formally retire Cavarretta's number. "Phil Cavarretta gave his heart and soul for 20 years to the Chicago Cubs," he wrote. "It seems as though it's time for the Cubs to give the Cavarretta family the honor it deserves by retiring No. 44. It might even be a nice omen for a team trying to get back to a World Series for the first time since a young man wearing No. 44 was playing first base."[10]

Both Claire and Cubs historian Ed Hartig have noted that even though the number was never officially retired, thanks to longtime Cubs clubhouse man Yosh Kawano no Cubs player wore number 44 until the team signed Burt Hooton in 1971. Claire quoted former Cubs manager Joey Amalfitano as saying, "Yosh didn't want the uniform used because he felt it should have been retired. It was kind of an unofficial retirement of a uniform in honor of Phil."[11]

After being fired, the 37-year-old veteran moved across town to play for the White Sox, hitting .316 in 71 games. His playing career came to an end on May 9, 1955, when the White Sox released him after he had appeared in six games.

At 5-feet-11-inches tall and 175 pounds, Cavarretta was hardly the prototypical slugging corner infielder. In 6,754 at-bats he hit 95 home runs (one every 71 at-bats) with a .416 slugging percentage. But he was a solid contact hitter, with a lifetime average of .293 and a .372 on-base percentage. "I was a disciplined, patient hitter," he said. His .355 batting average in 1945 remains as of 2014 the Cubs' single-season record for a left-handed hitter, and he ranks in the top ten in franchise history in runs, hits, RBIs, extra-base hits, triples, and walks.

Van Lingle Mungo was the victim of Cavarretta's sixth career home run on July 22, 1935, at Ebbets Field. Cavarretta's solo shot in the bottom of the tenth tied the score at 13-13 (Mungo had come on in relief in the eighth inning), but the Dodgers scored in the top of the 11th to win, 14-13. According to Cavarretta's son, Phil Jr., his father did not have fond memories of Mungo, who drilled him with a pitch in his first full season with the Cubs. "When he got back to the bench," said Phil Jr., "he expressed his frustration with Mungo to pitcher Charlie Root. 'Don't let it bother you,' said Root. 'Nobody really likes the guy. I'll get him for you later.'"[12]

With his boundless energy, constant hustle, and competitive fire, Cavarretta captured the hearts of Cubs fans. The Cubs' 1941 yearbook described him as "slim, swarthy, easy-going off the field, but possessed of one of the most fiery competitive temperaments in baseball." In a 1945 article in *The Sporting News,* Edgar Munzel wrote: "Phil definitely is a throw-back to the rugged hell-for-leather days. To him the opposition is the enemy and no quarter is asked and none given." The article quoted Cavarretta as saying: "Hustling was just born in me, I guess. By hustling you look good, you make your ball club look good and you make the fans feel like they're really getting their money's worth."[13]

It was during the 1938 World Series against the Yankees that Cavarretta got the chance to meet his boyhood hero, Lou Gehrig. "I got on base, I think it was the third game," he recalled. "He's holding me on first and I'm peeking at him, thinking, 'My God, this is my man.' He finally said, 'I've been watching you and I like the way you play. You're always hustling.' Then he said one more thing, and I'll never forget this as long as I live. He said, 'Don't change.' The rest of my career I always remembered that because I always gave one hundred percent, I always hustled, regardless of the score."

Andy Pafko, a Cubs outfielder from 1943 to 1951, had the locker adjacent to Cavarretta's. "I was honored

to be dressing next to the great Phil Cavarretta," he said. "I admired his hustle. He was a real competitor, and one of the most popular players in Chicago."[14]

Cavarretta was especially popular with Italian American fans. In 1935, the local Knights of Columbus sponsored Phil Cavarretta Day at Wrigley Field. He recalled that they presented him with "a nice automobile and a 16-gauge shotgun, which I still have." Even his parents became fans. "Once I went to the Cubs they took a little interest 'cause I was bringing in some money," he said. "I'd get paid on the first and the 15th, and I'd bring the check to my mom and dad."

Cavarretta remained in the game for many years after his playing days ended, working as a scout, coach, and minor-league manager. Married since 1936 to Chicago native Lorayne Clares, he had five children to support.[15] For 11 years between 1956 and 1971, he managed seven minor-league teams in five different leagues, from the Florida Instructional League to the Triple-A International League. He coached for the Detroit Tigers from 1961 to 1963 before scouting for them, and from 1973 to 1977 he was the minor-league hitting instructor for the New York Mets. He completed his career by serving as the Mets' hitting coach in 1978 under manager Joe Torre.

After retiring from baseball, Cavarretta and his wife lived for many years in Clearwater, Florida, before moving to Georgia, first to Villa Rica, then to Lilburn. He remained a loyal Cubs fan the rest of his life. On May 15, 1999, the 82-year-old Cubs legend returned to Wrigley Field to throw out the ceremonial first pitch. In an interview at that time he said, "Every day I wait for the Cubs games to come on cable TV. I watch all the games and I sit there and root for the Cubs."[16]

Phil Jr., who pitched in the minors in 1977-78, confirmed that his father loved the Cubs and watched the games. "But," he said, "he'd get aggravated when guys wouldn't play the game the way it's supposed to be played." He added that in retirement his father "played a little golf, did a little fishing. But mostly he spent time with the family. He was a good father, always there for you, always understanding."[17]

In 2001 Cavarretta, then living in Villa Rica, reflected on what baseball meant to him. "I don't know what I would have done if it hadn't been for baseball," he said. "It was a game that I was proud to be a part of, proud of so many things that I learned from the game itself and the people that were affiliated with the game."

After battling leukemia for several years, Cavarretta succumbed to complications from a stroke on December 18, 2010, in Lilburn, Georgia, at the age of 94. His remains were cremated. He was survived by his wife of 73 years; daughters Diana, Patti, Cheryl, and Lori; son Phil Jr.; and several grandchildren and great-grandchildren.

SOURCES

Cava, Pete, ed., *Tales From the Cubs Dugout* (Champaign, Illinois: Sports Publishing, Inc., 2000).

Golenbock, Peter, *Wrigleyville: A Magical History Tour of the Chicago Cubs* (New York: St. Martin's Press, 1996).

Hartig, Ed, "First Family: 1945 MVP Cavarretta Returns to Wrigley," *Vine Line*, July 1999, 15.

Munzel, Edgar, "Run-'em-out Phil in 11-Year Cub Run," *Sporting News*, May 31, 1945.

Chicago Cubs Yearbooks, 1941, '42, '51, '53.

Chicago Tribune

New York Times

The Sporting News

Claire, Fred, "Time for Cubs to Finally Honor Cavarretta," mlb.com, http://chicago.cubs.mlb.com/news/article. jsp?ymd=20101224&content_id=16367164&vkey=news_mlb&c_id=mlb

Interviews: Phil Cavarretta, Phil Cavarretta, Jr., Len Merullo, Andy Pafko.

Thanks to Cubs historian Ed Hartig for his assistance.

NOTES

1   Phil Cavarretta, telephone interview, April 29, 2001. Unless otherwise noted, all Cavarretta quotations are from this source.

2   Cava, *Tales From the Cubs Dugout*, 58.

3   Len Merullo, telephone interview, December 16, 2001.

4   *The Sporting News*, May 31, 1945. In his 20 years with the Cubs, Cavarretta played the outfield for parts of 13 seasons, in six of which he played the majority of his games in the outfield.

5   *The Sporting News*, July 25, 1940.

6   It was while he was managing that Cavarretta persuaded general manager Wid Matthews to close off a section of the center-field bleachers at Wrigley Field, arguing that the white shirts of fans in that area made it dangerous for hitters, who had a hard time seeing

the pitch against the white background. See Golenbock, *Wrigleyville*, 320, and Hartig, "First Family," 15.

7   *The Sporting News*, April 7, 1954.

8   *Chicago Tribune*, April 2, 1954.

9   In an email to the author (October 8, 2013), Cubs historian Ed Hartig, wrote, "I can only speculate that Cavarretta's signing with the White Sox likely had something to do with (the lack of a formal retirement ceremony)."

10 Claire, "Time for Cubs to Finally Honor Cavarretta."

11 In his October 8, 2013, email to the author, Hartig wrote: "I spoke with Hooton at the Cubs Convention several years ago. He recalled that Yosh Kawano called Cavarretta to ask permission to give the pitcher number 44. Cavarretta said it was OK."

12 Phil Cavarretta, Jr., telephone interview, December 20, 2013.

13 *The Sporting News*, May 31, 1945.

14 Andy Pafko, personal interview, April 21, 2001.

15 Some sources list her name as Loraine, but in his telephone interview on December 20, 2013, Phil Cavarretta, Jr. confirmed Lorayne as the correct spelling.

16 Hartig, "First Family," 15.

17 Phil Cavarretta, Jr., telephone interview, December 20, 2013.

George McQuinn

By C. Paul Rogers III

IT WAS A LONG JOURNEY FOR GEORGE McQuinn to the 1947 New York Yankees, where he became a key figure in their run to the pennant. In addition to his normal stellar play at first base, McQuinn batted .304 and drove in 80 runs, a significant upgrade from Nick Etten, a .232 hitter for the third-place Yankees in 1946. In late May McQuinn was batting a league-leading .392, and by the All-Star break he was still among the league leaders at .328. For his efforts, the fans chose McQuinn as the American League's starting first baseman in the All-Star Game. One sportswriter described his success as "the story book story behind the Yankees' surprising success … in 1947."[1]

McQuinn's contribution was perhaps equal parts unexpected and gratifying. It was unexpected because he had hit only .225 in 1946 for the cellar-dwelling Philadelphia Athletics, who released him after the season. It looked as though at the age of 36, without a job and with a bad back, his major-league career might be at an end. One article even referred to McQuinn as "the man nobody wanted."[2] New Yankees manager Bucky Harris, however, was an old fan of McQuinn's and the New Yorkers had a need at first base, so on January 25, 1947, the Yankees signed him as a free agent, setting the stage for his surprising landmark season.[3]

George Hartley McQuinn was born on May 29, 1910, in Arlington, Virginia, a suburb of Washington, DC. His parents were William McQuinn, an electrician, and Ada (Hartley) McQuinn, who was born in England but emigrated in 1899. The pair had seven children—five boys and two girls. George, the third son, began playing baseball at the age of 7. When he was 12 he bought a George Sisler model first baseman's glove, but McQuinn patterned himself after Joe Judge, the slick-fielding first baseman of the hometown Washington Senators.[4]

McQuinn starred in basketball and baseball at Washington-Lee High School. He was a left-handed pitcher as well as batter, but his high-school coach began playing him at first base full-time. McQuinn had an offer to play baseball at the College of William

and Mary but decided instead to try for a career in professional baseball.

In 1930 he was working as an elevator operator for the Chamber of Commerce in Washington and playing for a semipro team in Northern Virginia. After a tryout arranged by his semipro manager, the New Haven (Connecticut) Profs of the Class A Eastern League signed McQuinn to his first professional contract. Playing time was limited, however, and the league was a fast one for a 19-year-old. McQuinn could manage only two hits in 19 at-bats and in May New Haven released him.

Fortunately for McQuinn, he had made an impression on Joe Benes, one of the veteran infielders for the Profs. Benes recommended him to Yankees scout Gene McCann, who signed McQuinn to a contract with the Wheeling (West Virginia) Stogies, the Yankees' farm club in the Class C Middle Atlantic League.[5] McQuinn's .288 batting average for the Stogies earned him a promotion for 1931 to the Scranton Miners of the Class B

New York-Penn League, where he hit a strong .316 and drove in 101 runs while hitting just five home runs.

In 1932 McQuinn batted a combined .334 with 100 RBIs while splitting the season between the Albany (New York) Senators of the Eastern League and, after the league folded on July 17, the Binghamton (New York) Triplets of the New York-Penn League. That performance earned him a spring-training invitation in 1933 with the International League Newark Bears, the Yankees' top farm club. The Bears, however, had the veteran Johnny Neun at first base so they shipped McQuinn to the rival Toronto Maple Leafs. Despite an excellent start with the Leafs, he was sent back to Binghamton, where he batted a league-leading .357, drove in 102 runs, and won the league's Most Valuable Player award.

McQuinn played a full season with Toronto in 1934, hitting .331 in 138 games, before fracturing an ankle sliding into third base in the Junior World Series. By now some writers were wondering if the Yankees would consider trading Lou Gehrig to make room for McQuinn at first base.[6]

Yankees farm director George Weiss sent the Patient Scot, as the press sometimes called McQuinn, to Newark in 1935, where he hit .288 in 563 at-bats, subpar for him because of a sore shoulder. Defensively, he broke a 22-year-old International League record for first basemen by fielding .997 for the year.

McQuinn had yet to be invited to a Yankees' spring training, but he continued to attract attention from other organizations. Before the 1936 season, the Cincinnati Reds, looking to replace Jim Bottomley at first base, purchased McQuinn conditionally, meaning they could return him to the Yankees up until June 1. McQuinn, still just 25 years old, finally got his big-league chance and it was a flop. The Reds, under manager Charlie Dressen, immediately tried to get him to pull the ball rather than hit to all fields as was his custom. He was unable to adjust, and in 134 at-bats hit only .201 with no home runs, prompting the Reds to send him back to the Yankees on June 1.

McQuinn returned to Toronto and hit a reaffirming .329 in 410 at-bats. While there, he met Kathleen Baxter, originally from Belfast, Northern Ireland, on a blind date at the ballpark. They married after the 1937 season and eventually had two daughters, Virginia and Victoria.

Kathleen knew little about baseball. The first time she saw a game in which it rained, she was perplexed about why the team had removed the tarpaulin when the rain stopped. After the game, she asked George to explain why he had to play on a muddy field when it would have been so much cleaner to play on the canvas.[7]

With Lou Gehrig still going strong for the Yankees, McQuinn found himself back with Newark in 1937. Playing for what is widely regarded as the best minor-league team ever, he batted .330 and stroked 21 home runs, as the Bears won the pennant by 25½ games, finishing with a 109-43 record.[8] McQuinn later recalled that his friends used to kid him, saying, "Doesn't Gehrig ever have the mumps, whooping cough or measles? Why don't you send him a letter telling him he better take a vacation or else?"[9]

Under the rules then in place, McQuinn became eligible to be drafted by another major-league team after the 1937 season when the Yankees failed to place him on their big-league roster. As a result, the St. Louis Browns selected McQuinn with the first pick in the Rule 5 draft and installed him at first base to begin the 1938 season.

McQuinn soon discovered that the Yankees had made the Browns pay more than the $7,500 draft price for him, in violation of the draft rules. McQuinn wrote Commissioner Kenesaw Mountain Landis a letter of complaint and then showed up at his office in Chicago. Landis told McQuinn to go ahead and report to the Browns, but promised to investigate and get back to him. But McQuinn never did hear back from the Commissioner, which rankled him for many years.[10]

McQuinn made sure he did not flub his second chance at the big leagues. On Opening Day he clubbed a single, double, and triple against one of the best pitchers in the league, Cleveland's Johnny Allen. Typically a slow starter, he hovered around the .270 mark for the first two months of the season, before improving to .300. Then, on July 24, he had four hits in four at-bats against the Washington Senators, beginning a torrid 34-game hitting streak during which he batted .386 (56-for-145). For the season he was runner-up to Mel Almada on the seventh-place Browns with a .324 batting average, while slugging 12 home runs and driving in 82 runs, second in both categories to Harlond Clift.

Manager Gabby Street had scouted McQuinn at Newark and quickly lauded him as the best defensive first baseman in the league since George Sisler, and better than Jim Bottomley or Rip Collins of the Cardinals.[11]

The 1939 season brought more of the same as McQuinn led the Browns with a .316 average while playing in all 154 games. He improved his home run and runs batted in totals to 20 and 94 respectively for the last-place Browns. For his efforts, McQuinn was named to his first All-Star team, although he did not appear in the game.

After the season the Yankees sought to trade for McQuinn, who had been blocked in the minor leagues by Gehrig for all those years, to replace the ill Gehrig at first base. Yankees general manager Ed Barrow reportedly offered the Browns $75,000 plus Babe Dalhgren and other players for McQuinn. The American League, however, had instituted a bizarre rule barring trades with the pennant winner, which ended up quashing the deal.[12] Yankees general manager Ed Barrow later lamented that the failure to land McQuinn had cost the Yankees their fifth straight pennant in 1940.[13]

Thus, McQuinn found himself back with St. Louis in 1940. He slipped to a .279 average for the improved sixth-place Browns, but made his second All-Star team, although he again did not appear in the game. McQuinn, who was particularly adept at turning the 3-6-3 double play,[14] also led American League first basemen in fielding average.

Although only 5-feet-11, McQuinn quickly became known as the best fielding first baseman in the league and was often compared to George Sisler, Joe Kuhel, and Hal Chase. Veteran catcher Frank Mancuso called him the best first baseman he had ever seen.[15] As a result, the Rawlings Sporting Goods Company marketed a George McQuinn model first baseman's glove. Years later, it was reported that President George H.W. Bush, another slick-fielding first baseman from his days at Yale, kept his old first baseman's "claw" glove

in his desk drawer in the Oval Office at the White House. It was a George McQuinn model.[16]

McQuinn improved his batting average to .297 in 1941, with 18 homers and 80 runs batted in. The highlight of his season came on July 19, when he hit for the cycle. For the second consecutive year, McQuinn led American League first basemen in fielding percentage. After the season he was to be included in what would have been a blockbuster trade with the National League champion Brooklyn Dodgers. The deal would have sent McQuinn and third baseman Harlond Clift to the Dodgers for reigning National League MVP Dolph Camilli, Cookie Lavagetto, and cash. McQuinn and Clift, however, could not clear American League waivers so the deal did not happen.

A back ailment that was becoming chronic hampered McQuinn in 1942 and 1943; his batting average slipped to .262 in '42 and .243 in '43. It had gotten to the point that he needed to wear a brace in order to play. With World War II in full swing, McQuinn was ordered to take an Army pre-induction physical in June of 1943, but was rejected because of his back.[17]

The Browns were a veteran team and would lead the league in 4-Fs, medical discharges, and family-related deferments. While other teams were losing key players to the service, the Browns were relatively unaffected. They opened the 1944 season with 18 4-Fs and 13 were with the team for the long haul.[18] As a result, the 1944 Browns, playing in a weakened American League, won their first American League title in a thrilling pennant race that went down to the last day of the season. The Browns entered that day tied for first place with the Detroit Tigers, who were playing the Washington Senators in Detroit. The Browns were hosting the New York Yankees and learned in the fourth inning that the Tigers had lost. Although the Yankees got off to a 2-0 lead, the Browns came back to win 5-2 behind the stellar pitching of Sig Jakucki. With a runner on second and two out in the ninth the Yankees' third baseman Oscar Grimes hit a towering foul ball about ten feet outside of first base. McQuinn squeezed the ball for the final out and was immediately mobbed by fans and players spilling onto the field.

McQuinn held on to the ball that ended the game as if it were made of gold. In the clubhouse winning pitcher Jakucki approached McQuinn and said, "Look pal, that ball means a lot to me. How about giving it to me?"

McQuinn replied, "Well, let's be neighborly about this thing. I'll give you half of it." Browns' owner Don Barnes overheard the exchange and asked for a saw. Jakucki and McQuinn then spent ten minutes trying to saw the ball in two, but failed to make any headway. Finally batboy Bobby Scanlon flipped a coin to decide the winner. McQuinn won the flip and got the now thoroughly chewed up baseball.[19]

The 34-year-old McQuinn hit only .250 for the season but his 11 home runs were second on the team and he again led the league's first basemen in fielding average. He also made his fourth All-Star team, this time as the starting first baseman. He played the entire game, singling in the first inning off Bucky Walters to go 1-for-4, as the Americans went down to defeat, 7-1.

The Browns faced the St. Louis Cardinals, who had breezed to the National League pennant, in the only "All-St. Louis" World Series. In the fourth inning of the first game, with a man on, McQuinn blasted a towering drive off Mort Cooper onto the right-field roof to lead the Browns to a 2–1 victory. Then, in Game Two, McQuinn was involved in a play that is often considered the turning point in the entire Series. With the score tied 2-2, he led off the top of the 11th with a double off the screen in right field. Mark Christman attempted to sacrifice McQuinn to third by pushing a bunt toward third base, but Cardinals pitcher Blix Donnelly pounced off the mound and threw to Whitey Kurowski at third. Kurowski made a great stab of the ball and tagged McQuinn out by an eyelash. Observers were surprised that Donnelly had even elected to throw to third. Gene Moore, the next batter, lofted a long outfield fly that would have easily scored McQuinn but was instead just the second out of the inning. The Cardinals quickly scored the winning run in the bottom of the inning to tie the series at one apiece.[20]

The Browns won Game Three 6-2 and might well have been up three games to zero but for Donnelly's play at third in Game Two. But they hit only .183 and

lost Games Four, Five, and Six to lose the Series four games to two. McQuinn was the one bright spot, batting .438 with seven hits, seven walks, and five of the team's nine runs batted in. His home run in Game One was the only one the Browns hit.

McQuinn was again called for a pre-induction physical in early 1945 but was rejected under a new edict that ballplayers not fit for combat should not be drafted. McQuinn improved his batting average to .277 in 483 at-bats as the Browns finished a respectable third, six games behind the pennant-winning Detroit Tigers.

Shortly after the season, the Browns swapped McQuinn to the Philadelphia A's for first baseman Dick Siebert. The deal hit a snag when Siebert could not agree to terms with the Browns and retired from baseball, but Commissioner Happy Chandler ruled that the A's could keep McQuinn nonetheless.[21] The last-place A's may have regretted the commissioner's decision as McQuinn had his worst year in baseball in 1946, hitting only .225, with three home runs and just 35 RBIs. He struggled through some long slumps and incurred the ire of the Athletics fans. At one point, after striking out four times and popping up three times in a doubleheader, McQuinn decided to quit the game, but Kathleen talked him out of it, telling him he'd had too many good seasons not to be able to endure a bad one.[22]

The Athletics gave McQuinn his unconditional release on January 9, 1947. Connie Mack, the venerable manager of the Athletics, was heard to remark that McQuinn had "played baseball one year too long."[23]

That set the stage for McQuinn to sign with the Yankees, 17 years after he first became a Yankee farm-hand.[24] McQuinn did not accompany the team on its spring tour through Latin America in 1947, joining them when they returned to St. Petersburg, Florida. By that time the Yankees' lineup looked set, with Tommy Henrich at first base and Yogi Berra in right field. Charley Keller, however, pulled a muscle in early April, sending Henrich temporarily to left field and giving McQuinn an opening at first base. He began hitting well immediately, even against left-handers, and soon took over the first-base position, with Henrich occupying right field and Berra the catcher's spot.[25]

Early in the season McQuinn asked traveling secretary Arthur Patterson if he could room alone on the road. His chronic back pain made it hard for him to sleep at night, and he worried that his tossing and turning would disturb his roommate. He also found that being able to sprawl out in a double bed helped him sleep better.[26]

With his back responding, the 37-year-old McQuinn got off to a great start and by early June was leading the league with a .354 average. Only a few months after being released by the worst team in baseball, McQuinn was named as a starter for the American League All-Star team. He played the entire game at first base, going hitless in four at-bats.

Throughout his career, McQuinn had a reputation for having a dry sense of humor but being quiet and not very talkative. His Browns teammate Don Gutteridge recalled that McQuinn would say hello when he arrived for spring training and goodbye when he left in the fall.[27] Bobby Brown remembered that his nickname on the Yankees was Si, short for silent. Brown recalled McQuinn as a great teammate and a very nice man.[28] His typical postgame ritual on the road was to smoke an after-dinner cigar in the hotel lobby while watching the people go by, and then head to bed at 10 o'clock.[29]

McQuinn tailed off late in the year to a final .304 average — second highest on the team — with 13 home runs and 80 RBIs. Unlike 1944, however, he struggled in the World Series, hitting only .130 in 23 at-bats as the Yankees defeated the Brooklyn Dodgers in seven games.

Although he would turn 38 in May 1948, the Yankees wanted McQuinn back, and after a brief holdout, he signed for the '48 season. He got off to another exceptional start, with an average of .340 on May 31, and was again named the All-Star Game starter at first base for the American League, his sixth All-Star team. He played the entire game and was one of three players, along with Richie Ashburn and Stan Musial, with two hits as the American League won, 5–2. He also set an All-Star Game record with 14 putouts and tied a mark with 14 total chances. But he wore down over the long season and ended the campaign hitting .248 in 94 games

as the Yankees finished third in a tight, three-team pennant race.

The Yankees released McQuinn after the season, and he retired to Arlington, Virginia, to run a sporting-goods store bearing his name. He was lured back to baseball in 1950 by the Boston Braves organization with an offer to manage the Quebec Braves in the Class C Canadian-American League. The team finished first with a 97-40 record, won the semifinals four games to one, and swept the finals in four games against the Amsterdam (New York) Rugmakers. Along the way, McQuinn put himself into 74 games and hit .318 in 242 at-bats.

The Braves switched to the Provincial League, also Class C, in 1951 as McQuinn again managed the team, this time to a fourth-place finish. Although he was now 41 years old, he was still a playing manager, hitting .301 in 136 at-bats. McQuinn was back managing Quebec in 1952 and guided the Braves to a second-place finish, while appearing as a pinch-hitter 12 times, the final at-bats of his playing career.

McQuinn continued to manage Quebec through the 1954 season with remarkable success. In his five years leading the Braves, the club finished first twice, second once, third once, and fourth once, and won the league playoffs four times.

The Braves organization promoted McQuinn to manage the Atlanta Crackers in the Double-A Southern Association for 1955. With the club's record at 49-49 on July 16, McQuinn stepped down as manager. However, his magic touch returned in 1956. On July 1 of that year he took over the managerial reins of the Boise Braves in the Class C Pioneer League and led them to the pennant. McQuinn returned to Boise for 1957 but the team finished seventh. In 1958 he moved up to manage the Topeka Hawks in the Class A Western League, where the team also finished seventh in an eight-team circuit.

Now 48, McQuinn wanted to spend his summers closer to his Arlington home so he became a scout for the Washington Senators, concentrating on Virginia and West Virginia. He later scouted for the Montreal Expos before retiring from baseball in 1971 after 42 years in the game. He published a detailed guide to playing baseball in 1972 and delighted in giving it to any youngster who expressed an interest.

In an interview late in life, McQuinn lamented that Lou Gehrig probably cost him four years of his big-league career. He expressed some bitterness that the Yankees had never taken him to spring training, despite his outstanding years in the minor leagues.[30] McQuinn also had little use for Commissioner Landis, who refused to do anything when the Yankees violated baseball rules in sending him to the Browns in 1937.

But with the exception of his appeal to Landis, McQuinn was never one to make waves. During his minor-league career, his name was twice butchered by the teams he was playing for. In Scranton, the public-address announcer called him Mike McQuinn and later in Newark, an error led him to be listed on the roster as Jack. He never corrected either mistake and for the rest of his life was known as Mike to those who had known him in Scranton and Jack to those from Newark.[31]

McQuinn's major-league career spanned 12 years and four teams. He ended with a lifetime batting average of .276 with 1,588 hits in 1,550 big-league games. Although it was not as uncommon then as it is now, he walked more times (712) than he struck out (634). He is most remembered as a stalwart of some mediocre St. Louis Browns clubs in the late 1930s and early 1940s and as the star of the 1944 World Series. But he had a major impact on the '47 Yankees' run to the pennant after Yankees manager Bucky Harris plucked him off the scrap heap.

McQuinn died on December 24, 1978, in Alexandria, Virginia, of complications from a stroke. He was 68 years old.

SOURCES

Borst, Bill, *The Best of Seasons: The 1944 St. Louis Cardinals and St. Louis Browns* (Jefferson, North Carolina: McFarland & Co., Inc., 1995).

Borst, Bill, *Still Last in the American League* (West Bloomfield, Michigan: Altwerger & Mandel Publishing Co., 1992).

Cleve, Craig Allen, *Hardball on the Home Front,* (Jefferson, North Carolina: McFarland & Co., Inc., 2004).

Cobbledick, Gordon, "McQuinn Bolsters Three Positions," *Baseball Digest*, September, 1947.

Dahlgren, Matt, *Rumor in Town* (Ashland, Ohio: Woodlyn Lane, 2007).

Finoli, David, *For the Good of the Country—World War II Baseball in the Major and Minor Leagues* (Jefferson, North Carolina: McFarland & Co., Inc., 2002).

Goldstein, Richard, *Spartan Seasons: How Baseball Survived the Second World War* (New York: Macmillan Publishing Co., 1980).

Golenbock, Peter, *The Spirit of St. Louis: A History of the St. Louis Cardinals and Browns* (New York: Avon Books, Inc., 2000).

Gross, Milton, "The Man Nobody Wanted," in *Yankee Doodles* (Boston: House of Kent Publishing Co., 1948).

Gutteridge, Don, as told to Ronnie Joyner and Bill Bozman, *Don Gutteridge in Words and Pictures* (Dunkirk, Maryland: Pepperpot Productions, Inc., 2002).

Gutteridge, Don, with Ronnie Joyner and Bill Bozman, *From the Gas House Gang to the Go-Go Sox—My 50-Plus Years in Big League Baseball* (Dunkirk, Maryland: Pepperpot Productions, Inc., 2007).

Heidenry, John, and Brett Topel, *The Boys Who Were Left Behind* (Lincoln, Nebraska: University of Nebraska Press, 2006).

Heller, David Allan, *As Good As It Got: The 1944 St. Louis Browns* (Charleston, South Carolina: Arcadia Publishing, 2003).

Johnson, Lloyd, and Miles Wolff, eds., *The Encyclopedia of Minor League Baseball, Second Edition* (Durham, North Carolina: Baseball America, 1997).

Karst, Gene, and Martin Jones, eds., *Who's Who in Professional Baseball* (New Rochelle, New York: Arlington House, 1973).

Levitt, Daniel R., *Ed Barrow—The Bulldog Who Built the Yankees' First Dynasty* (Lincoln, Nebraska: University of Nebraska Press, 2008).

Linthurst, Randolph, *Newark Bears* (Trenton: White Eagle Printing Co., Inc., 1978).

Mayer, Ronald A., *The Newark Bears: A Baseball Legend* (East Hanover, New Jersey: Vintage Press, 1980).

Mead, William B., *Even the Browns: The Zany, True Story of Baseball in the Early Forties* (Chicago: Contemporary Books, Inc., 1978).

Porter, David L., *Biographical Dictionary of American Sports: Baseball, Revised and Expanded Edition G-P* (Westport, Connecticut: Greenwood Press, 2000).

Shatzkin, Mike, ed., *The Ballplayers* (New York: Arbor House, 1990).

Van Lindt, Carson, *One Championship Season: The Story of the 1944 St. Louis Browns* (New York: Marabou Publishing, 1994).

Vincent, David; Lyle Spatz, and David Smith, *The Midsummer Classic: The Complete History of the All-Star Game* (Lincoln, Nebraska: University of Nebraska Press, 2001).

George McQuinn clippings file, National Baseball Library.

Telephone interview by author with Dr. Bobby Brown, June 23, 2011.

NOTES

1   Milton Gross, "The Man Nobody Wanted," in *Yankee Doodles*, 98.

2   Gross, 97.

3   Cy Kritzer, "Bucky Played Hunch in Signing of McQuinn," *The Sporting News*, June 11, 1947, 6; Frances E. Stann, "McQuinn Feels Right at Home as Yank," *The Sporting News*, undated, from the George McQuinn clippings file, National Baseball Library.

4   Undated and unidentified clipping from the George McQuinn clippings file, National Baseball Library.

5   Frederick G. Lieb, " 'Forgotten Yankee' McQuinn Proves Star at 37," *The Sporting News*, undated, from the George McQuinn clippings file, National Baseball Library.

6   Michael F. Gaven, "George McQuinn, Kept Off Yankees for Eight Seasons by Gehrig, Getting His Chance With Browns Via Draft," *The Sporting News*, February 28, 1938.

7   Gross, 103.

8   Of the players who spent all or the bulk of the season with Newark, everyone but Jack Fallon had substantial major league careers. In addition to McQuinn, they included Joe Gordon, Charlie Keller, Babe Dahlgren, Atley Donald, Joe Beggs, Mario Russo, Buddy Rosar, Willard Hershberger, Bob Seeds, Spud Chandler, Jim Gleeson, Johnny Niggeling, Vito Tamulis, and Steve Sundra among others. Ronald A. Mayer, *The 1937 Newark Bears*, ix-xxiv.

9   Henry P. Edwards, January 29, 1939, American League Press Release in the George McQuinn clippings file, National Baseball Library.

10 St. Louis Browns general manager Bill DeWitt later admitted that the Yankees had made the Browns sell them first-baseman Harry Davis for $2,500 in order to obtain McQuinn. William B. Mead, *Even the Browns: The Zany, True Story of Baseball in the Early Forties*, 61-62.

11 The Old Scout, "Rookie McQuinn Ties Hornsby's Batting Streak," unidentified article dated August 25, 1938 in the George McQuinn clippings file, National Baseball Library.

12 Daniel R. Levitt, *Ed Barrow—the Bulldog Who Built the Yankees' First Dynasty*, 333; Frederick G. Lieb, " 'Forgotten Yankee' McQuinn Proves Star at 37," *The Sporting News*, undated, from the George McQuinn clippings file, National Baseball Library.

13 Joe King, "Flag No Surprise to McQuinn—He Knew It Back in January," unidentified article dated September 16, 1947 from the George McQuinn clippings file, National Baseball Library.

14 "McQuinn Sets Pace Again," unidentified clipping dated January 15, 1942 from the George McQuinn clippings file, National Baseball Library; Henry P. Edwards, January 29, 1939, American League Press Release in the George McQuinn clippings file, National Baseball Library.

15 Craig Allen Cleve, *Hardball on the Home Front*, 15.

16 ". . . It's a George McQuinn 'Claw,'" unidentified article dated October 19, 1989 from the George McQuinn clippings file, National Baseball Library.

17 Richard Goldstein, *Spartan Seasons*, 207; "Army Rejects Stephens and McQuinn of Browns," unidentified article dated June 29, 1943 from the George McQuinn clippings file, National Baseball Library..

18 John Heidenry and Brett Topel, *The Boys Who Were Left Behind*, 44.

19 John Heidenry and Brett Topel, 12-15.

20 Don Gutteridge with Ronnie Joyner and Bill Bozman, *From the Gas House Gang to the Go-Go Sox*, 164, 166; Heidenry and Topel, 95-96..

21 "McQuinn Stays With Athletics," unidentified article dated April 19, 1946 from the George McQuinn clippings file, National Baseball Library.

22 Gross, 102.

23 Gross, 98.

24 Rud Rennie, "McQuinn Hopes 17-Year Desire To Become Yankee Is Realized," unidentified article dated March 5, 1947 in the George McQuinn clippings file, National Baseball Library; Dan Daniel, "Merry-Go-ropund Brings Brass Ring for McQuinn," *The Sporting News*, April 23, 1947..

25 Dan Daniel, "McQuinn Named Yank 1st Sacker," unidentified article dated April 12, 1947 from the George McQuinn clippings file, National Baseball Library.

26 Gross, 101-102.

27 Don Gutteridge as told to Ronnie Joyner and Bill Bozman, *Don Gutteridge in Words and Pictures*, 73; Don Gutteridge with Ronnie Joyner and Bill Bozman, *From the Gas House Gang to the Go-Go Sox*, .173.

28 Author interview with Dr. Bobby Brown, June 23, 2011.

29 Gross, 106-107.

30 William B. Mead, , 41.

31 Gross, 106.

Howie Pollet
by Warren Corbett

LEFT-HANDER HOWIE POLLET WAS A pitching prodigy, but arm injuries stunted his career. Howard Joseph Pollet was born in New Orleans on June 26, 1921. The family name is French, but they pronounced it "pol-LET" rather than "Poh-LAY." His father, Jules, was a railroad detective; his mother, Rosalie, was Italian-American. Growing up in New Orleans, his next-door neighbor was Mel Parnell, who became a left-handed pitching star for the Boston Red Sox. Their fathers, both railroad men, were close friends.

Jules Pollet died when Howard was 15, leaving his widow with two younger sons, Wilson and Lloyd, and a daughter, Shirley. Howard worked in a gas station to help support the family. He also pitched for Fortier High School and American Legion Post 197. His Legion junior team played in the national championship game in 1937, but lost to a team from East Lynn, Massachusetts.

Pollet's boss at the gas station, Texaco executive Hugh McConaughey, recommended him to a friend in the oil business, Eddie Dyer, a former big-league pitcher also born in Louisiana and a longtime manager in the Cardinals' farm system. Dyer was named Houston's manager for the 1939 season and signed the teenager for a $3,500 bonus, beating out a half-dozen other clubs. Dyer became Pollet's mentor and lifelong business partner. Pollet later said he had used part of his baseball bonus to buy the Harvard Classics book collection.

The 17-year-old joined the Houston Buffaloes, a Cardinals farm club in the Class A Texas League, in 1939, but was soon sent down to New Iberia, Louisiana, in the Class D Evangeline League. He pitched a no-hitter in August and followed that with a one-hitter in his next start. He struck out 212 batters in 163 innings, a phenomenal accomplishment in that era. (No major-league starter struck out one batter per inning until 16 years later.) Pollet was deemed ready for the fast Texas League in 1940.

He was ready. Pollet won his first 12 decisions for Houston in 1940, celebrating his 19th birthday during the streak. He posted a 20-7 record with a 2.88 ERA.

He lost one game to Dizzy Dean, who was trying to come back from arm trouble with Tulsa.

Despite that strong showing, Pollet returned to Houston in 1941. The Cardinals had the majors' largest farm system and usually required their prospects to serve a long apprenticeship. He opened the season with three straight shutouts, the middle one a no-hitter against Shreveport. In August he won his 20th game, with a league-record 1.16 ERA. Cardinals general manager Branch Rickey watched that 20th win and broke his rule against calling up players in midseason, because Houston was 24 games in front of its nearest rival on the way to a third straight pennant.

The Cardinals were locked in a tight pennant race with the Brooklyn Dodgers. Manager Billy Southworth immediately put Pollet into the rotation. In his first start he was nursing a 3-2 lead over the Boston Braves when he let the potential tying and winning runs reach base in the ninth. Southworth came out to relieve him, but the rookie protested, "Hell, I'm not in a spot, Mr.

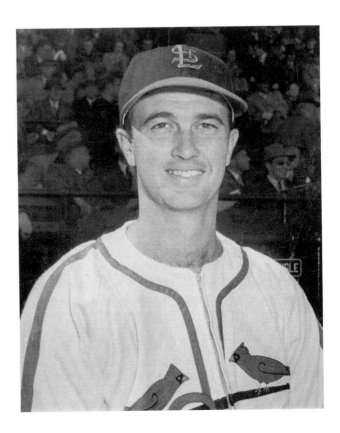

Southworth. I like spots like this." He stayed in the game and won.

Pollet started eight times down the stretch, winning five, losing two, and posting a 1.93 ERA. *Sporting News* publisher J.G. Taylor Spink dubbed him "the eleventh-hour sensation of this red-hot N.L. race." Despite his late-season heroics and those of 20-year-old outfielder Stan Musial, who batted .426 in 12 games, St. Louis finished 2½ games behind the Brooklyn Dodgers.

Rickey characteristically had plenty to say about the rookie: "He has inherent intellect. He was born with it and it shows in his pitching. What I mean is that he knows how to pitch and can put the ball just about where it should be pitched. ... No, Howard hasn't the greatest fastball, but it's a good one. It's the variations of his speed and curves that count. He uses three speeds on his fast one and his curve comes up at different paces. The sameness of his delivery also is a fine asset. He has a technique all his own."

Dick McCann of *The Sporting News* described the 20-year-old as "a soft-spoken, mild-mannered, honestly modest and quite model young man." Shortstop Marty Marion, who roomed with Pollet for a time, remembered him as "a good Catholic boy ... the calmest person I ever saw."

After the season Pollet married 18-year-old Virginia Clark, a Houston girl he had met at a skating rink. Described as "a vivacious blonde" and known as Ginger, she was studying piano at Loyola University in New Orleans. Howard (the name he preferred over "Howie") spent the balance of the offseason working as a department-store detective in New Orleans.

Pollet developed a sore arm during 1942 spring training and was in and out of the starting rotation in the first half of the season. He didn't start a game for seven weeks in July and August, but by mid-September was taking his regular turn. He pitched 27 times, only 13 of them starts, and registered an excellent 2.88 ERA and a 7-5 record.

The 1942 Cardinals won 106 games, but barely edged out Brooklyn in a classic pennant race. Another rookie, Johnny Beazley, joined veteran Mort Cooper as the aces of the pitching staff. In the World Series against the Yankees, Pollet relieved in the sixth inning of Game

Four with the score tied and threw one pitch to retire the side. He was replaced by a pinch-hitter as the Cardinals staged a winning rally in the top of the seventh.

Pollet was the pitcher of record when his club took the lead, but the three official scorers awarded the win to Max Lanier, who held the Yankees scoreless over the final three innings. The Cardinals won the Series in five games, and each player took home a full share of $6,192.53, much more than Pollet's annual salary.

World War II was under way and draft calls were claiming more and more ballplayers. Pollet went to work in a Houston defense plant in the offseason. When his draft board summoned him for a physical, he appealed for a deferment from military service because he was supporting his widowed mother and sister. (Being married didn't matter under the draft rules at the time unless a man had a child born before Pearl Harbor.)

Pollet's 1943 season showed every sign that he was living up to his promise. In July he had an 8-4 record with five shutouts. He had pitched three straight shutouts and 28 consecutive scoreless innings. He was chosen for the All-Star team, but his draft board had classified him 1-A, available for immediate induction. On the day the All-Star Game was played, Pollet enlisted in the Army Air Force. At the end of the season he was named the league's ERA champion at 1.75. (Ten complete games were required to qualify for the championship; Pollet completed 12 in his half-season.)

Pollet's military training took him to Miami Beach, Santa Ana, California, and Las Vegas, but he washed out of advanced gunnery school and never received a commission. In 1944 Private Pollet won 11 of 13 games for the San Antonio Aviation Cadet Center team. A Cardinal teammate, Sergeant Enos Slaughter, was San Antonio's star with a .414 average. Pollet went to the Pacific with military all-star teams in 1945 and continued to play exhibitions for the troops after the war ended. There is no mention in contemporary accounts of any combat service before he was discharged in November 1945.

Eddie Dyer had been named the Cardinals' manager for 1946. Pollet had settled in Houston, his wife's hometown as well as Dyer's. The men were so close that

Pollet had given Dyer his power of attorney while he was in the military service. When he rejoined the Cardinals in spring training, teammates called him "Eddie's boy."

He was Eddie's main man on the mound. In his first start Pollet tacked seven more scoreless innings onto the 28-inning streak he had left behind when he went into the Army three years earlier.

The Cardinals had a turbulent season. St. Louis had ten pitchers of prime age returning from military service, but two of them, Howard Krist and Johnny Grodzicki, never recovered from their war wounds. Left-hander Ernie White, a 17-game winner in 1941, had fought through a freezing winter in the Battle of the Bulge and come home with a dead arm. None of those three ever won another big-league game. Johnny Beazley, the rookie sensation of 1942, had ruined his arm pitching for an Army team in an exhibition against the Cardinals; his career was effectively over. Another prewar prospect, Hank Nowak, had been killed in action.

Two other pitchers, Max Lanier and Fred Martin, and second baseman Lou Klein defected to the Mexican League, which was tempting big-league players with fat salary offers. The Cardinals survived a scare when their superstar, Stan Musial, turned down a reported $50,000 signing bonus from the Mexicans, nearly four times his big-league salary.

After Lanier and Martin jumped the team, rookie manager Dyer said, "I felt like our pennant chances had been shot out from under us." As Dyer recalled it, Pollet came to his hotel room and said, "'Skipper, we're all going to have to carry a little extra load. I'll do my part. Give me a day's rest after I start a game and I can relieve if you need me. Then another day of rest and I can start again.' … Howie wasn't a robust fellow, but his heart was stout and I'll never forget it."

Pollet's friend Dyer took him up on that offer, and may have ruined his career. Pollet started 32 games, relieved in eight more and pitched a league-high 266 innings. His 2.10 ERA led the league as he finished 21-10. In August he was rushed into a game in relief without a proper warm-up and strained muscles behind his shoulder, but he didn't miss a start.

Two teams built by Branch Rickey, the Cardinals and Dodgers, finished tied for the National League lead. Both clubs had a chance to win the pennant on the final day, but both lost.

Pollet started the first playoff game in major-league history in a best-of-three series. He beat Brooklyn, 4-2. In Game Two, 15-game winner Murry Dickson and his roommate Harry Brecheen put the Dodgers away to send St. Louis to the World Series for the fourth time in five years.

Pollet opened the Series against the Boston Red Sox on four days' rest. He took a 2-1 lead into the ninth inning, but gave up the tying run with two out. Dyer sent him back to the mound in the tenth. Red Sox first baseman Rudy York had been embarrassed in his first three at-bats, but he told his teammates, "He's gonna throw me a changeup one time, and when he does, I'm gonna hit it." Pollet did and York did. His homer gave Boston a 3-2 victory.

During the game it was reported, Pollet was digging his fingernails into his palm to fight the pain in his shoulder. He said he lay awake all night afterward, hurting. The Series was tied at two games apiece when he started Game Five. Three of the first four Red Sox batters got base hits and Pollet was relieved after throwing only ten pitches. The Cardinals won the Series in seven games on Enos Slaughter's fabled "mad dash" from first to home with the winning run.

Pollet finished fourth behind Musial in the National League Most Valuable Player voting. At a dinner in Houston after the Series, Dyer said, "There was a lot of kidding among the Cardinals about Pollet being 'Eddie Dyer's boy.' Well, that suits me and I think it suits Howard, for Pollet is the type of man I'd like to have as a son or as a brother." But his future was in doubt at age 25.

Doctors treated Pollet's shoulder during the offseason and Dyer reported he was recovering. But he lost his first three starts in 1947 and uncharacteristically walked eight batters in his first victory. Later he said, "Every pitch hurt. I began to pitch with a half-motion, using my elbow instead of my back … and I began to feel a lump in my elbow. It frightened me. I was afraid I was through." He started 24 games, winning 9 and losing 11, and his ERA more than doubled to 4.34. After the season surgeons removed a bone spur from his elbow.

By this time Pollet had gone to work for Dyer's Houston insurance agency and was taking insurance courses at the University of Houston in the offseason. Another member of the 1946 championship team, utility infielder Joffre Cross, also began a long career with the firm. Cardinals pitcher George Munger later worked for Dyer in the winters.

A 1948 spring-training headline in *The Sporting News* asked, "Will Pollet and Musial Regain '46 Form?" Stan the Man had suffered from appendicitis and had batted "only" .312, 53 points below his MVP performance of 1946.

Musial rebounded with the best season of his career, leading the league in practically every batting category and falling just one home run short of the Triple Crown. Pollet's comeback attempt was not nearly as successful. He won his first four decisions, but was dropped from the rotation for nearly three weeks in July. Although he finished with a 13-8 record, his 4.54 ERA was 10 percent worse than the league average.

The 1949 season started no better. Pollet was battered for 11 runs in his first 6⅓ innings and was sent to the bullpen. Dyer, who had been sticking up for him, now said, "You've started your last game until you throw the damn ball hard." He waited 2½ weeks for his next start, and soon began to look like the 1946-model Pollet. In one stretch he won five straight games and allowed just four runs in 40 innings.

"I think I was too cautious about my arm last year," he told reporters. "I didn't dare try to break off my sharp curve until July. Now I throw hard and give it the full snap of my wrist without thinking. Most important, though, is that I have my control."

Back in top form, Pollet appeared in his only All-Star Game in July, but the American Leaguers torched him for three runs in his only inning. The Cardinals were in first place from August 17 until the last week of the season, when they lost four in a row and finished one game behind the Dodgers. Pollet apparently ran out of gas in September; he didn't start for 12 days before winning his 20th in the season's final game. He finished 20-9 with a league-leading five shutouts and a 2.77

ERA, third-best in the league. *The Sporting News* named him the NL Pitcher of the Year.

Pollet was a left-handed stylist rather than a power pitcher, and was known for sharp control and a fine changeup. His catcher in his early years with the Cardinals, Walker Cooper, said, "Pollet's change actually moved up and in on a right-handed hitter." Jackie Robinson credited him with "the best changeup in the league." Joe Garagiola, who caught Pollet on three teams, called him "an intelligent pitcher." In pregame meetings, Garagiola remembered, "He didn't say how he'd pitch the hitter, or what he'd throw him, but where to play the batter."

In a purple flight of fancy, longtime St. Louis writer Bob Broeg described Pollet as having "the sensitive features of a symphony violinist." Broeg soared on: "The virtuoso of variable velocities, he can throw his fast ball and curve at several disconcerting degrees of speed, keeps batters off stride constantly and he's got the courage to throw his change of pace and get it over the plate when he's behind in the ball and strike count."

Pollet earned a raise to a reported $25,000 in 1950, but had to hold out until the first week of spring training to get it. His 3.29 ERA was 30 percent better than the league average, but his record slipped to 14-13 as the Cardinals dropped to fifth place. That cost Eddie Dyer his job. St. Louis's attendance had fallen by more than 300,000 and owner Fred Saigh cut salaries across the board. When Pollet balked at a pay cut, Saigh called him "unreasonable." Pollet held out until just before Opening Day, and Saigh put him on the trading block.

After an 0-3 start in 1951, Pollet was swapped to the last-place Pittsburgh Pirates a few days before his 30th birthday with reliever Ted Wilks, outfielder Bill Howerton, and infielder Dick Cole for outfielder Wally Westlake and left-hander Cliff Chambers. He joined his former teammate, right-hander Murry Dickson, who had been sold to Pittsburgh in 1949.

On June 22, 1951, Pollet was warming up to start against Brooklyn when several lights in the Forbes Field outfield blinked out. After repairs were made, he delivered the first pitch at 10:44 P.M. The game was interrupted by rain after midnight, but Pollet came back to the mound after a 36-minute delay. Brooklyn won 8-4, with the last out recorded at 1:56 A.M. It was the latest completed game in major-league history to that point.

The highlight of Pollet's season came on August 28, when he stopped the New York Giants' 16-game winning streak with a six-hit shutout. The Giants were surging from behind to catch the Dodgers and win the pennant on Bobby Thomson's "shot heard 'round the world." At the other end of the standings, Pollet went 6-10 for Pittsburgh after the trade with an ugly 5.04 ERA. Dickson's 20 wins helped boost the Pirates to next-to-last. Sportswriter Milt Richman wrote that Pollet was "now considered strictly a junk pitcher."

Pittsburgh reclaimed last place in 1952 as Pollet lost 16 games against seven wins, with a 4.12 ERA. Dickson went from 20 wins to 21 defeats for a team that lost 112 games.

In June 1953 Pollet's ERA was above 10.00 when he was traded to another perennial loser, the Chicago Cubs, in the biggest deal of the year. Branch Rickey sent Pittsburgh's best player, Ralph Kiner, along with Pollet, catcher Joe Garagiola, and outfielder George Metkovich to Chicago for outfielder Gene Hermanski, catcher Toby Atwell, first baseman Preston Ward, third baseman George Freese, outfielder Bob Addis, pitcher Bob Schultz, and cash estimated at $100,000 to $150,000. Kiner had won or shared the NL's home-run championship in each of his first seven seasons, but Rickey wanted to dump his $65,000 salary. Rickey had told him, "We can finish last without you." He was right.

St. Louis Post-Dispatch writer J. Roy Stockton said, "Pollet is well over the hill." He was 32. He served as a spot starter and reliever for the Cubs over the next 2½ seasons until the club released him in the fall of 1955.

Pollet's former Cardinal teammate Marty Marion, manager of the White Sox, gave him a tryout the next spring. Chicago released him in May, but re-signed him a week later after trading two pitchers. The White Sox dropped Pollet for good in July, but he caught on with the Pirates. He wasn't ready to quit, as he told a reporter: "I have six children to support and they cost money. Our milk and food bill alone is $225 a month. And with September coming up, they'll all need new clothes." The Pirates were still where he had left them,

near the bottom of the league. He pitched creditably in relief, but was released after the season and retired. He had won 131 games and lost 116; his 3.51 ERA was 13 percent better than the league average.

Pollet returned to full-time work with the Eddie Dyer Insurance Agency. Dyer made Pollet and Joffre Cross partners in the business. Pollet's teammates had recognized his business knowledge; they elected him player representative for the Cardinals, Pirates, and Cubs. In those days the Players Association was a tame company union that did not even call itself a union. The player rep's job involved pressing such complaints as poor showers and inconvenient scheduling, according to historian Charles P. Korr.

Pollet went back to baseball in 1959 when the Cardinals' new manager, Houston resident Solly Hemus, named him pitching coach. In spring training *The Sporting News* credited him with "a new idea": counting pitches instead of innings in his pitchers' exhibition outings. Pitcher Jim Brosnan wrote, "Howie is a quiet, soft-spoken gentleman, a type not ordinarily given to accepting coaching jobs." Longtime reliever Lindy McDaniel said Pollet switched him from a side-arm delivery to overhand, enabling him to put more movement on the ball.

Hemus, a firebrand in the Leo Durocher mold, alienated many of the players and was fired midway through the 1961 season. His successor, Johnny Keane, was also a Houston resident and Pollet's friend. Keane led St. Louis to the world championship in 1964, but it was a year of tumult. Bing Devine, the general manager who built the championship team, was fired in midseason and the owner, August A. Busch, Jr., was planning to replace Keane with Durocher until the club got hot late in the season. After the Cardinals beat the Yankees in the World Series, Keane abruptly quit to become the Pinstripes' new manager.

Pollet left the Cardinals to join the Houston Astros as pitching coach in 1965, then went back to the insurance business. Eddie Dyer had died in 1964, and Pollet, Cross, and Eddie Dyer, Jr. ran the agency.

Howard Pollet died at the age of 53 on August 8, 1974, after a long illness. He was survived by Virginia, his wife of nearly 33 years, five sons, and two daughters.

SOURCES

Associated Press, stories in the *New York Times*, *New York World-Telegram*, *Washington Post*, and *Chicago Tribune*.

The Sporting News, various issues, 1939-1974.

Brosnan, Jim, *The Long Season* (New York: Harper & Row, 1960).

Giglio, James N., *Musial: From Stash to Stan the Man* (Columbia: University of Missouri Press, 2001).

Golenbock, Peter, *The Spirit of St. Louis* (New York: Spike/Avon Books, 2000).

James, Bill, and Rob Neyer, *The Neyer/James Guide to Pitchers* (New York: Fireside/Simon & Schuster, 2004).

Korr, Charles P., *The End of Baseball as We Knew It* (Urbana and Chicago: University of Illinois Press, 2002).

Moffi, Larry, "Mel Parnell," in *This Side of Cooperstown* (Iowa City: University of Iowa Press, 1996).

Turner, Frederick, *When The Boys Came Back* (New York: Henry Holt and Co., 1996).

U.S. Census, Orleans Parish, Louisiana, 1920.

Unidentified clippings in Howie Pollet player file, National Baseball Hall of Fame Library, Cooperstown, New York.

Early Wynn

By David Fleitz

CHICAGO FANS WERE OUTRAGED WHEN the White Sox traded their most popular player, Minnie Miñoso, to Cleveland in December 1957 with Fred Hatfield for Early Wynn and Al Smith. Wynn was a 37-year-old right-handed pitcher who had posted a losing record for the Indians that season, and his best days appeared to be behind him. However, Wynn joined with Billy Pierce to give the White Sox a formidable one-two punch at the top of their rotation, and his Cy Young Award-winning performance in 1959 led the club to its first American League pennant since 1919. Four years later, at age 43, he became the 14th member of baseball's 300-win club.

Early Wynn, Jr., whose family claimed Scotch-Irish and Native American descent, was born in Hartford, Alabama, on January 6, 1920, to Early Wynn, Sr. and his wife, Blanche. Hartford is a small town surrounded by peanut and cotton fields in Geneva County, which borders the Florida Panhandle in the southeastern part of the state. Early Sr. was an auto mechanic and a semipro ballplayer. Early Jr. earned ten cents an hour hauling 500-pound bales of cotton after school. He concentrated on baseball after breaking his leg in a high-school football practice, and at age 17 traveled to Sanford, Florida, to attend a baseball camp operated by the Washington Senators. Legend has it that Early, a husky 6-footer who weighed about 200 pounds, arrived at camp in his bare feet. He did not, Early told writer Roger Kahn years later. "[B]ut I was wearing coveralls."[1] A Washington scout, Clyde Milan, was impressed with Wynn's fastball and signed him to a contract. The young pitcher dropped out of high school and began his professional career in 1937 with Sanford, the Senators' farm team in the Class D Florida State League.

After a 16-11 season, Wynn advanced to the Charlotte Hornets of the Class B Piedmont League, where he remained for the next three years. The Senators gave him a trial in Washington at the end of the 1939 season, though Wynn was not yet ready for major-league action and went 0-2 in three games. He spent all of 1940 in

Charlotte, and then a good season at Springfield in the Class A Eastern League in 1941 (16-12, 2.56 earned-run average) brought him to Washington to stay. In 1942 he made 28 starts for the Senators, posting a 10-16 mark with a 5.12 ERA as a 22-year-old with little more than a fastball in his arsenal.

In 1939 Early married Mabel Allman, from Morganton, North Carolina, and the couple had a son named Joe Early Wynn. Tragically, the marriage ended prematurely. In December of 1942, Mabel was killed in an automobile accident in Charlotte, where the Wynns lived during the winter months. Early was left with a baby to raise, with the assistance of his relatives. He won 18 games for Washington in 1943, but fell to 8-17 in 1944 as he led the American League in losses. He married Lorraine Follin that September, shortly after entering the US Army. He served in the Tank Corps in the Philippines, spending all of the 1945 season and

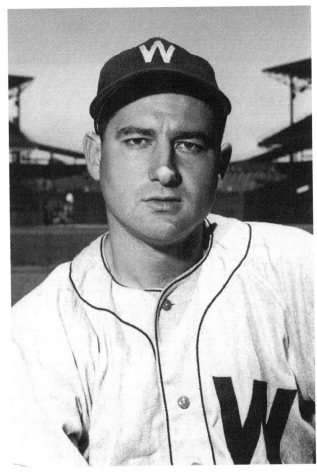

part of the next in the military before rejoining the Senators.

At this time, Wynn owned an impressive fastball, but had only a mediocre changeup to complement it. He was inconsistent, posting a 17-15 record in 1947 and an 8-19 mark in 1948. Still, he was undeniably talented, and the Cleveland Indians coveted his services. Bill Veeck, the Indians' owner, tried to acquire Wynn in a trade before the 1948 season, but was rebuffed by Washington owner Clark Griffith. In November 1948 Veeck acquired pitcher Joe Haynes, Griffith's son-in-law, from the Chicago White Sox. Veeck then offered Haynes to the Senators for Wynn, and Griffith agreed, sending first baseman Mickey Vernon with Wynn for Haynes, pitcher Ed Klieman, and first baseman Eddie Robinson.

The Indians figured that Wynn would become a big winner if he could develop more pitches, so the club assigned pitching coach Mel Harder to teach him how to throw a curve and a slider. "I could throw the ball when I came here [to Cleveland]," recalled Wynn years later in *The Sporting News*, "but Mel made a pitcher out of me."[2] By mid-1949 he had mastered the curve and slider, and began to use a knuckleball as an offspeed delivery. With a new array of pitches at his command, Wynn joined the ranks of top hurlers in 1950. He won 18 games and led the American League in earned-run average with a 3.20 mark.

Early, nicknamed Gus, got along well with his teammates, but was a grim, scowling presence on the mound. "That space between the white lines — that's my office, that's where I conduct my business," he told sportswriter Red Smith. "You take a look at the batter's box, and part of it belongs to the hitter. But when he crowds in just that hair, he's stepping into my office, and nobody comes into my office without an invitation when I'm going to work."[3] With his large frame, grizzled appearance, and willingness to knock down opposing hitters, Wynn stood out as one of the most intimidating pitchers in the game. Roger Kahn, in his book *A Season in the Sun*, described how the pitcher once brushed back his teenage son during a batting-practice session at Yankee Stadium. "You shouldn't crowd me," snarled the elder Wynn. As he explained to Kahn, "I've got a right to knock down anybody holding a bat."[4]

Wynn hated losing, and was never afraid to throw at batters who got too close to the plate, or hit line drives at him. Some called him a headhunter, but Early regarded close pitches as part of the game. "If they are going to outlaw the inside pitch," said Wynn in an article he wrote for *Sport* magazine in 1956, "they ought to eliminate line drives and sharp grounders hit through the pitcher's box." To those who suggested that he would throw at his own mother, Early famously replied, "I would if she were crowding the plate."[5] One day Mickey Mantle drilled a liner through the box for a single. Early then fired several pickoff attempts at Mantle's legs. "You'll never be a big winner until you start hating the hitter," he told rookie pitcher Gary Bell. "That guy with the bat is trying to take away your bread and butter. You've got to fight him every second."[6]

His toughness and durability made Wynn part of one of the greatest pitching rotations of all time in Cleveland, with Wynn, Bob Lemon, Bob Feller, and Mike Garcia all posting 20-win seasons during the early 1950s. Under the tutelage of Mel Harder and manager Al Lopez, Wynn won 20 games or more in a season four times for Cleveland, and anchored the rotation that led the Indians to the American League pennant in 1954. In the World Series that year Early lost to the New York Giants 3-1 in the second game, giving up three runs in seven innings. He did not have the chance to pitch again in the Series, as the Giants cruised to the title in four games.

Early and Lorraine made their permanent home in Nokomis, Florida, where they raised his son, Joe, and their daughter, Shirley. He spent his leisure hours hunting, driving powerboats, and flying his own Cessna 170 single-engine plane. Beginning in 1955, Wynn produced a regular column for the *Cleveland News*, titled "The Wynn Mill," and donated the money he earned from the effort to the Elks Club in Nokomis. Though he had dropped out of high school, Early wrote without the assistance of a ghostwriter, and his frank assessments of umpires, league policies, and his own management rankled Cleveland team officials and strained his relationship with general manager Hank Greenberg.

Wynn notched another 20-win campaign in 1956, but in 1957 he posted his first losing season in Cleveland (14-17, with his ERA leaping from 2.72 to 4.31) despite leading the league in strikeouts. The careers of both Bob Feller and Bob Lemon drew to a close during this time, and perhaps the Indians believed that the 37-year-old Wynn was fading as well. On December 4, 1957, the team traded Early to the Chicago White Sox. The White Sox inserted a clause in his contract that prohibited the pitcher from writing for newspapers, but the team compensated him for the lost income. Reunited with his old Cleveland manager Al Lopez, who had resigned and taken the Chicago job after the 1956 season, Early compiled a 14-16 record in 1958, leading the league in strikeouts again.

Wynn was still a tough competitor, sometimes throwing chairs in the locker room after losses. He hated to be taken out of games, though his advancing age often made it necessary to use relievers to finish his wins. In 1992 Al Lopez described Wynn's competitiveness to biographer Wes Singletary. "So this one day Early was arguing with the umpire," said Lopez, "when I came out there and he threw the ball at me, hitting me in the stomach. It was more of a flip/toss but the press played it up. I said give me the goddamned ball and don't be throwing it at me. After the game he came and apologized to me. I said, Early, I know how you feel but the people upstairs, the fans and media, they see that and think you're mad at me. I told him don't get mad at me, get mad at the guys who are hitting."[7]

Wynn had suffered from gout since the 1950 season and pitched in pain for the last half of his career. Still, he kept in good shape, and his fastball remained sharp as he approached his 40th birthday. Lopez kept Early at the top of the Chicago rotation, and in 1959, everything clicked for both Wynn and the White Sox. On May 1 the 39-year-old pitched a one-hit shutout against the Boston Red Sox and hit a home run that provided the only scoring in the 1-0 victory. He led the league in innings pitched, started that season's first All-Star Game for the American League, and won a league-leading 22 games, pitching the White Sox to their first American League flag in 40 years. Early's 21st win of the season, a 4-2 victory over Cleveland on September

22, clinched the pennant and set off a night of celebration on Chicago's South Side. At season's end, Wynn won the major-league Cy Young Award and finished third in the American League Most Valuable Player balloting behind teammates Nellie Fox and Luis Aparicio.

The White Sox faced the Los Angeles Dodgers in the 1959 World Series, and Early pitched seven shutout innings in the opening game, teaming with reliever Gerry Staley to defeat the Dodgers by an 11-0 score. However, he struggled in the fourth contest, played at the Los Angeles Coliseum before 92,650 fans. He failed to complete the third inning of a game that the White Sox eventually lost, 5-4, though Staley was the losing pitcher. In the sixth game, played in Chicago, a six-run Dodger explosion in the fourth inning knocked Wynn out of the game and saddled him with the Series-ending defeat.

Wynn's 13 wins in 1960 left him with 284 career victories, and the pitcher announced his intention of joining the 300-win club before his retirement. He pitched well in 1961, with eight wins in his ten decisions, but arm soreness, caused by gout, ended his season in July. He gave up eating meat in an attempt to control his gout problem, but the pain persisted, causing problems with his legs and right hand. He fell short of his 300th win in 1962, posting a 7-15 record while relying mostly on a slider and a knuckleball. His seventh win, a complete-game effort against the Senators on September 8, was the 299th of his career, but Early failed in three subsequent attempts to gain number 300. The White Sox were convinced that the 42-year-old pitcher had reached the end of the line, and in November the team released him.

The White Sox invited Wynn to their 1963 spring-training camp, but he failed to make the team. He returned home to Florida, where he stayed in shape and waited for a call from another club. A few teams offered Early one-game contracts, seeking to capitalize on his quest for 300 wins, but Wynn held out for a season-long deal. In June his old club, the Cleveland Indians, signed Early for the rest of the season and put him in the starting rotation. On July 13, in his fourth start of 1963, he pitched five innings against the Kansas

City Athletics and left the game with a 5-4 lead. Reliever Jerry Walker held the Athletics scoreless the rest of the way, giving Early his 300th, and final, win. He was the first man to win 300 games in the American League since Boston's Lefty Grove reached the mark in 1941.

Wynn started only one more game for Cleveland and retired at the end of the season. His career record stood at 300-244 with an ERA of 3.54. Early remained with the Indians, succeeding Mel Harder as Cleveland's pitching coach in 1964. He moved to the Minnesota Twins in 1967, and then managed in the minor leagues for one season. In 1972, in his fourth year of eligibility, Wynn was elected to the Baseball Hall of Fame. He had been disappointed in not gaining the honor earlier, once calling the institution the "Hall of Shame" in an interview. After his election, he told *The Sporting News*, "I would have been happier if I'd made it the first year. I don't think I'm as thrilled as I would have been if that had happened. But naturally I'm happy. So is my wife. We've had a long wait."[8]

Early Wynn worked as a broadcaster for the Toronto Blue Jays and the Chicago White Sox after his election to the Hall of Fame, and also owned a restaurant and bowling alley for a time. He fully expected to be the last of the 300-game winners, and often referred to himself in such terms in interviews. Nineteen years passed between Wynn's final victory in 1963 and Gaylord Perry's ascension to the 300-win club in 1982. As it was, Early saw six pitchers, including Perry, surpass his total during the 1980s and '90s. By the end of the 2013 season, Wynn was one of 24 pitchers with 300 wins or more.

Wynn retired during the mid-1980s and resided in Nokomis until his health began to fail after the death of his wife, Lorraine, in 1994. He suffered a heart attack and a series of strokes during the final years of his life, and spent his remaining days in an assisted-living center in Venice, Florida, where he died on April 4, 1999, at the age of 79.

This article originally appeared in the book *Go-Go To Glory—The 1959 Chicago White Sox* (ACTA, 2009), edited by Don Zminda.

SOURCES

Appel, Marty, and Burt Goldblatt, *Baseball's Best: The Hall of Fame Gallery* (New York: McGraw-Hill, 1980), 400-401.

Kahn, Roger. *A Season in the Sun* (Lincoln, Nebraska: University of Nebraska Press, 2000).

Kahn, Roger. "Early Wynn: The Story of a Hard Loser," *Sport*, March 1956.

Singletary, Wes. "Señor: The Managerial Career of Al Lopez," *The Sunland Tribune* (Journal of the Tampa Historical Society) 19, November 1993, 57-66.

Wynn, Early. "The Four Sides of the Beanball Argument: The Pitcher's Side," *Sport*, January 1956.

The Sporting News, May 14, 1942; October 7, 1959; June 15, 1963; February 5, 1972.

New York Times, April 6, 1999.

NOTES

1 Roger Kahn, "Early Wynn: The Story of a Hard Loser," *Sport*, March 1956.

2 *The Sporting News*, June 15, 1963, 7.

3 Red Smith, *Red Smith on Baseball* (New York: Ivan R. Dee, 2000), 325.

4 Roger Kahn, *A Season in the Sun* (Lincoln, Nebraska: University of Nebraska Press, 2000), 108.

5 Early Wynn, "The Four Sides of the Beanball Argument: The Pitcher's Side," *Sport*, January 1956.

6 *The Sporting News*, October 7, 1959.

7 Wes Singletary, "Señor: The Managerial Career of Al Lopez," *The Sunland Tribune* (Journal of the Tampa Historical Society) 19, November 1993, 57-66.

8 *The Sporting News*, February 5, 1972.

Art Passarella

By Rob Edelman

ACROSS THE DECADES, BASEBALL players from the celebrated to the obscure have traded in their spikes for movie or TV scripts. Some—Chuck Connors, Bob Uecker, and Greg Goossen come to mind—enjoyed careers in the entertainment industry as, respectively, the star of TV's *The Rifleman*, a sometime film and TV actor and full-time raconteur, and the longtime stand-in for Gene Hackman.

Such also was the case with Art Passarella, a big-league umpire from 1941-42 and 1945-53. After leaving the majors, Passarella regularly worked in front of the camera—and it is not surprising that a Google search for him results in as many showbiz as baseball-related hits. But Passarella did enjoy a healthy career in the majors, and he once offered a spot-on definition of an umpire: "...(W)hen the game starts there has to be a boss, a guy who has the say-so. History has shown that the umpire should have this authority. So I know where I stand and I call 'em as I see 'em regardless of what anybody else thinks."[1]

Arthur Matthew Passarella was born on December 23, 1909, in Rochester, New York. He was the eldest of four children—he had two brothers and a sister—and around his tenth birthday his family moved to Los Angeles.[2] Although many parents are averse to their offspring's desire for a career in the arts, Passarella's situation was the opposite. In his youth, he studied the violin for a decade and his father hoped that he would become a professional musician. But young Arthur had other ideas, wishing instead to be a major-league ballplayer. (A similar child-parental conflict was dramatized in the 1930s in playwright Clifford Odets' *Golden Boy*. Here, the father of Joe Bonaparte, the title character, pressures his son to be a classical violinist, but Joe yearns to take up prizefighting rather than ballplaying.)

In the early 1930s Passarella began playing semipro ball in the Los Angeles area and was proficient enough to sign a couple of professional contracts. Eventually, he rose to the Class B Decatur Commodores (Three-I League) but his baseball skills—not to mention a busted knee—prevented him from moving any higher.

So he switched to umpiring and, by 1937, was working semipro diamonds throughout Los Angeles. He also umpired a few games at a tryout at Wrigley Field, where he caught the attention of Russ Hall, a two-year big leaguer (1898, 1901) and secretary of the Association of Professional Ball Players of America. This led to Passarella's being hired to ump in the Class D Evangeline League for $80 per month; ten days later, his paycheck increased to $100 when he switched to the Class C Cotton States League. The Pine Bluff Judges were one of the league teams; while umping in the Arkansas town, Passarella met and began dating Elvina Laurich, whom *The Sporting News* described as "a woman fan [who] stood out as about the only one who didn't razz the umpire."[3] The two wed on March 14, 1938, in Garland, Arkansas, and purchased a home in Pine Bluff.[4]

Next, Passarella moved on to the Class A-1 Texas League, where he umped from 1938 to 1940. League President Alvin Gardner was impressed with Passarella, telling *The Sporting News* that he "learned faster than

any umpire ... in the league in years."[5] Connie Mack and Joe McCarthy observed him in exhibition games and liked what they saw. American League President Will Harridge sent Tommy Connolly, his supervisor of umpires, to check out Passarella, and Connolly also was impressed. So on November 10, 1940, Harridge announced the purchase of two new AL umpires, Ernie Stewart and Passarella. It was noted in *The Sporting News* that both would be "assigned to service for spring exhibition games, where their work will determine whether they will be retained or farmed out for seasoning."[6] Passarella's efforts were deemed sufficient and he made his AL debut on April 16, 1941. Two years later, he candidly recalled, "My first major-league game behind the plate is easy to remember. I walked out of the dugout and saw Bob Feller warming up. Boy, was I scared. I was my own worst enemy that day, nervous and unsure of myself. But I got by all right. Feller beat John Niggeling of the Browns and I didn't get into any trouble!"[7]

A couple of weeks after Passarella's hire, *The Sporting News* ran a feature article spotlighting his career—and his personality. "He will take a lot of color into major company," wrote reporter Flint Dupre. "Passarella once was credited in the box score with a run kicked in, which he doesn't consider exactly a high point in his short career. He explains that a man was on third base, when the pitcher threw the ball. 'The catcher dropped the throw and in trying to get out of the way, I kicked the ball into the dugout, with the runner from third scoring,' says Passarella. 'I was credited with a run kicked in and the players had considerable fun at my expense.' " The article also foreshadowed his future work as a mentor to wannabe umpires. "He aided a lot of kids in Dallas last winter," wrote Dupre, "and now is doing the same in San Antonio, where he is working in the capacity of a public relations man in a large hotel." Dupre also commented on his stature: "He looks like a small man, because of his build, but actually weighs 182 pounds and stands five feet 11."[8]

Passarella umped in the AL for the following two seasons. While quickly developing a reputation as a top-flight arbiter, he was prone to the kind of freak on-field mishaps that characterized his career. For example, during the 1942 season, a foul tip off the bat of the Red Sox' Bobby Doerr left him with a broken mask, a cut lip and nose, and a pair of chipped teeth.

At the start of the 1943 season, Passarella's AL career was halted temporarily—but not because of injury. On April 18 he became the first major-league arbiter to enter the US Army during World War II. After his induction in Chicago, he was dispatched to Camp Grant, Illinois, where he took his basic training in the Medical Corps. Almost immediately, he began umpiring games between competing camp teams. "After all," he noted, regarding his leave from the majors, "I'm the same as other American boys and I want to get this thing over and get back to baseball." Of military baseball, he observed that the "difference between our games and games in the fine big league parks is great—but it's still the National Pastime—make no mistake about that. The boys won't do without it."[9]

While in the service, Passarella held a range of jobs including work as an MP and guard in a POW camp. Most significantly, during the spring of 1944, he began directing an umpire school at Camp Grant. As reported in the *Toledo Blade*, the school was "believed to be the first of its kind in the country." Its purpose was to "train soldiers planning umpiring careers after the war. A boom in baseball and softball in the postwar period, camp officials said, would create many umpiring jobs."[10]

Passarella was discharged from the Army on December 11, 1944, and he resumed his big-league career at the start of the 1945 season. His return to the AL was not stress-free. On June 20 he was umpire-in-chief in a game between the Chicago White Sox and St. Louis Browns at Sportsman's Park in St. Louis. Karl Scheel, a 23-year-old former semipro hurler and ex-marine who was Chicago's batting practice pitcher, began goading the Browns' bench. In the eighth inning several St. Louis players charged the White Sox dugout and began badgering Scheel in what manager Jimmy Dykes called "the most brutal" attack he had ever witnessed on a ball field. During the melee, fans entered the field; Passarella and his fellow umps needed police assistance to restore order. He submitted a report of the incident to the American League office, which resulted in fines imposed on Browns manager Luke

Sewell and several players. Outraged, Browns president Don Barnes declared that Dykes also should have been censured because he "egged on Scheel." Sewell agreed. "It seems to me there was guilt on both sides," he declared.[11]

When Passarella was separated from the military, the AL already had the required 12 arbiters. But he was rehired; at the start of the 1945 campaign, the league employed 13 umps, but this changed on August 15 when Ernie Stewart was fired. The reason given was "disloyalty," with Harridge claiming that he was causing dissension among his fellow arbiters. For Stewart's part, he noted that he merely was attempting to win higher salaries for himself and his colleagues. Stewart reported that on July 20 Passarella and fellow ump Hal Weafer were discussing the low pay of umpires with Commissioner Happy Chandler. At this time, Stewart was brought into the conversation and was asked by the commissioner to sound out other arbiters on the subject. After reporting to Chandler, Stewart noted, Harridge "found out about this, it made him mad, and he fired me."[12] Harridge, however, did not fault Passarella, and that year he umpired in his first World Series; he went on to work two others, in 1949 and 1952, and umped in the 1947 and 1951 All-Star Games.

As time passed, Passarella developed his own on-field style—and it was anything but low-key. Lou Adamie, the scoreboard operator at Sportsman's Park, was famed for his ability to accurately call balls and strikes and post them on the board before the home-plate ump signaled his decision. "I merely study the mannerisms of the umpires," Adamie explained. "I usually can tell whether it's a ball or a strike, but I can't call 'em on my own, so I look for some telltale mannerism which tips me off." Adamie described Passarella as the "most jittery" of the big-league arbiters: an ump who "jumps when about to shout 'Steeeriiike.'"[13] Not surprisingly then, Passarella occasionally was excessively theatrical. On May 22, 1949, he inspected the glove of White Sox hurler Clyde Shoun and determined that the location of its light-tinted manufacturer's label was in violation of baseball's equipment code. Shoun disagreed. The problem was solved when the label was removed from the glove with a pair of shears, but only after Passarella,

as reported in *The Sporting News*, "put on a noisy, gesturing performance."[14] Leonard Koppett described Passarella as "talkative and friendly ... [and] one of the best umpires to be stuck in a club car with." But Koppett added that "players would accuse him of showboating, of putting on an act."[15]

Like any person whose workplace is a ball field, Passarella experienced his share of on-field close calls and injuries. On July 8, 1945, James P. Dawson, writing about a Yankees-Tigers contest in the *New York Times*, reported, "In the Tigers' half of the inning a line single by [Hal] Newhouser almost decapitated Art Passarella, working back of second. He ducked just in time."[16] Then on May 12, 1946, in a game pitting the Senators and Athletics, he suffered a broken jaw when he was hit by a foul ball off the bat of Washington's Mickey Vernon. Ten days later, he returned to the field as home-plate ump in an Indians-Red Sox game and, as reported in *The Sporting News*, his "mask was nipped by Johnny Lazor's seventh-inning foul, but he suffered no ill effects."[17] Four days after that, on May 26, Passarella left the field after colliding with the Senators' Buddy Lewis in the first inning of a Washington-Philadelphia game. He did so again on August 30 after suffering a second jaw injury. This time, he was hit by a foul tip at Fenway Park.

Passarella's calls occasionally were not the most popular—and he sometimes felt the brunt of fan frustration. Wrote Louis Effrat in the August 6, 1946 *New York Times*, "While the majority of 25,067 fans booed, Mayor William O'Dwyer presented the Mayor's Trophy to Manager Bill Dickey of the Yankees, immediately after the American League club had beaten the Giants 3-2... The disapproval ... was not against Dickey or the mayor, but in protest against the decision of plate umpire Art Passarella, who called Joe DiMaggio safe at home with the tie-breaking run." As reported in *The Sporting News* on July 9, 1947, "Although umpire Art Passarella was standing right behind the play, 36,752 Cleveland cash customers and manager Lou Boudreau protested his decision calling George Dickey of the White Sox safe on a steal of second, from which he scored the winning run [on] June 29. Boudreau contended Dickey slid into the ball, held by Lou, but the umpire didn't see it that way." If any umpire is around long enough, he likely will find himself at ground zero of a high-profile play. On August 19, 1951, Passarella was the first-base umpire when Eddie Gaedel came to the plate to pinch-hit for the Browns. Gaedel was of course only 3-feet-7-inches tall and weighed 65 pounds—and Passarella and home-plate ump Ed Hurley immediately halted the game. Zach Taylor, the St. Louis skipper, produced the player's contract that Gaedel had signed with Browns owner Bill Veeck, and so the umps allowed him to bat.

Even more significantly, Passarella was at the center of a controversial play that occurred in the fifth game of the 1952 World Series. The Yankees were playing the Dodgers, and Passarella was the first-base ump. The series was tied at two games apiece and the game—in which Brooklyn starter Carl Erskine retired 19 straight Yankees—was tied, 5-5, in the bottom of the tenth inning. Yankee hurler Johnny Sain led off against Erskine and grounded to Jackie Robinson at second. Robby fielded the ball and threw it to Gil Hodges, Brooklyn's first sacker. It seemed that Sain was safe, but Passarella called him out. Sain and first-base coach Bill Dickey vehemently protested, but to no avail. The Dodgers won the game in the next inning, with Duke Snider doubling home the winning run.

Afterward, photos of the play clearly indicated that Passarella had blown the call. For one thing, Sain's foot touched the bag before the ball reached Hodges. For another, before catching the ball, Hodges took his foot off the bag. Red Patterson, the Yankees PR director, admonished Passarella for making "two lousy calls on a single play."[18] The *St. Louis Post-Dispatch's* J. Roy Stockton labeled the call the "worst decision" of the Series. Passarella responded by declaring that "pictures don't always tell the true story. I was on top of the play and called it as I saw it. That's the way I called it, and I'll stick to it."[19]

Commissioner Ford Frick added some much-needed insight into the hullabaloo, declaring:

It looks like Passarella called a wrong play, but if he did he's only human. I assure you it's not the first wrong call ever made by an umpire, if it was that. What's all the shouting about? Players make mistakes, too. So do

officials. So does the commissioner. A player makes an error, another forgets to cover a base, a pitcher makes a wild pitch, a catcher lets the ball get away from him. Very little is said. But once an umpire makes a wrong call, he is crucified. Why? An umpire is only human. He can make mistakes, too. All I'm interested in is whether he was in the right position to make a call. The picture shows he was.[20]

As the years passed, it seemed that Passarella was increasingly victimized by controversy and physical injury. In 1951 an ankle injury he incurred was originally believed to be a sprain; in August it was diagnosed as a fracture, thus ending Passarella's season. Then in an April 23, 1952, Yankees-Red Sox game, he angered Boston catcher Sammy White after being hit by a foul tip off the bat of Gene Woodling. A momentarily stunned and staggering Passarella instinctively grabbed White's shoulder, which displeased the rookie backstop. Later in the game, a second foul tip, this one off the bat of Hank Bauer, crushed Passarella's mask, and the ump had to be treated with icepacks. The following day, when he was umping at third base, a screaming line drive forced him to sprawl over backward to avoid being hit. Then on July 2 he was hospitalized in New York after pulling a muscle in the previous day's Yankees-Red Sox contest. In a May 15, 1953, Browns-Senators game, Passarella tossed Browns manager Marty Marion and coach Bob Scheffing in the eighth inning after thinking that they were protesting a called strike on Bob Elliott, their third sacker. Marion immediately declared that he was playing the game under protest. The following day, Passarella acknowledged that upon further review Marion and Scheffing were not disputing his call, but the protest was voided because the Browns had won by a 4-0 score. Then on July 5, the ump was right in the middle of a bench-clearing ruckus that resulted when the Tigers' Johnny Bucha, attempting to score from third base on a fly ball, barreled into the Browns' Clint Courtney.

Passarella's plight was summed up in a promotion sponsored by the Simmons mattress company, whose ad campaign awarded Beautyrest mattresses to deserving consumers. One of the "winners" was Passarella. Under a photo of him jawing with a ballplayer and published in the April 13, 1953, *Life* magazine was a caption that read: "Who needs rest more than an umpire? Every day during the season, nine innings of baseball and ten innings of headaches! To Art Passarella of the American League, the Simmons Company presents a Beautyrest mattress."

Still, it was a bit of a shock when, on November 4, 1953, just over a month before his 45th birthday, Passarella announced that he had submitted his resignation to Harridge. He declined to comment on the reason why he quit, and it remained a mystery if he had done so on his own volition or if he was forced out by Harridge. Perhaps Passarella's resignation was linked to backlash relating to the Sain call. "Discussion of the game and the call persisted past the Series," wrote Roger Kahn, "and the umpire, Art Passarella, announced at length that he was 'resigning' from the American League staff. 'It turns out,' Dick Young said through a nasty smile, 'that Erskine didn't really retire 19 straight Yankees. He retired 18 Yankees and one umpire.'"[21]

Nonetheless, Passarella explained that he wished to remain connected to the sport. On the day his retirement was revealed, Eddie Joost was named skipper of the Philadelphia Athletics. A couple of months earlier, rumor had it that Joost was up for the appointment. *The Sporting News* reported that Passarella—perhaps with tongue implanted in cheek—told Joost, "If you ever get to be manager of this club, and don't hire me as a coach, I'll certainly be disappointed in you, Eddie."[22]

Passarella's final big-league appearance was on September 27, 1953. All told, he umpired in 1,668 major-league contests. (Some sources list the number as 1,670.) During his career he ejected players on 21 separate occasions. One whom he tossed twice—both times for bench jockeying—was Johnny Berardino, who eventually altered his name to John Beradino and also opted for a showbiz career, playing Dr. Steve Hardy on the long-running TV soap *General Hospital.*

One of the ejections was reported in *The Sporting News* on June 13, 1951:

Umpire Art Passarella chased Johnny Berardino, Browns veteran utility infielder, from the bench during the June 5 game with the Athletics, though Berardino claims he "didn't say a word." However, here's what

happened: After Passarella had made two trips to the Browns' dugout, warning the players to stop "riding" him, he pointed his finger menacingly at catcher Matt Batts and Berardino, and told them: "One more word out of either of you, and out you go!" All was silence for a few moments. Then suddenly, players in both the Browns' and A's dugouts broke out in loud guffaws. Members of the Athletics pointed to the Browns' bench and Passarella, glancing around, nearly blew a gasket when he saw what was going on. Berardino had slipped back to the trainer's room, obtained a piece of adhesive tape and there he was sitting in the front row of the dugout with the wide piece of white tape pasted across his mouth. It was only a "gag," but it was more than Passarella had asked for when he demanded silence from his tormentors.

After he exited the majors, the question facing Passarella was: How would he earn a living? (Certainly he was not meant to coach for Eddie Joost.) During the 1947-48 and 1948-49 offseasons, long before his retirement, he worked as an instructor at Bill McGowan's School for Umpires in Florida. In 1949-50 he opened his own arbiter academy. An advertisement in *The Sporting News* on December 7 featured a photo of the smiling ump and some inviting ad copy: "Art Passarella Says: Write me about my Umpire Training School. You will be amazed and interested in my proposition."

The instruction was held in Bartow, Florida, in conjunction with the Bartow Baseball School and the Gus Mauch Trainer's School. During the following offseason, the school was expanded to include a "Players' Division" for young baseball hopefuls, with instruction by pitcher Ed Lopat. After his retirement from the major leagues, Passarella continued his involvement with the school. Some of the advertising highlighted his participation, while others centered on Lopat and Mauch. The school's locations and affiliations also changed. For the 1952-53 offseason, the trio was connected to the St. Augustine Baseball School in St. Augustine, Florida, where Passarella now resided. But in 1953-54, only he and Lopat were involved. The ump's work was featured in a 1955 *Sports Illustrated* article on the proliferation of baseball academies. "[Passarella] trains them and if they show promise, he tries to get them jobs umpiring in Class D leagues," wrote James T. Farrell. "This year he took only four young umpires, all of whom admitted that they had once dreamed of becoming ballplayers before they realized they would never succeed. They took up umpiring to stay in baseball."[23]

Meanwhile, Passarella attempted to find other baseball-related work. He briefly considered a public-relations job but failed to secure a spot with the West Texas-New Mexico League. So he had no choice but to return to the Texas League, where was named umpire-in-chief for the 1954 campaign. But injuries still dogged him. Early in the season he was forced out of action after reinjuring his knee while ducking to avoid a line drive. In June he entered a Fort Worth hospital for a knee operation and was on the shelf for the rest of the season. That August he was removed from the league payroll.

Passarella then hired on as an agent at the St. Augustine branch of the Prudential Life Insurance Company and began hosting *Sports and Scores,* a television show, on WJHP-TV in St. Augustine. The 1955 season found him umping in the Pacific Coast League, where he yet again was felled by injuries. On June 8, in just his second week in the PCL, he suffered a mild concussion when Pete Milne of the Sacramento Solons crashed into him while running out a grounder. Meanwhile, Passarella's knee still bothered him; that August, he consulted with Dr. Bobby Brown, the former New York Yankee, who then was practicing in San Francisco. He underwent knee surgery early in the 1956 season and returned to action on June 16, only to suffer another season-ending leg injury on July 22.

Most significantly, Passarella at this juncture decided to try show business. Johnny Berardino, his old on-field nemesis, reportedly suggested this career change, telling him, "You've been acting all your life — as an umpire."[24] So in 1958, Berardino helped him find an agent and he began securing acting roles in films and on television series; this led to Passarella's entrance into the Screen Actors Guild. (Passarella's movie industry connection dates from the mid-1940s. On December 16, 1945, he, along with Red McDonald, Dewey Widner, and Spike Jordan, three PCL umps, officiated in a contest pitting

two teams comprised of major-league players in a benefit for a hospital Christmas fund. Jeanette MacDonald, Frances Langford, Carole Landis, Martha Raye, Kay Francis, and other "film celebrities" also participated in the event.)[25]

Early on, Passarella was the umpire on *Home Run Derby* (1960), a half-hour syndicated TV show that was the brainchild of Mark Scott, a part-time actor and play-by-play announcer for the PCL's Hollywood Stars. The program, filmed at Wrigley Field in Los Angeles, featured the era's top sluggers in one-on-one competitions that were the precursors of contemporary home-run hitting contests. The "derby" was divided into nine "innings," with three outs to an inning. The batter was not obliged to swing at every pitch; Passarella's job as "umpire-in-chief" was to determine if any pitches not swung at were strikes — and a strike (or any ball not hit over the fence) was the equivalent of an out.

In some of his acting assignments, Passarella was appropriately cast as an arbiter. He and Emmett Ashford were respectively the "1st Umpire" and "2nd Umpire" in a 1969 episode of the TV series *Ironside,* and he was behind the plate on several other shows, including *Guestward Ho!* (1961), a brief summer-replacement series titled *Summer Fun* (1966), *Nichols* (1971, in an episode titled "Peanuts and Crackerjacks"), and, most impressively, the John Ford-directed "Flashing Spikes," a 1962 *Alcoa Premiere* episode featuring James Stewart as an ex-major leaguer banned from baseball for accepting a bribe.

In the *Guestward Ho!* episode, Passarella played a Little League ump who tosses a female manager, played by Joanne Dru. In a UPI piece that appeared around the time the episode was aired, Passarella claimed that he was "type-cast as a hood ... a gangster. I'm always somebody's henchman. It's like when I went into the service, they made me an MP right away."[26] He observed that he had played thugs on *The Untouchables* and *Malibu Run* — but also a "hayseed" on *The Andy Griffith Show.* Other nonbaseball roles included "Prison Guard #2" on an episode of *Sea Hunt* (1959) and "Officer Sekulovich" on various mid-1970s episodes of *The Streets of San Francisco.* Passarella's character was named for series star Karl Malden, whose birth name was Mladen

Sekulovich, and he earned a steady paycheck as Malden's longtime stand-in. But perhaps his most intriguing small-screen appearance came in a 1963 installment of *General Hospital.* Passarella played a patient; this particular episode also featured Yogi Berra as Dr. Aloysius Sweeney, a brain surgeon.

Passarella umpired on the big screen in *Critics Choice* (1963), a Bob Hope-Lucille Ball comedy. He is not credited as having appeared in the film version of *Damn Yankees* (1958); however, according to the *American Film Institute Catalog of Feature Films,* "Modern sources add Nesdon Booth, Joseph Mell, Leo Theodore, and Art Passarella to the cast"—although Passarella cannot be spotted anywhere in the film. Easily his most memorable movie appearance was in *That Touch of Mink* (1962), a romantic comedy in which he worked the plate at Yankee Stadium and mixed with a quintet in the Bronx Bombers dugout. Two were "civilians": Cathy Timberlake (Doris Day), an unemployed "computer machine" operator; and Philip Shayne (Cary Grant), a wealthy mover and shaker. The remaining three were Roger Maris, Mickey Mantle, and Yogi Berra.

Passarella's film and television career was noted by industry types who were baseball buffs. A letter penned by longtime entertainment industry publicist Cliff Dektar and headlined "SHOW BIZ UMP," was published in the April 18, 1977, *Sports Illustrated.* "When Danny Kaye's show-biz types play Roy Clark's Tulsa Drillers ... they will need an umpire. I nominate Art Passarella, the retired American League ump who has been working off and on in show business for the last 20 years." Dektar added that Passarella was well-suited to acting because he "admits to being a ham as an umpire. ..."

Passarella was 71 when he died of a heart attack on October 12, 1981, in Hemet, California, where he and his wife, Elvina, had settled. So little was known about him that his brief *New York Times* obituary was filled with errors. For instance, it was stated that he was an AL arbiter from 1945-1953; not cited were the two seasons he spent in the majors prior to his military service. Also mentioned was that "for ten years, he appeared on television as Sergeant Sekulovich, alongside Karl Malden and Michael Douglas, in *The Streets of San Francisco.*" Not only was Passarella in just a handful of episodes, but the series itself lasted not quite six seasons, from September 1972 to June 1977.

Passarella was buried in Graceland Cemetery in Pine Bluff, Arkansas; Elvina died four years later, in 1985. Interestingly, Art's gravestone references his military service—it is noted that he was a "Sgt US Army"—but not his baseball or show-business careers.

SOURCES

Edelman, Rob, *Great Baseball Films* (New York: Citadel Press, 1994).

Kahn, Roger, *Memories of a Summer: When Baseball Was an Art, and Writing About It a Game* (New York: Diversion Books, 2012).

Koppett, Leonard, *All About Baseball* (New York: Quadrangle Books, 1974).

Birtwell, Roger, "Open season on Passarella in Red Sox-Yankee Games," *The Sporting News,* May 7, 1950.

Dawson, James P., "Yanks Lose, 3-2, in Tenth Inning," *New York Times,* July 8, 1945.

Dupre, Flint, "Passarella, New A.L. Umpire, Uses Color in Getting Up Ladder," *The Sporting News,* November 28, 1940.

Edelman, Rob, "Damn Yankees: A Washington Fan's Fantasy," *The National Pastime,* 2009.

Effrat, Louis, "Yanks Top Giants, 3-2, on Run in Ninth, *New York Times,* August 6, 1946.

Farrell, James T., "Get Your Mitt, Johnny—It's Time for Class!" *Sports Illustrated,* February 28, 1955.

Felker, Carl T., "Barnes Calls Browns' Brawl Fines 'Unfair.'" *The Sporting News,* June 28, 1945.

Ferdenzi, Til, "Ben Casey Beware! Yogi Winning Raves as Surgeon on Video," *The Sporting News,* August 24, 1963.

Gillespie, Ray, "Battler Clint Gets a New $1,000 Hint to Mind Manners," *The Sporting News,* July 15, 1953.

———, "Short Career of Midget in Brownie Uniform," *The Sporting News,* August 29, 1951.

Ruhl, Oscar, "From the Ruhl Book," *The Sporting News,* July 25, 1951.

———, "From the Ruhl Book," *The Sporting News,* April 30, 1958.

———, "Scoreboard Magician Beats Umps to Punch," *The Sporting News,* March 3, 1948.

Schumach, Murray, "Yankee Sluggers Make Film Debuts," *New York Times,* August 24, 1961.

Siler, Pfc. Tom, "Passarella Still Calling 'Em as He Sees 'Em, Views of Colonels, Captains Notwithstanding," *The Sporting News,* June 10, 1943.

St. Amant, Joe, "Ex-Ump Passarella Now an Actor," *Hammond* (Indiana) *Times,* May 1, 1961.

Stockton, J. Roy, "Highs and Lows of Yank-Dodger Slam-Bang," *The Sporting News*, October 15, 1952.

Zminda, Don, "Home Run Derby: A Tale of Baseball and Hollywood," *The National Pastime*, 2011.

"19th Hole: The Readers Take Over," *Sports Illustrated*, April 18, 1977.

Advertisement. *The Sporting News*, September 10, 1947

———. *The Sporting News*, December 10, 1947.

———. *The Sporting News*, October 27, 1948.

———. *The Sporting News*, December 7, 1949.

———. *The Sporting News*, December 28, 1949.

———. *The Sporting News*, September 13, 1950.

———. *The Sporting News*, October 3, 1951.

———. *The Sporting News*, October 29, 1952.

———. *The Sporting News*, November 26, 1952.

———. *The Sporting News*, September 9, 1953.

———. *The Sporting News*, September 30, 1953.

"A.L. Ump Assignments," *The Sporting News*, March 15, 1945.

"All Umpires Dissatisfied With Wages, Claims Ernie Stewart, Fired by A.L.,"

The Sporting News, August 23, 1945.

"American League," *The Sporting News*, July 9, 1947.

"Art Passarella, Ex-Umpire, Later Acted in Films and TV," *New York Times*, October 16, 1981.

"Art's Start in Army," *The Sporting News*, April 15, 1943.

"Berardino Puts on 'Gag'—Gets Thumb From Umpire," *The Sporting News*, June 13, 1951

"Big League Stars to Play in Coast Benefit Game," *The Sporting News*, December 13, 1945.

"Buffs' Radio Night Draws 11,483," *The Sporting News*, September 8, 1954.

"Camp Grant Starts School to Train Baseball Umpires," *Toledo Blade*, April 5, 1944.

"Caught on the Fly," *The Sporting News*, December 3, 1942.

———, *The Sporting News*, August 8, 1956.

"Decision on 'Battle of Dugout' In St. Louis Now Up to Harridge," *New York Times*, June 22, 1945.

"Firing of Umpire Creates Big Stir," *New York Times*, August 16, 1945.

"Frick Indicates Umpire Made Bad Call on Sain," *New York Times*, October 6, 1952.

"From Blue to Khaki," *The Sporting News*, April 29, 1943.

"Jaw Dislocated," *The Sporting News*, May 16, 1946.

"Major Flashes," *The Sporting News*, June 5, 1946.

"Major League Flashes," *The Sporting News*, July 9, 1952.

———. *The Sporting News*, May 27, 1953.

"Minor Meetings," *The Sporting News*, January 27, 1954.

"Obituaries," *The Sporting News*, October 31, 1981.

"Passarella an Insurance Agent," *The Sporting News*, November 24, 1954.

"Passarella Decides to Quit; On A.L. Ump Staff Since '41," *The Sporting News*, November 11, 1953.

"Passarella Gets His Umpiring Job Back," *Toronto Daily Star*. January 11, 1945.

"Passarella Joshed Joost: 'Hire Me as Coach, Eddie,'" *The Sporting News*, November 25, 1953.

"Passarella on Ump Faculty," *The Sporting News*, May 7, 1947.

"Passarella Out for Season," *New York Times*, August 29, 1951.

"Passarella Promoted," *Pittsburgh Press*, December 21, 1943.

"Russ Hall, Charity Leader, Dies; Served as Player, Pilot, Umpire," *The Sporting News*, July 8, 1937.

"Senators Defeat Athletics, 3 to 2," *New York Times*, May 27, 1946.

"Shoun in Stormy Debut, Loses Trademark on Glove," *The Sporting News*, June 1, 1949.

"Texas League," *The Sporting News*, May 5, 1954.

———, *The Sporting News*, May 12, 1954.

———, *The Sporting News*, May 26, 1954.

"Texas Releases 2 Umpires in League Economy Move," *The Sporting News*, June 16, 1954.

"To Celebrate National Beautyrest Month Simmons Announces: 1953 Beautyrest Award," *Life*, April 13, 1953.

"Tuning In," *The Sporting News*, May 26, 1955.

"Two New A.L. Umpires," *The Sporting News*, November 14, 1940.

"Ump Art Passarella Back With Army Sergeant Lingo," *The Sporting News*, December 21, 1944.

"Ump Passarella Suffers Mild Concussion in Field Mishap," *The Sporting News*, June 22, 1955.

"Umpires Only Human, Too, Says Frick, Defending Passarella on Disputed Call," *The Sporting News*, October 15, 1952.

"Woe for the Umpire," *Newsweek*, May 27, 1946.

afi.com/members/catalog/DetailView.aspx?s=&Movie=52519

arkbaseball.com/tiki-index.php?page=Art+Passarella

baseball-reference.com/bullpen/Art_Passarella

baseball-reference.com/bullpen/Evangeline_League

familysearch.org/pal:/MM9.1.1/XC8Z-DV8

imdb.com/name/nm0664819/

retrosheet.org/boxesetc/P/Ppassa901.htm

search.ancestry.com/cgi-bin/sse.dll?gl=allgs&gsln=Laurich&gspl=6&gss=seo&ghc=20

NOTES

1   Pfc. Tom Siler, "Passarella Still Calling 'Em as He Sees 'Em, Views of Colonels, Captains Notwithstanding," *The Sporting News*, June 10, 1943.

2   The 1910 United States Census lists "Arthur Passarella" with a 1910 birth year. His parents are "Robert Passarella" and "Lullu Passarella" and his residence is "Rochester, Ward 8, Monroe, New York." The 1930 United States Census lists "Arthur Passarella" and his three siblings (Matthew, Pauline, and John) as Los Angeles residents. Only here, his parents are "Rocco Passarella" and "Lulu Passarella." In the 1940 census, "Lulu Passarella" is listed as the "head of household." She died on December 21, 1953, and a brief obituary was published in *The Sporting News* on January 6, 1954.

3   Flint Dupre, "Passarella, New A.L. Umpire, Uses Color in Getting Up Ladder," *The Sporting News*, November 28, 1940.

4   Passarella's marriage to Elvina Laurich is duly noted in various sources. However, under "California, County Marriages 1850-1952," "Arthur Matthew Passarella" (birth year: 1909; father: "Rocco Passarella"; mother: "Lulu Matlie") is listed as having married Anna Mary Manguso in Los Angeles on January 25, 1931. "Arthur Matthew Passarella" (birth year: 1910; father: "Rocco Passarella"; mother: "Lulu Matalie") also is listed as having married Lucille Afton Cheshire in Los Angeles on October 28, 1934.

5   Dupre, "Passarella, New A.L. Umpire."

6   "Two New A.L. Umpires," *The Sporting News*, November 14, 1940.

7   Siler, "Passarella Still Calling 'Em."

8   Dupre, "Passarella, New A.L. Umpire."

9   Siler, "Passarella Still Calling 'Em."

10   "Camp Grant Starts School To Train Baseball Umpires," *Toledo Blade*, April 5, 1944.

11   Carl T. Felker, "Barnes Calls Browns' Brawl Fines 'Unfair'." *The Sporting News*, June 28, 1945.

12   "Firing of Umpire Creates Big Stir," *New York Times*, August 16, 1945.

13   Oscar Ruhl. "Scoreboard Magician Beats Umps to Punch," *The Sporting News*, March 3, 1948.

14   "Shoun in Stormy Debut, Loses Trademark on Glove," *The Sporting News*, June 1, 1949.

15   Leonard Koppett, *All About Baseball* (New York: Quadrangle Books, 1974).

16   James P. Dawson, "Yanks Lose, 3-2, in Tenth Inning," *New York Times*, July 8, 1945.

17   "Major Flashes," *The Sporting News*, June 5, 1946.

18   Roger Kahn, *Memories of a Summer: When Baseball Was an Art, and Writing About It a Game* (New York: Diversion Books, 2012).

19   "Umpires Only Human, Too, Says Frick, Defending Passarella on Disputed Call," *The Sporting News*, October 15, 1952.

20   Ibid.

21   Kahn, *Memories of a Summer*.

22   "Passarella Joshed Joost: 'Hire Me as Coach, Eddie,'" *The Sporting News*, November 25, 1953.

23   James T. Farrell, "Get Your Mitt, Johnny—It's Time For Class!" *Sports Illustrated*, February 28, 1955.

24   "Obituaries," *The Sporting News*, October 31, 1981.

25   "Big League Stars to Play in Coast Benefit Game," *The Sporting News*, December 13, 1945.

26   Joe St. Amant, "Ex-Ump Passarella Now an Actor," *Hammond (Indiana) Times*, May 1, 1961.

John Antonelli

by Jim Sweetman

JOHN LAWRENCE ANTONELLI, JR.[1] **WAS** a Memphis native who carved out a full life in baseball despite a series of setbacks, detours, and U-turns. A high-school pitching phenom, he suffered an elbow injury that forced him to become a full-time infielder, where he played for over 1,700 minor-league games. He then fought his way to the major leagues, played a full season, and then was sent back to the minors for good amid the flood of GIs returning from World War II. He was a player-manager at 19, shifted his sights to the field, and then returned to the dugout — twice. He left baseball to support his family, then after 19 years, returned to the game for a second career almost as successful as the first. Through it all, John maintained strong ties to his hometown.

Antonelli was born on July 15, 1915 in Memphis, Tennessee, to John Antonelli, Sr. and Vivian (Solari) Antonelli. John Sr. ran the Faust Cafe and was a New York native whose parents had emigrated from Italy. Vivian was a Memphis native and daughter of a local grocer. John and Vivian subsequently had two daughters, Vivian, who died in infancy, and Genevieve, who went on to become a physical-education teacher.[2]

John Jr. was a right-handed batter who stood around 5 feet 10 inches and weighed 165 pounds. His talent was evident from an early age. As a pitcher and roving fielder at the Catholic High School in Memphis, he helped lead his team to four city titles in five years. During the summers he played American Legion ball, where his pitching talent was similarly instrumental in his teams' successes in local and regional tournaments.[3] After completing high school in 1934, Antonelli got his first taste of the life of a baseball vagabond in semipro ball in Louisiana.[4] Shortly into his tenure, he injured his pitching arm. "I was really something," Antonelli later recalled. "I was a pitcher and I tore a nerve in my arm. So I became an infielder-outfielder."[5]

He returned to Memphis and in 1935 and signed with the local Chicks of the Southern Association when their third baseman went down with an injury.[6] Asked by a reporter if he had gotten a bonus, Antonelli replied, "I don't think anybody had ever heard of anything like that. Maybe I got a baseball."[7] Again, though, his tenure was short; after three games at Memphis he was released when the injured player returned; he managed only two hits in 11 at-bats. From there he found his way to Lexington (Tennessee) of the Kitty League, where he was asked to play shortstop as well as pilot the team — at the age of 19. Antonelli proved he was up to the task of managing older players, guiding his team to a first-half title while hitting .325 and playing nearly every position.[8] The team was known in the press as "Antonelli's Giants" (despite having no affiliation with the National League Giants.)[9] The team's second half was not as successful, ending with a 19-27 record for a last-place finish.

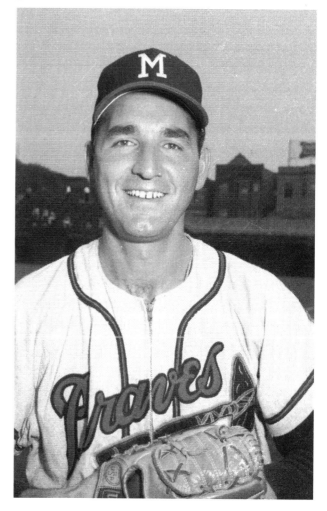

Antonelli returned to Lexington the following season but handed over the managerial reins to Rip Fanning. In July he was batting .369 and leading the voting for the league's all-star team, when he was injured in an outfield collision with a teammate.[10] Meanwhile, Fanning was having a rough go of it, with the team finishing fourth in the first half. Fanning was let go, and Antonelli replaced him upon returning from his injury.[11] He piloted the club to a second-place finish in the second half, missing the title by two games. He also maintained his hitting prowess, finishing the year with a .363 average.

Antonelli's performance sparked the interest of the St. Louis Cardinals, who bought his contract in 1937 to serve as player-manager of Union City, the Cardinals' Kitty League entry.[12] Antonelli played in 109 games, batting .298 and earning his second straight postseason all-star selection. He also led the club to a league-best 73-46 record. The next spring he was training with Union City alongside the Houston club, a Cardinals A1 affiliate. His play there caught the eye of Houston's management, who worked out a deal to bring him on as a utility infielder in exchange for pitcher Ed Hurley and outfielder Walter Schuerbaum.[13] Houston already had a player-manager, so John would have to temporarily put his managerial aspirations aside. He played in Houston for four seasons, putting up generally solid but unspectacular offensive numbers. He led the league in double plays in 1939 and his versatility made him popular with the fans, who rewarded him with two all-star selections plus one near-miss.

It was during his time in Houston that Antonelli married Amelia Gandi. They had a lot in common; Amelia was also a Memphis native and the child of Italian immigrants, including a father who ran a restaurant. Together they started a family, which included daughters Barbara and Joan. Their timing was fortuitous. With war already under way in Europe, the United States started a peacetime draft in 1940. However, men with families to support were largely exempt from induction. The draft was expanded after the attack on Pearl Harbor, but the deferments for men supporting families remained for much of the war. With the pool of available ballplayers shrinking due to both the draft

and voluntary enlistments, John's value as a ballplayer went up. Not only was there less competition for each roster spot, but also any team signing him could rest assured that he wouldn't be called away in the middle of the season for military duty.[14]

Antonelli's draft status proved to be an advantage in early 1942, when St. Louis's Double-A club in Columbus traded Morris "Buck" Jones, a single, draft-eligible outfielder, to Houston for Antonelli and first baseman Jack Angle, who was also married.[15] John mainly played second and third base at Columbus, and in both 1942 and 1943 he played well enough to keep his job but not well enough to earn a promotion. In 1944, however, he raised his batting average and slugging percentage, earning himself an All-Star selection and a September call-up to St. Louis, where he saw limited playing time. He did not make the World Series roster.

Antonelli stuck with the Cards, making the team in the spring of 1945, but saw action only twice in the season's first month. Then in May, St. Louis sent Antonelli and outfielder Glenn Crawford to the Philadelphia Phillies for outfielder Buster Adams. It was quite a change, moving from defending World Series champs to perennial cellar dwellers. The Phillies were so bad that in the spring of 1945 three minor leaguers refused to report when Philadelphia bought their contracts.[16] For John, though, the Phillies offered regular playing time (125 games over five months), something he was unable to get in St. Louis. His main contributions were strong defense and versatility—he played every infield position. His best performance at the plate came on June 17. Playing both ends of a double-header in New York that day, Antonelli punched out six singles in ten at-bats and drove in three runs.

Antonelli joined the Phillies for spring training in Florida in 1946. However, camp was swelled with players returning from the war. With so many players to evaluate, Antonelli got little playing time. When the team broke camp to start the season, it became clear that the there was no place for him on the major-league roster. However, Bucky Harris, who managed the Phillies in 1943, was then the general manager of the International League club in Buffalo, and he was looking for a hard-hitting outfielder and an infielder. So the Phillies sold

Antonelli and outfielder Coaker Triplett to Harris's club in a five-figure cash deal.[17]

Antonelli's major-league tenure—eight games in one season and 127 in another—was highly unusual. In fact, since 1900, only one other player has played at least 125 games in a season and recorded so few other appearances: Jim Doyle, who played seven games for Cincinnati in 1910 and 130 for the Cubs in 1911. Hughie Miller, who made it into a single game with the Phillies in 1911 and then 132 games with the 1914 St. Louis Terriers of the Federal League and another seven games with the same team in 1915, had a similar career profile, but no one else is really comparable.[18]

In Buffalo in 1946, Antonelli saw less playing time than in any other year in his career to that point. Three games into the next season, he was sent to Baltimore, where his playing time and production rebounded. That fall, Antonelli managed the US team in an Inter-American tournament at Caracas, Venezuela.[19] He was moved to Double-A Oklahoma City in early 1948, but rather than return to the Texas League, he bought out his contract to return to his hometown Memphis Chicks (now affiliated with the Chicago White Sox.[20] On July 9 of that year, Antonelli contributed a single and triple as the Chicks started a game against Nashville with nine straight hits. He ended the year batting. 329 with 32 doubles and 78 RBIs. The next season, though, his production again declined, due in part to injuries, and in November 1949 he was named player-manager of Hot Springs in the Class C Cotton States League. Unlike his first stint as player-manager, this time the 34-year-old Antonelli was the elder statesman, piloting a group of 20-somethings, none older than 26. He made it into only 20 games as a player, but managed his team to a 77-60 record and a postseason title.

As 1951 dawned, Antonelli was offered a chance to move up the ranks as a manager. At the same time, he was offered a full-time sales position with a wholesale liquor distributor. With a young family, John made the choice many players have made before and since, and chose the year-round job in his hometown. He told a reporter at the time: "It's tough traveling in the lower minors. ... I've lived more than six months away from home, excepting my two years with the Chicks."[21]

Although he kept his hand in with some scouting for the White Sox and conversations with former teammates, Antonelli was largely out of baseball.

While most ballplayers' stories end there, Antonelli still had a few chapters left to write. The Chicks folded in 1960, but baseball returned in 1968 when the New York Mets moved a Double-A team from Florida to become the Memphis Blues. Will Carruthers, Memphis's general manager and Antonelli's high-school baseball coach, was not happy with the team's performance during that first season. As part of his effort to bring in new blood, he asked Antonelli to come back as a coach. John agreed, starting out coaching first base at home games.[22] After his first game, Antonelli said, "It was the first time I had been in a baseball uniform in 19 years. Everything felt kind of funny. But after I got on the field, everything began to fall into place."[23] In the middle of the season, the team's manager was fired and his replacement was unable to join the club immediately. John managed the Blues during this gap, leading them to a 6-2 record. Later that season his former Catholic High teammates and friends held a commemorative day in his honor prior to a game.

After the end of that 1969 season, the Mets approached John about returning to full-time managerial duties. His daughters had grown up and struck out on their own. But that was not the only factor in his decision. "Working with those kids as a coach really did it," he told a reporter. "I really love to work with the young ball players."[24] When the Mets formally offered him the Blues' managerial job for 1970, he accepted.

Antonelli managed in Memphis for three seasons and demonstrated that he still had the ability to get the best from his players, finishing with winning records in two of those seasons. As a manager he was known for his good rapport with his players. In one often-told anecdote, when the Mets called up outfielder Dave Schneck from Memphis, John packed Schneck's bags and had them ready to go before he delivered the good news back at the team hotel.[25] He was also community-minded, initiating the practice of soliciting donations to charity for each of the team's victories. Even though Antonelli was generally soft-spoken, during games he was not afraid to put on a little show for the fans.

"When he'd get to battling an umpire really good, we'd move the ball bag over so he could do his thing," one of his former batboys told a reporter. "When he'd get thrown out, he'd come over and grab that bag and sling baseballs all over the field."[26]

The Mets took notice of Antonelli's skills. In 1971 they invited him to become an instructor in the Florida Instructional League. In November 1972 Hank Bauer, who had managed the Mets team at Triple-A Tidewater, resigned and the Mets promoted Antonelli to replace him. While his first season resulted in the now-familiar winning record, the 1974 Tides fell to a 57-82 mark. The next year the Mets moved Antonelli back to Double-A and their team in Jackson, Mississippi. There he led his charges to two nearly identical records (65-65 in 1975 and 69-66 in 1976). Then following the 1976 campaign, the Mets hired Bob Wellman, a successful manager from the Phillies system, to take over at Jackson. "I hate to leave Jackson," John said at the time, "but at my age the day-to-day grind of managing was getting a little tough."[27] Antonelli was kept on as an infield instructor, a job he held until his health began to fail in 1989. He also served as a scout and minor-league coach during that period, with stops in Tidewater, Lynchburg, Little Falls, Columbia, and Kingsport. Soon after the 1990 season began, John died at his Memphis home.[28]

When he returned to baseball full time in 1970, Antonelli told a reporter, "Sure, I'd like to be a big-league manager. I don't think I'm too old. I've got a lot of good years and this is my career now. I'd like to go all the way to the top."[29] John didn't make it back to the majors, but plenty of players whose careers he helped would probably consider him tops.

NOTES

1   John L. Antonelli the infielder is not to be confused with the pitcher Johnny A. Antonelli, who played more than a decade in the major leagues. Johnny's biography is part of SABR's BioProject: sabr.org/bioproj/person/e1774181.

2   Family information is generally based on US Census returns and Memphis City Directories.

3   David Bloom, "A Johnny Antonelli Day and a Lot of Days Past." *Memphis Commercial Appeal,* August 12, 1969; Will Carruthers, "Johnny Antonelli Going Up Slowly—But Surely," *Memphis Press-Scimitar,* February 12, 1940; Will Carruthers, "Antonelli Hangs Up Baseball Togs," *Memphis Press-Scimitar,* February 19, 1951.

4   Will Carruthers, " 'Jinx' Again Lays Heavy Hand on John Antonelli," *Memphis Press-Scimitar,* July 27, 1936.

5   Woodrow Paige, Jr., "Antonelli Upped Average Without Swinging a Bat," *Memphis Commercial Appeal,* February 15, 1970.

6   Carruthers (1936).

7   Bloom.

8   Carruthers (1936).

9   Richard Worth, *Baseball Team Names: A Worldwide Dictionary, 1869-2011* (Jefferson, North Carolina: McFarland & Co, 2013), 161.

10 Carruthers (1936).

11 *The Sporting News,* August 20, 1936, 12.

12 Richard S. Cox, "Antonelli, Veteran Pilot at 22, New Manager at Union City," *The Sporting News,* April 22, 1937, 6.

13 *The Sporting News,* April 7, 1938, 8.

14 For further discussion of draft deferments and professional baseball during the World War II era, see David Finoli, *For the Good of the Country: World War II Baseball in the Major and Minor Leagues* (Jefferson, North Carolina: McFarland & Co., 2002).

15 Bob Hooey, "Birds Give Up Bachelor for Two Married Men," *The Sporting News,* February 26, 1942, 2.

16 Stan Baumgartner, "Mother Ailing, Caulfield Stays With Oakland," *Philadelphia Inquirer,* May 11, 1945. See also James D. Szalontai, *Teenager on First, Geezer at Bat, 4-F on Deck: Major League Baseball in 1945* (Jefferson, North Carolina: McFarland, 2009) for a discussion of the state of the major leagues in 1945.

17 Art Morrow, "Phillies Sell Two, Show Direction of Baseball Winds," *Philadelphia Inquirer,* April 19, 1946; Cy Kritzer, "Bisons Name Kretlow to Pitch Int, Opener in His 1st Pro Start," *Buffalo Evening News* April 17, 1946; Cy Kritzer, "Baseball Bisons Buy Triplett and Antonelli From Phillies," *Buffalo Evening News,* April 18, 1946.

18 Author's analysis of major-league appearance statistics since 1900.

19 "Revolution Greets U.S. Team," *The Sporting News,* October 1, 1947, 37.

20 "Caught on the Fly," *The Sporting News,* March 10, 1948, 28.

21 Carruthers (1951).

22 Bobby Hall, "Blues Spice the Home Dish—John Antonelli Will Coach," *Memphis Commercial Appeal,* March 15, 1969, 21.

23 Bill E. Burk, "New Memphis Manager Ends Self-Exile," *The Sporting News,* February 7, 1970, 46.

24 Paige.

25 Murray Chass, "Schneck's Met Debut Like a Movie," *New York Times,* July 16, 1972, S2.

26 Bobby Hall, "Friends Remember Antonelli's Antics," *Commercial Appeal,* April 20, 1990.

27 "New Job For Antonelli," *The Sporting News*, October 30, 1976, 29.

28 Obituary, *The Sporting News*, June 4, 1990, 62.

29 Paige.

Ferris Fain

By Gregory H. Wolf

WHEN ASKED TO MAKE A LIST OF THE best hitters of the late 1940s and early 1950s, few would mention left-handed slugger Ferris Fain, but perhaps they should. Fain broke in with the Philadelphia Athletics as a 26-year-old rookie in 1947 and established a reputation as a daring first baseman with a discerning eye at the plate. The five-time All-Star won consecutive batting titles in 1951 and 1952, but was plagued by sore knees, a problem that eventually ended his big-league career after nine seasons. His hitting exploits were matched by his explosive personality. Fain, who was known as much during his playing days for his drinking and fighting as he was for his line drives, retired with a .290 batting average and his .424 on-base percentage ranked 12th highest in history at the time, 13th after the 2013 season.

Ferris Roy Fain was born on March 29, 1921, in San Antonio, Texas, the first of two sons born to Oscar and Ada Fain. Oscar was a construction worker and part-time boxer whose greatest claim to fame came as a jockey riding a horse named Duval to a second-place finish in the 1912 Kentucky Derby. "[He] was a pain in the ass to be around," Fain said bluntly about his alcoholic father, who taught him and his brother, Lafe, the art of fighting.[1] Fain's parents divorced when he was 12 years old. Ada took the two boys and settled in Oakland in 1933. "My mom was the glue that held the family together," Fain said. "She worked as a domestic and would bring us hand-me-downs from the people she worked for."[2]

Sports were a welcome diversion for the teenage Ferris growing up with limited means in a rough neighborhood. At Roosevelt High School he starred in basketball and football, but his passion was baseball. By his sophomore year, playing a smooth first base, Fain began attracting big-league scouts. Doc Silvey, a veteran scout for the San Francisco Seals of the Pacific Coast League, was hot on Fain's trial, too. "The Seals were paying me $200 a month under the table [by my senior year]," explained Fain. "The only restriction was that I did not play high-school football."[3] Concentrating just on baseball, Fain captained his high-school nine to consecutive berths in the Oakland city title series in 1938 and 1939.

After graduation in 1939, the 18-year-old Fain signed with Silvey and the Seals, and immediately joined the club. He had been working out with them for more than a year and knew the players. Described as a "mere boy," Fain took over first-base duties at the end of the season.[4] He batted .219 (7-for-32) for manager Lefty O'Doul. "Without a doubt [O'Doul] was the best baseball man I've ever known," said Fain. "[He] kind of adopted me and I looked up to him as a father figure. He could really teach."[5] In preparation for a chance as a starter in 1940, Fain played in local winter leagues. The "phenomenal young prospect" replaced Jack Burns in early May and never looked back.[6] Though he batted a modest .238, he was hailed as the "second Hal Chase" for his aggressive and exceptional defensive play at first base.[7]

Fain enjoyed a breakout season with a sub-.500 Seals team in 1941, batting .310 and leading the PCL with

122 runs scored. Seals beat reporter Jim McGee described him as the "backbone of the club"[8] who played first base with "catlike grace" and "uncanny judgment."[9] Fain's average inexplicably dropped almost 100 points to .216 in 1942 although he was healthy all season.

Despite his catchy name, Fain was known by myriad nicknames throughout his career. He acquired two of those sobriquets during his first few years with San Francisco. Seals trainer Bobby Johnson tabbed him Cocky because he thought the youngster had a lazy eye (though the moniker also aptly described Fain's boundless confidence in his abilities).[10] Longtime PCL pitcher Win Ballou, originally from Kentucky, gave Fain another nickname, Burrhead, because of his short, kinky black hair.[11] It had an unmistakable ring of racism, yet players and managers alike commonly used it throughout Fain's career.

Fain missed three seasons (1943-1945) when he served in the Army Air Force. Assigned to the 495th Squadron at McClellan Airfield, near Sacramento, Fain played for one of the strongest service teams on the Pacific Coast. He rose to the rank of sergeant, and was later stationed at Hickam Air Base in Hawaii. His base team included Joe DiMaggio, Red Ruffing, and Joe Gordon. "I believe that playing service ball made the difference in me going to the major leagues. That's because I got a chance to play against and with all these guys," said Fain.[12]

Fain returned to the Seals in 1946 and proved that his skills had not deteriorated during a three-year absence from Organized Baseball and that his season-long slump in 1942 was a fluke. Named to the midseason all-star team, Fain displayed a discerning eye, collecting 129 bases on balls, batting .301, and leading the league in both runs (117) and runs batted in (112), while clubbing just 11 home runs for the PCL champions. Fain also had a firmly established reputation as a no-nonsense brawler on the diamond. Scouts from no fewer than eight big-league teams flocked to Seals Stadium to watch the stocky left-handed hitting and fielding whiz. On the recommendation of veteran scout Harry O'Donnell, the Philadelphia Athletics' Connie Mack dispatched head scout Tom Turner to San Francisco.

Turner ultimately signed the 25-year-old after the A's selected him in the Rule 5 draft.

In what emerged as an almost annual tradition, Fain's contract squabbles with Mack and the A's began soon after he was drafted. "Connie wasn't exactly an easy negotiator," said Fain. "He sent me a contract for $600 per month. But I explained to him that I had made $5,500 with the Seals and an additional $1,000 for doing a nice job. I was not going to take a pay cut to play in the big leagues where it would cost me twice as much to live. He finally signed me to a contract for $6,500."[13]

Fain joined a moribund A's team that had not enjoyed a winning season since 1933. In his debut, on April 15, 1947, at Yankees Stadium (which also marked the first big-league regular-season game he ever attended), Fain beat out a bunt single off Randy Gumpert, his lone hit in four at-bats. Fain made a seamless transition to the big leagues, relying on his patience at the plate and his ability to make contact with the ball. "[Fain] stands deep in the batter's box, right foot planted firmly inside the line, left foot about one-third over and bat gripped with two inches of handle showing," wrote A's beat reporter Art Morrow. "He crouches from the knees and hunches at the shoulder."[14] Fain's aggressive, exuberant style of play was credited with energizing the A's, and Connie Mack lauded his "sheer spirit" on the field.[15] Fain finished the '47 season with a .291 batting average and boasted the league's second-best on-base percentage thanks to 95 walks, while the A's finished with a winning record (78-76). *The Sporting News* named him first baseman on its All-Rookie team.

Fain was one of the rare players who batted for average, drew an inordinate number of walks, and struck out infrequently. Fain credited O'Doul with teaching him discipline at the plate. "It used to be that I couldn't wait for my pitch. I'd lunge for anything. Lefty tied a rope around my middle, got behind the batting cage with the end of the rope, and every time I'd step in to meet one, I'd find myself on the dirt."[16] Fain annually ranked among the league leaders in walks and on-base percentage in each of his first seven seasons, and finished his career with an impressive .424 on-base percentage. He struck out only 261 times in 4,904 plate appearances.

Fain's chronic and ultimately career-ending knee pain began in his first season with the A's. In spring training he suffered from strained ligaments in his right knee, and by September doctors detected calcium deposits. After his rookie season, he underwent knee surgery to remove bone chips; however, he reinjured the same knee while pitching in a semipro game in Oakland and required a second surgery several months later.

Fain missed much of spring training in 1948 recuperating, but was in the lineup on Opening Day. Battling a tender knee, a broken middle finger on his throwing hand, and an eye infection, Fain managed to bat .281, draw at least 100 walks for the first of five times in his career, and drive in a career-high 88 runs in his sophomore campaign. Despite limited power (seven home runs in each of his first two seasons), Fain took most of his at-bats in the cleanup position. The A's enjoyed their best season (84-70) since 1932 and their glory days with Mickey Cochrane and Jimmie Foxx.

As patient as Fain was at the plate, he was equally aggressive playing first base. He was blessed with exceptional range and a powerful arm, and was known to charge to the first- and third-base sides of home plate on bunts and initiate a double play by throwing out the advancing runner at second base. "You never saw a guy who could make the plays like that guy can," said former A's Hall of Famer Al Simmons.[17] Art Morrow remarked that "no mere statistics could reflect [Fain's] value to the club."[18] While Fain's batting average slipped to .263 in 1949, his daring defensive play helped the A's become the first team in big-league history to complete more than 200 double plays in one season, finishing with 217 (followed by 208 in 1950 and 204 in 1951). Fain, second baseman Pete Suder, shortstop (and Fain's roommate) Eddie Joost, and third baseman Hank Majeski were hailed as one of the "greatest infields in the history of the Athletics."[19] "I never saw four guys with better arms than our infield," said Fain. "These guys all had rifles, and they were accurate. It got so that if a throw was beneath my waist at first base, I'd give them hell."[20] Fain set a record for double plays by a first baseman (194) in 1949 and led the league again in 1950. From 1948 to 1953, he led the league in assists four times

and was second the other two seasons. But Fain's aggressive play also occasionally led to miscues, and he led the league in errors by a first baseman five times.

Fain's desire to succeed was matched by his explosive temperament and low boiling point on and off the field. His reputation as a fighter followed him from San Francisco. In his rookie year he was involved in a highly publicized brawl with Boston Red Sox infielder Eddie Pellagrini in September, which resulted in a suspension. "[Fain] wanted to fight someone all the time," said teammate Gus Zernial.[21] The media referred to him as Fiery Ferris, Furious Ferris, Fearless Ferris, and the Firebrand, all of which attested to his will to win but also pointed at his combustible personality. Fain took defeat as a personal insult, prompting sportswriter Edgar Williams to dub him the "Angry Champion." "Some folks can shrug off a slump. I can't," Fain asserted. "If I'm not going well, I can't joke about it. I want to win whether I'm playing baseball or pinochle. I don't know how to play any other way than all-out, and if I get red-necked at times, I can't help it."[22]

In 1950 Fain was named to his first of five consecutive All-Star teams in an otherwise disappointing year for the A's. He raised his average to .282, smacked a career-best ten home runs, and walked 133 times (down from a career-high 136 the previous season), but the A's fell to last place with a dismal 52-102 record. The season also marked the end of Connie Mack's illustrious run of 50 years piloting the team. Days after the conclusion of the season, the rumor mill churned out reports of Fain's trade or sale to the Detroit Tigers or New York Yankees. The Yankees' Casey Stengel made it plain that he coveted the hot-blooded first-sacker, whom he saw as a throwback to an earlier era of baseball. "John McGraw (Stengel's manager when he played for the New York Giants) would have loved Fain. He's a guy who fights you for everything," said the "Old Perfessor."[23]

New A's manager Jimmy Dykes's feisty, hands-on approach to baseball was a great departure from Mack's staid demeanor. "I'm making [Fain] our field captain," said Dykes, wanting to create some excitement. "He's a real fighter … a holler guy. I predict he'll have a helluva year."[24] Off to a hot start, Fain belted 17 hits in 29 at-bats over a six-game stretch in May, propelling his average to .402. [He's] looser at the plate and swings more easily," wrote reporter Morrow, who also noted that batting second in the lineup seemed to relax Fain.[25] He was named to his second All-Star team and made his only career All-Star start, going 1-for-3 with a triple and an RBI. Fain's anger got the best of him on July 15 when he kicked the first-base bag in frustration after failing to beating out a groundball. He broke the metatarsal bone in his left foot and missed five weeks. He returned on August 21 and batted .364 over the rest of the season to capture his first batting title with a .344 mark (146-for 425). For the season he walked 80 times, and sported a .451 on-base-percentage (second to Ted Williams), but the A's still finished in sixth place (70-84). *The Sporting News* named Fain the "Outstanding Player of the Year."

A career .279 hitter prior to his breakout season, Fain offered several reasons for his success. "I didn't swing so hard at the ball. And I finally took Lefty O' Doul's advice and quit standing with my caboose sticking so far out."[26] The "Angry One" also began choking up on the bat more, but the primary reason for his success was freedom. "When Mr. Mack was my boss, we did everything by signs. He did our thinking," said Fain candidly. "He wanted us to wait out the pitcher and get the base on balls. Dykes gave me a free hand with the lumber."[27]

Fain's offseason was dominated by a contract holdout that played out in the press. "Just because they are on a shoestring, I can't see why a ballplayer should help them along," said Fain.[28] He finally signed in March 1952 for a reported $25,000 to become the highest paid A's player since Jimmie Foxx. In the first two months of the season, Fain was slowed by leg pain, and was batting only .245 at the end of May. In early June he cranked out 13 hits in 18 at-bats over five games, followed by a career-long 24-game hitting streak (37-for-99) to catapult him into the lead for the AL batting title. The A's won 21 games in July and 20 in August, the first time since their last pennant in 1931 that they won 20 games in two different months. Philadelphia wrapped up the season in fourth place. Fain played through a number of nagging injuries to his knees and hands to win his second consecutive batting title (.327). Along

with his career-high 176 hits, he also paced the junior circuit with 43 doubles and a .438 on-base-percentage. He placed sixth in the MVP voting for the second straight year.

Notwithstanding Fain's success, his life seemed to be careening out of control. His marriage to Jacqueline (Turner) Fain was in shambles. They had married while Fain was still with the Seals, and had three children. After the 1952 season, she filed for divorce. Fain's unpredictably violent temper was made worse by excessive drinking. "It was well known that he had a drinking problem," said Gus Zernial. But in the time-honored tradition of accepting alcohol abuse by teammates (especially those who performed on the field), Zernial added, "I don't think his drinking hurt us."[29] Fain revealed years later, however, that he could barely hold his bat during the final weeks of the season as a consequence of one late-night, alcohol-fueled eruption. "I was having some trouble beating out Dale Mitchell for the batting title because I had busted my little finger. We put out a story that I'd caught the finger in a car door. Actually, I broke it when I took a swing at some guy in a tavern fight. I missed the SOB and hit the bar instead."[30]

In the "biggest trade in the offseason," Fain was sent to the Chicago White Sox in January 1953 in exchange for slugging first baseman Eddie Robinson, shortstop Joe DeMaestri, and center fielder Ed McGhee. The A's publicly claimed they coveted the home-run threat Robinson provided (Fain hit just eight round-trippers combined in 1951 and 1952), but Fain's out-of-control behavior probably played a role in the first offseason trade of a reigning batting champion in AL history.[31] White Sox manager Paul Richards considered Fain "the best all-around first baseman in the league … [with] more than mechanical ability."[32] Fain became the highest-paid player in White Sox history when he inked a contract for a reported $35,000.[33] But he never got on track with the White Sox. He suffered a bruised right knee and then strained ligaments in his left knee during the first two months of the season. Fain's season was interrupted when he was involved in a barroom brawl after a game against the Washington Senators on August 2. He broke the ring finger on his left hand

and missed 22 games. He was also charged with assault.[34] He struggled in his return and finished with a .256 batting average in a forgettable season with the third-place White Sox.

With expectations tempered from his disastrous campaign in 1953, the 33-year-old Fain proved that he was still a dangerous hitter in 1954. Installed in the cleanup position, he seemed headed toward arguably the most productive season of his career. He played in 65 of the team's first 70 games, batted .302, and was among the league's leaders with 51 runs batted in (in just 235 at-bats). Then on June 27 he collided with catcher Sammy White of the Boston Red Sox, injuring his already fragile right knee and abruptly ending his promising season. A month later he underwent his third knee surgery and had cartilage removed.

Fain's long history of injuries cast doubt on his future. On December 6, 1954, the White Sox shipped him along with two throw-ins (pitcher Leo Cristante and first baseman Jack Phillips) to the Detroit Tigers for first baseman Walt Dropo, pitcher Ted Gray, and left fielder Bob Nieman. Fain saw little action in spring training with the Tigers and was still moving "rather gingerly" with a pronounced limp.[35] He clashed with manager Bucky Harris, who held him out of the Opening Day lineup. A shell of his former self, Fain batted .264 and was a liability in the field. The acquisition of first baseman Earl Torgeson at the June 15 trading deadline marked the end of the team's experiment with Fain, who was released on July 6. He got a second chance about a week later when he signed with the Cleveland Indians. "When Vic Wertz … came down with polio, [general manager] Hank Greenberg called me to play," explained Fain.[36] Fain filled in at first base and batted .254 as the Indians finished second to the Yankees. Fain posted a career-high .455 on-base percentage with the White Sox and Tigers, which would have led the league had he accumulated enough at-bats. (Wertz, diagnosed with a nonparalytic form of polio, recovered for the 1956 season.)

The Indians released Fain on November 2, 1955. Unable to catch on with another major-league team, Fain signed as a player-coach with the Sacramento Solons of the PCL. He batted just .252 and was released at the conclusion of the season, bringing his active playing career to an end.

In his nine-year big-league career, "Fearless Ferris" hit at a robust .290 clip, cranked out 1,139 hits, and sported an eye-popping .424 on-base percentage.

As impressive as the accomplishments of the five-time All-Star were on the field, he may be best remembered for his pugnacious behavior off the field. "If I had behaved more," Fain admitted, "I probably would have realized my dream of becoming a manager."[37]

In retirement, Fain settled down El Dorado County, California, located at the slopes of the Sierra Nevada Mountains. He worked in construction, built houses, and remarried, but also drifted away from baseball. His name surfaced again in 1985 when he was arrested for growing marijuana. He pleaded guilty, served four months under house arrest, and received five years' probation. He claimed he needed the money and grew the plants out of necessity. In his later years he was in declining health, had arthritis in both knees, and suffered from diabetes and gout. His name surfaced again three years later, in 1988, when agents raided his home and discovered a large-scale operation with more than 400 plants, processed pot, and ledgers detailing purchases and sales. Fain was arrested and spent 18 months in a state prison. "I grew 'em because, damn it, I was good at growing things, just like I was good at hitting a baseball," he told *Sacramento Bee* sports editor, Bill Conlin.[38]

On October 18, 2001, Ferris Fain died at the age of 80 in Georgetown, California. He had been suffering from leukemia. He was survived by his wife, Ruth, and was buried at the Georgetown Pioneer Cemetery. Fain played baseball and the game of life by his own rules, gave no quarter and expected none. "He was his own worst enemy," said his former roommate Eddie Joost.[39] On the field few players exhibited the tenacity and drive that made Fain one of the most exciting players of his era. "I've never seen a player who could outhustle the Burrhead," said Lefty O'Doul.[40]

SOURCES

Ferris Fain player file at the National Baseball Hall of Fame, Cooperstown, New York.

Ancestry.com

BaseballLibrary.com

Baseball-Reference.com

New York Times

Retrosheet.com

SABR.com

The Sporting News

NOTES

1 Charles Bricker, "Ferris Fain's story a complicated one," *San Jose Mercury News*. [no date]. Ferris Fain player file at the National Baseball Hall of Fame.

2 Herb Fagen, "Ferris Fain. Few Played The Game Any Better," *Oldtyme Baseball News*, Volume 7, Issue 5, 1996, 28.

3 Ibid.

4 *The Sporting News*, October 5, 1939, 16.

5 Fagen, 28.

6 *The Sporting News*, February 15, 1940, 3.

7 *The Sporting News*, June 6, 1940, 3.

8 *The Sporting News*, July 3, 1941, 2.

9 *The Sporting News*, September 4, 1941, 5.

10 Ibid.

11 Rich Marazzi, "Slick-fielding Ferris Fain was a bright light on a moribund Philly franchise," *Sports Collectors Digest*, August 29, 1997, 71.

12 Fagen, 28.

13 Fagen, 29.

14 *The Sporting News*, May 21, 1947, 12.

15 *The Sporting News*, August 20, 1947, 10.

16 *The Sporting News*, May 21, 1947, 12.

17 *The Sporting News*, March 16, 1949, 20.

18 *The Sporting News*, February 15, 1950, 13.

19 *The Sporting News*, July 20, 1949, 9.

20 Fagen, 29.

21 Richard Goldstein, "Ferris Fain, A.L. Batting Champion in the 1950s, Dies at 80." *New York Times*, October 27, 2001, D7.

22 Edgar Williams, "The Angry Champion," *Baseball Digest*, January 1953, 51-52.

23 "The Angry Champion," 52.

24 *The Sporting News*, March 28, 1951, 4.

25 *The Sporting News*, May 30, 1951, 19.

26 *The Sporting News*, February 6, 1952, 5.

27 Ibid.

28 *The Sporting News*, February 13, 1952, 26.

29 Frank Fitzpatrick, "Philadelphia A's star battled hurlers, demons, *Philadelphia Inquirer*, October 24, 2001, E7.

30 Dave Nightingale, "A Batting Champion Gone to Pot," *The Sporting News*, May 16, 1988, 18.

31 Nap Lajoie of Philadelphia won the batting title in the inaugural season of the AL, in 1901. He was traded in 1902 to the AL Cleveland Bronchos after playing just one game for the A's.

32 *The Sporting News*, February 4, 1953, 16.

33 *The Sporting News*, February 11, 1953, 14.

34 *The Sporting News*, August 2, 1953, 6.

35 *The Sporting News*, March 9, 1955, 27.

36 Marazzi, 70.

37 Goldstein, D7.

38 Nightingale, 19.

39 Goldstein, D7.

40 Williams, 53.

Frank Crosetti

By Tara Krieger

IN 37 SEASONS AS AN INFIELDER AND third-base coach for the Yankees, Frank Crosetti was on the field for 23 fall classics, of which New York won 17. After a while "The Crow" had collected so many rings that the Yankees started giving him engraved shotguns instead. Sandwiched between Tony Lazzeri and Joe DiMaggio as one of a troika of Bay Area Italians who came to the Bronx from the Pacific Coast League in the 1920s and '30s, Crosetti may not have been the most talented player in pinstripes—he is one of only two starting position players in his rookie season not in the Hall of Fame—but he was often the glue that held everyone together.[1]

Crosetti was a consummate professional, a sure-handed fielder, and as one writer put it, "one of the most annoying .245 batters that baseball ever had."[2] Perhaps the Yankees' success in his years with the team was no coincidence. "Crosetti is the sparkplug of the Yankees," Rogers Hornsby once said. "Without him they wouldn't have a chance. He is a great player and he is about the only one on the club who does any hollering."[3]

Crow's reputation as the Yankees' "holler guy" gave secondary meaning to a moniker that superficially seemed like a shortened version of his last name. Players grew accustomed to hearing his high-pitched voice cawing from all corners of the field.

It may have come about incidentally. During a frustratingly sluggish stretch in 1932, manager Joe McCarthy told the rookie Crosetti that Lou Gehrig looked too lackadaisical at first base. "When you get the ball in infield practice," McCarthy said, "fire it back hard at Gehrig. Holler at him. See if you can't wake him up."[4]

Obligingly, Crosetti obeyed. ("Although Gehrig was giving me dirty looks," he recalled. "I remember him saying, 'If I get ahold of you, I will break you in half!'—which he easily could have done!") Years later, McCarthy related that Gehrig was never the problem at all—it was Crosetti who had needed the extra mo-

tivation. Apparently it worked—his animated style on the field stuck.[5]

Off the field Crosetti had "the same approximate loquacity as the Sphinx," as *New York Times* columnist Arthur Daley once described him,[6] a trait he shared with the other two members of the Italian trio.

At least two oft-told stories illustrate this. In February 1936, Lazzeri and Crosetti took the rookie DiMaggio cross-country from San Francisco to St. Petersburg for spring training. The car was eerily silent for most of the three days of the trip. Crosetti and Lazzeri had taken turns behind the wheel, and toward the end of their trek, Lazzeri suggested, "Let the kid drive." Only then did DiMaggio reveal he didn't know how.[7]

Another story involved a St. Louis sportswriter who observed Lazzeri, Crosetti, and DiMaggio sitting together one day in the lobby of the Chase Hotel. Ninety minutes went by without a word until DiMaggio cleared his throat.

"What did you say?" asked Crosetti.

"Shut up," said Lazzeri. "He didn't say nothing."[8]

The younger son of Domenico Crosetti, who emigrated from near Genoa, Italy, around the turn of the 20th century, and Rachele Monteverde Crosetti, a California native whose parents were from the same region, Frank Peter Joseph Crosetti was born in San Francisco on October 4, 1910.

Because he suffered from poor health as a toddler, the family relocated to the more rural Los Gatos, and Domenico Crosetti—who would hold a number of unskilled odd jobs, including orchardist, gardener, and scavenger—started a vegetable farm. Frank's first baseball experiences were playing one-a-cat (a sort of hybrid of baseball and cricket) on that 12-acre plot. For a bat and ball, he and his brother, John, who was three years older, used a whittled-down board and the big end of a dried corncob.[9] No member of his family had ever seen a baseball game.[10]

Rachele Crosetti did not object to her son playing ball, but—even into Frank's professional days—she feared he would get hurt.[11] The family matriarch ran a stern but loving household, which included early curfews and church every Sunday. But she was always waiting for the Crosetti boys after school with a sandwich and eggnog.[12]

"My mother was on the strict side," Frank Crosetti wrote in 1997. "My brother and I probably resented it. But as we grew older we were thankful that she was. She was right, it kept us out of trouble, as it does not take much to go on the other side of the tracks."[13]

It didn't keep him in school, however. An unimpressive student, Crosetti, whose family moved to Santa Clara, then to the North Beach area of San Francisco, once skipped classes at Lowell High School for two weeks to watch the local Pacific Coast League team, the San Francisco Seals, play ball.[14] At 16, he dropped out.

After playing semipro ball for the Butte Mining League in Montana, Crosetti played winter ball in San Francisco at the Seals' Recreation Park, where Sam Fugazi, an unofficial Seals scout, invited him for a tryout with the professional club. The Seals appreciated Crosetti's talent but deemed him too small to be a regular, so team executive secretary George Putnam had bottles of milk delivered to his house every morning, and Crosetti put on ten pounds.[15] He wasted little time in grabbing his first headlines, hitting a grand slam off Joe Dawson of the Pittsburgh Pirates in a March 21, 1928, exhibition game against the reigning National League champions.

Crosetti batted a modest .248 in 96 games in 1928, mainly playing third base. The following year he was groomed to be a shortstop to replace Hal Rhyne, who had gone to the majors. Playing nearly the entire 180-plus-game schedule, Crosetti improved to .314 in 1929, and to .334 in 1930. In the latter season he hit 27 home runs, stole 18 bases, and led the league with 171 runs scored.

The slick-fielding leadoff hitter attracted the attention of major-league scouts, including Bill Essick of the New York Yankees. Convinced that he'd just seen the greatest shortstop in the game,[16] Essick persuaded Yankees owner Jacob Ruppert to open his wallet. On August 23, 1930, Crosetti became the property of the Yankees for what eventually amounted to a handful of marginal players—Julie Wera, Bill Henderson, and Sam Gibson—and $75,000 in cash.[17]

Still barely 20 years old, Crosetti remained with the Seals in 1931 for more seasoning at $1,000 a month, one of the league's highest salaries that season. He batted cleanup for the only time in his career and hit .343.

Crosetti was a "scared kid out of San Francisco"[18] who could barely put a sentence together when he met his idol and soon-to-be teammate Babe Ruth on a barnstorming tour that offseason,[19] but he headed to spring training in St. Petersburg in 1932 as the Yankees' leading shortstop candidate.[20] Manager Joe McCarthy drilled him hard—including subjecting him to a rigorous fielding drill in which coach Sunset Jimmy Burke would hit rapid-fire grounders just out of his reach[21]—but Crosetti impressed the skipper as "one of the fastest infielders around [with] a fine, sure pair of hands."[22] Lou Gehrig liked him ("because I kept quiet and didn't pop off"[23]), and double-play partner Lazzeri took him under his wing ("I looked up to him like a big brother"[24]).

Ultimately, McCarthy went with the veteran Lyn Lary at short and started Crosetti at third. Crosetti went 0-for-5 on Opening Day, April 12, against Philadelphia (his first big-league hit, a triple, came in the Yankees' next game) and was benched after batting just .228 in his first 29 games. He won the shortstop job later that summer when Lary stopped hitting, but the inflated expectations stemming from his purchase price and playing in the New York City fishbowl probably dogged Crosetti a bit in those early years.

Crosetti generally balked at interviews, though when he did talk—particularly as he got older –he wasn't shy about expressing opinions. As the last surviving member of the 1932 team, which decisively swept the Chicago Cubs in the World Series that year, he insisted that Babe Ruth had not "called his shot" in Game Three.

The Yankees may have considered trading Crosetti when Billy Werber outplayed him during 1933 spring training. Penciled in the lineup for the benefit of an interested Boston scout for a series of exhibitions as the team headed north, Crosetti turned on the spectacular, and the Yankees jacked up the price. The Red Sox took Werber for $40,000 less.[25]

And yet Crosetti endured relatively unimpressive seasons in 1933 and '34, and was often in danger of losing his job to another infielder. Before the 1935 season he worked out with University of California-Berkeley track coach Brutus Hamilton to become bigger, faster, and stronger,[26] and was assured by McCarthy he was the only shortstop candidate in the running.[27]

And he thrived—though his batting statistics were comparable to his previous season averages, he committed just 16 errors, after hovering around 40 in each of the prior two years, albeit in many fewer games.

Then on August 4, 1935, he blew out his left knee untying his shoes. Crosetti had strained it three weeks before in a collision with the White Sox' Luke Appling, but when he pulled his leg up to get undressed in his Pullman berth that night, some cartilage tore loose and he doubled over in pain. The prognosis: season-ending knee surgery.

Team president Ed Barrow offered Crosetti an invitation to spring training the next year on a provisional $1 contract. But Crosetti not only disposed of any doubt surrounding the status of his knee—securing an $11,000 raise at the start of the season—but he put together the best offensive season of his career, batting .288 with 15 home runs, 78 RBIs, and 18 stolen bases. He was selected to the American League All-Star team.

The surgery had actually helped his batting stance. "I am turned around more," Crosetti said. "And you will notice that I do not swing so hard. I do not fan so often. My timing is better."[28]

Actually, he did strike out quite a bit—83 times in 1936, second-most in the league, and he led the AL in strikeouts with 105 and 97 in 1937 and '38, respectively—but he also proved why traditional statistical categories may not tell the whole story. Crosetti took tremendous pride, for instance, in consistently leading the league in hit-by-pitched-balls, which Yankees coach Art Fletcher taught him how to execute without getting seriously injured.

And even though no one kept track of on-base percentage in those days, in hindsight, his knack for getting himself aboard explains how a career .245 hitter remained successful in the leadoff spot for the Yankees' four-straight World Series championship run from 1936 through 1939. Lifetime, Crosetti's OBP was .341—typically some 90 to 100 points higher than his season averages. His record of 757 plate appearances in 1938 was not eclipsed until 1962, after eight games were added to the major-league schedule.

Crosetti also mastered the hidden-ball trick, which he picked up while with the Seals from teammate-turned-umpire Babe Pinelli. The shape of the old glove, with the large hole above the wrist strap, allowed Crosetti to pretend to flip the ball to the pitcher, then quickly slip his left hand through the hole and pull the ball inside. The pitcher would fiddle with the rosin bag without returning to the rubber as Crosetti would politely ask the baserunner if he could clean the dirt from the base, tagging the startled man out as soon as he stepped off.[29]

Crosetti's shining moment (and greatest thrill) as a player was the 1938 World Series, the Yankees' second sweep of the Cubs. His defensive play, which included nailing a runner at the plate from the foul line in short left field, as well as coming "from nowhere" to turn a "certain single" up the middle into an out,[30] saved three runs in the Yanks' 3-1 victory in the opener. Crosetti's home run off Dizzy Dean in Game Two with two outs in the eighth proved the deciding blast in the 6-3 victory. Ol' Diz no longer had the same zip on his fastball, but he'd handcuffed the fearsome Yankees lineup on four hits — with the Cubs ahead, 3-2 — before Crosetti worked a ten-pitch at-bat into a two-run blast into the left-field seats.[31] Add a two-run double and a two-run triple in Game Four, and Crosetti tallied six RBIs for the Series.

He'd been no slouch in the regular season, either, leading the league in stolen bases (27), hitting 35 doubles (ninth in the league), and setting a record for shortstops by turning 120 double plays.[32] Much of his defensive success in 1938 could be attributed to the arrival of Joe Gordon at second base to replace a graying Lazzeri.

At that time Crosetti had been seeing Norma Devincenzi, whose family owned the apartment building in San Francisco where his brother, John, was a tenant. Crosetti asked her to come to Chicago for the World Series. When he subsequently had to have minor surgery in New York, she followed. He suggested that they get married, and on October 22, 1938, they quietly eloped at the Church of the Transfiguration in downtown Manhattan. Their union lasted until his death, 63 years later, along the way producing a daughter, Ellen, on October 4, 1941 (his 31st birthday), and a son, John, on October 5, 1943.[33]

Brimming with confidence from his marriage, his third straight championship, and another respectable year statistically, Crosetti staged a much-publicized holdout in the early days of spring training 1939, refusing to sign for less than $15,000. By mid-March, he'd caved for $14,000. In the rush to catch up in his conditioning, a process further delayed when he was hit in the leg by a thrown ball, Crosetti developed a sore arm and got off to a slow start. Eventually, he came around — and despite batting only .233, he scored 109 runs (the fourth straight season in triple digits) and was selected to the AL All-Star team (but didn't play). He also caught the

final out of the World Series, another sweep, this time of the Reds — though he went just 1-for-16 — as the Yankees took home their fourth consecutive championship.[34] He received a nice raise, signing for $18,000 by mid-February.

Then, abruptly, the honeymoon ended. Despite Yankees president Ed Barrow's new mandate that all players stay in shape during the offseason, Crosetti, determined to condition himself "slowly" so he wouldn't develop another sore arm, passed up that advice.[35] Yet again by mid-March, the sore arm returned. He couldn't hit anything and bobbled balls on plays he would normally make. After the Yankees lost seven straight in May, McCarthy benched him for a week in favor of Bill Knickerbocker (who couldn't hit or field much better). In August Crosetti was dropped to eighth in the batting order. The Yankees finished third and Crosetti hit .194.

Frank Graham of the *New York Sun* tried to excuse Crosetti's off year — Gordon had also been off all season, and Red Rolfe had been ill, so Crosetti "was trying to cover too much territory on legs that had been pounding the big-league trail for nine seasons."[36] But the talk now shifted to some kid named Phil Rizzuto who'd been tearing up the Yanks' Kansas City farm club. Only timing –the looming possibility that young, unmarried players like Rizzuto might be sent off to war –probably saved Crosetti from being dealt to another club that offseason.[37]

Determined to keep his job, Crosetti had worked furiously to stay in shape, running up the steep hills of San Francisco. He experimented batting left-handed in spring training, hoping it would raise his average.[38] And yet, while many of Crosetti's loyal teammates initially gave the usurper Rizzuto the cold shoulder, Crosetti actively helped the diminutive youngster. He taught Rizzuto how to position himself on each pitch, and how to bluff a bunt. He let him in on the secrets of being hit by a pitch and how to pull off the hidden-ball trick. "He made me look good — and here I am trying to take his job away," Rizzuto recalled years later.[39]

Rizzuto won the starting spot, but when he wasn't hitting by May, the Crow was waiting in the wings to reclaim the position. Then, on June 16, Crosetti was spiked in the throwing hand by Cleveland's Hal Trosky and had to miss some time, and Rizzuto took over again, for good. Crosetti found playing time later in the season at third base when Red Rolfe was hospitalized with chronic ulcerative colitis—but all told, his role was limited to 50 games. On the bench all five games of the Yankees' World Series victory over the Dodgers, Crosetti did what he did best off the field—he played the holler guy again.

The now reportedly "aging" Crosetti (he was only 31, but maybe his thinning hairline had something to do with it) broke camp as a utility infielder in 1942. He worked some with young Jerry Priddy, Rizzuto's minor-league partner up the middle who was being groomed for third base to replace the ailing Rolfe, but Priddy's bat stayed cold, and Crosetti became the starting third baseman. He did a formidable enough job that some Yankees were indignant that he didn't make the AL All-Star team. McCarthy, the AL manager, admitted that had he the choice, he would have chosen Crosetti over Cleveland third baseman Ken Keltner, but the Yankees already had nine representatives, and "we have no right to squawk over the omission of a tenth."[40]

Rolfe displaced Crosetti when he returned later that summer. Crosetti did get into the third game of the World Series, which the Yankees lost to the Cardinals. Playing third base, he shoved umpire Bill Summers over what he considered a bad call. Commissioner Kenesaw Mountain Landis fined Crosetti a reported $250 and suspended him for the first 30 days of the 1943 season.

In February 1943 Crosetti's father, Domenico, was struck by a car and killed. Barrow gave Crosetti permission to report to camp late, on April 10, to spend more time with his family. He didn't report until the beginning of May, however, due to a dispute over whether the Yankees should pay him for the first month of the season.[41] Barrow capitulated[42]—with the war sapping teams of talent, Crosetti would be needed to help fill the void left when Rizzuto joined the Navy. A bout with the flu days before his suspension ended left Crosetti weak and out of shape, however, and rookies Snuffy Stirnweiss and Billy Johnson had the left side

of the infield covered. Crosetti's return on May 21 went by almost unnoticed.

Still, Barrow and McCarthy recognized Crosetti's value on the bench, almost as a secret weapon. Despite continued interest from other teams over the years, Barrow refused to sell him. "I don't care how much they offer," Barrow said. "Nobody can buy Crosetti. He stays with the Yankees as long as I have anything to do with running them."[43] The feeling was mutual—for Crosetti, it was "the Yankees—or nothing."[44]

When Stirnweiss stopped hitting, Crosetti was back at short—and the Yankees turned a slim league lead into double digits for another pennant and a successful World Series rematch with the Cardinals. Crosetti reached base in each of the five games (5-for-18 with two walks), started the winning rally in the sixth inning of Game One with a leadoff single to center, and made game-saving defensive plays in Games Four and Five.

Working in a shipyard in Stockton, California, in the offseason gave Crosetti an occupational draft deferment as a defense worker, but tied him to his job. All he could do was wait patiently, playing semipro ball once or twice a week. When the draft board eased restrictions on men over 30 in July 1944, Crosetti jumped on a train to rejoin the Yankees, who hoped his presence would lead them to another pennant.[45] It didn't, but it gave Crosetti leverage when negotiating his 1945 contract. Again a late holdout, Crosetti signed for $15,000 two weeks before Opening Day. He didn't have the greatest season, but he was better than the alternative—Joe Buzas, who had iron hands.[46]

At 35, Crosetti was slowing down; the war was over, and Rizzuto and the rest of the major-league talent had returned. Crosetti batted .288 in 28 games off the bench in 1946. But his limited role was somewhat convenient, as the Yankees started traveling out west by airplane, and he was afraid to fly. ("It took me too long to accumulate what I have, and I am in no hurry to go where I can't spen[d] it," he said.[47]) He was granted permission to follow the team around by train.

Crosetti signed as a player-coach alongside new manager Bucky Harris for 1947 and got into three games, going hitless in his only at-bat. He went on the inactive list late that summer when the Yankees called up Jack Phillips and Allie Clark. He was making calls to the bullpen on Harris's behalf when the Yankees beat the Dodgers in the World Series.

At his request, Crosetti reported to spring training in 1948 as a player, not as a coach, though even that spring he was helping teammates, such as perfecting pitcher Joe Page's slider so that, as Page put it, it didn't "tear my arm apart."[48] He played in 17 games, in the last of which, on October 3 in Boston, he appeared as a defensive replacement at second base.

After that season—and for the next two decades—Crosetti coached full time. He waved home more than 16,000 men from the third-base coaching box and helped a slew of infielders realize their big-league talent. He also taught pitcher Ryne Duren—a hard-throwing, bespectacled righty whose control was purportedly as bad as his vision—to intimidate batters by firing his first warm-up pitch high over his catcher's head.

He was crafty in other ways, too. According to Rizzuto, "He could steal signs, and knew from the way the pitcher was holding the ball what he might be throwing, a curve or a fastball, and he'd be able to relay it to the batter."[49]

Crosetti lived in a somewhat old-fashioned manner—rising with the sun at 6 A.M., the first one in the clubhouse and the last one out, retiring no later than 9:30 or 10 P.M. (unless there was a night game). Baseball was all that mattered.

Whitey Ford recalled that after one long night of debauchery during spring training he returned to the hotel in Palm Beach with Mickey Mantle and Hank Bauer at 6:30 on a Sunday morning—in time to run into Crosetti on his way to church. When Crosetti asked where they'd been, they sheepishly said they'd just come from Mass. "He looked at us and laughed and went to church," Ford said. "Cro was a great guy. We didn't have to worry about him squealing."[50]

Yet when it came to behaving in a professional context, many saw Crosetti as being too tightly wound. He wouldn't hesitate to call out players for making mistakes if he thought they were not giving their all. When Phil Linz's infamous harmonica playing amid a losing streak started a fracas on the team bus in 1964,

Crosetti had little sense of humor about it, calling it the worst thing he'd ever witnessed in all his years with the club.[51]

And he hardly hid his disdain for the media or anything involving spectacle—pitcher Jim Bouton, who skewered him in his baseball exposé *Ball Four*, wrote that Crosetti's "twin fortes" were "saving baseballs ... to the point of jumping into the stands after them, and chasing photographers off the field."[52] Wrote Dan Daniel of Crosetti's reaction to seeing a pregame dog show on the field at Yankee Stadium: "His comments cannot be printed."[53]

Even after the Yankees would win the World Series, Crosetti wouldn't stick around to celebrate, preferring instead to jump into a car the next day and begin the drive back to Stockton to be with his family. In the offseason, he enjoyed fishing and hunting, biding his time until he could head to Florida for spring training.

When the Yankees needed a guide for young players first joining the team, they had Crosetti pen the 12-page pamphlet. It covered such topics as staying in peak physical condition, eating and sleeping well, hustling, keeping one's temper, and obligations as a teammate and as a public figure—which included choosing one's friends wisely and avoiding the temptations of drinking, carousing, gambling, and loose women. "It takes a man to say no, and it takes a man to realize 100% of his baseball is potential," he wrote, leaving one to wonder a bit about the wording.

In 1966 Crosetti published a youth instructional book titled *Frank Crosetti's Secrets of Baserunning and Infield Play*. It wasn't high literature, but, unlike many other books written by professional athletes, the words were all his, and not those of a ghostwriter or "co-author."[54]

Some called Crosetti the "perfect coach," because he never had any ambition whatsoever to manage.[55] He repeatedly spurned rumors that he was taking over for Casey Stengel ("I would not be manager of the Yankees if the job were offered to me."[56]), and also turned down offers to manage other major- and minor-league clubs.[57]

"You have to worry about 25 guys and make speeches and give out interviews and that doesn't appeal to me," Crosetti said. "Besides, who manages forever? You have a bad year, or don't win when the management thinks you should, and you're gone. Then how do you know you can get another job?

"I've been perfectly happy right where I am … at third base. You don't get a fat salary but you don't have problems either."[58]

As when he was a player, though, he refused to accept being short-changed. Crosetti was the ringleader in a 1962 suit filed on behalf of a couple of hundred contemporaries against the owners' pension committee. The Major League Baseball Players' Association, propelled by lucrative television and marketing deals, had met secretly the previous fall to raise the per-month pension rate to $250; players already retired more than ten years, however, like Crosetti, were frozen at $175. The players lost the suit and eventually settled for $750,000. Decades later, Crosetti was also one of a handful of old-time ballplayers who unsuccessfully brought what they hoped would be a class action against Major League Baseball for using their names and images in promotional materials.[59]

Not that Crosetti was ever in dire straits financially. His World Series checks alone totaled a reported $142,989.30—a stunning amount in an era when season salaries were still in the low five figures. He had also made a small fortune off shrewd real-estate investments—something he began doing while with the Seals when a banker friend advised him to acquire all the local real estate he could find in Depression-era San Francisco.[60]

By 1968, though, the Yankees' World Series bounty had dried up, and Crosetti longed to spend more time with his mother, children, and grandchildren on the West Coast. On October 4, his 58th birthday, he submitted a six-page handwritten letter of resignation.

"I was probably around too long anyway and people were getting tired of looking at me," he wrote. "They say a change once in a while is good for everyone—gives you a new lease on life."

He concluded: "This is not a good-bye—as I hate good-byes. Only a 'I'll see you later.' Come spring, the Cro will be back—only in another uniform. The old saying of years gone by probably will hold true of me also, 'Once a Yankee, always a Yankee!'"[61]

Specifics were unspoken in the letter, but Crosetti had all but signed to coach the expansion Seattle Pilots in 1969, thousands of miles closer to his home in Stockton, California. He grew fond of the Emerald City—despite there not being "enough traffic going around third base to suit me" for the victory-challenged Pilots[62]—and had planned on eventually transitioning into a scouting role with the organization. But Seattle finished dead last, and general manager Marvin Milkes, after supposedly promising Crosetti that he'd be there for more than one season, didn't renew his contract.[63] Crosetti felt betrayed, but before Christmas he'd been recruited by the Minnesota Twins.

Crosetti was in the coach's box along third as the Twins won the AL West division (and lost to Baltimore in the League Championship Series) in 1970. And he was there to shake hands with Harmon Killebrew for the slugger's 500th home run in 1971. Crosetti rarely shook hands after a player hit a round-tripper—Mickey Mantle's walk-off home run in the 1964 World Series and Roger Maris' 60th and 61st homers in 1961 being three other notable exceptions.

But after two seasons, he'd truly had enough. He retired and coached high-school ball—leading St. Mary's in Stockton to a 16-game undefeated season in 1972.

Although he never attended a Yankees Old Timers Day after he retired, Crosetti avidly followed the team from his home in Stockton and was a frequent visitor when the Yankees played Oakland each year, even appearing in the broadcast booth on occasion. Until a broken hip from a fall incapacitated him in January 2002, he went fishing regularly, and he rarely shied away from an opportunity to talk baseball or reminisce about his years in Pinstripes with those who would listen.

"He was Yankee all the way around," his wife, Norma, said after he died at age 91 on February 11, 2002. "He had no other team."[64]

The "old saying" had indeed held true.

SOURCES

Special thanks to the Baseball Hall of Fame for providing me a copy of Crosetti's player file, to Lawrence Baldassaro for sharing his research, and to Crosetti's grandson Michael McCoy for tracking down relatives to answer questions about his grandparents' history. All statistics, unless otherwise noted, are from baseball-reference.com.

Telephone interview by Ellen Biggs, Frank Crosetti's daughter, with Thomas Bourke on November 20, 2011.

A somewhat-abbreviated version of this biography appeared in the book *Bridging Two Dynasties: The 1947 New York Yankees,* edited by Lyle Spatz and published by the University of Nebraska Press in 2013.

NOTES

1 The Yankees lineup in the 1932 World Series featured Babe Ruth, Lou Gehrig, Tony Lazzeri, Earle Combs, Joe Sewell, and Bill Dickey (not to mention Red Ruffing, Lefty Gomez, and Herb Pennock on the mound). Ben Chapman was the other position player not enshrined in Cooperstown.

2 Arthur Daley, "End of the Trail," Sports of the Times, *New York Times,* January 20, 1947.

3 Daniel M. Daniel, "A Shoestring, A Slip and an Injured Right Knee Made Crosetti Yanks' Musketeer Number Three," *New York World-Telegram,* May 21, 1936.

4 Frank Crosetti as told to Al Hirshberg, "I Coach the Hot Corner," *Saturday Evening Post,* August 8, 1959.

5 Ibid.

6 Arthur Daley, "End of the Trail."

7 "Crosetti still has great range," *Sweet Spot,* December 1996/January 1997, Crosetti HOF file

8 Richard Goldstein, "Frank Crosetti, 91, a Fixture In Yankee Pinstripes, Is Dead," *New York Times,* February 13, 2002.

9 Gary Klein, "Frank Crosetti, 91; Yankee Player, Third-Base Coach," *Los Angeles Times,* February 13, 2002.

10 "Crosetti Eagerly Looks Forward To Joining Yankees This Spring," Associated Press report in *New York World-Telegram,* January 11, 1932.

11 Profile, *New York Mirror,* April 10, 1937.

12 Handwritten letter to "Richard," dated January 25, 1997. [Screenshot from eBay, but verified by Michael McCoy, Crosetti's grandson, to be his handwriting.]

13 Ibid.

14 Gary Klein, "Frank Crosetti, 91."

15 Ed R. Hughes, "Frisco to Fatten Up Gaunt Young Pitcher," *The Sporting News,* February 14, 1929.

16 Daniel, "Lou Gehrig, on Hitting Spree, Sets Flag Pace for Yankees," *New York World-Telegram,* June 18, 1935.

17 To put the amount spent on Crosetti in perspective—not that one can compare player purchases—Lefty Gomez had been acquired by the Yankees in 1929 (two months before the stock market crashed) for a mere $45,000.

18 Joseph M. Sheehan, "A Proper Yankee," Sports of the Times, *New York Times,* August 12, 1957.

19 "Crosetti Eagerly Looks Forward To Joining Yankees This Spring," Associated Press report in *New York World-Telegram,* January 11, 1932.

20 Tom Meany, "Crosetti Leading Candidate For Yankee Shortstop Berth," *New York World-Telegram,* March 9, 1932.

21 Tom Meany, "Crosetti and Saltzgaver Pass Critical Yankee Test," *New York World-Telegram,* March 3, 1932.

22 Meany, "Crosetti Leading Candidate For Yankee Shortstop Berth."

23 Stan Isaacs, "The 37 Seasons of Frank Crosetti," Out of Left Field, *Newsday,* April 9, 1968.

24 Paul Votano, *Tony Lazzeri: A Baseball Biography* (Jefferson, North Carolina: McFarland, 2005), 172.

25 Daniel M. Daniel, "A Shoestring, A Slip and an Injured Right Knee Made Crosetti Yanks' Musketeer Number Three," *New York World-Telegram,* May 21, 1936.

26 Daniel, "Lou to Stay At No. 4 in New Lineup," *New York World-Telegram,* March 12, 1935.

27 Daniel, "Yank Midway Combination May Rank Best in League," *New York World-Telegram,* April 6, 1935.

28 Daniel, "A Shoestring, A Slip and an Injured Right Knee."

29 Leo Trachtenberg, "Mr. Yankee, Frank Crosetti," *Yankees Magazine,* October 16, 1986.

30 "Crosetti New Hero of Yankees," United Press report in *New York World-Telegram,* October 6, 1938.

31 The oft-repeated story goes that as Crow was rounding the bases, Dean shouted, "Betcha ya couldn't a done that when I was good!" to which Crosetti responded, "You're damn right I couldn't." See Arthur Daley, "The Durable Crow," Sports of the Times, *New York Times,* November 7, 1960. According to Crosetti, however, the exchange never took place. "At least I didn't hear him," he recalled years later. "I was running with my head down. But it was true—I never could have gotten a loud foul off him when he had his fast ball." Dick Gordon, "Crosetti Vividly Remembers Glory Years of the Yankees." *Baseball Digest,* September 1970.

32 He also led AL shortstops in chances (905) and putouts (352); then again, he tied with Senators third baseman Buddy Lewis for the league lead in errors (47).

33 Several newspapers reported that the owner and operator of the PCL Oakland Oaks at the time, Victor "Cookie" Devincenzi, was Mrs. Crosetti's brother. However, when Crosetti's grandson, Michael McCoy, addressed the matter with his grandmother (in her late 90s in the fall of 2011), she said that none of her brothers ever worked in baseball.

34 Crosetti was also the first player to score on the infamous "Lombardi's snooze" play, in which Charlie Keller collided with Reds catcher Ernie Lombardi at home and knocked the ball from his hands. Crosetti, waiting on the other side of the plate, had motioned for Keller to slide. Dick Gordon, "Crosetti Vividly Remembers Glory Years of the Yankees," *Baseball Digest,* September 1970.

35 Daniel, "Crosetti Sees Good Season," *New York World-Telegram*, March 2, 1940.

36 Frank Graham, Setting the Pace, *New York Sun*, January 16, 1941.

37 Dan Daniel, Daniel's Dope, *New York World-Telegram*, November 27, 1940.

38 Apparently, Crosetti had originally batted lefty in semipro, until his brother informed him of a demand for right-handed hitters. "Crosetti Switches at Bat," *New York World-Telegram*, March 13, 1941.

39 Leo Trachtenberg, "Mr. Yankee."

40 Daniel, "Yanks Favor Crosetti for All-Star Berth," *New York World-Telegram*, June 26, 1942.

41 Crosetti had found a loophole—the baseball rulebook allowed a team to suspend a player for insubordination without pay, but the Yankees hadn't suspended him; the commissioner did.

42 Rud Rennie, "McCarthy's Susp[ects?] To Report to Club," *New York Herald-Tribune*, April 20, 1943. Clipping from Crosetti's HOF File with part of the headline cut off

43 Joe Williams, "Barrow Rates An Assist for Keeping Crosetti," *New York World-Telegram*, October 14, 1943.

44 Daniel, "Johnson Earns Yank Spurs," *New York World-Telegram*, June 22, 1943.

45 Crosetti's presence was so crucial that a group of Canadians wrote to Commissioner Landis protesting the "possible psychic effect" Crosetti would have on opponents; Crosetti was the "property of the United States Government," and the Yankees had "no business whatsoever obtaining unfair help." Letter from W.L. Brown to Commissioner Landis, September 4, 1944, Crosetti HOF player file.

46 Buzas started the first 12 games of the 1945 season at short, made six errors, and never used his glove in a major-league game again.

47 Dan Daniel, "Yankees, Dodgers, Giants Leaders In Air Argosies," *New York World-Telegram*, February 15, 1947.

48 Daniel, "Cards Still Haven't Seen Page's Top Series Form," *New York World-Telegram*, March 17, 1948.

49 Leo Trachtenberg, "Mr. Yankee."

50 "Crosetti still has great range," *Sweet Spot*, December 1996/January 1997, Crosetti HOF file.

51 According to David Halberstam in his book *October 1964* (New York: Random House, 1995), 283, Crosetti was not happy that Linz subsequently received an endorsement deal from a harmonica company—and from then on, when Crosetti would hit fungoes to fielders before the game, he would avoid hitting them to Linz. And Linz had little love for Crosetti, feeling that the coach held a double standard—riding hard the players who weren't stars, but allowing the Mickey Mantles and Whitey Fords to do as they pleased.

52 Jim Bouton, *Ball Four* (New York: Dell Publishing Co., 1971), 22.

53 Daniel, "Frisco Product Proven Maestro," *New York World-Telegram & Sun*, March 9, 1957.

54 Til Ferdenzi, "Crosetti Can Write Like Pro, And His New Book Proves It," *New York Journal-American*, July 2, 1966.

55 Harry Grayson, "Crosetti Most Typical Yankee," NEA wire report in *New York World-Telegram & Sun*, October 3, 1957.

56 Dan Daniel, "Three Managers on Shaky Side," *New York World-Telegram & Sun*, October 12, 1951.

57 Daniel, "Yankees Not Interested in Rudy York," *New York World-Telegram*, February 4, 1948 (turning down an offer to manage the Seattle PCL club); "No Orioles for Frank," *New York World-Telegram & Sun*, September 10, 1954 (turning down an offer to manage the Baltimore Orioles); John Carmichael, "Crosetti Happy To Remain Coach," *Pittsburgh Press*, April 1, 1967 (turning down an offer to manage Newark when it was a Yankees farm club). Crosetti did, however, take over as manager temporarily every so often, such as when Ralph Houk was suspended for seven games in 1961 after a tiff with an umpire. "Leaves from a Fan's Scrapbook," *The Sporting News*, October 18, 1961.

58 John Carmichael, "Crosetti Happy To Remain Coach," *Pittsburgh Press*, April 1, 1967.

59 The suit, *Gionfriddo v. Major League Baseball* (2001), was filed in a California court by Al Gionfriddo, Pete Coscarart, Dolph Camilli, and Crosetti—four high-profile ballplayers active before 1947, when a clause was inserted into all players' contracts to allow their image to be used commercially. They lost because the court concluded that "the public interest favoring the free dissemination of information regarding baseball's history far outweighs any proprietary interests at stake."

60 Daniel, "Frisco Product Proven Maestro," *New York World-Telegram & Sun*, March 9, 1957. The friend was Amadeo Giannini, who founded what is now Bank of America.

61 Jim Ogle, "Crosetti Ends 37 Years in Yankee Uniform," *Newark Star-Ledger*, April 19, 1968. Ogle was one of a handful of writers who suggested that the Yankees retire Crosetti's No. 2, which he had worn since 1945. "Ahh, that's a lot of bull," Crosetti told *Newsday*'s Stan Isaacs. "… I don't think any number should be retired. Maybe Ruth's—that's all because he was special—but the other numbers should be passed on to young players." Stan Isaacs, "The 37 Seasons of Frank Crosetti," Out of Left Field…, *Newsday*, April 9, 1968. Fitting that the number would eventually land with another great Yankees shortstop, Derek Jeter.

62 Joseph Durso, "Crosetti Returns to Stadium Soil," *New York Times*, June 14, 1969.

63 It was probably just as well, since the team would move to Milwaukee a few months later.

64 sportsillustrated.cnn.com/baseball/news/2002/02/12/crosetti_obit_ap

Johnny Sain

By Jan Finkel

First we'll use Spahn, then we'll use Sain,
Then an off day, followed by rain.
Back will come Spahn, followed by Sain
And followed, we hope, by two days of rain.
—Gerry Hern, Boston Post, *September 14, 1948*

NOBODY WOULD MISTAKE *POST* **SPORTS-**
writer Hern's famous lines for "Casey at the Bat" or even poetry except in the broadest sense, but it sums up most of what many people today know about Johnny Sain. That's unfortunate, because Sain was so much more than someone whose name, fortuitously for Hern, rhymed with "rain"—trainer of fighter pilots, ace pitcher, one of the great pitching coaches, and holder of a little-known but remarkable record attesting to his genius as a contact hitter.

He was born John Franklin Sain in the tiny town of Havana, Arkansas (population 375 in the 2010 census), on September 25, 1917, to Eva and John Sain. An automobile mechanic and a good left-handed pitcher at the amateur level, the elder Sain would profoundly affect his son's career, encouraging him early on and teaching him to throw a curve while varying his motions and speed.

No one showed much interest in young Johnny as a pitching prospect, and his journey to the majors became a six-year odyssey. According to author Al Hirshberg, Bill Dickey declined Johnny's father's request to talk to his son after watching him pitch in a high-school game because he didn't want to tell the boy he didn't have it. To make matters worse, Bill Terry tried soon after to talk him out of pursuing a baseball career.

Receiving little encouragement or interest, Sain began a long odyssey to the majors. After graduating from Havana High School in 1935, the 17-year-old Johnny reportedly signed a Class D contract from the Red Sox for $5. However, the Detroit Tigers signed him as an amateur free agent the next year. Whose property was he? It's a good question. He'd signed with the Red Sox first, but he was under age. He was of age

when he signed with the Tigers, but he'd already signed a contract with Boston.

In any case, Sain wound up in the Red Sox' farm system. Memphis native James "Doc" Prothro, manager of the Red Sox farm club in Little Rock, part of the Class A Southern Association, sent him to Osceola in the Class D Northeast Arkansas League for the 1936 season. The 18-year-old gave up a home run to the first batter he faced in a pro game, but still managed to win the contest and go 5-3 with a 2.72 ERA. The Red Sox dropped whatever association they had with Osceola in 1937, and the team began an affiliation with the St. Louis Browns. Despite the change in affiliation, Sain remained with Osceola, the only player from the 1936 roster to do so. The Indians slipped from second place to fifth (out of six) in 1937, and Sain's 5-8, 4.13 slate reflected the decline. Osceola left the league after the season, and Sain landed with the unaffiliated Newport Cardinals of the same league.

Coming into his own in 1938, Sain finished up 16-4 with a 2.72 ERA for Newport, good for a spot on the league's all-star team. Foreshadowing another of his talents, he also batted .257 with a home run and 14 RBIs. Remaining at Newport, now affiliated with the Detroit Tigers, who had originally signed him, Johnny had another strong year in 1939, his 18-10 mark accompanied by a 3.27 ERA; in addition, he and teammate Ed Hughes each set the league record for complete games with 27. Sain, who worked hard to become a good hitter and occasionally played in the outfield when not pitching, topped off his fine season with a .315 average, a pair of homers, and 20 RBIs.

Two good years with Newport weren't enough to get Sain to the majors, but he was unwittingly approaching the turning point in his career. It started innocuously on December 9, 1939, when Detroit traded second baseman Benny McCoy to the Philadelphia Athletics for outfielder Wally Moses. Citing corruption and cover-ups in the Tiger organization, Commissioner Kenesaw Mountain Landis nullified the trade and on January 14, 1940, granted free agency to 91 Detroit players and farmhands.[1] Sain was among the fortunate new free agents and one of 23 released players who made it to the majors, although in his case it would take two more years.

Accordingly, 1940 found Sain with the Nashville Volunteers, a Dodgers affiliate in the Southern Association. His 8-4 mark and 4.45 ERA pale beside the Vols' 101-47 record, good for a .682 winning percentage. The 1941 Vols, no longer a Brooklyn farm club, fell off to 83-70, in second place, and Sain fell much further to 6-12 and a 4.60 ERA. At this point Johnny didn't seem to be going anywhere, but the woeful Boston Braves, possibly on the advice of Pat Monahan, a longtime scout who worked for many teams, or Prothro, and hungry for pitchers, purchased his contract from Nashville and signed him to a major-league contract in March 1942.

Sain made his debut in the Braves' home opener on April 17, 1942—in relief—retiring all seven Giants batters he faced and striking out three in a 4-3 Boston win. For his efforts he was awarded (retroactively) the first save of his career. He picked up his first win on April 29 at Wrigley Field in relief of Al Javery. All told, he went 4-7 with a 3.90 ERA, mostly in relief, for Casey Stengel's last Boston team, a dismal unit that could manage only a 59-89 record and a seventh-place finish.

Even with World War II on, Sain was able to complete the season. Upon receiving his draft notice, he had enlisted for aviation training in the Navy on August 21. However, he didn't have to report until November 15, whereupon he was sent to Amherst College along with fellow big-league inductees Ted Williams, Johnny Pesky, Joe Coleman, and Buddy Gremp. Having completed preliminary ground training by May 1943, Sain was transferred to Chapel Hill, North Carolina, for preflight instruction. After a few months there, he moved on to Corpus Christi Naval Air Training Base and graduated as an ensign in August 1944. He wound up teaching flying at Corpus Christi through the end of the war, receiving his discharge on November 25, 1945.

The experience proved seminal for the young man, who noted, "I think learning to fly an airplane helped me as much as anything. I was twenty-five years old. Learning to fly helped me to concentrate and restimulated my ability to learn."[2] Shortly before his discharge, on October 1, Sain married Dallas native Doris May McBride. The couple had four children—John Jr., Sharyl, Rhonda, and Randy.

Service in the war benefited Sain in a variety of ways. For one thing, his arm got some rest. He threw whenever he could, though, and pitched on several teams against stiff competition that often included other major leaguers. He went 12-4 with the North Carolina Pre-Flight team, appropriately named the Cloudbusters, in 1943, but it was a war-relief game in Yankee Stadium on July 28 that stood out. The Cloudbusters were facing a team made up of reserves from the Yankees and Indians, whose regulars played a charity, regular-season doubleheader that same day. In the sixth inning, "Yank-Lands" third-base coach Babe Ruth left the box to pinch-hit. Seeing the game as a sort of audition in front of a number of big-league officials, Sain wanted to retire the 48-year-old Ruth, but catcher Al Sabo came out and told him not to throw Ruth any curves and risk embarrassing him. As Sain later said, "Taking away my curveball was like cutting off two of my fingers, but it was Babe Ruth in Yankee Stadium. Then, it became obvious that the home plate umpire wasn't going to call any strikes on him. So I threw five medium fastballs, almost batting practice pitches. Ruth took one, then hit a long foul ball and then walked on the last three pitches."[3] It was the Babe's last at-bat in an organized game.

Another benefit of the war years is that a maturing Sain came to realize and accept that although he was large for his era at 6-feet-2 and 180-200 pounds, he didn't have high-octane velocity. Accordingly, he'd have to rely on mechanics, finesse, and guile, letting batters hit the ball and letting his fielders do their jobs. Moreover, he changed his delivery. Through 1942 he constantly varied his arm action, even occasionally throwing from a crossfire motion. As Sain saw it, there were two problems with this approach: He risked hurting his arm, and it wasn't effective (63 walks in 97 innings with Boston in 1942 were ample proof). After the war he kept his windmill windup (he was one of the last pitchers to do so) and threw almost exclusively overhand, dropping down to side-arm on occasion if he was ahead of the hitter.

Finally, there was the curveball his father had taught Sain how to throw. Johnny had a good curve before the war, to be sure, but the knowledge of aerodynamics he'd absorbed as a pilot helped him turn his best pitch into so effective a weapon that he earned the nickname the Man of a Thousand Curves.

Showing no signs of rustiness after a three-year layoff, Sain became a star pitcher and Boston's staff ace in 1946. He turned in a 20-14 slate, a career-best 2.21 ERA, and a league-leading 24 complete games for the Braves, who took a big leap to 81-72 and fourth place under new manager Billy Southworth. Johnny also had the honor on May 11 of pitching the first night game in Boston big-league annals. Facing the Giants in a special "sateen" uniform designed to stand out under the lights, he lost to the Giants, 5-1, in front of 35,945 fans at Braves Field. The pitching highlight of Sain's year, however, came on July 12 at Cincinnati. In the first inning, Grady Hatton hit a pop fly that dropped among three Braves behind third base for a double. No other Red reached base as Johnny beat Ewell Blackwell, 1-0.

Life was improving for the Braves. Tommy Holmes was an effective contact hitter. Bob Elliott, a hustling, hard-hitting team player, was acquired from the Pirates over the winter and won the Most Valuable Player Award in 1947. And there was a decorated war hero, a southpaw who would be the perfect complement to Johnny Sain and a number of other pitchers over a long career—Warren Spahn.

Spahn and Sain became a factor in '47. Spahn had his first great year, going 21-10 with a 2.33 ERA, and Sain was close behind, turning in a 21-12 mark and 3.52 ERA (the relatively high ERA partially offset by an outstanding .346 batting average and only one strikeout in 107 at-bats). At 86-68, the Braves moved up another notch to third place. Sain even became a part of history on Opening Day, April 15, becoming the first major-league pitcher to face Jackie Robinson. Robinson went hitless in three trips to the plate as the Dodgers won, 5-3, at Ebbets Field.

Sain's reward for his fine early-season work was pitching in the All-Star Game at Wrigley Field. Replacing the Cardinals' Harry Brecheen in the seventh inning of a 1-1 contest, he contributed to his own undoing. He got George McQuinn to ground out. Bobby Doerr followed with a single, then stole second. Sain had Doerr picked off second but fired the ball into center field, sending Doerr to third. He struck out Buddy Rosar, but Stan Spence, batting for Spec Shea, singled, scoring Doerr with the go-ahead run. The American League held on for the 2-1 win, and Sain absorbed the loss. Nevertheless, it proved a good year, leaving the Braves and their fans reason to be optimistic.

The 1948 season *almost* brought baseball Nirvana to Boston and New England. The Red Sox finished 96-58, two games ahead of the hated Yankees. The bad news was that the Indians under the leadership of Lou Boudreau were also 96-58. The first playoff in American League history—a one-game affair—saw the Sox go down, 8-3, in Fenway Park as Boudreau put on a one-man show with two homers and four hits. However, the Braves, Boston's "other team" and a perennial poor cousin to the aristocratic Red Sox, took the National League flag with a 91-62 mark that would have been good only for fourth place in the American League.

The close pennant race gave rise to Gerry Hern's often quoted (and misquoted) lines about "Spahn and Sain." In a way Hern took advantage of a little poetic license. He got the Sain part right, but at 15-12 with a 3.71 ERA, Spahn actually had one of the least effective seasons of his brilliant career, a season more typical of a third or fourth starter than an ace. Vern Bickford (11-5, 3.27) and Bill Voiselle (13-13, 3.63) were a touch more effective.

As for Sain, he was in a class by himself, going 24-15 with a 2.60 ERA. He led the league in wins (24), games started (39), complete games (28), and innings pitched (314⅔). He pitched the Braves into first place on June 15, beating the Cubs, 6-3. It was a historic moment, as the game at Braves Field was the first to be televised in the Boston area. Appearing in the All-Star Game on July 13, he had three strikeouts (Vern Stephens, Bobby Doerr, and Hoot Evers, all in the fifth) over 1⅔ hitless innings. The year also included an extraordinary streak of personal endurance. From August 24 to September 21, Sain started and completed nine games, winning seven of them. Backed by Sain's efforts, and equally hot hurling from Spahn, the Braves took 21 of their final 27 games to coast to the National League pennant by 6½ games over St. Louis. *The Sporting News* rewarded Sain by naming him National League Pitcher of the Year, and he was runner-up to Stan Musial in voting for the NL Most Valuable Player Award.

The year wasn't all roses. During the season the Braves signed 18-year-old southpaw Johnny Antonelli for a sum reported to be at least $50,000. As a "bonus baby," Antonelli couldn't be sent to the minors for two years; but since he almost never pitched, he was taking a place on the roster that most players believed belonged to a proven veteran while pocketing more money than most could make in several seasons. Not surprisingly, the presence of Antonelli and other bonus babies made for tension in major-league clubhouses. All of the Braves were annoyed, none more so than Sain, who took his frustrations straight to owner Lou Perini in the front office. Mounting what he called the "Golden Staircase" that led to Perini's door, Sain told the boss that as a proven pitcher he deserved better treatment than an untried teenager. Perini listened, and before the All-Star

Game the Braves gave Johnny a new contract for the remainder of the season—and 1949 as well.

The World Series opened in Boston on October 6, with Sain drawing the nod against the Indians' Bob Feller. It was all a Series contest should be, as both pitchers were at the top of their craft. With the game scoreless in the bottom of the eighth, Bill Salkeld led off with a walk. Phil Masi ran for him, and Mike McCormick sacrificed Masi to second. Feller then intentionally walked Eddie Stanky, with utility infielder Sibby Sisti going in to pinch-run for him. With Sain at bat, Feller turned and fired to shortstop Lou Boudreau in an attempt to pick Masi off second. As the story goes, everyone in Braves Field thought Masi was out—everyone, that is, except second-base umpire Bill Stewart, who had the majority vote and called him safe. Sain lined out, but Tommy Holmes singled past third to score Masi from second and put Boston up 1-0. Sain shut down the Indians in the ninth, and Boston won. Sain had given up four hits on 95 pitches, Feller, two hits on 85 pitches in a game of exemplary efficiency.

After Cleveland won the next two contests, Johnny came back to face Steve Gromek in Game Four at Cleveland and pitched superbly in a 2-1 loss. The Braves staved off elimination in Game Five, but the Indians took Game Six back at Boston, and the Series. Sain was magnificent in defeat—two complete games, a shutout, a heartbreaking loss, nine strikeouts against no walks, nine hits allowed, and a 1.06 ERA.

All told, Sain was arguably the top pitcher in the National League from 1946 to 1948 with a 65-41 record and 2.77 ERA. Indeed, he fit in nicely with his American League counterparts Bob Feller (65-41, 2.75) and Hal Newhouser (64-38, 2.59). Johnny's decline, however, was swift and sudden. He was up and down—mostly down—from 1949 to 1951, going a combined 37-44 with an ugly 4.31 ERA. The kindest thing one can call the 1949 season is a disaster. Spent from his efforts of the year before and a sore shoulder that Sain blamed on his experimenting with a screwball during the spring, he suffered through a career-worst 17 losses (against just ten wins) with a horrendous 4.81 ERA. He had the dubious honor of leading the league in runs (150) and earned runs (130) allowed. For the only time in his career he walked more than he struck out (75 to 73), and he also surrendered more than a hit per inning (285 in 243 innings pitched), starting a pattern that would continue throughout the remainder of his career. True, he completed 16 of his 36 starts, but he was taking a beating most of the time. In short, there is no way to put the season in a positive light. The defending champs of the National League fell to fourth place with a 75-79 mark.

It wasn't just Sain's ailing shoulder at fault; almost everything went wrong for the Braves in 1949. Billy Southworth, whose demands were grudgingly accepted when his teams were winning, reportedly became intolerable during spring training. Claiming credit the players considered theirs and breaking rules that he set, Southworth put the defending National League champs through two-a-day sessions that totaled six hours and instituted a midnight curfew, complete with room checks by clubhouse attendant and watchdog Shorty Young. An early-to-bed, early-to-rise type, Sain usually retired by 9:30. Young checked on Sain just once, waking him out of a sound sleep. Furious, Sain said that if it ever happened again, he'd send the offender out the window. A rumor got out that Southworth had checked up on his star pitcher, that Sain had threatened to throw *him* out the window, and that Sain and Southworth weren't speaking. For his part, Sain said he never socialized with his managers.

Although Sain rebounded in 1950 with his fourth 20-win season (20-13), the won-lost record is deceptive. Even in a year replete with heavy hitters, his 3.94 ERA was well off the league pace. While he completed 25 of his 37 starts, he gave up 294 hits in 278⅓ innings. Particularly ominous was Sain's career-high and league-leading 34 home runs surrendered.[4] He was lucky to win more than he lost, largely because he was pitching for a team that went 83-71 in a nice recovery from the debacle of 1949.

All that kept Sain's 1951 season from being a repeat of 1949 was fewer innings pitched, because the figures were pretty proportional (195 hits in 160 innings and a 4.22 ERA with the Braves). It added up to a 5-13 slate when struggling Boston sold him to the Yankees for $50,000 and a young pitcher who would pay long-term

dividends to the Braves and haunt the Yankees a few years hence—Lew Burdette. Sain appeared in seven games for New York, starting four and completing one, while posting a 2-1 mark. The Yanks won the pennant, and Johnny was brought in to relieve starter Vic Raschi in the seventh inning of Game Six of the World Series with two on and nobody out. He retired the Giants without allowing an inherited runner to score, and worked out of a bases-loaded jam in the eighth. The Giants loaded the bases on three singles in the ninth before Bob Kuzava came in and surrendered two runs (both charged to Sain) but saved the game, 4-3, and the Series for the Yankees. It was hardly an auspicious start for Sain with a new team, especially one that had come to consider World Series titles their birthright (this was their third straight).

Making matters worse, the shoulder injury that had ruined Johnny's 1949 season had never completely gone away. With nothing to lose, he underwent a new radiation therapy from a doctor in Dallas, and was so pleased that he recommended it to others. Teammate Eddie Lopat tried it and was happy. In later years Whitey Ford had it done five times, and Mel Stottlemyre went Ford one better.

One of many keys to the Yankees' phenomenal success from the late 1940s to the mid-1960s was a genius for resurrecting the careers of players thought to be finished. Johnny Mize and Enos Slaughter, for example, had several productive years added to their careers, and Johnny Sain was a chief beneficiary among the pitching fraternity. How the Yankees did it was brilliant in its simplicity, and one wonders why nobody else figured it out. They made him a spot starter and reliever so that a bit fewer than half of his appearances were starts—16 of 35 in 1952 and 19 of 40 in 1953. He completed half of his starts, eight in 1952 and ten in 1953, and relieved superbly the rest of the time. In 1954, his last full year in pinstripes, all 45 of his appearances were in relief, and he saved a league-leading 22 games to become just the second pitcher (after Ellis Kinder of the Red Sox turned the trick the year before) to win 20 games in one season and save 20 in another. As of 2013, Wilbur Wood, Dennis Eckersley, John Smoltz, and Derek Lowe were the only other pitchers to accomplish the feat.

Adapting to his new role, Sain began to pay dividends in 1952 as both starter and reliever. On May 20 he scattered six hits to beat the White Sox, 4-3. He rescued the Yankees twice at Fenway Park on September 24, coming on in the ninth with the game tied and earning a 3-2 win in the opener of a doubleheader, then saving an 8-6 win in the nightcap. Two days later he got the win in relief in the Yankees' 11-inning pennant-clinching 5-2 win in Philadelphia. For the year he was 11-6 with a decent 3.46 ERA and seven saves. He pitched capably but didn't fare well in the World Series against the Dodgers. Taking over in the sixth inning of Game Five for starter Ewell Blackwell with the Yankees leading 5-4, he gave up the tying run in the seventh and the winning run in the 11th to take the 6-5 loss. The Yankees didn't use him again in their hard-fought seven-game win over their subway rivals.

Now a vital part of the Yankee machine, Sain was outstanding in 1953. Again dividing his duties between starting and relieving, he posted a 14-7 mark with nine saves and a 3.00 ERA while earning a spot on the All-Star team. Once again, the Yankees and Dodgers squared off in the World Series. Relieving starter Allie Reynolds in Game One with one out in the sixth and the Dodgers threatening, Sain stopped the damage, pitched the final 3⅔ innings, and picked up the 9-5 win, even contributing a double and a run scored. He was not as effective in his other appearance, in Game Four, but the Yankees nonetheless captured their fifth straight world championship.

By 1954 Sain was a full-time reliever, going 6-6 with a 3.16 ERA and the aforementioned 22 saves. The Yankees had their best season under Casey Stengel with a 103-51 record, but it was only second-best to the Indians' 111-43 mark, the American League record at the time. Johnny wouldn't get a chance to pitch in his fifth World Series.

Shortly into the 1955 season, after three appearances and a 6.75 ERA, the Yankees determined that Sain was finished. On May 11 New York traded Johnny and future Hall of Famer Enos Slaughter (he was hitting .111 at the time) to the Kansas City Athletics for journeyman

pitcher Sonny Dixon and cash. Sain appeared in 25 games for Kansas City, winning two and losing five while posting one save and an ERA of 5.44. He pitched his final game on July 15 and was released the next day.

For someone who toiled in the minors for six years, lost three more years to the war, and got started at an age when most players are entering their peak, Sain had a fine career: 139 wins against 116 losses,[5] a solid 3.49 ERA; an award as *The Sporting News* Pitcher of the Year; four 20-win seasons; three trips to the All-Star Game; four World Series; the league lead in wins once; the league lead in saves once; and league leads in other categories.

That's just the pitching side of the Sain ledger. An outstanding contact hitter, Johnny had always helped himself with the bat. He sported a .245 career average, led the league with 16 sacrifice hits in 1948 (the first pitcher to lead his league in an offensive category), led his league's pitchers in runs batted in five times, and struck out a mere 20 times in 774 lifetime at-bats. Those 20 strikeouts are extraordinary, the fewest for all hitters with between 500 and 800 at-bats from 1910 (when the National League began keeping strikeout records) and 1913 (when the American League followed suit) to the present.

While his playing days were over, Sain wasn't really through. He returned to Arkansas, to Walnut Ridge, and raised his children there. He'd had a prospering Chevrolet dealership in the town since 1952, but at heart he was a baseball man and was happy to get back into the game in 1959 as pitching coach for the Kansas City Athletics. Working with a veteran staff on a team that could do no better than 66-88, he got adequate seasons out of Ned Garver, Bud Daley, Ray Herbert, and Johnny Kucks. Sain resigned after the season to concentrate on business at home.

Catching on in the same capacity with the Yankees when Ralph Houk replaced the fired Casey Stengel for the 1961 season, Sain showed what he could do with good material. Persuading Houk to go with a four-man rotation, he transformed Whitey Ford from a perennially very good pitcher into a great one. Ford, who credited Sain with rejuvenating his career, posted a 25-4 mark and a 3.21 ERA in 1961, good enough to garner his only Cy Young Award; he followed that up with 17 wins in 1962 and 24 in 1963. Ralph Terry found his groove in 1962, leading the league with 23 wins. Jim Bouton, who called Sain "the greatest pitching coach who ever lived," had a career year in 1963 with a 21-7 slate and a 2.53 ERA.

Two contradictory versions exist as to why Sain and the Yankees parted company. Sain said in 1993 that he had heard that Houk was going to move into the Yankee front office, with Yogi Berra taking over as manager. Since Sain doubted that Berra would be effective managing recent teammates, he claimed he resigned. His misgivings were well-founded in that Berra was fired after one season despite leading the Yankees into the World Series.

The alternate version is that Houk showed his appreciation for Sain's helping him to three World Series appearances and two world championships in three years by firing him after the 1963 season. The move mystified many people, but Bouton offered a possible explanation: "What general—Houk started thinking of himself as a general—wants a lieutenant on his staff who's smarter than he is?"

After sitting out for a year, Sain joined the Minnesota Twins in 1965. Helping this club to its first pennant, he got Jim "Mudcat" Grant to achieve a 21-7 mark, good enough to lead the league in wins. Under Sain's tutelage, lefty Jim Kaat went 25-13 with a 2.75 ERA in 1966 to lead the American League in wins and help the Twins finish second. Twins manager Sam Mele was so happy with Sain's contribution that he fired him.

Sain moved from Minnesota to Detroit in 1967. Working with manager Mayo Smith's staff that year, he turned Earl Wilson into a 20-game winner for the first and only time in his career. In 1968, Sain crafted his masterpiece—Denny McLain, whose 31 wins were the most since Lefty Grove achieved the same total in 1931, and haven't been challenged since. With just six losses and a 1.96 ERA, McLain took home the Cy Young and Most Valuable Player awards. With lefty Mickey Lolich picking up three wins in the World Series, the Tigers beat the Cardinals and Bob Gibson. Sain kept McLain sufficiently focused in 1969 to go

24-9 and share the Cy Young Award with southpaw Mike Cuellar of the Orioles.

World Series victory aside, Sain and manager Mayo Smith were barely speaking. Sain's tenure with Detroit soured for good in 1969. One day Johnny took some time off to attend to some personal business. In his absence, Smith had the pitchers run, angering Sain, who asked Smith if he wanted to stick with what worked or with what hadn't worked for 25 years. Smith made his preferences clear on June 15, 1969, when he sold Sain favorite Dick Radatz to Montreal. By August 10, Sain was fired.

The rest of Sain's life was taking a bad turn as well. His marriage had fallen apart, as he later explained: "My first wife went back to college and got her degree at age 50 and it changed the tone of our relationship. My life in baseball seemed more and more trivial to her. The divorce was an enormous financial strain on me. I pretty much lost almost everything I had, to the point that I had to declare bankruptcy."

Attempting to dig out from under, Sain spent the 1970 season until late September as a roving minor-league pitching instructor for the California Angels, becoming friends with Angels minor-league manager Chuck Tanner. Next, Johnny was off to the White Sox, where he managed to stay for six years, in no small part because Tanner was manager the whole time and had the sense to let Sain go about his business. The approach produced incredible results. Wilbur Wood, who started out as a reliever, became a workhorse starter and won 20 games each year from 1971 to 1974. Wood's ERA in 1971 was a minuscule 1.91, and his work in 1972 earned him *The Sporting News* Pitcher of the Year Award. Reunited with Sain, Jim Kaat won 21 and 20 in 1974 and 1975, respectively. Stan Bahnsen, Rookie of the Year with the Yankees in 1968, reached his peak in 1972 with a 21-16 slate. Making Sain's achievement remarkable is that the White Sox usually were a middle-of-the-pack club during his tenure, while the Yankees, Twins, and Tigers had all been contenders or pennant winners.

The years on the South Side of Chicago paid an even greater dividend than all those 20-game winners. On July 3, 1972, now divorced, Sain was introduced to Mary Ann Zaremba, the 35-year-old widow of a

Chicago policeman, at a club in the suburbs. Johnny was smitten. Mary Ann remembered, "He called me the next day and said, 'You have to marry me.'" That seemed a little impetuous, so they compromised on a date at Comiskey Park on the Fourth. The date must have gone well, for they were married on August 24.

Sain coached the Atlanta Braves pitchers in 1977, but on a miserable team that went 61-101, he had only one first-rate pitcher, future Hall of Famer Phil Niekro. Stints with several clubs in Atlanta's farm system followed, and he went back to the Braves for one final fling from 1985 to 1986, where he was reunited with Chuck Tanner on a pair of second-division teams.

Most of Sain's coaching career followed a pattern: Almost immediate success, the lifelong loyalty and devotion of his pitchers that he reciprocated, inevitable conflict with management (and managers), and the search for another job. Often it seems to have been insecurity and jealousy on the manager's part, knowing that the pitchers listened to and respected Sain more than they did him. Sometimes a manager simply thought he knew more or better than Sain, and didn't want to be challenged.

On the flip side, some of the difficulty was Johnny's fault. To begin with, he encouraged pitchers to demand to be paid what they were worth, to mount the "Golden Staircase," as he had done back in 1948. Naturally, this didn't sit well with management. In the second place, he was extremely protective of his charges and wouldn't tolerate interference from anybody, including the manager. His refusal to speak ill of any of his pitchers led Detroit skipper Mayo Smith to conclude that he could never get a straight answer from Sain on a pitcher's physical condition, state of mind, or anything else. Ironically, Houk, Mele, and Smith all won a *Sporting News* Manager of the Year Award with Sain as their pitching coach, then left town not long after Sain's departure.

Always willing to stick up for his pitchers, he further endeared himself to hurlers by not making them run. Some baseball people found this strange, but Sain had two reasons for the tactic, one practical and the other philosophical or pedagogical. On the practical side he noted, "You don't run the ball up to home plate." On

the philosophical or pedagogical side, Sain said, "I've always felt that a lot of pitching coaches made a living out of running pitchers so they wouldn't have to spend that same time teaching them how to pitch." On the other hand, he believed that pitchers had to keep their arms strong, so he had them throw almost every day, even after a long stint on the mound the day or night before. To keep pitchers mentally focused, he had, as an example, Wednesday's pitcher chart pitches for Tuesday's game; that way, the pitcher could observe both his teammates and the opposing pitchers and hitters. It seems of obvious benefit, and most managers and pitching coaches now have their pitchers chart the game, but Sain seems to have been the first to make it a practice.

Finally, Sain brought his own brilliant creation to the table. Noted baseball author Roger Kahn described it in *The Head Game*:

The Yankees hired Sain in 1961 as pitching coach. He showed up with a briefcase full of inspirational books and tapes and a machine he was patenting as the "Baseball Pitching Educational Device," which everyone soon called "the Baseball Spinner." Baseballs were mounted on rotating axes—one axis per ball—and you could snap one in a variety of fastball spins and the other in rotations for sliders and curves. The baseballs were anchored. Except for rotating, they didn't move. Using John Sain's Baseball Pitching Educational Device, you could practice spinning your delivery at home or in a taxi or in a hotel room without endangering lamps, mirrors, or companions.

What Sain achieved as a pitching coach (sixteen 20-game winners in all or part of 17 seasons) is impressive, given the diversity of talents he worked with. Some, like Whitey Ford and Denny McLain, had experienced considerable success. On the other hand, Jim Bouton, Jim Kaat, Mudcat Grant, and Stan Bahnsen had yet to show how capable they were. Then there was Wilbur Wood, undergoing the transformation from reliever to starter.

The project that best epitomizes Sain at work has to be Denny McLain. The quintessential flake, McLain had all the tools to be a great pitcher except seriousness of purpose, sense, and maturity. Sain took Denny for what he was and worked his magic indirectly. Learning that McLain was working to obtain a pilot's license, Sain helped him prepare for the required tests, and even went up in the air with him. From that basis the two moved to McLain's pitching so smoothly that he was the best pitcher in the American League in 1968 and 1969, winning 55 games, a Most Valuable Player Award, and two Cy Youngs. At 25, he already had 114 wins under his belt and seemed on path for the Hall of Fame. What McLain's career might have been had he had Sain's guidance for a few more seasons is pure speculation, but the train wreck — erratic and criminal behavior; suspensions from baseball; prison for drug dealing, racketeering, and extortion; poor health in the form of obesity and heart trouble; and who knows what else — that has been McLain's life in the more than 40 years since is indisputable. Denny needed grounding, and Sain gave it to him for a magical couple of years.

Out of baseball, the Sains settled down to a quiet life in the Chicago suburb of Downers Grove, Illinois. John lectured and consulted with various teams and players, happy to talk with anybody who wanted to listen about the fine art of pitching. Mickey Lolich, a beneficiary of Sain's tutelage, could have been speaking for scores of pitchers when he described his mentor: "Johnny Sain loves pitchers. Maybe he doesn't love baseball so much, but he loves pitchers. Only he understands them."

Over the years there has been talk of enshrining coaches in the Hall of Fame. Writing of Sain in *Newsday*, Roger Kahn noted, "The Hall of Fame admits broadcasters, umpires, entrepreneurs, even newspaper writers. For goodness sake, let's enshrine a great coach."[6] Mike Shalin, Neil Shalin, and Brent Kelley, authors of books about players who were not in the Hall of Fame at the time of writing, have indicated support for the cause. Former White Sox GM Roland Hemond, Jim Bouton, Jim Kaat, and others have spoken up for Sain. There have been some letter-writing campaigns. Nevertheless, the movement has never gained sufficient traction.

Cooperstown notwithstanding, the Boston Braves Historical Association saw that Sain was honored for his years in their city. Sain, Warren Spahn, and Sibby Sisti were inducted into the Boston Braves Hall of Fame on October 16, 1994. Four years later, on October 4, 1998, the Association sponsored a 50th-anniversary celebration of the Braves' championship season. Bob Feller came to town, and the two aces revisited their pitching duel and the pickoff play that "failed."

After suffering a stroke on March 31, 2002, Sain spent his remaining years in ill health. On August 31, 2002, he became the seventh player inducted into the Braves' franchise Hall of Fame at Turner Field. Mary Ann wrote an acceptance speech for him; they couldn't attend the induction, but Hank Aaron read the speech at the ceremony in Atlanta.

Johnny Sain died on November 7, 2006, in Resthaven West Nursing Home in Downers Grove. Surviving him were Mary Ann, his four children, 11 grandchildren, and two great-grandchildren. Returning to Havana, he was buried in Walker Cemetery after a ceremony attended by many of his former pitching "pupils" and other friends he had made in the game. Several teams sent gorgeous floral arrangements; in death, all the hard feelings were forgotten.

The last pitcher to face Babe Ruth and the first to face Jackie Robinson, Sain started the first night game in Boston and the first game televised in New England, unleashed the potential of pitchers like Mudcat Grant, Jim Kaat, Earl Wilson, and Mickey Lolich, and coached probably the last 30-game winner. In the words of baseball historian Maxwell Kates "a veritable Forrest Gump in baseball history," Johnny Sain left a rich legacy.[7]

This article originally appeared in two different books: *Sock It To 'Em Tigers — The Incredible Story of the 1968 Detroit Tigers*, published by Maple Street Press in 2008; and *Spahn, Sain and Teddy Ballgame — Boston's Almost Perfect Baseball Summer of 1948*, published by Rounder Books in 2008.

ACKNOWLEDGMENTS

Gabriel Schechter, former research associate at the Hall of Fame, provided me with copies of the National and American Leagues' daily sheets detailing each of Sain's games and files of pitchers who came under Sain's tutelage.

Bob Brady sent me copies of the articles by Ed Rumill, thoroughly and thoughtfully reviewed my work, and provided me with invaluable material that I had missed.

Jim Sandoval and Rod Nelson, co-chairmen of SABR's Scouts Committee, guided me through the intricacies of scouts, contracts, and franchises—all as they applied to Sain.

Saul Wisnia and James Forr edited versions of this article. They made it better.

I'm grateful to everyone for their kindness, generosity, and friendship.

SOURCES

Allen, Thomas E., *If They Hadn't Gone: How World War II Affected Major League Baseball* (Springfield: Southwest Missouri State University, 2004).

Bailey, Jim, "Sain stood out as pitcher, excelled as coach." *Arkansas Democrat-Gazette.* November 16, 2006.

Eig, Jonathan, *Opening Day: The Story of Jackie Robinson's First Season* (New York: Simon & Schuster, 2007).

Fagen, Herb, "Johnny Sain Did It His Way … As a Pitcher and Coach," *Baseball Digest.* December 1993.

Gilbert, Bill, *They Also Served: Baseball and the Home Front: 1941-1945* (New York: Crown Publishers, 1992).

Hirshberg, Al, *The Braves: The Pick and The Shovel* (Boston: Waverly House, 1948).

_____, "What Really Happened to the Boston Braves?" *Sport.* January 1950.

James, Bill, and Rob Neyer, *The Neyer/James Guide to Pitchers: An Historical Compendium of Pitching, Pitchers, and Pitches* (New York, London, Toronto, and Sydney: Simon & Schuster, 2004).

Johnny Sain files at the National Baseball Hall of Fame and Museum in Cooperstown, New York.

Johnson, Lloyd, and Miles Wolff, eds. *The Encyclopedia of Minor League Baseball.* 3rd ed. (Durham, North Carolina: Baseball America, Inc., 2007).

Kaese, Harold, *The Boston Braves, 1871-1953* (Boston: Northeastern University Press, 2004). Reprint of 1948 original and 1954 reprint issued by Putnam.

Kahn, Roger, "A Slide Rule Can't Measure a Ballplayer," *New York Newsday.* July 29, 1994.

_____, *The Head Game: Baseball Seen From the Pitcher's Mound* (San Diego, New York, and London: Harcourt, Inc., 2001).

Kates, Maxwell, "Van Lingle Mungo." Baseball Analysts (baseballanalysts.com), November 13, 2006.

Kelley, Brent, *The Case For: Those Overlooked by the Baseball Hall of Fame* (Jefferson, North Carolina: McFarland, 1992).

McCann, Mike, "Mike McCann's Page of Minor League History," geocities.com/big_bunko/minor.html.

O'Donnell, Jim, "Mind over Batter: Ex-Major League Baseball Star and Coaching Legend Johnny Sain Never Was One to Do Things by the Book," *Chicago Tribune,* October 10, 1993. Reprint from *Chicago Tribune* archives at chicagotribune.com.

Peary, Danny, ed., *We Played the Game: 65 Players Remember Baseball's Greatest Era, 1947-1964* (New York: Hyperion, 1994).

Professional Baseball Players Database Version 6.0

Rumill, Ed, "Johnny Sain—Hero of the Hub," *Sport Pix,* February 1949.

_____, "Twenty for Sain, *Baseball Magazine,* January 1947.

Sandoval, Jim, and Bill Nowlin, eds., *Can He Play? A Look at Baseball Scouts and Their Profession* (Phoenix: Society for American Baseball Research, 2011), Electronic book.

Shalin, Mike, and Neil Shalin, *Out by a Step: The 100 Best Players NOT in the Baseball Hall of Fame* (London, South Bend, New York, and Oxford: Diamond Communications, 2002).

Siegel, Arthur, "Sain Is Product of Own Planning to Be Box Star," *Sports Parade.* October 13, 1948.

Thorn, John, and John Holway, *The Pitcher: The Ultimate Compendium of Pitching Lore: Featuring Flakes and Fruitcakes, Wildmen and Control Artists, Strategies, Deliveries, Statistics, and More* (New York, London, Toronto, Sydney, and Tokyo: Prentice Hall Press, 1988).

Tourangeau, Dixie, "Spahn, Sain, and the '48 Braves," *The National Pastime* 18 (1998), 17-20.

Vincent, David, Lyle Spatz, and David W. Smith, *The Midsummer Classic: The Complete History of Baseball's All-Star Game* (Lincoln and London: University of Nebraska Press, 2001).

Westcott, Rich, *Masters of the Diamond: Interviews with Players Who Began Their Careers More Than 50 Years Ago* (Jefferson, North Carolina: McFarland, 1994).

Wright, Craig R., and Tom House, *The Diamond Appraised* (New York and London: Fireside Books at Simon & Schuster, 1989).

sabr.org

baseballindex.org

baseball-reference.com

retrosheet.org

baseballlibrary.com

baseball-almanac.com

paperofrecord.com

proquest.com

NOTES

1   McCoy and Connie Mack made out nicely in the whole affair. Attracting bids from several clubs, McCoy signed with the Athletics for a $45,000 bonus and a two-year contract at $10,000 a year. Mack

kept Moses and obtained the second baseman he wanted in the first place.

2   Thomas E. Allen, *If They Hadn't Gone: How World War II Affected Major League Baseball* (Springfield: Southwest Missouri State University, 2004), 136.

3   Jim O'Donnell, "Mind Over Batter: Ex-major League Baseball Star And Coaching Legend Johnny Sain Never Was One To Do Things By The Book," *Chicago Tribune* (October 10, 1993).

4   Sain, Ken Raffensberger of the Reds, and Preacher Roe of the Dodgers all gave up 34 homers in 1950. It was the third highest number of home runs surrendered up to the time. Murry Dickson of the Cardinals gave up 39 in 1948, and Larry Jansen of the Giants was tagged 36 times in 1949. Jansen also gave up 31 homers in 1950.

5   Allen, 139. Allen projects a 45-33 slate with a 3.21 ERA for the three seasons Sain missed due to the war, but such projections seem to be enjoyable speculations.

6   *New York Newsday.* July 29, 1994.

7   Maxwell Kates, "Van Lingle Mungo." Baseball Analysts (www.base-ballanalysts.com), November 13, 2006.

Harry Brecheen

By Gregory H. Wolf

A TWO-TIME ALL-STAR, SLICK-FIELDING southpaw hurler Harry "The Cat" Brecheen broke in with the St. Louis Cardinals as a 28-year-old rookie in 1943 after a cup of coffee in 1940. He established himself as one of the National League's premier twirlers over a six-year period (1944-1949), during which he led the league in wins (96) and earned-run average (2.80) despite battling a chronically sore elbow. Brecheen, who pitched for three pennant winners, was recognized as a big-game pitcher. In the Cardinals' World Series victory over the Boston Red Sox in 1946, he became the first left-hander in big-league history to earn three wins in one Series. He compiled an impressive 4-1 record with a microscopic 0.83 ERA in 32⅔ innings in the fall classic. After hurling for the St. Louis Browns in his final season (1953), he remained with the club as it relocated to Baltimore, where he enjoyed a successful 14-year career as the Orioles' pitching coach.

Harry David Brecheen (pronounced Bruh-KEEN) was born on October 14, 1914, in Broken Bow, Oklahoma. He was the first of three children born to Texans Tom and Lucy (Tyree) Brecheen, who had settled in the small town near the Texas border when Oklahoma was still a territory. By the time Harry was 10, his family had relocated to Ada, then a city of fewer than 8,000 residents in the south-central part of the state. Harry was a scrawny kid and a natural left-hander who fought his teachers' attempts to make him write with his right hand. More interested in sports than school, little Harry seemingly always had a bat, glove, fishing rod, or gun in his hand while growing up on the family farm on the outskirts of the city.

Brecheen gathered most of his pitching experience in the local junior American Legion league where he supposedly won 65 games and lost just three times. Brecheen idolized Oklahoma native Carl Hubbell and hometown big leaguers Lloyd and Paul Waner, who generously supported baseball in Ada. The Tulsa Oilers of Class A Texas League invited 18-year-old Brecheen to try out with the club during spring training in 1933, but he was no match for seasoned players, many of whom had big-league experience.[1] He returned to Ada, married his high-school sweetheart, Vera Caperton, in the fall, and was lucky to find a job in construction during the harsh times of the Depression. Brecheen also pitched in local semipro leagues and soon earned the attention of scouts despite his small 5-foot-10, 160-pound stature. According to St. Louis sportswriter Bob Broeg, Brecheen turned down a $175-a-month contract from the St. Louis Cardinals and a similar offer from the New York Yankees, claiming he could earn money as a semipro.[2]

Brecheen commenced his grueling eight-year odyssey in the minor leagues in 1935 as a fastball-curveball artist with poor control. With the help of former big-league pitcher and Ada businessman Homer Blankenship, he signed with the Galveston (Texas) Buccaneers of the Class A Texas League but was soon transferred to the Greenville (Mississippi) Buckshots of the Class C East Dixie League. After another shot with the Buccaneers in 1936, Brecheen was sent to the Bartelsville (Oklahoma) Bucs in the Class C Western

Association and finished the season with a combined 6-22 record and 132 walks in 266 innings.

No one could have predicted Brecheen's stunning success in 1937 with the Portsmouth (Virginia) Cubs (Class B Piedmont League). He had learned to throw a screwball a few years earlier from big leaguer and fellow Oklahoman Cy Blanton of the Pittsburgh Pirates, but had been unable to get it over the plate. "I owe an awful lot to (Portsmouth catcher) Dick Luckey," Brecheen said. "Until I met him, I was just trying to throw the ball past hitters, always trying for strikeouts. But he worked on my control and showed me what it mean to think a game."[3] With his catcher's patience, Brecheen perfected his screwball so that it broke down and away from right-handed hitters and into left-handers (the opposite break of his curveball). He went 21-6 and walked only 69 in 249 innings. The St. Louis Cardinals, acting on the advice of Eddie Dyer, then the president of the Cardinals affiliate in the Piedmont League, drafted the wiry southpaw.

Brecheen joined an organization that he had once derided as a "chain gang" for its poor salaries and vast farm system.[4] He spent two years with the Houston Buffaloes of the Class A1 Texas League, going 13-10 in 1935 and improving to 18-7 in 1936, including a stretch of four consecutive shutouts and 38 consecutive scoreless innings.[5]

No team in the big leagues had a farm system as stacked with pitchers as the Cardinals in the late 1930s and early 1940s. Brecheen was also aware that Cardinals boss Branch Rickey preferred big, hard-throwing pitchers, like Mort Cooper and Max Lanier. After a productive spring, Brecheen made the Cardinals' Opening Day roster in 1940, but the southpaw's euphoria did not last long. After tossing 3⅓ innings (surrendering one unearned run) in three brief relief appearances, he was optioned to the Columbus Red Birds of the American Association, and didn't make it back to big leagues until 1943 — the year after Rickey left the club. The years 1940-1942 played like a broken record for Brecheen. "Stymied" (according to *The Sporting News*) by the surfeit of Cardinals pitchers, Brecheen annually participated in spring training, then was optioned to

Columbus, where he posted successive records of 16-9, 16-6, and 19-10.[6]

Brecheen was back in spring training with the reigning champion Cardinals in 1943 under vastly different circumstances. St. Louis had used its three options on Brecheen, and thus was forced to keep him on the big-league club or sell him. The club's decision was made easier by World War II, which had already begun playing havoc with the Cardinals' roster; among other things, the team lost 21-game-winner Johnny Beazley to the military.

Manager Billy Southworth saw the 28-year-old Brecheen as an ideal swingman. In his season debut, Brecheen tossed three innings of scoreless relief against the Chicago Cubs to notch his first big-league win. He extended his string of innings without allowing an earned run to 20⅔ (dating back to 1940) before yielding a run in a tough 1-0 loss on May 31 to the Brooklyn Dodgers in his first start and complete game. Pushed into the starting rotation with the loss of Howie Pollet to the war and Ernie White to injury, Brecheen won four of seven starts in August and limited opponents to a sparkling 1.89 ERA over 57 innings. While the Cardinals cruised to their second consecutive pennant, Brecheen posted a 9-6 record and a career-low 2.26 ERA in 135⅓ innings for the NL's best staff.

In the Cardinals' World Series rematch with the New York Yankees, Brecheen pitched three times, all in relief. After scoreless stints of one inning and two-thirds of an inning in losses in Games One and Three, he relieved Lanier to start the eighth inning in Game Four, with the score tied, 1-1. He surrendered a double to the first batter he faced, pitcher Marius Russo, who later scored the deciding run on Frank Crosetti's fly ball. The Yankees closed out the Series the next game.

Cardinals beat writer Roy Stockton began referring to rookie Brecheen as "The Cat" because of his quick, feline-like reflexes on the mound and excellent fielding.[7] "Harry the Cat" became such a recognizable nickname that papers did not need to mention Brecheen's surname. Brecheen led or co-led the NL with a 1.000 fielding percentage three times (1944, 1948, and 1950), and had four additional errorless seasons (1940, 1943, 1952, and 1953) in which he did not log enough innings to qualify for the crown. He committed only eight errors in more than 1,900 major-league innings.

Throughout Brecheen's career, sportswriters had a field day describing his appearance and small size. With blue eyes, dark blond hair and a weatherbeaten face, Brecheen was a "wiry [and] slender" country boy who felt at home in a Cardinals dugout filled with country boys like Lanier, Al Brazle, and Marty Marion.[8] Bob Broeg described Brecheen as a "hollow-cheeked, bandy-legged son of Oklahoma's red-clay country."[9] One of the most poetic characterizations came from syndicated columnist Red Smith, who saw Brecheen as "a scrawny little scrap of meat, just a fragment of whale bone and rawhide."[10] But Brecheen would not shy away from hitters. "[He] would buzz anybody," said teammate Chuck Diering. "He was a mean pitcher; a tough competitor."[11]

Brecheen got off to a hot start in 1944, shutting out the Chicago Cubs in his season debut and winning 13 of his first 15 decisions through August. He had an unflappable presence on the mound and rarely showed any emotion. "Deadpanned and apparently nerveless," wrote the United Press's Stan Mockler, "Brecheen has a reputation for having ice water in his veins."[12] After the loss of All-Star Red Munger to the war at midseason, Brecheen (16-5) formed the league's most formidable quartet of pitchers with Cooper (22-7), Lanier (17-12), and Ted Wilks (17-4); Brecheen's 2.85 ERA in 189⅓ innings was the highest of the lot. En route to their third consecutive pennant, the Cardinals became the first National League team to record 100 or more victories in three consecutive seasons. As a child, Brecheen had suffered a broken ankle and had a spinal malformation that kept him out of the war with a 4-F classification.

In October the Cardinals and the St. Louis Browns squared off in the Trolley Series with all games played in Sportsman's Park, which both teams called home, though the park was owned by the Browns. In an unexpectedly competitive World Series that the Cardinals won in six games, Brecheen tossed a complete-game victory in Game Four, winning 5-1. In trouble for most of the game, he yielded nine hits and walked four, but helped himself by recording three assists and one putout.

Brecheen started the 1945 campaign with two complete-game victories, but then came down with a sore elbow which bothered him for the rest of his career. Limited to just 43⅔ mostly ineffective innings by the All-Star break, Brecheen turned his season around in the second half. No longer capable of both starting and relieving because of elbow pain, Brecheen commenced one of the best stretches of his career, completing 11 of 13 starts (with just one relief appearance), winning 12 of 14 decisions, and carving out a microscopic 1.50 ERA in 113⅔ innings. Brecheen, early-season acquisition Red Barrett (21-9 with St. Louis) and rookie Ken Burkhart (18-8) kept the Redbirds in a tight race with the upstart Chicago Cubs, who eventually won the pennant. With a 15-4 record, Brecheen led the senior circuit with a .789 winning percentage and compiled the league's third-best ERA (2.52).

Brecheen's success resulted from exceptional control, a deceptive pitching motion, and his knee-buckling curve and screwball. Dizzy Dean was effusive in his praise of Brecheen: "For a little guy, Brecheen gets a lot on the ball. With the kind of control he's got, he could thread a needle with the ball. He's the nearest thing to Carl Hubbell. … Hub had a better screwball, but I don't think he threw that fast."[13] Brecheen would have been a darling to sabermetricians had such advanced metrics existed. For seven straight seasons (1944-1950) he ranked among the top eight NL pitchers allowing the fewest hits and walks (WHIP) per nine innings and the top ten for strikeout-to-walk ratio. "There's nobody I've seen with a finer pitching motion," said Brooklyn Dodgers star Pete Reiser. "Brecheen hides the ball well and he has fine deception."[14] Not a hard-throwing or overpowering pitcher like contemporaries Ewell Blackwell of the Cincinnati Reds or Kirby Higbe of the Brooklyn Dodgers, Brecheen threw a "sneaky-quick" side-arm fastball that caught batters off guard.[15] "Everybody says my screwball is my payoff pitch, but I really don't use it that often," Brecheen once revealed. "It just gives the batter one more delivery to worry about."[16]

With the conclusion of World War II, the Cardinals anticipated that pitchers Beazley, Murry Dickson, Howie Krist, Munger, and Pollet would be back with team in 1946; consequently, rumors swirled that Brecheen would be traded before Opening Day. However, when Eddie Dyer replaced Billy Southworth as manager of the club in the offseason, Brecheen was reunited with a strong supporter. "I can't say that I realized that Cat would become the great pitcher he has," said Dyer, who had a soft spot in his heart for the hurler he brought to the organization.[17] The Cardinals broke camp with what *Sporting News* publisher J.G. Taylor Spink called "the greatest bunch of hurlers ever assembled on one club."[18] The staff led in the NL in ERA for the fourth time in five years, but not all went according to plan. Lanier and Freddie Schmidt jumped to the outlaw Mexican League in late May, Munger's return was delayed until late August, and Beazley and Burkhart were plagued by arm woes. Brecheen, battling his own chronic elbow pain, pitched consistently all season, often on five or six days' rest, and finished with a deceptive 15-15 record. A hard-luck loser, Brecheen got three runs or fewer in 14 of those losses (20 runs total). He finished with the league's fifth best ERA (2.49) and led the loop with five shutouts. Saving his best for last, he tossed a four-hitter to defeat the Chicago Cubs, 4-1, in the next to last game of the season, thereby guaranteeing the Cardinals a share of the pennant. St. Louis lost the following day to set up a dramatic three-game playoff against the Dodgers. Brecheen came on in relief of road roommate and good friend Dickson with two outs in the ninth inning, protecting an 8-3 lead in Game Two. After surrendering an RBI single and issuing a walk, Brecheen struck out the last two batters to send the Cardinals to the World Series for the fourth time in five years.

Brecheen's performance in the World Series against the Boston Red Sox was arguably his crowning achievement in the big leagues. In Game Two he hurled a dominating four-hit, 3-0 shutout to even the Series at one game apiece. He struck out four and knocked in the game's first run with a single in the third inning. With the Cardinals facing elimination in Game Six, Brecheen limited Boston to just one run in a complete-game seven-hitter to earn the win, 4-1, and set up a winner-take-all Game Seven. Though Brecheen was suffering from a cold, Dyer called on his diminutive lefty one last time. With no outs in the eighth inning and runners on second and third, Brecheen relieved Dickson, who was nursing a 3-1 lead. He set down two batters then yielded a two-run double to Dom DiMaggio that tied the game, 3-3. But then in the bottom of the eighth, in one of the most memorable plays in the annals of the World Series, Enos Slaughter scored from first on Harry Walker's double with two outs to give the Cardinals a 4-3 lead. Brecheen, with his customary wad of chaw in his mouth, gave up two singles to lead off the ninth, but then secured the final two outs with runners on the corners, giving St. Louis its third title in five years. "The Cat's got a head, heart, and guts," said Dyer after the game.[19] With the dramatic victory, Brecheen became the first left-hander to win three games in one World Series, and the first pitcher of any kind to accomplish the feat since Stan Coveleski of the Cleveland Indians in 1920. Mickey Lolich (1968) and Randy Johnson (2001) are the only other left-handers among the 13 pitchers to win three games in one World Series. "Brecheen is a remarkable pitcher," gushed *The Sporting News*. "He doesn't throw hard and his curveball doesn't break much. But what a gamester he is."[20]

With the addition of a "tantalizing slider" to his pitching arsenal, the hero of the '46 World Series opened the 1947 season with seven consecutive complete games, winning five of them.[21] He was named to the first of two All-Star teams, joining Cardinals starters Marion (SS) and Slaughter (LF) and backups Stan Musial (1B), Whitey Kurowski (3B), and Munger. Brecheen pitched the fourth through sixth innings, yielding five hits and one run. Despite persistent elbow pain since early July, Brecheen won his first three starts after the Midsummer Classic to push his record to 12-5. He struggled the last two months to finish with a 16-11 record while the aging Cardinals fell to second place behind their archrivals, the Brooklyn Dodgers.

At the age of 33 and plagued by an elbow that puffed up like a balloon after every start, Brecheen needed some extra time between starts during the cold weather of the early weeks of the 1948 season. He responded to

Dyer's gift by opening the season with three consecutive shutouts, the third of which was his only career one-hitter, a 5-0 victory over the Philadelphia Phillies. He ran his streak of scoreless innings to a personal-best 32 in his fourth consecutive complete-game victory, 8-3. "I can snap off a sharper curve [and] that gives me an effective counter for batters looking for a screwball," said Brecheen, who added that he was pain-free for the first time in more than four years.[22] The Cardinals were in an exciting pennant race with the Dodgers and Boston Braves, but lacked the pitching depth, long the hallmark of the great Cardinals teams, to overtake their competition. Brecheen won 11 of his last 14 decisions en route to a career year for a second-place club. His 20 wins and 21 complete games trailed only Johnny Sain, and the Cat led the NL in ERA (2.24) and shutouts (7) while surrendering only six home runs in a career-high 233⅓ innings. Surprisingly, Brecheen, who was never a big strikeout pitcher, led the NL with 149 punchouts, including two games with a career-high ten. (He had also struck out ten in a game in 1946). He was named to his second and final All-Star Game, joining starters Musial, Slaughter, and Red Schoendienst (2B), but did not pitch.

With the oldest pitching staff in the big leagues in 1949, the Cardinals mounted their last serious challenge for the pennant until 1964. Brecheen (14-11) and Brazle (14-8) were the grizzled veterans at 34 and 35 respectively; Munger (15-8) was 30 and Pollet (20-9) was the youngster at 28. The 34-year-old Brecheen won three of four starts between September 8 and 25 to maintain the Cardinals' precarious 1½-game lead over the Dodgers and Phillies. But after emerging victorious so often in close games and races, the Cardinals saw their luck run out. They lost their next four games (including one by Brecheen) and needed a victory and a loss by the Dodgers in the last game of the season to set up another playoff with Brooklyn for the pennant. The Dodgers won. Brecheen made a career-high 31 starts and logged over 200 innings for the fourth consecutive and final time in his career.

As the effects of age and ongoing elbow problems took their toll, Brecheen saw increasing duty out of the bullpen during his last three years with the Cardinals

(1950-1952). His workload steadily decreased from 163⅓ to 100⅓ innings. In 1950 he posted his first losing record (8-11) as the Cardinals fell into the second division for the first time since 1938.

Brecheen's value to the Cardinals, however, could not be measured in wins and losses. Always a student of the game, he mentored prospects and veterans alike. "The Cat has a great knack of working with young pitchers and imparting his knowledge," said Fred Saigh, who purchased the Cardinals from Sam Breadon after the 1947 season.[23] In 1952 Eddie Stanky (the Cardinals' third manager in three years) named Brecheen "pitcher-coach."[24] Considered washed up as a player, Brecheen surprised his skipper and teammates by winning five straight decisions in midsummer, including his 25th and final shutout (a masterful three-hitter against the Cincinnati Reds) as part of a streak of 24 scoreless innings.

Brecheen was involved in a contractual brouhaha after the 1952 season when he signed with the St. Louis Browns on October 30. The Cardinals, who had placed him on waivers at the end of the season, claimed that the Browns had tampered with Brecheen before his official release, and filed a formal complaint with the commissioner's office, which was eventually dismissed. "[Browns manager Marty] Marion wanted me over here to pitch for him," said Brecheen. "Eddie [Stanky] is going to concentrate on using his young pitchers next summer so there would be no place on his pitching staff."[25] It was a fortuitous move with long-term consequences. Though he went just 5-13 for a team that lost 100 games, Brecheen was arguably the Browns' most effective pitcher, posting a staff-best 3.07 ERA in 117⅓ innings. He retired after the season to become the team's pitching coach.

In his 12-year big-league career, Brecheen established his reputation as a big-game pitcher. "(He) was a real pressure guy," said Joe Cronin of the Red Sox. "When he walked out onto the field, you knew a 'take-charge' guy was in the game."[26] In addition to his brilliance in the World Series, Brecheen compiled a 133-92 record and impressive 2.92 ERA in 1,907⅔ innings in the regular season. He won 114 games and logged 1,715 innings in eight minor-league seasons.

In 1954 the St. Louis Browns were sold and relocated to Baltimore, where they were renamed the Orioles in honor of the city's team in the International League. While the Browns were arguably the worst team in American League history, the Orioles developed into a model franchise grounded on fundamentals and smart pitching. During Brecheen's 14-year tenure as pitching coach, the Orioles' staff ranked in the top four in ERA (the AL expanded from eight to ten teams in 1961) for ten consecutive years (1957-1966) and led the league four times. In an era defined by hard-throwing strikeout pitchers (especially the 1960s), Brecheen preferred fundamentally sound pitchers with good control. He mentored many young pitchers who eventually became All-Stars, including Jim Palmer, Dave McNally, Steve Barber, Chuck Estrada, and Milt Pappas; and also helped seasoned veterans. He converted 36-year-old Hoyt Wilhelm into a starter in 1959 and the knuckleballer promptly led the league in ERA; under the Cat's guidance, Robin Roberts, considered washed up in 1961, enjoyed a rebirth. In Baltimore's four-game sweep of the Los Angeles Dodgers in the 1966 World Series, the Orioles yielded just two earned runs in 36 innings.

As he had every offseason throughout his life in baseball, Brecheen returned to Ada with his wife and son, Steve, in retirement. The couple enjoyed traveling throughout the Southwest. An avid hunter and fisherman, Brecheen never lost his passion and interest for baseball. He participated in occasional reunions and old-timer's games for the Cardinals and Orioles, and was a fixture at local sandlots mentoring youngsters. In 1997 he was inducted into the Oklahoma Sports Hall of Fame.

In declining health in his later years, Harry Brecheen died at the age of 89 on January 17, 2004, at a nursing facility in Bethany, Oklahoma. He had been preceded in death by his wife of 63 years, and was buried at Rosedale Cemetery in Ada.

SOURCES

Newspapers

New York Times

The Sporting News

Online

Ancestry.com

BaseballLibrary.com

Baseball-Reference.com

Retrosheet.org

SABR.org

Other

Harry Brecheen player file, National Baseball Hall of Fame, Cooperstown, New York.

NOTES

1 Associated Press, *San Antonio Light*, April 25, 1933, 6A.
2 Bob Broeg, "Keep Your Eye on the Cat," *Sport*, October 1947, 32.
3 Broeg, 33.
4 Broeg, 32.
5 *The Sporting News*, May 8, 1941, 1.
6 *The Sporting News*, March 26, 1942, 15.
7 *The Sporting News*, July 1, 1943, 5.
8 Ibid.
9 Broeg, 31.
10 Red Smith, "Views of Sport. The Cat of the Cardinals," *New York Herald Tribune*, May 1948 (undated clipping from Brecheen's Hall of Fame player file).
11 Gene Fehler, *When Baseball Was Sill King. Major League Players Remember the 1950s* (Jefferson, North Carolina: McFarland, 2012), 232.
12 Stan Mockler, "The 'Cat' o' Nine Innings," May 1949 (Unattributed article, player's Hall of Fame file).
13 Ibid.
14 Ibid.
15 Ibid.
16 Ibid.
17 Broeg, 33.
18 *The Sporting News*, April 18, 1946, 5.
19 *The Sporting News*, November 6, 1946, 7.
20 *The Sporting News*, November 20, 1946, 6.
21 *The Sporting News*, June 4, 1947, 7.
22 *The Sporting News*, September 22, 1948, 11.
23 *The Sporting News*, October 3, 1951, 15.
24 *The Sporting News*, January 30, 1952, 13.
25 *The Sporting News*, November 5, 1952, 8.
26 *The Sporting News*, June 6, 1951, 1.

Lou Boudreau

by Ralph Berger

IN 1942, THE CLEVELAND INDIANS CHOSE their slow-footed, hard-hitting, slick-fielding 24-year-old shortstop Lou Boudreau to become player-manager of the ballclub. In his seventh season at the helm, he led the Indians to a World Series title. Perhaps the best shortstop of the 1940s and a great defensive player and batting champion, in that glorious season he also led by example, hitting .355 with 106 runs batted in. He did not have such a season again, but then again, not many people do.

Louis Boudreau Jr. was born on July 17, 1917, in Harvey, Illinois, to Louis Boudreau Sr., of French descent, and Birdie (nee Henry) Boudreau, of Jewish and German descent. Although his mother was Jewish, Lou and his older brother Albert were raised as Christians. His father was a machinist and a semipro baseball player.[1]

Lou's father, a good third baseman for a semipro team in Kankakee, Illinois, instilled in Lou a gift for leadership, the drive to excel, and confidence in his ability. He would take young Lou Jr. out to the park and hit him 100 ground balls and count the errors he made. Lou's parents were divorced when he was seven, and Lou split time with his parents thereafter. His mother married again, to a man who didn't like sports and paid scant attention to Lou.

Lou went to Thornton Township High School, a school without a baseball team. Boudreau instead became a very good basketball player, an excellent passer and playmaker. At Thornton he met his wife-to-be, Della DeRuiter. They married in 1938.

In 1936, Boudreau entered the University of Illinois, where he majored in physical education and captained both the basketball and baseball teams. Boudreau led Illinois to the Big Ten basketball title in 1937, and was a 1938 All-American. Basketball took a huge toll on his ankles, eventually leading to arthritis. Lou had to tape them before every game of his baseball career. The ankles also earned him a 4-F classification during World War II.

As a college baseball player he averaged about .270 and .285. But all that practice with his dad fielding ground balls showed as he fielded his third base position excellently. The Cubs and Indians both pursued Boudreau and he also fielded offers to act in a movie and to play for $150 a game with Caesar's All-Americans, a Hammond, Indiana, team in the National Basketball League, a forerunner of the NBA,. But Boudreau felt he owed his loyalty to Cleveland's Cy Slapnicka, who had done his best to help him maintain his amateur status at Illinois.

The Indians assigned Boudreau in 1938 to a Class C club in the Western Association: he sat on the bench for a week and then was shipped to Cedar Rapids in the Class B Three-I League. After hitting .290 in 60 games, the third baseman was called up to the Indians. He sat on the bench observing Hal Trosky, Ken Keltner, Jeff Heath, Earl Averill, and a young pitcher named Bob Feller. Boudreau played first base and went to bat twice, grounding out and walking.

In 1939, Lou trained with the Indians in New Orleans. Manager Oscar Vitt advised Boudreau to move to the shortstop position, because young Ken Keltner looked to have a lock on third base. Ex-big leaguer Greg Mulleavy, the regular shortstop at Buffalo, was kind enough to take Boudreau under his wing and teach him the job. Lou batted .331 with 17 homers and 57 RBIs in 117 games, earning an August 7 recall to the parent club. Boudreau played 53 games at shortstop for the Indians in 1939, batting .258 with 19 runs batted in. Lou was now in the big leagues for good, but unfortunately lost his father that year. Lou Sr. never got to see his son play in the majors.

The 1940 season looked promising but would be tumultuous for the Cleveland Indians. Feller opened the season with a 1-0 no-hitter, and the Indians were in contention for the pennant all season long. But the season was marred by a rebellion of Cleveland ballplayers (not including Boudreau) who were unhappy with Vitt, who'd been known to bad-mouth his players with derogatory remarks. The ten players, thereafter known as the "Crybabies," complained to owner Alva Bradley in early June. Nothing was done and Vitt remained the manager for the rest of the season. The story hit the newspapers immediately, but the Indians continued to play well and went into Detroit on August 22 with a 5 ½ game lead over the second-place Tigers.

Boudreau kept his views to himself, but later wrote, "Had I been asked my opinion, I would have urged them to either wait till the end of the season, or to meet with Vitt himself and not with Bradley. But I wasn't asked, I didn't volunteer and the veterans did what they felt they had to do." [2]

The Indians didn't win the pennant that year, losing to Detroit by one game. Boudreau had a good season despite all the turmoil, batting .295, clouting nine homers, and driving in 101 runs. Defensively Lou led all shortstops in the American League.

In 1941, Lou was back at shortstop under popular manager Roger Peckinpaugh. Despite the switch, neither the Indians nor Boudreau fared as well as in 1940. Lou's average fell to .257 with 10 homers and 56 runs batted in, though he led the league with 45 doubles.

After just a single season, Peckinpaugh was promoted to general manager and while a search was underway for a new manager, Lou sent a letter requesting an interview. On November 24, Lou presented his case. Initially, the vote was 11-1 against him, but George Martin, president of Sherwin Williams Paint Company, felt that a young man would be more desirable at this point than the tried and true. The directors finally agreed on Boudreau, backing him up with a staff of older and more experienced coaches: Burt Shotton, Oscar Melillo, and George Susce.

Bradley introduced Lou to the press as the new manager, and one wag wrote, "Great! The Indians get a Baby Snooks for a manager and ruin the best shortstop in baseball." The general feeling around the city was that Boudreau would not be able to handle both being a ballplayer and a manager, but the press was generally kind.

Soon after Boudreau's hiring, the Japanese attacked Pearl Harbor. Two days later Bob Feller joined the Navy, and Boudreau, like his counterparts on the other teams, spent the next four years not knowing who their players were going to be.

Not all of the Indians were happy with the new manager. During his first spring training, Boudreau had three players walk into his office (Ben Chapman, Gee Walker, and Hal Trosky) to tell him they had asked for the job and could do a better job than he would. During some conferences on the mound, veteran pitchers would give Boudreau a variation of "Listen, college boy, you play shortstop and I'll do the pitching." Especially troublesome was Jim Bagby Jr., who Boudreau considered "the nastiest pitcher [I] ever played behind." When Boudreau would boot a ball, he would hear razzing about going back to college to learn how to play shortstop.

Without Feller, the 1942 Indians went 75-79, 28 games behind the Yankees. Playing in 147 games, Boudreau batted .283, batting in 58 runs. Boudreau felt that the hardest part of his new job was having the sense of when to take a pitcher out. Though he was still learning, he proved able to manage the club and still play good ball at shortstop.

The 1943 club finished 82-71, still 15 ½ games out of first place at season's end. Boudreau played in 152 games and batted .286 with 154 hits and 67 runs batted in. He led all league shortstops in fielding, and made his fourth All-Star team.

In 1944, the Indians slumped to 72-82, though Boudreau personally had a fine season, leading league batters at .327 and knocking in 27 runs. The next season he suffered a broken ankle and hit .306 in just 97 games, and the Indians finished 73-72. More importantly, the war ended in late summer, and Boudreau looked forward to the 1946 season and the return of real major-league ball.

With all the stars now returned to baseball in 1946, the fans turned out en masse. As usual Ted Williams was tearing up the league. The Indians went into Boston on July 14, for a doubleheader. In the opening game Boudreau went 5-for-5 with four doubles and a homer. Williams went 4-for-5 with three homers, all to right field. The Tribe lost the game, 11-10. Between games Boudreau came up with the famous Williams shift. When Williams came to bat with the bases empty, Boudreau yelled, "Yo," and all the fielders shifted to the right side of the field. Williams laughed, got back in the box, and promptly grounded out to Boudreau, playing in the second baseman's position. It wasn't the first time a shift had been employed, but against a star of Ted Williams' magnitude, it captured attention.[3]

The Indians went 68-86 in 1946. Boudreau hit .293, with 151 hits, six homers, and 62 runs batted in. On June 21, 1946, Bill Veeck became the principal owner of the Cleveland Indians, and vowed to make changes. The Tribe improved to 80-74 in 1947, and Boudreau batted .307, banging out 165 hits with four homers, and 67 RBIs. The nucleus was there and Bill Veeck turned loose his bloodhounds, sniffing out trades that would turn things around. First they acquired second baseman Joe Gordon from the Yankees, along with third baseman Eddie Bockman. The Indians added Gene Bearden to the pitching staff and Hal Peck to the outfield.

The Indians made history in 1947 by signing the American League's first black ballplayer, Larry Doby. Doby had been a second baseman for the Newark Eagles of the Negro National League. Boudreau tried to defuse any tensions about a black ballplayer coming on the roster by personally taking Doby around the clubhouse and introducing him. Some shook his hand while others refused, but Boudreau tried to make Doby's joining the team as painless as possible.

Veeck thought the Indians needed a new manager. After that year's World Series, Veeck proposed a deal with the St. Louis Browns that involved Boudreau. Lou also told Veeck that were he deposed as manager he would not play shortstop and would request a trade. These rumors did not sit well in Cleveland, and Veeck received more than 4,000 letters protesting any change. The *Cleveland News* ran a front-page ballot to elicit fans' opinions, and 100,000 responses ran 10-1 for Lou Boudreau. Veeck yielded.

Boudreau and Veeck reconciled, and Lou was set as manager for the 1948 season.

Boudreau was upbeat about the 1948 season but knew he had to produce a winner or his tenure as manager would be up. The Indians remained in or near first place all season, locked in a tight three-team race with the Yankees and Red Sox. They added a new pitcher in July by the name of Satchel Paige, an aged but legendary hurler from the Negro Leagues. J. Taylor Spink, in *The Sporting News*, accused Veeck of signing Paige only as a publicity stunt. But Paige proved his worth, and eventually Spink apologized to Veeck. Boudreau used Paige sparingly as a starter and a reliever, and he had a 6-1 mark in the heat of the pennant race.

Boudreau experienced some hard times during the '48 campaign. Veeck had brought Hank Greenberg into the Indians organization to serve as Veeck's right-hand man and confidant. This dismayed Boudreau, who at best never had Veeck's ear, and now had to go through another channel before conferring with him. Greenberg and Veeck were always questioning Boudreau's moves. Every morning during home stands Boudreau had to trudge up to Veeck's office, where Veeck and Greenberg would fire questions at him. Even on the road he could not escape the telephone constantly ringing with questions from his two bosses.

Nothing was going to stop Boudreau from driving his team to the 1948 American League pennant, not even the plethora of injuries that befell him. During a hard collision at second base, Lou sustained a shoulder contusion, a bruised right knee, a sore thumb, and a sprained ankle. Managing from the dugout while icing down his injuries during a doubleheader against the Yanks, he watched the Indians fall behind, 6-1. The Indians bounced back and scored three runs to make it 6-4. The Indians then loaded the bases, and Lou called time. After selecting his bat he announced himself as a pinch hitter. Injuries or no injuries, he was going to take matters into his own hands. Boudreau ripped a single between the legs of Joe Page, tying the game. The Indians went on to sweep the doubleheader, 8-6 and 2-1.

As the season neared its end in 1948, Boudreau saw that some of his players were becoming a little too anxious. He feared that one or more of his players would say something in anger, sparking an incident that would upset the club. He asked reporters not to come into the clubhouse and they complied, showing the journalistic mores that existed at that time. Red Smith said that during the season "Boudreau managed like mad."

At the conclusion of the 1948 schedule the Indians and the Red Sox were tied for first place. Some critics said that Boudreau could have avoided the need for a playoff game had he used Paige more, but instead a single-game playoff at Fenway Park determined the American League champion. Boudreau selected Gene Bearden start the game. Bearden had been a sailor on the *USS Helena* when it was torpedoed by a Japanese submarine and had been catapulted overboard. For two years he was in a hospital where they put a steel plate into his head and a metal hinge on one of his knees. Fully recovered, in 1948 he pitched the most important game of his life. Many question the choice of a left-hander in Boston with its looming left-field wall, but Boudreau felt that a knuckleball pitcher had a better chance against Boston's powerhouse team. Feller called the decision "a stroke of genius and a shock to all of us."

Boudreau took matters into his own hands and had a 4-for-4 performance that included two homers. When the final out was made and the Indians triumphed, 8-3, Boudreau on his gimpy ankles rushed over to his wife. Bearden was on the shoulders of his mates, and, Bill Veeck, another casualty of World War II, hobbled out

at top speed on his prosthetic leg to join the joyous mob. During his incredible season, Boudreau had slammed out 199 hits, belted 18 homers, and drove in 106 runs with a .355 average, all while guiding his team as manager. Boudreau was voted the Most Valuable Player in the American League in 1948.

The Indians capped off their 1948 season beating the Boston Braves and winning the World Series in six games. Boudreau batted .273 in the series with three runs batted in and fielded flawlessly. Lou Boudreau remains the only manager to win a World Series and win the Most Valuable Player Award in the same season.

Bill Veeck tore up Boudreau's old contract and gave him a raise to $62,000 a year. Still, when the Indians failed to repeat in 1949, Boudreau knew his time was coming to an end. He felt that Hank Greenberg had a lot to do with his fate as manager. Boudreau didn't mind Greenberg's second guessing, but was upset that Greenberg never gave him reasons for disagreeing. Veeck was distant with Boudreau in 1949, never having much to say to him. Lou, playing all four infield positions, batted .284, with four homers and 60 RBIs.

Lou's last season in Cleveland was 1950. Playing in only 81 games, he batted .269, with just one homer. Ellis Ryan took over as principal owner from Bill Veeck and put Greenberg in charge. As expected, on November 10, the Indians released Boudreau after 12 years as a player and nine as manager. The Red Sox acquired him in 1951 as a utility infielder. Playing in 82 games, he batted .267, with five homers and 47 runs batted in. After the 1951 season, the Red Sox named Boudreau manager. He played four games for the club in 1952, but was a bench-manager for the rest of his career.

Boudreau managed the Red Sox from 1952 through 1954, an event-filled period for the franchise. The team had spent a lot of money on amateur players in recent years, and Boudreau presided over the transition. Bobby Doerr had recently retired, Johnny Pesky and Vern Stephens were traded, and Ted Williams spent most of two seasons in the Marines In the spring of 1953 center fielder Dom DiMaggio suffered an eye injury and was replaced by Tommy Umphlett; when Umphlett got hot, DiMaggio stayed on the bench. DiMaggio was unhappy, but Lou felt that he had slowed down and was letting too many balls drop in center field. DiMaggio retired, and remained bitter at Boudreau for the rest of his life.

Boudreau also chose to move promising rookie Jimmy Piersall from the outfield to shortstop in 1952, a shift that Piersall later claimed led to bizarre behavioral problems and eventual nervous breakdown. When Piersall recovered, Boudreau kept him in the outfield, and Piersall played another 15 seasons. Though the Red Sox posted a surprising 84-69 record in 1953, their regression the next year (69-85) led to Boudreau's dismissal.

After being fired by the Red Sox in 1954, Boudreau got a job as manager of the Kansas City Athletics, a bad club recently transplanted from Philadelphia. He lasted three years at Kansas City; the team finished sixth once and eighth twice during his tenure.

Boudreau was fired in August 1957. Not long after, Jack Brickhouse approached Lou about being the color man for the Chicago Cubs broadcast team. He auditioned and got the job. Lou was no Demosthenes, and he stumbled over difficult names of players, but his knowledge of the game and his uncanny ability to anticipate what would happen in certain situations was noted. For over two years Boudreau was the Cubs color man, but by 1960, Lou was back into the managing business for the team, while Charlie Grimm was shifted from skipper to the radio booth. A poor team, the Cubs finished in last place 35 games behind the Pittsburgh Pirates. In 1961, Lou was back in the broadcasting booth.

Della Boudreau stayed home and raised four children. Older son Louis joined the Marine Corps and was wounded in Vietnam. James was a fairly good left-handed pitcher who played in the minors but hurt his arm and gave up baseball. Lou's daughter Sharyn married Tigers pitcher Denny McLain, who had numerous legal trouble during after his career, including two stints in prison. Older daughter Barbara married Paul Golazewski, a former quarterback at Illinois.

Lou was a part of the Cubs broadcast team for 30 years. When the station chose not to pick up his contract for the 1988 season, Lou was 71 years old, and finally retired, after having been a player, manager, and broadcaster for 50 years.

On July 27, 1970, Lou was inducted into the Baseball Hall of Fame in Cooperstown, New York. Bowie Kuhn, the Commissioner of Baseball, introduced Boudreau: "There are hitters in the Hall of Fame with higher batting averages, but I do not believe there is in the Hall of Fame a baseball man who brought more use of intellect and advocation of mind to the game than Lou Boudreau."

Bob Feller, a close friend of Boudreau, said, "Boudreau was one of the most talented players in baseball in his time, in addition to being one of the classiest human beings you'd ever want to meet." Feller added, "Even before he was manager, as a 21-year-old shortstop he was our on field leader. Boudreau drew people to him. He had the looks of a matinee idol."

Lou Boudreau Jr. left his mark on baseball through his intelligence and innovativeness as a manager and by his sterling play at shortstop and his all-out competitiveness. He died in Frankfort, Illinois, on August 10, 2001, at age 84. Della had preceded him in death in 1999. Boudreau was survived by four children and ten grandchildren. Lou Boudreau is interred in the Pleasant Hill Cemetery in Frankfort, Illinois.

SOURCES

Louis Boudreau and Russell Schneider, *Covering All the Bases* (Champaign, Illinois: Sagamore Publishing, 1993).

Gordon Cobbledick, "The Cleveland Indians" in Ed Fitzgerald, ed., *The Book of Major League Baseball Clubs: The American League* (New York: A. S. Barnes, 1952).

Robert Feller and Bill Gilbert, *Now Pitching Bob Feller* (New York: Citadel Press, 1990).

David Halberstam, *Summer of '49* (New York: William Morrow and Company, Inc., 1989).

Donald Honig, *The American League: A Pictorial History* (New York: Crown Publishers Inc., 1983).

Peter S. Horvitz and Joachim Horvitz, *The Big Book of Jewish Baseball* (New York: S.P.I Books, 2001).

Franklin A. Lewis, *The Cleveland Indians* (New York: Putnam, 1949).

William Marshall, *Baseball's Pivotal Era, 1945-1951* (Lexington: University Press of Kentucky, 1999).

Joseph Thomas Moore, *Pride against Prejudice: The Biography of Larry Doby* (New York: Greenwood Press, 1988).

Red Smith, *On Baseball* (Chicago: Ivan R. Dee, 2000).

NOTES

1   Most of the material from Boudreau's early life is from Louis
    Boudreau and Russell Schneider, *Covering All the Bases* (Champaign,
    Illinois: Sagamore Publishing, 1993).

2   Boudreau and Schneider, 28.

3   Though the Williams shift was a success, its origins are unclear.
    In *Great Baseball Feats, Facts and Firsts*, David Nemec says it was
    used against another player named Williams, Ken Williams of the
    St. Louis Browns. Rob Neyer argues that the shift was used some
    years earlier, against Cy Williams of the Phillies. And finally, Glenn
    Stout, editor of *Great American Sportswriting*, says that Jimmie
    Dykes, manager of the Chicago White Sox in 1941, was the first to
    use a shift against Ted Williams. In any case, left-handed-hitting
    Williamses seem to have cornered the market on shifts.

Frankie Gustine

By Gregory H. Wolf

"BASEBALL HAD ALWAYS BEEN IN MY blood," said versatile infielder Frankie Gustine, who signed with the Pittsburgh Pirates as a 16-year-old athletic prodigy in 1936. One of the most popular Pirates of his era, Gustine debuted as a September call-up in 1939 and was named to three consecutive NL All-Star teams (1946-1948) as a second baseman and third baseman. A rough-and-tumble hustler whose play harkened back to an earlier generation, he was known for his infectious, competitive spirit, and was recognized as the cornerstone of the Pirates' infield throughout the 1940s.

Frank William Gustine (pronounced with a hard "G") was born on February 20, 1920, in Hoopeston, founded as a small railroad outpost in east-central Illinois about five miles from the Indiana border. He was the second of two children born to Harry and Zelda (Forshier) Gustine, both native Illinoisans. Marjorie, Frankie's only sibling and one year younger, developed a serious case of whooping cough as a toddler and ultimately went deaf. Around 1927, in search of proper medical care and education for her, the Gustines moved to the Englewood neighborhood on the south side of Chicago, which is where Frankie grew up. His father worked as a machinist in a factory while his mother was a waitress in a local school. Frankie was an athletic youngster who dreamed about playing big-league baseball. "I kept scrapbooks of all the stars and gave special prominence to Pie Traynor because he was my idol," said Gustine.[1]

As a youth Gustine gravitated to third base and modeled his game after his hero. According to his family, he spent his summers back in Hoopeston, where he began to play baseball for the American Can Company in a local industrial league by the age of 12. At Parker High School in Chicago, Gustine excelled as a forward in basketball and played on the tennis and golf teams, but his passion was baseball. He made a name for himself as a bullet-throwing third sacker and occasional second baseman and shortstop on his school team, which also included future big-league pitcher

Bob Carpenter; he was also a standout in local late-summer and fall sandlot leagues. The nearby University of Chicago recruited the prized athlete and offered him a basketball scholarship, but he turned it down to concentrate on baseball. Gustine's big break came from his next-door neighbor, Sam Roberts, an unofficial scout for the Pittsburgh Pirates and a good friend of Traynor. "I was a 14-year old kid … in 1934 when I first met Pie," Gustine recalled.[2] Traynor promised to keep close tabs on the youngster's development. Two years later, Traynor, then manager of the Pirates, met Gustine again under much more serious circumstances. "Traynor talked to me for about two hours at the Pirates' hotel and it was the thrill of my life. He invited me to go out to Wrigley Field and work out the next day," Gustine told sportswriter Dick Farrington. "I guess he liked me, because before he left town with his team, he had my mother sign a contract so I could report to the

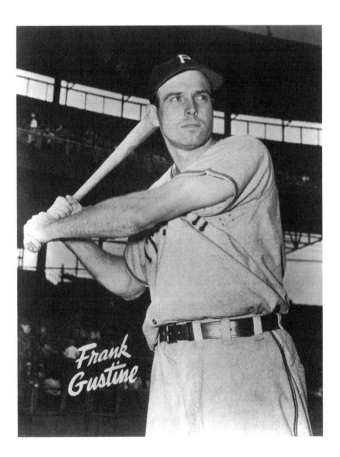

Hutchinson farm club of the Pirates in the spring of 1937."[3]

While his classmates were anxiously awaiting graduation from high school, Gustine was preparing for spring training with the Hutchinson (Kansas) Larks in the Class C Western Association less than two months after his 17th birthday. In his first year of professional ball he displayed the infield versatility that would eventually lead him to a big-league career spanning 12 seasons. Gustine began the 1937 campaign as a third baseman for the Paducah Indians of the Class D Kentucky-Illinois-Indiana (Kitty) League, and then was recalled in midseason to Hutchinson, for whom he played shortstop. He batted a combined .256. The Larks' youngest fielder the following season, Gustine showed more pop in his bat in 1938 and swiped 34 bases while playing third base "brilliantly," in the words of The Sporting News.[4]

Praised as having all the "making[s] of another great third sacker" for the Pittsburgh Pirates, Gustine celebrated his 19th birthday with an invitation to the team's spring training in San Bernardino, California.[5] Gustine impressed his hero Traynor with his athleticism; but the future Hall of Famer already had an established third baseman, Lee Handley, who was just 25 years old. Consequently, Gustine was assigned to the Gadsden (Alabama) Pilots of the Class B Southeastern League. Big, strong, and about the same size as Traynor, the 6-foot-tall, 170-pound Gustine held his own against considerably older competition, improving his batting average to .300 and demonstrating his superior arm from the hot corner. He was named to the league's all-star team.

Gustine made an unusually big jump from Class B to the major leagues in September 1939 when the Pirates tabbed him to replace the injured Handley. He debuted at third base in a doubleheader against the New York Giants on September 13 at Forbes Field, where he connected for a single in seven at-bats. Though Gustine hit only .186 (13-for-70) in his trial, The Sporting News noted that he "did a few fancy tricks around the hot corner."[6]

Most sportswriters thought that Gustine was still one or two years away from being major-league ready,

but when he arrived at the Pirates' spring training in 1940, new manager and former All-Star second baseman Frankie Frisch tutored him in the art of fielding at the position. By the sixth game of the season, Gustine had replaced veteran Pep Young at second base. Sportswriters had a field day with the 20-year-old Gustine, whom they often described as a "boy,"[7] or "cherubic faced,"[8] and jokingly made references to him not yet needing to shave. Fans loved him because of his youthful energy and competitive approach to the game. The name "Frankie" even seemed to suggest an adolescent-like exuberance and enthusiasm. In the course of his career, teammates also called him Gus.

Gustine's bat was red-hot to start the 1940 season. By the end of June he owned a .326 average. Pirates beat writer Charles J. Doyle wrote gushingly that Gustine was "playing a Johnny Evers engagement around the bag." Doyle was effusive in his praise of the youngster: "His judgment in playing hitters smacks of a [Billy] Herman, and his snap throws and sure hands make him a standout in the art of starting and pivoting double-play numbers."[9] Gustine continued to bat well over .300 through mid-August but suffered a sprained ankle and was hobbled the final six weeks of the season, finishing with a .281 average accompanied by a career-high 32 doubles. Noted for his "smoothness and finish" in the field, Gustine was named the second baseman on The Sporting News All-Rookie team.[10] Sportswriters coined the term "pulling a Gustine" to refer to players who experienced unexpected success jumping from the lower-level minors to the big leagues.[11]

Sportswriter John Drebinger of the New York Times caused a stir in 1941 when he called Gustine the best second baseman in baseball.[12] Gustine was a classic contact hitter with an orthodox swing, and was acknowledged as a good bunter with excellent speed. But throughout the '41 season he battled a number of injuries that limited his effectiveness at the plate and in the field. A tricky grounder from the Brooklyn Dodgers' Dixie Walker split his right index finger on July 27. Gustine missed two weeks, but the finger and a twisted ankle suffered in August bothered him for the remainder of the season. In spite of the injuries, Gustine was described as a pronounced star around the middle of the infield who had the rare quality of making other infielders play better, especially rookie Alf Anderson, who filled in at times for injured shortstop Arky Vaughan.[13] When Handley's season prematurely ended due to injury, Gustine belted two triples in his first full game playing third base on September 12. He batted .333 (36-for-108) in his last 30 games to finish the season with a respectable .270 average for the fourth-place Pirates.

Frisch considered Gustine a selfless team player whose all-out hustling was in the mold of his own St Louis Cardinals Gas House Gang clubs a decade earlier. Gustine respected Frisch's desire to win. "He's a wonder and lashes a whip," Gustine said of the Fordham Flash, who didn't take lightly to losing.[14] Gustine's son Bob added, "Our father would come home after a tough loss and tell us how Frisch made all the players just sit on the stools in front of their lockers with their heads down. No one was allowed to talk while Frisch reminded them of all their mistakes. He liked Frisch, but he also said that Frisch made the players feel miserable."[15]

The world of baseball changed after the attack on Pearl Harbor on December 7, 1941. Heeding the call to duty, many players and coaches enlisted while others were drafted in the ensuing years, depleting big-league rosters. In the offseason Gustine attempted to enlist in the Navy, but was classified as 1-B (available, but fit for only limited duty) and eventually 4-F because of a diagnosed hernia. The 1942 season proved to be frustrating for both the Pirates and Gustine. While rumors of Gustine's impended draft into the Army circulated in the press, the second baseman slumped at the plate, batting just .229 for the fifth-place Bucs. Gustine's draft status was a constant topic throughout the war years; his hernia, however, bothered him for the remainder of his playing days.

In many ways Gustine's scrappy determination, willingness to play through injuries, and winning attitude symbolized Pittsburgh, a gritty industrial city and the world's leading producer of steel and glass. And in no season was that more apparent than 1943. With players lost to injury and the war effort, Frisch counted on Gustine's versatility to provide him flexibility with his infield. For the first time in his big-league career,

Gustine was moved to shortstop because of his superior arm. He juggled duties at shortstop (68 games) and second base (40 games) throughout the season. In late April he fractured the middle finger on his right hand fielding a grounder.[16] Although the injury affected his throwing accuracy the entire season, Gustine went on a hitting tear in June, cranking out 23 hits in 48 at-bats (.479) over a ten-game span from June 6 to 16, including three games with four hits. "Gustine's consistent hitting, base running, and general heads-up play is one of the bright spots" in Pittsburgh, announced *The Sporting News*.[17] On August 15 he suffered a serious knee injury when his "left leg folded" as he attempted to steal third base. He resumed play in the field only in late September, and was limited to just 112 games that season. Charles J. Doyle writing for *The Sporting News* captured Gustine's essence as a player: "Gustine stood out as a symbol of this great team play. … Scorning physical ills, [he] moved back and forth from second to short at the call of his manager. Not once did he say that his broken finger was bothering him or that he should have rested."[18]

During the offseason, Gustine lived in Chicago with his parents. He kept in shape by working out at the University of Chicago, and held various jobs, including serving as a deputy clerk in a Chicago court. With his short brown hair, blue eyes, and soft-spoken air, Gustine was an eligible bachelor. His life changed when he met Mary Alice Gormley, a native Pittsburgher who lived just blocks away from Forbes Field. They married on November 25, 1944, at St. Paul's Cathedral in Pittsburgh. Teammate Jim Russell was his best man. Frankie and Mary Alice Gustine had five children (Frank Jr., Joanne, Robert, Mark, and Mary Louise) and adopted Pittsburgh as their hometown. Their sons recalled how their father was an approachable player, always willing to sign autographs for kids and take the time to talk to people on the streets. Gustine became close friends with not only Traynor but also Honus Wagner (later serving as a pallbearer for both) and players like Russell and Vaughan. According to his sons, Gustine often told a comical story about how Wagner constantly tried to set him up with his daughter.

A notoriously streaky hitter, Gustine struggled at the plate for much of 1944, batting under .200 as late as August 18. A surge in the final third of the season (.301 in his last 47 games) pushed his average to a season ending .230. Despite his offensive inconsistencies, Gustine sacrificed personal accolades by playing out of position at shortstop and remained the infield leader of what Charles J. Doyle called the "strongest part of the club" that finished a surprisingly strong second.[19]

Playing shortstop primarily but also seeing action at second base for the third consecutive season in 1945, Gustine finally put together an offensively consistent campaign, keeping his average around .280 the entire year. On May 24 against the Boston Braves at Forbes Field, he experienced arguably his strangest game as a big leaguer. When Frisch had used all three of his catchers by the end of the ninth inning with the game tied, 7-7, Gustine donned the tools of ignorance for the final two innings. With two outs and the bases loaded in the top of the 11th inning, Braves center fielder Carden Gillenwater attempted to steal home just as Pirates rookie pitcher Ken Gables unloaded a pitch low and away. In the words of Charles J. Doyle, "Gustine was able to nail it and dive head-first into the speedboy to thwart the winning run."[20] The Pirates' Johnny Barrett ended the game a few minutes later with a walk-off home run.

For the first time in his career, Gustine was a contract holdout in 1946, signing just two weeks before the start of the season for a reported $9,000 and an additional $1,000 "if he plays regularly."[21] Gustine moved back to second base with the return of sure-armed Billy Cox from the military. In great health, Gustine got off to another fast start, boasting a .338 average on June 15 courtesy of a 16-game hitting streak (tied for the longest in the NL that season). He was rewarded by being named to the NL All-Star squad as a backup to starter Red Schoendienst. He struck out and drew a walk in his two plate appearances in the AL's convincing 12-0 victory. In an almost annual tradition, Gustine struggled down the stretch. He lacerated his foot on August 11 when teammate Russell inadvertently spiked him. An infection ensued and it became difficult to put pressure

on the foot. Gustine played through the pain, but batted just .175 thereafter to finish with a .259 average.

An era came to a close during the 1946 season as the Dreyfuss family, owners of the Pirates since 1900, sold the team to a group led by Indianapolis banker Frank McKinney, and the new ownership made substantial changes in 1947. First-year manager Billy Herman moved Gustine to third base. To accommodate the pull-hitting slugger Hank Greenberg, acquired in the offseason, the dimensions of left and left center field in Forbes Field were reduced, resulting in an offensive explosion. (The Pirates belted a team-record 156 home runs, shattering their previous high of 86 in 1930.) Known throughout his career as a spring hitter, Gustine got off to another torrid start. In July he put together a career-best 21-game hitting streak (39-for-85, .459) to push his average to .335. In the first year fans voted for All-Star Game participants, Gustine came in a close second in the third-base voting to eventual MVP Bob Elliott of the Boston Braves. (Gustine went 0-for-2 in the game.) He cooled off on August, but finished his most successful season by leading the NL in games (156), and setting career highs in runs (102), hits (183), and average (.297).

"You won't find two finer fellows in baseball than Greenberg and Gustine," Jackie Robinson told *The Sporting News* during his second month in the major leagues after breaking the color barrier in 1947.[22] Gustine and Robinson first came into contact with each other in 1946 during a segregated barnstorming tour;[23] however, Robinson's compliment probably stems from a game on May 17 at Forbes Field during which he was hit on the arm by an inside pitch from Fritz Ostermueller in the first inning. Gustine reached first base on a walk in the bottom half of the frame and told Robinson, "I'm sure he didn't mean it."[24] The events were widely circulated in an article by Wendell Smith of the *Pittsburgh Courier* (an African-American paper) the following day. Director Brian Helgeland took liberty with this event in his Hollywood film *42* (2013) by portraying Robinson as getting beaned in the temple by a malicious Ostermueller.

Praised as "the best third sacker in the league" in the first four months of 1947, Gustine underwent a double hernia operation in the offseason.[25] "Every year in the last months of the season, I'd get that tired feeling," said Gustine whose stellar play earned a hefty salary increase to a reported $15,000 in 1948.[26] As if on cue, Gustine rapped 50 hits in his first 30 games to pace the NL in hitting with a .427 mark on May 25. Seemingly at the top of his game, he was voted to his third consecutive All-Star Game. "There hasn't been a more popular Pirate since Traynor," wrote Bucs beat reporter Les Biederman. "No one can remember when fans at Forbes Field—or any other park—booed him."[27] But Gustine's second half was as frustrating as his first half was promising. He batted under .200 after the All-Star Game and ultimately lost his starting position in September. With trade rumors intensifying during his slump, Gustine's tenure in Pittsburgh came to a close when he and pitcher Cal McLish were sent to the Chicago Cubs on December 8 for pitcher Cliff Chambers and catcher Clyde McCullough.

Only 29 years old, Gustine seemingly had several more years of baseball ahead of him, but his career came to an unexpected early end. Like many players before him, he spent his twilight days on an undignified baseball odyssey. Gustine struggled with the Cubs in 1949 (batting .226), was optioned to the Los Angeles Angels of the Pacific Coast League, and ultimately was placed on waivers. The Philadelphia Athletics claimed him on September 14, but then traded him three months later in a multi-player deal to the St. Louis Browns. In a gesture of good will, the Browns kept Gustine on their roster long enough in 1950 for him to earn status as a ten-year man for his baseball pension.[28] On May 22 Gustine was unconditionally released.

The Associated Press reported in 1950 that Gustine had been diagnosed with "nervous fatigue."[29] A noted workaholic, Gustine had little time in the offseason to recover physically from his annual injuries. In 1947 he became the head basketball coach at Waynesburg College, located about 50 miles south of Pittsburgh. He commuted daily from the October until the beginning of spring training, before resigning in 1950 for health reasons.

Gustine remained a popular fixture in Pittsburgh for three decades after his retirement. In 1952 he opened Frankie Gustine's Restaurant and Bar just blocks from Forbes Field. Decorated with Pirates memorabilia, the establishment, which billed itself as a "Major League Atmosphere with Minor League Prices," was in business until 1982 and became a hangout for Pirates players in the 1950s and 1960s before Three Rivers Stadium opened in 1970. A successful real-estate developer, Gustine was later part owner of the Sheraton Inn at Station Square, located in one of the most popular tourist areas in Pittsburgh.

Second only to Gustine's passion for baseball was his love of basketball. He turned down an offer to play professional basketball for the Pittsburgh Raiders in the National Basketball League (a forerunner to the NBA) in 1944, but played informally against high-school and semipro teams throughout his baseball career, much to the chagrin of manager Frisch. According to his sons, in retirement Gustine found a like-minded fanatic in Pirates shortstop Dick Groat, a former All-American basketball player at Duke. "Our father would come home and tell us that he and Groat scored 50 against some high-school team. Then he'd say that Groat had 44," his son Frank said jokingly. In 1962 Gustine was lured back to the hardwood when he became head basketball coach for Point Park College in Pittsburgh. He resigned in 1967 in order to establish the school's baseball program. Beginning with a limited fall schedule in 1967 and continuing through spring 1974, Gustine laid the foundations for one of the most successful programs in the NAIA. He led the Pioneers to a 103-46 record, including two district championship and a fourth-place finish in the 1974 NAIA World Series.[30]

Gustine was in Davenport, Iowa, to take part in the maiden voyage of a riverboat casino owned by his business partner John E. Connelly, when he died of a heart attack on April 1, 1991. He was 71 years old. Services were held at St. Margaret of Scotland Parish in Green Tree and Gustine was buried at Resurrection Cemetery in Coraopolis, Pennsylvania. Gustine's 12 years in the big leagues and his lifelong service to and interest in sports may best be summed up by a remark from his mentor Pie Traynor from the late 1940s: "I consider Gustine one of the best team men and hustlers in the game."[31]

SOURCES

Newspapers

Pittsburgh Post Gazette

The Sporting News

Websites

Ancestry.com

BaseballAlmanac.com

BaseballCube.com

BaseballLibrary.com

Baseball-Reference.com

SABR.com

Interviews

The author expresses his sincere gratitude to Frankie Gustine's sons, Frank Gustine, Jr. and Robert Gustine, whom he interviewed in August 2013. They provided many insights to their father's playing career and personality, and helped ensure the factual accuracy of this biography.

NOTES

1   *The Sporting News*, November 11, 1947, 11.

2   Ibid.

3   *The Sporting News*, June 27, 1940.

4   *The Sporting News*, March 16, 1939, 2.

5   *The Sporting News*, January 26, 1939, 7.

6   *The Sporting News*, December 21, 1939, 5.

7   *The Sporting News*, February 14, 1940, 10.

8   *The Sporting News* June 27, 1940, 3.

9   *The Sporting News*, June 13, 1940, 5.

10   *The Sporting News*, October 17, 1940, 5.

11   *The Sporting News*, August 29, 1940, 14.

12   *The Sporting News*, May 29, 1941, 2.

13   *The Sporting News*, July 10, 1941, 3.

14   *The Sporting News*, December 11, 1941, 12.

15   Interview with Frankie Gustine's sons, Frank Gustine and Robert Gustine, in August 2013. All quotations from them are from these interviews.

16   *The Sporting News*, April 22, 1943, 10.

17   *The Sporting News*, June 17, 1943, 5.

18   *The Sporting News*, July 22, 1943, 2.

19   *The Sporting News*, September 13, 1944, 4.

20   *The Sporting News*, May 31, 1945, 9.

21   *The Sporting News*, April 4, 1946, 15.

22   *The Sporting News*, May 28, 1947, 9.

23   Thomas Barthel, *Baseball Barnstorming and Exhibition Games, 1901–1962* (Jefferson, North Carolina: McFarland, 2007), 221.

24   Jonathan Eig, *Opening Day. The Story of Jackie Robinson's First Season* (New York: Simon and Schuster, 2008), 140.

25   *The Sporting News*, November 12, 1947, 10.

26   Ibid.; *The Sporting News*, February, 4, 1948, 10.

27   *The Sporting News*, May 12, 1948, 17.

28   "Teams Down to 25-Limit" (UP), *Bend* (Oregon) *Bulletin*, May 14, 1950, 9.

29   "Training Camp News" (AP), *Ludington* (Michigan) *Daily News*, April 4, 1950, 8.

30   Point Park University Athletics. pointpark.edu/Athletics/MensSports/Baseball/BaseballNews2012/media/Athletics/Baseball/naiaopeningrdinfopacket.pdf

31   *The Sporting News*, December 15, 1948, 3.

Claude Passeau

By Gregory H. Wolf

ON BASEBALL'S BIGGEST STAGE, Chicago Cubs right-hander Claude Passeau tossed the game of his life: a one-hit shutout against the Detroit Tigers in Game Three of the 1945 World Series. Though often overlooked in discussions about the best pitchers of his era, Passeau was a durable workhorse and five-time All-Star who averaged 15 wins and 252 innings over a ten-year stretch (1936-1945) for the perennially underachieving Philadelphia Phillies and Chicago Cubs.

Claude William Passeau was born on April 9, 1909, in Waynesboro, Mississippi, the only child of Claude and Juanita (Pope) Passeau. The elder Passeau, a sawyer and miller by trade, moved the family from one small town to the next in the southeastern part of the state in search of work. By 1920 the family had settled about five miles off the Gulf Coast in the small, picturesque town of Moss Point, where Passeau's grandmother ran a boarding house. Claude dabbled in sports at Moss Point High School, and graduated in 1928. "I'd rather fish and hunt than I would play baseball, at least at that time," said Passeau, claiming that he was the 12th man on a 12-man team.[1]

Passeau had scholarship offers to attend Louisiana State University and Millsaps College, and chose the latter, located in Jackson on the southern edge of the Mississippi Delta. Passeau gradually filled out his big, 6-foot-3 frame and became an excellent athlete. He earned three letters each in baseball, basketball, football, and track before graduating with a degree in agricultural science in 1932; however, he was initially reluctant to play baseball because of a gruesome hunting accident he suffered as a 16-year-old. He had accidentally discharged a shotgun and the blast tore through his left hand and part of his wrist. After surgery, his third and fourth fingers were permanently flexed toward the palm of his hand. The baseball coach invited him to throw batting practice one day. "I didn't even know how to stand on the mound. I just threw hard and of course the batters didn't like it," he recalled.[2]

In 1929 Passeau played semipro baseball in Inverness, Mississippi, under the alias Newburn to keep his college eligibility. "Late that season, Eddie Goosetree, scout for the Tigers, came upon us and signed me to an Evansville [Hubs] contract," Passeau told Dick Farrington of *The Sporting News*. "I didn't report … and explained that I wanted to go back to college."[3]

Passeau agreed to report to the Fort Smith (Arkansas) Twins of the Class C Western Association in 1930, but quit after just nine days because of homesickness. He returned to the semipro circuit and "worked under more pseudonyms than a carnival wrestler."[4] "I'd play somewhere about 30 to 45 days and then I'd move on to another league, another town, and just disappear after two or three paydays," said Passeau. He recalled that he used about six different aliases.[5]

After graduating from college in 1932 and no longer concerned about his eligibility, Passeau spent three frustrating years battling control problems in the Detroit Tigers farm system. He bounced around with seven different teams in lower-level leagues, posting a combined 30-30 record, and struggled in his 18 games in A-ball. Passeau was given his unconditional release

during spring training with the Milwaukee Brewers of the American Association in 1935.[6]

Undeterred by the "no prospect" label given to him by Tigers scout Billy Doyle, the 26-year-old Passeau signed with the Des Moines Demons in the Class A Western League for the 1935 season.[7] Unexpectedly, Passeau harnessed his speed and developed into the circuit's best pitcher. He struck 68 batters over a five-game span en route to the league high in strikeouts (239) and wins (20). Passeau got another chance when Pittsburgh Pirates scout Bill Hinchman signed him to a contract in late July.

Passeau was a September call-up with the Pirates in 1935 and made his big-league debut in the last regular-season game, a start against the Cincinnati Reds at Crosley Field on September 29. The big Mississippian got tagged with the loss by surrendering seven hits and four runs in just three innings. "My arm was shot," said Passeau, after pitching 244 innings in a short Class A season before moving to the big leagues.[8] Passeau was a throw-in when the Pirates traded catcher Earl Grace to the Philadelphia Phillies for their catcher, Al Todd, in the offseason. Coincidentally, the Phillies had the chance to sign Passeau after his release from the Tigers organization, but scout Patsy O'Rourke considered him a "wild man" with poor control.[9]

Passeau arrived with high expectations at Phillies spring training in Winter Haven, Florida. Manager Jimmie Wilson and Philadelphia sportswriters labeled him the "rookie most likely to succeed."[10] With only one winning season since their unceremonious trade of the legendary Grover Cleveland Alexander after the 1917 season, the Phillies were in dire need of pitching. Passeau picked up his first two big-league wins toiling out of the bullpen, which was his role through June. In the second game of a doubleheader on July 4, Passeau hurled a seven-hit shutout against the Dodgers in his first start as a Phillie. He won four more times that month, splitting his time between starts and relief outings. "Passeau looks like he is going to be a big winner," wrote Philadelphia sportswriter James C. Isaminger.[11] The stout right-hander was one of the lone bright spots on the league's worst staff. He appeared in 49 games (third-most in the league), tied for the

team high in wins (11) and logged in excess of 200 innings for the first of ten consecutive seasons. "[Passeau] is looked upon by all National League managers as a brilliant pitching prospect," wrote Tom Swope of the *Cincinnati Enquirer*.[12]

"The Phils young pitching staff should be better," declared an Associated Press report during spring training in 1937.[13] Manager Wilson boasted three prized, strong young arms, Passeau and Bucky Walters, both 28 years old, and 23-year-old Hugh Mulcahy. Phillies hurlers suffered from playing in the Baker Bowl, which was described by *New York Times* sportswriter Roscoe McGowen as a "hat box ball park."[14] It was a pitcher's nightmare with its short 280-foot right-field fence, which artificially inflated ERAs. Passeau proved to be one of the most durable pitchers in the league, pacing the senior circuit in innings (292⅓) and starts (34), and appearing in a career-high 50 games. Though he yielded a league-high 348 hits, he still managed a 14-18 record for the seventh-place Quakers, as they were colloquially called. Trade rumors swirled constantly around the Phillies' "Big Three" pitching core, but financially strapped team owner Gerald Nugent, long renowned for selling his most talented players, rejected all offers—until he needed the money.

Passeau's stock in trade was a high, sailing heater, a curveball, and a change-of pace. According to *The Sporting News*, he was able to make his fastball sail by placing his index and middle fingers against the seams and folding back the knuckle of his ring finger to grip the ball. The movement of the ball was described as "strangely mystifying" and resembling a spitter.[15] "I have a great habit of blowing in my hands when I get ready to deliver the ball," said Passeau. "And because the ball does sail, the batters think I am doing something illegal."[16] Opposing managers routinely requested that the home-plate umpire examine balls thrown by Passeau, as well as his cap and glove. Passeau was also accused of throwing a "sweat spitter."[17] "Lots of times I would get in a jam and I might have a scuffed ball. I'd throw it out and get a new one because a smooth one would sail better," said Passeau. "That's a reason why umpires used to check me so often. They thought I cheated because the ball would kind of knuckle up there."[18]

Passeau forged a psychological edge with his dastardly pitch. He was fidgety on the mound, and consciously tugged at his cap and pants, and altered his glove to give the impression that he was doing something illegal. Even though no incriminating evidence was ever found on Passeau during a game, the charges of throwing a spitball continued until his retirement.

Passeau endured a nightmarish season in 1938 as the Phillies won only 45 times. On a woefully inept staff that lost Walters to the Cincinnati Reds at the trading deadline, the overworked Passeau suffered from the strains of starting and relieving. (From 1936 through 1938 he appeared in 143 games, more than any other pitcher in the NL.) Passeau finished with an unsightly 11-18 record, but three of the wins occurred during a dominating ten-day stretch in July. Passeau made a "'declaration of independence' at being released from the telephone-booth proportions of the Baker Bowl," wrote the AP's Sid Feder cleverly with a nod to American history about the big right-hander's five-hit victory over the Boston Bees on July 1.[19] [The Phillies had ended their tenure at Baker Bowl on June 30 and started playing their home games at Shibe Park, the Athletics' ballpark.] Following a second complete-game victory over the Bees, on July 4 in the City of Brotherly Love, Passeau tossed a career-long 16-inning complete game to defeat the Brooklyn Robins 4-3 in front of just 1,277 spectators at Shibe Park.

In defiance of the oddsmakers, Passeau opened the season in a Phillies uniform in 1939. He was "faster than light" in his first start, striking out a career-high 11 in a no-decision against the Dodgers. As the Phillies got off to another horrible start, the only question about Passeau's imminent trade was to whom—the Cardinals, Cubs, or Giants? On May 29 the Phillies finally sent Passeau to the Cubs in exchange for pitchers Ray Harrell and Kirby Higbe, center fielder Joe Marty, and a cash sum reported to be between $25,000 and $50,000.[20]

A .500 team at the time of the trade, the reigning NL pennant winners were hard pressed for quality pitchers with only Bill Lee and Larry French as reliable starters. Edward Burns of the *Chicago Daily Tribune* championed the acquisition of Passeau, whom he de-

scribed as "one of the league's better right hand pitchers" despite a 38-56 career record.[21] In his first start with the North Siders, Passeau limited the Dodgers to just four hits and struck out seven in seven innings in a 3-2, 14-inning loss. He gave the Cubs a much needed shot in the (pitching) arm and proved to be the team's most durable and effective hurler, capable of starting and relieving. The Cubs moved to within 6½ games of the league lead behind Passeau's complete-game victory over the Cincinnati Reds on September 2, but finished the season in fourth place. At the age of 30, Passeau enjoyed his first winning season (15-13) and led the National League in strikeouts (137).

Passeau had a reputation as one of the fiercest competitors in baseball with a temper to match. In his return to Shibe Park, on July 13, 1939, he got into a fight with his former roommate, Hugh Mulcahy, who had dusted him off with two inside pitches. The two pitchers tangled when Passeau bunted and was tagged out by Mulcahy. In the ensuing brawl, benches cleared, and Passeau was cold-cocked. In his next start Passeau was ejected in the fifth inning when he argued with the first-base umpire after being called out on a close play. "Claude Passeau's southern blood didn't boil over today" wrote Edward Burns. "For the first time in three starts, Claude avoided the heave-ho," and tossed a complete-game victory over the Dodgers to push the Cubs briefly into second place.[22]

Once described as the "picture of an athlete," Passeau had the physique of a boxer.[23] At 6-feet-3 and 200 pounds, he was strong, lithe, and extremely quick. Dark-complexioned with dark hair, Passeau had a wide face, a squared jaw, and blue-gray eyes with which he stared down batters and runners on first base. "The guy's murderous mien would scare us," wrote Edward Burns. "We think it's those iron jaws and merciless eyes that scare opposing batsmen more than Claude's pitching."[24]

In Passeau's first five full seasons with the Cubs (1940-1944), the team posted a losing record each year and finished in fifth and sixth place twice each and in fourth place once. "I thought we had a pretty good ballclub," said Passeau, "but we always found a way to lose."[25]

The rubber-armed Passeau was manager Gabby Hartnett's jack-of-all-trades in 1940. He appeared in 46 games (third-most in the league), completed 20 of 31 starts, and won 20 games for the first and only time in his career. In a 12-day stretch in August he won five consecutive games, including two shutouts. Notwithstanding his success, Cubs beat reporter Irving Vaughan opined that Passeau "can rightly claim that he and lady luck are almost total strangers."[26] Passeau suffered from the league's second worst defense (in terms of fielding percentage) and a notably inconsistent offense (they scored three runs or fewer in ten of his 13 losses).

As the Cubs fell on hard times after 14 consecutive winning seasons (1926-1939), Passeau became one of the team's enforcers. He had a penchant for throwing inside, regularly dusting off batters, and worked quickly (complete-game victories under two hours were de rigueur). *The Sporting News* asserted that Passeau's "temper make[s] many of the game's best hitters duck in terror of his high hard one."[27] Although he paced the circuit in hit batsmen just once (1938), Passeau was one of the instigators in the team's beanball wars with the Dodgers in the early 1940s. In a highly publicized event on July 19, 1940, at Wrigley Field, Passeau flung his bat at pitcher Hugh Casey of the Dodgers after being dusted off twice and then hit in the back by a pitch in the eighth inning. That precipitated a bench-clearing brawl. Rumors later surfaced that Dodgers manager Leo Durocher had ordered Casey to plunk Passeau.

"Passeau is undoubtedly the most underrated flinger in the loop" wrote Dan Daniel of the *New York World-Telegram* in 1941.[28] He was the Cubs' only reliable starter. Passeau's record dropped to 14-14, but he led the staff in practically every meaningful pitching category. One of the best hitting pitchers of his generation (a .192 average with 15 home runs and 80 RBIs for his career) Passeau clouted his only grand slam—off his nemesis Casey—and a career-best five runs batted in on May 19 in a complete-game drubbing of the Dodgers, 14-1,

Passeau was named to the first of five All-Star squads in 1941 and was involved in one of the midsummer classic's greatest moments. Just two days before the All-Star Game, he tossed a complete game on two days' rest and arrived in Detroit feeling the effects of overwork. Passeau entered the game in the seventh inning. With two outs and two men on in the ninth, Ted Williams victimized Passeau by launching a dramatic walk-off home run at Briggs Stadium to give the AL an exciting 7-5 victory.

While in 1942 the Cubs sank to depths not experienced in 17 years Passeau was recognized as one of the National League's best pitchers. "It's a pity Claude Passeau is working for a club so lowly as the Cubs," wrote Joe King of the *New York World-Telegram*. "For service to his team Passeau isn't surpassed by anyone—he holds the pitching staff together."[29] At the age of 33, Passeau seemed more durable than ever although he was no longer expected to relieve ten to 15 times per year. In the first half of the season, he won a career eight straight starts (all complete games) en route to a 19-14 record accompanied by 24 complete games (in 34 starts). He redeemed himself in the All-Star Game, surrendering just one hit in two scoreless innings in the NL's 3-1 loss.

Slugging outfielder Bill Nicholson, second-year pitcher Hi Bithorn, and Passeau were among the few highlights on an underachieving Cubs squad in 1943 that had been widely expected to compete for the pennant largely because of an expected potent offense that never materialized. Passeau won 15 games, highlighted by two early-season extra-inning affairs. On May 5 he held the St. Louis Cardinals to just one run in a 14-inning complete game at Wrigley Field to earn his first victory of the season; in his last start of the month, he hurled a 13-inning complete game and drove home Lou Novikoff with two outs in the ninth to defeat the Boston Braves, 4-3.

During his playing days, Passeau was a successful farmer and business man in Lucedale, Mississippi, and was often counted among the few baseball players who did not need to play for the money. He owned a 600-acre farm on which he cultivated tung oil trees, and a John Deere farm-equipment dealership. In November 1938 he married Agnes Bernyce Spafford, with whom he had two children, Claude Jr. and Patricia. Passeau was classified 4-F because of his deformed hand, and was not required to serve in the military in World War II.

The Cubs were accustomed to Passeau's annual late arrival at spring training in order to finish planting on the farm; however, they were surprised by his unexpected announcement that he would not return to the team in 1944. But the tug of pitching and the intervention of the Cubs' otherwise aloof owner, Philip K. Wrigley, was too much for him to ignore. "Needless to say," wrote Irving Vaughan of the *Chicago Daily Tribune*, "[Passeau] was welcomed like a long lost uncle with a bank roll."[30] Having missed all of spring training and the first week of the season, Passeau struggled in his return, and didn't win his first game until June 2. The 35-year-old gradually rounded into shape to win his final seven decisions in the last four weeks of the campaign en route to a 15-9 record.

The atmosphere at the Cubs' 1945 spring-training facility in French Lick, Indiana (where they met because of wartime travel restrictions), was positive despite the club coming off its fifth consecutive losing season. Former Cubs first baseman Charlie Grimm had taken over the team in 1944 after 11 games, and the players responded to his laid-back style of leadership. The mood soured that spring, though, when Passeau reported elbow pain for the first time in his career. Doctors discovered bone chips and ordered x-ray treatment instead of potential season- and career-ending surgery. Passeau felt well enough to toss a shutout in his first start and later won a career-best nine consecutive decisions to push his record to 10-2 and keep the Cubs in an unexpected pennant race. To alleviate the pain in his shoulder and bicep muscles caused by the bone growths, Passeau submitted to hourlong massages before each start. His courage and desire to win were not lost on beat reporter Edward Burns, who noted "Passeau has been a vital factor in the Cubs' success this season."[31]

As the Cubs clung to a precarious lead in September and eventually secured the pennant by three games over the St. Louis Cardinals, Passeau won three consecutive decisions, highlighted by back-to-back four-hit shutouts. Aptly nicknamed "Mr. Chips" (because of his bone chips) by "Jolly Cholly" Grimm, Passeau won 17 games, posted the second-best ERA in the NL (2.46),

and led the league with five shutouts. He had an uncanny ability of avoiding the gopher ball despite pitching his home games in a home-run-friendly park, yielding just four in 227 innings.

The 1945 World Series matched the Cubs and the Detroit Tigers with the first three games scheduled at Briggs Stadium in accordance with wartime travel restrictions still in effect though the war had just ended. With the Series tied at one game apiece, Passeau pitched the game of his life in front of 55,500 spectators on October 5. "I felt so good," he said, "I began to tease the Detroit hitters, I am naturally fidgety. I noticed it annoyed them so I put it on more than ever."[32] On baseball's biggest stage, Passeau tossed his only career one-hitter, surrendering a single to his former roommate from the Tigers farm system, Rudy York, in the second inning. Passeau also knocked in the third and final run on a deep fly ball to center field allowing catcher Mickey Livingston to score. "[Passeau displayed] good speed, sharp breaking curve ball, perfect control, and an un-ruffled demeanor, plus a slider," wrote syndicated columnist Grantland Rice.[33] Passeau struggled with his control in Game Six, issuing six walks and three earned runs in 6⅔ innings before yielding to reliever Hank Wyse, yet was in line for the victory until the Cubs bullpen squandered the lead in the eighth inning of an eventual 8-7 victory in 12 innings. In the Cubs' demoralizing 9-3 Game Seven defeat at Wrigley Field, Passeau tossed one inning of relief, yielding the final two Tigers runs.

Passeau shrugged off the pangs of defeat to win seven of his first nine decisions in 1946 and was selected to the All-Star squad for the final time. "I didn't have any business pitching," said Passeau, who had lost a tough two-hit complete game to the Cardinals, 1-0, four days before the All-Star Game. "Nobody wanted to start the game, so I said 'Give me the ball'."[34] He took the mound for the first three innings, surrendered a two-run home run to Charlie Keller, and was charged with the loss in a 12-0 thrashing. In August Passeau strained his back fielding a grounder against the Cardinals. He was eventually diagnosed with two ruptured discs which required surgery in the offseason.

Notwithstanding his injury, Passeau happened to be one of the best fielding pitchers of his era. He led pitchers in fielding percentage (1.000) five times and established a major-league record by fielding 273 consecutive chances without committing an error (September 21, 1941, to May 28 1946). His pickoff move to first base was acknowledged as one of the best in baseball.[35]

The offseason back operation in February effectively ended Passeau's big-league career. He struggled in his return to the team in late June 1947 and made just six starts among his 19 appearances. At a press conference on the eve of the Cubs' final home series of the season, general manager James T. Gallagher signaled a decisive youth movement and an unceremonious end to an era in Cubs baseball by announcing the unconditional release of veterans Passeau, Stan Hack, Bill Lee, and Billy Jurges, each at least 37 years old.[36] Passeau posted a 162-150 record accompanied by 3.32 ERA in 2,719⅔ innings in his 13-year big-league career.

Passeau served as a roving pitching instructor in the Cubs farm system in 1948 and 1949 and also managed two lower-level minor-league teams on an interim basis. He retired from baseball in 1949 and returned to Mississippi. He continued to operate his successful farm and John Deere dealership until his death. He was elected county sheriff and served two four-year terms (1968-1976). In 1964 Passeau was selected in the inaugural class to the Mississippi Sports Hall of Fame. He never lost his passion for baseball, and occasionally participated in old-timer's and reunion games. "I didn't enjoy my baseball career like I should have," said Passeau in a serious moment in 1974. "I was so intent about it, so sincere. I worked as hard as I could because I never felt it was a cinch."[37]

Passeau died on August 30, 2003, in Lucedale at the age of 94. He was preceded in death by Bernyce, his wife of 64 years. They are both buried at Magnolia Cemetery in their home town.

SOURCES

Websites

Ancestry.com

BaseballAlmanac.com

BaseballCube.com

BaseballLibrary.com

Baseball-Reference.com

SABR.org

Newspapers

Chicago Daily Tribune

New York Times

The Sporting News

Other

Claude Passeau player file, National Baseball Hall of Fame, Cooperstown, New York

NOTES

1   Rick Hines, "Claude Passeau. Ex-Cub ace recalls major league career," *Sports Collectors Digest*, March 8, 1991, 200.

2   Hines, 200.

3   *The Sporting News*, January 1, 1939.

4   Ibid.

5   Hines, 200.

6   *The Sporting News*, October 10, 1945, 4.

7   Associated Press, "Today by Knight," *Charleston* (West Virginia) *Gazette*, July 28, 1935, 1.

8   John C. Skipper, *Take Me Out to the Cubs Game* (Jefferson, North Carolina: McFarland, 2000), 16.

9   United Press, "Passeau Rated 'Wild Man' by Scout Patsy O'Rourke," *Pittsburgh Press*, August 12, 1945, 31.

10 Associated Press, "Phillies," *New York Times*, March 5, 1936, 29.

11 *The Sporting News*, December 31, 1936, 1.

12 *The Sporting News*, January 14, 1937, 4.

13 Associated Press, "Wilson Counting Heavily on Pair of Former Grays," *Gazette and Bulletin* (Williamsport, Pennsylvania), March 16, 1937, 8.

14 Roscoe McGowen, "Passeau Pitches Phillies to Victory Over Dodgers With Aid of Two Homers," *New York Times*, July 4, 1937, C5.

15 "Passeau Delivery Stirs Inquiry," 1939 (unknown source, in Passeau's Hall of Fame file).

16 *The Sporting News*, January 19, 1939, 3.

17 "Say Passeau Uses A 'Sweat Spitter,'" 1940 (unknown source, in Passeau's Hall of Fame file).

18 Hines, 201.

19 Sid Feder, Associated Press, "Jimmy Foxx Threatens Runs-Batted-In Record," *The Day* (New London, Connecticut), July 2, 1938, 8.

20 The Old Scout, "Phillies' Deal Stirs Surmises," 1939 (Unknown source, in Passeau's Hall of Fame file).

21 Edward Burns, "Cubs Get Passeau; Trade Three to Phillies," *Chicago Daily Tribune*, May 30, 1939, 21.

22 Edward Burns, "Cubs Climb Into 2d Place; Best Dodgers, 4-2," *Chicago Daily Tribune*, July 19, 1939, 21.

23 *The Sporting News*, January 19, 1939, 3.

24 *The Sporting News*, September 20, 1945, 7.

25 Hines, 201.

26 Irving Vaughan, "Passeau Runs Into More Hard Luck—And Reds—So Cubs Lose," *Chicago Daily Tribune*, June 30, 1940, A1.

27 *The Sporting News*, May 21, 1942, 1.

28 Dan Daniel, "Dan's Dope," *New York World Telegram*, June 1941.

29 Joe King, "Ott Candidate For Best Player Award," *New York World-Telegram*, August 17, 1942 (unknown source, in Passeau's Hall of Fame file).

30 Irving Vaughan, "Cubs Perk Up; Passeau in Fold," *Chicago Daily Tribune*, April 29, 1944, 17.

31 *The Sporting News*, September 20, 1945.

32 *The Sporting News*, October 11, 1945, 1.

33 Grantland Rice, "Tigers Trek From Bench To Plate and Vice Versa In Futile Bid," *Ottawa Citizen*, October 6, 1945, 10.

34 Hines, 201.

35 Bill James and Rob Neyer, *The Neyer/James Guide to Pitchers* (New York: Fireside, 2004), 337.

36 James Segreti, "Cubs Release Passeau, Hack," *Chicago Daily Tribune*, September 27, 1947, 19.

37 United Press International, "Claude Passeau Now Sheriff," *Daily News* (Springfield, Massachusetts), June 19, 1974, 40.

Eddie Basinski

By Dave Eskenazi, Steve Rudman, and Mark Armour

EDDIE BASINSKI ALWAYS CONCEDED that he never looked much like a baseball player. He sported a slender frame and bottle-thick steel-rimmed classes, prompting many fans to view him as a Mr. Peepers in flannels and Brooklyn Dodgers president and general manager Branch Rickey to describe him as "the escaped divinity student."[1]

"Inside, I had the same competitive fire that Michael Jordan, Lou Gehrig, and Joe DiMaggio had," Basinski once told an interviewer. "I just didn't look the part, and people didn't like it."[2]

But they loved the view when Eddie Basinski played baseball. Although he didn't get much of a shot at the major leagues—he played in 203 games with the Dodgers and Pittsburgh Pirates in 1944-45 and part of 1947—he was a minor-league legend good enough to make the Pacific Coast League Hall of Fame, an accolade he earned mainly because of his slick fielding, which was the result of his remarkably quick reflexes.

Apart from Basinski's scholarly, if not dweebish, appearance, the other thing that stamped him as a baseball odd duck was that he came to the game as a trained—starting at age 5—classical violinist who occupied a chair in the Buffalo Symphony Orchestra, earning him the nickname "The Fiddler." As a college freshman, Basinski played in the last chair. By his junior year, he had challenged and outplayed 40 other violinists to become a concertmaster.

For all of his natural musical talent (he was also a near virtuoso on the piano), Basinski didn't have much when it came to baseball. But he practiced baseball fundamentals as religiously as he practiced the violin, which was the main reason he ultimately carved out a 16-year professional career, most of it with the Portland Beavers, some of it with the Seattle Rainiers.

Edwin Frank Basinski was born on November 4, 1922, to Walter and Sophie Basinski, part of a large working-class Polish family in Buffalo, New York. He had two older brothers and four younger sisters, according to the 1940 US Census. His father, Walter, a former Navy man who plied his trade as a machinist,

ran his house like a military encampment. At age 4, Basinski had scarlet fever, which caused his terrible eyesight—20-800, according to Basinski.[3]

Walter believed that if Eddie was going to make anything of himself in life he needed an honest trade. Further, he considered baseball a frivolous waste of time that had no place in his son's development. Eddie thought otherwise, but had to sneak out of the house just to play and risked a whipping if his father found out.

Through considerable cajoling, Basinski ultimately received his father's permission to try out for his high-school baseball team, but failed to earn a spot because the school's coach, Pop Yerke, couldn't conceive of a skinny, bespectacled kid like Eddie playing ball.

So Basinski took to the Buffalo sandlots, playing and practicing with a small core of players that included future Hall of Famer Warren Spahn, one of Basinski's closest childhood friends.

"The city park was next to the street I lived on," Basinski told author Craig Allen Cleve, who wrote

Hardball on the Home Front: Major League Replacement Players of World War II. "There were five aspiring baseball hopefuls who practiced every day there. We rotated our practices so that each player got 30 swings of batting practice. We were able to complete the rotation three times before it got dark."[4]

If no one else showed at the park, Basinski still had his own training routine. He practiced baserunning and sliding and even stood a bat on end in front of the backstop, and then went into the outfield to practice making throws at the plate. "I had something going for me in baseball," Basinski told Cleve. "I was quick on my feet. I could leap. I had long arms. I thought this is it for me. There isn't any other way. For me, it was trying to find some way to gain some sort of recognition, so I wasn't just one of those Polish punks over there from Kaiser town in Buffalo. None of us were going anywhere. Sports was the only avenue I had at that time."[5]

Basinski didn't play baseball at the University of Buffalo, either, because the school, although it had an excellent engineering program, had no baseball team. So Basinski lettered in tennis and cross-country and continued to practice baseball, hoping to play one day in one of Buffalo's semipro AA leagues. In 1943 Basinski earned a degree in mechanical engineering and went to work for the Curtiss-Wright Company in Buffalo, one of the country's leading aircraft manufacturers and a primary producer of US warplanes, including the P-40 Warhawk and the C-46 cargo plane.

Also in 1943, the 6-foot-1, 175-pound Basinski finally broke into Buffalo's AA league, playing shortstop and batting cleanup, and people began to take notice of his superb fielding and timely hitting. Dick Fisher, who owned a Buffalo sporting-goods store and bird-dogged the city's sandlots for major-league teams, lobbied on Basinski's behalf. At the end of 1943, an all-star team composed of Buffalo's best AA players, Basinski included, assembled to play similar teams in New York and Pennsylvania. One such outfit from Oil City, Pennsylvania, boasted a 19-game winning streak. Fisher persuaded Brooklyn Dodgers president Branch Rickey to send a scout to the Buffalo-Oil City game.

Buffalo hammered Oil City, 9-1, with Basinski delivering a two-run triple and pair of three-run homers, accounting for eight of his team's nine runs. A perfect performance under perfect circumstances resulted in the Dodgers signing Basinski to a contract that included a $5,000 signing bonus. Basinski joined the Dodgers for two weeks in early 1944 so that the club could take a look at him and figure out at which minor-league level he ought to play. At the end of the two weeks, with the Dodgers at Crosley Field in Cincinnati, manager Leo Durocher called on Basinski to bat eighth and play second base. The date was May 20, 1944. Basinski had not played baseball in high school, college or the minor leagues, and had only one limited season in a Buffalo semipro league.

Ripley's Believe It or Not called his jump from semipro ball to the majors "a 10 million to one shot."[6] In his second time up, Basinski looked at Reds left-hander Bob Katz's first pitch and drilled the second one off the wall in left for a triple. After he nailed a runner at first by ten feet and handled seven chances, Durocher began calling him "Bazooka."[7]

By the first of June, Basinski was hitting better than .300 and making both Durocher and Rickey look like the smartest men in the history of baseball. Whenever Basinski made a key play in the infield, announcer Red Barber would enthuse, "The violin is playing sweetly today!"

Basinski's teammates ribbed him mercilessly about playing the violin, one reason that Basinski never brought his prized violin to the Dodgers' Ebbets Field clubhouse. In fact, Durocher grew skeptical that he could actually play. So Basinski made Durocher a bet: He would play the violin in front of Leo and anybody else Leo wanted. If they like what they heard, Leo would pay Basinski $1,000. Durocher thought that over and accepted.

A few weeks later, Basinski showed up in the clubhouse and played selections from Cole Porter, Irving Berlin, and Victor Herbert. He also threw in a Strauss waltz. "Well, I'll be a son of a bitch. The kid can play," marveled Durocher. "A lot of people think musicians are pantywaists," Basinski said. "That's a bunch of nonsense."[8]

Unfortunately for Basinski, he couldn't sustain his hot hitting and finished the season at Double-A Montreal, where he hit .244. He played 108 games for the Dodgers in 1945, hitting .262 as the team's most frequently used shortstop (star Pee Wee Reese was serving in the military). Although there was no All-Star Game that season due to the war, the Associated Press named two unofficial teams after polling managers, and selected Basinski and the Cardinals' Marty Marion as the two NL shortstops.

With Reese back on board in 1946, Basinski spent the year with St. Paul of the American Association, where he hit .252 in full-time play. Then Basinski went to Pittsburgh in a December 5, 1946, trade for pitcher Al Gerheauser. After Basinski hit only .199 in 56 games for the 1947 Pirates, his major-league career came to an end and his PCL career began at age 24 when the New York Yankees, who had acquired him from the Pirates, sent him to the Portland Beavers.

"When I got out here (Pacific Northwest) I was floored by the beauty," Basinski told *The Oregonian*. "And the people were just great. Buffalo neighborhoods were divided among ethnic groups, and gangs guarded their turf. Somebody who didn't belong there was beaten up. Back there you'd introduce yourself and … they'd immediately categorize you. That didn't happen in Portland. It finally dawned on me, and I said, `Hey, this is America!'"9

The Yankees wanted Basinski after the 1947 season, but he instead arranged to stay in Portland. "I knew there was an awful lot of politics up there," he recalled. "When I turned the Yankees down, it was probably a terrible mistake. They won a lot of pennants after that. I would have been part of those great teams and made all that money. A lot of players who are just average players are highlighted because they won pennants."10

In Portland, Basinski became a second baseman, and spent just over ten seasons with the Beavers, hitting between .240 and .278 while annually ranking among the top defensive players in the league. In 1950 Basinski played in every inning of the 202-game Pacific Coast League schedule. He played in 557 consecutive games at one point. "I would have broken Hugh Luby's consecutive-game streak at second base—886

games—had not Walt Dropo deliberately cut me down on a tag at second base. He was out by thirty feet—embarrassed, I guess—and he cut me down with a three-inch gash on my left shin."11

In 1950 the *Oregonian* newspaper named him the club's most valuable player. He became a fan favorite—in 1955, in a newspaper poll to name Portland's all-time team, Basinski got more votes than anybody else. That probably figured, given that Basinski often trotted out his violin and performed home-plate recitals on Sundays between games of doubleheaders. "One time I got a tremendous ovation, and had a good doubleheader, too," he said.12

Basinski figured that he would end his career with the Beavers. But on April 25, 1957, the Beavers waived the 34-year-old in a cost-cutting move, leaving him available for any team willing to pay the waiver price. The Rainiers acted swiftly, largely to add to their infield depth and also because of Basinski's ability as a clutch hitter. When Basinski left Portland, he had played in 557 consecutive games and couldn't understand his release. "I was shocked when Portland waivered me out," Basinski told *The Oregonian*. "I'll never understand why the club let me go. I had the second-best spring training of my life."13

Basinski's most notable series for the Rainiers came when they faced the Beavers for the first time in an early-season seven-game series. Basinski went 7-for-14, while missing four of the seven contests with an eye injury. After appearing in seven games for the Beavers, Basinski played in 129 games for the 1957 Rainiers, who went 87-80 under Lefty O'Doul, in his last year of managing. He hit .271 with a .712 OPS and often helped rookie Maury Wills with infield fundamentals. "I had more fun and enjoyed baseball more with Lefty O'Doul. I had admired him all the years playing against him [O'Doul had managed several PCL teams during Basinski's career], and he was very complimentary to me. He used to say, 'That god-damn Basinski. If it wasn't for him, we would have won a lot more games.' His hit-and-run sign for me was playing the violin left-handed in the third-base coach's line."14

Basinski posted a good year for Seattle in 1958 when he hit .301 with 47 RBIs (Basinski hit the first double of the season, winning 13 car washes from a Rainiers sponsor), but the Rainiers, despite 19-year-old sensation Vada Pinson hitting .343 in 124 games, flailed under manager Connie Ryan, finishing 68-86, at one point losing 14 consecutive games, just three shy of Sacramento's 1925 league record of 17.

Despite Basinski's numbers, the Rainiers figured that he didn't have much left and sold him to Vancouver. In fact, he didn't have much left. Basinski played in just 43 games and hit .138 for the 1959 Mounties. "He was unathletic looking," recalled Mounties radio announcer Jim Robson, "but the kind of guy you want on your team. He undoubtedly helped the young infielders develop."[15] One of those infielders was Brooks Robinson.

During his PCL career, Basinski compiled 1,544 hits, 109 homers, and 634 RBIs, all while batting .260. He led the PCL in games played in 1950 and in at-bats in 1951.

After his career ended, Basinski settled in Oregon with his wife and two sons. He became an accounts manager for Consolidated Freightways in Portland, where he worked for 31 years, retiring in 1991. He took up bowling and golf in retirement. He had the honor of being inducted into the Oregon Sports Hall of Fame in 1987, the Brooklyn Dodgers Hall of Fame in 1996, and the Pacific Coast League Hall of Fame in 2006. In 1984, he was named to the all-time PCL All-Star team. In 2014 the 91-year-old Basinski resided in Milwaukie, Oregon, a suburb of Portland.

"I don't look like a big strong guy, but I was an iron man with Portland. My looks were always against my ability. I looked like a damn doctor or a preacher, and the glasses didn't help. But man, I had the fire, and I wanted to be a perfectionist."

"I settled in Portland, married there, had a couple of boys. I think that had a lot to do with turning down the Yankees. I'm sure it was a mistake as far as money, but I had the great love and devotion of Portland all those years."[16] Though he would occasionally be asked to play his violin for a baseball audience, he did so reluctantly. "I'm a perfectionist," he admitted," and if I can't play well then I prefer not to do it."[17]

A version of this article, written by Dave Eskenazi with help from Steve Rudman, first appeared at sportspressnw.com on March 5, 2013. Mark Armour expanded Dave's article for this book.

NOTES

1   Craig Allen Cleve, *Hardball on the Home Front: Major League Replacement Players of World War II* (Jefferson, North Carolina: McFarland, 2004), 119.

2   Cleve, *Hardball on the Home Front*, 119.

3   Eddie Basinski, interview with Chris Potter, youtube.com, 2011.

4   Cleve, *Hardball on the Home Front*, 120.

5   Cleve, *Hardball on the Home Front*, 120.

6   Eddie Basinski, interview with Chris Potter, youtube.com, 2011.

7   David Eskenazi, "Wayback Machine: Eddie Basinski, 'The Fiddler,'" SportsPressNW.com, March 5, 2013.

8   Daniel J. Wakin, "Ballplayers Who Hit the Right Notes," *New York Times*, June 24, 2011.

9   Eskenazi, "Wayback Machine."

10 Larry Stone, "'Those were the most wonderful days I believe I ever had,'" in Mark Armour (ed.), *Rain Check* (SABR, 2006), 101.

11 Cleve, *Hardball on the Home Front*, 140.

12 Eskenazi, "Wayback Machine."

13 Eskenazi, "Wayback Machine."

14 Dobbins, *The Grand Minor League—An Oral History of the Old Pacific Coast League* (Emeryville, California: Woodford Press, 1999), 143.

15 Dick Dobbins, *The Grand Minor League*, 105.

16 Stone, "'Those were the most wonderful days I believe I ever had,'" 101.

17 Dobbins, *The Grand Minor League*, 154.

Ernie Lombardi

By Joe Wancho

IT IS ONE OF THOSE RECORDS THAT MAY never be equaled, much less broken. For 75 years a handful of pitchers have come close to tying Johnny Vander Meer's record of pitching two consecutive no-hitters. But it has proven elusive for even the most elite hurlers throughout major-league history.

His first no-hitter came on June 11, 1938, at Crosley Field, Vander Meer's home ballpark in Cincinnati. Many games of this variety require great defense and timely hitting. Cincinnati's left-handed hurler was the beneficiary of both against the opponent, the Boston Bees. In the fourth inning Vander Meer walked right fielder Gene Moore, one of his three walks that day. The next batter was Johnny Cooney. The hit-and-run play was on. Cooney popped out to catcher Ernie Lombardi. Moore was steaming toward second base, and then tried to scamper back to the first-base bag, but he was doubled off when Lombardi alertly threw to first baseman Frank McCormick to complete the double play. In the fifth inning Vander Meer walked Tony Cuccinello. Lombardi made a snap throw to first base and caught Cuccinello leaning toward second base. "Lom would pick about six to seven guys a year off first base, throwing side-arm behind left-handed hitters," said Vander Meer. [1]

But the Reds backstop was not through. With the home team clinging to a lead of a single run, Lombardi connected for a two-run home run in the bottom of the sixth inning. It provided the final margin of victory in the 3-0 Reds win. It was just another day at the office for the lumbering catcher.

Vander Meer next toed the rubber on June 15 against the Brooklyn Dodgers, the first night game at Ebbets Field, and in New York City. Vander Meer was not as sharp on this night; he walked eight Dodgers, three in the ninth inning to load the bases with one out. A force out at home plate accounted for the second out, and Leo Durocher's line out to center fielder Harry Craft ended the game. Vander Meer etched his name in major-league history with the 6-0 victory and his second consecutive no-hitter.

Home-plate umpire Bill Stewart was as close to the action as one could get without having to purchase a ticket. He offered a different perspective on the game. "Give some credit to Lombardi," said Stewart. "Sure, Vander Meer had to pitch perfectly to get his no-hitters. But what about the guy who told the kid what to pitch? If Lombardi had guessed wrong on one hitter, if he had called for a fastball when a curve was the smart pitch, Vander Meer never would've made it. Lombardi's judgment was just as perfect and just as important as Vander Meer's pitches." [2]

Ernesto Natali Lombardi was born on April 6, 1908, in Oakland, California. He was one of four children born to Mr. and Mrs. Domenic Lombardi. Ernie had three sisters, Stella, Rena, and Rose. Domenic Lombardi emigrated from Italy and owned a small grocery store.

Ernie was a common sight to customers, working at his post behind the counter.

Lombardi, who would grow to be 6-feet-3 as an adult, was taller than most children around his age. He spent much of his time playing sandlot baseball at Bay View Park. When he was 12, he played for a semipro team, Ravoli's Meat Market. Coaches took notice of Lombardi's strong arm, and his career as a catcher began. A scout from the Oakland Oaks tried to sign Ernie but the youngster refused because he did not want to leave the Bay Area to play for one of Oakland's farm clubs. However, after a short stint running the grocery store while his father was away, Lombardi changed his mind and contacted the Oaks. He realized that he might prefer a career in professional baseball over that of a grocer.

After a brief stop in Ogden, Utah, Lombardi honed his craft back home in Oakland. From 1928 through 1930, he smoked the ball in Pacific Coast League parks, posting batting averages of .377, .366, and .370. His defensive ability was also supreme. He registered an amazing 95 assists in 1929, and topped that mark with 102 in 1930.

Lombardi possessed some distinctive physical characteristics, including a pair of huge hands and a bigger-than-normal nose. There is a picture of Lombardi holding seven baseballs in one hand. His nose was said to be just as enormous. "They first began kidding me about the nose and calling me 'Schnozz' back in the Coast League," he said. "But the funny thing was, I didn't get too much razzing from the bench jockeys. Mostly, it came from the fans."[3] Lombardi was good-natured about the kidding he received, and often showed off a self-deprecating humor of his own.

The Brooklyn Dodgers sent Hank DeBerry, Eddie Moore, and $50,000 to Oakland for Lombardi on January 19, 1931. Brooklyn skipper Wilbert Robinson favored seasoned veterans over green kids, which left Ernie the bench watching Al Lopez handle most of the catching chores. But Lombardi produced when he was given the opportunity, hitting .275 in 43 starts at catcher. He demonstrated a strange batting grip in which he clamped his left index finger over the little finger of his right hand. It is the same grip a golfer

employs, although Lombardi never once stepped on the links. Apparently, the grip worked just dandy for him.

Lombardi's stay in Brooklyn was short, and on March 14, 1932, he was part of a six-player deal that sent him to Cincinnati. He started instantly with the Reds, batting over .300 in six of his first seven seasons there. Although Lom had success at most of the venues in the National League, he seemed to thrive at the Baker Bowl in Philadelphia.

Lombardi enjoyed some of his biggest career days at the Philadelphia bandbox, at the expense of the Phillies. On May 8, 1935, he tied a league record with four doubles in a game as the Reds pasted the Phils, 15-4. On May 9, 1937, Lombardi became the second Red to tally six hits in a nine-inning game. In a 21-10 shellacking of the Phillies, Ernie stroked two doubles, drove in five runs, and scored three runs.

Between 1932 and 1937 Cincinnati finished in the cellar four times and the manager seat was more like a carousel. Bill McKechnie came to the Queen City and took the reins before the 1938 season. "I liked to play for Bill," said Lombardi. "He was quieter than other managers. But all he had to do was look out at you over the top of his glasses and you'd know you'd done something wrong."[4]

"Deacon Bill" guided the Reds to a fourth-place finish in 1938, his first year at the helm. That was just a preview of coming attractions. One reason for the Reds' sudden surge in the standings was Lombardi. Although he had been a starter since being acquired from Brooklyn, Lombardi finally received some notice for his abilities when he led the circuit that season with a .342 batting average. He smashed 19 home runs, had 95 RBIs, and hit 30 doubles. He was the starting catcher for the National League team in the All-Star Game. (On the negative side, Lombardi set a National League record for the most double plays hit into in a season with 30. The record stood for 70 years until Houston's Miguel Tejada broke it in 2008.) Lombardi was honored by both the Baseball Writers Association of America and *The Sporting News* as the National League's Most Valuable Player.

As the double-play mark suggests, one aspect missing from Lombardi's skill set was speed. Although he was

THE MAN, THE SONG, THE PLAYERS

a smart baserunner, he was not a fast one; in fact, he is widely recognized as one of the slowest runners in baseball history. It was often said that Lombardi doubled to left and beat out a single. However, Lom hit rifle shots, and there were no cheap hits in his arsenal. Many times infielders would station themselves on the grass behind the dirt infield. The joke was that the opposing team's insurance policy would not cover all the potential damage caused by Ernie's hitting ability.

Behind the plate, however, Lombardi was as agile as they come. He possessed a strong throwing arm, and moved with ease to catch pop flies around home plate. He was so skilled that sometimes he looked almost nonchalant working behind the dish.

The Reds won the pennant in 1939 and 1940. Bucky Walters won 49 games and Paul Derringer 45 in the two seasons to lead a solid staff. "You could sit in a rocking chair and catch them guys," said Schnozz. [5] In contrast, Lombardi felt that Vander Meer was hard to catch because he was a hard thrower and erratic. You could never tell where the ball was going to end up. Once Pepper Martin of St. Louis was on third base, dancing around in an attempt to distract Vander Meer. His strategy worked, and Vander Meer uncorked a pitch way outside. Lombardi just reached for the ball with his bare hand and snagged it. "Listen, if you're going to sit back there and catch me barehanded, the least you could do after you throw the ball back to me is shake your hand a little like I had something on the pitch," Vander Meer told Lombardi. "You're making me look bad." [6]

It is unfortunate, even unfair, that a player can be best remembered for one single play in his career. Ernie Lombardi is one such player. On October 8, 1939, at Crosley Field, the Reds and New York Yankees were playing Game Four of the World Series. The Yankees held a commanding 3-0 lead in the Series, and were looking to sweep the Reds. But the Reds would not bow, and the game was tied, 4-4, heading into extra innings. Walters, pitching in relief, walked Frank Crosetti to lead off the tenth. After a sacrifice, Charlie Keller reached on an error by shortstop Billy Myers. Joe DiMaggio laced a shot that fell in front of right fielder Ival Goodman. Goodman bobbled the ball, and

by the time he threw home, Crosetti had scored the go-ahead run and Keller was making his way to the plate. Keller crashed into Lombardi, who fell back and lost control of the ball. Lombardi lay sprawled out on the ground behind the plate, the ball lying two feet away. DiMaggio kept coming toward home. Ernie regained his senses, grabbing the baseball in a futile attempt to tag DiMaggio. But the runner slid over the catcher's hand, and was called safe. The play was referred to as "Lombardi's Snooze." The Yankees wrapped up the Series with the 7-4 victory. The next year at spring training, Keller denied that he had touched Lombardi, and that the big catcher had just fallen backward.

"Ernie was wronged," recalled Joltin' Joe. "He WAS knocked out in a collision with Charley Keller, who scored, and I saw immediately that something was haywire. I kept running and never stopped. Keller gave Ernie more than just a bump, as they described it. He put Ernie out of commission." [7] Vander Meer had a different take on the play. "The throw from the outfield came in a short hop and hit Lom in the cup. You just don't get up too quick. Somebody put out the word that 'Lombardi went to sleep, took a snooze.' He was paralyzed. He couldn't move. Anybody but Lombardi, they would have had to carry him off the field." [8] Bucky Walters said, "It was a silly rap. But the Yankees beat us four straight and they had to pick on something, I guess. You can blame part of the thing on me. I was pitching, and I should have been behind home plate, backing up Lombardi. But the run didn't mean anything, anyway." [9]

The 1940 season offered a different climax. Powered by a 23-8 record in September, the Reds coasted to their second pennant in a row. They had 100 wins, besting second-place Brooklyn by 12 games. But Lombardi badly sprained his right ankle on September 15 at Brooklyn. His season was over, and when it was time for the World Series, backup Jimmie Wilson caught most of the games, with Lom able to catch in only one. Behind two wins each from Walters and Derringer, the Reds topped the Detroit Tigers in seven games.

In Lombardi's ten years with the Reds, he hit over .300 in seven. By all accounts he was a terrific teammate and a good-hearted person. Like most people, he had his peculiarities. He did not believe in signing autographs. It wasn't until a youngster asked if he was illiterate that Lombardi, to dispute the point, signed the scrap of paper.

Lombardi towered over many of the other players, and was somewhat of a gentle giant. However, there were instances when he could get riled. Tony Cuccinello was a prankster and particularly apt at pulling off the hidden-ball trick. "There was a close play at second and I missed (Lombardi) sliding in. The pitcher was standing nearby. While Ernie's getting up I told the pitcher to stay off the rubber. I had the ball in my glove. The pitcher went toward the mound, picked up the rosin bag and looked in at the catcher like he's looking for the sign and Ernie walked off the bag. When I had enough room I ran over to him and showed him the ball. Oh, he was mad. He said to me, 'You tag me and I'll punch you right in the nose.' I never tagged him. He just walked back to the dugout."[10]

Lombardi's batting average plummeted to .264 in 1941. Differences with general manager Warren Giles and the dramatic drop in his hitting prompted Cincinnati to sell Lombardi to the Boston Braves before the 1942 season.

The Braves, who were piloted by Casey Stengel, were an atrocious bunch. First baseman Max West was the leading power hitter with 16 home runs and 56 RBIs. Lombardi, in only 309 at-bats was credited under the rules of the day with leading the league in hitting with a .330 average. During a game with the Reds, Cincinnati catcher Ray Lammano told him, "Man, you're driving McKechnie crazy with the way you're hitting. He's pulling his hair out."[11] Lombardi earned a spot on the National League All-Star squad.

Despite the fine year he had in Boston, Lombardi asked the Braves to trade him and held out until a deal could be completed. On April 27, 1943, he got his wish. He was dealt to the New York Giants for catcher Hugh Poland and infielder Connie Ryan. "To say that I'm highly pleased to become a Giant doesn't adequately express my feelings," said Lom. "I've had my eye on that left-field scoreboard in the Polo Grounds for a long time. Now, I'm going to see what can be done about it as a home-field target."[12]

In 1944 Lombardi married Berice Ayers of Oakland, California. They had no children.

With World War II raging and many leading players in the armed forces, many of the major-league teams were filled with aging veterans or players who might still be in the minors under normal circumstances. Billy Jurges, Dick Bartell, and Joe Medwick had all seen better days, and player-manager Mel Ott was also past his prime. Others, like Mickey Witek and Johnny Rucker, had major-league jobs but saw their careers end shortly after the war ended. For Lombardi, whose Selective Service number was 4,541, the chances of being drafted seemed unlikely. He was called to take his draft physical in September 1943, but was turned down by the Army.

The playing field was balanced in the major leagues with many of the teams being forced to field patchwork lineups. The Giants were not competitive during this period, often placing in the second division. But on April 30, 1944, all of the Giants had their hitting shoes on as they thrashed the Dodgers, 26-8. Lombardi posted a career high with seven RBIs. In two of the three years he started for the Giants, Lombardi batted over .300. But before the 1946 season, with Lombardi aging, the Giants purchased Walker Cooper from St. Louis to assume the catching burden. Lombardi played two more years, retiring after the 1947 season. In 17 seasons, he had a career batting average of .306, with 190 home runs, and 990 RBIs. He returned to the Pacific Coast League and played one final year of professional baseball in 1948, with Oakland and Sacramento. In 2003 Lombardi was inducted into the Pacific Coast League Hall of Fame.

Unfortunately for Lombardi, his life after baseball was not a comfortable one. He held different jobs on the West Coast, unable to settle into a steady profession. He lived the life of a recluse, still haunted by the "Lombardi Snooze" moniker. In April of 1953, he and his wife were visiting relatives in Castro Valley, California. Ernie used the bathroom, said he was not feeling well, and went to lie down in a bedroom. Bernice, his wife, checked on him a short time after and discovered that he had cut his throat with a razor he found in the bathroom. He struggled with emergency personnel, saying that he wanted to die. Lombardi was saved from his suicide attempt and entered a private sanitarium.

Year after year, Lombardi was passed over for entry into the Baseball Hall of Fame. The Veterans Committee also passed over Schnozz. Lombardi was disgruntled about his exclusion. He vowed that he would not attend the induction ceremonies even if he was elected. He re-entered the baseball world when he took a job as a press-box attendant at Candlestick Park in San Francisco. It was more of a public-relations position, but Lombardi loved to talk baseball, specifically about his playing days.

Lombardi died on September 26, 1977, after a long illness. He was survived by his three sisters. Bernice had preceded him in death in 1973. Lombardi finally received the call from Cooperstown, posthumously, in 1986. One of his peers, Birdie Tebbetts, a good catcher in his own right, had been elected to the Veterans Committee and led a personal crusade to get Lombardi elected. The "Snooze play" and Lombardi's attempted suicide were major roadblocks. Lombardi was inducted into the Hall of Fame along with Bobby Doerr and Willie McCovey.

Lombardi was inducted into the Cincinnati Reds Hall of Fame in 1958. In 2004 a full-size bronze statue of Ernie was dedicated outside Great American Ballpark, joining those of Frank Robinson, Joe Nuxhall, and Ted Kluszewski at the entrance to the ballpark.

SOURCES

Tebbetts, Birdie, and James Morrison, *Birdie* (Chicago: Triumph Books, 2002).

baseball-almanac.com/

baseball-reference.com/

cincinnati.reds.mlb.com/index.jsp?c_id=cin&tcid=mm_cle_sitelist

milb.com/content/page.jsp?sid=l112&ymd=20061214&content_id=148680&vkey=league3

retrosheet.org/

sabr.org

NOTES

1 James W. Johnson, *Double No-Hit* (Lincoln: University of Nebraska Press, 2012), 3.

2 Lombardi's Hall of Fame player file.

3 Jack Zanger, *Great Catchers of the Major Leagues* (New York: Random House, 1970), 125.

4 Zanger, 129.

5 Zanger, 131.

6 Norman L. Macht and Dick Bartell, *Rowdy Richard* (Berkeley, California: North Atlantic Books, 1987), 319.

7 Art Rosenbaum, "One Out From Hall of Fame, *San Francisco Chronicle*, September 28, 1977.

8 Dave Kindred, "Ernie Lombardi a Bitter Recluse Because of 'Snooze,'" *Louisville Courier-Journal*, February 8, 1977.

9 Kindred.

10 Macht and Bartell, 95.

11 Zanger, 134.

12 Lombardi's Hall of Fame player file.

Hugh Mulcahy

By C. Paul Rogers III

ONE CAN SENSIBLY ARGUE THAT HUGH Mulcahy was one of the hardest-luck pitchers in baseball history. At first glance a pitcher with a 45-89 career record and a lifetime earned-run average of 4.49, one who was twice the league leader in losses, is not exactly a player one thinks of as a victim of bad luck. On the contrary, when a pitcher wins barely half as many games as he loses during his career, one might consider him pretty lucky just to play the nine big-league seasons that Mulcahy put in between 1935 and 1947. But luck is often in the eyes of the beholder, and a closer examination of Mulcahy's career suggests that he indeed might have been one of the game's unluckiest ballplayers.

During his four principal years in the big leagues, 1937 through 1940, Mulcahy's Philadelphia Phillies finished seventh once and in the cellar three times, losing 92, 105, 106, and 103 games.. Toiling for the woeful Phillies as one of their most used pitchers, he lost 20 games in 1938 and 22 in 1940 — and was tabbed by sportswriters with the moniker "Losing Pitcher," supposedly because his name appeared so often in the newspaper box score with an "LP" beside it. (If such a label was actually deserved by Mulcahy, it could have been applied equally to fellow Phillies pitchers Bucky Walters, Kirby Higbe, and Claude Passeau, who each compiled similarly mediocre won-lost records — Walters went 11-21 in 1936 — before each had the good fortune to be traded away to better clubs in the National League.) In addition to these burdens, Mulcahy became the first major-league player drafted into the armed services for World War II when he was inducted on March 8, 1941, nine months *before* Pearl Harbor. He would serve 53 months, including a year in New Guinea and the Philippines, before receiving his honorable discharge on August 5, 1945. He lost to all intents and purposes, five full seasons of baseball.

Of course many ballplayers lost years to the war, including well-known stars like Joe DiMaggio, Bob Feller, Hank Greenberg, and Ted Williams. And many baseball fans are familiar with the unlucky tale of Cecil Travis, who entered the war after completing one of the greatest seasons ever by a shortstop, only to lose four years of his career and end up with frostbitten feet in the Battle of the Bulge, which curtailed his playing days. But each of those players had either already enjoyed many prime seasons or returned young enough to regain the skills that made him a great player to begin with. Not so for Mulcahy. Whatever developing potential he had that might finally have brought him stardom in 1941 and beyond was never realized.

Here's the way Red Smith, writing in 1947 after the Pirates had released the veteran pitcher (shortly after the Phillies had also released him), described Mulcahy's fate:

"Chances are there has not been in modern times another ballplayer with ability comparable with Mulcahy's who put so much into baseball and took so little out, that is, no one who wasn't at least partly at fault, no one at once so deserving and unlucky. In a strictly professional sense, Mulcahy is the major war casualty among big-league players. He didn't get shot,

like John Grodzicki or young Bob Savage. He wasn't knocked out of the skies and imprisoned like Phil Marchildon. But those fellows were young enough to come back and start over. Mulcahy only lost a career that seemed just about to come full flower when he had to give it up [for military service]."[1]

If not for the years lost to the war, how good might Hugh Mulcahy have become? Anybody's guess would be mere speculation, but it's worth noting that Mulcahy's three former Phillies peers—Walters, Higbe, and Passeau (of whom only Higbe would lose any years to the war, and only two at that)—all went on to All-Star-caliber pitching careers, and each would post a 20-victory season the very year after leaving the Phillies. So who's to say that Mulcahy wouldn't have fared just as well?

Thus, life seems to have dealt Hugh Mulcahy a tough hand: He pitched for an awful club, got tagged with an ignominious nickname, was the first major-league World War II draftee, and spent 4½ "prime" years in military service, effectively ruining his big-league career. However, Mulcahy himself thought otherwise.

In correspondence when he was 87 years old, living in suburban Pittsburgh and suffering from cancer, he preferred to view himself as a fortunate man. Fortunate to break into the majors with the Phillies, where manager Jimmie Wilson straightened out his pitching delivery, he became a workhorse, and was named to the 1940 National League All-Star team. Fortunate to survive World War II, particularly the stint in New Guinea, where his outfit was ravaged by a tropical disease that proved nearly fatal for many of them. And fortunate, after his playing days were over, to secure a job in baseball as a respected pitching coach and minor-league administrator. In other words, as Mulchahy saw it, it was a life blessed by a lot of good luck, not bad.[2]

Hugh Noyes Mulcahy was a Massachusetts native, born on September 9, 1913, in the Brighton section of Boston. He played shortstop in grade school and high school, where he was named to the all-city team in Boston. After a prep-school year as an outfielder at Dean Academy in Franklin, Massachusetts, he tried his hand at pitching in 1932 with Allston of the semipro

Boston Twilight League, where he won eight and lost 12. That earned him a tryout with the New York Giants in 1933 and assignment to North Attleboro (Massachusetts), of the New England League, which was being revived after a three-year hiatus. The league was shaky and so was the franchise, shifting to Lawrence, Massachusetts, and then to Woonsocket, Rhode Island. After compiling an 8-4 record, Mulcahy jumped the Woonsocket club because it couldn't meet payroll and finished the year in Saranac, New York, hurling for a semipro team for $8 a week and room and board.

The New York Giants organization eventually paid Mulcahy some of what Woonsocket owed him by giving him a glove, a pair of spikes, and some other equipment. Mulcahy signed with Manchester in the Northeastern League for 1934 and compiled a solid 14-10 record, allowing only 140 hits in 199 innings pitched, before finishing the year with Reading in the faster New York-Penn League.

His performance with Manchester earned him an invitation to the 1935 spring training with the Washington Senators in Biloxi, Mississippi. There, Mulcahy's big-league career almost ended before it began. As he picked up a bat near the batting cage, a foul tip clobbered him right between the eyes: A doctor told him that an inch either way would have resulted in the loss of an eye. In typical fashion, Mulcahy chose to focus on his good fortune of the ball not blinding an eye rather than his misfortune of being in the wrong place at the wrong time.[3]

Mulcahy did not stick with the Senators, but was assigned to Albany in the top-drawer International League. There he struggled somewhat, posting a 4-2 record but with a 5.12 earned-run average. After about six weeks, however, the owner of the Albany club, Joe Cambria, was convinced that Hugh had big-league ability and traveled to Philadelphia to try to peddle him to the pitching-poor Phillies. Cambria told Phillies manager Jimmie Wilson that he had a prospect who was 6-feet-2 and could throw hard, but needed to be taught how to pitch.[4]

Wilson was a veteran catcher who knew something about pitching. That very year he converted third baseman Bucky Walters into a starting pitcher. Walters would go on to lead the 1939 and 1940 Cincinnati Reds to the National League pennant, winning 27 games in '39 and 22 in '40. Wilson brought Mulcahy in for a workout, saw his potential, and purchased him for the big-league club. Hugh joined the team in St. Louis, but it quickly became apparent that he did not know how to balance himself while standing on the pitching rubber and had little idea where the ball was going. Wilson and coach Hans Lobert worked with Mulcahy on all aspects of pitching, even changing his sidearm delivery to three-quarters. They urged him to take advantage of his natural throwing style and to point his left foot at the batter so as to utilize his leverage off the mound.

As a result Mulcahy took no real windup but simply reared back, pointed his left foot, and fired fastballs. He was on the wild side but his ball moved, so Wilson advised him to just aim for the center of the plate and it would find the corners. He developed a curve but relied mainly on the heater early in his career.[5]

Mulcahy made his big-league debut amid memorable circumstances in Pittsburgh's Forbes Field. Pitching in relief, he retired in succession future Hall of Famers Paul Waner, Lloyd Waner, and Arky Vaughn. He finished the season with the Phillies, winning one while losing five, mostly in relief. Wilson even started Mulcahy in right field in one game; he threw a runner out on the bases while going 0-for-4 at the plate. Wilson later told Mulcahy, "You're not a good hitter, Hughie, but you're plenty dangerous."[6]

The following spring Wilson wanted Mulcahy to work on his new mechanics and sent him to Hazleton of the New York-Penn League for the 1936 season. There Hugh blossomed, winning 25 games and earning the league's Most Valuable Player Award (beating out, among others, future Hall of Famer Rabbit Maranville). He certainly had an opportunity to fix his mechanics, pitching an astounding 325 innings in 46 games. Not only that, he appeared in three more games and logged another 21⅔ innings for the Phillies in a late-season call-up.[7] On September 24 Mulcahy showed his potential in no uncertain terms, pitching 13 innings and allowing only eight hits as he beat the Brooklyn Dodgers, 4-2.

Mulcahy stuck with the Phillies in 1937 and quickly became a mainstay of the staff. Managers did not coddle young pitchers in those days, so Mulcahy led the league with 56 appearances as a starter and in relief, totaling 216 innings and tying the great Christy Mathewson for the most appearances by a pitcher in a National League season. As a result, the press began to call Mulcahy "Iron Man."[8] He put together an 8-18 won-loss record for the seventh-place Phillies, who finished 34½ games behind the pennant-winning New York Giants. It would be the Phillies' only finish out of the basement during Mulcahy's four principal years with the club.

He threw his first big-league shutout that year, a four-hitter against the Cincinnati Reds. Mulcahy managed to lose another game on one pitch. On June 17 against the Cubs, he entered the game with two on, one out, and the winning run at the plate. Billy Jurges was the batter and he bunted the first pitch down the third-base line. Mulcahy recalled that he and third sacker Pinky Whitney played "Alphonse and Gaston" with the ball and Jurges ended up safe at first. Manager Jimmie Wilson then brought in lefty Wayne LaMaster to face the next batter, Augie Galan. Although Galan was a switch-hitter, he was a weaker right-handed batter. Not this day, however. Augie hit LaMaster's first pitch for a triple to score Jurges with the winning run, giving Mulcahy a one-pitch defeat.

Late in life, Mulcahy remembered little about the "losing pitcher" moniker and recalled the writers of the day more often referring to him as a workhorse. Given his endurance, "workhorse" certainly would have been an appropriate nickname. In 1938, only his second full year in the majors, Mulcahy appeared in 46 games, starting 34, and pitching 267 innings while compiling a 10-20 record for a team that finished in the cellar 24½ games out of *seventh* place. Jimmie Wilson had little tolerance for the nickname, saying, "Call him Losing Pitcher Mulcahy if you like, but he's one hell of a pitcher."[9] At the end of the season, Wilson told Mulcahy that in winning ten games for a 45-105 team, he should consider himself a 20-game winner.[10]

The highlight of Mulcahy's 1938 season undoubtedly occurred on September 16 in the second game of a doubleheader against the Cincinnati Reds at

Philadelphia's Shibe Park. Mulcahy took a no-hitter into the eighth inning before Ernie Lombardi broke it up with a single. He ended up with a three-hitter and a 2-1 victory over the club that would win the pennant the next two years. According to contemporary press accounts, Mulcahy was "jinxed" by a female fan after he flied out to Harry Craft in the bottom of the seventh. While he was jogging back to the dugout, the fan leaned out of a box seat and yelled, "Keep it up, Hughie; it'll be a no-hitter," thus breaking the baseball code of silence concerning no-hitters in progress.[11] Sure enough the next batter, Lombardi, singled.

Mulcahy also distinguished himself in 1938 by tying for the National League lead in fielding his position by not committing an error for the entire season. Not bad work on a club that was the worst-fielding team in the league, with 201 miscues.

The following year, 1939, turned out to be another losing season, with Mulcahy hampered by a sore shoulder in spring training and again late in the year. A slow start led to a 9-16 record in 226 innings for a dismal team that finished with a 45-106 record, *50½ games out of first place* and 18 games behind the seventh-place Boston Bees. Mulcahy again showed flashes of brilliance, beating the defending champion Cubs at Wrigley Field, 4-1, on a five-hitter, on May 3, and again on a two-hit shutout at Wrigley on June 24. After the first win, Cubs manager Gabby Hartnett said that every team in the league would like to have Mulcahy.[12]

In 1939 the Phillies began playing a few night games in Shibe Park, which they shared with the Athletics of the American League. Not surprisingly, the Phils lost their first four night games at home before Mulcahy beat the Dodgers 3-2 on August 8, posting the Phillies' first home night-game victory.

In 1940 Mulcahy seemed to put it all together, even though the Phils were again headed for the cellar by a wide margin. Bolstered by a new changeup, he got off to a fine start. In a memorable game on May 23, however, he lost to the Cubs 4-3 in 13 innings when roommate and close friend Morrie Arnovich slipped on the wet outfield grass and failed to catch a drive by Al Todd that would have been the third out. Afterward, Arnovich was inconsolable, even though Hugh told him, "Forget

it. I know how you feel and know you tried your damnedest. You'll make up for it."[13]

Earlier Mulcahy had shut out the St. Louis Cardinals in Philadelphia, 4-0, driving in three of the runs himself. In fact, he remembered winning four or five games in 1940 with his hitting. For the year he batted .202, more than respectable for a pitcher. He also received some notoriety for his pitching notebook, which had a page for every batter in the league. A distinctive feature of the book was that at the top of each page, Hugh had written the same rule number one for every batter: "Don't Walk Him"—a testament to his continuing control problems.[14]

On June 30 Mulcahy was named to the National League All-Star team along with teammates Kirby Higbe and Pinky May. Phillies manager Doc Prothro was even included as one of the All-Star coaches.

Mulcahy's selection was not without some irony. In those days all eight league managers participated in selecting the All-Star squad. Just three days before the team was announced, Hugh lost to Bill Terry's New York Giants, 7-0, as Prince Hal Schumacher shut out the Phils on three hits. Mulcahy and his successor, Lloyd Brown, gave up 15 hits (in just an hour and 42 minutes), all singles. Nonetheless, Terry was quoted after the game as viewing Mulcahy as the number-one hurler in the league, remarking, "That's a funny thing, but when I was asked to make out my list of 25 players for the National League team this year I immediately named Mulcahy. … I hope Mul can lick the American Leaguers, but in our own league we'll take him apart every chance we get. That's what we're out here for."[15]

National League manager Bill McKechnie may not completely have agreed with Terry, however, as Mulcahy did not pitch in the game, which the National League won, 4-0. Paul Derringer, Bucky Walters, Whitlow Wyatt, Larry French, and Carl Hubbell held the American League to three hits. Only the two Phils chuckers, Mulcahy and Higbe, failed to see action.

Still, on July 31 Hugh beat the Cubs 7-3 for his 12th win of the season (and fifth in a row), and the press touted his chances as "better than fair" to become the first Phillies hurler to win 20 or more games since Grover Cleveland Alexander (with 30 victories) did so in 1917.[16] But it was not to be. Mulcahy embarked on a 12-game losing streak, including several one-run defeats, before shutting out Carl Hubbell and the Giants on four hits in the last game of the season. It gave Hugh a 13-22 record for the year and was the last game he would pitch in the big leagues for five years.

That win, and an earlier 3-2 victory over Hubbell, were two of Mulcahy's biggest thrills as a big leaguer, given that Hubbell had been Hugh's baseball hero. "To me he was the greatest man in the world besides my dad and I never dreamed I'd even meet him, much less beat him," Mulcahy told a Philadelphia sportswriter in 1946.[17]

Despite that disappointing record in 1940, Mulcahy had a fine year by any other measure. He started 36 games and completed 21, third most in the league. His 280 innings were fifth in the league and his 3.60 ERA was well below the league average. That he got little hitting support is all too apparent, given the Phillies' league-worst .238 batting average. The team managed just 50 wins and finished 50 games behind the pennant-winning Reds.

Pitching for an outfit like the Phillies, it was better to not take oneself too seriously, and Mulcahy did not. He was known as a low-key guy with a self-deprecating sense of humor. With tongue planted firmly in cheek, he actually responded to a reporter's questioning about the keys to losing in the April 28, 1938, *Philadelphia Evening Bulletin.* According to Hugh, it was important to (1) try new stuff out until you walk the batter; (2) always stay behind in the count; and (3) be sure not to bear down on the Medwicks, Mizes, and DiMaggios, guys who can beat you.[18]

One could push him too far, however, as his old friend Claude Passeau learned one July evening during the 1939 season. Passeau had been Hugh's pitching mate with the Phillies until his trade to the Cubs earlier in the year. They were mound opponents in Shibe Park on July 13, at a time when the Phillies harbored ill feelings against Cubs manager Gabby Hartnett for failing to play the Phils' Morrie Arnovich in the All-Star Game the previous week. Arnovich, the Phillies' only All-Star representative, was hitting a cool .383 to lead the league at the time. In the fourth inning Passeau

tapped a roller down the first-base line. As Mulcahy pounced on the ball and raced over to apply the bare-hand tag, Passeau responded by trying to knock the ball out of his right hand with a chop above the wrist. Mulcahy reacted immediately, swinging and missing at his friend Passeau's chin and precipitating a bench-clearing brawl.

Both pitchers were kicked out of the game. Afterward, Passeau visited the Phillies clubhouse and apologized to Hugh, and the two remained good friends. Mulcahy was fined $25 and referred to as One Punch Mulcahy in the *Philadelphia Inquirer,* which also quoted him as saying, "It was worth $25 to relieve my mind and show the Cubs that we weren't going to take anything laying down. I like to win and when I felt Passeau trying to knock the ball out of my hand I saw red."[19]

After the 1940 season, Phillies owner Gerald Nugent announced that to make ends meet, he had to sell one of his star pitchers, Mulcahy or Kirby Higbe, a flaky fastballer who had thrown 283 innings and led the league in strikeouts while compiling a 14-19 record. The asking price for either was a hefty $150,000 plus players in return.[20] Several clubs were interested and Nugent eventually made a deal with the Dodgers: Higbe for $100,000 cash and three players, pitchers Vito Tamulis and Bill Crouch and catcher Mickey Livingston. So Mulcahy stayed in Philadelphia. It turned out to be a wonderful deal for the Dodgers and not so good for the futile Phillies. Higbe led Brooklyn to the 1941 pennant with a 22-9 record, while by March of that year Mulcahy was hurling for Uncle Sam when he was pitching at all.

The details of Mulcahy's military induction suggest more bad luck and unfortunate timing. Only six days before his March 8 induction, he had signed a new Phillies contract that included a $3,000 raise, placing his salary in the relatively rarefied air above $10,000. He received his induction notice the day before he was to leave for spring training in Miami Beach and so got to trade his princely new baseball salary for Army pay of $30 a month. He had previously asked for a six-month deferment to help pay for a home he had purchased for his parents (whom he was partially supporting), but his draft board denied the request, although it told him he was not likely to be called until the following September. Further, he was 27 when he was drafted, very close to the 28-year-old draft age limit of the time.[21]

Mulcahy certainly kept a stiff upper lip when drafted, saying "Personally, I think this conscription bill is a great thing for the young men of today." He also showed his sense of humor, reportedly saying, "At last I'm on a winning team."[22] According to teammate Bobby Bragan, "Hugh Mulcahy was a hero in the minds of all ballplayers at that time."[23] Later on, baseball writer Arthur Mann penned a song for a sportswriters' banquet that paid homage to Mulcahy and others who went: "Bless 'em all, bless 'em all, let their names echo out in the hall; start with Mulcahy, the first to go in, shout 'Captain Greenberg' and set up a din. ..."[24]

Mulcahy's induction was initially for just one year, until he reached 28, and so he stood to miss only one baseball season. After ten months in the service, he was discharged on December 5, 1941, along with all other conscriptees who were 28 or older. But two days later Pearl Harbor changed all that for Mulcahy and thousands of other soldiers, and he was quickly back in the Army. By the time Mulcahy was finally discharged, in August 1945, he was within a month of his 32nd birthday and had missed almost five full seasons of what should have been his prime baseball years.

During the 1942 season, teams hosted war relief games and on May 17 Mulcahy, on furlough from Camp Edwards in Massachusetts, pitched batting practice in Shibe Park, threw out the first pitch, and was presented with $250 worth of war bonds as well as a silver platter from the American Legion. Four days later he pitched against Bob Feller in an Army-Navy exhibition game before a Red Sox-Athletics game, beating Feller's team 5-0 in a five-inning game.[25]

It was not until Mulcahy was transferred to 2nd Army Headquarters in Memphis, Tennessee, in June 1943, that he had any real opportunity to play baseball. Pitching for the 2nd Army team, Hugh shed his civilian "losing pitcher" tag, winning 15 of 16 decisions for a team that went 45-5 and won the unofficial Southern Army baseball championship. In a playoff with Fort Oglethorpe (40-10), he matched up against the Cardinals' 1942 World Series hero Johnny Beazley and

won 1-0 on a three-hitter when his catcher, Ken Silvestri of the New York Yankees, hit one past everyone on the fenceless field and scored standing up.[26]

Interestingly, Mulcahy's old New York Giants bugaboo followed him even to the 2nd Army in Memphis. In spite of defeating Hubbell on those two occasions in 1940, his overall record against the Giants before entering the service was a sad three wins and 16 losses. His one defeat for the 2nd Army was against a service team featuring Giants star hurler Hal Schumacher. His tour of duty in Memphis was nothing but a success on other fronts, however, for it was there that he married the former Ruth Hamilton of Beaver, Pennsylvania, on July 12, 1943.[27] The two had met when Philadelphia sportswriter Stan Baumgartner introduced them at Forbes Field in Pittsburgh before Mulcahy was drafted.[28] The couple's first child, Hugh Jr., was born while Mulcahy was overseas. The couple later had a second son whom they named David.

While in Memphis Mulcahy received a transfer to the 8th Army and was assigned as player-manager of the 8th Army team known as the Chicks (after the minor-league Memphis Chicks). The Army Chicks won the Southern Army championship and Mulcahy beat the minor-league Chicks 5-1 before shipping overseas to New Guinea in August 1944. Six months in various spots on the New Guinea coast left little time for baseball, but plenty of time for intestinal illness. He did manage to participate in a New Guinea Series in the fall of 1944 with other professional ballplayers stationed in the area.[29] The weakened unit transferred to battle-scarred Leyte in the Philippines and had to build living quarters out of the jungle in intense heat. The 8th Army had some fine major-league ballplayers, including Silvestri, Al Flair, and Erv Dusak, and several minor leaguers including Al Kozar, who would go on to play with the Washington Senators after the war. With the help of the locals, they knocked down enough coconut trees to clear space for a ballfield.

Variously known as Mulcahy's Marauders and Mulcahy's Wanderers as well as the 8th Army Chicks, they began playing other US military teams on Leyte and other islands. They won all of their 16 games, with Hugh winning seven. But the heat at Leyte (reportedly as high as 135 degrees) was so intense that the games were played at twilight and pitchers rarely went longer than a few innings.[30] The labor was strenuous as well; Mulcahy injured his back while clearing the field at Leyte before one game and had to watch from the sidelines.[31]

By the summer of 1945 Mulcahy had a Bronze Star, three campaign ribbons, and more than enough points for a discharge. He actually delayed his departure from the Philippines for a week, hoping to pitch for the 8th Army Chicks in the Philippines World Series in Manila's Rizal Stadium. In the bloody battle for Manila earlier that spring, Rizal Stadium had been a prime battle site. After the Japanese were defeated, the Corps of Engineers removed from the stadium more than 800 booby traps and a dead Japanese soldier, shot between third and home. Torrential rain, however, flooded the field and washed out the series.[32]

Mulcahy soon departed the Philippines, arriving in San Francisco on July 27. He was discharged on August 5, and after a visit with his parents and a reunion with his wife (as well as getting to see his 4-month-old son for the first time), on August 11 he rejoined the Phillies, 4½ years older and 35 pounds lighter.[33] Chuck Klein, now a coach, was the only member of the team left from 1940.[34] The owner (Bob Carpenter), the general manager (Herb Pennock), and the manager (Ben Chapman) were all new. The Phillies fans, however, remembered Mulcahy and gave him a rousing welcome. If, given all the new faces, he had any doubt that he was back with the Phillies, the club confirmed that nothing had really changed, losing a doubleheader to the Cubs, 4-3 and 12-6.[35]

Mulcahy first took the mound on August 26, pitching six innings and giving up nine hits and four runs but, alas, losing to the Boston Braves in the first game of a doubleheader, 6-5. His luck had not changed in his years away; two Phillies errors led to three unearned runs and wiped out a 2-1 lead in the sixth.[36] For the rest of the year, he appeared in four more games, starting three and compiling a 1-3 record with a respectable 3.81 earned-run average, leading to high hopes for 1946.

It was not to be, however. Mulcahy struggled with his control (a problem throughout his career) and his endurance in 1946, appearing in 16 games with a 2-4 record and a 4.45 ERA. Manager Chapman seemed to lose confidence in him as the season wore on, and Hugh suffered from a lack of work. In the offseason he decided a change of scenery might help; he requested and received his release from the Phillies and shortly thereafter signed with the Pittsburgh Pirates to be near his wife's hometown.[37] He made the Pirates out of spring training but was released on May 11. His old Phillies club knocked him out of the box in the fifth inning on April 30.[38] His final big-league appearance was an ineffectual two-inning relief job against the Boston Braves on May 8. Reflecting back on his postwar efforts, Hugh thought that perhaps he should have come up with a knuckleball or some other trick pitch.[39]

At the time, however, he was not ready to give up the ghost. He signed with the Oakland Oaks of the Pacific Coast League and finished the year there in undistinguished fashion before returning to Memphis in 1948 to pitch for the Chicks of the Southern Association. With Memphis he performed very well, compiling a 14-7 record and earning an invitation to spring training in 1949 with the Chicago White Sox, the Chicks' parent club. But he did not stick with the big-league club and again threw for the Chicks in 1949, putting together a 14-11 record and a 3.05 earned-run average for a seventh-place team.[40] He started 1950 with the Syracuse Chiefs of the International League, but finished the year with Memphis again. He finally called it quits in 1951 after going 9-15 with the Albany Senators, then of the Eastern League, completing a circle that began 16 years earlier when he wore an Albany uniform on his way up to the majors.[41]

The White Sox, impressed by Mulcahy's even disposition, patience, and knowledge of the game, hired him as a minor-league pitching instructor and scout. During his major-league career, Hugh had often taken young pitchers under his wing and helped them with their mechanics. He stayed in the White Sox system for the rest of his career, retiring more than 20 years later. He ran the White Sox' minor-league training camp for years and in 1955 invented a catching machine that returned the ball automatically to the pitcher. The invention was to combat an age-old spring-training problem: more pitchers needing to throw than catchers available to catch them.[42]

In 1963 Mulcahy co-managed the Middlesboro (Kentucky) Cubsox in the Rookie-classification Appalachian League. The following year he co-managed the Clinton, Iowa, Cubsox in the Class A Midwest League for most of the summer. The team finished second in a ten-team league with a 77-48 record.[43]

Mulcahy made it back to the big leagues for a time in 1970 as the White Sox pitching coach and was named White Sox Man of the Year in 1974 for his work in developing young pitchers in the club's farm system.[44]

In retirement, he lived quietly in the present and without regret, playing golf and enjoying his family. He had two sons (neither of whom played baseball seriously) six grandchildren, and three great-grandchildren. For many years he was a volunteer for the Meals on Wheels program, often delivering meals to people his junior in age.[45]

Mulcahy left a positive mark throughout his life. He was remembered fondly by former teammates like Danny Litwhiler, Pinky May, Frank Hoerst, and Kirby Higbe as not only an ace pitcher but also as "a fine gentleman" and friend.[46]

Rather than lament his fate pitching for the downtrodden Phillies of the late 1930s and his early induction into the military, Mulcahy chose to view his glass as half full rather than half empty. On the latter issue, he noted, "A lot of guys went to the war and didn't come back. I came back and had a long career in baseball. I feel I was fortunate, not cheated." He added with a chuckle, "You never know, six more months with the Phillies and I might have gotten hit with a line drive."[47]

Mulcahy also believed that he was quite fortunate to break in with the Phillies, where he got proper instruction and an opportunity to pitch. He recalled financially strapped Phillies' owner Gerald Nugent as "a real fine man," and manager Jimmie Wilson and coaches Hans Lobert and Dick Spalding as "real pros."[48]

That Mulcahy remembered Nugent fondly is a testament to his genuine good nature. Before the 1937 season he received a contract with a check and a small raise from Nugent. Hugh was so pleased that he sent Nugent a thank-you note. Nugent responded by sending back a letter that read: "Thank you very much for your nice letter, but please return the check. It was made out for the wrong amount."[49]

Mulcahy died on October 19, 2001, in Beaver, Pennsylvania, a little more than a month after his 88th birthday.

Note: An earlier version of this article appeared in the Summer 2001 issue of *Elysian Fields Quarterly* under the title "Hard Luck Mulcahy."

SOURCES

Baseballprospectus.com/article.php?articleid-11024.

Baseballinwartime.blogspot.com/2010/09/hugh-mulcahy.

Blake, Mike, *Baseball Chronicles—An Oral History of Baseball Through the Decades* (Cincinnati: Betterway Books, 1994).

Bloodgood, Clifford, "Hard Luck Guy," *Baseball Magazine*, February 1940.

Bloomfield, Gary, *Duty, Honor, Victory*—America's *Athletes in World War II* (Guilford, Connecticut: The Lyons Press, 2003).

Finoli, David, *For the Good of the Country—World War II Baseball in the Major and Minor Leagues* (Jefferson, North Carolina: McFarland & Co., Inc., 2002).

Gilbert, Bill, *They Also Served—Baseball and the Home Front, 1941-1945* (New York: Crown Publishers, Inc., 1992).

Goldstein, Richard, *Spartan Seasons—How Baseball Survived the Second World War* (New York: Macmillan Publishing Co., 1980).

Higbe, Kirby, with Martin Quigley, *The High Hard One* (New York: Viking Press, Inc., 1967).

Honig, Donald, *The Philadelphia Phillies—An Illustrated History* (New York: Simon & Schuster, 1992).

Jackson, W. Robert, "For Mulcahy, Numbers Lied," *USA Today Baseball Weekly*, May 30, 1995, 38.

Kaufman, James K., and Alan S. Kaufman, *The Worst Baseball Pitchers of All-Time* (New York: Citadel Press, 1995).

Kuklick, Bruce, *To Everything a Season—Shibe Park and Urban Philadelphia 1909-1976* (Princeton: Princeton University Press, 1991).

Lewis, Allen, *The Philadelphia Phillies—A Pictorial History* (Virginia Beach: JCP Corp. of Virginia, 1981).

Lieb, Frederick, and Stan Baumgartner, *The Philadelphia Phillies* (Kent, Ohio: Kent State University Press, 2009, reprint of 1948 version by A.S. Barnes & Co.).

Litwhiler, Danny, with Jim Sargent, *Danny Litwhiler—Living the Baseball Dream* (Philadelphia: Temple University Press, 2006).

Mead, William B., *Even the Browns—The Zany, True Story of Baseball in the Early Forties* (Chicago: Contemporary Books, Inc., 1978).

Hugh Mulcahy clippings file, National Baseball Library, Cooperstown, New York.

Hugh Mulcahy clippings file, Temple University Palen Library Urban Archives, Philadelphia.

Hugh Mulcahy correspondence with author (on file with author).

Roberts, Robin, and C. Paul Rogers, III, *The Whiz Kids and the 1950 Pennant* (Philadelphia: Temple University Press, 1996).

Rogers, C. Paul III, "Hard Luck Mulcahy," *Elysian Fields Quarterly*, Summer, 2001).

Sargent, Jim, "Mulcahy Was First Major Leaguer Drafted Into Army," *Sports Collectors Digest*, November 17, 2000.

Smith, Red, *Red Smith on Baseball* (Chicago: Ivan R. Dee, 2000).

Stang, Mark, *Phillies Photos — 100 Years of Philadelphia Phillies Images* (Wilmington, Ohio: Orange Frazer Press, Inc., 2008).

Szalotiai, James, *Teenager on First, Geezer at Bat, 4-F on Deck* (Jefferson, North Carolina: McFarland & Co., Inc., 2009).

Van Blair, Rick, *Dugout to Foxhole — Interviews with Baseball Players Whose Careers Were Affected by World War II* (Jefferson, North Carolina: McFarland & Co., Inc., 1994).

Westcott, Rich, and Frank Bilovsky, *The New Phillies Encyclopedia* (Philadelphia: Temple University Press, 1993).

Westcott, Rich, *Philadelphia's Old Ballparks* (Philadelphia: Temple University Press, 1996).

Westcott, Rich, *Tales From the Phillies Dugout* (Sports Publishing, LLC, 2003).

NOTES

1 Red Smith, *Red Smith on Baseball*, 36; Red Smith, "Mulcahy Loses His Last Decision in the Majors," *Philadelphia Inquirer*, May 14, 1947, 24.

2 Hugh Mulcahy correspondence with the author, March 7, 2000; John Perutto, "Memorial Day Remembrance — Hugh Mulcahy, baseballprospectus.com/article.php?articleid=11024..

3 W. Robert Jackson, "For Mulcahy, Numbers Lied, *USA Today Baseball Weekly*, May 30, 1995; Stan Baumgartner, "'Ugly Duckling' Becomes Cock of Walk," *The Sporting News*, June 29, 1939.

4 Stan Baumgartner, "Phillies Secure Mulcahy, Albany Right-hander, for Eddie Boland and Money," *The Sporting News*, July 10, 1935.

5 Stan Baumgartner, "'Ugly Duckling' Becomes Cock of Walk," *The Sporting News*, June 29, 1939; W. Robert Jackson, "For Mulcahy, Numbers Lied," *USA Today Baseball Weekly*, May 30, 1995; Jim Sargent, "Mulcahy Was First Major Leaguer Drafted Into Army, *Sports Collectors Digest*, November 17, 2000, 110; Hugh Mulcahy correspondence with the author, March 7, 2000.

6 Hugh Mulcahy correspondence with the author, March 25, 2000.

7 Official records show 22⅔ innings, but appear to have mistakenly assigned him nine innings in the September 20 game; he did pitch in the bottom of the ninth inning, but allowed a double, a walk, and a game-winning single before recording an out.

8 "Mulcahy of Phils Real 'Iron Man,'" *Philadelphia Evening Bulletin*, December 22, 1937; Mulcahy also remembered being called "work-horse" as a result of all the innings he pitched. Hugh Mulcahy correspondence with author, March 7, 2000.

9 Red Smith, 37.

10 David Finoli, *For the Good of God and Country*, 51.

11 Franklin W. Yeutter, "Mulcahy Praised by McKechnie After Reds and Phils Split, *The Sporting News*, September 17, 1938.

12 Frank Yeutter, "Hartnett Admires Phils' Hustling," *The Sporting News*, May 4, 1939.

13 Frank Yeutter, "Cubs Win When He Sprawls in 13th," *Philadelphia Inquirer*, May 24, 1940.

14 Unidentified clipping dated May 22, 1940, from the Hugh Mulcahy clipping file, National Baseball Library.

15 Frank Yeutter, "Mulcahy Beaten by 15 Singles," *The Sporting News*, June 28, 1940.

16 Ted Meier, "Mulcahy May Be Phillies' First 20-Game Winner in 24 Years," *Philadelphia Evening Bulletin*, July 30, 1940.

17 W. Robert Jackson, "For Mulcahy, Numbers Lied," *USA Today Baseball Weekly*, May 30, 1995; Jim McLoughlin, "Mulcahy Hits Road Back to Fitness, *The Sporting News*, January 17, 1946.

18 "Phil Hurler Tells How to Lose Them, *Philadelphia Evening Bulletin*, April 28, 1938.

19 Stan Baumgartner, "'One-Punch' Mulcahy Fined $25 by Frick," *Philadelphia Inquirer* July 15, 1939. Mulcahy was quoted in *The Sporting News* as saying, "I got pretty mad when he rapped me. I just started punching." Frank Yeutter, "Mulcahy Knocks Down Passeau But Chicago Outpoints Phillies," *The Sporting News*, July 14, 1939; Hugh Mulcahy correspondence with the author, April 29, 2001. ("We always remained good friends.")

20 "Mulcahy or Higbe Will Be Traded," unidentified clipping dated November 7, 1940, from Hugh Mulcahy clippings file, Temple University Paley Library Archives. According to news reports, the Dodgers had been after Mulcahy all season. "Brooklyn Seeking Mulcahy of Phils," unidentified clipping dated May 13, 1940, from Hugh Mulcahy clippings file, Temple University Paley Library Archives

21 William B. Mead, *Even the Browns*, 28; "Hugh Hopes to Play for Uncle Sam," unidentified clipping dated March 9, 1941 in Hugh Mulcahy clippings file, Temple University Paley Library Archives.

22 *Philadephia Inquirer*, October 31, 1948; James D. Szalontai, *Teenager on First, Geezer at Bat, 4-F on Deck*, 112.

23 Gary Bedingfield, "Hugh Mulcahy: Among the First to Go!" baseballinwartime.com/player_biographies/mulcahy_hugh.htm

24 Red Smith, 37.

25 Gary Bedingfield, "Hugh Mulcahy: Among the First to go!"baseballinwartime.com/player_biographies/mulcahy_hugh.htm; Richard Goldstein, *Spartan Seasons*, 67; Ed Pollock, "Playing the Game," *Philadelphia Evening Bulletin*, May 19, 1942.

26 "Mulcahy's Team Wins Army Game," unidentified clipping dated September 15, 1943 in Hugh Mulcahy clippings file, Temple University Paley Library Archives.

27 "Hugh Mulcahy Now a Bridegroom," unidentified clipping dated July 13, 1943, in Hugh Mulcahy clippings file, Temple University Paley Library Archives.

28 Dick Conners, "Hugh Heading Back to Game," *The Sporting News*, July 12, 1945.

29 Gary Bloomfield, *Duty, Honor, Victory—America's Athletes in World War II*, 193.

30 "Mulcahy Out of Army; Phils Awaiting Visit," unidentified clipping dated August 6, 1945, from Hugh Mulcahy clippings file, Temple University Paley Library Archives. One might question the actual temperature, since the average high temperature in Leyte in the summer is about 90 degrees.

31 "Mulcahy Hurt in Leyte Baseball," unidentified clipping dated May 5, 1945, from Hugh Mulcahy clippings file, Temple University Paley Library Archives.

32 Gary Bedingfield, "Hugh Mulcahy: Among the First to Go! baseballinwartime.com/player_biographies/mulcahy_hugh.htm; Richard Berholz, "Mulcahy Decorated on Way Back," unidentified clipping dated July 2, 1945, from Hugh Mulcahy clippings file, Temple University Paley Library Archives.

33 Hugh Mulcahy correspondence with the author, March 7, 2000; Jim McLoughlin, "Mulcahy Hits Road Back to Fitness," *The Sporting News*, January 17, 1946, 3. Other articles had him 15 pounds underweight upon his return from the war. Bill Dooly, "Mulcahy Rejoins Phils 15 Pounds Underweight," *The Sporting News*, August 16, 1945; Dick Conners, "Hugh Heading Back to Game," unidentified clipping dated July 12, 1945, from Hugh Mulcahy clippings file, Temple University Paley Library Archives.

34 Bill Dooly, "Mulcahy on Way Home to Join Phillies Staff; Earns Army Discharge," unidentified clipping dated June 27, 1945, from Hugh Mulcahy clippings file, Temple University Paley Library Archives.

35 Don Donaghey, "Flag-Hungry Cubs Stand By as Mulcahy is Honored Then Beat Phils Twice," unidentified article dated August 13, 1945, from Hugh Mulcahy clippings file, Temple University Paley Library Archives.

36 Don Donaghey, "Phils Play Doubleheader with Giants Tonight, Ending Home Stay," unidentified clipping dated August 25, 1945, from Hugh Mulcahy clippings file, Temple University Paley Library Archives.

37 Frank Yeutter, "Mulcahy Set Free by Phils to Pitch for Rival Team," *Philadelphia Inquirer*, January 30, 1947.

38 "Pittsburgh Pirates Drop Hugh Mulcahy," unidentified clipping dated May 12, 1947, from Hugh Mulcahy clippings file, Temple University Paley Library Archives.

39 Hugh Mulcahy correspondence with the author, March 7, 2000.

40 At one point he won five in a row for the Chicks, including a 4-1 12-inning game and a five-hit shutout. *Phildaephia Inquirer*, August, 14, 1949.

41 Dick Conners, "Hugh Mulcahy Back at Albany After an Absence of 16 Years," *The Sporting News*, March 7, 1951.

42 "Hugh Mulcahy Invents Automatic Catcher; Demonstration Model Being Turned Out," *Philadelphia Inquirer*, January 16, 1955.

43 The Chicago White Sox and Chicago Cubs jointly operated the Middlesboro and Clinton franchises, so each organization named a co-manager.

44 Press Release, Chicago White Sox, November 11, 1974, in Hugh Mulcahy clippings file, National Baseball Library.

45 W. Robert Jackson, "For Mulcahy, Numbers Lied," *USA Today Baseball Weekly*, May 30, 1995.

46 Danny Litwhiler with Jim Sargent, *Danny Litwhiler—Living the Baseball Dream*, 1, 50; Rick Van Blair, *Dugout to Foxhole*, 133; Kirby Higbe with Martin Quigley, *The High Hard One*, 48, 54-55.

47 William B. Mead, 29.

48 Hugh Mulcahy correspondence with the author, March 7, 2000.

49 Mike Blake, *Baseball Chronicles*, 67.

Roy Campanella

By Rick Swaine

ROY CAMPANELLA WAS THE SIXTH acknowledged black player to appear in the major leagues in the 20th century, debuting with the Brooklyn Dodgers a year after Jackie Robinson broke the color barrier. Campanella went on to become the second black player, after Robinson, to win the Most Valuable Player award, and eventually became the second black Hall of Famer, again following in Robinson's footsteps. Campanella, however, holds the distinction of being the first black player to capture the MVP award twice, and at the time of his death in June 1993 he was the only black player to own three MVP trophies.

Campanella spent his entire big-league career with the Dodgers, taking over as their regular catcher during the 1948 campaign and serving in that capacity through 1957, the franchise's last season in Brooklyn. In those years the Dodgers won five National League pennants and a world championship. Prejudice and tragedy limited his major-league career to a mere ten seasons, the color of his skin delaying his debut until he was 26 years old, and an automobile accident prematurely ending his playing days at the age of 35.

In fact, Campanella made the fewest major-league plate appearances of any Hall of Fame position player. Yet statistical guru Bill James rated him the third best catcher of all time behind top-ranked Yogi Berra and runner-up Johnny Bench, and ahead of such stalwarts as Mickey Cochrane, Carlton Fisk, Bill Dickey, and Gabby Hartnett.

Baseball-Reference.com lists Campanella's height at 5-feet-9 and his playing weight at 190 pounds, which may have been close to the truth when he started out. The 1954 *Baseball Almanac* and the 1955 *Who's Who in Baseball* list him at 205 pounds, which was still probably a generously low estimate considering that Campy himself pegged his weight at 215 to 220 pounds shortly before he signed with the Dodgers. Roger Kahn, author of *The Boys of Summer*, likened Campanella to a little sumo wrestler. Despite his roly-poly appearance, the squatty catcher was extremely muscular with massive arms and a bulky torso. At the plate he was a dead pull hitter with a distinct uppercut. He was graceful behind the dish, supplementing surprising agility with a cannon-like arm. He was considered an astute handler of pitchers, both white and black—knowing when to provide encouragement and when to provide a good kick in the butt.

Roy was also tough as nails. As a Negro Leaguer, he purportedly caught four games in one day—an early doubleheader in Cincinnati and a twi-nighter in Middletown, Ohio. And he claimed to have caught three doubleheaders in one day in winter ball. He endured repeated injuries to his fingers, hands, and legs—occupational hazards of working behind the bat—but in his last appearance he establish a since-broken major-league record for durability by catching at least 100 games in nine straight seasons, a remarkable achievement prior to the new generation of catcher's mitts that allow receivers to protect their throwing hand by catching one-handed.

The popular catcher was often described as gentle, unassuming, jovial, and full of life. He was a cheerleader, almost childlike in his enthusiasm. Although Campy and Jackie Robinson were teammates for nine years when there were only a handful of other black major leaguers, they were not particularly close. In fact, there were even a few well-publicized feuds over the years. Robinson was sometimes frustrated with Campanella's reluctance to help carry the banner for their race. "There's a little Uncle Tom in Roy," he once remarked.[1]

Despite their differences, however, Campy deeply respected Jackie and fully appreciated the sacrifices he'd made. "Jackie made things easy for us," he said. "[Because of him] I'm just another guy playing baseball."[2]

Roy Campanella was born on November 19, 1921, in Philadelphia. He had no known middle name. At the time of Roy's birth his family lived in the Germantown section of the city, but they moved to an integrated section in the northern part of the city known as Nicetown when Roy was 7 years old. He was the product of an interracial marriage, an African-American mother and a father of Sicilian descent—something of a novelty in those days. He attended Gillespie Junior High and Simon Gratz High School, although he left high school before graduating. Growing up, the light-complexioned youngster was tauntingly called "half-breed" by kids of both races, which helped him develop into a pretty good scrapper. In fact, he briefly fought as a Golden Gloves boxer. Roy, the baby of the family, had three older siblings. His brother, Lawrence, about ten years older, wasn't around very much when Roy was growing up. His sisters, Gladys and Doris, were both excellent female athletes.

John Campanella, Roy's father, made his living selling vegetables and fish out of a truck and later operated a grocery store while Roy's mother, Ida, ran the household. Growing up in the middle of the Depression, Roy had to work as a youngster. He helped his father, sold newspapers, shined shoes, and had a milk route as a teenager.

Through high school Roy attended integrated schools and played for integrated football, basketball, and baseball teams. Though blacks were in the minority, he was invariably chosen as the captain, whatever the sport. He participated in other sports, but baseball was his passion. He watched many a game at nearby Shibe Park from the top of an adjacent building. By the time he entered high school, he'd abandoned his early aspirations to be an architect and was determined to be a professional ballplayer.

Gradually word of his prowess on the diamond spread. While in high school, he was reportedly offered an opportunity to work out with the Phillies, but the club rescinded the invitation when they discovered he was black.

At the tender age of 15 in 1937, Campanella began his professional baseball career with a top-notch semipro team, the Bacharach Giants. Mama Campanella didn't want her baby to play pro ball with grown men, but when they promised to pay him more for a weekend of catching than his father made in a week, a compromise was reached. Despite his youth, Campanella performed so impressively for the Bacharach Giants that the Baltimore Elite Giants of the Negro National League soon signed him to spell veteran receiver and manager Biz Mackey on weekends. Roy was an indifferent student to begin with, but after he spent his summer vacation barnstorming with the Elite Giants, schoolwork could no longer hold his attention. As soon as he turned 16, Roy quit school to play baseball full time. By 1939 the precocious 17-year-old youngster had taken over the regular catching chores and helped lead the Giants to playoff victories over the Newark Eagles and Homestead Grays. Soon he was challenging the legendary Josh Gibson's status as the best catcher in Negro baseball. While still a teenager, he won MVP honors as the star of the 1941 Negro League East-West All-Star Game.

Campanella had married a Nicetown girl, Bernice Ray, in 1939 and they had two girls. With three dependents his draft status was 3-A when World War II broke out, so he was never called for active duty, although he was required to work in war-related industry for a time.

During the 1942 Negro League season, Campanella jumped to the Monterrey Sultans of the Mexican League after a contract dispute with the Elite Giants.

He remained in Mexico for the 1943 season before returning to Baltimore for the 1944 and 1945 campaigns.

In October 1945 Campanella caught for a black all-star team organized by Effa Manley against a squad of major leaguers managed by Charlie Dressen in a five-game exhibition series at Ebbets Field. Dressen, a Dodgers coach at the time, approached Campanella to arrange a meeting with Dodgers general manager and part-owner Branch Rickey later that month. Campanella spent four hours listening to Rickey, whom he later described as "the talkingest man I ever did see," and politely declined when Rickey asked if he was interested in playing in the Brooklyn organization.[3] Campy thought he was being recruited for the Brooklyn Brown Dodgers, a new Negro League outfit that Rickey was supposedly starting. A few days later, however, he ran into Jackie Robinson in a Harlem hotel. After Robinson confidentially told him he'd already signed with the Dodgers, Campy realized that Rickey had been talking about a career in Organized Baseball for him. Afraid that he'd blown his shot at the big leagues, he fired off a telegram to Rickey indicating his interest in playing for the Dodgers just before he left on a barnstorming tour through South America.

The 1946 spring-training season was already under way by the time Campanella returned from South America and reported to the Dodgers office in Brooklyn. The Dodgers didn't quite know what to do with him or Don Newcombe, another Negro League star they'd signed. Robinson and former Homestead Grays hurler Johnny Wright were already slated for Montreal, and most of the organization's other minor-league franchises were located in the South or the Midwest. They tried to send Campanella and Newcombe to Danville of the Class B Illinois-Indiana-Iowa (Three I) League, but the circuit wouldn't accept black players. The Dodgers then checked with their Nashua, New Hampshire, farm club in the New England League, a lesser regarded Class B circuit, where young general manager Buzzy Bavasi welcomed the opportunity to add two such talented black players to their roster.

Like most of the first generation of black players to cross the color line, Campanella took a steep pay cut to enter Organized Baseball and was forced to start at a level far below his ability. A top star in the Negro leagues, he found himself competing against a bunch of inexperienced kids, most of whom would never rise above Class A ball. Furthermore, he would be making only $185 a month for six months at Nashua rather than the $600 a month he'd been earning with the Baltimore Elite Giants.

Campanella hit .290 and drove in 96 runs in 1946 to win the New England League MVP award. Early in the season, Nashua manager Walter Alston, who doubled as the club's first baseman, asked Campy to take over the team for him if he ever got tossed out of a game. His reasoning was that Roy was older than most of the players and they respected and liked him. Sure enough, in a June contest Alston was ejected in the sixth inning and Campy became the first black man to manage in Organized Baseball. Moreover, his strategic move resulted in a comeback victory when he called on the hard-hitting Newcombe to pinch-hit and was rewarded with a clutch home run.

Roy's experience in Nashua also changed his parents' life. Fences around the New England League were virtually unreachable, and a local poultry farmer offered 100 baby chicks for every Nashua home run. At the end of the season, Campy collected 1,400 chicks as reward for his 14 homers (a team-leading 13 in the regular season and one in the playoffs). He had them shipped to his father, who promptly began a farming business on the outskirts of Philadelphia.

Campanella went to spring training with the Dodgers in Havana before the 1947 season. He was listed on the Montreal roster, along with Robinson, Newcombe, and Roy Partlow, a left-handed pitcher. Jackie, of course, was promoted to the Dodgers, Newcombe was sent back to Nashua, and Partlow was released, leaving Campanella the only black player in the International League. That season, while Robinson was burning up the basepaths as the first black player in the majors in the 20th century, Campanella was winning the International League MVP award. Veteran catcher Paul Richards, then managing Buffalo in the International League, called him "the best catcher in the business—major or minor leagues."[4] With his extensive Negro League experience and a Triple-A

MVP award under his belt, the 26-year-old receiver was ready for major-league duty.

Unfortunately, the Brooklyn Dodgers weren't yet ready for him. Brooklyn's regular catcher was Bruce Edwards, who in 1947 posted an excellent .295 batting mark, drove in 80 runs, and finished fourth in National League MVP balloting., the highest ranking of any Dodger. In addition, Edwards was a fine defensive backstop and was almost two years younger than Campy.

According to popular legend, Rickey wanted Campanella to break the racial barrier in the American Association, the Midwestern Triple-A circuit, before he became established with the Dodgers. Therefore he attempted to conceal Roy's skills from the press by carrying him on the preseason roster as an outfield candidate—a position for which Campanella was clearly ill-suited. A less Machiavellian, but plausible, explanation might be that Rickey didn't want to cause dissension or put too much pressure on Campanella by replacing the popular Edwards. Whatever the reason, the Dodgers brought Campanella to camp as an outfielder and even tried him out at third base.

But Edwards had injured his arm in the offseason, and it failed to come around in the spring of 1948. Manager Leo Durocher, back in command of the Dodgers after a year's suspension, fully appreciated Campanella's talents and wanted to insert him in Edwards' place behind the plate. But Rickey did not want to put the rookie catcher's skills on display. The issue apparently became a source of friction between Durocher and Rickey.

Though Campanella broke camp with the Dodgers, the plan was to send him down to their St. Paul American Association farm club when rosters had to be trimmed to 25 players on May 15. He made his big-league debut against the New York Giants at the Polo Grounds on Opening Day. Gil Hodges, who hadn't made the move to first base yet, started behind the plate in place of Edwards, but went out for a pinch-hitter in the top of the seventh. In the bottom half of the inning, Campanella took over behind the plate with the Dodgers down 6-5. With ace reliever Hugh Casey on the mound, the Giants went scoreless for the final three innings while the Dodgers scored two runs to win the

game. Campanella got to the plate in the top of the eighth inning and was promptly drilled by Giants reliever Ken Trinkle—the type of welcome that many more black hitters would receive in the early days of baseball's integration era.

Campanella made his second big-league appearance three days later, replacing Hodges to finish up a 10-2 Phillies blowout. Then on April 27, after a pair of losses, Durocher defied Rickey and started Campy at catcher in Boston. He went hitless but acquitted himself well behind the plate. Though Brooklyn lost, wildman Rex Barney held the Braves to three runs with Campanella calling the pitches. Rickey was reportedly incensed and ordered Durocher not to put Campanella behind the plate again. This time Leo complied. Campy warmed the bench until he was farmed out to St. Paul on May 15.

The American Association's first black player broke the color barrier with a disastrous performance, going hitless and fanning twice in four at-bats, and making an error on a pickoff attempt. But he was soon terrorizing the opposition. In 35 games, Campy batted .325, slammed 13 homers, and drove in 39 runs, forcing the struggling Dodgers to recall him.

When Campanella joined the Dodgers' lineup on July 2, 1948, the defending National League champions had lost five straight and were languishing in seventh place with a 27-34 record. From that point on they won 57 while losing 36, a .613 pace—better than the .591 overall winning percentage posted by the pennant-winning Braves. Even more remarkable was the fact that the Dodgers won 50 of the 73 games that Campanella started after his recall, an incredible .685 mark. His installation behind the plate was the last in a series of moves orchestrated by Durocher to turn the club around. Three days earlier Gil Hodges, who had acquitted himself well behind the plate filling in for the injured Edwards, was shifted to first base, allowing Jackie Robinson to move over to his natural second-base position. Unfortunately for Durocher, he didn't stay around long enough to enjoy the results, as he left the Dodgers to take over the reins of the New York Giants a week after Campanella's recall.

For his rookie year, Campanella batted .258 with 9 homers in 83 games and led National League catchers in percentage of runners caught stealing. He even garnered eight points in the MVP voting despite playing only half the season.

In 1949 Campanella hit .287 with 22 home runs and 82 runs batted in, cementing his hold on the Dodgers' first-string catching job. During the campaign, pitcher Don Newcombe was called up from the minors, combining with Campanella to form the major leagues' first black battery. The pair had developed an excellent rapport at Nashua three years earlier and, under Roy's expert handling, the volatile young flamethrower quickly became the ace of the staff. Both Campanella and Newcombe made the 1949 National League All-Star squad, joining Robinson and Cleveland's Larry Doby in becoming baseball's first black All-Stars. Campanella replaced starting catcher Andy Seminick in the fourth inning and went the rest of the way, beginning a streak in which he would catch every All-Star inning for the National League until Smoky Burgess relieved him in the eighth inning of the 1954 contest. Campanella also displayed his toughness that season when, after a beaning by Bill Werle of the Pirates, he rejected the doctor's recommendation to take a few days off and rejoined the lineup the next day.

Campanella upped his homer total to 31 in 1950 and batted .281, firmly establishing himself as the best catcher in the National League, if not all of major-league baseball. He caught all 14 innings in that summer's All-Star Game. In September he suffered a compound fracture from a foul tip off his right thumb and missed starting 11 consecutive games behind the plate — the Dodgers dropping seven of them. Campy's absence probably cost Brooklyn the pennant as they ended up losing to the Phillies on the last day of the season to finish two games off the pace.

In spring training before the 1951 season, Campy took another foul tip on the right thumb that chipped the bone and forced him to play in pain all year. Later, a beaning by Turk Lown of the Cubs sent him to the hospital for five days with a concussion and he experienced dizziness for weeks thereafter. Nevertheless, he batted a career-high .325 with 33 homers and 108 runs batted in, and finished third in the league in doubles, slugging, and OPS. On the last day of the regular season,

which ended in a tie between the Dodgers and the New York Giants, Campanella aggravated a leg injury he had received in a collision at home plate a few days earlier. He gamely struggled through the first game of the three-game playoff series, but realized he was hurting the team and sat out the last two contests. It's widely believed that if Campanella had been behind the plate for the third game, he would have been able to nurse his pal Newcombe through the ninth inning — and Bobby Thomson would never have come to the plate to hit his historic pennant-winning home run. In MVP voting Campanella beat out Stan Musial of the Cardinals for the National League award. In the American League Yogi Berra of the Yankees captured his first MVP award. It was the first year in history that catchers won the annual award in both leagues.

Campanella followed his brilliant 1951 campaign with a disappointing performance in 1952. After he had endured numerous minor injuries early in the season, a foul tip chipped a bone in his left elbow in July. He played with the injury for ten days before his arm had to be placed in a cast for nearly two weeks. His season average fell to .269 and he hit only 22 home runs. In the Dodgers' seven-game World Series loss to the Yankees, he managed only six singles.

In 1953 Campanella reported to spring training in great shape and stayed remarkably healthy through the season. And what a great season it was. He batted .312 and his 41 home runs and league-leading 142 RBIs established all-time highs for major-league catchers that stood until 1970. Campanella's home-run total was the third highest in the league and he ranked third in slugging and fourth in OPS as he led the Dodgers to their second straight National League pennant. But in the first game of the World Series, Allie Reynolds of the Yankees hit him on the hand with a pitch and he was unable to properly grip the bat through the club's second straight seven-game Series defeat. His second National League MVP award, however, was a foregone conclusion.

In spring training before the 1954 campaign, Campanella injured his left wrist and hand when he slid awkwardly trying to break up a double play. The bone on the heel of his hand was fractured and pieces that chipped off were impinging on the nerve. Surgery was recommended, but Campanella tried to play with the painful condition. He finally agreed to an operation in early May. Initial estimates put the recovery time at eight to ten weeks, but Campy returned to action in less than a month. Numbness in the hand bothered him all year, however, resulting in a dismal .207 batting average with 19 homers. Campanella's value to the Dodgers, even at less than full strength, was demonstrated by the fact that the club posted a .623 winning percentage for the 106 games he started, compared with .542 without him. At season's end, the Dodgers trailed the Giants by five games. Insult was added to injury when their crosstown rivals defeated the Cleveland Indians to capture the world-championship banner that had proved so elusive to the Dodgers. After the season Campanella submitted to further surgery on the hand to remove scar tissue and repair nerve damage.

It was feared that Campanella's hand problems could mean the end of his career, or at least drastically curb his productivity. But the 33-year-old veteran made a miraculous comeback in 1955. At midseason he was leading the league in hitting when he was hit on the left kneecap by a foul tip that broke a bone spur loose from his patella. The knee was in a cast for more than two weeks and he missed his first All-Star Game since 1949, although he was picked for the team. Nevertheless, Campy was still challenging for the batting title late in the season, when the rigors of catching every day caused his hands to start bothering him again and his hitting fell off. He still finished with a .318 batting average, slammed 32 home runs, and knocked in 107 runs, despite sitting out more than 30 games. He again drove the Dodgers to the National League pennant, and led them to victory over the Yankees in the World Series. In National League MVP balloting he prevailed for a third time. In the American League, Yogi Berra also captured his third MVP trophy. Four years after Campy and Yogi became the first catchers to win MVP honors in the same season, they became the second and last duo to accomplish the feat through the 2013 season.

But thousands of games behind the bat had taken a toll, and Campanella's 1956 season was ruined by more hand problems. His twice-operated-on glove hand, which had begun tormenting him again late the previous year, still ached. Then he broke his thumb when he slammed his right hand against the hitter's bat while attempting a pickoff throw to first. That injury kept him out 15 days and bothered him all year. He ended the campaign with a .219 batting average, but still managed 20 homers as the Dodgers captured their last pennant in Brooklyn. In the World Series, another seven-game loss to the Yankees, he hit only .182 with no homers and seven strikeouts.

Campanella decided to undergo another operation after the 1956 campaign to relieve the pain in his left hand, but the Dodgers insisted that he go on their offseason exhibition tour of Japan first, which drastically cut into his recovery period. With his hands still troubling him in 1957, he missed more than 50 games and hit .246 while belting just 13 home runs, and failed to make the All-Star squad for the first time since his rookie year. Brooklyn fell to third place in the National League amid persistent rumors of a move to the West Coast. Shortly after the Dodgers' last game, it was officially announced that the franchise would relocate to Los Angeles for the 1958 season.

Campy loved playing in Brooklyn and like most of the Dodger veterans hated the prospect of moving. But his hands were feeling better than they had in years and he was starting to warm up to the idea of taking aim at the 295-foot left-field fence of the Los Angeles Coliseum, an oval-shaped football stadium that would serve as the club's makeshift home field.

But in January 1958, just before he was due to report for spring training, Campanella was permanently disabled in a traffic accident. He had successfully invested in a liquor store in central Harlem, called Roy Campanella Choice Wines and Liquors, earlier in his career and worked there in the offseason. He normally left for home in the early afternoon, but on that fateful day he'd stayed in town to plug a YMCA fund-raising drive on a local television show. The appearance was canceled, but he stayed to help close up the liquor store before leaving for his home in Glen Cove, on the North Shore of Long Island. The Chevy station wagon Campy normally drove was in the shop for repairs, and he was driving a much lighter rental car when he lost control of the vehicle on an icy street. He hit a telephone pole and the car flipped over, pinning him under the steering wheel. Roy's neck was broken and his spinal cord was severely damaged, paralyzing him from the chest down.

Roy Campanella, once the best catcher in the National League, if not all of major-league baseball, would spend the rest of his life in a wheelchair.

The Dodgers continued to pay Campanella his salary while he was hospitalized for surgery and rehabilitation for almost a year after the accident. Though he never got a chance to play for the Dodgers in Los Angeles, a crowd of 93,103 fans, the largest in baseball history, jammed the Los Angeles Coliseum on May 7, 1959, for a benefit exhibition game between the Yankees and Dodgers—a tribute to the former Brooklyn great.

Campanella's personal life began to unravel in the wake of his accident. His teenage marriage to Bernice Ray had quickly ended in divorce. With Roy away so much of the time, traveling the Negro League circuit or playing winter ball in the Caribbean, Bernice continued to live with her parents and the couple had gradually drifted apart. In 1945 Roy married Ruthe Willis, a fine athlete herself. They had two sons and a daughter together and Ruthe's son from a previous marriage also lived with them.

But Ruthe was unable to adjust to Roy's physical disability. In 1960 he sued for a legal separation, a messy affair that kept the city's tabloid press busy. In 1963 Ruthe suffered a fatal heart attack at the age of 40 before a divorce was finalized. On May 5, 1964, Roy married Roxie Doles, who remained at his side for the remainder of his life.

After enduring years of therapy, Campanella regained some use of his arms. He eventually was able to feed himself, shake hands, and even sign autographs with the aid of a device strapped to his arm, though he remained dependent on his wheelchair for mobility. Through it all he managed to maintain the positive, upbeat attitude that was his trademark and became a universal symbol of courage. In 1969, the same year he was inducted into the Hall of Fame, he received the Bronze Medallion from the City of New York, the highest honor the city confers upon civilians, awarded

for exceptional citizenship and outstanding achievement. Three years later the Dodgers retired his uniform number 39 along with Robinson's number 42 and Sandy Koufax's 32.

Though Campanella stayed in New York, continuing to operate his liquor store and hosting a radio sports program called "Campy's Corner," he remained a part of the Dodgers family. He worked in public relations, helped with scouting, and served as a special instructor and adviser at the club's Vero Beach spring-training facility. In 1978 he moved to Los Angeles and took a job as assistant to the Dodgers' director of community relations, Don Newcombe, his former teammate and longtime friend.

On June 26, 1993, Campanella succumbed to a heart attack in Woodland Hills, California. He lived to be 71, far exceeding the normal life expectancy for someone in his condition. In 2006 he was honored with a US postage stamp bearing his image, and later that year the Dodgers announced the creation of the Roy Campanella Award, to be given annually to the Dodger who best exemplifies Campanella's spirit and leadership.

Roy Campanella's lifetime batting average for 10 major-league seasons was .276 and he hit 242 home runs while driving in 856 runs in 1,215 games. His 1953 totals of 41 homers and 142 RBIs stood as single-season highs for a catcher until Johnny Bench hit 45 homers and drove in 148 runs in 1970. Bench, however, played a 162-game schedule rather than the 154 contests played in 1953, and had 86 more at-bats than Campanella.

Campanella shone just as brightly on defense. Sportswriters often referred to him as "The Cat" because of his feline-like quickness blocking stray pitches or pouncing on bunts in front of home plate. He led National League catchers five times in percentage of runners caught stealing, and his career rate of 57 percent is the best all-time among catchers who appeared in more than 100 games.

But the most revealing statistic is the three Most Valuable Player awards Campanella earned in his all-too-brief career. When he was honored for the third time, in 1955, Stan Musial was the only other National Leaguer to have accomplished the feat, while Joe DiMaggio, Jimmie Foxx, and Yogi Berra were the only

American Leaguers to have done so. Since then, only the names of Mickey Mantle, Mike Schmidt, Barry Bonds, Alex Rodriguez, and Albert Pujols have been added to the exclusive list.

Nonetheless, Campanella's career is sprinkled with what-ifs. It's fair to say that, even with the premature end to his career, Campy's third place ranking on Bill James's catchers list might have been higher if he hadn't been denied the opportunity to play in the major leagues at an earlier age. It's also probably realistic to assume that he wouldn't have had to wait six years after gaining eligibility to be elected to the Hall of Fame.

If circumstances had been right, Campanella could have been the first black player in the big leagues. Back in 1943, he had been invited to Forbes Field to work out for the Pittsburgh Pirates, but team president William Benswanger succumbed to peer pressure and canceled the tryout.

And if not for the accident, Campanella might well have become the major league's first black manager. Before joining the Dodgers he managed the Caracas club in the Venezuelan Winter League for a few seasons. In 1946 the 25-year-old skipper's charges included Newcombe, Sam Jethroe, Harry Simpson, and Luis Aparicio, Sr., father of the Hall of Fame shortstop. Before his accident the Dodgers had already approached Campanella about a future coaching or managing in the minor leagues after his career ended.

In his autobiography *It's Good to Be Alive*, Campanella reminisced about the happiest days of his life in Brooklyn: "That's where I wanted to finish my playing career. I got my wish all right, but in a much different way."

This article was adapted from the author's book *The Black Stars Who Made Baseball Whole: The Jackie Robinson Generation in the Major Leagues* (Jefferson, North Carolina: McFarland, 2004).

SOURCES

Campanella, Roy, *It's Good to Be Alive* (New York: Dell, 1959).

Campanella, Roy II, "Roy Campanella" in *Cult Baseball Players*, Danny Peary, ed. (New York: Simon and Schuster, 1990), 251-9.

Golenbock, Peter, *Bums: An Oral History of the Brooklyn Dodgers* (New York: Putnam's, 1984).

James, Bill, *The New Bill James Historical Baseball Abstract* (New York: Simon and Schuster, 2001).

Kahn, Roger, *The Boys of Summer* (New York: Harper and Row, 1971).

Moffi, Larry, and Jonathan Kronstadt, *Crossing the Line: Black Major Leaguers, 1947-1959* (Jefferson, North Carolina: McFarland, 1994).

Peterson, Robert W., *Only the Ball Was White* (Englewood Cliffs, New Jersey: Carol Publishing, 1970).

Tygiel, Jules, *Baseball's Great Experiment: Jackie Robinson and His Legacy* (New York: Oxford University Press, 1997).

The Sporting News, March 24, 1948, 22.

Clark, Dick, and Larry Lester, *The Negro Leagues Book* (SABR, 1994, statistical section)

NOTES

1   Roger Kahn, *The Boys of Summer*, 327.

2   Larry Moffi and Jonathan Kronstadt, *Crossing the Line*, 27.

3   Roy Campanella, *It's Good to Be Alive*, 109.

4   Jules Tygiel, *Baseball's Great Experiment*, 223.

Johnny Kucks

By Alan Cohen

EVERYONE HAS HIS BASEBALL DREAM when growing up, but few get the opportunity to realize that one special moment.

On October 12, 1956, the New York Yankees and the Brooklyn Dodgers played the seventh game of the World Series. The Yankees had lost the first two games but had come back to win the next three before losing Game Six to the Dodgers and Clem Labine. Manager Casey Stengel, after conferring with Yogi Berra, elected to go with Johnny Kucks in Game Seven. The reasoning was that Kucks was superior to the other Yankees pitchers (Whitey Ford and Tom Sturdivant were also candidates for the start) in one specific area: He could, as Stengel liked to say, throw ground balls.[1] In Yankee tradition, Frank Crosetti, the team's third-base coach, placed a baseball into one of Kucks' shoes by his locker. Years later, Kucks said, "My first inclination was to put it in somebody else's shoe."[2] It turned out to be the game of Johnny's life. He shut out the Dodgers, 9-0, and the Yankees were world champions for the seventh time in ten years.[3]

John Charles Kucks, Jr. (pronounced "Cooks") grew up in Jersey City, right across the Hudson River from New York. He was born in nearby Hoboken on July 27, 1932, the youngest of seven children born to John and Millie Kucks. His father, a butcher by trade, was the foreman of the Cudahy Meat Packing Plant in Hoboken. Kucks pitched at William L. Dickinson High in Jersey City, where he went 32-9 with five one-hitters.[4]

Through 1950, the New York Giants' affiliate in the Triple-A International League played in Jersey City and Kucks grew up rooting for both the Jersey City Giants and the New York Giants. He played sandlot ball for the Cloverdale A.C. Kucks was first recruited by the Phillies, but after they withdrew a bonus offer to him, he signed with scouts Paul Krichell and Frank O'Rourke of the Yankees for a reported $13,000 on January 1, 1952. (Some accounts have the figure at $18,000.) With the Norfolk Tars of the Class B Piedmont League, Kucks won 15 of his first 17 decisions, including 11 in a row, and finished 20-6 with a 2.55 ERA. He had four shutouts, led the league's pitchers with 60 assists, and paced his team with 118 strikeouts. as the Tars finished in first place. In the playoffs he posted another win, beating Richmond 5-3, but the Tars lost the series in five games. At the end of the season, Kucks was named to the league's All-Star team.

Kucks spent 1953 and '54 in the US Army, and while in the service pitched effectively for squads at Fort Dix, New Jersey, and in Germany, posting a 25-6 record. After his discharge Kucks was invited to the Yankees' instructional school in 1955, stayed around for spring training, and pitched his way onto the team, perfecting his changeup with the help of pitching coach Jim Turner.[5] He so impressed everyone in spring training that this verse, attributed to "Yankee Frankovic," appeared in the *Cleveland Plain Dealer*:

Yank pitching rook, one
Johnny Kucks
Is looking like one million
Bucks
And kindly let me hear no
More
If possible of one Herb Score [6]

While this may have been a bit overstating the case (Score went on to win the Rookie of the Year award in 1955), Kucks did effectively jump directly from Class B to the major leagues with a sensational spring. When he joined the Yankees, his roommate was Bob Grim, who had, like Kucks, flourished in the Yankees' instructional school, making the squad in 1954.

Manager Casey Stengel said of Johnny, "This here Kucks, with a natural sinker, and the ability to field well and hold men on bases, is justifying my decision not to ship him to Denver. I have great faith and confidence in this Kucks kid, and Ol' Case ain't wrong all the time. I have been known to make the right decisions very often."[7]

On April 23, 1955, at Yankee Stadium in New York, Kucks made his first major-league start. Facing the Boston Red Sox, he pitched into the sixth inning before being relieved by Tom Morgan. The Yankees had staked Kucks to a 3-0 lead and he was credited with the win as the Yankees pulled away for a 7-2 victory.

After failing to go the distance in his first two starts, Kucks gained his first complete-game win on May 21, defeating Baltimore 9-4 at Yankee Stadium. On June 1 he limited Kansas City to two hits in eight innings before being removed for a pinch hitter, as the Yankees defeated the A's 3-1 for Kucks' fourth win of the season, against one loss.

However, Kucks was erratic in his next ten appearances, and he took a 6-4 record into his start at Kansas City on July 24. For eight innings, he and the A's Arnie Portocarrero matched each other pitch for pitch, and the game was scoreless. A double by Mickey Mantle and a homer by Yogi Berra gave the Yanks the lead in the top of the ninth inning, and Kucks shut down the A's in their half of the inning to gain his first major-league shutout.

In the World Series Kucks pitched in relief in the third and fourth games (each lost by the Yankees) and was not involved in either decision. He remembered many years later giving up a home run to Duke Snider

in Game Four.[8] Kucks had entered the game in the bottom of the fifth inning with none out and the Dodgers' Jim Gilliam at second base. The Dodgers had a 4-3 lead. A single by Pee Wee Reese and Snider's three-run-homer gave Brooklyn a 7-3 lead and the Dodgers went on to win the game, 8-5, and even the Series at two games apiece. The Dodgers won the Series in seven games.

In his rookie season, Kucks pitched in 29 games, 13 as a starter, and compiled an 8-7 record with a 3.41 ERA. In high school, he had met Barbara Daum, a cheerleader, and they were married on October 6, 1955. Shortly after the wedding the couple joined the Yankees as they visited Japan. The honeymoon began in Honolulu en route to stops in Japan, Okinawa, and Guam, and continued for more than 50 years until Barbara died after a long illness in 2006. They had two daughters, Laura-Jean and Rebecca, and four grandchildren, Kierstin, Kelly, Katie, and Jessica.

Kucks did find some time to pitch during the trip to Japan and posted a 3-0 record with a 0.33 ERA in his three games.[9] He also found time to work on a slider.

In 1956 Kucks surprised everyone. In spring training, he was not expected to be a part of the rotation, but after Tommy Byrne became ill, Kucks became the number two starter behind Whitey Ford and kept the Yankees out in front as they broke open the pennant race and won by nine games over Cleveland. He was at his best against the teams contending with the Yankees, defeating Cleveland four of the first five times he faced the Tribe. His 18-9 record placed him second on the team in victories, behind Ford. He pitched 12 complete games and had three shutouts. Stengel selected Kucks for the American League All-Star team, but he did not appear in the game.

By the end of May, Kucks had won six of his first eight decisions with four complete games, and the Yankees led the league by 6½ games. On June 10 he shut out Cleveland and his two wins against the Tribe that month were key to the Yankees' maintaining a two-game lead over the Indians as the season entered July.

In July the Yankees sprinted away from the field. Kucks won four straight games during the month, including a 4-0 shutout of Detroit on July 17. By the end of the month, his record stood at 14-6, and the Yankees had a nine-game lead. Kucks's best performance during the regular season came in his 17th win, on August 24, a four-hit, 2-0 shutout of third-place Chicago to keep the Yankees eight games ahead.[10]

It appeared a certainty that Kucks would win 20 games (he had 18 victories on September 3), but he developed a sore elbow and lost his last two decisions. The injury cost him his place in the starting rotation,[11] in during the first two games of the World Series, he pitched in relief. Over the next four games, he was a spectator as Ford, Sturdivant, Larsen (the perfect game), and Turley (losing 1-0) pitched complete games. When Game Seven came around, Kucks ended the season with his own complete game as the Yankees won, 9-0. It was, said Kucks, "my career season."[12] His side-arm sinker was so effective that 16 of the Dodgers' outs, including the first eight, came on groundballs. Kucks also kept the Dodgers off-stride with his slider, a pitch that he had not used in September because it aggravated the pain in his elbow.

There was a tense moment in the bottom of the first inning. Pee Wee Reese walked and Duke Snider singled, and the Dodgers had runners on first and second with one out. Kucks remembered, "I turned to get the rosin bag and I see (Whitey) Ford and Tom Sturdivant warming up in the bullpen. I thought, 'They really have a lot of faith in the big guy.'"[13] He got Jackie Robinson to ground into a double play, and from then on it was clear sailing. The game ended when Jackie Robinson swung at a third strike in his last major-league at-bat. It was Kucks's only strikeout of the game.

Only nine pitchers have hurled shutouts to win Game Seven of a World Series. Kucks's gem did not get as much acclaim as some of the others because it came on the heels of Don Larsen's perfect game in Game Five. Both men received bonus gifts. "Larsen got a car (after being chosen Series MVP)," Kucks told the Associated Press in 2000. "I got a fishing rod."[14] He was honored in Jersey City after the Series and received several gifts, including a gold watch and a key to the city.[15]

Kucks gained notice the following season—for being in the wrong place at the wrong time. On the evening of May 15, 1957, he and his wife were part of a group of Yankees couples including Yogi Berra, Whitey Ford, Mickey Mantle, Hank Bauer, and their wives, that was celebrating Billy Martin's 29th birthday. After dinner at Danny's Hideaway, the group went club-hopping, and arrived at the Copacabana sometime after midnight. Accounts of what happened that evening are such that the facts did not get in the way of a good story. During Sammy Davis, Jr.'s act, an altercation broke out between the Yankees and a group of bowlers seated at an adjoining table. In the aftermath, Bauer was accused of punching one of the bowlers, but the charges were eventually dropped. The Yankees players maintained that a bouncer had knocked out the bowler. Berra, Bauer, Mantle, Ford, and Martin were fined $1,000 each by the Yankees while Kucks, because he was earning far less than the established veterans, and, to quote the ever quotable Yogi, "done nuthin' to nobody," was docked $500.[16] Subsequently, the fines were rescinded by Yankees owner Dan Topping.

Kucks was never able to come close to duplicating his 1956 form. In 1957 he went 8-10 and in 1958 was 8-8 with four saves in 34 games, including 15 starts. The highlight of the latter season came on June 3 when he shut out Chicago, 13-0, allowing only two hits, to put his record at 4-1. In that year's World Series, won by the Yankees in seven games over the Milwaukee Braves, he appeared twice in relief, but was not involved in any decisions.

In 1958 Virgil Trucks, then 41, joined the Yankees for a short while. An oft-told story has it that manager Stengel at one point wanted Kucks to come in from the bullpen, but the bullpen coach had thought pitching coach Jim Turner said Trucks over the phone to the bullpen. Once Trucks's name had been announced, he was ordered into the game by the umpire.[17] In 1969 Dave Frishberg used the names of the two players in his song "Van Lingle Mungo."

In May 1959, the Yankees sent Kucks, pitcher Tom Sturdivant, and infielder Jerry Lumpe to Kansas City for third baseman Hector Lopez and pitcher Ralph

Terry. In his time with the Yankees, Kucks had gone 42-35 with six saves and an ERA of 3.82.

Kucks remained with the A's through 1960, posting a combined 12-21 record. The highlight of his first season was a 2-1 win over the Yankees on August 1 in which he scattered seven hits.

But in 1960 Kucks's sinker failed him as he yielded 22 homers in 114 innings. He did not win his first game of the season until June 12, when he won in relief. On July 26, manager Bob Elliot gave him an opportunity to start and he had his best outing of the season, pitching a complete game, as the A's defeated Baltimore 2-1. He remained in the rotation but did not fare well, winning only one of his remaining 11 starts and finishing the season at 4-10 with an ERA of 6.00. In his last appearance in the major leagues, on September 25, 1960, he lasted only four innings and was not involved in the decision as the A's lost to the Tigers. For his major-league career, Kucks was 54-56 with a 4.10 ERA.

After the season Kucks was optioned to Rochester in the International League, where he posted a 10-14 record in 1961. At the end of that season, he was sold to the Baltimore Orioles and shortly thereafter was traded to the Cardinals. He spent 1962 with the top Cardinals farm team, the Atlanta Crackers, where he posted a 14-7 record during the regular season and won three games and lost two in the playoffs. In the Junior World Series opener he defeated Louisville, 5-1, allowing only four hits, but was out-dueled, 2-1, in the fifth game of the series. Atlanta won the Junior Series in seven games, and over his last 27 innings in the playoffs, Kucks allowed only two earned runs. .

Kucks hoped that his performance with Atlanta would entice a major-league club to draft him in the off-season, but he was not chosen. He was conditionally purchased by the New York Mets (managed by Casey Stengel) and assigned to the Buffalo roster on January 9, 1963. Kucks attempted to make it back to the majors during spring training, but did not make the club. He was sent back to Atlanta. He got off to a 5-8 start with the Crackers but won his last eight decisions to finish at 14-9 with a 2.77 ERA, and keep alive the hope of a return to the major leagues. On July 26 he had his best performance of the season, shutting out Syracuse 1-0.

The game at Atlanta followed a seven-hour plane flight from Rochester and the heat was typical of Atlanta in late July. Commenting that he tended to perform better when tired, he said, "When I'm pretty well bushed, I don't throw quite as hard and when I take a little off the pitch the sinker sinks better."[18]

Kucks won the opener of the first round of the International League playoffs, defeating the Toronto Maple Leafs 9-1. Atlanta swept Toronto in four games and moved on to meet Indianapolis for the league championship. Kucks lost twice as Indianapolis won the series in five games. In what was to be his final professional appearance, he pitched the final inning of the last game of the series and was not involved in the decision.

The Cardinals switched their Triple-A affiliation from Atlanta to Jacksonville in 1964, and Kucks went to spring training with the Jacksonville Suns. But that spring he tore a nerve in his arm, and did not return to the mound. He accepted a position as a roving pitching instructor and scout in the Cardinals organization for the 1964 season.

In retirement, Kucks lived in Hillsdale, New Jersey. While still playing, he had begun training in the brokerage business and took correspondence courses with the New York School of Finance during his days in Kansas City. In 1964, after leaving the Cardinals organization, he earned his broker's license, went to work for Golkin, Bomback and Company, and stayed with them through 1973, working out of the firm's Jersey City office.[19] For 20 years afterward, he was an account executive for several steamship companies.[20] He also managed the Jersey City team in the Atlantic Collegiate Baseball League from 1967 through 1970.

In 1992. Kucks was inducted into the Hudson County (New Jersey) Hall of Fame. In his later years, he also provided care for his wife, Barbara, who died in 2006. Kucks died of cancer on October 31, 2013.

SOURCES

Barra, Allen, *Yogi Berra: Eternal Yankee* (New York, W.W. Norton, 2009).

Daniel, Dan, "Howard, Kucks, Sturdivant Pick of Yank Rookie Crop," *The Sporting News*, April 13, 1955, 11.

Daniel, Dan, "Ol' Casey Chuckles Over the Guys who 'Pitied My Pitching,'" *The Sporting News*, June 8, 1955, 7.

Daniel, Dan, "Pat-on-the-Back Strategy Paid Off for Case on Kucks," *The Sporting News*, May 16, 1956, 7.

Daniel, Dan, "Hats Off," *The Sporting News*, September 12, 1956, 21.

Daniel, Dan, "Glamour Went to Larsen but Kucks Took 'Big One,'" *The Sporting News*, October 17, 1956, 11.

Eck, Frank, "Yankees' Kucks Is Rookie With Poise," *Aberdeen* (South Dakota) *Daily News*, April 7, 1955, 14.

Levin, Jay, "Johnny Kucks, Yankees 1956 World Series Hero and Hillsdale Resident, Dies at 81," *The Record* (Hackensack, New Jersey), November 2, 2013.

Madden, Bill, "Johnny Kucks, World Series Hero for the Yankees in 1956, Dead at 80," *New York Daily News*, November 1, 2013.

Noble, Marty, "Showing Appreciation for 1956 Series Hero Kucks," MLB.com, November 3, 2013.

Rolfe, Shelley, "Yanks' Cheap Bonus Baby Gives Tars Top Pitching," *Richmond* (Virginia) *Times-Dispatch*, July 3, 1952, 27.

Rosenthal, Harold, "Phils Cooled on Kucks as Kid Prospect," *The Sporting News*, October 31, 1956, 5.

Weber, Bruce, "Johnny Kucks, Who Pitched Yankees to Title, Dies at 81," *New York Times*, November 1, 2013.

Newspapers:

Cleveland Plain Dealer

New York Times

New York World Telegram

Richmond (Virginia) *Times-Dispatch*

The Record (Hackensack, New Jersey)

The Sporting News

Ancestry.com

Baseball-Reference.com

GenealogyBank.com

NewspaperArchive.com

Interview with Johnny Kucks by Thomas Harris, September 8, 1993 (Baseball Hall of Fame, SABR Oral History Collection)

NOTES

1   Allen Barra, *Yogi Berra: Eternal Yankee* (New York, W.W. Norton, 2009), 227.

2   Associated Press, "Memories: Last Subway Series Was One to Remember." *Erie* (Pennsylvania) *Times-News*, October 19, 2000.

3   Marty Noble, "Showing Appreciation for 1956 Series Hero Kucks," MLB.com, November 3, 2013.

4   Dan Daniel, *The Sporting News*, May 16, 1956, 7.

5   Dan Daniel, *The Sporting News*, April 13, 1955, 11.

6   James E. Doyle, *Cleveland Plain Dealer*, April 5, 1955,

7   Dan Daniel, *The Sporting News*, June 8, 1955, 7.

8   Thomas Harris interview with Johnny Kucks.

9   *New York Times*, January 30, 1956, 32.

10 Joseph M. Sheehan, "Kucks of Bombers Takes 17th, 2-0," *New York Times*, August 25, 1956, 8.

11 Harold Rosenthal, *The Sporting News*, October 31, 1956, 5.

12 Bill Madden, "Johnny Kucks, World Series Hero for the Yankees in 1956, Dead at 80," *New York Daily News*, November 1, 2013.

13 Associated Press, "Memories: Last Subway Series Was One to Remember," *Erie* (Pennsylvania) *Times-News*, October 19, 2000.

14 Bruce Weber, "Johnny Kucks, Who Pitched Yankees to Title, Dies at 81," *New York Times*, November 1, 2013.

15 *New York Times*, October 18, 1956, 43.

16 Barra, 238.

17 Leonard Koppett, *New York Times*, September 15, 1964, 42.

18 *The Sporting News.* August 10, 1963, 38.

19 *New York Herald Tribune*, September 22, 1964.

20 Joe Chessari, "Where's What's-His-Name," *The Record* (Hackensack, New Jersey), March 31, 1990.

Virgil Trucks

By Gregory H. Wolf

THE LAST-PLACE DETROIT TIGERS WENT to New York to meet the reigning World Series champion Yankees in August 1952. After Detroit lost the first game of the series, Virgil Trucks started Game Two. The veteran right-hander came in with a 4-15 record, but he had pitched a no-hitter and a one-hitter for two of his victories. On August 25 Trucks had his fastball humming and threw his second no-hitter of the season; however, the game was marked by controversy involving an error, an official scorer, and even a phone call to the fielder involved. In an interview with the author, Virgil Trucks recalled this exceptional game:

"In the [third] inning, Phil Rizzuto hit a groundball to Johnny Pesky. We thought he'd thrown him out at first, but the umpire called him safe. When I walked off the field, on the scoreboard you could see there was an error. When I went back onto the field to start the third inning, there had been a hit put up. … The scorer that day was John Drebinger [of the *New York Times*], and the sportswriters were getting on him for changing it from an error to a hit. He called down to the bench and talked to Johnny Pesky; Pesky said that it was nothing but an error. The ball was not stuck in his glove, he said; he just could not get a grip on it. Drebinger accepted his word. When I went out in the eighth inning, they announced over the PA system what [Drebinger had] done and it had been corrected as an error. They put an error back on the board and it was still a no-hitter."[1]

Right-hander Virgil "Fire" Trucks set down the Yankees in order in the eighth and ninth to join Johnny Vander Meer and Allie Reynolds as the only pitchers to throw two no-hitters in the same season. (Nolan Ryan joined them in 1973, and in 2010 Roy Halladay tossed a no-hitter in the regular season and the postseason.) With 19 losses and just five victories for the year, Trucks provided some of the few highlights for a Tigers team that finished the season in eighth place at 50-104, the first time in franchise history that the Tigers lost 100 games or finished last in the AL.[2]

Virgil Oliver Trucks was born on April 26, 1917, to Lula Belle and Oliver Trucks in Birmingham, Alabama. Raised at home by his mother and by Aunt Fannie, an African American nanny, Virgil was the fourth of 13 children. He had eight brothers and four sisters.[3] Virgil's first encounters with baseball were as a toddler with his father. Oliver operated a company store for the Tennessee Coal and Iron Company in Birmingham and played for the company baseball team in a local sandlot league. Virgil recalled that his father, an accomplished pitcher, was offered a minor-league contract by the Nashville Vols of the Southern Association and "probably could have made the major leagues, but with four kids at the time, he couldn't leave home." He snuck into his father's games and also into Rickwood Field, where the Birmingham Barons of the Southern Association and the Black Barons of the Negro Leagues

played. By the age of 10, Virgil was playing youth ball, and he progressed through the American Legion leagues during his high-school years.

Virgil developed a reputation after high school as a strong-throwing infielder and outfielder. Playing for company teams including A.C.I., Hightower, and then Stockham Pipe in the Birmingham City League, Trucks caught the attention of scouts. Eddie Goostree, a roving scout for the Detroit Tigers, signed Trucks to a contract as an outfielder in 1937 and awarded him a $100 bonus.[4]

Because he had not been assigned to a team by May, Trucks decided to play semipro ball for Shawmut in the Chattahoochee Valley League, a textile league. Brunner Nix, a Shawmut catcher, thought Trucks would make a great pitcher because of his arm strength. "Nix more or less worked with my control," Trucks said. "I could throw pretty hard, but was a little bit wild. He got me to the point that I got the ball more over the plate. He taught me about spinning the curveball."

At the conclusion of Shawmut's season, Andalusia of the Class D Alabama-Florida League called: "They came and asked me if I would play for them in the [league championship] series," Trucks remembered. "They'd pay me $35 a game and expenses. I pitched and won the opening game, 3-0; I pitched another game and won 5-0. They wanted me to sign a contract with them. They said they'd give me $700. And I just let that fly by because I had already signed a contract with the Detroit Tigers." But ultimately he signed with Andalusia and was now under contract with them and the Tigers.

Back home in Birmingham during the offseason, Trucks wasn't sure what to do or which contract was valid. "I started to get contracts from Beaumont, Texas, which was the Detroit farm club," he said. "And then I got one from Andalusia. I'd just send them back, saying it was not enough money. I thought they'd come and arrest me for taking their money." So he decided to ignore the problem altogether and contacted Fob James, manager of the Lanett, Alabama, team in the same semipro league where he had played in 1937. In an exhibition game against the Atlanta Crackers of the Southern Association, Trucks met manager Paul Richards, who later played a pivotal role in his career. "Paul wanted to sign me also," Trucks said, but his

conscience bothered him and his pitching suffered. "I finally confessed to James what I had done. I said that I don't know who I belong to and I keep getting contracts. … I went to see him [later] and he said that you are the property of Andalusia. I asked how that could be since I signed with Detroit first. He said that Detroit pigeon-holed the contract." "Pigeon-holing" was a practice of not submitting contracts to major-league baseball.

Trucks earned his national reputation as a strikeout artist while pitching for the Andalusia Bulldogs in 1938. Jack House, sportswriter for the *Birmingham News*, saw him pitch and gave him the apt moniker "Fire," which stayed with Trucks his entire life. *The Sporting News* ran front-page headlines about his pitching exploits and his new record for most strikeouts in a season in Organized Baseball with 420, breaking Hoss Radbourn's record set in 1884.[5] (Later research has established that Matt Kilroy struck out 513 for Baltimore of the American Association in 1886.) Trucks was 25-6, pitched two no-hitters, had a 1.25 ERA, and wound up in a *Ripley's Believe It or Not* comic strip.[6] Yam Yaryan, manager and part-time catcher of the Andalusia Bulldogs, suggested that Trucks alter his birth date to appear two years younger. Throughout his playing career, 1919 was given as his year of birth.

After seeing Trucks pitch for Andalusia, Eddie Goostree helped secure the sale of his player rights to Detroit. Trucks reported to the Tigers' Beaumont Exporters, a team in the Class A-1 Texas League, in 1939, but due to his inconsistent pitching he was demoted to Class D, the Alexandria Aces of the Evangeline League. He had the opportunity to pitch regularly, regained his confidence, and finished with a 13-5 record. Trucks reported back to Beaumont to start the 1940 season and pitched consistently, though not spectacularly, for manager Al Vincent, including his third no-hitter. His 12-11 record earned him a trial at the Tigers' spring training in 1941.[7]

Trucks reported to the Tigers in Lakeland, Florida, with a rebellious reputation due to his attitude and clashes with Vincent, which resulted in disciplinary actions and fines on several occasions. At the end of spring training he was optioned to the Buffalo Bisons of the Double-A International League, managed by the recently promoted Vincent. They reconciled their differences, prompting Trucks to comment, "I was just a thrower until Vincent's coaching began to set in."[8] His 12 wins and league-leading 204 strikeouts earned him a September call-up.

On September 27, 1941, Trucks made his major-league debut in the top of the fifth inning with the Tigers down 8-4 at home against the Chicago White Sox. "I learned something and it taught me a lesson that I remembered for the rest of my career," he said. "I had a guy steal home on me from third base." With no one out and a player on third, Trucks was stunned when the player broke for home. "The first time I looked," Trucks said, "he was almost at the plate. I wanted to hurry up my throw, but that would have been a balk. He'd have been safe anyway. He stole home without a tag! With him on third base, I took my windup. I should have glanced at him, but I didn't." And that was the last time someone stole home with Trucks on the mound. Just over two months later, Pearl Harbor was bombed and Trucks wondered what would happen to his baseball career.

In 1942 Trucks arrived at spring training anticipating being in the starting rotation. He made his first career start in the fourth game of the season, losing 7-6 to the Browns in St. Louis. In his second start, on his birthday, he notched his first career win, but afterward lost his place in the rotation due to wildness. After being idle for a month Trucks had another poor start, on May 22, and manager Del Baker considered demoting him. Pitching for his future, Trucks tossed a complete-game four-hit victory and followed it with his first career shutout, a six-hit gem against the Athletics at Philadelphia to cement not just his spot on the team, but also in the rotation. By September *The Sporting News* considered him the best hurler on the staff.[9] He finished his rookie season with a team-high 14 wins and a 2.74 ERA.

Because of wartime travel restrictions, the Tigers conducted spring training in Evansville, Indiana in 1943, and new manager Steve O'Neill had big aspirations. However, the Tigers duplicated their fifth-place finish from the year before. In establishing himself as

a big-league starter, Trucks put up even better numbers in his second full season, including 16 wins.

Trucks' will to succeed and ability to navigate through unwritten rules of baseball etiquette helped ease his transition to the major leagues. The Tigers had an older staff in 1941 and "rookie pitchers were teased and aggravated," he said. Furthermore, Trucks was a Southerner with an accent. "Some of the players didn't like Southern ballplayers," he recalled, "and they stayed away from us."

At the end of the 1943 season Trucks took his military physical and decided to enlist in the Navy with the hope of being assigned to the Great Lakes Naval Training Station, outside Chicago, and playing Navy baseball for coach Mickey Cochrane.[10] "I never got to play for Mickey when he was at Detroit and I always admired him," Trucks recounted in an interview. The 1944 Great Lakes Bluejackets were a powerhouse, winning 48 of 50 games against major-league, minor-league, college, and industrial-league teams. With a starting lineup comprising major leaguers, including Billy Herman, Gene Woodling, and Schoolboy Rowe, and superior minor leaguers, they had a reputation as a "17th major league team."[11] Typically two or three games were played each week at the base in front of 10,000 to 12,000 sailors, which provided a major-league atmosphere.[12] The Bluejackets played 14 of the 16 major-league teams, beating all except the Brooklyn Dodgers. Trucks pitched 48 innings against major-league teams, gave up just 21 hits and five earned runs, and won all four of his decisions; cumulatively, he was 10-0 with 161 strikeouts in 113 innings.

The Navy's Admiral Chester Nimitz challenged the Army to a Military Service World Series in Hawaii. Both rosters comprised major-league stars, but the Navy squad, managed by Bill Dickey, may have been the most talented service team ever assembled; it included Phil Rizzuto, Johnny Mize, Dom DiMaggio, Pee Wee Reese, Johnny Vander Meer, and Virgil Trucks.[13] In front of 20,000 servicemen at Furlong Field in Honolulu, Trucks threw a four-hit shutout in game one.[14] The Army and Navy decided to play all seven games regardless of the outcome and the Navy proceeded to win the first six and lose game seven when

Trucks gave up a home run to Ferris Fain in the last inning.[15] Trucks was on active duty in 1944 and 1945 in Hawaii and several islands in the South Pacific, where he played baseball against local military base teams.

In the summer of 1945 Trucks aggravated his already injured knee on Guam, and was ultimately discharged. "There was a minor-league catcher at the rehab center. He and I got together and I'd throw to him every day and run a bit. That's all the training I had for the World Series."

Trucks was discharged near the end of the baseball season. He met the Tigers in St. Louis to play the final two games. A win against the Browns would give the Tigers the pennant. And in dramatic fashion, Trucks was chosen to start the first game. "I had just gotten out of the service three days before I joined the ballclub," Trucks said. "Paul Richards was one of the coaches and catchers on the ballclub. He warmed me up a little and said that I was available to pitch if the Tigers wanted to use me." After a rainout, his start was pushed to Sunday. Trucks pitched three-hit ball for 5⅓ innings, giving up just one run. Hank Greenberg's grand slam with two outs in the ninth won the game and propelled the Tigers to the World Series.

Owing to an exemption that allowed returning servicemen to join their teams at any point in the season and sill be eligible for the World Series, Trucks was on the roster.[16] The Tigers, led by a pitching staff that outfielder Hub Walker called TNT (Trout, Newhouser, and Trucks),[17] were set to play the Chicago Cubs. In the first game, in Detroit, the Tigers and AL MVP Newhouser were pummeled, 9-0, which seemed to affirm the team's collective nickname as "nine old men."[18]

Trucks started the pivotal Game Two and pitched the most important game of his life: a complete-game 4-1 victory. "That was the greatest thrill I think I've had in baseball," he said. Cubs manager Charlie Grimm said, "Virgil Trucks was faster than anyone we saw all year in the National League."[19] The Tigers went on to win the World Series in seven games. Sportswriter Frederick G. Lieb maintained that Detroit won because "Trucks tipped [the] pitching scale at the last minute."[20]

The Tigers finished a distant second to the Red Sox in 1946 and Yankees in 1947, and a disappointing fifth in 1948 while Trucks struggled to find his prewar form. He won 14, 10, and 14; however, his ERA rose dramatically, his control suffered, he gave up an uncharacteristic number of home runs, and at times lost his spot in the starting rotation. At the conclusion of the 1947 season, the Tigers dangled him unsuccessfully in several trade attempts and manager Steve O'Neill expressed his disappointment in Trucks' pitching: "He hasn't measured up to specifications in the postwar era."[21] Trucks admitted, "I had a miserable season."[22] Back problems limited his motion, and his weight, which he fought with his entire career, rose to 220, about 20 pounds over his typical playing weight. One critic commented, "Trucks' chief pitching flaw is that he throws everything with the same tempo and at the same height."[23]

At 32 Trucks got off to the best start of his career in 1949, which helped end the trade rumors. He won his first four starts, including three complete games. He exhibited better control and location of his pitches and developed a good changeup. Importantly, he was pitching late into games, underscoring his improved conditioning. In a span of five starts in late May and early June, Trucks pitched four complete games, including three extra-inning games, and then followed those with two consecutive shutouts. Trucks attributed his transformation into one of the major leagues' foremost winners to "an entirely new attitude," support from new manager Red Rolfe, who took him off the trading block, and help from pitching coach Ted Lyons.[24] "Ted Lyons," Trucks recalled, "helped me to learn how to throw different pitches. He helped me mostly to improve my slider and curveball, and how to grip the ball. The slider is gripped entirely differently than any other pitch. It's pitched with half of the ball outside of your hand and fingers." Trucks finished the season at 19-11 with a 2.81 ERA and led the league in shutouts with six and strikeouts with 153. One of the season's highlights was his first All-Star Game, which he won by pitching the second and third innings.

With high expectations, Trucks started 1950 where he left off the previous year. After his sixth start, an 11-inning shutout on May 13, he felt pain in his right arm for the first time in his life. Concerned and confused, he shrugged it off and made his next scheduled start, but didn't survive the third inning. After diathermy treatment didn't help,[25] he was sent to Dr. Robert F. Hyland in St. Louis. "He gave me ten days of X-ray treatment," Trucks said. "One beep each day on my upper arm, which was a pulled tendon. He told me when I left after ten days, if I try to throw and it hurts, then quit for the year. I went back and tried to throw. It hurt so, I didn't throw. It probably saved my career by listening to him." Trucks missed the rest of the season.

Based on his performance in 1950, Trucks' 1951 salary was slashed by 25 percent and reported to be $15,000.[26] After Trucks failed to show his usual velocity in the spring, manager Rolfe proceeded cautiously with his comeback. Rolfe relegated Trucks to the bullpen, where he struggled. On May 27 he won his first start of the year; it was his first win in 12½ months. He entered the starting rotation in mid-July and came on strong at the end of the season, recording complete games in five of his last six starts, including a 14-inning marathon. Manager Rolfe said, "He's a better pitcher now than when he won 19 games … [has] better control and a curve. He can set up his hitters better."[27]

Trucks' 1952 season is one of the most incongruous and surprising ones imaginable. The Tigers suffered through the worst season in franchise history and Trucks had a 5-19 record. Deeper research reveals that not all those losses were his fault; the Tigers scored 0, 1, or 2 runs in 15 of his starts. Among his five wins were two no-hitters, a one-hitter, a two-hitter through 7⅔ innings, and a six-hitter. After his first no-hitter, Trucks remarked, "Before my arm trouble, I depended mostly on my fastball. Now I am using curves and sliders … but my fastball has [also] returned."[28]

In December Trucks was traded to the St. Louis Browns. "I thought [the trade] was awful," he said. "I would have loved to stay with Detroit my entire career." In 1953 he arrived in San Bernardino, California, at the Browns' spring-training facility in "better shape than he has been in five years"[29] and looking "like the old Trucks."[30] Manager Marty Marion was upbeat about the Browns, who had finished last or second-to-last in six of the previous seven seasons, and praised Trucks: "I'm counting on Trucks as the Browns' number-one stopper."[31] He was tabbed the Opening Day starter

against his former team. In overpowering fashion, the 36-year-old Trucks threw a four-hit shutout.

After two months Trucks was the Browns' most effective pitcher, but they were in last place. Owner Bill Veeck, in financial difficulty, was fighting with the commissioner and the other owners, who had blocked his attempt to relocate his franchise. After being offered to several teams, Trucks was sent to the Chicago White Sox in June, primarily in order to infuse the Browns with needed cash to meet operating expenses. "I was traded five times," Trucks recounted, "and Veeck was the only man who ever came to me, called me into his office, and told me that I was traded. I think Bill Veeck was one of the greatest guys that ever owned a ballclub. He gave me the absolute truth. He said [the American League] will not let him move the ballclub; the owners wouldn't approve of it. He's got to meet the payroll, so he's selling me and Bob Elliott to the White Sox for $100,000 [actually $75,000] and getting a couple of ballplayers in trades." During his brief tenure with the Browns, Trucks had his first African American teammate, Satchel Paige, whom he saw pitch two decades earlier in Birmingham in Negro League games. Paige and Trucks formed a strong friendship that carried into their post-baseball days.

The White Sox, Indians, and Yankees were in an exciting three-team battle for the AL pennant. The acquisition of Trucks paid instant dividends. After a no-decision in his first start, Trucks won his next eight starts. *The Sporting News* called him the "AL's most effective pitcher"[32] and teammate Minnie Miñoso called him "sensational."[33] Though the White Sox finished in third place, Trucks and Billy Pierce proved to be one of baseball's best 1-2 punches. Trucks won 15 games for the White Sox, which gave him a season total of 20, his career high. At 36, he was among the league leaders in almost every major pitching category.

Trucks started 1954 where he left off the previous year, winning 10 of his first 13 starts. As a 37-year old, he relied less on his fastball and credited his success to a more mature approach. Trucks also revealed that he learned a new pitch: "Paul Richards [the White Sox manager] taught me his 'slip pitch,' which I used as a changeup."[34] He was named to his second All-Star

Game, pitched a hitless and scoreless ninth inning (earning a save), and helped the American League defeat the National League, 11-9, in front of almost 70,000 spectators at Municipal Stadium in Cleveland. With a record of 17 wins and just five defeats in mid-August, Trucks appeared to be headed for 20 wins again, but a series of nagging injuries and his teammates' untimely hitting affected his performance. Trucks closed out the season 2-7. Again, he was among the league leaders in every major statistical category. After the season, Trucks signed a contract reported at $35,000 and exclaimed that it was the "highest salary I ever received."[35]

After a slow start in 1955, Trucks was reportedly in general manager Frank Lane's doghouse for not performing up to expectations[36] and new manager Marty Marion's for his lack of focus. "He [Marion] didn't pitch me like he should have in 1955," Trucks said. "He'd skip me … and I didn't like that. He wasn't my kind of manager." Trucks' and Marion's antagonism traced back to their time together on the Browns. An outspoken critic of Marion, Trucks resented that his manager demanded that the 45-year-old Satchel Paige take part in all of the running and training exercises scheduled for pitchers. Now, as a 38-year-old, Trucks was obviously slowing down, but his competitive spirit was not. He was not ready to back down from any challenge in the clubhouse or on the field. In response to claims that he used the brushback pitch too much, Trucks replied, "I believe it is necessary and legitimate [when batters are] crowding the plate."[37] He finished with a 13-8 record.

After expressing his desire to pitch, but not as both a starter and a reliever ("I'm too old for that."[38]), Trucks was traded back to the Tigers for Bubba Phillips in December 1955. Manager Bucky Harris hoped to squeeze what he could out of the former Tiger star: "We realize Trucks has quite a few years on him, but all we want is one more good season."[39] The oldest player on the roster, Trucks had developed a knuckleball while barnstorming in previous years and honed it in spring training,[40] but a series of injuries limited his effectiveness. He made just 16 starts and won only six games. It was clear that Trucks had lost his velocity and that his days as a starter were over. In December

1956 the Tigers traded him in an eight-player deal to the Kansas City Athletics. It was his fourth trade and fifth team in five years.

With his typical optimism, Trucks arrived at spring training with the A's claiming, "The club is 50 percent better than it was last year and the pitching staff is 100 percent improved."[41] Privately, however, he told friends and family that this would be his last season. After getting pummeled in spring training, Trucks was assigned to the bullpen, where he pitched in a career-high 48 games and won nine to lead the team.

Lured back to the A's in 1958, Trucks pitched well, with an ERA hovering near 2.00 after 16 appearances. His effectiveness caught the eyes of the Yankees, who had attempted to acquire him the previous season to shore up their bullpen. They traded for him in June and Trucks went on to pitch in 25 games for the Bronx Bombers. Though "totally surprised" by the trade, Trucks could not replicate the same success he had with the A's. He was hit hard in a few initial outings before finding a groove in late July and August. After a couple of poor outings in September, he apparently lost manager Casey Stengel's confidence. The Yankees won the pennant, but Trucks was left off the World Series roster. Trucks had a poor relationship with Stengel and commented, "I disliked him in every sense." Trucks was persuaded to serve as the batting-practice pitcher for the Yankees in the World Series, which they won in thrilling fashion, over the Milwaukee Braves in seven games.

Approaching his 42nd birthday, Trucks held out to begin the 1959 season, and ultimately signed in March after taking a 25 percent pay cut, the maximum allowed.[42] Out of shape and still disappointed at being left off the World Series roster, he struggled in spring training and was released in April. Trucks said, "I just lost the desire to play even though I felt fine. There was nothing wrong with me physically. My arm was all right. I just couldn't get myself motivated to play." Bill Durney, general manager of the Miami Marlins in the International League, persuaded Trucks to attempt a comeback and offered him a $5,000 bonus no matter how he pitched.[43] After a few uninspired performances, Trucks ended his professional playing career.

In an 18-year major-league career during which he lost practically two full seasons to military service, Trucks won 177 games and lost 135, recorded 33 shutouts, and compiled a 3.39 ERA. He won another 65 games in the minor leagues. Though it is impossible to know how Trucks would have pitched in 1944 and 1945, or if he would have been injured, it is not far-fetched to assume that he would have won another 30 to 38 games based on his performance before and after his military service. Had that been the case, he would have finished with career numbers similar to those of his peers and Hall of Famers Hal Newhouser and Bob Lemon. Trucks was considered one of the hardest throwers in major-league history. (Ted Williams thought Trucks was the fastest pitcher he ever faced, and supposedly an Army radar gun clocked him at 105 miles per hour.)[44] Trucks was also remarkably resilient and suffered just one debilitating arm injury. Commenting on his delivery, Trucks said, "I was primarily an overhand pitcher. I never dropped down to side-arm. That was a reason I lasted so long. Because of throwing overhand, I could follow through; your arm follows through to where you are not putting a lot of pressure on it."

Throughout his playing career, Trucks held a variety of jobs and had a number of business interests to augment his income and support his family. He directed youth programs, worked for railways and shipyards, operated baseball camps, owned a beer distributorship, and even served in the emergency police reserve in Detroit as a volunteer in case of a nuclear attack on the city.[45] But the most lucrative opportunity for extra income during the offseason was barnstorming.[46]

Trucks' return to the major leagues in 1960 was the result of a botched barnstorming tour showcasing him and Satchel Paige. "Paige had a barnstorming tour all set up. Just he and I were going to be the ones who pitched on the tour. We had a busload of young ballplayers from Cuba. We opened the season out in Kansas and went south until we got to Mexico." Unfortunately, Trucks and Paige were not paid as promised, Paige quit, and the Castro revolution in Cuba forced the players to return home.

In 1960 Trucks hooked on with the Pirates as a batting-practice pitcher, and stayed with the team until 1963. Throughout the 1960s and early 1970s, he had jobs in and outside of baseball. He operated baseball camps for Pirates, scouted Pittsburgh and Western Pennsylvania for the Seattle Pilots, served as a pitching coach for his former team, the Triple-A Buffalo Bisons, in 1971, and also served as a roving scout for the Braves and Tigers from 1970 through 1974. In 1974 he retired from baseball and returned to Alabama, where he spent most of his time.

At the age of 95, Trucks died in 2013 in Calera, Alabama, south of Birmingham, and was buried in the Alabama National Cemetery in Montevallo. He was survived by his fourth wife, Anne, whom he married in 2003. He had five children from previous marriages, Jimmie, Carolyn, Virgil, Darryl, and Wendy, as well as grandchildren and great-grandchildren.

Looking back on his career and accomplishments, Trucks was insightful. "I would do it all over again," he responded when asked about his military service. He had no second thoughts about losing almost two years of his prime. Always known for his humor, he continued, "Why wasn't I traded to [the Yankees] in 1941? Because I'd definitely be in the Hall of Fame if I had been traded to [them]."

NOTES

1   The author interviewed Virgil Trucks on September 19, 2011. All quotations from Trucks are from the author's interview with him unless otherwise noted.

2   All season and career statistics have been verified with baseballreference.com. All games statistics have been verified with retrosheet.org/.

3   Virgil Trucks' autobiography is an insightful and thorough book about his life and times. See Virgil O. Trucks, with Ronnie Joyner and Bill Bozman, *Throwing Heat: The Life and Times of Virgil Fire Trucks* (Dunkirk, Maryland: Pepperpot, 2004).

4   Trucks, 11–12.

5   *The Sporting News,* August 25, 1938, 1, and September 1, 1938, 1.

6   See Trucks, 27 for a reprint of the Ripley strip.

7   *The Sporting News,* September 12, 1940, 5.

8   *The Sporting News,* July 10, 1940, 5.

9   *The Sporting News,* September 3, 1942, 3.

10 Trucks, 77.

11 Trucks, 79.

12 *The Sporting News*, July 6, 1944, 17.

13 Trucks provides the starting lineup for both squads in his autobiography, page 81.

14 *The Sporting News*, September 28, 1944, 12.

15 Trucks, 82.

16 *The Sporting News*, October 4, 1945, 4.

17 *The Sporting News*, October 11, 1945, 7.

18 Fredrick G. Lieb, *The Detroit Tigers* (New York: Putnam, 1946), 263.

19 *The Sporting News*, October 11, 1945, 4

20 *The Sporting News*, October 18, 1945, 2. For an excellent history of the Tigers team in 1945, see Burge Carmon Smith's *The 1945 Detroit Tigers: Nine Old Men and One Left Arm Win t All* (Jefferson, North Carolina: McFarland and Co.), 2010.

21 *The Sporting News*, November 11, 1947, 9.

22 *The Sporting News*, December 24, 1947, 10.

23 *The Sporting News*, May 5, 1948, 11.

24 *The Sporting News*, June 29, 1949, 9.

25 *The Sporting News*, July 12, 1950, 20.

26 *The Sporting News*, January, 31, 1951, 8.

27 *The Sporting News*, October 3, 1951, 15.

28 *The Sporting News*, May 28, 1952, 13.

29 *The Sporting News*, February 25, 1953, 29.

30 *The Sporting News*, April 1, 1953, 22.

31 *The Sporting News*, April 22, 1953, 8.

32 *The Sporting News*, August 5, 1953, 4.

33 Minnie Miñoso and Herb Fagen, *Just Call Me Minnie: My Six Decades in Baseball* (Urbana, Illinois: Sagamore, 1994), 89.

34 The Sporting News, November 24, 1954, 21.

35 Ibid.

36 *The Sporting News*, May 11, 1955, 18.

37 *The Sporting News*, September 28, 1955, 14.

38 *The Sporting News*, November 30, 1955, 36.

39 *The Sporting News*, December 7, 1955, 6.

40 *The Sporting News*, April 11, 1956, 7.

41 *The Sporting News*, March 20, 1957, 27.

42 *The Sporting News*, February 25, 1959, 6.

43 Trucks, 248-9.

44 Doug Segrest,"5 Questions: Former major leaguer Virgil Trucks," *Birmingham* (Alabama) *News,* December 18, 2009. blog.al.com/birmingham-news-sports/2009/12/5_questions_former_major_leagu.html

45 *The Sporting News*, December 20, 1951, 15.

46 Arguably the most definitive book about barnstorming is Thomas Barthel's *Baseball Barnstorming and Exhibition Games 1901-1962. A History of Off-Season Major League Play* (Jefferson, North Carolina: McFarland, 2007). Barthel provides a comprehensive list of barnstorming teams and rosters.

Contributors

Mark Armour is the director of SABR's Baseball Biography Project, and the author or editor of six books on baseball. His forthcoming book *Champions* (written with Dan Levitt) will be published by the University of Nebraska Press in 2015.

Lawrence Baldassaro is professor emeritus of Italian at the University of Wisconsin-Milwaukee. He has written for several baseball journals and has been a regular contributor to the Milwaukee Brewers magazine since 1990. He is the editor of *Ted Williams: Reflections on a Splendid Life* and co-editor, with Richard Johnson, of *The American Game: Baseball and Ethnicity*. His latest book is *Beyond DiMaggio: Italian Americans in Baseball*.

Ralph Berger held a Bachelor of Arts Degree from the University of Pennsylvania and a Master of Public Administration degree from Temple University, and earned a Certificate in Human Resources from the University of Michigan. He wrote over 50 biographies for SABR. He lived with his beautiful wife Reina in Huntingdon Valley, Pennsylvania. A lifelong fan of the Fightin' Phillies, he endured as a Philly fan for eons.

Alan Cohen is a retired insurance underwriter who has been a member of SABR since 2011. He has written 15 biographies for the SABR bio-project. A native of Long Island, he now resides in West Hartford, Connecticut with his wife Frances, two cats and a dog. He graduated from Franklin and Marshall College in 1968. His article about the Hearst Sandlot Classic, which launched the careers of 89 major leaguers, appeared in the Fall, 2013 edition of the *Baseball Research Journal*. During the baseball season, he serves as the datacaster (stringer) for the New Britain Rock Cats of the Eastern League.

Warren Corbett is a contributor to SABR's Biography Project and the author of *The Wizard of Waxahachie: Paul Richards and the End of Baseball As We Knew It*. He lives in Bethesda, Maryland.

Rob Edelman teaches film history courses at the University at Albany. He is the author of *Great Baseball Films and Baseball on the Web*, and is co-author (with his wife, Audrey Kupferberg) of *Meet the Mertzes*, a double biography of *I Love Lucy's* Vivian Vance and fabled baseball fan William Frawley, and *Matthau: A Life*. He is a film commentator on WAMC (Northeast) Public Radio and a Contributing Editor of *Leonard Maltin's Movie Guide*. He is a frequent contributor to *Base Ball: A Journal of the Early Game*, and has written articles for and chapters in a host of baseball publications. His essay on early baseball films appears on the DVD *Reel Baseball: Baseball Films from the Silent Era, 1899-1926*, and he is an interviewee on the director's cut DVD of *The Natural*.

Dave Eskenazi is a Seattle native and lifelong Seattle resident. He works in the financial services industry, and shares his affection for Seattle, Northwest, and West Coast sports history via historical displays, articles, documentaries, public speaking, and collaboration with Steve Rudman on "The Wayback Machine" on sportspressnw.com.

A retired English professor, **Jan Finkel** joined SABR in 1994 and has been chief editor of the Biography Project since 2002. He lives with his wife Judy on Deep Creek Lake in the mountains of western Maryland, where he outwits an occasional largemouth, and passes his time contemplating great books and baseball, often simultaneously.

David Fleitz, a computer systems analyst from Pleasant Ridge, Michigan, has written eight books on baseball history, including biographies of Shoeless Joe Jackson, Louis Sockalexis, and Cap Anson. David's latest work, *Napoleon Lajoie: King of Ballplayers*, was published by McFarland in 2013.

James Forr has authored or contributed to six books on baseball history, including *Pie Traynor: A Baseball Biography* (with David Proctor), which was a finalist for the 2010 Casey Award. James lives in Scottsdale, Arizona.

Jerry Grillo is the husband of Jane, the father of Samantha and Joey, and also a longtime journalist and occasional playwright who lives in Sautee Nacoochee, Georgia, a beautiful rural mountain community about 15 miles from Johnny Mize's hometown, and seven or eight miles from the house where Claire Merritt Hodgson Ruth once lived.

Eric Hanauer is a widely published writer and underwater photographer, with nearly 1,000 magazine articles and three books. His scuba diving adventures have taken him to some 50 countries around the world. For 35 years his day job was associate professor of physical education at California State University Fullerton, where he also coached swimming and water polo, and introduced the scuba diving program. His main claim to fame was developing the grab start. He owes all that his to lack of baseball skill as a youth, which led him to the water as a second choice. Hanauer is a lifelong Cubs fan, ever since his first Wrigley Field game at the age of nine. For more, see his website, www.ehanauer.com.

Mark Hodermarsky is an English teacher at Saint Ignatius High School in Cleveland where he taught a baseball literature course for 20 years. He has written or edited five sports books, including *Baseball's Greatest Writers*, and has reviewed baseball books for the *Cleveland Plain Dealer*. Hodermarsky's most memorable baseball moment occurred on May 15, 1981 when his son was born while Tribe pitcher Lenny Barker hurled a perfect game.

Joanne Hulbert is co-chair of the Boston Chapter, and co-chair of SABR's Baseball Arts Committee. She is an avid collector of baseball poetry and songs, and resides in Holliston, Massachusetts, in the part of town known as Mudville since the 1850s. She has been there long enough to know the importance of baseball to poetry and music.

Bill Johnson is a retired Naval Flight Officer living in Cedar Rapids, Iowa. Since joining SABR in 1994, he has focused on Iowa's baseball heritage, including several essays for the BioProject. He is also co-author of the book *Norway Baseball: Gone But Not Forgotten*, with Shona Frese.

James W. Johnson is a retired journalism professor at the University of Arizona. He is also a veteran newspaperman, having worked at the *Philadelphia Inquirer*, the *Oregonian*, the *Providence Journal*, the *Arizona Republic*, the *Arizona Daily Star* and the *Oakland Tribune*. His book, *DeGrazia: The Man and the Myth*, about the acclaimed Southwest artist, was released February 27, 2014 by the University of Arizona Press. It was his seventh book. He also co-authored a biography of the late Congressman Mo Udall as well as *Double No-hit: Johnny Vander Meer's Historic Night Under the Lights*, *The Dandy Dons: Bill Russell, K.C. Jones, Phil Woolpert*, and *One of College Baseball's Greatest and Most Innovative Teams*, and *The Wow Boys: A Coach, a Team and a Turning Point in College Football*. He currently is at work on a book, *The Black Bruins*, about four African-Americans, including Jackie Robinson, who played football for UCLA in the late '30s. He lives in Tucson.

Greg King, a co-founder of SABR's Sacramento Chapter in 1994, was born in Southern California and received a master's degree in public history from the University of California, Santa Barbara. Growing up following the Dodgers as he did, Greg has not been inclined to switch his allegiance to their arch-rivals the Giants merely due to a move to the northern part of the state and a drought between World Series championships for the Boys in Blue.

Norm King is retired and lives in Ottawa, Ontario. He delights in having the time to do research for SABR, and was thrilled to have that research used by Jonah Keri in his history of the Montreal Expos. Norm still misses his 'spos, and looks forward to the day he will hear an umpire yell "Au jeu" again at the beginning of a ball game.

Tara Krieger joined SABR in 2005, after years of studying unusual names and statistics in baseball encyclopedias. She has previously been on staff as a writer at *Newsday* and *The Poughkeepsie Journal*, and as an editor at MLB.com. She currently works as an attorney in New Jersey.

Len Levin is old enough to have seen a few of these players in action. A retired newspaper copy editor in Providence, Rhode Island, he now does a lot of editing for SABR writing projects and has a part-time job editing the decisions of the Rhode Island Supreme Court.

Bill Nowlin has spent 43 years in the music business, so when Lyle Spatz suggested a BioProject "team book" centered on Dave Frishberg's song "Van Lingle Mungo," it didn't take a lot of arm-twisting. A co-founder of Rounder Records, Bill helped shepherd over 3,000 record albums into release. He interviewed Dave to kick off the project, though was pleased when Stew Thornley offered to write the Frishberg bio. Stew was VP of SABR before Bill was first elected to the position in 2004.

Armand Peterson is a retired engineer and manager, living in Maple Grove, Minnesota. He's been hooked on baseball since he saw some cousins play a town team game on a hardscrabble field in eastern South Dakota when he was nine years old. He was a Yankees and Mickey Mantle fan in his youth — thanks to indoctrination by his baseball-playing cousins — but switched his allegiance to the Minnesota Twins when the Senators moved to Minnesota in 1961. Since retirement he has co-authored *Town Ball: The Glory Days of Minnesota Amateur Baseball*, and written two other SABR biographies.

Paul Rogers is a law professor at Southern Methodist University, where he served as dean for nine years. When not writing about antitrust law or legal history, he has co-authored four baseball books, including two with his boyhood hero Robin Roberts, *The Whiz Kids and the 1950 Pennant* and *Throwing Hard Easy*. His most recent collaboration is *Lucky Me — My 65 Years in Baseball* with Eddie Robinson. He is also president of the Ernie Banks-Bobby Bragan DFW SABR Chapter, has authored a score of biographies for the SABR BioProject, and in 2014 served as a judge for the Casey Award.

Steve Rudman is co-founder of Sportspress Northwest, a web site devoted to analytical coverage of sports in Washington state and throughout the Pacific Northwest. He has been a daily columnist for *The Seattle Post-Intelligencer*, research director of ESPN, creator of "Wow!Stats," a Universal Press Syndicate newspaper feature, and the author/co-author of three books, including *100 Years of Washington Football* and *The Great Book of Seattle Sports Lists*.

Jim Sargent, a longtime Tigers fan who grew up in Flint, Michigan, completed the MA and PhD in History at Michigan State University. He taught American History on the college level for 40 years, since 1977 at Virginia Western Community College in Roanoke. Retired since 2010, Jim and his wife Betty live in Roanoke. A SABR member for many years, Jim enjoys writing profile articles as well as books about baseball.

Rick Swaine is a semi-retired CPA who lives near Tallahassee, Florida. A past contributor to various SABR publications, he enjoys writing about baseball's unsung heroes. He teaches a class in baseball history for FSU's Oscher Lifelong Learning Institute and still plays competitive baseball in various leagues and senior tournaments.. His recently released *Baseball's Comeback Players* (McFarland 2014) is his fourth historical baseball book.

Jim Sweetman is a lifelong Phillies fan, despite growing up on the edge of the New York media market in central New Jersey and living for the past 25 years just outside Washington, D.C. Since 1994, he's operated www.broadandpattison.com, a web site providing daily slices of Phillies history, for which he has conducted extensive reviews of contemporary press accounts. He holds Bachelors' and Masters' degrees from Rutgers University and an MBA from James Madison University. He is a senior official with the U.S. Government Accountability Office, where he manages efforts to evaluate the efficiency and effectiveness of government programs, primarily those dealing with information technology.

Stew Thornley is a former class clown and juvenile delinquent. He is no longer a juvenile.

Joseph Wancho is a long-suffering Cleveland Indians fan and resides in Westlake, Ohio. A SABR member since 2005, he served as Editor for *Pitching to the Pennant*, a Bio Project book on the 1954 Indians (University of Nebraska Press, 2014).

A lifelong Phillies fan who also follows the San Francisco Giants, **Charlie Weatherby** is a Wilmington, Delaware, native who is a social work supervisor at the Independent Adoption Center, a domestic open adoption program. He is also a softball fanatic and manages the Marin Joe's Giants Over-40 club, has a pitching record of 931-465, and counts 80 championships during the last 40 years. A periodic contributor to SABR's

BioProject, he now lives in Novato, California, with his wife, Sara Duggin, and their cat, Panther.

A lifelong Pirates fan, **Gregory H. Wolf** was born in Pittsburgh, but now resides in the Chicagoland area with his wife, Margaret, and daughter, Gabriela. A Professor of German and holder of the Dennis and Jean Bauman endowed chair of the Humanities at North Central College in Naperville, Illinois, he recently served as editor of the SABR book, *Thar's Joy in Braveland. The 1957 Milwaukee Braves* (April 2014) and is currently editing a SABR book on the 1929 Chicago Cubs.

Join SABR today!

If you're interested in baseball—writing about it, reading about it, talking about it — there's a place for you in the Society for American Baseball Research.Our members include everyone from academics to professional sportswriters to amateur historians and statisticians to students and casual fans who merely enjoy reading about baseball history and occasionally gathering with other members to talk baseball.

SABR members have a variety of interests. There are dozens of groups devoted to the study of areas related to the game, from Baseball and the Arts to Statistical Analysis to the Deadball Era to Women in Baseball. In addition, many SABR members meet formally and informally in regional chapters throughout the year, and hundreds come together for the annual national convention, the organization's premier event. These meetings often include panel discussions with former major league players and presentations by members.

Why join SABR? Here are some benefits of membership:

- Two issues of the *Baseball Research Journal*, which includes articles on history, biography, statistics, personalities, book reviews, and other aspects of the game.
- One issue of *The National Pastime*, which focuses on baseball in the region where that year's national convention is held.
- Regional chapter meetings, which can include guest speakers, presentations and trips to ballgames
- "This Week in SABR" e-newsletters every Friday, with the latest news in SABR and highlighting SABR research
- Online access to back issues of *The Sporting News* and other periodicals through Paper of Record
- Access to SABR's lending library and other research resources
- Online member directory to connect you with an international network of passionate baseball experts and fans
- Discount on registration for our annual conferences
- Access to SABR-L, an e-mail discussion list of baseball questions and answers that many feel is worth the cost of membership itself
- The opportunity to be part of a passionate international community of baseball fans

SABR membership is on a "rolling" calendar system; that means your membership lasts 365 days no matter when you sign up! Enjoy all the benefits of SABR membership by signing up today at SABR.org/join or by clipping out the form below and mailing it to SABR, 4455 E. Camelback Rd., Ste. D-140, Phoenix, AZ 85018.

✂ --

SABR MEMBERSHIP FORM

Dues payable by check, money order, Visa, MasterCard or Discover Card; online at http://store.sabr.org; or by phone at (602) 343-6455
Mail to: SABR, 4455 E. Camelback Rd., Ste. D-140, Phoenix, AZ 85018

	Annual	3-year	Senior	3-yr Sr.	Under 30
U.S.:	❏ $65	❏ $175	❏ $45	❏ $129	❏ $45
Canada/Mexico:	❏ $75	❏ $205	❏ $55	❏ $159	❏ $55
Overseas:	❏ $84	❏ $232	❏ $64	❏ $186	❏ $55

Add a Family Member: $15 each family member at same address
(list on back)
Senior: 65 or older before end of the current year
All dues amounts in U.S. dollars or equivalent

Participate in Our Donor Program!
I'd like to designate my gift to be used toward:
❏ General Fund ❏ Endowment Fund ❏ Research Resources
❏ Other: _____
❏ I want to maximize the impact of my gift; do not send any donor premiums
❏ I would like this gift to remain anonymous.
Note: Any donation not designated will be placed in the General Fund.
SABR is a 501 (c) (3) not-for-profit organization & donations are tax-deductible to the extent allowed by law.

NAME _____

ADDRESS _____

CITY _____ STATE _____ ZIP _____

HOME PHONE _____ BIRTHDAY _____

EMAIL _____
(Your e-mail address on file ensures you will receive the most recent SABR news.)

Dues _____ $

Donation _____ $

Total Enclosed _____ $

Do you work for a matching grant corporation? Call (602) 343-6455 for details.
❏ Check/Money Order Enclosed   ❏ VISA, Master Card, Discover

CARD # _____

EXP DATE _____   SIGNATURE _____

SABR BioProject Books

In 2002, the Society for American Baseball Research launched an effort to write and publish biographies of every player, manager, and individual who has made a contribution to baseball. Over the past decade, the BioProject Committee has produced over 2,200 biographical articles. Many have been part of efforts to create theme- or team-oriented books, spearheaded by chapters or other committees of SABR.

THE YEAR OF THE BLUE SNOW:
The 1964 Philadelphia Phillies
Catcher Gus Triandos dubbed the Philadelphia Phillies' 1964 season "the year of the blue snow," a rare thing that happens once in a great while. This book sheds light on lingering questions about the 1964 season—but any book about a team is really about the players. This work offers life stories of all the players and others (managers, coaches, owners, and broadcasters) associated with this star-crossed team, as well as essays of analysis and history.
Edited by Mel Marmer and Bill Nowlin
$19.95 paperback (ISBN 978-1-933599-51-9)
$9.99 ebook (ISBN 978-1-933599-52-6)
8.5"x11", 356 pages, over 70 photos

DETROIT TIGERS 1984:
What a Start! What a Finish!
The 1984 Detroit tigers roared out of the gate, winning their first nine games of the season and compiling an eye-popping 35-5 record after the campaign's first 40 games—still the best start ever for any team in major league history. This book brings together biographical profiles of every Tiger from that magical season, plus those of field management, top executives, the broadcasters—even venerable Tiger Stadium and the city itself.
Edited by Mark Pattison and David Raglin
$19.95 paperback (ISBN 978-1-933599-44-1)
$9.99 ebook (ISBN 978-1-933599-45-8)
8.5"x11", 250 pages (Over 230,000 words!)

SWEET '60: The 1960 Pittsburgh Pirates
A portrait of the 1960 team which pulled off one of the biggest upsets of the last 60 years. When Bill Mazeroski's home run left the park to win in Game Seven of the World Series, beating the New York Yankees, David had toppled Goliath. It was a blow that awakened a generation, one that millions of people saw on television, one of TV's first iconic World Series moments.
Edited by Clifton Blue Parker and Bill Nowlin
$19.95 paperback (ISBN 978-1-933599-48-9)
$9.99 ebook (ISBN 978-1-933599-49-6)
8.5"x11", 340 pages, 75 photos

RED SOX BASEBALL IN THE DAYS OF IKE AND ELVIS: The Red Sox of the 1950s
Although the Red Sox spent most of the 1950s far out of contention, the team was filled with fascinating players who captured the heart of their fans. In Red Sox Baseball, members of SABR present 46 biographies on players such as Ted Williams and Pumpsie Green as well as season-by-season recaps.
Edited by Mark Armour and Bill Nowlin
$19.95 paperback (ISBN 978-1-933599-24-3)
$9.99 ebook (ISBN 978-1-933599-34-2)
8.5"x11", 372 pages, over 100 photos

THE MIRACLE BRAVES OF 1914
Boston's Original Worst-to-First Champions
Long before the Red Sox "Impossible Dream" season, Boston's now nearly forgotten "other" team, the 1914 Boston Braves, performed a baseball "miracle" that resounds to this very day. The "Miracle Braves" were Boston's first "worst-to-first" winners of the World Series. Refusing to throw in the towel at the midseason mark, George Stallings engineered a remarkable second-half climb in the standings all the way to first place.
Edited by Bill Nowlin
$19.95 paperback (ISBN 978-1-933599-69-4)
$9.99 ebook (ISBN 978-1-933599-70-0)
8.5"x11", 392 pages, over 100 photos

THAR'S JOY IN BRAVELAND!
The 1957 Milwaukee Braves
Few teams in baseball history have captured the heart of their fans like the Milwaukee Braves of the 1950s. During the Braves' 13-year tenure in Milwaukee (1953-1965), they had a winning record every season, won two consecutive NL pennants (1957 and 1958), lost two more in the final week of the season (1956 and 1959), and set big-league attendance records along the way.
Edited by Gregory H. Wolf
$19.95 paperback (ISBN 978-1-933599-71-7)
$9.99 ebook (ISBN 978-1-933599-72-4)
8.5"x11", 330 pages, over 60 photos

NEW CENTURY, NEW TEAM:
The 1901 Boston Americans
The team now known as the Boston Red Sox played its first season in 1901. Boston had a well-established National League team, but the American League went head-to-head with the N.L. in Chicago, Philadelphia and Boston. Chicago won the American League pennant and Boston finished second, only four games behind.
Edited by Bill Nowlin
$19.95 paperback (ISBN 978-1-933599-58-8)
$9.99 ebook (ISBN 978-1-933599-59-5)
8.5"x11", 268 pages, over 125 photos

CAN HE PLAY?
A Look At Baseball Scouts and their Profession
They dig through tons of coal to find a single diamond. Here in the world of scouts, we meet the "King of Weeds," a Ph.D. we call "Baseball's Renaissance Man," a husband-and-wife team, pioneering Latin scouts, and a Japanese-American interned during World War II who became a successful scout—and many, many more.
Edited by Jim Sandoval and Bill Nowlin
$19.95 paperback (ISBN 978-1-933599-23-6)
$9.99 ebook (ISBN 978-1-933599-25-0)
8.5"x11", 200 pages, over 100 photos

SABR Members can purchase each book at a significant discount (often 50% off) and receive the ebook editions free as a member benefit. Each book is available in a trade paperback edition as well as ebook suitable for reading on a home computer or Nook, Kindle, or iPad/tablet.

To learn more about becoming a member of SABR, visit the website: sabr.org/join

The SABR Digital Library

The Society for American Baseball Research, the top baseball research organization in the world, disseminates some of the best in baseball history, analysis, and biography through our publishing programs. The SABR Digital Library contains a mix of books old and new, and focuses on a tandem program of paperback and ebook publication, making these materials widely available for both on digital devices and as traditional printed books.

CLASSIC REPRINTS

BASE-BALL: How to Become a Player
by John Montgomery Ward
John Montgomery Ward (1860-1925) tossed the second perfect game in major league history and later became the game's best shortstop and a great, inventive manager. His classic handbook on baseball skills and strategy was published in 1888. Illustrated with woodcuts, the book is divided into chapters for each position on the field as well as chapters on the origin of the game, theory and strategy, training, base-running, and batting.
$4.99 ebook (ISBN 978-1-933599-47-2)
$9.95 paperback (ISBN 978-0910137539)
156 pages, 4.5"x7" replica edition

BATTING
by F. C. Lane
First published in 1925, Batting collects the wisdom and insights of over 250 hitters and baseball figures. Lane interviewed extensively and compiled tips and advice on everything from batting stances to beanballs. Legendary baseball figures such as Ty Cobb, Casey Stengel, Cy Young, Walter Johnson, Rogers Hornsby, and Babe Ruth reveal the secrets of such integral and interesting parts of the game as how to choose a bat, the ways to beat a slump, and how to outguess the pitcher.
$14.95 paperback (ISBN 978-0-910137-86-7)
$7.99 ebook (ISBN 978-1-933599-46-5)
240 pages, 5"x7"

RUN, RABBIT, RUN
by Walter "Rabbit" Maranville
"Rabbit" Maranville was the Joe Garagiola of Grandpa's day, the baseball comedian of the times. In a twenty-four-year career that began in 1912, Rabbit found a lot of funny situations to laugh at, and no wonder: he caused most of them! The book also includes an introduction by the late Harold Seymour and a historical account of Maranville's life and Hall-of-Fame career by Bob Carroll.
$9.95 paperback (ISBN 978-1-933599-26-7)
$5.99 ebook (ISBN 978-1-933599-27-4)
100 pages, 5.5"x8.5", 15 rare photos

MEMORIES OF A BALLPLAYER
by Bill Werber and C. Paul Rogers III
Bill Werber's claim to fame is unique: he was the last living person to have a direct connection to the 1927 Yankees, "Murderers' Row," a team hailed by many as the best of all time. Rich in anecdotes and humor, Memories of a Ballplayer is a clear-eyed memoir of the world of big-league baseball in the 1930s. Werber played with or against some of the most productive hitters of all time, including Babe Ruth, Ted Williams, Lou Gehrig, and Joe DiMaggio.
$14.95 paperback (ISNB 978-0-910137-84-3)
$6.99 ebook (ISBN 978-1-933599-47-2)
250 pages, 6"x9"

ORIGINAL SABR RESEARCH

INVENTING BASEBALL: The 100 Greatest Games of the Nineteenth Century
SABR's Nineteenth Century Committee brings to life the greatest games from the game's early years. From the "prisoner of war" game that took place among captive Union soldiers during the Civil War (immortalized in a famous lithograph), to the first intercollegiate game (Amherst versus Williams), to the first professional no-hitter, the games in this volume span 1833–1900 and detail the athletic exploits of such players as Cap Anson, Moses "Fleetwood" Walker, Charlie Comiskey, and Mike "King" Kelly.
Edited by Bill Felber
$19.95 paperback (ISBN 978-1-933599-42-7)
$9.99 ebook (ISBN 978-1-933599-43-4)
302 pages, 8"x10", 200 photos

NINETEENTH CENTURY STARS: 2012 EDITION
First published in 1989, Nineteenth Century Stars was SABR's initial attempt to capture the stories of baseball players from before 1900. With a collection of 136 fascinating biographies, SABR has re-released Nineteenth Century Stars for 2012 with revised statistics and new form. The 2012 version also includes a preface by John Thorn.
Edited by Robert L. Tiemann and Mark Rucker
$19.95 paperback (ISBN 978-1-933599-28-1)
$9.99 ebook (ISBN 978-1-933599-29-8)
300 pages, 6"x9"

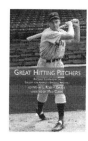

GREAT HITTING PITCHERS
Published in 1979, Great Hitting Pitchers was one of SABR's early publications. Edited by SABR founder Bob Davids, the book compiles stories and records about pitchers excelling in the batter's box. Newly updated in 2012 by Mike Cook, Great Hitting Pitchers contain tables including data from 1979-2011, corrections to reflect recent records, and a new chapter on recent new members in the club of "great hitting pitchers" like Tom Glavine and Mike Hampton.
Edited by L. Robert Davids
$9.95 paperback (ISBN 978-1-933599-30-4)
$5.99 ebook (ISBN 978-1-933599-31-1)
102 pages, 5.5"x8.5"

THE FENWAY PROJECT
Sixty-four SABR members—avid fans, historians, statisticians, and game enthusiasts—recorded their experiences of a single game. Some wrote from inside the Green Monster's manual scoreboard, the Braves clubhouse, or the broadcast booth, while others took in the essence of Fenway from the grandstand or bleachers. The result is a fascinating look at the charms and challenges of Fenway Park, and the allure of being a baseball fan.
Edited by Bill Nowlin and Cecilia Tan
$9.99 ebook (ISBN 978-1-933599-50-2)
175 pages, 100 photos

SABR Members can purchase each book at a significant discount (often 50% off) and receive the ebook editions free as a member benefit. Each book is available in a trade paperback edition as well as ebooks suitable for reading on a home computer or Nook, Kindle, or iPad/tablet.

To learn more about becoming a member of SABR, visit the website: sabr.org/join